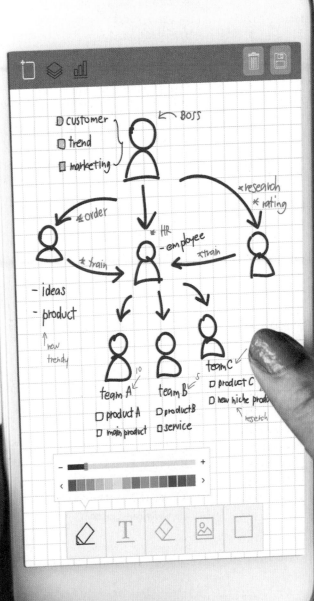

ORGB6

Debra L. Nelson, Oklahoma State University and James Campbell Quick, University of Texas, Arlington

Senior Vice President, Higher Education Product Management: Erin Joyner

Senior Product Manager: Michael Giffen

Content Developer: Patricia Hempel

Product Assistant: Nick Perez

Marketing Manager: Audrey Jacobs

Content Project Manager: Colleen A. Farmer

Content Manager: Julia Chase

Sr. Art Director: Bethany Bourgeois

Text Designer: Tippy McIntosh

Cover Designer: Lisa Kuhn, Curio Press, LLC / Chris Miller, Cmiller Design

Cover Image: Rawpixel Ltd/Alamy Stock Photo

Interior Design Image: Vital9s/Shutterstock.com

Back Cover and Special Page Images:

Computer and tablet illustration: © iStockphoto. com/furtaev; Smart Phone illustration: © iStockphoto.com/dashadima; Feedback image: © Rawpixel.com/Shutterstock.com

Intellectual Property Analyst: Diane Garrity

Intellectual Property Project Manager: Nick Barrows

Production Service: MPS Limited

For product information and technology assistance, contact us at
Cengage Customer & Sales Support, 1-800-354-9706

For permission to use material from this text or product, submit all requests online at **www.cengage.com/permissions** Further permissions questions can be emailed to **permissionrequest@cengage.com**

Library of Congress Control Number: 2017957886

Student Edition ISBN: 978-1-337-40783-0
Student Edition with Online ISBN: 978-1-337-40781-6

Cengage
20 Channel Center Street
Boston, MA 02210
USA

Cengage is a leading provider of customized learning solutions with employees residing in nearly 40 different countries and sales in more than 125 countries around the world. Find your local representative at **www.cengage.com.**

Cengage products are represented in Canada by Nelson Education, Ltd.

To learn more about Cengage platforms and services, visit **www.cengage.com**

To register or access your online learning solution or purchase materials for your course, visit **www.cengage.com**

Printed in the United States of America
Print Number: 01   Print Year: 2019

NELSON / QUICK
ORGB⁶ BRIEF CONTENTS

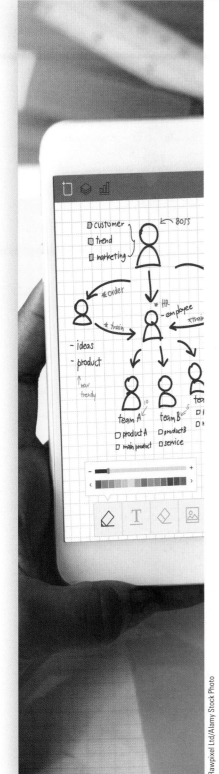

Rawpixel Ltd/Alamy Stock Photo

PART 1 INTRODUCTION

1 Organizational Behavior and Opportunity   2

2 Challenges for Managers   16

PART 2 INDIVIDUAL PROCESSES AND BEHAVIOR

3 Personality, Perception, and Attribution   34

4 Attitudes, Emotions, and Ethics   52

5 Motivation at Work   70

6 Learning and Performance Management   86

7 Stress and Well-Being at Work   104

PART 3 INTERPERSONAL PROCESSES AND BEHAVIOR

8 Communication   124

9 Work Teams and Groups   142

10 Decision Making by Individuals and Groups   160

11 Power and Political Behavior   180

12 Leadership and Followership   198

13 Conflict and Negotiation   218

PART 4 ORGANIZATIONAL PROCESSES AND STRUCTURE

14 Jobs and the Design of Work   236

15 Organizational Design and Structure   252

16 Organizational Culture   272

17 Career Management   290

18 Managing Change   310

Endnotes   329

Index   363

CONTENTS

Part 1
INTRODUCTION

Dimitri Otis/Getty Images

1 Organizational Behavior and Opportunity   2

1-1 Human Behavior in Organizations   2

1-2 Behavior in Times of Change   5

1-3 The Organizational Context   6

1-4 The Formal and Informal Organization   7

1-5 Diversity of Organizations   9

1-6 Change Creates Opportunities   9

1-7 Learning about Organizational Behavior   13

2 Challenges for Managers   16

2-1 Competing in the Global Economy   16

2-2 Cultural Differences and Work-Related Attitudes   21

2-3 The Diverse Workforce   22

2-4 Ethics, Character, and Personal Integrity   28

2-5 Ethical Dilemmas Facing the Modern Organization   29

Part 2
INDIVIDUAL PROCESSES AND BEHAVIOR

Gandee Vasan/Getty Images

3 Personality, Perception, and Attribution   34

3-1 Individual Differences and Organizational Behavior   34

3-2 Personality and Organizations   36

3-3 Application of Personality Theory in Organizations   40

3-4 Social Perception   45

3-5 Barriers to Social Perception   47

3-6 Attribution in Organizations   50

4 Attitudes, Emotions, and Ethics   52

4-1 Attitudes   52

4-2 Attitude Formation   54

4-3 Job Satisfaction   56

4-4 Organizational Citizenship versus Counterproductive Work Behavior   57

4-5 Persuasion and Attitude Change   59

4-6 Emotions and Moods at Work   61

4-7 Ethical Behavior   63

4-8 Factors That Affect Ethical Behavior   65

5 Motivation at Work 70

5-1 Motivation and Work Behavior 70

5-2 Maslow's Need Hierarchy 73

5-3 McClelland's Need Theory 75

5-4 Herzberg's Two-Factor Theory 77

5-5 Two New Ideas in Motivation 78

5-6 Social Exchange and Equity Theory 79

5-7 Expectancy Theory of Motivation 82

5-8 Cultural Differences in Motivation 84

6 Learning and Performance Management 86

6-1 Behavioral Models of Learning in Organizations 86

6-2 Social and Cognitive Theories of Learning 91

6-3 Goal Setting at Work 92

6-4 Performance: A Key Construct 94

6-5 Performance Feedback 96

6-6 Rewarding Performance 98

6-7 Correcting Poor Performance 99

7 Stress and Well-Being at Work 104

7-1 What Is Stress? 104

7-2 Four Approaches to Stress 105

7-3 The Stress Response 107

7-4 Sources of Work Stress 107

7-5 The Consequences of Stress 111

7-6 Individual Differences in the Stress–Strain Relationship 114

7-7 Preventive Stress Management 116

Part 3
INTERPERSONAL PROCESSES AND BEHAVIOR

Klaus Vedfelt/Taxi/Getty Images

8 Communication 124

8-1 Interpersonal Communication 124

8-2 Communication Skills for Effective Managers 129

8-3 Barriers and Gateways to Communication 130

8-4 Civility and Incivility 132

8-5 Nonverbal Communication 134

8-6 Positive, Healthy Communication 137

8-7 Communicating through New Technologies and Social Media 138

9 Work Teams and Groups 142

9-1 Groups and Work Teams 142

9-2 Why Work Teams? 143

9-3 Group Behavior 145

9-4 Group Formation and Development 146

9-5 Task and Maintenance Functions 150

9-6 Factors That Influence Group Effectiveness 151

9-7 Empowerment and Self-Managed Teams 154

9-8 Upper Echelons: Teams at the Top 156

10 Decision Making by Individuals and Groups 160

10-1 The Decision-Making Process 160

10-2 Models and Limits of Decision Making 162

10-3 Individual Influences on Decision Making 165

10-4 The Group Decision-Making Process 170

10-5 Diversity and Culture in Decision Making 175

10-6 Participation in Decision Making 176

11 Power and Political Behavior 180

11-1 The Concept of Power 180

11-2 Forms and Sources of Power in Organizations 181

11-3 Using Power Ethically 184

11-4 Symbols of Power 186

11-5 Political Behavior in Organizations 188

11-6 Managing Political Behavior in Organizations 192

12 Leadership and Followership 198

12-1 Leadership versus Management 199

12-2 Early Trait Theories 200

12-3 Behavioral Theories 201

12-4 Contingency Theories 204

12-5 Recent Leadership Theories 210

12-6 Emerging Issues in Leadership 212

12-7 Followership 214

12-8 Guidelines for Leadership 215

13 Conflict and Negotiation 218

13-1 The Nature of Conflicts in Organizations 218

13-2 Causes of Conflict in Organizations 221

13-3 Forms of Group Conflict in Organizations 224

13-4 Individual Conflict in Organizations 225

13-5 Conflict Management Strategies and Techniques 229

13-6 Conflict Management Styles 232

Part 4 ORGANIZATIONAL PROCESSES AND STRUCTURE

Henrik Sorensen/Riser/Getty Images

14 Jobs and the Design of Work 236

14-1 Work in Organizations 236

14-2 Traditional Approaches to Job Design 239

14-3 Alternative Approaches to Job Design 244

14-4 Contemporary Issues in the Design of Work 248

15 Organizational Design and Structure 252

15-1 Key Organizational Design Processes 253

15-2 Basic Design Dimensions 258

15-3 Five Structural Configurations 259

15-4 Contextual Variables 261

15-5 Forces Reshaping Organizations 267

15-6 Emerging Organizational Structures 269

15-7 Factors That Can Adversely Affect Structure 270

16 Organizational Culture 272

16-1 Levels of Organizational Culture 272

16-2 Functions of Organizational Culture 277

16-3 The Relationship of Culture to Performance 278

16-4 The Leader's Role in Shaping and Reinforcing Culture 279

16-5 Organizational Socialization   281

16-6 Assessing Organizational Culture   283

16-7 Changing Organizational Culture   284

16-8 Challenges to Developing a Positive, Cohesive Culture   286

17 Career Management   290

17-1 Occupational and Organizational Choice Decisions   291

17-2 Foundations for a Successful Career   296

17-3 The Career Stage Model   297

17-4 The Establishment Stage   298

17-5 The Advancement Stage   299

17-6 The Maintenance Stage   305

17-7 The Withdrawal Stage   306

17-8 Career Anchors   308

18 Managing Change   310

18-1 Forces for Change in Organizations   310

18-2 The Scope of Change   315

18-3 Resistance to Change   316

18-4 Lewin's Model for Managing Change   318

18-5 Determining the Need for Organization Development Interventions   320

18.6 Group-Focused Techniques for OD Intervention   321

18-7 Individual-Focused Techniques for OD Intervention   323

Endnotes   329

Index   363

1 | Organizational Behavior and Opportunity

LEARNING OBJECTIVES

1-1 Define organizational behavior.

1-2 Identify four action steps for responding positively in times of change.

1-3 Identify the important system components of an organization.

1-4 Describe the formal and informal elements of an organization.

1-5 Identify factors that contribute to the diversity of organizations in the economy.

1-6 Describe the opportunities that change creates for organizational behavior.

1-7 Demonstrate the value of objective knowledge and skill development in the study of organizational behavior.

After finishing this chapter go to **PAGE 15** for **STUDY TOOLS**

DimitriOtis/DigitalVision/Getty Images

1-1 HUMAN BEHAVIOR IN ORGANIZATIONS

Human behavior in organizations is complex and often difficult to understand. Organizations have been described as clockworks in which human behavior is logical and rational, but they often seem like snake pits to those who work in them.[1] The clockwork metaphor reflects an orderly, idealized view of organizational behavior devoid of conflict or dilemma because all the working parts (the people) mesh smoothly. The snake pit metaphor, on the other hand, conveys the daily conflict, distress, and struggle in organizations. Each metaphor reflects reality from a different perspective—the organization's versus the individual's. The snake pit metaphor expresses the dark side of human behavior, which is seen at its extreme in cases of road rage and workplace violence. Workplace incivility has become commonplace in many organizations,

with an estimated 50 percent of workers saying that they experience uncivil behavior weekly. Incivility has negative affective, cognitive, and behavioral consequences for instigators, targets, and witnesses of such negative behaviors.[2] In contrast, the clockwork metaphor expresses the view of organizations as healthy and productive systems in which individuals have a clear sense of the shared vision and values, are personally invested in outcomes, feel that their contributions are significant, and receive support and respect from the organization's leadership.[3]

This chapter serves as an introduction to the complex subject of organizational behavior. The first section provides an overview of human behavior in organizations, its interdisciplinary origins, and its responses to change. The second section presents an organizational context within which behavior occurs. The third section

Organizations have been described as clockworks, but they often seem like snake pits.

highlights the **opportunities** that exist in times of **change** and **challenge** for people at work.[4] The fourth section addresses the ways people learn about organizational behavior and explains how the text's pedagogical features relate to the various learning styles. The final section presents the plan for the book.

We can define **organizational behavior** as the study of individual behavior and group dynamics in organizations. The study of organizational behavior is primarily concerned with the psychosocial, interpersonal, and behavioral dynamics in organizations. However, organizational variables that affect human behavior at work are also relevant to the study of organizational behavior. These organizational variables include jobs, the design of work, communication, performance appraisal, organizational design, and organizational structure.

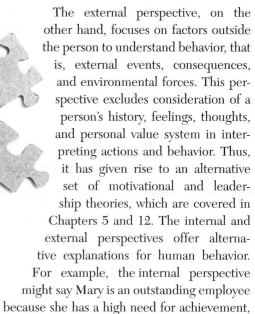

Cristalov/Shutterstock.com

1-1a Understanding Human Behavior

The vast majority of theories and models of human behavior fall into two basic categories: that of an internal perspective and that of an external perspective. The internal perspective looks at workers' minds to understand their behavior. It is psychodynamically oriented, and its proponents understand human behavior in terms of the thoughts, feelings, past experiences, and needs of the individual. The internal perspective explains people's actions and behavior in terms of their histories and personal value systems. The idea of this perspective is that internal processes of thinking, feeling, perceiving, and judging lead people to act in specific ways; therefore, people are best understood from the inside, and their behavior is best interpreted alongside their thoughts and feelings. The internal perspective has given rise to a wide range of motivational and leadership theories.

The external perspective, on the other hand, focuses on factors outside the person to understand behavior, that is, external events, consequences, and environmental forces. This perspective excludes consideration of a person's history, feelings, thoughts, and personal value system in interpreting actions and behavior. Thus, it has given rise to an alternative set of motivational and leadership theories, which are covered in Chapters 5 and 12. The internal and external perspectives offer alternative explanations for human behavior. For example, the internal perspective might say Mary is an outstanding employee because she has a high need for achievement, whereas the external perspective might say it is because she is extremely well paid for her work. Kurt Lewin combined both perspectives with his claim that behavior is a function of both the person and the environment.[5]

1-1b Interdisciplinary Influences

Organizational behavior is a blended discipline that has grown out of contributions from numerous earlier fields of study. The sciences of psychology, sociology, engineering, anthropology, management, and medicine have all contributed to our understanding of human behavior in organizations.

Psychology, the science of human behavior, was developed during the closing decades of the nineteenth century. Psychology traces its origins to philosophy and the science of physiology. One of the most prominent early psychologists, William James, held a degree in medicine (MD). Since its beginnings, psychology has branched into a number of specialized fields, including clinical, experimental, military, organizational, and social psychology. Organizational psychology frequently overlaps with organizational behavior; for instance, both investigate work motivation.[6] Johnson & Johnson, Valero Energy, and Chaparral Steel all used longstanding psychological research to develop their sophisticated personnel selection methods.[7]

Sociology, the science of society, has contributed greatly to our knowledge of group and intergroup dynamics. Because sociology takes society rather than the individual as its point of departure, sociologists focus on the variety of roles within a society or culture,

opportunities Favorable times or chances for progress and advancement.

change The transformation or modification of an organization and/or its stakeholders.

challenge The call to competition, contest, or battle.

organizational behavior The study of individual behavior and group dynamics in organizations.

psychology The science of human behavior.

sociology The science of society.

the norms and standards of behavior in groups, and the consequences of compliant and deviant behavior. Individuals have a role set that is determined by their social position, and roles affect how people interact within organizations. The Professional Role Behaviors Survey, for example, studied how the roles of various medical practitioners changed during hospital restructuring and these changes influenced organizational behavior and culture.[8]

Engineering is the applied science of energy and matter. It enhances our understanding of the design of work. Frederick Taylor took basic engineering ideas and applied them to human behavior at work, influencing the early study of organizational behavior.[9] With his engineering background, Taylor placed special emphasis on human productivity and efficiency in work behavior. Job preparation and performance shifted from a long apprenticeship and a creative, problem-solving approach to work to training in and automated performance of simplified tasks. A study published in 1990 showed that Taylor's notions of performance standards and differential piece-rate systems were still shaping organizational goal-setting programs at Black & Decker, IBM, and Weyerhaeuser at that time.[10]

Anthropology, the science of human learned behavior, is especially important to our understanding of *organizational culture*. In fact, anthropological research has been used to examine the effects of efficient organizational cultures on organizational performance[11] and the ways pathological personalities may lead to dysfunctional organizational cultures.[12] In one case study, Schwartz used a psychodynamic, anthropological mode of inquiry to explore corporate decay at General Motors and NASA.[13]

Management, originally called *administrative science*, is the study of overseeing activities and supervising people in organizations. It includes the design, implementation, and management of various administrative and organizational systems. March and Simon take the human organization as their point of departure to investigate administrative practices that enhance the effectiveness of the system.[14] Management is the first discipline to take the modern corporation as the unit of analysis, a viewpoint that distinguishes its contribution to the study of organizational behavior.

Medicine, the applied science of treating diseases to enhance an individual's health and well-being, focuses on both physical and psychological health as well as industrial mental health.[15] As modern care defeats acute diseases, medical attention is shifting to more chronic diseases such as hypertension and to issues involved in occupational health and well-being.[16] These trends have contributed to the growth of corporate *wellness programs* such as Johnson & Johnson's "Live for Life Program." Moreover, *ergonomics* has gained increasing attention as a way to prevent medical problems resulting from poor design of workstations, resulting in the loss of billions of dollars from higher healthcare costs and lower worker productivity.[17] Such costs can be cut nearly in half by implementing the results of medical research into better workplace design.[18]

1-2 BEHAVIOR IN TIMES OF CHANGE

Early research of individuals and organizations in the midst of environmental change found that people often experience change as a threat and respond by relying on well-learned and dominant forms of behavior.[19] That is, people often become rigid and reactive in the midst of change, rather than open and responsive. This behavior works well in the face of gradual, incremental change. However, rigid and well-learned behavior may be a counterproductive response to significant change, such as outsourcing. Prompted by dramatic advances in Internet and networking technology, outsourcing has been unavoidable in much of American industry.[20] Yet factors such as employee attrition and the potential for data loss have caused many companies to modify their outsourcing strategies to keep both talent and information within the organization.[21] Big changes disrupt people's habitual behavior and force them to learn new skills, often creating discomfort and discontent. To such employees, Eric Brown, CEO of PlusFactor recommends looking for the positive opportunities in change and viewing challenge as a good rather than bad experience. His action steps for adapting to change are to (1) have a positive attitude, (2) ask questions, (3) listen to the answers, and (4) be committed to success.[22]

Success is never guaranteed, however, and change sometimes results in failure. Some of the world's greatest leaders, such as Winston Churchill, experienced dramatic failures before they achieved lasting success. It was their capacity to learn from the failure and to respond positively to new opportunities that helped them overcome early setbacks. Knowing this, one venture capitalist with whom the authors have worked likes to ask an executive who is seeking to build a business to tell him about his or her greatest failure. He wants to hear

engineering The applied science of energy and matter.

anthropology The science of human learned behavior.

management The study of overseeing activities and supervising people in organizations.

medicine The applied science of healing or treating diseases to enhance an individual's health and well-being.

Habits Can Be Good to Have

Product packaging often focuses on developing novel, innovative, and markedly distinctive designs, shapes, and colors that "stand out" for the consumer. This may actually be counterproductive given how people are hard wired. Our brains are designed, especially in stressful or dangerous times, to reduce information intake and increase control. The brain is not designed to be open and creative when it is in a hurry. This has important consequences in how people form and maintain habits, which are behaviorally efficient and demand less energy. So, with repeated responses to familiar and similar objects, the brain requires less information and uses less power to get to the same recognition level or conclusion that would be required if the habit were not formed and in place. Thus, implicit memory has power and helps the brain lead to recognition efficiency. This level of cognitive and behavioral efficiency may become compromised in new and changed environments and circumstances.

SOURCE: S. Berinato, "The Science: How Habit Beats Novelty," *Harvard Business Review*, January–February 2017, pp. 60–61.

maxim ibraginov/Shutterstock.com

how the executive responded to the failure and what he or she learned from the experience.

So change carries both the risk of failure and the opportunity for success; our behavior often determines the outcome. Moreover, success can come through the accumulation of small wins and through the use of microprocesses, as has been found with middle managers engaged in institutional change. Finally, companies can improve their performance in the emerging China market during uncertain times and economic transitions by engendering trust between the business and state bureaucrats.[23,23a]

1-3 THE ORGANIZATIONAL CONTEXT

A complete understanding of organizational behavior requires an understanding of both human behavior and of the organizational context—that is, the specific setting—within which behavior is acted out.

1-3a Organizations as Open Systems

Just as two different perspectives offer complementary explanations for human behavior, two views shape complementary explanations of organizations. Organizations are open systems of interacting components, including people, tasks, technology, and structure. These internal components also interact with components in the organization's task environment.

task An organization's mission, purpose, or goal for existing.

people The human resources of an organization.

Today, the corporation is the dominant organizational form for much of the Western world, but other organizational forms have dominated other societies. Religious organizations, such as the temple corporations of ancient Mesopotamia and the churches in colonial America, can often dominate society.[24] So can military organizations, such as the clans of the Scottish Highlands and the regional armies of the People's Republic of China.[25] All of these societies are woven together by family organizations, which themselves may vary from nuclear and extended families to small, collective communities.[26] The purpose and structure of religious, military, and family organizational forms varies, but people within different organizations often behave alike. In fact, early discoveries about power and leadership in work organizations were remarkably similar to findings about power and leadership within families.[27]

Because organizations are so varied in function, manufacturing products such as aircraft components or delivering services such as money management, for example, we must first understand the open system components of an organization and its task environment in order to see how the organization performs.

Accordingly, Katz and Kahn in one study, and Leavitt in another, established open system frameworks for understanding organizations.[28] The four major internal components are task, people, technology, and structure. These four components, along with the organization's inputs, outputs, and key elements in the task environment, are depicted in Figure 1.1. The **task** of the organization is its mission, purpose, or goal for existing. The **people** are the human resources of the organization.

FIGURE 1.1 AN OPEN-SYSTEMS VIEW OF ORGANIZATION

Task environment:
Competitors
Unions
Regulatory agencies
Clients

Inputs:
Material
Capital
Human

Structure

Task

Technology

People
(Actors)

Outputs:
Products
Services

Organizational boundary

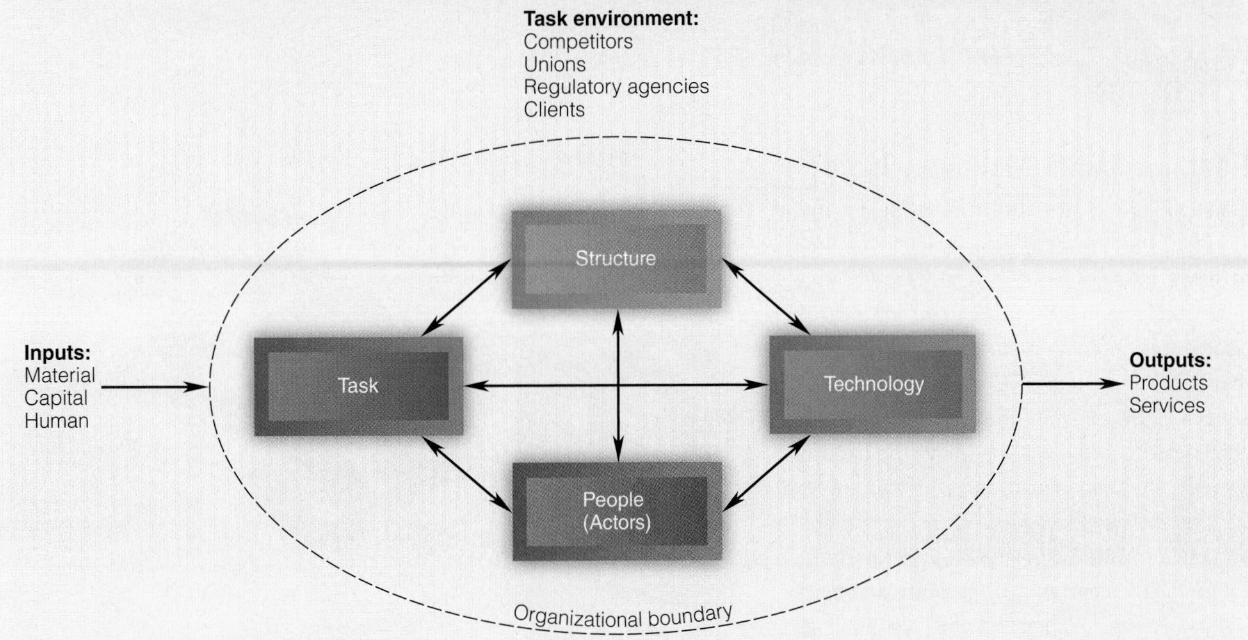

SOURCE: Based on H. Leavitt, "Applied Organizational Change in Industry: Structural, Technological, and Humanistic Approaches," in J. G. March, ed., *Handbook of Organizations* (Chicago: Rand McNally, 1965), 1145. Reprinted by permission of James G. March.

The **technology** is the wide range of tools, knowledge, and/or techniques used to transform inputs into outputs. The **structure** involves the systems of communication, authority and roles, and workflow.

In addition to these major internal components, the organization as a system also has an external task environment composed of different constituents such as suppliers, customers, and federal regulators. Thompson describes the task environment as that element of the environment related to the organization's degree of goal attainment, or its basic task.[29] A number of organizations are using or considering the use of Twitter as a way of networking into elements of their task environments.[30] For example, NASA uses Twitter to update followers on the status of upcoming shuttle flights.

The organization system works by taking inputs, converting them into throughputs, and delivering outputs to its task environment. *Inputs* are the human, informational, material, and financial resources used by the organization. *Throughputs* are the materials and resources as they are transformed by the organization's technology component. Once the transformation is complete, they become *outputs* for customers, consumers, and clients. The actions of suppliers, customers, regulators, and other elements of the task environment affect the organization and the behavior of people at work. The role of modern corporations has expanded to include corporate social responsibility. Customers expect these organizations to be good corporate citizens, creating social value as well as financial wealth for their shareholders.[31] Organizational transparency contributes to trust in organization–stakeholder relationships, which is good for the health and well-being of the organization.[31a]

1-4 THE FORMAL AND INFORMAL ORGANIZATION

The open systems view of organizations suggests that they are designed like clockwork (recall the clockwork metaphor described at the beginning of this chapter), with a neat, precise, interrelated functioning. The **formal organization** is the official, legitimate, and most visible part of the organization, and it enables people to think of organizations in logical and rational ways. The snake pit

technology The tools, knowledge, and/or techniques used to transform inputs into outputs.

structure The systems of communication, authority and roles, and workflow.

formal organization The official, legitimate, and most visible part of the system.

Google's Racial Makeup…Is Up

People are at the heart of Google's success. The company has searched its soul to move minority workers from 37 percent of their workforce in 2012 to 43.1 percent in 2016. Google does employ more men (70.8 percent) than the U.S. average (53.2 percent) and fewer women (29.2 percent) than the U.S. average (46.8 percent). Google is way above the national average for Asian employees (33.5 percent vs. 5.2 percent) while being behind the national average for White (56.9 percent vs. 78.7 percent), Latino (5.2 percent vs. 16.6 percent), and Black (2.4 percent vs. 12.3 percent) employees. But, all their minority trend lines from 2012 to 2016 are positive (up).

SOURCE: E. McGirt, "Google Searches Its Soul," *Fortune*, Feb. 1, 2017, p. 54.

lightpoet/123RF

metaphor mentioned earlier originates from the study of the **informal organization**, which is unofficial and less visible. The **Hawthorne studies**, conducted during the 1920s and 1930s, first suggested the importance of the informal elements. During the so-called interview study, the third of the four Hawthorne studies, the researchers began to fully appreciate the informal elements of the Hawthorne Works as an organization.[32] The formal and informal elements of the organization are depicted in Figure 1.2.

Because the formal and informal elements of an organization can sometimes conflict, we must understand both. Such conflicts erupted in many organizations during the early years of the twentieth century and were embodied in the union–management strife of that era. Sometimes these formal–informal conflicts escalated into violence.

informal organization The unofficial and less visible part of the system.

Hawthorne studies Studies conducted during the 1920s and 1930s that suggested the importance of the informal organization.

For example, supervisors at the Homestead Works of U.S. Steel during the 1920s were issued pistols "just in case" they felt it necessary to shoot unruly, dangerous steelworkers. However, during that same era, the progressive Eastman Kodak

FIGURE 1.2 FORMAL AND INFORMAL ORGANIZATION

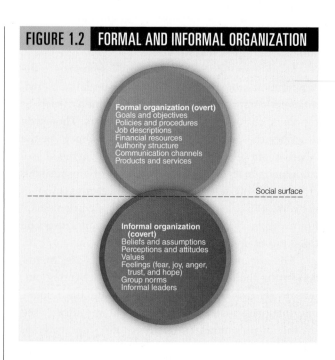

Formal organization (overt)
Goals and objectives
Policies and procedures
Job descriptions
Financial resources
Authority structure
Communication channels
Products and services

Social surface

Informal organization (covert)
Beliefs and assumptions
Perceptions and attitudes
Values
Feelings (fear, joy, anger, trust, and hope)
Group norms
Informal leaders

company provided financial backing for employees' neighborhood communities, such as Meadowbrook in Rochester, New York. Kodak's concern for employees and attention to informal issues made unions unnecessary at the company.

Monkey Business Images/Shutterstock.com

The open systems view of an organization suggests that it is designed and run like clockwork.

The informal elements of the organization are often points of diagnostic and intervention activities in organizational development, though the formal elements must always be considered because they provide the context for the informal.[33] It is the informal elements involving people's feelings, thoughts, and attitudes about their work that most affect their behavior and performance, but individual behavior plays out in the context of both the formal and informal elements of the system, becoming, in the process, organizational behavior. Employees' moods, emotions, and dispositions all influence critical organizational outcomes such as job performance, decision making, creativity, turnover, teamwork, negotiation, and leadership.[34]

1-5 DIVERSITY OF ORGANIZATIONS

Most attempts to explain or predict organizational behavior rely heavily on factors within the organization and give less weight to external environmental considerations.[35] Yet organizational behavior always occurs in the context of a specific organizational setting, so students can benefit from being sensitive to that industrial context and from developing an appreciation for the diversity of various organizations.[36]

Large and small organizations operate in each sector of the economy: the private, manufacturing, service, government, and nonprofit sectors. In the private sector are a great variety of organizations that play an important role in the economy. The manufacturing sector includes the production of basic materials, such as steel, and the production of finished products, such as automobiles and electronic equipment. The service sector includes transportation, financial services, insurance, and retail sales. The government sectors, which provide essential infrastructure, and nonprofit organizations are important to our collective well-being because they meet needs that other sectors do not address. For example, in France, the not-for-profit Action Tank has discovered a solution for poor consumers who find access to even low-cost products and services out of their reach.[37]

Hundreds of small, medium-sized, and large organizations contribute to the economic health and human welfare of the United States. Throughout this book, we provide examples from a variety of organizations to help you develop a greater appreciation for your own organization and for others in the diverse world of private business enterprises and nonprofit organizations.

1-6 CHANGE CREATES OPPORTUNITIES

Global competition, which is a leading force driving change at work, has increased significantly during the past few decades, especially in industries such as banking, finance, and air transportation. As a result, change has accelerated and, with it, both opportunities and risks. Corporate competition creates performance and cost pressures, changes that have a ripple

FAST FACT

The Cost of Ignoring Older Employees

When companies do not pay attention to older employees, they pay a price. This conclusion was based on a study of 666 Australian workers between the ages of 45 and 75. In workplaces that were most unfavorable to older employees, engagement levels were 19 to 20 percent lower than those whose workplaces were most helpful. This has financial implications because organizations lose money when workers are disengaged.

SOURCE: R. Feintzeig, "Companies Suffer When They Ignore Older Employees, Study Says; When workplaces are less friendly to that group, engagement among veteran workers drops," *Wall Street Journal*, 3 Jan 2017.

> Winning in a competitive industry can be a transient victory; staying ahead of the competition requires constant change.

effect on people and their behavior at work. Although one such risk for employees is the marginalization of part-time professionals, good management practice can ensure their integration.[38] Furthermore, although competition may lead to downsizing and restructuring, it also provides the opportunity for revitalization.[39] And small companies don't necessarily lose in this competitive environment. Scientech, a small power and energy company, needed to enhance its managerial talent and service quality to meet the challenges of growth and big-company competitors, and it consequently improved its performance. Thus, competition spurred its increased success.

Product and service quality are the major ways that companies can win in a competitive environment. IBM, Control Data Services, Inc., Northwest Airlines (now Delta), and Southwest Airlines all used problem-solving skills to achieve high-quality products and services in their attempts to deal with competitive forces. Change in

the coffee industry has been a key stimulus for both Caribou Coffee and Starbucks as they innovate and improve.

Too much change, however, leads to chaos, and too little change leads to stagnation. Also, winning in a competitive industry can be a transient victory; staying ahead of the competition requires constant change.

1-6a Global Competition in Business

Managers and executives in the United States face radical change in response to increased global competition. According to noted economist Lester Thurow, this competition is characterized by intense rivalry between the United States, Japan, and Europe in core industries.[40] As a result, all categories of employees face increased pressure to be productive and to add value to the firm. Moreover, corporate warfare and competition make employment uncertain for people in companies or industries that pursue cost-cutting strategies to achieve economic success. Five months after taking over as CEO of Microsoft, Satya Nadella notified employees of impending organizational changes, not limited to job cuts, required for the technology giant to return to its core business.[41] The global competition in the automotive industry among Japanese, U.S., and European car companies exemplifies the intensity that other industries can expect in the future.

In the midst of this international competition, managers must at the same time pay attention to changes and pressures within their own countries. This was exemplified in the in-depth study of a "whole-system" change program in the Scottish national healthcare system where the multilevel dynamics underlying organizational change and adaption were examined.[42] Managers must work across inter-organizational boundaries to ensure effective adaptation in bringing about successful organizational change. Global, economic, and organizational changes have dramatic effects on the study and management of organizational behavior.

1-6b Customer Focused for High Quality

Global competition has challenged organizations to become more customer focused, to meet changing product and service demands, and to exceed customers' expectations of high quality. Quality has

Managers must work across inter-organizational boundaries to ensure successful organizational change.

DENYS Rudyi/123RF

the potential to give organizations in viable industries a competitive edge against international competition. By aiming to be number one in experience, for example, Caribou Coffee competes with a customer-focused, high-quality approach.

Quality has become a rubric for products and services of high status. *Total quality* is defined in many ways.[43] *Total quality management (TQM)* is the total dedication to continuous improvement and to customers so that the customers' needs are met and their expectations exceeded. This customer-oriented philosophy of management has important implications for virtually all aspects of organizational behavior. Quality cannot be optimized because customer needs and expectations are always changing, but it is embedded in highly successful organizations. Part of what has catapulted Toyota to the top of the auto industry is its attention to quality and detail throughout the organization. Even though TQM consulting has experienced a boom-to-bust cycle, the main concepts underlying its initial rise in popularity are here to stay.

Quality improvement enhances the probability of organizational success in increasingly competitive industries. One study of 193 general medical hospitals examined seven TQM practices and found them positively related to the financial performance of the hospital.[44] Indeed, quality improvement is an enduring feature of an

TABLE 1.1	CONTRASTING SIX SIGMA AND TOTAL QUALITY MANAGEMENT
Six Sigma	**Total Quality Management**
Executive ownership	Self-directed work teams
Business strategy execution system	Quality initiative
Truly cross-functional	Largely within a single function
Focused training with verifiable return on investment	No mass training in statistics and quality Return on investment
Business results oriented	Quality oriented

SOURCE: M. Barney, "Motorola's Second Generation," *Six Sigma Forum Magazine* (May 2002): 13.

organization's culture and of the economic competition we face today. It leads to competitive advantage through customer responsiveness, results acceleration, and resource effectiveness.[45] In evaluating quality improvement ideas for people at work, three key questions should be asked: (1) Does the idea improve customer response? (2) Does the idea accelerate results? (3) Does the idea increase the effectiveness of resources? A "yes" answer means the idea should be implemented to improve quality.

Six Sigma is a philosophy for company-wide quality improvement developed by Motorola and popularized by General Electric. Characterized by its customer-driven approach, through its emphasis on using quantitative data to make decisions and its priority of saving money,[46] it has evolved into a high-performance system for executing business strategy. Part of its quality program is a twelve-step problem-solving method specifically designed to lead a Six Sigma "Black Belt" to significant improvement within a defined process. It tackles problems in four phases: (1) measure, (2) analyze, (3) improve, and (4) control. In addition, it forces executives to align the right objective and targets, and it forces quality improvement teams to mobilize for action in order to accelerate and monitor sustained improvement. Six Sigma is set up so that that it can be applied to a range of situations, from manufacturing settings to service work environments. Table 1.1 contrasts Six Sigma and TQM.

Any quality control method has some success and some failure, and some methods may work better in a given organization than others due to differences in organizational culture. One study, with a strong emphasis on exploring

Making Good Decisions and Forecasts

Computer-driven algorithms are adept at making decisions and providing forecasts, frequently of better quality than produced by unaided human intuition and judgment. Despite the evidence, researchers have found that when people have some experience with algorithms and have found them imperfect, they develop "algorithm aversions." One way to overcome this aversion has been tested and relies on giving algorithm users some degree of control over the machine. While tinkering with the algorithm may ultimately degrade its performance to some degree, the study results suggest that even these slightly flawed results are better than human prediction alone. In addition, they concluded that people value the ability to put their own imprint on a forecast, even if that is a small imprint, and do value to power of the algorithm more in making good quality decisions and forecasts.

SOURCE: J. Dietvorst, J. P. Simmons, and C. Massey, "Algorithms: People Like the Illusion of Control," *Harvard Business Review*, January–February 2017, p. 26.

Martin Barraud/Caiaimage/Getty Images

Quality is a customer-oriented philosophy of management with important implications for virtually all aspects of organizational behavior

statistical modeling techniques, compared Six Sigma to two other methods for quality improvement (specifically, Taguchi's methods and the Shainin system) and found it to be the most complete strategy of the three.[47] On the other hand, statistical data on the actual economic effect of Six Sigma is lacking, and the method has come under some critique.[48] It is important for managers to consider which of a variety of options is best for their organization.

1-6c Behavior and Quality at Work

Whereas total quality may draw on reliability engineering or just-in-time management, total quality improvement can succeed only when employees have the skills and authority to respond to customer needs.[49] Total quality has important direct effects on the behavior of employees at all levels in the organization, not just on employees working directly with customers. Thus, chief executives can advance total quality by engaging in participative management, being willing to change things, focusing quality efforts on customer service (not cost cutting), including quality as a criterion in reward systems, improving the flow of information regarding quality-improvement successes or failures, and being actively and personally involved in quality efforts. While serving as chair of Motorola, George Fisher emphasized the behavioral attributes of leadership, cooperation, communication, and participation as important elements in the company's Six Sigma program.

Quality improvement is crucial to competitive success. The U.S. Department of Commerce sponsors an annual award in the name of Malcolm Baldrige, former

secretary of commerce in the Reagan administration, to recognize companies excelling in quality improvement and management. The Malcolm Baldrige National Quality Award examination evaluates an organization in seven categories: leadership, information and analysis, strategic quality planning, human resource utilization, quality assurance of products and services, quality results, and customer satisfaction. Hospitals and health systems that have won the Malcolm Baldrige Award have excelled by integrating innovation into every aspect of healthcare delivery, from leadership and goal-setting to patient care.[50]

According to George H. W. Bush, "Quality management is not just a strategy. It must be a new style of working, even a new style of thinking. A dedication to quality and excellence is more than good business. It is a way of life, giving something back to society, offering your best to others."[51]

Quality is one watchword for competitive success. Organizations that do not respond to customer needs find their customers choosing alternative product and service suppliers who are willing to exceed customer expectations. Keep in mind, however, that total quality isn't a panacea for all organizations, and it doesn't guarantee unqualified success.

1-6d Managing Organizational Behavior in Changing Times

Over and above the challenge of quality improvement to meet international competition, managing organizational behavior during changing times is challenging for at least three other reasons: (1) the increasing globalization of organizations' operating territory, (2) the increasing diversity of organizational workforces, and (3) the continuing demand for higher levels of moral and ethical behavior at work.

Each of these three issues is explored in detail in Chapter 2 and highlighted throughout the text as they appear intertwined with contemporary organizational practices. For example, the issue of women in the workplace concerns workforce diversity and at the same time overlaps with the globalization issue. Gender roles are often defined differently in various cultures, and sexual harassment often plagues organizations in the United States, Europe, Israel, and South Africa.

1-7 LEARNING ABOUT ORGANIZATIONAL BEHAVIOR

The study of organizational behavior is based on scientific knowledge and applied practice. It involves abstract ideas, such as valence and expectancy in motivation, as well as concrete matters, such as observable behaviors and medical symptoms of distress at work. Therefore, learning about organizational behavior includes at least three activities, as shown in Figure 1.3. First, the science of organizational behavior requires the mastery of a certain body of **objective knowledge**. Objective knowledge results from research, experimentation, and scientific observation. Second, the practice of organizational behavior requires **skill development** based on knowledge and an understanding of oneself in order to master the abilities essential to success. Third, both objective knowledge and skill development must be applied in real-world settings.

Learning can be challenging and fun if student diversity is addressed in the learning process, when students have more options and can take greater responsibility as coproducers.[52] Teaching and learning styles should be aligned carefully, and educators should be aware that teaching is no longer merely verbal and visual but has now become virtual.[53] If you are a visual learner, use charts, maps, PowerPoint slides, videos, the Internet, notes, or flash cards and write things out

FIGURE 1.3 LEARNING ABOUT ORGANIZATIONAL BEHAVIOR

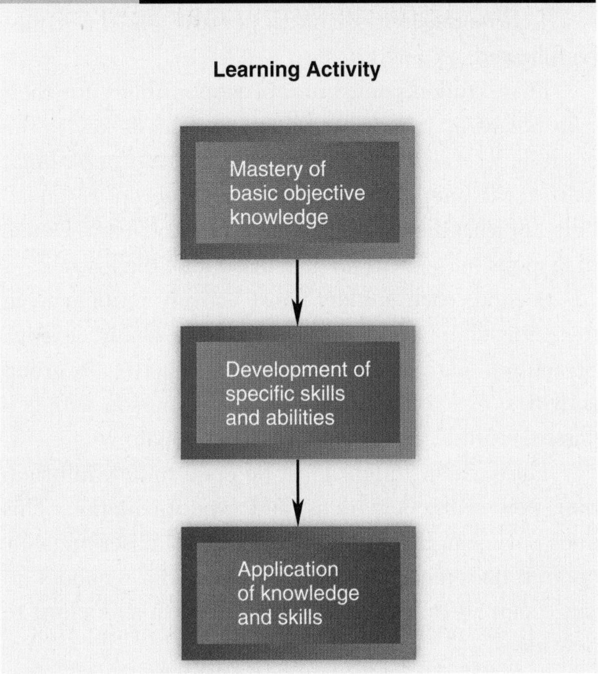

Learning Activity

Mastery of basic objective knowledge

↓

Development of specific skills and abilities

↓

Application of knowledge and skills

for visual review. If you are an auditory learner, then listen, take notes during lectures, consider taping them so that you can fill in gaps later, review your notes frequently, and recite key concepts aloud. If you are a tactile learner, trace words as you are saying them, write down facts several times, and make study sheets.

1-7a Objective Knowledge

In any field of study, objective knowledge is developed through basic and applied research. Since the early research on scientific management, research on organizational behavior has continued to provide objective knowledge involving theories, conceptual models, and various research findings. In this book, the objective knowledge in each chapter is reflected in the supporting notes. Mastering the concepts and ideas that come from these notes enables you to discuss intelligently topics such as motivation and work behavior[54] as well as stress and health.[55]

We encourage instructors and students of organizational behavior to think critically about the objective knowledge that has been gained in the study of organizational behavior. Only by engaging in critical thinking can one question or challenge the results of specific research or consider how such research should be applied in a particular work setting. Rote memorization does not prepare students to appreciate the complexity of specific theories or the intricacies of interrelated concepts, ideas, and topics. Critical thinking, by contrast, enables students to identify inconsistencies and limitations in the current body of objective knowledge.

Critical thinking, based on knowledge and understanding of basic ideas, leads to inquisitive exploration and is a key to accepting the responsibility of coproducer in the learning process. A questioning, probing attitude is at the core of critical thinking. The student of organizational behavior

objective knowledge Knowledge that results from research and scientific activities.

skill development The mastery of abilities essential to successful functioning in organizations.

FIGURE 1.4 LEARNING FROM STRUCTURED ACTIVITY

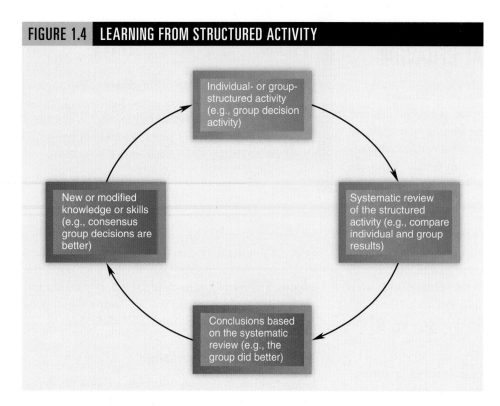

should evolve into a critical consumer of knowledge related to organizational behavior—one who is able to intelligently question the latest research results and distinguish plausible, sound, new approaches from fads that lack substance or adequate foundation. Ideally, the student of organizational behavior develops into a scientific, professional manager who is knowledgeable in the art and science of organizational behavior.

1-7b Skill Development

Learning about organizational behavior requires doing as well as knowing. Furthermore, the development of skills and abilities requires that students be challenged by the instructor and by themselves. The "What About You?" features on the Chapter Review Cards give you a chance to learn about yourself, challenge yourself, and apply what you are learning.

The U.S. Department of Labor tries to ensure that people acquire the necessary skills to be successful in the workplace.[56] The essential skills identified by the department are (1) resource management skills, such as time management; (2) information management skills, such as data interpretation; (3) personal interaction skills, such as teamwork; (4) systems behavior and performance skills, such as cause–effect relationships; and (5) technology utilization skills, such as troubleshooting. Many of these skills, such as decision making and information management, are directly related to the study of organizational

behavior.[57] Employers increasingly demand that workers possess effective teamwork and collaboration skills. Eighty percent of employers surveyed cited the ability to work in groups as a highly desirable attribute of recruits.[58]

Developing skills is different from acquiring objective knowledge because it requires structured practice and feedback. A key function of experiential learning is engaging the student in individual or group activities that are systematically reviewed, leading to new skills and understandings. However, objective knowledge acquisition and skill development are interrelated, as shown in Figure 1.4. The student engages in an individual- or group-structured activity and then systematically reviews that activity, gaining new or modified knowledge and skills.

If skill development and structured learning occur in this way, there should be an inherently self-correcting element to learning because of the modification of the student's knowledge and skills over time.[59] To ensure that skill development does occur and that the learning is self-correcting as it occurs, three basic guidelines must be followed.

First, students must accept responsibility for their own behavior, actions, and learning. This is key to the coproducer role in the learning process. A group cannot learn for its members. Members must accept responsibility for what they each individually do and learn. Denial of responsibility helps no one, least of all the learner.

Second, each student must actively participate in the individual- or group-structured learning activity. Structured learning is not passive; it is active. In group activities, everyone suffers if just one person adopts a passive attitude. All must actively participate.

Third, each student must be open to new information, new skills, new ideas, and experimentation. This does not mean that students should be indiscriminately open. It does mean that students should have nondefensive, open attitudes so that they can learn and adjust to new ideas.

BY THE NUMBERS

pio3/Shutterstock.com

1920s
supervisors at U.S. Steel issued pistols

$18.9 trillion
U.S. GDP in 2016

3
activities involved in learning organizational behavior

12
steps in the GE Six Sigma problem-solving method

47%
of the U.S. GDP comes from the service sector

1-7c Application of Knowledge and Skills

Understanding organizational behavior includes an appreciation and understanding of working realities as well as of science and of oneself. One of the advantages of structured, experiential learning is that a person can explore new behaviors and skills in a comparatively safe environment. Fortunately, losing your temper in a classroom activity and learning about the potentially adverse impact on other people will have dramatically different consequences from losing your temper with an important customer in a tense work situation. Thus, learning spaces that offer the interface of student learning styles with institutional learning environments give learners safe spaces to engage their brains to form abstract hypotheses, to actively test these hypotheses through concrete experiences, and to reflectively observe the outcomes in behavior and experience.[60] The ultimate objective of skill application and experiential learning is that one transfers the process employed in learning from structured activities in the classroom and learning spaces to learning from unstructured opportunities in the workplace.

Although organizational behavior is an applied discipline, students are not "trained" in organizational behavior. Rather, they are "educated" in organizational behavior and are coproducers in learning. The distinction between these two modes of learning is found in the degree of direct and immediate applicability of either knowledge or skills. As an activity, training ties objective knowledge or skill development more directly to specific applications. By contrast, education enhances a person's residual pool of objective knowledge and skills that may then be selectively applied later—sometimes significantly later—when the opportunity presents itself. Hence, education is consistent with the concept of lifelong learning. Especially in a growing area of knowledge such as organizational behavior, the student can think of the first course as the outset of lifelong learning about the subject.

> Learning about organizational behavior requires doing as well as knowing.

STUDY TOOLS 1

LOCATED AT BACK OF THE TEXTBOOK
☐ Rip Out Chapter Review Card

LOCATED AT WWW.CENGAGE.COM/LOGIN
☐ Gain unique perspectives on key concepts with new Concept Clip videos in the e-book

☐ Review key term flashcards and create your own

☐ Increase your comprehension with online homework and quizzes

2 | Challenges for Managers

LEARNING OBJECTIVES

2-1 Describe the factors that affect organizations competing in the global economy.

2-2 Explain how cultural differences form the basis of work-related attitudes.

2-3 Describe the challenges and positive influences diversity brings to today's business environment.

2-4 Discuss the role of ethics, character, and personal integrity in the organization.

2-5 Explain five issues that pose ethical dilemmas for managers.

After finishing this chapter go to **PAGE 33** for **STUDY TOOLS**

Key challenges that managers face today stem from the fact that business is increasingly global in scope.[1] Globalization is driven by the spread of economic logics centered on freeing, opening, deregulating, and privatizing economies to attract investment as well as technological innovations that are revolutionizing communication.[2] The resulting challenges for managers can be viewed as both opportunities and threats.

Chief executive officers of U.S. corporations have cited three challenges managers must overcome to remain competitive: (1) globalizing the firm's operations to compete in the global village; (2) leading a diverse workforce; and (3) encouraging positive ethics, character, and personal integrity.[3]

2-1 COMPETING IN THE GLOBAL ECONOMY

Only a few years ago, business conducted across national borders was referred to as *international* activity, a term implying that the individual's or the organization's nationality is held strongly in consciousness.[4] *Globalization*, by contrast, suggests that the world is free from national boundaries and is borderless.[5] U.S. workers now compete with workers in other countries. Organizations from other countries, such as the auto manufacturers Honda, Toyota, Nissan, and Daimler Benz, are establishing subsidiaries in the United States.

Similarly, what were once called *multinational organizations* (organizations that did business in several countries) are now referred to as **transnational organizations**, indicating that the global viewpoint supersedes national issues.[6] Transnational organizations such as 3M, Dow Chemical, and Coca-Cola operate worldwide across long distances and employ a multicultural mix of workers.

2-1a Social and Political Changes

Social and political upheavals have led organizations to change the way they conduct business as a result of thinking globally. Toyota, for example, is one Japanese company thinking big, thinking globally, and thinking differently by learning to speak to the 60-million-strong Generation Y, or so-called millennials.[7]

Business ventures in China have become increasingly attractive to U.S. companies. One challenge U.S. managers have tackled is understanding the Chinese way of doing business, ways that have been shaped by the Communist Party, socialism, feudalistic values, and *guanxi* (building networks for social exchange). Once *guanxi* is established, individuals can ask favors of each other with the expectation that the favor will be returned. Thus, many Chinese use *guanxi*, or personal connections, to conduct business or obtain jobs.

The concept of *guanxi* is not unique to China. There are similar concepts in many other countries, including Russia and Haiti. It is a broad term that can mean anything from strongly loyal relationships to ceremonial gift giving, sometimes seen as bribery. *Guanxi* is more common in societies with underdeveloped legal support for private businesses.[8]

What major challenges must managers overcome to remain competitive?

Americans can learn to build their own *guanxi* in order to interact effectively with Chinese managers. This would involve understanding the Chinese chain of command and negotiating slow, general agreements. Using the foreign government as a local franchisee may be effective in China. For example, KFC's operation in China is a joint venture between KFC (60%) and two Chinese government bodies (40%).[9]

The opening of trade barriers is a third issue that affects organizations competing in a global economy. In 1993, the European Union integrated fifteen nations into a single market by removing trade barriers. At that time, the member nations

transnational organization
An organization in which the global viewpoint supersedes national issues.

guanxi The Chinese practice of building networks for social exchange.

Companies like Coca-Cola are transnational and are recognized around the world.

their products, and many companies located plants in Mexico to take advantage of low labor costs. Prior to NAFTA, Mexico placed heavy tariffs on U.S. exports. The agreement immediately eliminated many of these tariffs and provided that the remaining tariffs be phased out over time.

Given these changes, managers must think globally and adopt a long-term view. Entering global markets requires long-term strategies.

2-1b Cultural Differences

Managers need to not only understand the climate and culture of their own organizations,[10a] they must also understand cultural differences and diversity. Whether managing culturally diverse individuals within a single location or managing individuals at remote locations around the globe, organizations must appreciate the differences among cultures. Edgar Schein suggests that to understand an organization's culture or, more broadly, any culture, one should dig below the surface of visible artifacts and uncover the basic underlying assumptions at the core of the culture.[11]

Microcultural differences (i.e., differences within cultures) are key to our understanding of the global work environment.[12] One such difference is the gap between generations, which Toyota, as previously mentioned, is addressing by learning to speak to the 60-million-strong millennial Generation Y.[13]

When considering differences among cultures, symbols are extremely important because they can generate misunderstanding or inhibit communication if they are interpreted incorrectly. Consider the thumbs-up sign, which means approval in the United States but is an obscene gesture in Australia. Consider also the Windows icon representing a manila file folder, which is meaningless to Europeans who have never used such folders.[14]

Do cultural differences translate into differences in work-related attitudes? To answer this question, the pioneering Dutch researcher Geert Hofstede, with his colleagues, surveyed 160,000 managers and employees of IBM working in sixty different countries. Thus, the researchers were able to study individuals from the same company in the same jobs but living in different countries. They found that national culture explains more differences in work-related attitudes than does age, gender, profession, or position in the organization. Five dimensions of cultural differences that formed the basis for work-related attitudes were identified (Figure 2.1).[15]

of the European Union were Austria, Belgium, Denmark, Finland, France, Germany, Greece, Ireland, Italy, Luxembourg, the Netherlands, Portugal, Spain, Sweden, and the United Kingdom. By 2007 Bulgaria, Cyprus, the Czech Republic, Estonia, Hungary, Latvia, Lithuania, Malta, Poland, Romania, Slovakia, and Slovenia had also joined. Europe's integration provides many opportunities for U.S. organizations to engage 494 million potential customers. Companies such as Ford Motor Company and IBM, which entered the market early with wholly-owned subsidiaries, were able to capitalize on their much anticipated head start.[10] Competition within the European Union will intensify, however, as will competition from Japan and the former Soviet nations.

The United States, Canada, and Mexico dramatically reduced trade barriers with the North American Free Trade Agreement (NAFTA), which took effect in 1994. Organizations found promising new markets for

FIGURE 2.1 HOFSTEDE'S DIMENSIONS OF CULTURAL DIFFERENCES

Individualism ⟷ Collectivism

High power distance ⟷ Low power distance

High uncertainty avoidance ⟷ Low uncertainty avoidance

Masculinity ⟷ Femininity

Long-term orientation ⟷ Short-term orientation

SOURCE: Based on Academy of Management, P.O. Box 3020, Briarcliff Manor, NY 10510-8020. Cultural Constraints in Management Theories. G. Hofstede, Academy of Management Executive 7 (1993).

Management careers have taken on a global dimension in that working in transnational organizations may give managers the opportunity to work in other countries. **Expatriate managers**, those who work in a country other than their home country, benefit greatly from knowledge of cultural differences.

International executives are executives whose jobs have international scope, whether they have an expatriate assignment or deal with international issues.

FAST FACT

Immigrants Fuel Start-Up Take Offs

Foreign-born workers are important contributors to new-business creation. Immigrants account for 27 percent of entrepreneurs, a number that has risen sharply since the 1990s. Twenty-six percent of employees in new firms are immigrants, and 37 percent of new firms are started by at least one immigrant. The positive impact of immigrants on start-ups is impressive by the numbers. While immigrant entrepreneurs risk failure as do native-founded firms, those immigrant entrepreneurial firms that survive show faster employment and payroll growth. The conclusion is that non-native (immigrant) entrepreneurs are very successful and have a positive economic and human impact on the U.S. economy.

SOURCE: S.P. Kerr and W.R. Kerr, "Entrepreneurship: How Immigrants Fuel Start-Ups," *Harvard Business Review*, January–February 2017, p. 26.

What kind of competencies should an individual develop to prepare for an international career? Some key competencies are integrity, insightfulness, risk taking, courage to take a stand, and ability to bring out the best in people. Learning-oriented attributes of international executives include cultural adventurousness, flexibility, openness to criticism, desire to seek learning opportunities, and sensitivity to cultural differences.[16]

Further, strong human capital generally has a positive effect on internationalization.[17] Notice that all these qualities are based on core competencies and the ability to learn from experience.

Because workplace customs vary widely, understanding cultural differences becomes especially important for companies that are considering opening foreign offices. It is wise to do the research in advance. Consulate offices and companies operating within the foreign country provide excellent information about national customs and legal requirements. Table 2.1 presents a business guide to cultural differences in three countries: Japan, Mexico, and Saudi Arabia.

Another reality affecting global business practices is the cost of layoffs in other countries. As the economy has become more global, downsizing has presented challenges worldwide. For example, dismissing a forty-five-year-old middle manager with twenty years of service and a $50,000 annual salary varied in cost from a low of $13,000 in Ireland to a high of $130,000 in Italy.[18] Laying off this manager in the United States would have cost approximately $19,000. The wide variability in costs stems from the various legal protections that certain countries give workers. In Italy, laid-off employees must receive a so-called notice period payment (one year's pay if they have nine years or more of service) plus a severance payment (based on pay and years of service). U.S. companies operating overseas often adopt the European tradition of training and retraining workers to avoid overstaffing and potential layoffs. Appreciating the customs and rules for doing business in another country is essential to global success.

expatriate manager A manager who works in a country other than her or his home country.

©Artishok / shutterstock 125877440

TABLE 2.1 BUSINESS GUIDE TO CULTURAL DIFFERENCES

Country	Appointments	Dress	Gifts	Negotiations
Japan	Punctuality is a necessity. It is considered rude to be late.	Conservative dress is the norm for men and women in large to medium-sized companies, though pastel shirts are common. One may be expected to remove shoes in temples and homes, as well as in some ryokan (inn) style restaurants. In that case, slip-on shoes should be worn.	Important part of Japanese business protocol. Gifts are typically exchanged among colleagues on July 15 and January 1 to commemorate midyear and the year's end, respectively.	Business cards (*mishit*) are an important part of doing business and key for establishing credentials. One side of your card should be in English and the other in Japanese. It is an asset to include information such as membership in professional associations.
Mexico	Punctuality is not always as much of a priority. Nonetheless, Mexicans are accustomed to North Americans arriving on time, and most Mexicans in business, if not government, will try to return the favor.	Dark, conservative suits and ties are the norm for most men. Standard office attire for women includes dresses, skirted suits, or skirts and blouses. Femininity is strongly encouraged in women's dress.	Not usually a requirement in business dealings, though presenting a small gift is generally appreciated as a gesture of goodwill. If giving a gift, be aware that inquiring about what the receiver would like to receive may offend.	Mexicans avoid directly saying "no." A "no" is often disguised in responses such as "maybe" or "we'll see." You should also use this indirect approach in your dealings. Otherwise, your Mexican counterparts may perceive you as being rude and pushy.
Saudi Arabia	It is customary to make appointments for times of day rather than precise hours. The importance Saudis attach to courtesy and hospitality can cause delays that prevent keeping to a strict schedule.	The only absolute requirement of dress code is modesty. For men, this means covering everything from navel to knee. In public, women are required to cover everything except the face, hands, and feet by wearing an *abaya* (standard black cloak) and headscarf.	Should only be given to the most intimate of friends. For a Saudi to receive a present from a lesser acquaintance is so embarrassing that it is considered offensive.	Business cards are common but not essential. If used, the common practice is to have both English and Arabic printed on the same side so that neither language is perceived as less important by being on the reverse of the same card.

SOURCE: Adapted from information obtained from business culture guides accessed online at http://www.ExecutivePlanet.Com.

CULTURAL DIFFERENCES AND WORK-RELATED ATTITUDES

Hofstede's work has implications for work-related attitudes. We'll now take a closer look at how his five dimensions of cultural differences are manifest in a variety of countries.

2-2a Individualism versus Collectivism

In cultures where **individualism** predominates, the social framework is loose and employees put loyalty to themselves and their families ahead of loyalty to their company and work group. Cultures characterized by **collectivism**, on the other hand, are tightly knit social frameworks in which individual members depend strongly on others and group decisions are valued and accepted.

North American and European cultures are individualistic in orientation. Managers in Great Britain and the Netherlands, for example, emphasize and encourage individual achievement. In contrast, in collectivist cultures, such as Israeli *kibbutzim* and Japan, people view group loyalty and unity as paramount. Collectivistic managers seek to fit harmoniously within the group and encourage their employees to do the same. The world's regions are patterned with varying degrees of this cultural difference.

2-2b Power Distance

Power distance relates to the acceptance of the unequal distribution of power. In countries with a high power distance, bosses are afforded more authority, which is seldom bypassed, titles are used, and formality is the rule. Managers and employees in such countries see one another as fundamentally different kinds of people. India, Venezuela, and Mexico all demonstrate high power distance.

In societies with low power distance, people believe in minimizing inequality. People at various power levels in these countries are less threatened by and more willing to trust one another. Managers and employees judge each other on a basis of equality. Managers are given authority only if they have expertise. Employees frequently bypass the boss in order to get work done in countries with a low power distance, such as Denmark and Australia.

2-2c Uncertainty Avoidance

Cultures with high **uncertainty avoidance** are concerned with security and tend to avoid conflict. People in such cultures tend to seek consensus in an effort to

In feminine cultures, relationships and concern for others are emphasized. Nations with feminine cultures include Denmark, Sweden, the Netherlands, and Norway.

Kichigin/Shutterstock.com

moderate the threat of life's inherent uncertainty. Cultures with low uncertainty avoidance tolerate ambiguity better. People are more willing to take risks and are more comfortable with individual differences. Conflict is seen as constructive, and people accept dissenting viewpoints. Accordingly, Norwegians and Australians value job mobility because they have low uncertainty avoidance; Japan and Italy are characterized by high uncertainty avoidance, and so, not surprisingly, their cultures emphasize career stability.

2-2d Masculinity versus Femininity

In cultures characterized by traditional **masculinity**, assertiveness and materialism are valued. Men, the idea goes, should be assertive, tough, and decisive, whereas women should be nurturing, modest, and tender.[19] Money and possessions are very important in this viewpoint, and performance is what counts. Achievement is admired. Cultures characterized by traditional **femininity** emphasize relationships and concern for others. Men and women are expected to

individualism A cultural orientation in which people belong to loose social frameworks and their primary concern is for themselves and their families.

collectivism A cultural orientation in which individuals belong to tightly knit social frameworks and depend strongly on extended families or clans.

power distance The degree to which a culture accepts unequal distribution of power.

uncertainty avoidance The degree to which a culture tolerates ambiguity and uncertainty.

masculinity A cultural orientation in which assertiveness and materialism are valued.

femininity A cultural orientation in which relationships and concern for others are valued.

> In cultures with low power distance, managers are more likely to consult employees and work with them to achieve harmonious results.

assume both assertive and nurturing roles. Quality of life is very important, and people and the environment are emphasized.

2-2e Time Orientation

Cultures also differ in **time orientation**. A culture's values may be oriented toward the future (long-term orientation) or toward the past and present (short-term orientation).[20] In China, which has a long-term orientation, values such as thrift and persistence, which look toward the future, are emphasized. Russians generally have a short-term orientation and particularly value respect for tradition (past) and meeting social obligations (present).

Hofstede found the United States to be the most individualistic country of any he studied. It ranked among the countries with weak power distance, and its level of uncertainty avoidance indicated a tolerance of uncertainty. The United States also ranked as a masculine culture with a short-term orientation. These values have shaped U.S. management theory, so Hofstede's work casts doubt on the universal applicability of U.S. management theories. Because these dimensions vary widely, management practices should be adjusted to account for cultural differences. Managers in transnational organizations must learn as much as they can about other cultures in order to lead their culturally diverse organizations effectively.

time orientation Whether a culture's values are oriented toward the future (long-term orientation) or toward the past and present (short-term orientation).

diversity All forms of difference among individuals, including culture, gender, age, ability, religion, personality, social status, and sexual orientation.

2-2f Developing Cross-Cultural Sensitivity

In today's multicultural environment, it is imperative that organizations help their employees recognize and appreciate cultural differences. One way companies do this is through cultural sensitivity training. IBM's cultural sensitivity program, Global Citizens Portfolio, consists of flexible spending accounts that employees can use to enhance their training and in turn benefit the company.[21] Another way to develop sensitivity is by using cross-cultural task forces or teams. The Milwaukee-based GE Medical Systems Group (GEMS), with 19,000 employees working worldwide, has developed a vehicle for bringing together managers from each of its three regions (the Americas, Europe, and Asia) to work on a variety of business projects. Their Global Leadership Program forms several work groups made up of managers from various regions and has them work together on important projects, such as worldwide employee integration, to increase employees' sense of belonging throughout the GEMS international organization.[22] Because cultural differences are constantly in flux, it is important for managers to foster up-to-date knowledge of relevant cultural trends.

The globalization of business affects all parts of the organization, but particularly human resource management. Human resource managers must adopt a global view of human resource planning, recruitment and selection, compensation, and training and development. This means that they must possess a working knowledge of the legal systems in various countries as well as of global economics, culture, and customs. Not only do HR managers prepare U.S. workers to live outside their native country, but they also help foreign employees interact with U.S. culture. Global human resource management is a complex field, one that is critical to organizations' success in the global marketplace.

2-3 THE DIVERSE WORKFORCE

Cultural differences contribute a great deal to the diversity of the workforce, but other forms of diversity are important as well. **Diversity** encompasses all forms of difference among individuals, including surface-level differences such as gender, national origin, age, and race and deep-level differences such as personality, religion, social status, and sexual orientation. Largely because of demographic changes in the working population, diversity has garnered increasing attention in recent years. Managers feel that dealing with diversity is a paramount concern for two reasons: first, they need to motivate diverse work groups, and, second, they must communicate with employees who have different values and language skills.

Several demographic trends are affecting organizations. By the year 2020, the workforce will be more culturally diverse, more female, and older than ever. Thus, workforce demographic change and diversity are critical challenges for the study and management of organizational behavior.[23] The theories of motivation, leadership, and group behavior based on research in a workforce of one composition may not be applicable in a workforce of a very different composition.[24] This may be especially problematic if ethnic, gender, and/or religious differences lead to conflict between leaders and followers in organizations. Still another factor in diversity involves individuals with disabilities because recent legislation and new technologies have helped more **disabled workers** enter the workforce. Hence, learning to work together with an open mind is an increasingly important skill. Alcon Laboratories, the Swiss-owned and Fort Worth-based international company whose mission is to improve and preserve eyesight, is an example of the kind of organization that offers diversity training to help employees learn to work together.

2-3a Ethnic Diversity

The globalization of business is not the only force promoting cultural and ethnic diversity in the workplace. Changing domestic demographics also affect organizations' cultural diversity. By 2020, minorities will constitute more than one-half of the new entrants to the U.S. workforce. Yet African Americans and Hispanic Americans are overrepresented in declining occupations, thus limiting their opportunities. Further, African Americans and Hispanic Americans tend to live in a few large cities that are facing severe economic difficulties and high crime rates. Minority workers are less likely to be prepared because they are less likely to have had satisfactory schooling and on-the-job training, which will likely put them at a disadvantage within organizations. It need not be this way. For example, Coca-Cola has made substantial progress on diversity by monitoring its human resource systems, and companies such as Motorola already recognize and meet these needs by focusing on basic skills training.[25]

In sum, the globalization of business and changing demographic trends present organizations with a culturally diverse workforce, creating both challenge and risk. The challenge is to harness the wealth of differences provided by cultural diversity. The risk is that prejudices and stereotypes may prevent managers and employees from developing synergies to benefit the

Women are creating businesses at a faster rate than ever before.

organization. Diversity of the workforce was a major factor in the innovation that drove the dot-com boom in Silicon Valley, illustrating that the benefits of a diverse workforce make good management of these challenges and risks important.[26]

2-3b Gender Diversity

The number of women in the U.S. labor force reached its peak in 1999 with a rate of 60%. Since then, the participation rate for women (as for men) declined to 57.2% in 2013.[27]

Women are better prepared to contribute in organizations than ever before because they earn 51% of all doctorates, 60% of master's degrees, and 57% of all bachelor's degrees.[28] But their share of authority and compensation is not increasing commensurately with their education and participation in the workforce. Half of the males in the workforce occupy line positions, compared to only one-quarter of women in business.[29] American Express is an exception to the rule. Rated as one of the top 50 companies for executive women in 2015 by the National Association for Female Executives (NAFE), American Express not only places women in top positions, it also provides them training and experiences that expand their skills.[30] Nonetheless, median weekly earnings for women persist at a level of 81% of their male counterparts' earnings.[31] Because benefits are tied to compensation, women also receive fewer benefits.

The **glass ceiling** is a transparent barrier that keeps women from rising above a certain level in organizations. In the

glass ceiling A transparent barrier that keeps women from rising above a certain level in organizations.

United States, it has been rare to find women in positions above middle management.[32] Although growth in opportunities for women to attain executive positions has recently stagnated, the situation is improving for women in the boardroom. Women currently hold 23.4% of board seats in S&P 500 companies, up from 15% in 2010.[33] Research has shown that companies that have gender-diverse board leadership performed better across dimensions of corporate social performance (CSP).[34] The ultimate glass ceiling may well be the professional partnership. Although women account for 34% of legal professionals, they account for only 21% of the partners.[35] Women are preserving their professional identities during pregnancy through strategies such as keeping up the same work pace and not asking for special accommodations.[35a]

Globally, the leadership picture for women is improving. For example, the number of female political leaders has grown dramatically worldwide in recent decades. In the 1970s, there were only five such leaders. In the 1990s, twenty-one female leaders came into power, and today women around the world are leading major global companies. Note, however, that these global female business leaders do not come predominantly from the West. In addition, a large number of women have founded entrepreneurial businesses.

Removing obstacles to women's success presents a major challenge for organizations. If they do not help the increasing numbers of female employees achieve their potential, they risk underutilizing the talents of half the U.S. workforce. Therefore, it is wise for organizations to develop policies that promote equity in pay and benefits, to encourage benefit programs of special interest to women, and to provide equal starting salaries for jobs of equal value. Corporations that shatter the glass ceiling share several practices:

1. Upper managers demonstrate support for the advancement of women.

2. Leaders incorporate practices into their diversity management programs to ensure that women perceive the organization as attractive.[36]

3. Women are represented on standing committees addressing key strategic business issues and are targeted for participation in executive education programs.

4. Systems are put in place to identify women with high potential for advancement.[37]

Companies such as IBM and Ernst & Young work for diversity not only by offering excellent programs for advancing and developing women executives, but also by judging supervisors based on their active support for such endeavors.[38]

2-3c Age Diversity

The graying of the U.S. workforce is another source of workplace diversity. Older Americans, aged 65 or older, number 41 million, or 13% of the U.S. population. That equates to more than one in every eight individuals. The number of middle-aged Americans (aged 45 to 64 years) increased by 33% during the same period. The 65 and over population is projected to increase to 80 million by 2040.[39]

This change in worker profile has profound implications for organizations. The job crunch among

HOT TREND

Women Make Gains Toward Winning CEO Jobs

When proxy statements appeared in 2016, 13 women were president or chief operating officer of an S&P 500 company. This number is up from just nine when the 2006 proxy statements appeared a decade earlier. The numbers are still small, but they are growing. Women represent the strongest internal contenders for the corner office at a small but growing number of major U.S. companies. The ultimate prize is the CEO job. Nearly all of the 15 women appointed CEO at S&P 500 companies between 2012 and fall 2016 ascended internally. Research looks at gender asymmetry, with men winning promotion based on potential while women win promotion based on actual results. That is why the line and operational jobs are so critical for women's success in ascent to the CEO position. Interestingly, at Kohl's, the *two* leading contenders for the CEO spot are both women.

SOURCE: J.S. Lublin, "Women Make Gains toward Winning CEO Job; There are strong internal candidates to lead Tupperware, Kohl's, Abercrombie, Verizon," *Wall Street Journal*, 17 Jan. 2017.

middle-aged workers will intensify as companies seek flatter organizational structures and eliminate middle-management jobs. Older workers are often higher paid, and companies that employ large numbers of aging baby boomers may find these pay scales a handicap to competitiveness.[40] Paid volunteerism, however, can be a draw to younger generations.[41] Conversely, a more experienced, stable, reliable, and healthier workforce can pay dividends to companies. A recent study showed that age diversity among employees in Western companies had a positive impact on profitability.[42] The baby boomers are well trained and educated, and their knowledge is a definite asset to organizations.

The aging workforce is increasing intergenerational contact at work.[43] As organizations flatten, workers traditionally segregated by old corporate hierarchies find themselves working together. Four generations are cooperating: the *silent generation* (people born from 1930 through 1945), a small group that includes most organizations' top managers; the *baby boomers* (people born from 1946 through 1964), whose substantial numbers give them a strong influence; the *baby bust generation*, popularly known as *Generation X* (those born from 1965 through 1976); and the subsequent generation, tentatively called *Generation Y*, *millennial*, or the *baby boomlet* (those born after 1976).[44] The millennial often bring new challenges to the workplace because of their early access to technology and their continuing connection to parents.[45]

The differences in attitudes and values among these four generations can be substantial, and managers struggle to integrate their workers into a cohesive group. Most leadership positions are currently held by members of the silent generation. Baby boomers tend to (1) regard the silent generation as complacent, (2) strive for moral rights in the workplace, and (3) take a more activist position regarding employee rights. The baby busters, newer to the workplace, are often impatient, want short-term gratification, and value a greater balance between family and work. They scorn the achievement orientation and materialism of the baby boomers. Members of Generation Y, on the other hand, place high importance on independence and creativity, and they are less inclined to settle for work that is not in line with their values.

Younger workers may have false impressions of older workers, viewing them as resistant to change, unable to learn new work methods, less physically capable, and less creative than younger employees. Research indicates, however, that older employees are more satisfied with their jobs, more committed to the organization, and more internally motivated than their younger cohorts.[46] Research also indicates that direct experience with older workers reduces younger workers' negative beliefs.[47] Motivating aging workers and helping them maintain high levels of contribution to the organization is a key task for managers.

2-3d Ability Diversity

Employees with different abilities present yet another form of diversity. Individuals with disabilities are an underutilized human resource. An estimated 50 million individuals with disabilities live in the United States, and their unemployment rate is estimated to exceed 50%.[48] Nevertheless, they have entered the workforce in greater numbers since the Americans with Disabilities Act went into effect in the summer of 1992. The act defines a person with a disability as "anyone possessing a physical or mental impairment that substantially limits one or more major life activities."[49] Under this law, employers are required to make reasonable accommodations

Erase Your Past and Act Your Age

Dmytro Zinkevych/Shutterstock.com

Age bias is real and one of the unconscious stereotypes that plays in many minds in the workplace. Experienced and seasoned professionals must learn to negotiate in this reality without losing their integrity through the process. There are several recommended ways of achieving both objectives. First, erase dates on your work history before the year 2000. Design your resumé so that those years do not appear. The lessons learned during those years are the tuition more experienced professionals pay for their advanced mastery, so do not forget that. There are three tips for experienced professionals managing around age bias. First, be specific about using a new technology or learning from a younger colleague or boss. Second, be passionate because that is the one thing younger candidates have since they lack experience. Third, be your age and act your age rather than attempting to mimic younger generations. Career moves are for older employees too. Go for it!

SOURCE: E. McGirt, "Facebook: Iterating Diversity?" *Fortune*, Feb. 1, 2017, p. 55.

McJOBS is a plan by McDonald's to recruit, train, and retain individuals with disabilities.

to permit workers with disabilities to perform jobs. The act's protection encompasses a broad range of illnesses that produce disabilities, including acquired immune deficiency syndrome (AIDS), cancer, hypertension, anxiety disorders, dyslexia, blindness, and cerebral palsy, to name only a few.

Some companies recognized the value of employing workers with disabilities long before the legislation. In 1981, McDonald's created McJOBS, a corporate plan to recruit, train, and retain individuals with disabilities, which has hired more than 9,000 mentally and physically challenged individuals.[50] Its participants include workers with visual, hearing, or orthopedic impairments; learning disabilities; and developmental disabilities. McJOBS holds sensitivity training sessions with managers and crew members before workers go onsite to help workers without disabilities understand what it means to be a worker with a disabling condition. Most McJOBS

workers start part-time and advance according to their abilities and the opportunities available.

2-3e Sexual Orientation and Gender Identity

Another type of workplace diversity is sexual orientation and gender identity. Increasing numbers of employees identify as gay, lesbian, bisexual, or transgender (LGBT). Because many in the LGBT community are not "out," the exact population cannot be determined. Nearly 49 percent of bisexual employees reported that they had not come out to anyone at their workplace. A recent Gallup poll, however, found that 4.1 percent of Americans identify as LGBT. Another study found that an estimated 9 million individuals or 4 percent of the U.S. population is lesbian, gay, or bisexual.

LGBT workers present organizations with opportunities and challenges. Sixty-six percent of Fortune 500 companies offer domestic partner health benefits, and 89 percent have nondiscrimination policies that include sexual orientation. While gay and transgender employees have become more commonplace in organizations, they still experience unfair treatment including discrimination, harassment, or violence in the workplace.[51] Organizations that treat all employees fairly and respectfully despite their sexual identity will have an advantage in attracting and recruiting potential employees, customers, and clients. Research has found a positive connection between companies' adoption of LGBT-friendly policies and their stock price. The decision to offer LGBT-friendly HR policies often depends on external factors such as state and local policies and pressure to match competitor

offerings. The demographic composition of the board can also affect whether companies offer HR benefits to same-sex employees. Companies that have more women board members are more likely to adopt LGBT-friendly HR policies.[52] Dallas-based AT&T was listed as number one of the top ten companies for LGBT employees for its employee development practices especially designed to promote inclusion of LGBT employees as well as women, veterans, and people with disabilities.[53]

TABLE 2.2 THE BENEFITS AND PROBLEMS OF DIVERSITY	
Benefits	**Problems**
> Attracts and retains the best talent	> Resistance to change
> Improves marketing efforts	> Lack of cohesiveness
> Promotes creativity and innovation	> Communication problems
> Results in better problem solving	> Interpersonal conflicts
> Enhances organizational flexibility	> Slower decision making

2-3f Valuing Diversity

Diversity involves more than culture, gender, age, ability, and personality. It also encompasses religion, social status, and sexual orientation. These diversity types lend heterogeneity to the workforce.

Managers must combat prejudice and discrimination to manage diversity. *Prejudice* is an attitude, whereas *discrimination* describes behavior. Both diminish organizational productivity in that they present obstacles to promoting and compensating good workers fairly. Discrimination poses challenges to an organization's ability to attract and recruit prospective workers, retain good human talent, and maintain positive work environments that employees perceive as fair and inclusive.[54] The potential for unfair treatment increases as the workforce becomes increasingly diverse. Combating stereotypes is essential. For example, a recent study revealed that male bosses sometimes hold certain stereotypes that negatively influence their interaction with female employees of color.[55] Open communication can help clarify misperceptions and clear the way for advancement.

Diversity helps organizations in many ways. Some organizations recognize the potential benefits of aggressively working to increase the diversity of their workforces. Yum! Brands' Kentucky Fried Chicken (KFC) tries to attract and retain female and minority-group executives. A president of KFC's U.S. operations said, "We want to bring in the best people. If there are two equally qualified people, we'd clearly like to have diversity."[56]

In an effort to understand and appreciate diversity, Alcon Laboratories developed a diversity training class called Working Together. The course takes advantage of two key ideas. First, people work best when they are valued and when diversity is taken into account. Second, when people feel valued, they build relationships and work together as a team.[57] Even majority-group managers may be more supportive of diversity training if they appreciate their own ethnic identity. One evaluation of diversity training found that participants preferred training with a traditional title and a broad focus.[58] Further, women were found to react more positively to diversity training than were men. A conclusion from the evaluation was that companies should measure the effects of training so that they can monitor its positive payoffs.

Managing diversity helps companies become more competitive, but effective diversity management involves more than simply being a good corporate citizen or complying with affirmative action.[59] Managing diversity requires a painful examination of employees' hidden assumptions. Having empathy, being able to see and understand the viewpoints of others, is an essential component of Emotional Intelligence (EI) and important for developing and maintaining relationships with others, whether minority or majority. Biases and prejudices about people's differences must be uncovered and dealt with so that differences can be celebrated and used to their full advantage.

2-3g Diversity's Benefits and Problems

Although diversity has the potential to enhance organizational performance, it may pose some problems as well. Table 2.2 summarizes the main benefits and

> The toughest problems for managers to resolve include employee theft, environmental issues, comparable worth of employees, conflicts of interest, and sexual harassment.

problems with diversity at work. The first main benefit of diversity management is that it helps firms attract and retain the best available human talent. The companies topping the lists of the best places to work are usually excellent at managing diversity. A second benefit is that diversity aids marketing efforts. Just as workforces are diversifying, so are markets. A diverse workforce, therefore, can improve a company's marketing plans by drawing on insights from various employees' cultural backgrounds. Third, diversity promotes creativity and innovation. The most innovative companies, such as Hewlett-Packard, deliberately build diverse teams to foster creativity. Fourth, diversity improves problem solving. Diverse groups bring more expertise and experience to bear on problems and decisions, and they encourage higher levels of critical thinking. Fifth, diversity enhances organizational flexibility because it makes an organization challenge old assumptions and become more adaptable. These five benefits add up to competitive advantage for companies with well-managed diversity.

We must also recognize diversity's potential problems. Five problems are particularly notable: resistance to change, lack of cohesiveness, communication problems, interpersonal conflicts, and slower decision making. People are attracted to and are more comfortable with others like themselves. Thus, it stands to reason that workers may resist diversity efforts when they are forced to interact with others unlike themselves. Managers should be prepared for this resistance rather than naively assuming that everybody supports diversity. Another difficulty with diversity is the issue of cohesiveness, that invisible glue that holds a group together. Cohesive groups have higher morale and better communication, but diverse groups take longer to achieve cohesiveness, so they may also take longer to develop high morale.

Another obstacle to performance in diverse groups is communication. Culturally diverse groups may encounter special communication barriers. Misunderstandings can lower work group effectiveness by creating conflict and hampering decision making.[60]

consequential theory An ethical theory that emphasizes the consequences or results of behavior.

Scottish philosopher Adam Smith presented a doctrine of natural liberty.

Heartland Arts/Shutterstock.com

2-4 ETHICS, CHARACTER, AND PERSONAL INTEGRITY

Managers frequently face ethical dilemmas and tradeoffs. Merck & Company is an example of a company that manages ethical issues well, and its emphasis on ethical behavior has consistently earned it a place on *Business Ethics'* list of top 100 corporate citizens.[61] For many organizations, however, unethical conduct sometimes occurs despite their best attempts to prevent such problems. The toughest problems for managers to resolve include employee theft, environmental issues, comparable worth of employees, conflicts of interest, and sexual harassment.[62] Ethical leadership can be a powerful antidote for these problems, contributing to group ethical voice and to positive ethical performance.[62a]

Ethical theories help us understand, evaluate, and classify moral arguments; make decisions; and then defend conclusions about what is right and wrong. Ethical theories can be classified as consequential, rule-based, or character theories.

2-4a Consequential Theories of Ethics

Consequential theories of ethics emphasize the consequences or results of behavior. John Stuart Mill's *utilitarianism*, a well-known consequential theory, suggests that the consequences of an action determine whether it is right or wrong.[63] Good is the ultimate moral value, and we should maximize good effects for the greatest number of people. But do good ethics make for good business? Right actions do not always produce good consequences, and good consequences do not always follow right actions. And how do we determine the greatest good? The protection of what is good for minorities is critically important in a free, good society.

Corporations and business enterprises tend to subscribe to consequential ethics, partly due to the persuasive arguments of the Scottish moral philosopher Adam Smith.[64] He believed that the self-interest of human beings is God's providence, not the government's. Smith set forth a doctrine of *natural liberty*, presenting the classical argument for open-market competition and free trade. Within this framework, people should be allowed to pursue what is in their economic self-interest, and the natural efficiency of the marketplace will then serve the well-being of society. However, Smith was mindful of the interests of others and argued for three key virtues: prudence, which is good self-care; justice, which is doing no harm to others, and beneficence, which is doing good for others.[65]

2-4b Rule-Based Theories of Ethics

Rule-based theories of ethics emphasize the character of the act itself, not its effects, in arriving at universal moral rights and wrongs.[66] Moral rights, the basis for legal rights, are associated with such theories. In a theological context, the Bible, the Talmud, and the Koran are rule-based guides to ethical behavior. Immanuel Kant worked toward the ultimate moral principle in formulating his *categorical imperative*, a universal standard of behavior.[67] Kant argued that individuals should be treated with respect and dignity and that they should not be used as a means to an end. He argued that we should put ourselves in the other person's position and ask whether we would make the same decision if we were in that person's situation.

2-4c Character Theories of Ethics

Virtue ethics, of which **character theories** of ethics are a type, offer an alternative to understanding behavior in terms of self-interest or rules. Character theories of ethics emphasize the character of the individual and the intent of the actor instead of the character of the act itself or its consequences. These virtue-ethics theories are based on Aristotle's view of ethics, which focused on an individual's inner character and virtuousness rather than on outward behavior. Thus, the good person who acted out of virtuous and right intentions was one with integrity and ultimately good ethical standards. Robert Solomon is the best known advocate of this Aristotelian approach to business ethics.[68] He advocates a business ethics theory centered on the individual within the corporation, emphasizing personal virtues as well as corporate roles. Solomon's six dimensions of virtue ethics are community, excellence, role identity, integrity, judgment (*phronesis* in Greek),

and holism. We previously noted Smith's three key virtues. At the heart of character and virtue ethics is emotional intelligence, a central component in leader and follower development. The Goolsby Leadership Academy at the University of Texas at Arlington emphasizes the development of emotional competencies, such as empathy, compassion, and self-control. For the emotionally competent person of good character, integrity comes first.[69] Organizational factors may negatively affect an otherwise virtuous individual. Workers who experience increased anxiety and feel threatened at work may engage in unethical behavior despite having good intentions.[70]

2-4d Cultural Relativism

Cultural relativism contends that there are no universal ethical principles and that people should not impose their own ethical standards on others. Local standards guide ethical behavior. Cultural relativism encourages individuals to operate under the old adage of "When in Rome, do as the Romans do." Unfortunately, people who adhere strictly to cultural relativism may avoid difficult ethical dilemmas by denying their own accountability.

2-5 ETHICAL DILEMMAS FACING THE MODERN ORGANIZATION

People need ethical theories to guide them through complex, difficult, and often confusing moral choices and ethical decisions. Contemporary organizations experience a wide variety of ethical and moral dilemmas. In this section,

rule-based theory An ethical theory that emphasizes the character of the act itself rather than its effects.

character theory An ethical theory that emphasizes the character, personal virtues, and intent of the individual.

we address employee rights, sexual harassment, organizational justice, and whistle-blowing. We conclude with a discussion of social responsibility and codes of ethics.

2-5a Employee Rights

Managing the rights of employees at work creates many ethical dilemmas in organizations. Drug testing, free speech, downsizing and layoffs, and due process are but a few of the employee rights issues that managers face.

These dilemmas include privacy issues related to technology. Many feel that computerized monitoring constitutes an invasion of privacy. Using employee data from computerized information systems presents many ethical concerns. New software allows employers to tap into their employees' address books and e-mail contacts to obtain new potential clients and discern who in the company might be best suited to approach them.[71] Safeguarding the employee's right to privacy while preserving access to the data for those who need it forces managers to balance competing interests.

The reality of AIDS in the workplace also illustrates the difficulties managers face in balancing various interests. Managers may encounter a conflict between the rights of HIV-infected workers and the rights of their coworkers who feel threatened. But laws protect HIV-infected workers. The Americans with Disabilities Act (ADA) requires employees to treat HIV-infected workers as disabled individuals and to make reasonable accommodations for them. But ADA cannot encompass all of the ethical dilemmas involved.

Confidentiality may also present challenges. Employers are not required to make concessions to coworkers, but they are obligated to educate, reassure, and provide emotional support to them. Some employees with HIV or AIDS fear stigmatization or reprisals and do not want their condition known by their coworkers. Management should discuss the ramifications of trying to maintain confidentiality and should assure affected employees that every effort will be made to prevent negative consequences for them in the workplace.[72]

2-5b Sexual Harassment

According to the Equal Employment Opportunity Commission, sexual harassment is unwelcome verbal or physical sexual attention that affects an employee's job conditions or creates a hostile working environment.[73] Supreme Court rulings tend to blame companies when managers create a sexually hostile working environment. Sexual harassment is more likely to occur in some organizations than in others—for example, in male-dominated workplaces.[74] In some organizations, employees risk their jobs by complaining of sexual harassment or are not taken seriously, and perpetrators are rarely punished. While there has been progress since the 1990s in addressing sexual harassment, the problem continues. Emerging evidence suggests that bystander interventions can be effective in preventing and/or managing incidences of workplace sexual harassment.[75] Everyone in the workplace has responsibility for this endemic problem. Managers can defend themselves by demonstrating that they took action to eliminate workplace harassment and that the complaining employee did not take advantage of company procedures to deal with harassment. Even the best sexual harassment policy, however, will not absolve a company when harassment leads to firing, demotions, or undesirable working assignments.[76]

There are three types of sexual harassment. *Gender harassment* includes crude comments or behaviors that convey hostility toward a particular gender. *Unwanted sexual attention* involves unwanted touching or repeated pressures for dates. *Sexual coercion* consists of implicit or explicit demands for sexual favors by threatening negative job-related consequences or promising job-related rewards.[77] Recent theory has focused attention on the aggressive behavior of sexual harassers.[78]

Sexual harassment costs the typical *Fortune* 500 company $6.7 million per year in absenteeism, turnover, and lost productivity. Valeant Pharmaceuticals International paid out millions to settle four sexual harassment complaints against former CEO Milan Panic. Plaintiffs

Sexual harassment costs the typical *Fortune 500* company $6.7 million per year in absenteeism, turnover, and lost productivity.

may now sue for compensatory and punitive damages in addition to back pay. And these costs do not take into account the negative publicity that sexual harassment cases may attract. Moreover, victims of sexual harassment who do not report the problem are less satisfied with their work, supervisors, and coworkers, and they may psychologically withdraw at work. They may suffer poorer mental health and even exhibit symptoms of post-traumatic stress disorder in conjunction with the harassment experience. Some victims report alcohol abuse, depression, headaches, and nausea.[79]

Several companies have created comprehensive sexual harassment programs. Atlantic Richfield (ARCO), owned by British Petroleum and a player in the male-dominated energy industry, has a handbook on preventing sexual harassment that includes phone numbers of state agencies where employees can file complaints. The openness seems to work. Lawsuits rarely happen at ARCO. When employees make sexual harassment complaints, the company investigates thoroughly. ARCO fired the captain of an oil tanker for sexually harassing coworkers. Not all sexual behavior among employees is harmful or harassing in nature. Workplace interactions between organizational members that have sexual connotations but not perceived by any of the parties as being threatening or harassing are considered social sexual behavior. Examples of social sexual behavior include flirting, sharing sexual stories or jokes, complimenting physical appearance, or gentle touching. Social sexual behavior in the workplace can have numerous psychological, emotional, and relational benefits for those involved. Among the benefits are increased self-esteem, energy, vigor, and creativity. There is also evidence that social sexual behavior can enhance group cohesion and camaraderie.[80]

2-5c Organizational Justice

Organizational justice also generates moral and ethical dilemmas at work. **Distributive justice** concerns the fairness of outcomes individuals receive. For example, during former President George H. W. Bush's 1992 visit, Japanese CEOs questioned the distributive justice of keeping American CEOs' salaries so high while many companies were struggling and laying off workers.

Procedural justice concerns the fairness of the process by which outcomes are allocated. The ethical questions in procedural justice examine the process by which an organization distributes its resources. Has the organization used the correct procedures in allocating resources? Have the right considerations, such as competence and skill, been brought to bear in the decision

---

The Rooney Rule…at Facebook and in the UT System

Dan Rooney, the late owner of the Pittsburgh Steelers, advocated for procedural justice at least, and distributive justice as well, for minority candidates in head coaching and senior football operation job searches. The Rooney Rule has opened doors for minority candidates well beyond senior jobs in football. Facebook uses a Diverse Slate Approach based on the Rooney Rule. Chancellor William McRaven of The University of Texas system uses the Rooney Rule for dean-level positions and above within the entire UT universe of academic and medical campuses. Facebook goes beyond the Rooney Rule to ensure organizational justice for all concerned. Specifically, the company does training at surfacing and thus helping to manage unconscious bias. Negative stereotypes related to competency and performance can compromise the fairness and justice in hiring and advancement processes for minority candidates.

SOURCE: E. McGirt, "Facebook: Iterating Diversity?" *Fortune*, Feb. 1, 2017, p. 55.

---

process? And have the wrong considerations, such as race and gender, been excluded from the decision process? One study of work scheduling found that advance notice and consistency, two dimensions of procedural justice, reduced voluntary turnover.[81] Some research suggests cultural differences in the effects of distributive and procedural justice.[82]

2-5d Whistle-Blowing

Whistle-blowers are employees who inform authorities of wrongdoings by their companies or coworkers. Depending on their situations, whistle-blowers may be perceived as either public heroes or vile wretches. Those seen as heroes generally report serious and high-magnitude ethical breaches widely perceived as abhorrent.[83]

distributive justice The fairness of outcomes that individuals receive in an organization.

procedural justice The fairness of the process by which outcomes are allocated in an organization.

whistle-blower An employee who informs authorities of the wrongdoings of her or his company or coworkers.

Others may see the whistle-blower as a wretch if they feel the act of whistle-blowing is more offensive than the situation reported. One of the most well-known whistle-blowers, Edward Snowden is hailed as a hero by some for revealing the extent of the U.S. government domestic surveillance program. However, others consider Snowden a disgruntled NSA contractor who participated in industrial espionage.[84]

Whistle-blowing is a powerful influence on corporate America because committed organizational members sometimes engage in unethical behavior in an intense desire to succeed. Organizations can manage whistle-blowing by explaining the conditions that are appropriate for disclosing wrongdoing. Clearly delineating wrongful behavior and the appropriate ways to respond are important organizational actions.

2-5e Corporate Social Responsibility

Corporate **social responsibility** is an organization's obligation to behave ethically in its social environment. Ethical conduct at the individual level can translate into social responsibility at the organizational level. Multiple stakeholders in society expect organizations to engage in socially responsible actions. Servant leaders play an important role in creating, implementing, and sustaining socially responsible behaviors.[85]

Current concerns include protecting the environment, promoting worker safety, supporting social issues, and investing in the community, among others. Some organizations, such as IBM, loan executives to inner-city schools to teach science and math. Some companies have even tried to build a brand around social responsibility, such as the Just Coffee Cooperative, which sponsors trips to coffee-producing regions in order to build customer loyalty to the cause and their brand.[86] Firms that are seen as socially responsible have a competitive advantage in attracting applicants.[87] American Apparel, however, tried to build a brand around the fact that they produce garments locally rather than in foreign sweatshops but found that, as attractive as its ethics might have been to customers, sex appeal was more effective in actually selling its product.[88]

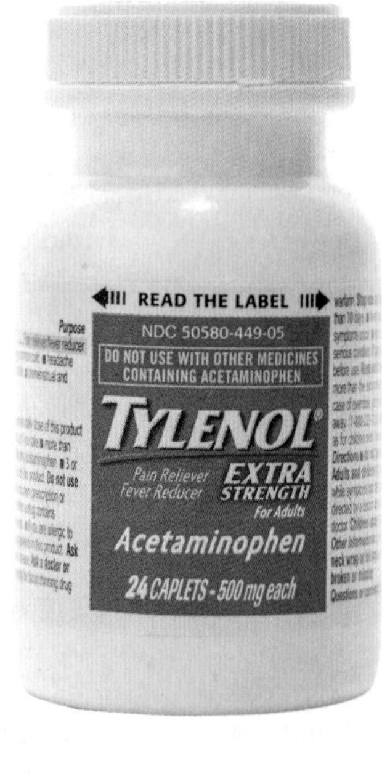

social responsibility The obligation of an organization to behave ethically in its social environment.

FIGURE 2.2 THE FOUR-WAY TEST

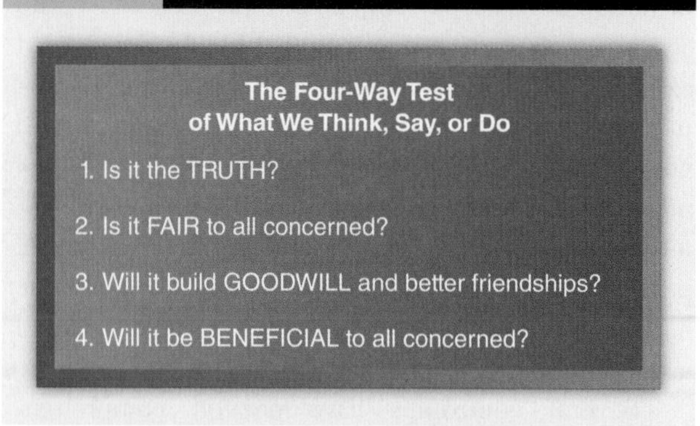

The Four-Way Test
of What We Think, Say, or Do

1. Is it the TRUTH?

2. Is it FAIR to all concerned?

3. Will it build GOODWILL and better friendships?

4. Will it be BENEFICIAL to all concerned?

2-5f Codes of Ethics

Most mature professions guide their practitioners' actions and behavior with codes of ethics. For example, the Hippocratic oath guides doctors. A profession's code of ethics becomes a standard against which members can measure themselves in the absence of internalized standards.

A similar professional code of ethics does not exist for business. However, Rotarian Herbert J. Taylor developed the four-way test, shown in Figure 2.2, in a major business turnaround during the 1930s as a way to create strategic advantage through good character and moral behavior. Now used in more than 166 nations by 1.2 million Rotarians, this test focuses the questioner on key ethical and moral questions.

Beyond the individual and professional level, corporate culture is another excellent starting point for addressing ethics and morality. Sometimes regulations articulate a corporation's ethics. For example, the Joint Ethics Regulation (DOD 5500.7-R, August 1993) specifies the ethical standards that all U.S. military personnel must follow. In other cases, corporate ethics appear as a credo. Johnson & Johnson's credo, shown in Figure 2.3, helped hundreds of employees ethically address criminal tampering with Tylenol products.

Individual codes of ethics, professional oaths, and organizational credos must all be anchored in a moral, ethical framework because ethical theories are the only way to question and improve our current standards. However, even though a universal right and wrong may exist, it would be hard to agree on a single code of ethics to which all individuals, professions, and organizations can subscribe.

FIGURE 2.3 THE JOHNSON & JOHNSON CREDO

We believe our first responsibility is to the doctors, nurses, and patients, to mothers and all others who use our products and services. In meeting their needs everything we do must be of high quality. We must constantly strive to reduce our costs in order to maintain reasonable prices. Customers' orders must be serviced promptly and accurately. Our suppliers and distributors must have an opportunity to make a fair profit.

We are responsible to our employees, the men and women who work with us throughout the world. Everyone must be considered as an individual. We must respect their dignity and recognize their merit. They must have a sense of security in their jobs. Compensation must be fair and adequate, and working conditions clean, orderly, and safe. Employees must feel free to make suggestions and complaints. There must be equal opportunity for employment, development, and advancement for those qualified. We must provide competent management, and their actions must be just and ethical.

We are responsible to the communities in which we live and work and to the world community as well. We must be good citizens—support good works and charities and bear our fair share of taxes. We must encourage civic improvements and better health and education. We must maintain in good order the property we are privileged to use, protecting the environment and natural resources.

Our final responsibility is to our stockholders. Business must make a sound profit. We must experiment with new ideas. Research must be carried on, innovative programs developed and mistakes paid for. New equipment must be purchased, new facilities provided, and new products launched. Reserves must be created to provide for adverse times. When we operate according to these principles, the stockholders should realize a fair return.

SOURCE: "Our Credo," http://www.jnj.com/wps/wcm/connect/c7933f004f5563df9e22be1bb31559c7/jnj_ourcredo_english _us_8.5x11_cmyk.pdf?MOD=AJPERES.

STUDY TOOLS 2

LOCATED AT BACK OF THE TEXTBOOK

☐ Rip out chapter review card

LOCATED AT WWW.CENGAGE.COM/LOGIN

☐ Gain unique perspectives on key concepts with new Concept Clip videos in the e-book

☐ Review key term flashcards and create your own

☐ Increase your comprehension with online homework and quizzes

3 | Personality, Perception, and Attribution

LEARNING OBJECTIVES

3-1 Describe individual differences and explain why they are important in understanding organizational behavior.

3-2 Articulate key personality traits and explain how they influence behavior in organizations.

3-3 Discuss how personality theories may be applied in organizations.

3-4 Define social perception and explain the factors that affect it.

3-5 Identify five common barriers to social perception and explain the difficulties they cause.

3-6 Explain the attribution process and how attributions affect managerial behavior.

After finishing this chapter go to **PAGE 51** for **STUDY TOOLS**

3-1 INDIVIDUAL DIFFERENCES AND ORGANIZATIONAL BEHAVIOR

Over the next two chapters, we'll explore the concept of **individual differences**. Individuals are unique in terms of their skills, abilities, personalities, perceptions, attitudes, emotions, and ethics. Hence, individual differences represent the essence of the challenge of management. Managers must often work with people who possess a multitude of varying characteristics, so the more managers understand individual differences, the better they can work with others.

interactional psychology
The psychological approach to understanding human behavior that involves knowing something about the person and about the situation.

individual differences
The way in which factors such as skills, abilities, personalities, perceptions, attitudes, values, and ethics differ from one individual to another.

The basis for understanding individual differences stems from Kurt Lewin's early contention that behavior is a function of the person and the environment.[1] He expressed this idea in an equation: $B = f(P, E)$, where B = behavior, P = person, and E = environment. Lewin's idea has been developed further by the **interactional psychology** approach.[2] Basically, this approach says that we must know something about the person and something about the situation in order to understand human behavior. There are four basic propositions of interactional psychology:

Gandee Vasan/Stone/Getty Images

1. Behavior is a function of continuous, multidirectional interaction between the person and the situation.

2. The person is active in this process, both changing his or her situations and being changed by them.

3. People vary in many characteristics, including cognitive, affective, motivational, and ability factors.

4. Two aspects of a situation are important: the objective situation and the person's subjective view of the situation.[3]

The interactional psychology approach points out the need to study both persons and situations. The *person* consists of individual elements such as personality, perception, attribution, attitudes, emotions, and ethics. The *situation* consists of the environment the person operates in, including the organization, work group, personal life situation, job characteristics, and other environmental influences. The effect of personal and environmental differences on organizational behavior is shown visually in Figure 3.1. In this chapter, we'll address skills and

> Individuals are unique in terms of their skills, abilities, personalities, perceptions, attitudes, emotions, and ethics.

abilities, personality, perception, and attribution. Chapter 4 will deal with attitudes, emotions, and ethics.

3-1a Skills and Abilities

Many skills and abilities influence work outcomes. Nearly 100 years ago, Charles Spearman introduced the concept of *general mental ability (GMA)* as a measure of an individual's innate cognitive intelligence.[4] GMA, which includes a person's skills and abilities, is the single best predictor of work performance across many occupations and across different cultures.[5]

3-2 PERSONALITY AND ORGANIZATIONS

What makes an individual behave consistently in a variety of situations? **Personality** is the relatively stable set of characteristics that influences an individual's behavior and lends it consistency. Although researchers debate what determines personality, we conclude that it has several origins. One determinant is heredity. Researchers have found that identical twins who were separated at birth and raised in very different situations nevertheless shared personality traits and job preferences. In fact, about half of the variations in traits such as extraversion, impulsiveness, and flexibility were shared by identical twins who grew up separately.[6] Thus, genes appear to influence personality.

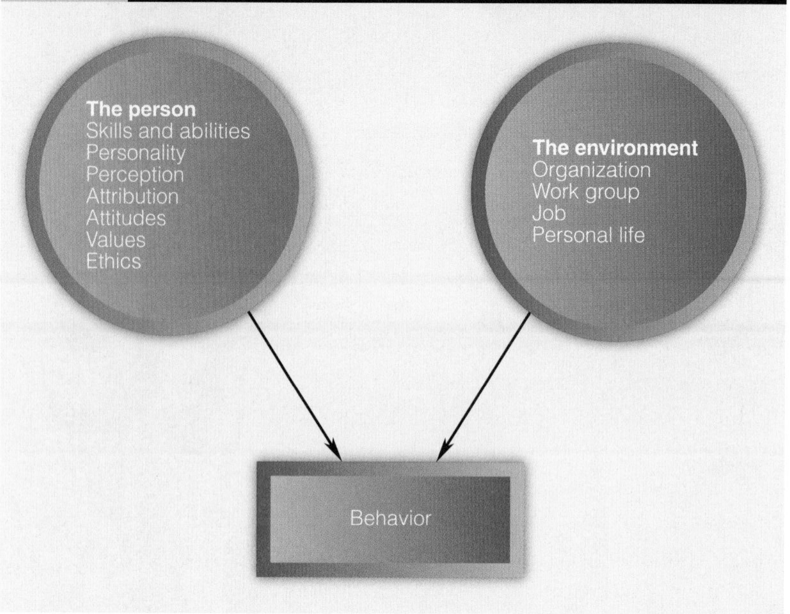

Environment also determines personality, shaping it through family influences, cultural influences, educational influences, and other environmental factors. Two major theories of personality are the trait theory and the integrative approach. Each theory has influenced the study of personality in organizations.

3-2a Trait Theory

Some early personality researchers believed that we must break down behavior patterns into a series of observable traits in order to understand individuals. According to **trait theory**, the combination of these traits forms an individual's personality. Gordon Allport, a leading theorist, saw traits as broad, general guides that lend consistency to behavior.[7] Thousands of traits have been identified over the years. Raymond Cattell, another prominent theorist, identified sixteen traits that formed the basis for differences in individual behavior. He described traits in binary pairs such as self-assured/apprehensive, reserved/outgoing, and submissive/dominant.[8]

One popular personality classification involves the so-called Big Five. These traits (described in Table 3.1) include extraversion, agreeableness, conscientiousness, emotional stability, and openness to experience.[9] The Big Five are broad, global traits associated with behaviors at work. For example, from preliminary research, we know that introverted and conscientious employees are less likely to be absent from work.[10] Individuals with high agreeableness tend to rate others more leniently on peer evaluations, while those with high conscientiousness tend to be tougher raters.[11] In terms of work stress, employees who are extraverted, conscientious, and open to experience fare better. They're less likely to let stress result in a negative mood.[12] Across many occupations, conscientious people are more motivated and perform better than others.[13]

personality A relatively stable set of characteristics that influence an individual's behavior.

trait theory A personality theory that advocates breaking down behavior patterns into a series of observable traits in order to understand human behavior.

FIGURE 3.1 | VARIABLES INFLUENCING INDIVIDUAL BEHAVIOR

The person
Skills and abilities
Personality
Perception
Attribution
Attitudes
Values
Ethics

The environment
Organization
Work group
Job
Personal life

Behavior

TABLE 3.1 | THE BIG FIVE PERSONALITY TRAITS

Extraversion	The person is gregarious, assertive, and sociable (as opposed to reserved, timid, and quiet).
Agreeableness	The person is cooperative, warm, and agreeable (rather than cold, disagreeable, and antagonistic).
Conscientiousness	The person is hardworking, organized, and dependable (as opposed to lazy, disorganized, and unreliable).
Emotional stability	The person is calm, self-confident, and cool (as opposed to insecure, anxious, and depressed).
Openness to experience	The person is creative, curious, and cultured (rather than practical with narrow interests).

SOURCES: P. T. Costa and R. R. McCrae, *The NEO-PI Personality Inventory* (Odessa, Fla.: Psychological Assessment Resources, 1992); J. F. Salgado, "The Five Factor Model of Personality and Job Performance in the European Community," *Journal of Applied Psychology* 82 (1997): 30–43.

But different patterns of the Big Five traits are related to high performance in different occupations and work situations. For customer service jobs, individuals high in emotional stability, agreeableness, and openness to experience perform best. Managers with emotional stability and extraversion are top performers.[14] People who are emotionally stable (as opposed to neurotic) hold up better in decision making under time and social pressure, and people who are more agreeable have a tougher time making decisions under pressure.[15] Studies have also shown that an extreme amount of any trait harms organizations. Interestingly, highly conscientious and emotionally stable individuals perform worse on the job than those with more moderate levels of both traits. The reasons could be that very conscientious individuals may be overly rigid, inflexible, and compulsive, paying too much attention to small details at the expense of larger goals. And, a pronounced lack of conscientiousness can be a distinct disadvantage when trying to develop a network of relationships to support one's career goals.[16] It seems that any Big Five trait maximized or minimized can become a liability at work.

The Big Five framework is helpful for understanding cultural differences and has held up well when applied to Western cultures, particularly among Spanish and Mexican populations.[17] But it remains to be seen whether the Big Five traits will emerge in studies of non-Western cultures.[18] Personality traits are also relevant to *cultural intelligence*, which, in the workplace, means how we adapt to cultural differences.[19]

But the trait approach has many critics. Some theorists argue that simply identifying traits is not enough because personality is dynamic and never completely stable. Further, early trait theorists tended to ignore the influence of situations.[20] The trait theory also tends to ignore process, that is, how we get from a trait to a particular outcome.

3-2b Integrative Approach

In response to the criticisms of trait theory, researchers have taken a broader, more **integrative approach** to the study of personality.[21] This integrative approach focuses on both personal dispositions and situational variables as combined predictors of behavior. *Dispositions* are the tendencies of an individual to respond to situations in consistent ways. They include emotions, cognitions, attitudes, expectations, and fantasies.[22] Influenced by both genes and experiences, dispositions can be modified.

A recent study of how personality affects status offers a good example of how an integrative approach can be applied to better understand organizations. The study looked at a variety of personality variables that affected not only the actual status held by an individual,

High Core Self-Evaluation Can Pay Off!

Core self-evaluation (CSE) reflects an individual's fundamental concept of himself or herself. Do people with positive CSE earn more money? A recent study showed that high CSE was correlated with income, but CSE alone didn't predict income. When the researchers added in networking ability, they found a winning formula. Income was highest for individuals who had both high CSE and strong networking ability.

Having a positive view of self leads to setting and achieving challenging goals, and networking ability means being willing to draw on social connections to achieve these goals. The combination is powerful.

SOURCE: R. A. Venz and E. Gardiner, "It Pays to Be Well-Connected: The Moderating Role of Networking Ability on the Relationship Between Core Self-Evaluations and Income," *Personality and Individual Differences*, 110 (2017): 85–89.

but how that individual perceived his or her status as well as how the person's status was viewed by others. The most important variable was leadership identity, though the leader's self-perception was determined largely by emotional stability and agreeableness. Meanwhile, extraversion and conscientiousness most affected how the leader was perceived by others.[23]

3-2c Personality Characteristics in Organizations

Managers should learn as much as possible about personality in order to understand and better relate to their employees, which is why we devote much attention to the subject of personality in this text. Although researchers have identified hundreds of personality characteristics, we have selected a few with particularly strong influences on individual behavior in organizations. *Core self-evaluation (CSE)* involves a broad set of personality traits that articulates an individual's concept of himself or herself.[24] CSE is concerned with people's locus of control, self-esteem, generalized self-efficacy, and emotional stability. It predicts both goal-directed behavior and performance, even in non-U.S. cultures (e.g., Japan).[25] All these aspects of CSE will be examined shortly. In addition to the traits associated with CSE, we will consider the personality traits of self-monitoring and positive/negative affect.

Can managers predict the behavior of their employees from their personalities? Not completely. Recall that the interactional

integrative approach
The broad theory that describes personality as a composite of an individual's psychological processes.

psychology model (Figure 3.1) requires both dispositional and situational variables to predict behavior. As we consider the following personality variables, then, keep in mind that they are only one piece of the personality puzzle.

When weighing the role of situation, it is important to understand that situations vary in strength. **Strong situations** overwhelm the effects of individual personalities. These situations are interpreted in the same way by different individuals, evoke agreement on the appropriate behavior in the situation, and provide cues to appropriate behavior. For example, at performance appraisal sessions, employees know to listen to their bosses and to contribute when asked to do, so this is a strong situation.

Weak situations are open to many interpretations. They provide few cues to appropriate behavior and no obvious rewards for any particular behavior. Individual personalities thus have a greater influence in weak situations than in strong situations. An informal meeting without an agenda might be a weak situation. Because organizations present combinations of strong and weak situations, personality affects behavior more in some situations than in others.[26]

Following are explanations of the various aspects of personality involved in CSE plus the traits of self-monitoring and positive/negative affect. Locus of control, self-efficacy, self-esteem, and the effects of emotional stability together constitute the core self-evaluations. CSE is a strong predictor of both job satisfaction and job performance, next only to GMA. Employees with high CSE are more likely to offer suggestions and ideas for improving the organization in which they work, and this helps companies prevent crises, improve processes, and perform better overall.[27]

LOCUS OF CONTROL An individual's generalized belief about internal (self) versus external (situation or others) control is called **locus of control**. People who believe they control what happens to them have an internal locus of control, whereas people who believe that circumstances or other people

Rasulov/Shutterstock.com

control their fate have an external locus of control.[28] In an organization, people with an internal locus of control (called *internals*) often report higher job satisfaction, exhibit superior job performance, are more likely to assume managerial positions, and tend to prefer participative management styles more than those with an external locus of control (*externals*).[29]

Internals and externals have similar positive reactions to being promoted, including high job satisfaction, job involvement, and organizational commitment. However, internals remain happy long after the promotion, whereas externals' joy over the promotion is short-lived. This might occur because externals do not believe their own performance led to the promotion.[30]

Knowing about locus of control can prove valuable to managers. Because internals believe they control what happens to them, they will want to exercise control in their work environments. Internals don't react well to close supervision, so managers should give them considerable voice in how work is performed. Externals, by contrast, may appreciate more structured work settings and prefer not to participate in decision making.

SELF-EFFICACY People's **general self-efficacy** is their overall view of themselves as being able to perform effectively in a wide variety of situations.[31] Employees with high general self-efficacy have more confidence in their job-related abilities and other personal resources (e.g., energy, influence over others) that help them function effectively on the job. People with low general self-efficacy often feel ineffective at work and may express doubts about performing new tasks well. Previous success or performance is one of the most important determinants of self-efficacy. People who trust their own efficacy tend to attempt difficult tasks, persist in overcoming obstacles, and experience less anxiety when faced with adversity.[32] Because they are confident in their capability to provide meaningful input, they value the opportunity to participate in decision making.[33] High self-efficacy has also been related to higher job satisfaction and performance.[34]

Another form of self-efficacy, called *task-specific self-efficacy*, describes a person's belief that she or he can perform a specific task. ("I believe I can do this sales presentation today.") In contrast, general self-efficacy is broader. ("I believe I can perform well in just about any part of the job.")

SELF-ESTEEM Self-esteem is an individual's general feeling of self-worth. Individuals with high

---

strong situation
A situation that overwhelms the effects of individual personalities by providing strong cues for appropriate behavior.

locus of control An individual's generalized belief about internal control (self-control) versus external control (control by the situation or by others).

general self-efficacy An individual's general belief that he or she is capable of meeting job demands in a wide variety of situations.

self-esteem An individual's general feeling of self-worth.

self-esteem have positive feelings about themselves, perceive themselves to have strengths as well as weaknesses, and believe their strengths are more important than their weaknesses.[35] Individuals with low self-esteem view themselves negatively. They are more strongly affected by what other people think of them, and they compliment individuals who give them positive feedback while cutting down people who give them negative feedback.[36]

Evaluations from others affect our self-esteem. You might be liked for who you are, or you might be liked for your achievements. Being liked for who you are is more stable, and people with self-esteem stemming from this type of reaction from other people are usually able to be less defensive and more honest with themselves. Being liked for your achievements is more unstable; self-esteem resulting from this type of reaction waxes and wanes depending on the magnitude of achievements.[37]

Self-esteem affects attitudes and behavior in organizations. People with high self-esteem perform better and are more satisfied with their jobs.[38] They tend to seek out higher-status jobs.[39] A work team made up of individuals with high self-esteem is more likely to succeed than a team with low or average self-esteem.[40]

High self-esteem, however, can be too much of a good thing. People with inflated self-esteem may brag inappropriately when they find themselves in stressful situations.[41] Very high self-esteem may also lead to overconfidence and relationship conflicts.[42] Such individuals may shift their social identities to protect themselves when they do not live up to some standard. For example, if Denise outperforms Teresa on a statistics exam, Teresa may convince herself that Denise is not really a good person to compare herself with because Denise is an engineering major and Teresa is a physical education major. Teresa's high self-esteem protects her from this unfavorable though, in truth, valid comparison,[43] which might otherwise prompt her to improve her knowledge of statistics.

Self-esteem may be strongly affected by situations. Success tends to raise self-esteem, whereas failure lowers it. Managers should thus encourage employees to raise their self-esteem by giving them appropriate challenges and opportunities for success.

SELF-MONITORING Self-monitoring—the extent to which people base their behavior on cues from other people and situations—has a huge impact on behavior in organizations.[44] High self-monitors pay attention to what is appropriate in particular situations and to the behavior of other people, and they behave accordingly. Low self-monitors, by contrast, pay less attention to situational cues and act from internal states instead. As a result, low self-monitors behave consistently across situations.

> Individuals with positive affect are more likely to help others at work and engage in more organizational citizenship behaviors . . . and have fewer absentee days.

High self-monitors, because their behavior varies with the situation, appear more unpredictable and less consistent but in practice are actually more effective at work because they respond appropriately to changes in the organizational situation. For example, one study of managers at a recruitment firm found that high self-monitors were more likely to offer emotional help people dealing with work-related anxiety. Low self-monitors, on the other hand, were unlikely to offer such emotional support.[45]

According to our research, high self-monitors get promoted because they accomplish tasks by meeting the expectations of others and because they seek out central positions in social networks.[46] They are also more likely to use self-promotion to make others aware of their skills and accomplishments.[47] However, the high self-monitors' flexibility may not be suited for every job, and the tendency to move may not fit every organization.[48]

Because high self-monitors base their behavior on cues from others and from the situation, they demonstrate higher levels of managerial self-awareness. This means that, as managers, they assess their own workplace behavior accurately.[49] Managers who are high self-monitors are also good at reading their employees' needs and changing the way they interact with employees.[50]

We can further speculate that high self-monitors respond more readily to work group norms, organizational culture, and supervisory feedback than do low self-monitors, who adhere more to internal guidelines for behavior ("I am who I am"). In addition, high self-monitors may support the trend toward work teams because they can easily assume flexible roles.

POSITIVE/NEGATIVE AFFECT Individuals who focus on the positive aspects of themselves, other people, and the world in general are said to have **positive affect**.[51] In contrast, those

self-monitoring The extent to which people base their behavior on cues from other people and situations.

positive affect An individual's tendency to accentuate the positive aspects of herself or himself, other people, and the world in general.

who accentuate the negative in themselves, others, and the world are said to possess **negative affect** (also called *negative affectivity*).[52] Individuals with positive affect are more satisfied with their jobs.[53] They are also more likely to help others at work and engage in more organizational citizenship behaviors.[54] Employees with positive affect have fewer absentee days.[55] Positive affect has also been linked to more life satisfaction and better performance across a variety of life and work domains.[56] Individual affect influences the work group as well. Positive individual affect produces positive team affect, which promotes cooperation and reduces conflict.[57] In particular, leader affectivity influences the affectivity of his or her subordinates. Thus, positive affect is a definite asset in work settings. Managers can encourage it by allowing people to participate in decision making and by providing pleasant working conditions.

3-2d Proactive Personality

Proactive personalities identify opportunities and act on them; they show initiative, take action, and persevere until they effect change. People who are not proactive fail to identify, let alone seize, opportunities to effect change.[58] Proactivity has been positively related to job performance, career success, and job search success.[59] Additionally, leaders who identify themselves as proactive are viewed as more charismatic by their subordinates.[60]

3-3 APPLICATION OF PERSONALITY THEORY IN ORGANIZATIONS

To apply personality theories in their organizations, managers first must measure the personalities of their organizations' members. Projective tests, behavioral measures, and self-report questionnaires can all be used to measure personality.

3-3a Common Personality Measurement Tools

During **projective tests**, individuals are shown a picture, abstract image, or photo and are asked to describe what they see or to tell a story about it. The rationale behind projective tests is that each individual responds to the stimulus in a way that reflects his or her unique personality. The Rorschach ink blot test is commonly used to assess personality.[61] Like other projective tests, however, it has low reliability. The individual being assessed may look at the same picture and see different things at different times. In addition, the assessor might apply her or his own biases in interpreting the information about the individual's personality.

Behavioral measures of personality examine an individual's behavior in a controlled situation. We might assess a person's sociability, for example, by counting the number of times he or she approaches strangers at a party. The behavior is scored to produce an index of personality. Some potential problems with behavioral measures include the observer's ability to stay focused and the way the observer interprets the behavior. Additionally, some people behave differently when they know they are being observed.

The most common method of assessing personality is the **self-report questionnaire**. An individual responds to a series of questions, usually in an agree/disagree or true/false format. One of the more widely recognized questionnaires is the *Minnesota Multiphasic Personality Inventory (MMPI)*, a comprehensive test assessing a variety of traits that can help diagnose several neurotic or psychotic disorders. Another self-report questionnaire, the *NEO Personality Inventory*, measures the Big Five traits. Self-report questionnaires also suffer from potential biases. It is difficult to view your own personality objectively. People often answer the questionnaires in terms of how they want to be seen rather than as they really are.

3-3b Carl Jung and the Myers-Briggs Type Indicator® Instrument

Another approach to applying personality theory in organizations is the Jungian approach and its measurement tool, the *Myers-Briggs Type Indicator® (MBTI)*. This instrument was developed to measure ideas about individual differences advocated by the Swiss psychologist Carl Jung. Many organizations use the MBTI instrument, and we will focus on it as an example of how some organizations use personality concepts to help employees appreciate diversity.

Jung built his work on the notion that people are fundamentally different but also fundamentally alike. His classic treatise *Psychological Types* proposed that the

negative affect An individual's tendency to accentuate the negative aspects of himself or herself, other people, and the world in general.

projective test A personality test that elicits an individual's response to abstract stimuli.

behavioral measures Personality assessments that involve observing an individual's behavior in a controlled situation.

self-report questionnaire A common personality assessment that involves an individual's responses to a series of questions.

The Myers-Briggs Type Indicator is a common way to measure differences in individuals.

TABLE 3.2	TYPE THEORY PREFERENCES AND DESCRIPTIONS
Extraversion	**Introversion**
Outgoing	Quiet
Publicly expressive	Reserved
Interacting	Concentrating
Speaks, then thinks	Thinks, then speaks
Gregarious	Reflective
Sensing	**Intuition**
Practical	General
Specific	Abstract
Feet on the ground	Head in the clouds
Details	Possibilities
Concrete	Theoretical
Thinking	**Feeling**
Analytical	Subjective
Clarity	Harmony
Head	Heart
Justice	Mercy
Rules	Circumstance
Judging	**Perceiving**
Structured	Flexible
Time oriented	Open ended
Decisive	Exploring
Makes lists/uses them	Makes lists/loses them
Organized	Spontaneous

SOURCE: Adapted from *Introduction to Type*®, Sixth Edition by Isabel Briggs Myers. Copyright 1998, 2011 by CPP, Inc. All rights reserved.

population was made up of two basic types: Extraverted types and Introverted types.[62] He went on to identify two types of Perceiving (Sensing and Intuition) and two types of Judgment (Thinking and Feeling). Perceiving (how we gather information) and Judging (how we make decisions) represent the two universal basic mental functions.

Jung suggested that human similarities and differences could be understood by combining preferences. We prefer and choose one way of doing things over another. We are not exclusively one way or another; rather, we have a preference for Extraversion or Introversion, just as we have a preference for right-handedness or left-handedness. Jung's type theory argues that no preferences are better than others. Differences are to be understood, celebrated, and appreciated.

During the 1940s, the mother-daughter team of Katherine Briggs and Isabel Briggs Myers became fascinated with individual differences among people and with Jung's work. They developed the **Myers-Briggs Type Indicator® (MBTI) instrument** to put Jung's type theory into practical use. The MBTI instrument is used extensively in organizations as a basis for understanding individual differences. More than 2 million people complete the instrument per year in the United States, and it is frequently used by *Fortune* 500 companies.[63] The MBTI instrument has been used in career counseling, team building, conflict management, and understanding management styles.[64]

THE PREFERENCES There are four scale dichotomies in type theory: extraversion/introversion, sensing/intuition, thinking/feeling, and judging/perceiving. Table 3.2 shows these preferences. The combination of these preferences makes up an individual's psychological type.

Myers-Briggs Type Indicator® (MBTI) instrument An instrument developed to measure Carl Jung's theory of individual differences.

Who Says Introverts Can't Be Leaders?

Do you have to be an extravert to be a leader? Some of the most influential leaders in business and politics would disagree—they're introverts!

> Elon Musk, founder and CEO of SpaceX and Tesla Inc.

> Former U.S. president Barack Obama

> Wendy Kopp, founder of Teach for America

> Warren Buffett, famous investor and philanthropist, CEO of Berkshire Hathaway

> Hillary Clinton, former Secretary of State

> Mark Zuckerberg, cofounder of Facebook

Introverted leaders may succeed because of their natural capacity for introspection and thoughtful communication. They spend a lot of time listening and are more open to others' ideas, collaborating with others before making important decisions. Rather than interacting with a great number of people, introverts form genuine, deep ties to a smaller network of people they can rely on.

It's important to remember that introversion means getting energy from time alone. It has nothing to do with social skills; in fact, many of the leaders mentioned above have great social skills.

SOURCE: S. Cole, "7 Famous Leaders Who Prove Introverts Can Be Wildly Successful," *Fast Company*, http://www.fastcompany.com/3032028/the-future-of-work/7-famous-leaders-who-prove-introverts-can-be-wildly-successful, accessed June 18, 2014.

Kathy Hutchins/Shutterstock.com

VASILIS VERVERIDIS/123RF

Everett Collection Inc/Alamy Stock Photo

KATHY WILLENS/POOL/EPA/Newscom

JStone/Shutterstock.com

Frederic Legrand - COMEO/Shutterstock.com

EXTRAVERSION/INTROVERSION The **Extraversion/Introversion** preference represents where you find energy. Jung's theory holds that the Extraversion/Introversion preference reflects the most important distinction among individuals. The Extraverted type (E) is energized by interaction with other people. The Introverted type (I) is energized by time alone. Extraverted types typically have a wide social network, whereas Introverted types have a more narrow range of relationships. As articulated by Jung, this preference has nothing to do with social skills. Many introverts have excellent social skills but prefer the internal world of ideas, thoughts, and concepts. Extraverts represent approximately 49 percent of the U.S. population, and introverts represent about 51 percent, indicating a fairly even split.[65] Our U.S. culture rewards and nurtures extraverts. In work settings, extraverts prefer variety and do not mind being interrupted by phone calls or visits. They communicate freely but, on the negative side, may say things that they regret later.

Introverts prefer to concentrate quietly and think things through privately. They are detail oriented and do not mind working on a project for a long time; but they dislike telephone interruptions and may have trouble recalling names and faces.

Extraversion Being energized by interaction with other people.

Introversion Being energized by spending time alone.

Sensing Gathering information through the five senses and focusing on what actually exists.

Intuition Gathering information through a "sixth sense" and focusing on what could be.

SENSING/INTUITION The **Sensing/Intuition** preference represents perception or information gathering. The Sensing type (S) pays attention to information gathered through the five senses and to what actually exists. The Intuitive type (N) pays attention to a "sixth sense" and to what could be rather than to what actually exists.[66] Approximately 70 percent of people in the United States are Sensing types.[67]

At work, Sensing types prefer specific answers to questions and can be frustrated by vague instructions. They like jobs yielding tangible results and would rather use established skills than learn new ones. Intuitive types like solving new problems and are impatient with routine details. They enjoy learning new skills more than actually using them. They tend to think about several things at once and may appear absentminded. They like figuring out how things work just for the fun of it.

THINKING/FEELING The **Thinking/Feeling** preference describes the way we prefer to make decisions. The Thinking preference (T) makes decisions in a logical, objective fashion, whereas the Feeling preference (F) makes decisions in a personal, value-oriented way. The general U.S. population is divided 40/60 on the Thinking/Feeling type preference, respectively. But, interestingly, the majority of males are Thinking types, whereas the majority of females are Feeling types. It is the one preference in type theory that has a strong gender difference. Thinking types tend to analyze decisions, while Feeling types sympathize. Thinking types try to be impersonal, whereas Feeling types base their decisions on how the outcome will affect the people involved.

In work settings, Thinking types tend to show less emotion. They also tend to be less comfortable with others' emotional expressions and respond more readily to other people's thoughts. They tend to be firm minded and like putting things into a logical framework. Feeling types, by contrast, are comfortable with emotion in the workplace. They enjoy pleasing people and receiving frequent praise and encouragement.

JUDGING/PERCEIVING The **Judging/Perceiving** dichotomy reflects one's orientation to the outer world. The Judging preference (J) loves closure. They prefer to lead planned, organized lives and like making decisions. On the other hand, Perceivers (P) prefer flexible and spontaneous lives and like to keep options open. Imagine two people, one with a preference for Judging and the other for Perceiving, going out for dinner. J asks P to choose a restaurant, and P suggests ten alternatives. J just wants to decide and get on with it, whereas P wants to explore all the options.

Judging types love getting things accomplished and delight in checking off completed tasks on their calendars. Perceiving types generally adopt a wait-and-see attitude, collecting new information instead of drawing conclusions. Perceiving types are curious and welcome new information. They may start many projects without finishing them.

THE SIXTEEN TYPES The preferences combine to form sixteen distinct types, as shown in Table 3.3. For example, the ESTJ type has Extraversion, Sensing, Thinking, and Judging preferences. ESTJs see the world as it is (S); make decisions objectively (T); and like structure, schedules, and order (J). Combining these qualities with their preference for interacting with others makes them ideal managers. ESTJs are dependable, practical, and able to get any job done. They are conscious of the chain of command and see work as a series of goals to be reached by following rules and regulations. They may have little tolerance for disorganization and have a high need for control. Research results from the *MBTI Atlas* show that most of the 7,463 managers studied were ESTJs.[68]

The MBTI instrument has been found to have good reliability and validity as a measurement instrument for identifying type.[69] There are no good or bad types; each has its own strengths and weaknesses. Type influences learning style, teaching style, and choice of occupation. A study of the MBTI types of engineering students at Georgia Tech determined that STs and NTs were more attracted to engineering. Es and Fs were more likely to withdraw from engineering courses.[70] Type can also determine an individual's decision-making and management styles.

HOW COMPANIES USE MBTI Recent studies have focused on the relationship between type and specific managerial behaviors. The Introverted type (I) and the Feeling type (F), for example, appear to be more effective at participative management than their counterparts, the Extraverted type and the Thinking type.[71] Companies such as AT&T, ExxonMobil, and Honeywell use the MBTI instrument in their management development programs to help employees understand the different viewpoints of others in the organization. The MBTI instrument can also be used for team building, and resources are available to help managers learn how to do so effectively.[72]

> **Thinking** Making decisions in a logical, objective fashion.
>
> **Feeling** Making decisions in a personal, value-oriented way.
>
> **Judging** Preferring closure and completion in making decisions.
>
> **Perceiving** Preferring to explore many alternatives with flexibility and spontaneity.

TABLE 3.3 CHARACTERISTICS FREQUENTLY ASSOCIATED WITH EACH TYPE

Sensing Types		Intuitive Types	
ISTJ	**ISFJ**	**INFJ**	**INTJ**
Quiet, serious, earn success by thoroughness and dependability. Practical, matter-of-fact, realistic, and responsible. Decides logically what should be done and works toward it steadily, regardless of distractions. Takes pleasure in making everything orderly and organized—work, home, and life. Values traditions and loyalty.	Quiet, friendly, responsible, and conscientious. Committed and steady in meeting obligations. Thorough, painstaking, and accurate. Loyal, considerate, notices and remembers specifics about people who are important, concerned with how others feel. Strives to create an orderly and harmonious environment at work and at home.	Seeks meaning and connection in ideas, relationships, and material possessions. Wants to understand what motivates people and is insightful about others. Conscientious and committed to firm values. Develops a clear vision about how best to serve the common good. Organized and decisive in implementing his or her vision.	Has an original mind and great drive for implementing ideas and achieving goals. Quickly sees patterns in external events and develops long-range explanatory perspectives. When committed, organizes a job and carries it through. Skeptical and independent, has high standards of competence and performance for self and others.
ISTP	**ISFP**	**INFP**	**INTP**
Tolerant and flexible, quiet observer until a problem appears, then acts quickly to find workable solutions. Analyzes what makes things work and readily gets through large amounts of data to isolate the core of practical problems. Interested in cause and effect, organizes facts using logical principles, values efficiency.	Quiet, friendly, sensitive, and kind. Enjoys the present moment, and the immediate environment. Likes to have his or her own space and to work within a selected time frame. Loyal and committed to personal values and to people who are important to him or her. Dislikes disagreements and conflicts, does not force opinions or values on others.	Idealistic, loyal to values and to people who are important to him or her. Wants an external life that is congruent with values. Curious, quick to see possibilities, can be a catalyst for implementing ideas. Seeks to understand people and to help them fulfill their potential. Adaptable, flexible, and accepting unless a value is threatened.	Seeks to develop logical explanations for everything that interests him or her. Theoretical and abstract, interested more in ideas than in social interaction. Quiet, contained, flexible, and adaptable. Has unusual ability to focus in depth to solve problems in area of interest. Skeptical, sometimes critical, always analytical.
ESTP	**ESFP**	**ENFP**	**ENTP**
Flexible and tolerant, takes a pragmatic approach focused on immediate results. Finds theories and conceptual explanations boring. Wants to act energetically to solve the problem. Focuses on the here and now, spontaneous, enjoys each moment that he or she can be active with others. Enjoys material comforts and style. Learns best through doing.	Outgoing, friendly, and accepting. Exuberant lover of life, people, and material comforts. Enjoys working with others to make things happen. Brings common sense and a realistic approach to his or her work and makes work fun. Flexible and spontaneous, adapts readily to new people and environments. Learns best by trying a new skill with other people.	Warmly enthusiastic and imaginative. Sees life as full of possibilities. Makes connections between events and information very quickly, and confidently proceeds based on the patterns he or she sees. Wants a lot of affirmation from others, and readily gives appreciation and support. Spontaneous and flexible, often relies on his or her ability to improvise and verbal fluency.	Quick, ingenious, stimulating, alert, and outspoken. Resourceful in solving new and challenging problems. Adept at generating conceptual possibilities and then analyzing them strategically. Good at reading other people. Bored by routine, will seldom do the same thing the same way, apt to turn to one new interest after another.
ESTJ	**ESFJ**	**ENFJ**	**ENTJ**
Practical, realistic, matter-of-fact. Decisive, quickly moves to implement decisions. Organizes projects and people to get things done, focuses on getting results in the most efficient way possible. Takes care of routine details. Has a clear set of logical standards, systematically follows them and wants others to do so also. Forceful in implementing plans.	Warmhearted, conscientious, and cooperative. Wants harmony in the environment, works with determination to establish it. Likes to work with others to complete tasks accurately and on time. Loyal, follows through even in small matters. Notices what others need in their day-to-day lives and tries to provide it. Wants to be appreciated for who he or she is and for his or her contribution.	Warm, empathetic, responsive, and responsible. Highly attuned to the emotions, needs, and motivations of others. Finds potential in everyone, wants to help others fulfill their potential. May act as a catalyst for individual and group growth. Loyal, responsive to praise and criticism. Sociable, facilitates others in a group, and provides inspiring leadership.	Frank, decisive, assumes leadership readily. Quickly sees logical and inefficient procedures and policies, develops and implements comprehensive systems to solve organizational problems. Enjoys long-term planning and goal setting. Usually well informed, well read, enjoys expanding knowledge and passing it on to others. Forceful in presenting ideas.

NOTE: I = Introversion; E = Extraversion; S = Sensing; N = Intuition; T = Thinking; F = Feeling; J = Judging; and P = Perceiving.

SOURCE: Adapted from *Introduction to Type*, Sixth Edition by Isabel Briggs Myers. Copyright 1998 by Peter B. Myers and Katharine D. Myers. All rights reserved.

Hewlett-Packard and Armstrong World Industries use the MBTI instrument to show teams that diversity and differences lead to successful performance.

Managers value type theory for its simplicity and accuracy. But information from the MBTI instrument can be misused in organizational settings.[73] Some inappropriate uses include labeling one's coworkers, claiming results as a convenient excuse that one simply can't work with a particular coworker, and avoiding responsibility for learning to work flexibly with others. Although personality type is not an excuse for inappropriate behavior, if used well, type theory helps managers develop interpersonal skills. It also helps in building teams that capitalize on individuals' strengths and foster appreciation of individual team members' differences.

3-4 SOCIAL PERCEPTION

Perception is another psychological process that creates individual differences. As the primary vehicle through which we come to understand ourselves and our world, perception adds meaning to information gathered via the five senses of touch, smell, hearing, vision, and taste. Virtually all management activities rely on perception. Here, we focus specifically on **social perception**, or the process of interpreting information about another person.

The *selection interview* highlights the importance of perception. The consequences of a bad match between an individual and the organization are devastating for both parties, so accurate data must be gathered. First interviews are typically brief, and the candidate is usually one of many seen by an interviewer during a day. The interviewer often makes an accept or reject decision in the first four to five minutes based on her or his perception of the candidate.[74]

Social perception affects how people perceive each other when going through a life change such as pregnancy. Pregnant women are often viewed negatively in the workplace due to stereotypes, and women work hard to maintain their professional images by maintaining their work pace, going the extra mile, and not requesting accommodations.[75] They want to avoid being perceived as less capable, less career oriented, and less committed to the organization. Having to worry about how others see them can lead to burnout. The women do not see themselves as different

> Although personality type is not an excuse for inappropriate behavior, if used well, type theory helps managers develop interpersonal skills.

professionally during a pregnancy; it's the changing perceptions of others that make working during pregnancy a challenge.

Perception is often culturally determined. Based on our cultural backgrounds, we tend to perceive things in certain ways. Read the following sentence: *Finished files are the result of years of scientific study combined with the experience of years.* Now quickly count the number of *Fs* in the sentence. Individuals who speak English as a second language see all six *Fs*. Most native English speakers report that there are three *Fs* because they are culturally conditioned to ignore unimportant words like *of*.[76] Culture can affect our interpretation of the data we gather as well as the meaning we add to it. In other words, our culture can affect our social perception. Valuing diversity, including cultural diversity, has been recognized as a key to international competitiveness, so managers need good social perception skills.[77]

Three major categories of factors influence our perception of others: characteristics of ourselves as perceivers, characteristics of the target person we are perceiving, and characteristics of the situation in which the interaction takes place. Figure 3.2 models social perception.

3-4a Characteristics of the Perceiver

Several characteristics of the perceiver can affect social perception. The perceiver uses *perceptual lenses* to shape his or her view of the target, especially if it is a new encounter. Perceptual lenses are filters used by the perceiver to make a quick initial assessment. The most often used lenses

social perception The process of interpreting information about another person.

FIGURE 3.2 A MODEL FOR SOCIAL PERCEPTION

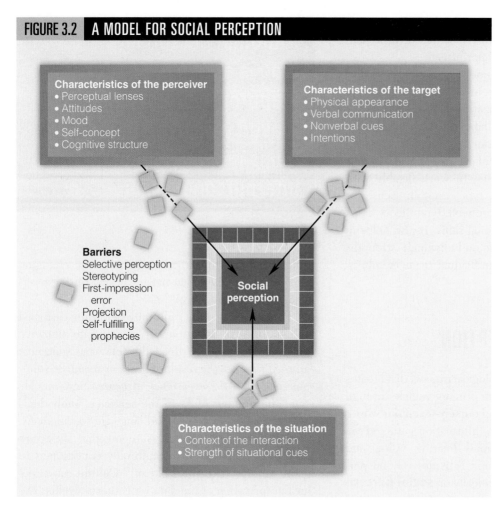

remember information that matches our mood state better than information that is inconsistent with it. When in a positive mood, we form more positive impressions of others. When in a negative mood, we tend to evaluate others unfavorably.

Another factor that can affect social perception is the perceiver's *self-concept*. An individual with a positive self-concept tends to notice positive attributes in another person. In contrast, a negative self-concept can lead a perceiver to pick out negative traits in another person. The better we understand ourselves, the more accurate our perceptions of others.

Cognitive structure, an individual's pattern of thinking, also affects social perception. Some people tend to perceive physical traits such as height, weight, and appearance more readily. Others focus on central traits, or personality dispositions. Cognitive complexity allows a person to perceive multiple characteristics of another person rather than attending to just a few traits.

3-4b Characteristics of the Target

Characteristics of the target (the person being perceived) influence social perception in various ways. *Physical appearance* plays a big role in our perception of others. The perceiver will notice physical features such as height, weight, estimated age, race, and gender. Clothing says a great deal about a person. Blue pinstriped suits, for example, suggest banking or Wall Street. Perceivers tend to notice physical appearance characteristics that contrast with the norm, that are intense, or that are new or unusual.[80] A loud person, one who dresses outlandishly, a very tall person, or a hyperactive child will be noticed because he or she contrasts

include the trust lens (are you friend or foe?), the power lens (are you useful to me?), and the ego lens (which of us is superior?). You can use knowledge of perceptual lenses to ensure that you're perceived accurately. For the trust lens, project warmth and competence through appropriate eye contact, smiling, and good posture. For the power lens, make yourself instrumental through assurances that you can help the perceiver reach mutual goals. For the ego lens, be modest and inclusive, and create a sense of "us."[78]

The perceiver's *attitudes* also affect social perception. Suppose you are interviewing candidates for a very important position in your organization—a position that requires negotiating contracts with suppliers, most of whom are male. You may feel that women are not capable of holding their own in tough negotiations. This attitude will doubtlessly affect your perceptions of the female candidates you interview.

Mood can have a strong influence on the way we perceive someone.[79] We think differently when we are happy than we do when we are depressed. We also

with what is commonly encountered. Novel individuals such as newcomers or minorities also attract attention.

Physical attractiveness often colors our entire impression of another person. Interviewers rate attractive candidates more favorably and award them higher starting salaries.[81] But people who are perceived as physically attractive face some nonbeneficial stereotypes as well.

Verbal communication from a target affects our perception of him or her. We listen to the topics discussed and his or her tone of voice and accent, and we make judgments based on this input.

Nonverbal communication conveys a great deal of information about the target. Eye contact, facial expressions, body movements, and posture all are deciphered by the perceiver in an attempt to form an impression of the target. Awareness of cultural differences is particularly important when it comes to nonverbal communication because some nonverbal signals mean very different things in different cultures. The "okay" sign in the United States (forming a circle with the thumb and forefinger) is an insult in South America. Facial expressions, however, seem to have universal meanings. Individuals from different cultures can recognize and decipher expressions the same way.[82]

The *intentions* of the target are inferred by the perceiver who observes the target's behavior. We may see our boss appear in our office doorway and think, "Oh no! She's going to give me more work to do." Or we may perceive that her intention is to congratulate us on a recent success. In any case, the perceiver's interpretation of the target's intentions affects the way the perceiver views the target.

3-4c **Characteristics of the Situation**

The situation in which the interaction between the perceiver and the target takes place, the *social context*, also influences perception. Meeting your professor in his or her office affects your impression

Stefan Randholm/Flickr/Getty Images

The way you dress influences how people perceive you.

differently than meeting your professor in a local restaurant would. Social context is very important in Japan. Business conversations after working hours or at lunch are taboo. If you try to talk business during these times, you may be perceived as rude.[83]

The *strength of situational cues* also affects social perception. As discussed earlier in the chapter, some situations provide strong cues about appropriate behavior. In these situations, we assume that the individual's behavior can be accounted for by the situation and may not reflect the individual's disposition. This is the **discounting principle** in social perception.[84] For example, you may encounter an automobile salesperson who has a warm and personable manner, asks about your work and hobbies, and seems genuinely interested in your taste in cars. Yet you probably cannot assume that this behavior reflects the salesperson's personality because of the influence of the situation. This person is trying to sell you a car and probably treats all customers in this manner.

3-5 BARRIERS TO SOCIAL PERCEPTION

It would be wonderful if all of us had accurate social perception skills. Unfortunately, barriers often prevent us from perceiving others accurately. Five barriers to social perception are selective perception, stereotyping, first-impression error, projection, and self-fulfilling prophecies.

Selective perception is our tendency to prefer information that supports our viewpoints. Individuals often ignore information that threatens their viewpoints. Suppose, for example, that a sales manager is evaluating the performance of his employees. One

discounting principle
The assumption that an individual's behavior is accounted for by the situation.

selective perception The tendency to select information that supports our individual viewpoints while discounting information that threatens our viewpoints.

Guys Don't Cry at Work

No one enjoys getting negative feedback, and everyone reacts differently. How do feedback providers evaluate employees' reactions to the feedback? Does it depend on gender? Men who cry at work may be seen as behaving against the

stereotype of being dominant and strong. Atypical behavior such as crying may work against them.

In one study, participants watched videos of males or females receiving a negative performance review. After viewing the video, participants rated the employee's performance and leadership ability, and they were asked to write a recommendation letter for the employee. Results showed that when women cried, it did not affect perceptions of the performance or leadership ability. Not so for the men. Men who cried were seen as atypical, were rated lower in both performance and leadership ability, and were given less positive recommendation letters.

Gender bias at work affects men too. Sexism based on stereotypes goes both ways.

SOURCE: D. Motro and A.P.J. Ellis, "Boys, Don't Cry: Gender and Reactions to Negative Performance Feedback," *Journal of Applied Psychology*, 102 (2017), 227–235.

employee does not get along well with colleagues and rarely completes sales reports on time. This employee, however, generates the most new sales contracts in the office. The sales manager may ignore the negative information, choosing to evaluate the salesperson only on contracts generated. The manager is exercising selective perception.

A **stereotype** is a generalization about a group of people. Stereotypes reduce information about other people to a workable level so that it can be compiled efficiently. Stereotypes become even stronger when they are shared with and validated by others.[85] Some stereotypes are accurate and serve as useful perceptual guidelines, but, of course, many are inaccurate and do much harm, generating false impressions that may never be tested or changed.

Stereotypes about different generations present challenges in the workplace. Older workers may see Millennials and Generation Z employees as entitled and unfocused, but

stereotypes of older workers also exist. Ageism is prejudice or discrimination either for or against an age group. With four generations in the workforce, employees use stereotypes as shortcuts to categorize their coworkers, and these stereotypes can lead to misunderstandings and even obstacles to performance. Managers can create positive intergenerational climates by encouraging interactions between the coworkers of different generations, promoting cross-generational mentoring relationships, and creating a work environment that is inclusive and healthy for people of all ages.[86]

Attractiveness is a powerful stereotype. We assume that attractive individuals are also warm, kind, sensitive, poised, sociable, outgoing, independent, and strong. However, a study of romantic relationships showed that most attractive individuals do not fit the stereotype apart from possessing good social skills and being popular.[87] Some individuals may seem to us to fit the stereotype of attractiveness because our behavior elicits from them behavior that confirms the stereotype. Consider, for example, a situation in which you meet an attractive fellow student. Chances are that you respond positively to this person because you assume she or he is warm, sociable, and so on. Even though the person may not possess these traits, your positive response may bring out these behaviors in the person. Thus, your interaction may be channeled to confirm the stereotype.[88]

Stereotyping pervades work life. When an individual's behavior contrasts with a stereotype of his or her group, he or she is treated more positively (given more favorable comments or pats on the back). For example, a female softball player might receive more applause for a home run hit than a male teammate because some people may stereotype women as less athletic than men and hold female players to a lower standard. Either way, the contrast is still part of stereotyping.[89]

First impressions are lasting impressions, so the saying goes. We tend to remember what we perceive first about a person, and sometimes we are quite reluctant to change our initial impressions.[90] **First-impression** occurs when we observe a very brief bit of a person's behavior in our first encounter and infer that this behavior reflects what the person is really like. Such primacy effects can be particularly dangerous in interviews, given that we form first impressions quickly and that these impressions may be the basis for long-term employment relationships.

What factors do interviewers rely on when forming first impressions? Perceptions of the candidate, such as whether they like the person, whether they trust the person, and whether or not the person seems credible, all influence the interviewer's decision. Something as

stereotype A generalization about a group of people.

first-impression Forming lasting opinions about an individual based on initial perceptions.

Stereotypes about Gender and "Smarts" Start Early

There is a common stereotype that extremely high intellectual ability is a male trait. Because of this stereotype, women may not pursue careers in fields that require high levels of "smarts." Researchers wanted to learn children's perceptions of who is "really, really smart," so they showed five-year-olds pictures and asked which person in the photo was "really, really smart." Five-year-olds associated "smart" with their own gender. Boys said the man was the smart one; girls said the woman was the smart one.

At age 6, things changed. Boys still said males were smarter, but girls were less likely to say females were smarter, and they began to show less interest in games meant for smart people. These beliefs persisted despite the fact that at that age, girls outperform boys in school.

It's no wonder fewer girls are interested in STEM (science, technology, engineering, and math) disciplines. Not only does the "science is male" stereotype keep women from entering STEM careers; it may also be that the "smart is male" stereotype is a culprit.

Researchers are now studying what can be done to reverse this trend. One idea is to show more examples of brilliant women to children at younger ages.

SOURCES: L. Bian, S. Leslie, and A. Cimpian, "Gender Stereotypes About Intellectual Ability Emerge Early and Influence Children's Interests," *Science*, 355 (2017): 389–391.

seemingly unimportant as the pitch of your voice can leave a lasting impression.

Speakers with lower vocal pitch are believed to be more competent, more dominant, and more assertive than those with higher voices. Men whose voices are high enough that they sound feminine are judged the least favorably of all by interviewers. This finding is ironic, given that research has found that students with higher vocal pitch tend to earn better grades.[91]

Projection, also known as the *false-consensus effect*, causes inaccurate perceptions of others. When we project, we assume that our own beliefs and values are commonly held and normative, and we overestimate the number of others who share them. People who are different are viewed as unusual and even deviant. Projection occurs most often when you surround yourself with others similar to you. You may overlook important information about others when you assume we are all alike and in agreement.[92]

Self-fulfilling prophecies, also called the *Pygmalion effect*, interfere with social perception in that our expectations affect the way we interact with others such that we provoke the very response we expect. Early studies of self-fulfilling prophecy were conducted in elementary school classrooms. Teachers were given bogus information that some of their pupils had high intellectual potential. These pupils were chosen randomly; there were really no differences among the students. Eight months later, the "gifted" pupils scored significantly higher on an IQ test. The teachers' expectations elicited growth from these students because they had given them tougher assignments and more feedback on their performance.[93]

A manager's expectations of an individual affect both the manager's behavior toward the individual and the individual's response. For example, suppose your initial impression is that an employee has the potential to move up in the organization. Chances are you will spend a great deal of time coaching and counseling the employee, providing challenging assignments, and grooming the individual for success. Managers can harness the power of the Pygmalion effect to improve productivity in the organization simply by expecting positive results from a group of employees.[94]

3-5a Impression Management

Most people want to make favorable impressions on others. This is particularly true in organizations where individuals compete for jobs, favorable performance evaluations, and salary increases. The process by which individuals try to control the impressions others have of them is called **impression management**. Individuals use

projection Overestimating the number of people who share our own beliefs, values, and behaviors.

self-fulfilling prophecy Allowing expectations about people to affect our interaction with them in such a way that those expectations are fulfilled.

impression management The process by which individuals try to control the impressions others have of them.

several techniques to control others' impressions of them.[95]

Some impression management techniques are *self-enhancing*. Name-dropping, or mentioning an association with important people in the hope of improving one's image, is often used. Controlling one's appearance is another self-enhancing technique for impression management. Individuals dress carefully for interviews because they want to "look the part" in order to get the job. Self-descriptions, or statements about one's characteristics, are used to manage impressions as well.

Another group of impression management techniques are *other-enhancing*. They focus on the individual on whom one is trying to make an impression rather than on oneself. People often use flattery and favors to win approval. Agreeing with someone's opinion can create a positive impression. People with disabilities, for example, often use other-enhancing techniques. They may feel that they must take it upon themselves to make others comfortable interacting with them. Impression management techniques help them prevent potential avoidance by others.[96]

Leaders, as the face of organizations, engage in impression management. If the company is in a highly publicized decline and their own compensation depends on company performance, leaders increase their impression management behaviors.[97] And firms often tailor their impression management techniques to different stakeholders such as local press, international press, and financial analysts, to manipulate each group's view of the company's performance.[98]

So impression management does seem to influence others' impressions. As long as the impressions conveyed are accurate, this process benefits organizations. If the impressions are found to be false, however, the result is a strongly negative overall impression. Furthermore, excessive impression management can lead to the perception that the user is manipulative or insincere.[99]

3-6   ATTRIBUTION IN ORGANIZATIONS

Human beings are innately curious. We want to know *why* people behave the way they do. We also seek to understand and explain our own behavior. **Attribution theory** explains how we pinpoint the causes of our own

attribution theory A theory that explains how individuals pinpoint the causes of their own and others' behavior.

behavior (and therefore our performance) and that of other people.[100]

3-6a   Internal and External Attributions

We can attribute events to an internal source of responsibility (something within the individual's control) or an external source (something outside the individual's control). Suppose you perform well on an exam. You might say you aced the test because you are smart or because you studied hard; this internal attribution credits your ability or effort. Alternatively, you might make an external attribution for your performance by saying it was an easy test or that you had good luck.

Attribution patterns differ among individuals.[101] Achievement-oriented individuals attribute their success to ability and their failures to lack of effort—both internal causes. Failure-oriented individuals attribute their failures to lack of ability and may develop feelings of incompetence (or even depression) as a result.[102] Women managers are less likely to attribute their success to their own ability. This may be because they are adhering to social norms that compel women to be modest or because they believe that success has more do to with hard work than ability.[103]

Attribution theory has many applications in the workplace. The way you explain your own behavior affects your motivation. If you believe careful preparation and rehearsal led to your successful presentation, you're likely to take credit for the performance and to have a sense of self-efficacy about future presentations. If, however, you believe that you were just lucky, you may not be motivated to repeat the performance because you believe you had little influence on the outcome.

Lots of attributions are made during employment interviews when candidates are asked to explain the causes of previous performance. Candidates want to give interviewers reasons to hire them ("I work well with people, so I'm looking for a managerial job"). Research shows that successful candidates make different attributions for negative outcome than unsuccessful ones. Successful candidates are willing to make internal attributions for negative events. Unsuccessful candidates blame negative outcomes on things beyond their control, giving interviewers the impression that they failed to learn from the event and that they will likely blame others when something goes wrong in the workplace.[104]

3-6b Attributional Biases

The attribution process may be affected by two very common problems: The first is the tendency to make attributions to internal causes when focusing on someone else's behavior, known as the **fundamental attribution error**.[105] The other error, **self-serving bias**, occurs when focusing on one's own behavior. Individuals tend to make internal attributions for their own successes and external attributions for their own failures.[106] In other words, when we succeed, we take credit for it; when we fail, we blame the situation on other people.

Both biases were illustrated in a study of healthcare managers asked to cite the causes of their employees' poor performance.[107] The managers claimed that internal causes (their employees' lack of effort or lack of ability) explained their employees' poor performance. When the employees were asked to pinpoint the cause of their own performance problems, they blamed a lack of support from the managers (an external cause), which illustrates self-serving bias.

There are cultural differences in these two attribution errors. In fatalistic cultures, such as India, people tend to believe that fate is responsible for much that happens. People in such cultures tend to emphasize external causes of behavior.[108] In China, people are taught that hard work is the route to accomplishment. When faced with either a success or a failure, Chinese individuals first reflect on whether they tried hard enough or whether their attitude was correct. Thus, in analyzing a cause, they first look to their own effort.[109]

The way individuals interpret the events around them has a strong influence on their behavior. People in general try to understand the causes of behavior so that they can predict and control future behavior, and managers certainly do this. Hence, they use attributions in all aspects of their jobs. Especially in evaluating performance and rewarding employees, managers must determine the causes of behavior and a perceived source of responsibility.

Attribution theory explains how performance evaluation judgments can lead to differential rewards. A supervisor attributing an employee's good performance to internal causes such as effort or ability may give a larger raise than a supervisor attributing the good performance to external causes like help from others or good training. Managers are often called on to explain their own actions as well, and in doing so they make attributions about the causes of their own behavior. We continue our discussion of attributions in Chapter 6.

Are successes from luck or skill?

John Lund/Heather Hryciw/Blend Images/Getty Images

fundamental attribution error The tendency to make attributions to internal causes when focusing on someone else's behavior.

self-serving bias The tendency to attribute one's successes to internal causes and one's failures to external causes.

STUDY TOOLS 3

LOCATED AT BACK OF THE TEXTBOOK

☐ Rip out chapter review card

LOCATED AT WWW.CENGAGE.COM/LOGIN

☐ Gain unique perspectives on key concepts with new Concept Clip videos in the e-book

☐ Review key term flashcards and create your own

☐ Increase your comprehension with online homework and quizzes

4 | Attitudes, Emotions, and Ethics

LEARNING OBJECTIVES

4-1 Explain the ABC model of an attitude.

4-2 Describe how attitudes are formed.

4-3 Identify sources of job satisfaction and commitment.

4-4 Distinguish between organizational citizenship and workplace deviance behaviors.

4-5 Identify the characteristics of the source, target, and message that affect persuasion.

4-6 Discuss the definition and importance of emotions at work.

4-7 Contrast the effects of individual and organizational influences on ethical behavior.

4-8 Identify the factors that affect ethical behavior.

alphaspirit/123RF

After finishing this chapter go to **PAGE 69** for **STUDY TOOLS**

 4-1 ## ATTITUDES

An **attitude** is a psychological tendency expressed when we evaluate a particular entity with some degree of favor or disfavor.[1] Since we respond favorably or unfavorably toward many things such as coworkers, our own appearance, or politics, we have attitudes toward many things. Attitudes are closely linked to behavior in general, so they are an important factor in organizational behavior. Managers complain about workers with "bad attitudes" and conduct "attitude adjustment" talks. Poor performance attributed to bad attitude can often stem from lack of motivation, minimal feedback, lack of trust in management, or other problems. On the positive side, recognition and praise from colleagues and supervisors can positively impact an individual's attitudes and job performance.[2]

Thus, managers should understand the antecedents to attitudes as well as their consequences. They also need to understand the different components of attitudes, how attitudes are formed, the major attitudes that affect work behavior, and how to use persuasion to change attitudes.

4-1a The ABC Model

An individual does not have an attitude until he or she responds to an entity (person, object, situation, or issue) on an affective, behavioral, or cognitive basis. We can break attitudes down into three components, as depicted in Table 4.1. These three components compose what we call the *ABC model* of an attitude.[3]

Affect is the emotional component of an attitude. It refers to an individual's feeling about something or someone. Statements such as "I like this" or "I prefer that" reflect the affective component of an attitude. Affect can be measured by self-report questionnaires as well as physiological indicators such as blood pressure, which show emotional changes by measuring physiological arousal.

The second component is *behavioral intent* toward an object or person. Here, it is important to note that

> ## We may be supportive, passive, or hostile, depending on our attitude.

a behavioral intent may not actually lead to a particular behavior. But often it does. Our attitudes toward women in management, for example, may be inferred from observing the way we treat a female supervisor. We may be supportive, passive, or hostile, depending on our attitude. The behavioral component of an attitude is measured by observing behavior or by asking a person about behavior or intentions.

The third component of an attitude, *cognition* (thought), reflects a person's perceptions or beliefs. Cognitive elements are evaluative beliefs measured by attitude scales or by asking about thoughts. The statement "I believe Japanese workers are

> **attitude** A psychological tendency expressed by evaluating something with a degree of favor or disfavor.
>
> **affect** The emotional component of an attitude.

TABLE 4.1 THE ABC MODEL OF AN ATTITUDE

	Component	Measured By	Example
A	Affect	Physiological indicators Verbal statements about feelings	I don't like my boss.
B	Behavioral intent	Observed behavior Verbal statements about intentions	I want to transfer to another department.
C	Cognition	Attitude scales Verbal statements about beliefs	I believe my boss plays favorites at work.

SOURCE: Adapted from M. J. Rosenberg and C. I. Hovland, "Cognitive, Affective, and Behavioral Components of Attitude," in M. J. Rosenberg, C. I. Hovland, W. J. McGuire, R. P. Abelson, and J. H. Brehm, eds., *Attitude Organization and Change* (New Haven, Conn.: Yale University Press, 1960).

industrious" reflects the cognitive component of an attitude.

The ABC model shows that we must assess all three components to understand an attitude. Suppose, for example, you want to evaluate your employees' attitudes toward *flextime* (flexible work scheduling). You would want to determine how they feel about the policy (affect), whether they would participate in it (behavioral intention), and what they think about it (cognition). The most common method of attitude measurement, however, is the attitude scale, which measures only the cognitive component.

4-1b Cognitive Dissonance

As rational beings, people prefer consistency (consonance) between their attitudes and behavior. Anything that disrupts this consistency causes tension (dissonance), which motivates individuals to change either their attitudes or their behavior to maintain consistency. The tension produced by a conflict between attitudes and behavior is **cognitive dissonance**.[4]

Suppose, for example, a salesperson is required to sell damaged televisions for the full retail price without revealing the damage to customers. She believes, however, that this is unethical, which creates a conflict between her attitude

cognitive dissonance A state of tension produced when an individual experiences conflict between attitudes and behavior.

(concealing information from customers is unethical) and her behavior (selling defective TVs to uninformed customers). Uncomfortable with the dissonance, she will try to resolve the conflict. She might change her behavior by refusing to sell the defective TV sets. Alternatively, she might rationalize that the defects are minor and that the customers won't be harmed by not knowing about them. These are attempts by the salesperson to restore equilibrium between her attitude and behavior, thereby eliminating the tension from cognitive dissonance.

Managers need to understand cognitive dissonance because employees often find themselves in situations in which their attitudes conflict with their behavior. Employees who display sudden shifts in behavior may be attempting to reduce dissonance. Some employees find the conflicts between strongly held attitudes and required work behavior so uncomfortable that they leave the organization to escape the dissonance.

4-2 ATTITUDE FORMATION

Attitudes are learned. Our responses to people and issues evolve over time. Two major influences on attitudes are direct experience and social learning.

Direct experience with something strongly influences attitudes toward it. How do you know that you like biology or dislike math? You have probably formed these attitudes from experience studying the subjects. Research has shown that attitudes derived from direct experience are stronger, held more confidently, and more resistant to change than attitudes formed through indirect experience.[5] These attitudes are powerful because of their availability; they are easily accessed and

A salesperson who tries to sell a damaged product for full price may experience cognitive dissonance.

active in our cognitive processes.[6] When attitudes are available, we can call them quickly into consciousness.

In **social learning**, the family, peer groups, religious organizations, and culture shape an individual's attitudes indirectly.[7] Children adopt certain attitudes when their parents reinforce attitudes they approve. This is evident from the fact that very young children express political preferences similar to those held by their parents. Later, peer pressure molds attitudes through group acceptance of individuals who express popular attitudes and through sanctions, such as exclusion from the group, placed on individuals who espouse unpopular attitudes. Substantial social learning occurs through *modeling*, in which individuals acquire attitudes by observing others. After overhearing other individuals expressing opinions or watching them engage in behaviors that reflect an attitude, the observer adopts the attitude.

Culture also plays a definitive role in attitude development. Consider, for example, the contrast in the North American and European attitudes toward vacation and leisure. The typical vacation in the United States is two weeks. In Europe, longer vacations are the norm. In some countries, *holiday* means everyone taking a month off. The European attitude is that an investment in longer vacations is important to health and performance.

4-2a Attitudes and Behavior

The correspondence between attitude and behavior has concerned organizational behaviorists and social psychologists for quite some time. Can attitudes predict behaviors such as being absent from work or quitting your job? Some studies suggested that they can, because attitudes and behavior are closely linked, while others found no relationship at all. Researchers also focused on when attitudes predict behavior and when they do not. Attitude–behavior correspondence depends on five things: attitude specificity, attitude relevance, timing of measurement, personality factors, and social constraints.

Individuals possess both general and specific attitudes. You may favor a woman's right to reproductive freedom (a general attitude) and prefer pro-choice political candidates (a specific attitude) without attending pro-choice rallies or donating to Planned Parenthood. That you don't perform these behaviors appears to weaken the link between your attitude and behaviors. However, given a choice between a pro-choice and an anti-abortion political candidate, you will probably vote for the pro-choice candidate. In this case, your attitude seems quite predictive of your behavior. The more specific the attitude, the stronger is its link to behavior.[8]

Another factor that affects the attitude–behavior link is relevance.[9] Attitudes that address an issue in which we have some self-interest are more relevant for us, and our subsequent behavior is consistent with our expressed attitude. Consider a proposal to raise income taxes for those earning $150,000 or more. If you are a student, you may not find the issue of great personal relevance. Individuals in that income bracket, however, might find it highly relevant. Their attitude toward the issue would be strongly predictive of whether they would vote for the tax increase.

The timing of the measurement is still another factor affecting attitude–behavior correspondence. The shorter the time is between the attitude measurement and the observed behavior, the stronger the relationship. For example, voter preference polls taken close to an election are more accurate than earlier polls.

Personality factors also influence the attitude–behavior link. One personality disposition that affects the consistency between attitudes and behavior is *self-monitoring*. Recall from the discussion of personality characteristics in Chapter 3 that low self-monitors rely on their internal states when making decisions about behavior, while high self-monitors are more responsive to situational cues. Low self-monitors therefore display greater correspondence between their attitudes and behaviors.[10] High self-monitors may display little correspondence between their attitudes and behavior because they behave according to signals from others and from the environment.

Finally, *social constraints* affect the relationship between attitudes and

social learning The process of deriving attitudes from family, peer groups, religious organizations, and culture.

Learning from Observing a Model

For an individual to learn from observing a model, four processes must take place:

1. The learner must focus attention on the model.

2. The learner must retain what was observed from the model. Retention is accomplished in two basic ways:

   - The learner "stamps in" what was observed by forming a verbal code for it.

   - The learner forms a mental image of himself or herself behaving like the model—what is known as *symbolic rehearsal*.

3. The learner must reproduce the behavior through practice.

4. The learner must be motivated to learn from the model.

behavior.[11] The social context provides information about acceptable attitudes and behaviors.[12] New employees in an organization are exposed to the attitudes of their work group.[13] A newcomer from Saudi Arabia may hold a negative attitude toward women in management because this attitude prevails in his home culture. He sees, however, that his work group members respond positively to their female supervisor. His own behavior may therefore be compliant because of social constraints even though it is inconsistent with his attitude and cultural belief system.

4-2b Work Attitudes

Attitudes at work are important because, directly or indirectly, they affect work behavior. Chief among the things that negatively affect employees' work attitudes are demanding jobs over which employees have little control.[14] A study concerned with how to prevent turnover in nursing found that commitment to the profession was one factor, but nurses' attitudes were significantly affected by whether or not they had flexibility in their schedules, could get enough time off, and had opportunities to learn new skills and advance. A major factor was the tension between patient care and hospital profits. The nurses in this study said that they felt called to make a difference in their patients' lives, but sometimes worried they could not offer patients adequate care and attention due to competing interests.[15] In contrast to the nursing situation in that study, another study found that a positive psychological climate was enough to generate positive attitudes and good performance in various jobs.[16]

4-3 JOB SATISFACTION

Job satisfaction is a pleasurable or positive emotional state resulting from the appraisal of one's job or job experiences.[17] It has been treated both as a general attitude and as satisfaction with five specific dimensions of the job: pay, the work itself, promotion opportunities, supervision, and coworkers.[18]

An individual may hold different attitudes toward various aspects of a job. For example, an employee may like her job responsibilities but be dissatisfied with the opportunities for promotion. Characteristics of individuals also affect job satisfaction.[19] Those with high negative affectivity are more likely to be dissatisfied with their jobs. Challenging work,

job satisfaction A pleasurable or positive emotional state resulting from the appraisal of one's job or job experiences.

valued rewards, opportunities for advancement, competent supervision, and supportive coworkers are dimensions of the job that can lead to satisfaction. What may surprise you is that pay is only marginally related to job satisfaction. Well-paid individuals are only slightly more satisfied than relatively poorly paid individuals.[20]

There are several measures of job satisfaction. One of the most widely used measures comes from the *Job Descriptive Index (JDI)*. This index measures the specific facets of satisfaction by asking employees to respond "yes," "no," or "cannot decide" to a series of statements describing their jobs. Another popular measure is the *Minnesota Satisfaction Questionnaire (MSQ)*.[21] This survey also asks employees to respond to statements about their jobs using a five-point scale that ranges from very dissatisfied to very satisfied. Figure 4.1 presents some sample items from each questionnaire.

Managers and employees believe that happy or satisfied employees are more productive at work. Most of us feel more satisfied than usual when we believe that we are performing better than usual.[22] But research on the relationship between job satisfaction and performance has shown it to be more complex than that. If job satisfaction always improved performance, then the manager's job would simply be to keep workers happy. Although this may be the case for certain individuals, research has shown that job satisfaction for most people is only one of several causes of good performance. Another view holds that good performance causes satisfaction, yet some high performers are not satisfied with their jobs. It is important to consider all of the potential variables when considering job satisfaction.[23]

The lack of a clear relationship between satisfaction and performance can be explained by the intervening role of rewards. Employees who receive valuable rewards are more satisfied. In addition, employees who receive rewards that are contingent on performance (the higher the performance, the larger the reward) tend to perform better. Rewards thus influence both satisfaction and

dotshock/Shutterstock.com

FIGURE 4.1   SAMPLE ITEMS FROM SATISFACTION QUESTIONNAIRES

Job Descriptive Index

Think of the work you do at present. How well does each of the following words or phrases describe your work? In the blank beside each word given below, write

_____Y_____ for "Yes" if it describes your work
_____N_____ for "No" if it does NOT describe it
_____?_____ if you cannot decide

WORK ON YOUR PRESENT JOB:

_____ Routine
_____ Satisfying
_____ Good

Think of the majority of the people who you work with now or the people you meet in connection with your work. How well does each of the following words or phrases describe these people? In the blank beside each word, write

_____Y_____ for "Yes" if it describes the people you work with
_____N_____ for "No" if it does NOT describe them
_____?_____ if you cannot decide

COWORKERS (PEOPLE):

_____ Boring
_____ Responsible
_____ Intelligent

Minnesota Satisfaction Questionnaire

1 = Very dissatisfied
2 = Dissatisfied
3 = I can't decide whether I am satisfied or not
4 = Satisfied
5 = Very satisfied

On my present job, this is how I feel about:

_____ The chance to work alone on the job (independence)
_____ My chances for advancement on this job (advancement)
_____ The chance to tell people what to do (authority)
_____ The praise I get for a good job (recognition)
_____ My pay and the amount of work I do (compensation)

SOURCE: The Job Descriptive Index is copyrighted by Bowling Green State University. The complete forms, scoring key, instructions, and norms can be obtained from the JDI Office, Department of Psychology, Bowling Green State University, Bowling Green, OH 43403. Minnesota Satisfaction Questionnaire from D. J. Weiss, R. V. Davis, G. W. England, and L. H. Lofquist, *Manual for the Minnesota Satisfaction Questionnaire* (University of Minnesota Vocational Psychology Research, 1967).

performance. The key to influencing both satisfaction and performance through rewards is that the rewards are valued by employees and are tied directly to performance.

4-4 ORGANIZATIONAL CITIZENSHIP VERSUS COUNTERPRODUCTIVE WORK BEHAVIOR

Job satisfaction encourages **organizational citizenship behavior (OCB)**—behavior that is above and beyond the call of duty. Satisfied employees are more likely to help their coworkers, make positive comments about the company, and refrain from complaining when things at work go poorly.[24] Going beyond the call of duty is especially important to organizations using teams, as employees in teams depend on extra help from each other to get things accomplished.

Satisfied workers are more likely to want to give something back to the organization—that is, to engage in OCBs because they want to reciprocate their positive experiences.[25] Often, employees may feel that their OCBs are not recognized because they occur outside the confines of normal job responsibilities, but they do indeed influence performance evaluations. Employees who help others, suggest innovations, and develop their skills receive higher performance ratings.[26]

OCBs can be directed at different facets of an organization, determined according to individual attitudes. For example, affect tends to direct OCBs toward other people, while cognition directs OCBs toward the organization.

Performing OCBs at work has multiple benefits for employees. OCBs help individuals see their work as more meaningful and promote employee well-being. You might think that performing these extra behaviors depletes employees' energy. Research shows the opposite—that OCBs actually enhance employee energy and vigor.[27]

When OCBs are the norm within a team, members are more likely to engage in OCBs. The impact of one person's OCB can spread throughout an entire team and spill over into the organization.[28] It should be recognized, though, that employees who over-engage in OCBs can become exhausted because of the toll it takes on their personal energy resources.[29] Organizations can help individuals avoid fatigue and

> **organizational citizenship behavior (OCB)** Behavior that is above and beyond the call of duty.

exhaustion from OCBs by providing a supportive environment, encouraging strong teamwork, and by not pressuring employees for OCBs.[30] The impact of one worker's OCBs can thus spread throughout an entire department.

Researchers have found a strong link between job satisfaction and organizational performance, although, as mentioned earlier, the relationship between the two factors is more complex than one might think. Nevertheless, overall, companies with satisfied workers have better performance than companies with dissatisfied workers.[31] This may be due to the more intangible elements of performance, such as OCB, that contribute to organizational effectiveness but aren't necessarily captured by measuring individual job performance.

Job satisfaction connects to other important outcomes. Dissatisfied workers are more likely to skip work and quit their jobs, driving up the cost of turnover. Furthermore, dissatisfied workers report more psychological and medical problems than do satisfied employees.[32]

One factor that leads to dissatisfaction at work is a misfit between an individual's values and the organization's values, or a lack of *person–organization fit*. People who feel that their values don't mesh with the organization's values experience job dissatisfaction and eventually leave the organization.[33]

Like all attitudes, job satisfaction is influenced by culture. A recent study of job satisfaction rates in forty-nine countries found a close link between job characteristics and job satisfaction in countries with higher incomes, higher individualism, and lower power distance than in countries with lower incomes, lower individualism (higher collectivism), and higher power distance.[34] As employees from different cultures may have differing job expectations, there may be no single prescription for increasing the job satisfaction of a multicultural workforce. Researchers found in China's hotel and restaurant industry that high-performance human resource practices such as promotions from within, flexible job assignments, long-term results-oriented appraisals, and job security fostered service-oriented OCBs. Such OCBs were in turn linked to lower turnover and higher productivity at the organizational level.[35]

Nature Improves Work Attitudes

Managers who want to improve employees' job satisfaction and organizational commitment may want to redesign their workplaces. Research has shown that exposure to nature and being in sunlight while at work improved work attitudes, and even indirect sunlight boosted employees' moods at work. Natural elements in the workplace can be views out of windows, office plants, or simple things such as nature scenes as art or screen savers.

Amazon is bringing nature to downtown Seattle by constructing Spheres, which use natural elements to inspire employees. Set to open in 2018, the spheres will be filled with botanical gardens and tree canopies three stories high, along with indoor creeks. Employees will be able to hold meetings, take breaks, and eat lunch in the spheres, and hopefully come up with more creative ideas.

David Ryder/Getty Images News/Getty Images

SOURCE: M. An, S.M. Colarelli, K. O'Brien, and M.E. Boyajian, "Why We Need More Nature at Work: Effects of Natural Elements and Sunlight on Employee Mental Health and Work Attitudes," *PLOS One*, May 2016, http://journals.plos.org/plosone/article?id=10.1371/journal.pone.0155614; N. Wingfield, "Forget Beanbag Chairs. Amazon Is Giving Its Workers Treehouses," *New York Times*, July 10, 2016, https://www.nytimes.com/2016/07/11/technology/forget-beanbag-chairs-amazon-is-giving-its-workers-treehouses.html.

When employees are dissatisfied with their jobs, they are more likely to engage in **counterproductive work behavior (CWB)**, which is defined as any voluntary, attitude-driven behavior that violates organizational norms and causes some degree of harm to the organization, coworkers, or supervisors.[36] CWB can include calling in sick when you're not, coming in late, putting little effort into your work, taking property from work without permission, gossiping about others, and sabotaging others' projects. Negative events in the business world, such as downsizing and technological insecurities, are generally considered responsible for spikes in counterproductive work behavior. Layoffs, for example, may inspire employees to develop negative attitudes, to feel anger and hostility toward the organization, and to retaliate. Even when an employee keeps her job but believes the procedure used to determine the layoff is unfair, she may still take revenge against the manager. Perceived unfairness at work is a major cause of deviance, sabotage, and retaliation. Managers must prevent and manage CWB to keep it from damaging performance. One way to do that is to encourage positive attitudes among employees by providing a supportive organizational climate. Communicating to employees that their contributions are valued and that the company cares about their well-being can help prevent CWB.[37]

4-4a Organizational Commitment and Job Satisfaction

The strength of an individual's identification with an organization is known as **organizational commitment**. There are three kinds of organizational commitment: affective, continuance, and normative. **Affective commitment** is an employee's intention to remain in an organization because of a strong desire to do so. Affective commitment encompasses loyalty and a deep concern for the organization's welfare based on three factors: a belief in the goals and values of the organization, a willingness to put forth effort on behalf of the organization, and a desire to remain a member of the organization.[38]

Continuance commitment is an employee's tendency to remain in an organization because he cannot afford to leave.[39] Sometimes employees believe that they will lose a great deal of their investments in time, effort, and benefits if they leave. **Normative commitment** is a perceived obligation to remain with the organization. Individuals who experience normative commitment stay with the organization because they feel they should.[40]

Certain organizational conditions, such as participation in decision making and job security, encourage commitment. And so do job characteristics such as autonomy, responsibility, role clarity, and interesting work.[41] Affective

> Affective and normative commitments are related to lower rates of absenteeism, higher quality of work, increased productivity, and overall performance.

and normative commitments are related to lower rates of absenteeism, higher quality of work, increased productivity, and overall performance.[42] Managers should encourage affective commitment in particular because committed individuals expend more task-related effort and are less likely to leave the organization.[43]

Managers can increase affective commitment by communicating their appreciation of employees' contributions and concern for employees' well-being.[44] Affective commitment also increases when the organization and employees share the same values and when the organization emphasizes values like moral integrity, fairness, creativity, and openness.[45] Negative experiences at work, such as perceived age discrimination, diminish affective commitment.[46]

4-5 PERSUASION AND ATTITUDE CHANGE

The days of command-and-control management, in which executives simply told employees what to do, are over. Modern managers must instead aim to change employee attitudes and thus need to be skilled in the art of persuasion.[47] Through persuasion, one individual (the source) tries to change the attitude of another person (the target) in regard to a certain issue (the message). Certain characteristics of the source, target, and message affect the persuasion process.

counterproductive work behavior Behavior that violates organizational norms and causes harm to the organization and/or employees.

organizational commitment The strength of an individual's identification with an organization.

affective commitment Organizational commitment based on an individual's desire to remain in an organization.

continuance commitment Organizational commitment based on the fact that an individual cannot afford to leave.

normative commitment Organizational commitment based on an individual's perceived obligation to remain with an organization.

FIGURE 4.2 THE ELABORATION LIKELIHOOD MODEL OF PERSUASION

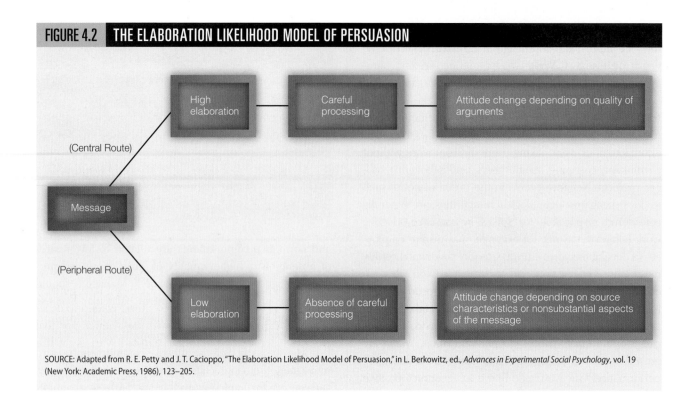

SOURCE: Adapted from R. E. Petty and J. T. Cacioppo, "The Elaboration Likelihood Model of Persuasion," in L. Berkowitz, ed., *Advances in Experimental Social Psychology*, vol. 19 (New York: Academic Press, 1986), 123–205.

4-5a Source Characteristics

Three major characteristics of the source affect persuasion: expertise, trustworthiness, and attractiveness.[48] A source who is perceived as an expert is particularly persuasive. Testimonials, for example, are the third most effective technique in advertising, after corporate responsibility and emotional appeal. Endorsers of a product are effective when they are perceived as trustworthy, attractive, or similar to the consumer, or when they represent an image the consumer would like to adopt.[49]

4-5b Target Characteristics

Individuals with low self-esteem are more likely to change their attitudes in response to persuasion than are individuals with high self-esteem. Individuals who hold very extreme attitudes are more resistant to persuasion, and people who are in a good mood are easier to persuade.[50] Undoubtedly, individuals differ widely in their responsiveness to persuasion. Managers must recognize these differences and realize that their attempts to change attitudes may not be universally accepted.

4-5c Message Characteristics

Suppose you want to persuade your employees that an unpopular policy is a positive change. Should you present one side of the issue or both sides? Given that your employees are already negatively inclined toward the policy, you will have more success in changing their attitudes if you present both sides. This shows support for one side of the issue while acknowledging that another side does exist. Moreover, refuting the other side rather than ignoring it makes it harder for the targets to hang on to their negative attitudes.

Persuasion is a delicate skill. Undisguised deliberate attempts at changing attitudes may drive employees' attitudes in the opposite direction. This is most likely to occur when the target of the persuasive communication feels her or his freedom is threatened.[51] Less threatening approaches are less likely to elicit negative reactions. The emotional tone of the message is also important. Messages framed with the same emotion as that felt by the receiver are more persuasive.[52]

4-5d Cognitive Routes to Persuasion

The source, target, and message characteristics are weighed differently in the two cognitive routes to persuasion, the central route and the peripheral route, as shown in the *elaboration likelihood model* of persuasion in Figure 4.2.[53] The routes are differentiated by the amount of elaboration, or scrutiny, that the target is motivated to give to the message.

The *central route* to persuasion involves direct cognitive processing of the message's content. In this route, individuals think carefully about issues that are personally relevant. The listener may nod his head at strong arguments and shake his head at weak ones.[54] Logical and convincing arguments are needed to change attitudes by this route.

In the *peripheral route* to persuasion, the individual is not motivated to pay much attention to the message's content because she is distracted or perceives the message as personally irrelevant. Instead, she is persuaded by characteristics of the persuader such as expertise, trustworthiness, and attractiveness. The individual may also be persuaded by statistics, the number of arguments presented, or the method of presentation—none of which relate to the actual content of the message.

The elaboration likelihood model shows that the target's level of involvement with the issue is important. That involvement also determines which route to persuasion will be more effective. In some cases, attitude change comes about through both the central and the peripheral routes. To cover all of the bases, managers should structure the content of their messages carefully, develop their own effective persuasive attributes, and choose a method of presentation that will appeal to the audience.[55]

4-6 EMOTIONS AND MOODS AT WORK

Emotions are discrete and fairly short-lived feelings that have a specific, known cause. An emotion like anger, for example, may arise because a colleague was rude to you. Or you may feel happy because you got a promotion. *Moods*, on the other hand, are typically classified as positive or negative and are made up of various emotions. Moods typically last longer than emotions and don't have a specific cause. Traditional management theories did not place a premium on studying the effects of employees' moods and emotions because they were thought to be bad for rational decision making at work. Ideas about management centered around the stereotypical ideal employee who kept his emotions in check and behaved in a totally rational, nonemotional manner. Research has proven that emotions and cognitions are intertwined and that both are normal parts of human functioning and decision making.[56]

4-6a Emotions

Emotions (e.g., anger, joy, pride, hostility) are short-lived, intense reactions to an event. Employees have to cope with both positive and negative events at work on a daily basis, and these events, in turn, lead to emotions. When events at work are positive and goals are being met, employees experience positive emotions. But when events at work are perceived as negative, the opposite can be true.[57] Emotions, in turn, impact both work attitudes and work behaviors.

Different emotions relate to specific facets of job satisfaction. Gratitude, for example, may be related to satisfaction with coworkers or satisfaction with supervisors. Interest, a feeling of curiosity or fascination, may relate to satisfaction with the work itself.[58] Positive emotions produce better cognitive functioning, physical and psychological health, and coping mechanisms.[59] Individuals differ in their capacity to experience both positive emotions (e.g., happiness, pride) and negative emotions (e.g., anger, fear, guilt).[60] People who experience positive emotions tend to do so repeatedly.[61] Overall, people who experience positive emotions are more successful across a variety of life domains and report higher life satisfaction. Negative emotions, on the other hand, lead to unhealthy coping behaviors and lowered cardiovascular function and physical health.[62]

4-6b Moods

Moods are feeling states that are more enduring than emotions and have no clear cause. Moods are one level above emotions since they are made up of a variety of emotions. Individuals experiencing a strongly positive mood at work feel excited, enthusiastic, and peppy, while individuals experiencing a less positive mood feel dull and sluggish. Individuals experiencing a negative mood at work feel distressed, hostile, or jittery, while those experiencing a less negative mood are calm and relaxed.[63]

Moods may be particularly important in the workplace because they last longer than emotions. Positive moods at work lead to better work performance and OCBs and decrease counterproductive work behavior.[64] Positive moods at work lead to better work performance and more OCBs, whereas negative moods lead to absenteeism and turnover intentions.[64] Awareness of whether you are a morning person or an evening person in terms of your energy can allow you to better regulate your mood. Individuals are more energetic at their preferred times of day, and in better moods. It takes emotional intelligence, as discussed in the next section, to become self-aware of one's

emotions Mental states that include feelings, physiological changes, and the inclination to act.

Google's SIYLI Develops Emotional Intelligence and Mindfulness

Google uses its Search Inside Yourself Leadership Institute (SIYLI) to train leaders in mindfulness practices and emotional intelligence skills. Based on studies of neuroscience, the program is focused on helping leaders become more resilient, more creative, and happier. SIYLI's cofounder and chair, Chade-Meng Tan, is a Google engineer who believes work should be fun and enjoyable, and that it should create the conditions for world peace. Meng, also known as Google's Jolly Good Fellow, connected with emotional intelligence guru Daniel Goleman and mindfulness pioneer Jon Kabat Zinn to create the program, which was tested and refined at Google over a four-year period.

SIYLI is an intense two-day experience in which participants learn to train their attention, develop self-knowledge and self-mastery, and create useful mental habits. More than a thousand Google employees have been through SIYLI training, and there's a lengthy waitlist to get in. Now, SIYLI is offered worldwide to the public and in-house to companies such as Ford and American Express. Maybe Meng's vision of creating world peace is not so far-fetched.

SOURCE: silyi.org

Daniel Goleman

moods and energy and use this awareness to improve performance.[65]

4-6c Emotional Contagion at Work

Emotions have far-reaching influence on workplace behavior. They drive employee decision making and are even used as a manipulative tool to ensure desired outcomes from conflicts or negotiations.[66] The influence of emotion at work is extended by **emotional contagion**, which is the dynamic process through which emotions are transferred from one person to another, either consciously or unconsciously, through nonverbal channels.

Emotions need to be managed at work because they spread easily. Emotional contagion occurs primarily through nonverbal cues and the basic human tendency to mimic each other's facial expressions, body language, speech patterns, vocal tones, and even emotions. Contagion affects any job involving interpersonal interaction.

emotional contagion A dynamic process through which the emotions of one person are transferred to another, either consciously or unconsciously, through nonverbal channels.

Positive emotions that travel through a work group due to emotional contagion produce cooperation and task performance.[67] The opposite occurs when negative emotions destroy morale and performance.

When organizations and their employees experience change and/or huge losses, they may struggle to recover. Good leaders can help by using compassion to heal and rebuild employee morale.[68] Organizations need to give employees a comfortable place to share their mutual grief and trauma. These issues can be resolved by caring leaders who are willing to share their emotions with employees.

4-6d Emotional Intelligence

Emotional intelligence (EI) is the ability to recognize and manage emotion in oneself and in others. EI is made up of several types of abilities: perceiving, understanding, facilitating, and regulating emotion.[69] This type of intelligence is thought to be an important ability for many types of jobs and to be a fundamental aspect of leadership (see Chapter 12 for more information). EI seems to facilitate job performance in a sequential fashion. Having the ability to perceive

of coworkers and bosses are essential in understanding our own emotional intelligence.

4-6e Emotional Labor

It is clear that moods and emotions impact employees and organizations a great deal. Positive moods and emotions bring about positive outcomes. This can be particularly true for highly interpersonal jobs like customer service representatives, flight attendants, and, oftentimes, professors, who are expected to express positive emotions and suppress any anger or hostility they may be feeling. *Emotional labor* is the work that employees do to control their feelings and expression of emotions in the workplace and is a type of emotion regulation.[71]

Often organizations have specific rules regarding emotional expression called *display rules*. There are two primary types of emotional labor used to meet these display rules: deep acting and surface acting. *Deep acting* involves attempting to feel the emotion one is displaying. Picturing a beautiful mountain vista or thinking about a pleasant memory are examples of deep acting. *Surface acting* is faking an emotion to meet the display rules. Surface acting causes *emotional dissonance*, or a discrepancy between one's felt emotion and one's expressed emotion. Surface acting can result in negative outcomes such as burnout, negative mood, and work withdrawal. Deep acting, in general, seems to have positive consequences and has been related to positive mood at work as well as high-quality customer service performance and reduced burnout.[72]

4-7 ETHICAL BEHAVIOR

Ethics is the study of moral values and moral behavior. **Ethical behavior** involves acting in ways consistent with one's personal values and the commonly held values of the organization and society.[73] Paying attention to ethical issues pays off for companies. In the early 1990s, James Burke, then CEO of Johnson & Johnson, put together a list of companies committed to ethics. The group included Johnson & Johnson, Coca-Cola, Gerber, Kodak, 3M, and Pitney Bowes. A recent study showed that over a forty-year period, the market value of these organizations grew at an annual rate of 11.3 percent, as compared to 6.2 percent for the Dow Jones industrials as a whole.[74] Doing the right thing can have a positive effect on an organization's performance.[75]

> **ethical behavior** Acting in ways consistent with one's personal values and the commonly held values of the organization and society.

emotions allows one to better understand emotions, which then increases emotion regulation. Being able to regulate your emotion, in turn, helps as you display appropriate emotions in the workplace, which allows you to perform better at work. Emotional intelligence helps you avoid amygdala hijacks, in which the emotional brain runs away with the rational brain. Jet Blue flight attendant Steven Slater's famous rant and exit from the airplane is a well-documented example of an amygdala highjack. Such losses of self-control, if frequent or extreme enough, can cost you your career!

Although self-report measures are often used to measure EI, they are not always accurate, since individuals do not always have a good perspective as to their own abilities. Studies indicate that colleagues are quite accurate in rating an individual's emotional intelligence. Whereas others tend to rate us on our behavior, we tend to rate ourselves on our intentions.[70] Because emotional intelligence shows in our work behavior, the perceptions

Ethical behavior in firms can also lead to practical benefits, particularly by attracting new talent. Firms with better reputations attract more applicants, creating a larger hiring pool, and evidence suggests that respected firms can choose higher-quality applicants.[76] For example, Timberland's strong value system helps the company attract and recruit the best talent and maintain a solid reputation with investors.

Failure to handle situations ethically can hurt companies. Employees who are laid off or terminated are very concerned about the quality of treatment they receive. Honestly explaining the reasons for the dismissal and preserving the dignity of the employee will reduce the likelihood of employees initiating a claim against the company. One study showed that less than 1 percent of employees who felt the company was being honest filed a claim. More than 17 percent of those who felt the company was being less than honest filed claims.[77] Conversely, ethical actions can be a boon to organizations. Australia's former prime minister, Kevin Rudd, apologized publicly for the ill treatment of Aborigines on the part of the national government. Even before the issue of financial compensation was addressed, this action built trust and hope among Australians of all races.[78]

Unethical behavior by employees can affect individuals, work teams, and even the organization. Organizations thus depend on individuals to act ethically. For this reason, more and more firms are starting to monitor their employees' Internet usage. Although some employees complain that this monitoring violates their privacy,

the courts tend to disagree, arguing that companies have the right to monitor employees' use of company-owned hardware and software.

Michael Smyth was fired from his job with Pillsbury Company after employees read inflammatory comments he made in several e-mails to his supervisor. Smyth sued for wrongful termination, claiming that the firm had violated his right to privacy after telling employees their e-mail would remain confidential. Despite these promises, the court ruled that Smyth had no reasonable expectation of privacy while using the firm's equipment. Further, it said, Smyth's right to privacy was outweighed by the firm's need to conduct business in a professional manner. Only future court cases will clarify where a firm's effort to monitor potentially unethical behavior actually violates its own ethical code.[79] Nonetheless, today's high-intensity business environment only increases the need for strong ethics programs.

Managers often struggle to align the ideal of ethical behavior with the reality of everyday business practices. Violations of the public's trust are costly. When Mattel recalled 20.5 million toys that were manufactured in China because they contained lead, its public image suffered greatly. The company attempted to undo the damages through a national advertising campaign.[80] Firms can experience lower accounting returns and slow sales growth for as long as five years after having been convicted of illegal corporate behavior.[81]

Individuals face complex ethical issues at work. A one-week review of *The Wall Street Journal* revealed

FAST FACT

What Is a B Corp?

B Corps (Certified Benefit Corporations) are companies that use the power of business as a force for good. To be designated a B Corp, a company must meet tough standards in environmental performance, social responsibility, accountability, and transparency. Today, there are more than one thousand certified B Corps in more than thirty countries representing sixty different industries. B Corps aim not only to be the best in the world but also to be the best for the world. For example, when compared to other sustainable businesses, B Corps are more likely to donate at least 10 percent of their profits to charity, use on-site renewable energy, and use suppliers from low-income communities. B Corps you may recognize include Ben & Jerry's, Patagonia, Warby Parker, and Klean Kanteen, among others.

SOURCE: bcorporation.net

TABLE 4.2   ETHICAL ISSUES FROM ONE WEEK IN THE LIFE OF *THE WALL STREET JOURNAL*

1. Stealing	Taking things that don't belong to you
2. Lying	Saying things you know aren't true
3. Fraud and deceit	Creating or perpetuating false impressions
4. Conflict of interest and influence buying	Bribes, payoffs, and kickbacks
5. Hiding or divulging information	Concealing information that another party has a right to know or failing to protect personal or proprietary information
6. Cheating	Taking unfair advantage of a situation
7. Personal decadence	Aiming below excellence in terms of work performance (e.g., careless or sloppy work)
8. Interpersonal abuse	Behaviors that are abusive of others (e.g., sexism, racism, emotional abuse)
9. Organizational abuse	Organizational practices that abuse members (e.g., inequitable compensation, misuses of power)
10. Rule violations	Breaking organizational rules
11. Accessory to unethical acts	Knowing about unethical behavior and failing to report it
12. Ethical dilemmas	Choosing between two equally desirable or undesirable options

SOURCE: Kluwer Academic Publishers and Journal of Business Ethics, 11, 1992, 255–265, A Menu of Moral Issues: One Week in the Life of The Wall Street Journal, J. O. Cherrington and D. J. Cherrington, with kind permission from Springer Science+Business Media B.V.

more than sixty articles dealing with ethical issues in business.[82] As Table 4.2 suggests, few of these issues are clear-cut. They depend on the specifics of the situation, and their interpretation depends on the characteristics of the individuals examining them. Consider lying, for instance. Many business people tell white lies. Is this acceptable? The perception of what constitutes ethical versus unethical behavior in organizations varies among individuals.

 ## 4-8 FACTORS THAT AFFECT ETHICAL BEHAVIOR

Two sets of factors—individual characteristics and organizational factors—influence ethical behavior.[83] In this section, we'll look at the individual influences on ethical behavior. Ethical decision making requires three qualities of individuals[84]:

1. The competence to identify ethical issues and evaluate the consequences of alternative courses of action.

2. The self-confidence to seek out different opinions about the issue and decide what is right in terms of a particular situation.

3. Tough-mindedness—the willingness to make decisions when all that needs to be known cannot be known and when the ethical issue has no established, unambiguous solution.

Which individual characteristics lead to these qualities? According to our model, they are value systems, locus of control, Machiavellianism, and cognitive moral development. Figure 4.3 illustrates these, as well as the organizational influences, which we will examine throughout the remainder of the book.

4-8a Values

Different values generate different ethical behaviors. **Values** are enduring beliefs that a specific mode of conduct or end state of existence is personally or socially preferable to an opposite or converse mode of conduct or end state of existence.[85] This definition was proposed by Rokeach, an early scholar of human values. As individuals grow and mature, they learn values, although these may change as an individual develops a sense of self. Cultures,

> **values** Enduring beliefs that a specific mode of conduct or end state of existence is personally or socially preferable to an opposite or converse mode of conduct or end state of existence.

FIGURE 4.3 **INDIVIDUAL/ORGANIZATIONAL MODEL OF ETHICAL BEHAVIOR**

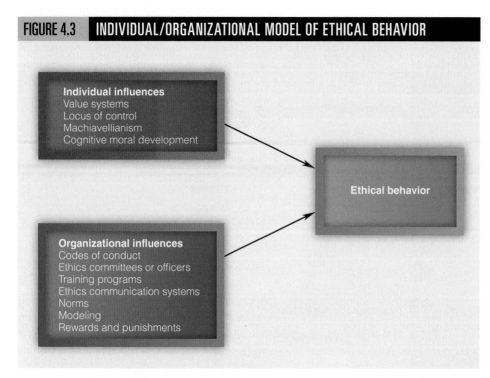

happiness, self-respect, and wisdom.

Age also affects values. Baby boomers' values contrast with those of the baby busters, who are beginning to enter the workforce. The baby busters value family life and time off from work and want to balance work and home life. This contrasts with the more driven, work-oriented value system of the boomers. The baby boomers place a huge emphasis on achievement values at work. Their successors in Generations X and Y are markedly different. Generation X values self-reliance, individualism, and balance between family and work life. Generation Y values freedom in scheduling and embraces a work-to-live mind-set rather than the live-to-work approach of the baby boomers.[87]

WORK VALUES Work values influence individuals' perceptions of right and wrong on the job.[88] Four work values are achievement, concern for others, honesty, and fairness.[89] *Achievement* is a concern for the advancement of one's career; it drives people to work hard and seek opportunities to develop new skills. *Concern for others* is shown in caring, compassionate behaviors such as encouraging others or helping them with difficult tasks. These behaviors also constitute organizational citizenship. *Honesty* is providing accurate information and refusing to mislead others for personal gain. *Fairness* means remaining impartial while recognizing different points of view.

Individuals rank these values in terms of their relative importance in their work lives.[90] Employees who share their supervisor's values are more satisfied with their jobs and more committed to the organization.[91] Values also have profound effects on job choice. Although traditionally pay and advancement potential have had the strongest influences on job choice decisions, one study found that three other work values—achievement, concern for others, and fairness—had greater influence.[92] This means that organizations recruiting job candidates should pay careful attention to individuals' values and to the messages their organizations send about company values.

societies, and organizations shape values. Parents and other respected role models influence value development by providing guidance about what is right and wrong. Like general beliefs about right and wrong, values form the basis for ethical behavior. Though values vary widely among individuals, we use them to evaluate our own behavior and that of others.

INSTRUMENTAL AND TERMINAL VALUES Rokeach distinguished between two types of values: instrumental and terminal. **Instrumental values** shape the acceptable behaviors that can be used to achieve some goal or end state. Instrumental values identified by Rokeach include ambition, honesty, self-sufficiency, and courage. **Terminal values** influence the goals to be achieved or the end states of existence. Rokeach identified happiness, love, pleasure, self-respect, and freedom among the terminal values. Table 4.3 gives a complete list of instrumental and terminal values. Terminal and instrumental values work in concert by providing individuals with goals to strive for and acceptable ways to achieve those goals.

Americans' rankings of instrumental and terminal values have been remarkably stable over time.[86] The highest ranked instrumental values were honesty, ambition, responsibility, forgiveness, open-mindedness, and courage. The highest ranked terminal values were world peace, family security, freedom,

instrumental values
Values that shape the acceptable behaviors that can be used to achieve some goal or end state.

terminal values Values that influence the goals to be achieved or the end states of existence.

TABLE 4.3	INSTRUMENTAL AND TERMINAL VALUES	
INSTRUMENTAL VALUES		
Honesty	Ambition	Responsibility
Forgiveness	Open-mindedness	Courage
Helpfulness	Cleanliness	Competence
Self-control	Affection/love	Cheerfulness
Independence	Politeness	Intelligence
Obedience	Rationality	Imagination
TERMINAL VALUES		
World peace	Family security	Freedom
Happiness	Self-respect	Wisdom
Equality	Salvation	Prosperity
Achievement	Friendship	National security
Inner peace	Mature love	Social respect
Beauty in art and nature	Pleasure	Exciting, active life

SOURCE: Based on *The Nature of Human Values* by Milton Rokeach.

CULTURAL DIFFERENCES IN VALUES Organizations facing the challenges of an increasingly diverse workforce and a global marketplace must understand culture's influence on values. Doing business in a global marketplace often means encountering a clash of values among different cultures. Consider loyalty, for example. In Japan, loyalty means "compassionate overtime." Even when you have no work yourself, you should stay late to provide moral support for your peers who are working late.[93] In contrast, Koreans value loyalty to the person for whom one works.[94] In the United States, family and other personal loyalties are held above loyalty to the company or one's supervisor.

Cultures differ in the individual contributions they value at work. Collectivist cultures like China and Mexico value a person's contributions to relationships in the work team. By contrast, individualist cultures (the United States, the Netherlands) value a person's contribution to task accomplishment. Both collectivist and individualist cultures, however, value rewards based on individual performance.[95] Iran's collectivist managers demonstrate little tolerance for ambiguity, high need for structure, and willingness to sacrifice for the good of society—all values they derive from Islam, which promotes belonging, harmony, humility, and simplicity.[96]

Values also affect individuals' views of what constitutes authority. French managers value authority as a right of office and rank. Their behavior reflects this value, as they tend to exercise power based on their position in the organization. By contrast, managers from the Netherlands value group inputs to decisions and expect employees to challenge and discuss their decisions.[97]

We may be prone to judging the value systems of others, but we should resist this tendency. Tolerating diverse values can help us understand other cultures. The value systems of other nations are not necessarily right or wrong; they are merely different.

4-8b Locus of Control

Another individual influence on ethical behavior is locus of control. Recall from Chapter 3 that individuals with an internal locus of control believe that they control events in their lives and that they are responsible for their own experiences. Those with an external locus of control believe that outside forces such as fate, chance, or other people control what happens to them.[98]

Internals are more likely than externals to take personal responsibility for the consequences of their ethical or unethical behavior. Externals are more apt to believe that external forces caused their ethical or unethical behavior. Research has shown that internals make more ethical decisions than do externals.[99] Internals also are more resistant to social pressure and are less willing to hurt another person even if ordered to do so by an authority figure.[100]

4-8c Machiavellianism

Machiavellianism also influences ethical behavior. Niccolò Machiavelli was a sixteenth-century Italian statesman famous for writing *The Prince*, a guide for acquiring and using power.[101] He suggested that manipulating others was the best way to achieve power. **Machiavellianism**, then, is a personality characteristic involving one's willingness to do whatever it takes to get one's own way.

A high-Mach individual operates from the notion that it is better to be feared than loved. High-Machs tend to be deceitful, have a cynical view of human nature, and care little for conventional notions of right and wrong.[102] They are skilled manipulators, relying on their persuasive abilities. Low-Machs, in contrast, value loyalty and relationships. They are less willing to manipulate others for personal gain and are concerned with others' opinions.

Machiavellianism A personality characteristic involving one's willingness to do whatever it takes to get one's own way.

"The first method for estimating the intelligence of a ruler is to look at the men he has around him."

—Niccolo Machiavelli
(1469–1527)
The Prince

High-Machs believe that the desired ends justify any means, so they feel it's fine to manipulate others in order to achieve a goal.[103] They are emotionally detached from other people and focus on the objective aspects of situations. High-Machs are also more likely to engage in ethically questionable behavior.[104] Employees can counter Machiavellian individuals by focusing on teamwork instead of one-on-one relationships where high-Machs have the upper hand. Making interpersonal agreements public reduces their susceptibility to Machiavellian manipulation.

4-8d Cognitive Moral Development

An individual's level of **cognitive moral development** also affects ethical behavior. Psychologist Lawrence Kohlberg proposed that as individuals mature, they move through a series of six

cognitive moral development
The process of moving through stages of maturity with regard to making ethical decisions.

stages of moral development (Table 4.4).[105] With each successive stage, they become less dependent on other people's opinions of right and wrong and less self-centered (focusing less on their own interests). At higher levels of moral development, individuals are concerned with broad principles of justice and with their self-chosen ethical principles. Kohlberg's model focuses on the decision-making process and on how individuals justify ethical decisions. His cognitive developmental theory explains how people decide what is right and wrong and how the decision-making process changes through interaction with peers and the environment.

Cognitive moral development occurs at three levels, each consisting of two stages. At Level I, called the *premoral level*, a person's ethical decisions are based on rewards, punishments, and self-interest. In Stage 1, people obey rules to avoid punishment. In Stage 2, people obey rules only if it is in their immediate interest to do so.

At Level II, the *conventional level*, people focus on the expectations of others. In Stage 3, individuals try to live up to the expectations of people close to them. In Stage 4, they broaden their perspective to include the laws and norms of the larger society. They fulfill duties and obligations to contribute to society.

At Level III, the *principled level*, universal values determine what is right. The individual sees beyond laws, rules, and the expectations of other people. In Stage 5, individuals are aware that people have diverse value systems. They uphold their own values even if others disagree. Individuals in Stage 5 make decisions based on principles of justice and rights. For example, someone who decides to picket an abortion clinic just because his religion bans abortion is not a Stage 5 individual. A person who arrives at the same decision through a complex decision process based on justice and rights may be a Stage 5 individual. The key is the process rather than the decision itself. In Stage 6, the individual follows self-selected ethical principles. Stage 6 individuals act according to their own self-selected ethical principles, even when these principles conflict with a law.

TABLE 4.4	KOHLBERG'S STAGES OF COGNITIVE MORAL DEVELOPMENT	
Level I	Premoral	Reward, punishment, self-interest
Level II	Conventional	Expectations of other people and society
Level III	Principled	Universal values and personal ethical principles

As individuals mature, their moral development passes through these stages in an irreversible sequence. Research suggests that most adults are in Stage 3 or 4. Most adults thus never reach the principled level of development (Stages 5 and 6).

Kohlberg's model of cognitive moral development has been supported by a great deal of research since it was proposed more than thirty years ago. Individuals at higher stages of development are less likely to cheat, more likely to engage in whistle-blowing, and more likely to make ethical business decisions.[106]

But Kohlberg's model has also been criticized. Carol Gilligan, for example, argues that the model does not take gender differences into account. Kohlberg's model was developed from a twenty-year study of eighty-four boys.[107] Gilligan contends that women's moral development follows a different pattern, one based not on individual rights and rules but on responsibility and relationships. Women and men face the same moral dilemmas but approach them from different perspectives—men from the perspective of equal respect and women from the perspective of compassion and care. But researchers who reviewed the research on these gender differences concluded that the differences may not be as strong as Gilligan originally suggested.[108]

In general, though, evidence supports the idea that men and women view ethics differently. A large-scale review of sixty-six studies found that women were more likely than men to perceive certain business practices as unethical. Young women were more likely than young men to see breaking the rules and acting on insider information as unethical. Both sexes agreed that collusion, conflicts of interest, and stealing are unethical. It takes about twenty-one years for this gender gap to disappear. Men seem to become more ethical with more work experience; the longer they are in the workforce, the more their attitudes resemble those held by women. That said, age and experience are related for both sexes. Experienced workers of either sex are more likely to think that lying, bribing, stealing, and colluding are unethical.[109]

Individual differences in values, locus of control, Machiavellianism, and cognitive moral development all influence ethical behavior in organizations. Organizations might use this knowledge to promote ethical behavior by hiring individuals who share the organization's values or hiring only internals, low-Machs, and individuals at higher stages of cognitive moral development. Such strategies, however, obviously present both practical and legal problems.

Training may be a safer way to use this knowledge. Evidence suggests that training can increase cognitive moral development. Organizations could help individuals move to higher stages of moral development by providing educational seminars. That said, values, locus of control, Machiavellianism, and cognitive moral development are fairly stable in adults.

The best way to use the knowledge of individual differences may be to recognize that they help explain why ethical behavior differs among individuals and to focus managerial efforts on creating a work situation supporting ethical behavior.

Most workers are responsive to external influences. They do not act as independent ethical agents but look to their organization for guidance. Managers can offer such guidance by exercising the organizational influences listed in Figure 4.3. They can encourage ethical behavior through codes of conduct, ethics committees, ethics communication systems, training, norms, modeling, and rewards and punishments, as shown in Figure 4.3. We discuss these areas further in Chapter 16.

STUDY TOOLS 4

LOCATED AT BACK OF THE TEXTBOOK
☐ Rip out chapter review card

LOCATED AT WWW.CENGAGE.COM/LOGIN
☐ Gain unique perspectives on key concepts with new Concept Clip videos in the e-book

☐ Review key term flashcards and create your own

☐ Increase your comprehension with online homework and quizzes

5 | Motivation at Work

LEARNING OBJECTIVES

 5-1 Define motivation and articulate different views of how individuals are motivated at work.

5-2 Explain Maslow's hierarchy of needs and its two main modifications.

5-3 Discuss how the needs for achievement, power, and affiliation influence an individual's behavior in the workplace.

5-4 Describe the two-factor theory of motivation.

5-5 Explain two new ideas in human motivation.

5-6 Describe the role of inequity in motivation.

5-7 Describe the expectancy theory of motivation.

5-8 Describe the cultural differences in motivation.

After finishing this chapter go to **PAGE 85** for **STUDY TOOLS**

5-1 MOTIVATION AND WORK BEHAVIOR

Motivation is the process of arousing and sustaining goal-directed behavior. Motivation theories attempt to explain and predict observable behavior. They may be broadly classified into internal, process, and external theories. *Internal theories* of motivation give primary consideration to variables within the individual that lead to motivation and behavior. Maslow's hierarchy of needs is a good example of an internal theory. *Process theories* of motivation, such as expectancy theory, emphasize the nature of the interaction between the individual and the environment. *External theories* of motivation focus on the elements in the environment, including the consequences of behavior, as the basis for understanding and explaining people's

behavior at work. A review of motivation related to work over the past century categorized the theories, findings, and advances according to their primary focus on (a) motives and traits (content); (b) features of the job, work role, and work environment (context); and (c) the mechanisms and processes involved in choice and striving (processes).[1] This is the first of three chapters addressing the full set of motivation theories, research, and practice, the other two being Chapters 6 and 14.

A comprehensive approach to understanding motivation, behavior, and performance must consider all three elements of the work situation and how they interact.

motivation The process of arousing and sustaining goal-directed behavior.

Compulsive Behavior as Adaptive, Even Pragmatic

Compulsive behavior is often thought of as odd, irrational, even crazy and self-destructive. Not so fast! Compulsive behavior may be a form of self-reassurance that is adaptive, even pragmatic, and all too human. About 18 percent of the adult population suffers

lightwise/123RF

from anxiety intense enough to be considered a disorder. This compares to only 7 percent who suffer from major depression. This may well be accurately characterized as the age of anxiety. Neuroimaging research of the brain has found that the roots of compulsion lie in brain areas that can trigger anxiety. Hence the deeper motivations for compulsive behaviors may not be as crazy or irrational as would appear on the surface. The hard-wiring for compulsive behavior suggests that, while the behavior may not lead to a sense of joy or euphoria, the behavior can reduce anxiety and therefore the degree to which a person suffers.

SOURCE: S. Begley, "How Compulsions Help Us Manage Our Age of Anxiety: Neuroimaging and other brain-based studies suggest that compulsive behavior is a form of self-reassurance that can help us function," *Wall Street Journal*, 19 Jan. 2017.

5-1a Internal Needs

Philosophers and scholars have theorized for centuries about human needs and motives. During the past century, researchers have focused on motivation in a business context.[2] Max Weber, an early German sociologist, argued that the meaning of work lies not in the work itself but in its deeper potential for contributing to a person's ultimate salvation.[3] Weber, and later Milton Blood, understood this *Protestant ethic*, with its foundations in Calvinist thought, as the fuel for human industriousness. The Protestant ethic encouraged hard work on the grounds that prosperous workers were more likely to find a place in heaven.

psychoanalysis Sigmund Freud's method for delving into the unconscious mind to better understand a person's motives and needs.

self-interest What is in the best interest of and benefit to an individual.

Sigmund Freud proposed a more complex motivational theory, suggesting that a person's organizational life was founded on the compulsion to work and the power of love.[4] He emphasized the unconscious mind's influence on human motivation. **Psychoanalysis** is Freud's method for delving into the unconscious mind to better understand a person's motives and needs. Thus, the psychoanalytic approach can help explain irrational and self-destructive behaviors such as suicide or workplace violence.[5] Analyzing a person's unconscious needs and motives can help us understand such traumatic work events. The psychoanalytic approach also helps explain deviant behavior in the workplace.

Freud's thought served as the basis for subsequent *need theories* of motivation. Research suggests that people's deeper feelings transcend culture, with most people caring deeply about the same few things. Factors that make employees motivated and loyal to the organization include fair compensation and the trust and respect of their supervisors. Intrinsic motivation varies by the individual and has a positive effect on individual personality traits. For example, an employee who performs a work task for the pure satisfaction of doing so tends to be more conscientious, open to experience, and agreeable the following day.[6] Managers who are more supportive and less controlling appear to elicit more intrinsic motivation from their employees.

5-1b External Incentives

Most economic assumptions about human motivation emphasize financial incentives. The Scottish political economist and moral philosopher Adam Smith argued that a person's **self-interest** was determined by God, not the government.[7] Smith laid the cornerstone for the free enterprise system of economics when he formulated the so-called invisible hand and the free market to explain the motivation for individual behavior. The "invisible hand" refers to the unseen forces of a free market system that shape the most efficient use of people, money, and resources for productive ends. Smith assumed that people are motivated by self-interest for economic gain to provide the necessities and conveniences of life. Thus, employees are most productive when motivated by self-interest.

The more collective wealth an economy can produce, the better individuals can fulfill their self-interest. Technology and labor efficiency are two ways of promoting greater collective wealth. Technology is crucial to Smith's view because he believed that the productivity of a nation's labor force determines its wealth. Therefore, a more efficient and effective labor force yields greater abundance for the nation. Technology acts as a force multiplier for the productivity of labor.[8]

Frederick Taylor, the founder of *scientific management*, also examined labor efficiency and effectiveness.[9] His goal was to change the relationship between management and labor from one of conflict to one of cooperation.[10] Taylor believed the basis of the conflict was the division of the profits. Instead of continuing this conflict, labor and management should work together to enlarge total profits.

Early organizational scholars assumed that people were motivated by self-interest and economic gain. Consequently, they developed differential piece-rate systems of pay emphasizing external incentives. Modern management practices, such as employee recognition programs, flexible benefit packages, and stock ownership plans, stem from Smith's and Taylor's original theories. They emphasize external incentives, which may take either strictly economic form or more material form, such as outstanding employee plaques. Whataburger has developed the WhataGames in which the best employees compete for bragging rights and medals.[11] This training-and-loyalty exercise reduces turnover and builds commitment.

Some approaches, however, suggest that economic motives alone are not sufficient and need to be combined with other external motives. The Hawthorne studies, mentioned in Chapter 1 as the first to recognize informal aspects of an organization, also studied what motivates people to be productive. They confirmed the positive effects of pay incentives on productivity but also demonstrated the importance of social and interpersonal motives.[12] Other people constitute yet another external motive. Executives have recently championed so-called enlightened self-interest. Self-interest is concern for one's own needs; enlightened self-interest recognizes others' interests as well.

In still other approaches, external and internal motivations are combined. Psychological ownership considers both psychological needs and external incentives to motivate workers. One study of 800 managers and employees in three different organizations found that "feelings of ownership" of an organization increased organizational citizenship behavior.[13]

5-2 MASLOW'S NEED HIERARCHY

Abraham Maslow, a psychologist, proposed a theory of motivation that went beyond just physical and economic needs to emphasize psychological and interpersonal needs as well. The core of Maslow's theory is a hierarchy of five categories of need.[14] Although he recognized that factors other than one's needs (e.g., culture) determine behavior, his theory focused on specifying people's internal needs. As shown in Figure 5.1, Maslow labeled the five levels of his *need hierarchy* as physiological needs, safety and security needs, love (social) needs, esteem needs, and the need for self-actualization. He conceptually derived the five need categories from the early thoughts of William James and John Dewey, coupled with the psychodynamic thinking of Sigmund Freud and Alfred Adler.[15]

One distinguishing feature of Maslow's need hierarchy is the *progression hypothesis*, which suggests that as

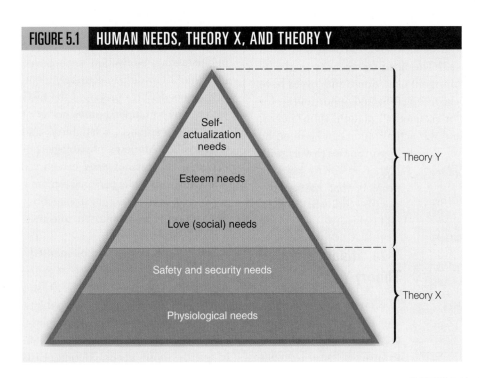

FIGURE 5.1 HUMAN NEEDS, THEORY X, AND THEORY Y

- Self-actualization needs
- Esteem needs
- Love (social) needs — Theory Y
- Safety and security needs
- Physiological needs — Theory X

Self-interest is concern for one's own needs; enlightened self-interest recognizes others' interests as well.

Sergey Nivens/Shutterstock.com

one level of need is met, a person progresses to the next higher level of need as a source of motivation. Hence, people progress up the hierarchy as they successively gratify each level of need. Maslow understood the lowest level of ungratified needs to motivate behavior.

Managers can make the most of Maslow's need hierarchy for success in their teams by recognizing that each individual has a unique set of needs and therefore gearing incentives to meet various needs. The physiological need for sleep is instrumentally important for employee performance, safety, health, and even employee attitudes.[16] The need for security might be filled by a good retirement plan. Some employees have a high need for social interaction, and opportunities for after-work tennis or racquetball may fill those needs. Needs for status and self-actualization can be filled by opportunities to work with higher-ups or to work on projects that particularly suit the individual's skills and interests.[17]

Theory X A set of assumptions managers might apply to individuals who are motivated by lower-order needs.

Theory Y A set of assumptions managers might apply to individuals who are motivated by higher-order needs.

ERG theory A theory that organizes human needs into the categories of existence, relatedness, and growth.

5-2a Theory X and Theory Y

Maslow's need hierarchy has been applied to organizational behavior in two key ways. Douglas McGregor strove to explain motivation by grouping the physiological and safety needs as lower-order needs and the social, esteem, and self-actualization needs as upper-order needs. According to McGregor's theory, managers can make one of two sets of assumptions about an individual depending on the factors that motivate his or her behavior. McGregor's **Theory X** assumptions are appropriate for employees motivated by lower-order needs, while **Theory Y** assumptions apply to employees motivated by higher-order needs. These assumptions are listed in Table 5.1 and have been mapped onto Maslow's hierarchy, from which they derive, in Figure 5.1.[18] McGregor understood the responsibility of management to be the same under both sets of assumptions. Specifically, "Management is responsible for organizing the elements of productive enterprise—money, materials, equipment, people—in the interest of economic ends."[19] Trust in top level leaders has been found to trickle-up from trust in direct supervisors, hence making these relationships a key to the benefits of having employees' trust.[20] Employees are more likely to identify with and motivated to achieve organizational outcomes when leaders formulate messages appropriately.[21] Whole Foods founder and CEO John Mackey relies on Maslow's hierarchy of needs in motivating employees.[22]

5-2b ERG Theory

Clayton Alderfer recognized Maslow's contribution to understanding motivation yet believed that the original need hierarchy didn't accurately identify and categorize human needs.[23] He proposed the **ERG theory** of motivation, which grouped human needs into only three basic categories: existence, relatedness, and growth.[24] Alderfer classified Maslow's physiological and physical safety needs in an *existence need* category. The interpersonal safety, love, and interpersonal esteem needs were reclassified in a *relatedness need* category. Finally, a *growth need* category encompassed Maslow's self-actualization and self-esteem needs.

ERG theory also supplemented Maslow's original progression hypothesis with a *regression hypothesis*. Alderfer's regression hypothesis suggests that when people are frustrated by their inability to meet needs at the next higher level in the hierarchy, they regress to the next lower category of needs and intensify their desire to gratify those needs. Hence, ERG theory explains

TABLE 5.1 McGREGOR'S ASSUMPTIONS ABOUT PEOPLE

Theory X	Theory Y
> People are by nature indolent. That is, they work as little as possible.	> People are not by nature passive or resistant to organizational needs. They have become so as a result of experience in organizations.
> People lack ambition, dislike responsibility, and prefer to be led.	> The motivation, the potential for development, the capacity for assuming responsibility, and the readiness to direct behavior toward organizational goals are all present in people. Management does not put them there. It is a responsibility of management to make it possible for people to recognize and develop these human characteristics for themselves.
> People are inherently self-centered and indifferent to organizational needs.	
> People are by nature resistant to change.	> The essential task of management is to arrange conditions and methods of operation so that people can achieve their own goals best by directing their own efforts toward organizational objectives.
> People are gullible and not very bright, the ready dupes of the charlatan and the demagogue.	

SOURCE: Excerpted by permission of the publisher, from the "MacGregor's Assumptions about People" from Management Review, November 1957, American Management Association, New York, NY. All rights reserved. www.amanet.org

both progressive need gratification and regression when people face frustration.

5-3 McCLELLAND'S NEED THEORY

A second major need theory of motivation focuses on personality and learned needs. Henry Murray developed a long list of motives and manifest needs in his early studies of personality.[25] Inspired by Murray's work, David McClelland identified three learned, or acquired, needs, called **manifest needs** because they are easily perceived.[26] These are the needs for *achievement*, *power*, and *affiliation*. Some individuals have a high need for achievement, while others have a moderate or low need for achievement. The same is true for the other two needs. A manager may have a strong need for power, a moderate need for achievement, and a weak need for affiliation. Different needs are dominant in different people, and each need has different implications for people's behavior. Companies such as American Express recognize the importance of such diverse employee needs by creating and maintaining family-friendly policies.

5-3a Need for Achievement

The **need for achievement** encompasses excellence, competition, challenging goals, persistence, and overcoming difficulties.[27] People with a high need for achievement thus seek performance excellence, enjoy difficult and challenging goals, persevere, and are competitive. The *Murray Thematic Apperception Test (TAT)*, a projective test such as those discussed in Chapter 3, was used as an

> **manifest needs** Learned or acquired needs that are easily perceived.
>
> **need for achievement** A manifest need that concerns excellence, competition, challenging goals, persistence, and overcoming difficulties.

FAST FACT

Achieving Immigrants on the Move

Between 1990 and 2010 the number of immigrants worldwide with a college degree rose by 130 percent, while the number with less education rose by only 40 percent. Highly skilled immigrants increasingly head to the United States and other English-speaking countries; they have a positive impact. This is in the context of a rather stable number of immigrants worldwide. Only 3 percent of people live outside their country of birth, and this number has been constant since 1960. Skilled and talented immigrants make up 50 percent of Silicon Valley's entrepreneurs and technology workers. The lesson to learn is that greater skills and achievement lead to more and better employment opportunities.

SOURCE: S.P. Kerr, W. Kerr, C. Ozden, and C. Parsons, "Talent: Global Brain Drain," *Harvard Business Review*, March-April 2017, p. 34.

FIGURE 5.2 NEED THEORIES OF MOTIVATION

	Maslow	McGregor	Alderfer	McClelland
Higher order needs	Self-actualization		Growth	Need for achievement
	Esteem — Self / Interpersonal	Theory Y		Need for power
	Belongingness (social and love)		Relatedness	Need for affiliation
Lower order needs	Safety and security — Interpersonal / Physical	Theory X		
	Physiological		Existence	

early measure of the achievement motive. It was further developed by McClelland and his associates, although it has been criticized, and alternative instruments have been developed.[28]

McClelland found that people with a high need for achievement perform better than those lacking such a need. Such individuals share these three characteristics: First, they set goals that are moderately difficult yet achievable. Second, they like to receive feedback on their progress toward these goals. Third, they do not like having external events or other people interfere with their progress toward the goals.

In addition, high achievers (1) often hope and plan for success; (2) may be quite content to work alone or with other people, whichever is more appropriate to their task; and (3) like being very good at what they do so and, accordingly, tend to develop expertise and competence in their chosen endeavors. Groups consisting of high-achieving members may experience conflict over how to get work tasks accomplished as members attempt to demonstrate their individual task-related contributions.[29] The need for achievement is consistent across countries for adults who are employed full-time, but researchers have found international differences in the tendency for achievement.[30] Achievement tendencies are highest in the United States, an individualistic culture, and lowest in collectivist societies such as Japan and Hungary.[31]

need for power A manifest need that concerns the desire to influence others, change people or events, and make a difference in life.

5-3b Need for Power

The **need for power** includes the desire to influence others, the urge to change people or events, and the wish to make a difference in life. The need for power is interpersonal because it involves influence over other people. McClelland distinguishes between *socialized power*, which is used for the benefit of many, and *personalized power*, which is used for individual gain. The former is a constructive force, while the latter may be a very disruptive or even destructive force.

AP Images/Sean Kardon

David McClelland

According to McClelland's research, the best managers have a very high need for socialized power as opposed to personalized power.[32] They are concerned for others; have an interest in organizational goals; and want to be useful to the larger group, organization, and society. For example, the CEO of Management Sciences for Health, Jonathan D. Quick, MD, displayed a high need for interactive, or socialized, power on the McClelland need profile while showing a very low need for imperial power, both of which are strong positive traits.

TABLE 5.2	THE MOTIVATION-HYGIENE THEORY OF MOTIVATION
Motivation factors that contribute to job satisfaction when they are present:	**Hygiene factors that contribute to job dissatisfaction when they are absent:**
> Achievement	> Company policy and administration
> Recognition of achievement	> Supervision
> Work itself	> Interpersonal relations
> Responsibility	> Working conditions
> Advancement	> Salary
> Growth	> Status
> Salary	> Security

5-3c Need for Affiliation

The **need for affiliation** is an urge to establish and maintain warm, close, intimate relationships with others.[33] People with a high need for affiliation are motivated to express their emotions to others and expect them to do the same in return. They find conflicts disturbing and are strongly motivated to work through any such barriers to closeness. The need for relationships is important not only in McClelland's theory but also in each of the theories we have discussed so far.

Over and above these three needs for achievement, power, and affiliation, Murray's manifest needs theory also included the need for autonomy. This is the desire for independence and freedom from constraints. People with a high need for autonomy prefer to work alone and to control the pace of their work. They dislike bureaucratic rules, regulations, and procedures.

Figure 5.2 shows the parallel structures of Maslow's, McGregor's, Alderfer's, and McClelland's theories of motivation.

5-4 HERZBERG'S TWO-FACTOR THEORY

In developing his *two-factor theory of motivation*, Frederick Herzberg departed from need-based theories and examined the critical incident experiences of people at work.[34] Herzberg's original study included 200 engineers and accountants in western Pennsylvania during the 1950s. He asked them to describe two important incidents at their jobs: one that was very satisfying and made them feel exceptionally good at work and another that was very dissatisfying and made them feel exceptionally bad.

Herzberg and his colleagues believed that people had two sets of needs: one based on avoiding pain and one stemming from the desire for psychological growth. Conditions in the work environment would affect one or the other of these two needs. Work conditions related to satisfaction of the need for psychological growth were labeled **motivation factors**. Work conditions related to dissatisfaction caused by discomfort or pain were labeled **hygiene factors**. Motivation factors relate to job satisfaction, and hygiene factors relate to job dissatisfaction.[35] Table 5.2 lists the motivation factors and hygiene factors included in the following discussion.

5-4a Motivation Factors

Job enrichment involves building motivation factors into a job and, according to Herzberg, creates job satisfaction. In his original research, Herzberg identified motivation factors as responsibility, achievement, recognition, advancement, and the work itself. When these factors are present, they improve a worker's effort and performance. Table 5.2 lists salary as a motivational factor based on some studies. Acceptance of this idea has led many organizational reward systems to include financial benefits such as stock options as part of an employee's compensation package.

Motivation factors lead to positive mental health. They challenge people to grow, contribute to the work environment, and invest themselves in the organization. The absence of these factors does not lead to dissatisfaction, but rather to feelings of neutrality.

need for affiliation A manifest need to establish and maintain warm, close, intimate relationships with other people.

motivation factor A work condition that satisfies the need for psychological growth.

hygiene factor A work condition that generates dissatisfaction due to discomfort or pain.

iQoncept/Shutterstock.com

Motivation factors are the more important of the two sets of factors because they directly affect a person's drive to do a good job. When they are absent, a person lacks the motivation to perform well and achieve excellence.

5-4b Hygiene Factors

Hygiene factors are completely distinct from the motivation factors and are unrelated to the drive to achieve and do excellent work. While motivation factors create job satisfaction if present or feelings of neutrality if absent, absent or insufficient hygiene factors result in job dissatisfaction. Herzberg's hygiene factors include company policy and administration, technical supervision, interpersonal relations with one's supervisor, working conditions, salary, and status. Good hygiene factors cannot stimulate psychological growth or human development, but they are necessary to prevent job dissatisfaction.

When these hygiene factors are poor or absent, the dissatisfied employee complains about poor supervision, poor medical benefits, or whatever hygiene factor is poor. One method that employees use to determine the quality of supervision they receive is by the level of fairness they perceive the supervisor uses when enacting company policies. However, the supervisor's motives may have a greater impact on employee perceptions of workplace fairness.[36] Even in unfair work environments, employees and managers can still enact fairness for the good of the workplace.[37] Even in the absence of good hygiene factors, employees may still be very motivated to perform their jobs well if the motivation factors are present.

eustress Healthy, normal stress.

Two conclusions can be drawn. First, hygiene factors are important to a certain level but unimportant beyond that threshold. Second, the presence of motivation factors is essential to enhancing employee motivation to excel at work.

5-4c Critique of the Two-Factor Theory

One critique of the theory surrounded the classification of the two factors. Some data have shown that a factor may not fit exclusively into either the hygiene or motivation categories. For example, employees generally classify pay as both a hygiene factor and a motivation factor. A second critique of the theory does not account for individual differences. Differences in age, sex, social status, education, or occupational level may influence the classification of factors. A third concern is that intrinsic job factors like the workflow process may be more important in determining satisfaction or dissatisfaction on the job. Finally, much of the supporting data for the theory is based on the *critical-incident technique*. Despite the critiques, Herzberg's was the first motivation theory developed specifically to predict motivation in work settings, thus having important implications for the design of work as we will discuss in Chapter 14.[38]

 5-5 TWO NEW IDEAS IN MOTIVATION

Two new ideas in motivation have emerged in the past decade. One centers on eustress, strength, and hope. This idea comes from the new discipline of *positive organizational behavior*. A second new idea centers on positive energy and full engagement, translating what was learned from high-performance athletes for the use of *Fortune* 500 executives and managers. In addition, supporting a family (family motivation) provides a powerful source of motivation that can boost performance in the workplace, even when a person's intrinsic motivation is low, by providing energy.[39] However, family motivation does not reduce work stress.

5-5a Eustress, Strength, and Hope

Eustress (for "euphoria + stress") is healthy, normal stress. Stress is the energy we experience when confronted with a challenging or difficult situation. Such situations can produce *distress*, a negative response such as frustration or fear, which leads to unhealthy and unproductive results, or eustress, a positive response to challenges that generates energy and motivates an individual to achieve. Eustress leads us to invest in strengths, find meaning in work, display courage and principled action, and draw on positive emotions at work.[40] This positive perspective on organizational life encourages optimism, hope, and health for people at work. Instead of focusing on the individual's needs or the rewards or punishment meted out in the work environment, the idea of encouraging eustress is to focus on the individual's interpretation of or response to events. An assumption underlying eustress is that although things happen that are out of our control, we can control our response to a situation. Thus, we can control distress by reframing our perspective on a situation. Eustress is a healthy and positive motivational force for individuals who harness its energy for productive work and organizational contributions.

5-5b Positive Energy and Full Engagement

The second new concept in motivation, Jim Loehr's *full engagement* idea, uses lessons learned from professional athletes.[41] The central tenets are that an individual should manage energy rather than time and should strategically disengage from certain activities to balance the power of full engagement.[42] This approach suggests that individuals do not need to be activated by unmet needs but are already activated by their own physical, emotional, mental, and spiritual energy. Managers should therefore help individuals learn to manage their energy so that they can build positive energy and capacity for work.

Loehr's concept stresses the role of energy recovery in overall performance. Some individuals work best by putting forth productive energy for short periods and then taking time to rest and reenergize. This mimics the human body's potential to build or enhance its capacity, enabling the individual to sustain a high level of performance in the face of increasing work demands. Organizations with high levels of employee engagement have strong financial performance, even in volatile economic conditions.[43]

5-6 SOCIAL EXCHANGE AND EQUITY THEORY

Equity theory is a social exchange process approach to motivation that focuses on the interaction between an individual and the environment. In contrast to needs theories based on internal motivation, equity theory is concerned with the social processes that influence motivation and behavior. Power and exchange are important considerations in understanding human behavior.[44] Accounting for such external factors, Amitai Etzioni developed three categories of exchange relationships that people have with organizations: committed, calculated, and alienated involvements.[45] Committed relations have high positive intensity, calculated relationships have low positive or low negative intensity, and alienated relationships have high negative intensity. Committed relationships may characterize a person's involvement with a religious group, and alienated relationships may characterize a person's incarceration in a prison. These three categories will be discussed further in Chapter 11.

5-6a Demands and Contributions

Calculated involvements are based on the notion of social exchange in which each party in the relationship demands certain things of the other and contributes accordingly to the exchange. Business partnerships and commercial deals are both calculated involvements. When both parties to the exchange benefit, the relationship has a positive orientation. When losses occur or conflicts arise, the relationship has a negative orientation. Figure 5.3 offers a model for examining calculated exchange relationships.

DEMANDS Each party to the exchange makes demands on the other. The organization expresses its

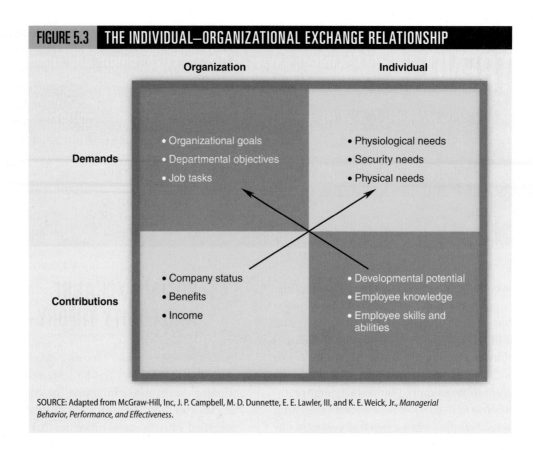

FIGURE 5.3 THE INDIVIDUAL–ORGANIZATIONAL EXCHANGE RELATIONSHIP

	Organization	Individual
Demands	• Organizational goals • Departmental objectives • Job tasks	• Physiological needs • Security needs • Physical needs
Contributions	• Company status • Benefits • Income	• Developmental potential • Employee knowledge • Employee skills and abilities

SOURCE: Adapted from McGraw-Hill, Inc, J. P. Campbell, M. D. Dunnette, E. E. Lawler, III, and K. E. Weick, Jr., *Managerial Behavior, Performance, and Effectiveness*.

demands on the individual in the form of goal or mission statements, job expectations, performance objectives, and performance feedback. The individual expresses demands, or needs, in the form of expectations of the organization. Employee need fulfillment and the feeling of belonging are both important to a healthy exchange and to organizational membership.[46] These needs may be viewed from the perspective of Maslow, Alderfer, Herzberg, or McClelland. When employees are well taken care of by the company, they take care of the business even in very difficult times.

CONTRIBUTIONS Just as each party to the exchange makes demands on the other, each also contributes to the relationship. These contributions are the basis for satisfying the demands expressed by the other party. Employees satisfy organizational demands through a range of contributions, including their skills, abilities, knowledge, energy, professional contacts, and native talents. As people grow and develop over time, they are able to increasingly satisfy the range of demands and expectations placed on them by the organization.

In a similar fashion, organizations contribute to the exchange relationship to meet individual needs. These contributions include salary, benefits, advancement opportunities, security, status, and social affiliation. Some organizations are richer in resources and better able to meet employee needs than other organizations. One of the concerns that both individuals and organizations have is whether the relationship is a fair deal or an equitable arrangement for both members of the relationship. Social exchange relationship perceptions are influenced by executive leadership style, organizational culture, and employment approach, which in turn have an effect on commitment and performance, though not organizational citizenship behavior (OCB), discussed in Chapter 4.[47]

AnneRosukon/Shutterstock.com

5-6b Adams' Theory of Inequity

Ideas about social process and exchange advocated by Etzioni and others provide a context for understanding fairness, equity, and inequity in work relationships. Stacy Adams developed the idea that **inequity** in the social exchange process is a particularly important motivator.

inequity A situation in which a person perceives that he or she is receiving less than he or she is giving or is giving less than he or she is receiving.

FIGURE 5.4   EQUITY AND INEQUITY AT WORK

	Person	Comparison other
(a) Equity	$\dfrac{\text{Outcomes}}{\text{Inputs}}$	$=$ $\dfrac{\text{Outcomes}}{\text{Inputs}}$
(b) Negative Inequity	$\dfrac{\text{Outcomes}}{\text{Inputs}}$	$<$ $\dfrac{\text{Outcomes}}{\text{Inputs}}$
(c) Positive Inequity	$\dfrac{\text{Outcomes}}{\text{Inputs}}$	$>$ $\dfrac{\text{Outcomes}}{\text{Inputs}}$

Adams' *theory of inequity* suggests that people are motivated when they find themselves in situations of inequity, or unfairness.[48] Inequity occurs when a person receives more or less than she believes she deserves based on her effort and/or contribution. Inequity creates tension, which in turn motivates a person to take action to resolve the inequity.

A perception of inequity arises when people consider their inputs (their contributions to the relationship) and their outcomes (the organization's contributions to the relationship) according to an input/outcome ratio, which they compare to that of a generalized "other," or *comparison other*. Figure 5.4 shows two inequity scenarios for a single situation, one negative and one positive. The negative inequity in (b) could occur, for example, if the comparison other earned a higher salary, while inequity in (c) could occur if the person had more vacation time, all else being equal in both cases. Although not illustrated in the example, nontangible inputs such as emotional investment and nontangible outcomes such as job satisfaction may enter into a person's equity equation.

Pay inequity has been a thorny issue for women in some companies. Eastman Kodak and other companies have made real progress in addressing the issue of pay equity.[49] Globalization also presents a challenge for pay equity. As organizations grow internationally, they may have trouble determining pay and benefit equity/inequity across national borders.

Adams considers a situation in which there is inequity in only one variable to be a first level of inequity. A more severe, second level of inequity would occur, for example, in a situation where the inputs of a person experiencing negative inequity, as in Figure 5.4(b), are also greater than those of the comparison other. Inequalities in one (inputs or outcomes) coupled with equality in the other (inputs or outcomes) are experienced as a less severe inequity than inequalities in both inputs and outcomes. One drawback of Adams's theory is that it does not provide a way of determining whether some inputs or some outcomes are more important than others.

5-6c The Resolution of Inequity

Once a person establishes the existence of an inequity, she might use a number of strategies to restore equity. Adams's theory provides seven basic strategies for restoring equity: (1) alter the person's outcomes, (2) alter the person's inputs, (3) alter the comparison other's outcomes, (4) alter the comparison other's inputs, (5) change who is used as a comparison other, (6) rationalize the inequity, and (7) leave the organizational situation.

Each of the first four strategies could involve a wide variety of tactics. For example, if an employee has a strategy to increase his income by $11,000 per year to restore equity, the tactic might be a meeting between the employee and his manager concerning the issue of salary equity. Another tactic would be for the person to work with the company's compensation specialists.

The selection of a strategy and a set of tactics is a sensitive issue with possible long-term consequences. In this example, a strategy aimed at reducing the comparison other's outcomes may have the desired short-term effect of restoring equity but reduce morale and productivity in the long term. The equity theory does not include a hierarchy predicting which inequity-reduction strategy a person will or should choose, but it is nevertheless a reminder of the importance of fairness. Pay dispersion (the amount of allowable differences between employee pay) has the ability to enhance or diminish employee motivation. Employees will generally be motivated when pay dispersion strategies are based on performance.[50]

5-6d New Perspectives on Equity Theory

Equity theory has been revised in light of new theories and research. One important theoretical revision proposes three types of individuals based on preferences for equity.[51] **Equity sensitives** prefer equity based on the originally formed theory. In other words, they want the relationship between their own input and output to be equal to that of

equity sensitive An individual who prefers an equity ratio equal to that of his or her comparison other.

> People believe there is a correlation between the effort they put forth, the performance they achieve, and the outcomes they receive.

their comparison other. Equity sensitivity contributes to the extent to which employees feel obligated to help in the workplace. Equity sensitive employees who monitor resources they receive from their supervisors may feel less obligated to engage in helping behaviors if they perceive they have been provided with fewer resources.[52] **Benevolents** are comfortable with an equity ratio less than that of their comparison other.[53] These people may be thought of as givers. **Entitleds** are comfortable only with an equity ratio greater than that of their comparison other.[54] These people may be thought of as takers.

Equity in pay is an important factor in motivation because pay is often thought to relate to a person's self-imposed performance expectations. But one study suggests that a person's organizational position also influences self-imposed performance expectations and may be a more important factor than pay.[55] Specifically, a two-level move up in an organization with no additional pay creates a higher self-imposed performance expectation than a one-level move up with modest additional pay. Similarly, a two-level move down in an organization with no reduction in pay creates a lower self-imposed performance expectation than a one-level move down with a modest decrease in pay.

benevolent An individual who is comfortable with an equity ratio less than that of his or her comparison other.

entitled An individual who is comfortable with an equity ratio greater than that of his or her comparison other.

Unfortunately, inequity and organizational injustice can also generate dysfunctional behavior.[56] More seriously, workplace injustice can trigger aggressive reactions that harm both individuals and the organization. Fortunately, only a small number of individuals respond to such unfairness through dysfunctional behavior.[57]

Increasing, decreasing, or constant experiences of inequity over time may have very different consequences for people.[58] Equity theory can help companies implement two-tiered wage structures such as the one used by American Airlines in the early 1990s. In a two-tiered system, one group of employees receives different pay and benefits than another group of employees. Such a system can, however, generate perceptions of inequity, especially where the value of equal pay for equal work is strongly held. Research suggests that unions and management may want to consider work location and employment status (part-time versus full-time) prior to implementing a two-tiered system.[59]

5-7 EXPECTANCY THEORY OF MOTIVATION

In addition to individual needs and social exchange, motivation can also be explained in terms of an individual's perception of the performance process. Victor

Most motivation theories in use today have been developed by and about Americans.

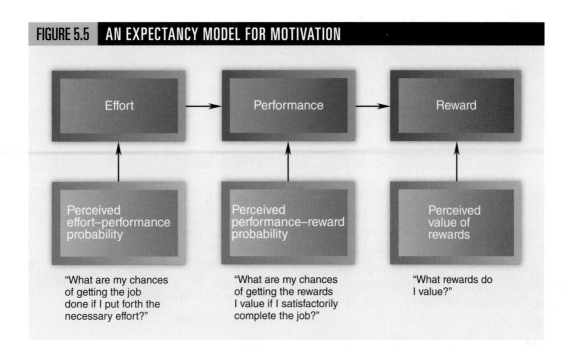

FIGURE 5.5 AN EXPECTANCY MODEL FOR MOTIVATION

Effort → Performance → Reward

Perceived effort–performance probability
"What are my chances of getting the job done if I put forth the necessary effort?"

Perceived performance–reward probability
"What are my chances of getting the rewards I value if I satisfactorily complete the job?"

Perceived value of rewards
"What rewards do I value?"

Vroom's *expectancy theory* of motivation is a cognitive process theory founded on two basic notions. First, Vroom assumes that people expect certain outcomes of behavior and performance, which may be thought of as rewards, or consequences of behavior. Second, people believe there is a correlation between the effort they put forth, the performance they achieve, and the outcomes they receive. Expectancy theory has been used in a wide variety of contexts, including test-taking motivation among students.[60]

The key constructs in the expectancy theory of motivation are the valence of an outcome, expectancy, and instrumentality.[61] **Valence** is the value, or importance, one places on a particular reward. **Expectancy** is the belief that effort leads to performance (e.g., "If I try harder, I can do better"). **Instrumentality** is the belief that performance is related to rewards (e.g., "If I perform better, I will get more pay"). Figure 5.5 models the expectancy theory notions of effort, performance, and rewards.

Valence, expectancy, and instrumentality all influence a person's motivation. The perceived relationship between effort and performance varies from person to person and from activity to activity. One person might believe that an increase in effort has a direct, positive effect on performance. Another person might have a very different set of beliefs about the link between effort and performance. In a similar fashion, people's beliefs about the link between performance and reward vary. From a motivation perspective, it is the person's belief about the relationships between these constructs that is important, not the actual nature of the relationship.

Managers can use expectancy theory to design *motivation programs*.[62] Sometimes called *performance planning* or *evaluation systems*, these motivation programs are meant to enhance a person's belief that effort will improve performance and therefore lead to better pay. Valence and expectancy are particularly important in establishing priorities for people pursuing multiple goals.[63]

Valence is the third key idea within the expectancy theory of motivation. Different people value different rewards. One person prefers salary to benefits, whereas another person prefers just the reverse. In fact, employees vary greatly with respect to the link between work and pay, as well as how much they value money.[64]

5-7a Motivational Problems

Expectancy theory attributes motivational problems to three basic causes: disbelief in a relationship between effort and performance, disbelief in a relationship between performance and rewards, and lack of desire for the rewards offered. If the motivational problem stems from the person's belief that effort will not improve performance,

valence The value or importance one places on a particular reward.

expectancy The belief that effort leads to performance.

instrumentality The belief that performance is related to rewards.

FAST FACT

How American Workers Got Lazy

American workers' job change rate is down 50 percent of what it was 15 years ago. Entrepreneurship has plunged dramatically too, with only 7 to 8 percent of U.S. companies being start-ups. During the 1980s start-ups composed 12 to 13 percent of U.S. companies. Since Alexis de Tocqueville visited and wrote about his view of America, Americans have been known for their restlessness, a signature American trait. Americans have displayed a willingness to move, take risks, and adapt to change, thus producing a dynamic economy and a tradition of innovation from Ben Franklin to Steve Jobs. Have Americans become complacent? During one recent 12-month period, the percentage of Americans who moved from one dwelling to another was at the lowest point since 1948, the year such data began being collected. Important questions include, Have Americans run out of gas? Have they lost their motivation and will to achieve?

Tero Vesalainen/Shutterstock.com

SOURCE: M. Rees, "How American Workers Got Lazy," *Wall Street Journal*, 28 Feb. 2017.

---

the solution lies in altering this belief. The person can be shown how an increase in effort or an alteration in the kind of effort put forth can be converted into improved performance.

If the motivational problem is related to the person's belief that performance will not result in rewards, the solution also lies in altering that belief. The person can be shown how an increase in performance or a somewhat altered form of performance will be converted into rewards. If, however, the motivational problem is related to the value placed on certain rewards, there are two possible solutions: to alter the value placed on the rewards or to alter the rewards themselves.

Research results on expectancy theory have been mixed.[65] The theory predicts job satisfaction accurately, but its complexity makes it difficult to test the full model, and the measures of instrumentality, valence, and expectancy have only weak validity.[66] In addition, measuring expectancy constructs is time-consuming, and the values for each construct change over time for an individual. Finally, the theory assumes that the individual is totally rational and acts as a minicomputer, calculating probabilities and values. In reality, the theory may be more complex than the way people typically function.

moral maturity The measure of a person's cognitive moral development.

5-7b Motivation and Moral Maturity

Expectancy theory predicts that people will work to maximize their personal outcomes. This is consistent with Adam Smith's idea of working for one's own self-interest. Both suggest that people work to benefit themselves alone. Expectancy theory cannot explain altruistic behavior. Therefore, it may be necessary to consider an individual's **moral maturity** in order to understand altruistic, fair, and equitable behavior. Moral maturity is the measure of a person's cognitive moral development, as discussed in Chapter 4. Morally mature people behave based on universal ethical principles, while morally immature people behave based on egocentric motivations.[67]

5-8 CULTURAL DIFFERENCES IN MOTIVATION

Most motivation theories in use today have been developed by and about Americans.[68] When researchers have examined the universality of these theories, they have found cultural differences, at least with regard to Maslow's, McClelland's, and Herzberg's theories. For example, while self-actualization is the pinnacle need for Americans in Maslow's need hierarchy, security may be the most important need for people in cultures with a high need to avoid uncertainty.[69] Although achievement is an important need for Americans, research suggests that other cultures do not value achievement as much as Americans do.

The two-factor theory has been tested in other countries as well. Results in New Zealand did not replicate the results found in the United States; supervision and interpersonal relationships were important motivators in New Zealand, as opposed to the importance of hygienic factors as in America.[70] Researchers examining equity theory in cross-cultural contexts have suggested reexamining equity preferences, selection of referent others, and reactions to inequity.[71] Finally, expectancy theory may hold up well in cultures that value individualism but break down in more collectivist cultures that value cooperative efforts. In collectivist cultures, rewards are more closely tied to group and team efforts, and expectancy theory is ill equipped to deal with such differences.

STUDY TOOLS 5

LOCATED AT BACK OF THE TEXTBOOK
☐ Rip out chapter review card

LOCATED AT WWW.CENGAGE.COM/LOGIN
☐ Gain unique perspectives on key concepts with new Concept Clip videos in the e-book
☐ Review key term flashcards and create your own
☐ Increase your comprehension with online homework and quizzes

6 | Learning and Performance Management

LEARNING OBJECTIVES

6-1 Describe behavioral theories of learning.

6-2 Describe social and cognitive theories of learning.

6-3 Explain how goal setting can be used to direct learning and performance.

6-4 Define performance and identify the tools used to measure it.

6-5 Explain the importance of performance feedback and how it can be delivered effectively.

6-6 Identify ways managers can reward performance.

6-7 List several strategies for correcting poor performance.

After finishing this chapter go to **PAGE 102** for **STUDY TOOLS**

6-1 BEHAVIORAL MODELS OF LEARNING IN ORGANIZATIONS

Learning is a change in behavior acquired through experience. It helps guide and direct motivated behavior. Learning may begin with the cognitive activity of developing knowledge about a subject, which then leads to a change in behavior. Alternatively, the behaviorist approach to learning assumes that observable behavior is a function of its consequences. Behaviorists argue that learning stems from classical and operant conditioning. Machine learning is a subfield of computer science that evolved from the study of pattern recognition and computational learning theory in artificial intelligence.[1] The concept of machine learning is extrapolated from human learning, the principle focus of the first section in this chapter.

6-1a Classical Conditioning

Classical conditioning is the process of modifying behavior by pairing a conditioned stimulus with an unconditioned stimulus to elicit an unconditioned response. Its discovery is largely the result of Russian physiologist Ivan Pavlov's research in the early 1900s, Pavlov's professional exchanges with Walter B. Cannon and other American researchers brought his ideas to prominence in the United States.[2]

Classical conditioning builds on the natural reaction of an unconditioned response to an unconditioned stimulus. In dogs, this might be the natural production of saliva (unconditioned response) in response to the presentation of meat (unconditioned stimulus). By presenting a conditioned stimulus (e.g., a ringing bell) simultaneously with the unconditioned stimulus (meat), the researcher made the dog develop a conditioned response (salivation). After enough trials, the dog salivated at the sound of a bell, even when no meat was presented.

As demonstrated by B. F. Skinner, classical conditioning may occur similarly in humans.[3] For example, people working at a computer terminal may get lower back tension

> **Reinforcement and punishment are used to manage good and bad behavior.**

(unconditioned response) from poor posture (unconditioned stimulus). If they become aware of that tension only when the manager appears (conditioned stimulus), then they may develop a conditioned response (lower back tension) to the appearance of the manager.

But classical conditioning has limited applicability to human behavior in organizations for three reasons. First, humans are more complex than dogs and less amenable to simple cause-and-effect conditioning. Second, the behavioral environments in organizations are complex and not very amenable to single

learning A change in behavior acquired through experience.

classical conditioning Modifying behavior by pairing a conditioned stimulus with an unconditioned stimulus to elicit an unconditioned response.

stimulus–response manipulations. Third, the human capacity for decision making can override simple conditioning.

6-1b Operant Conditioning

Operant conditioning is the process of modifying behavior by following specific behaviors with positive or negative consequences.[4] These consequences influence behavior through three strategies: reinforcement, punishment, and extinction. Management pioneer Fred Luthans and his colleagues used *organizational behavior modification (OBM)* to shape behavior in a variety of organizations.[5] OBM employs three types of consequences: financial reinforcement, nonfinancial reinforcement, and social reinforcement. A major review of OBM's influence in organizations found that it had significant and positive influence on task performance in both manufacturing and service organizations but that the effects were most powerful in manufacturing organizations.[6] In a study of pay for performance, more productive employees chose performance-based compensation over fixed compensation when given a choice.[7] However, regardless of which pay scheme employees chose, all produced more under a pay-for-performance scheme. And while attitudes about pay for performance continue to vary according to cultural values, research suggests that its use may be rising cross-culturally.[8]

operant conditioning
Modifying behavior through the use of positive or negative consequences following specific behaviors.

positive consequences
Results of a behavior that a person finds attractive or pleasurable.

negative consequences
Results of a behavior that a person finds unattractive or aversive.

6-1c Reinforcement Theory

Reinforcement theory holds that reinforcement enhances desirable behavior, whereas punishment and extinction diminish undesirable behavior. This theory is central to the design and administration of organizational reward systems, which are a key factor in attracting and retaining top employees. Strategic rewards help motivate behavior, actions, and accomplishments, all of which advance the organization toward specific business goals.[9] In addition to cash rewards such as bonuses, strategic rewards include training and educational opportunities, stock options, and recognition awards such as travel.

Reinforcement and punishment represent the positive and negative consequences of behavior. **Positive consequences** are the results that the person finds attractive or pleasurable. They might include a pay increase, bonus, promotion, transfer to a more desirable geographic location, or praise from a supervisor. **Negative consequences** are the results that the person finds unattractive or aversive. They might include disciplinary action, an undesirable transfer, a demotion, or harsh criticism from a supervisor. The recipient of the consequences defines them as positive or negative. Therefore, individual personality differences as well as gender and cultural differences may be important in their classification.

Following a specific behavior with a positive or negative consequence either reinforces or punishes that behavior.[10] Thorndike's *law of effect* states that behaviors followed by positive consequences are more likely to recur and behaviors followed by negative consequences are less likely to recur.[11] Figure 6.1 shows how positive and negative consequences may be applied or withheld in the strategies of reinforcement and punishment.

FIGURE 6.1 | REINFORCEMENT AND PUNISHMENT STRATEGIES

	Reinforcement (desirable behavior)	Punishment (undesirable behavior)
Positive consequences	Apply	Withhold
Negative consequences	Withhold	Apply

SOURCE: Table from Organizational Behavior Modification by Fred Luthans and Robert Kreitner. Copyright © 1985, p. 58 by Scott Foresman and Company and the authors. Reprinted by permission of the authors.

The Natural Consequences of Solving Important Problems

While reinforcement theory is helpful in shaping behavior in organizations, there are some problems that demand creativity and exploratory behavior. These problems have many of their own natural consequences as the person working on them will likely experience repeated failures before achieving success. Therefore, it is crucial to maintain persistence in the presence of what might feel like a punishing process. For example, Einstein encountered numerous false starts and outright errors between 1912 and 1915 while forging his general theory of relativity (GTR). He often felt like he was groping in the dark for a truth he believed existed but could not express.

Danish mathematician Piet Heim used one of his rhyming aphorisms to express the challenge that important problems are only solved through trial and error, often many errors, before final success. "Problems worthy of attack/Prove their worth by hitting back." To learn and to solve challenging and complex problems calls the problem solver to continually move beyond negative consequences and failure in seeking the final solution.

SOURCE: F. Wilczek, "The Power of Learning by Doing: From the Beatles to Einstein, the key to creativity is often going for it and learning from your mistakes," *Wall Street Journal*, 18 Jan. 2017.

REINFORCEMENT

Reinforcement is a strategy to cultivate desirable behavior by either bestowing positive consequences or withholding negative ones. Positive reinforcement occurs when a positive consequence (like a bonus) follows a desirable behavior (like a successful business year). Marriott International provides positive reinforcement by honoring ten to twenty employees each year with its J. Willard Marriott Award of Excellence. Each recipient receives a medallion engraved with the words that express the basic values of the company: dedication, achievement, character, ideals, effort, and perseverance. A recent field experiment examining the reward practices of an Israeli high-tech manufacturing factory sought to better understand the type of short-term bonus (monetary or nonmonetary) with the most positive effect on worker productivity and the circumstances under which short-term bonuses reinforced employee behavior. One group of employees was incentivized with monetary bonuses in the form of cash and family meal vouchers; the other group, with nonmonetary bonuses in the form of a note providing them with positive feedback. Employees who received monetary and nonmonetary bonuses increased their productivity by over 5%. Similarly, productivity decreased for both sets of employees once they were no longer being incentivized for their performance. However, the performance decrease took longer for the employees who had been incentivized with a simple note acknowledging their good performance than those who received cash or the meal voucher.[12]

Negative reinforcement occurs when managers withhold a negative consequence after an employee demonstrates a desirable behavior. For example, a manager who reduces an employee's pay (negative consequence) if the employee comes to work late (undesirable behavior) refrains from doing so when the employee is on time (desirable behavior). The employee avoids the negative consequence (a reduction in pay) by exhibiting the desirable behavior (being on time to work).

> **reinforcement** A strategy to cultivate desirable behavior by either bestowing positive consequences or withholding negative consequences.

TABLE 6.1 SCHEDULES OF REINFORCEMENT

Schedule	Description	Effects on Responding
Continuous	Reinforcer follows every response.	Steady, high rate of performance as long as reinforcement follows every response. High frequency of reinforcement may lead to early satiation. Behavior weakens rapidly (undergoes extinction) when reinforcers are withheld. Appropriate for newly emitted, unstable, low-frequency responses.
Intermittent	Reinforcer does not follow every response.	Capable of producing high frequencies of responding. Low frequency of reinforcement precludes early satiation. Appropriate for stable or high-frequency responses.
Fixed ratio	A fixed number of responses must be emitted before reinforcement occurs.	A fixed ratio of 1:1 (reinforcement occurs after every response) is the same as a continuous schedule. Tends to produce a high rate of response that is vigorous and steady.
Variable ratio	A varying or random number of responses must be emitted before reinforcement occurs.	Capable of producing a high rate of response that is vigorous, steady, and resistant to extinction.
Fixed interval	The first response after a specific period of time has elapsed is reinforced.	Produces an uneven response pattern varying from a very slow, unenergetic response immediately following reinforcement to a very fast, vigorous response immediately preceding reinforcement.
Variable interval	The first response after varying or random periods of time have elapsed is reinforced.	Tends to produce a high rate of response that is vigorous, steady, and resistant to extinction.

SOURCE: F. Luthans and R. Kreitner, *Organizational Behavior Modification* (Glenview, Ill.: Scott, Foresman, 1985). Copyright © by Scott Foresman and Company and the authors. Reprinted by permission of the authors.

When managers design organizational reward systems, they consider not only the type of reinforcement but also how often to provide it, according to continuous or intermittent schedules, as shown in Table 6.1.

6-1d Punishment

Punishment is a strategy to discourage undesirable behavior. One way to punish a person is to follow an undesirable behavior with a negative consequence. For example, a professional athlete who is excessively offensive to an official (undesirable behavior) may be ejected from the game (negative consequence). The other way to punish a person is to withhold a positive consequence following an undesirable behavior. For example, a salesperson who puts little

punishment A strategy to discourage undesirable behavior by either bestowing negative consequences or withholding positive consequences.

extinction A strategy to weaken a behavior by attaching no consequences to it.

effort into his pitch (undesirable behavior) won't likely receive a large commission check (positive consequence).

Punishment sometimes has unintended results. Because punishment is discomforting to the individual being punished, it can bring about negative psychological, emotional, performance, or behavioral consequences (such as workplace deviance), especially when applied too often. Being aware of this potential consequence of a generalized negative response and decreased motivation to work better, some managers use the threat of punishment—rather than actually applying the punishment—to scare workers into greater effort whenever possible.[13]

EXTINCTION An alternative to punishing undesirable behavior is **extinction**—a strategy to weaken a behavior by attaching no consequences (either positive or negative) to it. This strategy may require time and patience, but the absence of consequences eventually weakens a behavior. Extinction may be most effective when used in conjunction with the positive reinforcement of desirable behaviors. For example, complimenting a sarcastic colleague for constructive comments (reinforcing desirable behavior) while ignoring sarcastic comments (extinguishing undesirable behavior) may prove doubly effective. Extinction is not always the best strategy, however. In cases of dangerous or seriously undesirable behavior, punishment might better deliver a swift, clear lesson.

6-2 SOCIAL AND COGNITIVE THEORIES OF LEARNING

In addition to behaviorist theory, social and cognitive theories of learning have been proposed.

6-2a Bandura's Social Learning Theory

Albert Bandura's social learning theory offers a complementary alternative to Pavlov's and Skinner's behaviorist approaches.[14] Bandura asserts that learning occurs when we observe other people and model their behavior. Because employees look to their supervisors for acceptable norms of behavior, they are likely to pattern their own actions after the supervisor's. Central to Bandura's social learning theory is the notion of **task-specific self-efficacy**, an individual's internal expectancy to perform a specific task effectively. Individuals with high self-efficacy believe that they have the ability to get things done. Self-efficacy is higher in a learning context than in a performance context, especially for individuals with a high learning orientation.[15] There are four sources of task-specific self-efficacy: prior experiences, behavior models (witnessing the success of others), persuasion from other people, and assessment of current physical and emotional capabilities.[16] Evidence suggests that self-efficacy leads to high performance on a wide variety of physical and mental tasks.[17] Employees with high self-efficacy are more likely to learn new things and seek out variety in conducting their job tasks.[18] Prior success can also enhance one's self-efficacy. For example, women who trained in physical self-defense increased their self-efficacy in self-defense and new tasks.[19]

Alexander Stajkovic and Fred Luthans drew on Bandura's ideas of self-efficacy and social learning to expand their original work in behavioral management and OBM into a comprehensive framework for performance management.[20] Bandura saw the power of social reinforcement, recognizing that financial and material rewards often follow or coincide with the approval of others, whereas punishments often follow social disapproval. Thus, Stajkovic and Luthans saw that self-efficacy and social reinforcement influence behavior and performance at work and have suggested that managers can be confident that employees with high self-efficacy will perform well.

Managers can empower employees and help them develop self-efficacy by providing job challenges, offering coaching and counseling for improved performance, and rewarding employees' achievements. Managers can also remove organizational barriers that stand in the way of employees making progress in meaningful work.[21] Given the increasing diversity of the workforce, managers may want to target their efforts toward women and minorities, who tend to have lower than average self-efficacy.[22]

> Managers can empower employees and help them develop self-efficacy by providing job challenges, offering coaching and counseling, and rewarding employees' achievements.

6-2b Cognitive Theories of Learning

The cognitive approach to learning is based on the *Gestalt* school of thought and draws on Jung's theory of personality differences, discussed in Chapter 3. Recall the distinction between introverts (who need to study, concentrate, and reflect) and extraverts (who need to interact with other people). Introverts learn best alone, whereas extraverts learn best by exchanging ideas with others.

The personality functions of intuition, sensing, thinking, and feeling all have learning implications, which are listed in Table 6.2. Each person has a preferred mode of gathering information and a preferred mode of evaluating and making decisions about that information. For example, an intuitive thinker may want to skim research reports about implementing total quality programs and then, based on hunches, decide how to apply the research findings to the organization.

> **task-specific self-efficacy**
> An individual's internal expectancy to perform a specific task effectively.

TABLE 6.2 PERSONALITY FUNCTIONS AND LEARNING

Personality Preference	Implications for Learning by Individuals
Information gathering	
Intuitors	Prefer theoretical frameworks. Look for the meaning in material. Attempt to understand the grand scheme. Look for possibilities and interrelations.
Sensors	Prefer specific, empirical data. Look for practical applications. Attempt to master details of a subject. Look for what is realistic and doable.
Decision making	
Thinkers	Prefer analysis of data and information. Work to be fair-minded and evenhanded. Seek logical, just conclusions. Do not like to be too personally involved.
Feelers	Prefer interpersonal involvement. Work to be tenderhearted and harmonious. Seek subjective, merciful results. Do not like objective, factual analysis.

SOURCE: From Type Talk at Work by Otto Kroeger and Janet Theusen, copyright © 1992 by Janet Theusen and Otto Kroeger. Used by permission of Delacorte Press, an imprint of The Random House Publishing Group, a division of Random House, Inc.

A sensing feeler may prefer viewing videos of interviews with people in companies that implemented total quality programs and then identify people in the organization most likely to be receptive to the approaches presented.

6-3 GOAL SETTING AT WORK

Goal setting is the process of establishing desired results that guide and direct behavior. Goal-setting theory is based on laboratory studies, field research experiments, and comparative investigations by Edwin Locke, Gary Latham, John M. Ivancevich, and others.[23] Goals crystallize the sense of purpose and mission that drives success.

6-3a Characteristics of Effective Goals

Various organizations define the characteristics of effective goals differently. As one example, Sanger-Harris, a former retail organization, used SMART goals. SMART stands for Specific, Measurable, Attainable, Realistic, and Time-bound. Specific and challenging goals focus attention on exactly what will be accomplished and inspire peak performance. People who set specific, challenging goals consistently outperform those with easy or unspecified goals, as Figure 6.2 shows. Subconscious thought may have a positive effect as well. Two studies of subconscious motivation found that goals that were ingrained but not explicitly expressed significantly enhanced task performance for difficult conscious goals, though not for easy goals.[24]

Measurable, quantitative goals provide opportunities for feedback about goal progress. Qualitative goals are also valuable. The Western Company of North America (now part of BJ Services Company) allows about 15% of a manager's goals to be of a qualitative nature.[25] An example of a qualitative goal is improving customer relations. To assess its progress, this qualitative goal might be quantified using measures like the number of complaints or the frequency of compliments.

Time-bound goals enhance measurability. Many organizations work on standardized cycles of time, such as quarters or years. If there is any uncertainty about the time period of the goal effort, the time limit should be explicitly stated.

The prioritizing of goals allows efficient resource allocation. As time, energy, or other resources become available, a person can work through her list of goals in order of importance.[26] Priority helps direct a person's efforts and behavior.

Goal setting can serve three functions. First, it can increase work motivation and task performance.[27] Second, it can reduce stress caused by conflicting or confusing expectations.[28] Third, it can improve the accuracy and validity of performance evaluation.[29] Let's look at each of these functions in some detail.

6-3b Goals Increase Work Motivation and Task Performance

Goals often increase employee effort and motivation, which in turn improve task performance. The higher the goal is, the better the performance. People work harder

goal setting The process of establishing desired results that guide and direct behavior.

FIGURE 6.2 GOAL LEVEL AND TASK PERFORMANCE

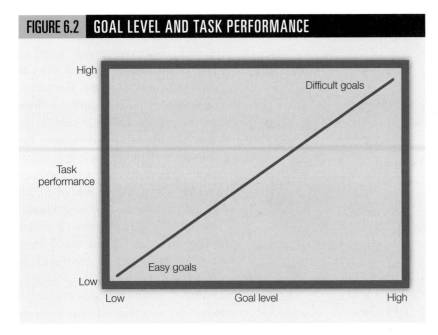

to reach difficult goals. Figure 6.2 depicts this positive relationship.

Managers who use goal setting should ensure employee participation, supervisory commitment, and useful performance feedback. Participation encourages employees to accept and commit to the goal, two prerequisites to goal accomplishment. Employee participation is especially important in the accomplishment of difficult goals.[30] And when a difficult goal is assigned, acceptance and commitment are considered essential prerequisites to accomplishment.

Supervisory goal commitment reflects an organization's commitment to goal setting. Indeed, organizational commitment is a prerequisite for successful goal-setting programs such as *management by objectives (MBO)*, discussed shortly.[31] The organization commits to the program, and the supervisors and employees commit to its specific work goals.

The supervisor also provides employees with interim performance feedback on their progress toward goals. Such performance feedback is most useful for goals that are specific, and specific goals improve performance most when interim feedback is given.[32] When approached correctly, even negative performance feedback can improve performance.[33] For example, assume an insurance salesperson has a goal of selling $500,000 worth of insurance in six months but has sold only $200,000 after three months. During an interim performance feedback session, the supervisor helps the salesperson identify his problem—that he is not focusing his calls on the likeliest prospects—and

gets him back on track to achieve his goal. Feedback is most helpful when it provides practical advice and is timely.

6-3c Goals Reduce Role Stress, Conflict, and Ambiguity

Goal setting also reduces the *role stress* associated with conflicting and confusing expectations because it clarifies the task–role expectations for employees. Supervisors, coworkers, and employees all provide task-related information. A fourteen-month evaluation found that goal setting reduced conflict, confusion, and absenteeism.[34]

Because goal setting improves role clarity, it generally improves communication between managers and employees.[35] This is why FedEx encourages managers to include communication-related targets in their annual MBO goal-setting process.[36]

6-3d Goals Improve Performance Evaluation

The third major function of goal setting is improving the accuracy and validity of performance evaluation. One of the best methods for this is **management by objectives (MBO)**—a goal-setting program based on interaction and negotiation between employees and managers.

According to Peter Drucker, who developed the concept of MBO over fifty years ago, the objectives-setting process begins with the employee writing a so-called employee's letter to the manager. The letter explains the employee's general understanding of the scope of the manager's job as well as the scope of the employee's own job. The employee lays out a set of specific objectives to be pursued over the next six to twelve months, and after some discussion and negotiation, the manager and the employee finalize these items into a performance plan.

Drucker considers MBO a participative and interactive process. This does not mean that goal setting begins at the bottom of the organization.

management by objectives (MBO)
A goal-setting program based on interaction and negotiation between employees and managers.

It means that goal setting is applicable to all employees; both lower-level organizational members and professional staff influence the goal-setting process.[37] Most goal-setting programs are designed to enhance performance, especially when incentives are associated with goal achievement.[38]

The two central ingredients in goal-setting programs are planning and evaluation. The *planning* component consists of organizational and individual goal setting, two essential and interdependent processes.[39] In planning, individuals and departments usually develop operational and tactical plans to support the corporate objectives. The idea is to formulate a clear, consistent, measurable, and ordered set of goals to articulate *what* to do. Operational support planning then determines *how* to do it. The concept of *intention* encompasses both the goal (*what*) and the pathways that lead to goal attainment (*how*).[40]

The *evaluation* component of goal setting consists of interim reviews conducted by managers and employees and formal performance evaluation. The interim reviews are designed to help employees take self-corrective action.

marigranula/123RF

The formal performance evaluation occurs at the close of a reporting period, usually once a year. Based on goal orientation theory, four types of feedback seeking were developed: self-positive, self-negative, other-positive, and other-negative.[41] If the goal was improved performance, the following feedback seeking patterns worked best. Self-negative feedback seeking was positively related to job performance, role clarity, and social integration, while self-positive feedback seeking was negatively related, and other-positive feedback seeking was positively related to job performance.

Because goal-setting programs are somewhat mechanical by nature, they are most valuable and easily implemented in stable, predictable industrial settings. They are less useful in small, unpredictable organizations. Neither individual personality differences nor gender nor cultural differences appear to threaten the success of goal-setting programs, making them useful tools for a large, diverse workforce.[42]

Goal setting can increase work motivation and task performance, reduce stress, and improve the accuracy of performance evaluation.

FAST FACT

Rethinking the Annual Performance Review

Traditional performance appraisals have been abandoned by more than 33 percent of U.S. companies. These companies are moving instead to frequent development focused conversations between managers and employees. These conversations take time and patience yet yield management and leadership development opportunities for employees. Training of employees, and even managers, in some performance based activities is warranted and useful. However, much work performance that demands creativity and agility requires education and development. That is why over one-third of U.S. companies are moving to developmental approaches rather than traditional performance appraisals.

SOURCE: P. Cappelli and A. Tavis, "Rethinking the Annual Performance Review," *Harvard Business Review*, December 2016, p. 20.

6-4 PERFORMANCE: A KEY CONSTRUCT

Performance is most often called *task accomplishment*, the term *task* coming from Frederick W. Taylor's conception of a worker's required activity.[43] Since Taylor's time in the early 1900s, there has been an extensive body of applied research on the constructs of performance management and performance appraisal.[44] Principle concerns over the past century have included purposes for evaluating performance, training, and reactions to appraisals, as well as demographic differences and cognitive processes. Hence, outcomes and effort are both important to good performance.

Predicting job performance has also been a concern for over a century. Early World War I–era theories focused on intelligence and *general mental ability* (*GMA*). Research has found GMA highly predictive of job knowledge in both civilian and military jobs.[45] Researchers have found mixed EI (emotional intelligence) to be a valid predictor of job performance. Mixed EI consists of personality traits, such as extraversion and conscientiousness, as well as affect and self-perceived abilities.[46] But before job performance can be predicted, it must be defined.

6-4a Performance Management

Performance management is a process of defining, measuring, appraising, providing feedback on, and improving performance.[47] Defining performance in behavioral terms is an essential first step in the process. Done well, the performance management process leads to increased employee engagement, whereby workers know exactly what's expected of them and have the skills and abilities to meet those expectations.[48] Once defined, performance can be measured and assessed so that workers can receive feedback and managers can set goals to improve performance. Positive performance behaviors should be rewarded, and poor performance behaviors should be corrected.

6-4b Defining Performance

Managers must clearly define performance if their employees are to perform well at work. Most work performance is multidimensional. For example, a sales executive's performance will require administrative, financial, and interpersonal skills. Knowing the skills and behaviors needed to succeed in a position is a prerequisite to measuring and evaluating job performance.

Although different jobs require varying skills and behaviors, *organizational citizenship behavior (OCB)* spans many jobs. Recall from Chapter 4 that OCB is behavior above and beyond the call of duty. Employee involvement programs enhance OCB by engaging employees in the work environment.[49] OCB emphasizes collective performance rather than individual performance. It is but one of many dimensions to consider when defining the requirements of a specific job.

Performance appraisal is the evaluation of a person's performance. Accurate appraisals help supervisors fulfill their dual roles as evaluators and coaches. As the latter, a supervisor encourages growth and development. As the former, a supervisor makes judgments about employees' roles in the organization. Keeping an employee's position within the company in mind lends greater contextual significance to the appraisal process.[50]

Performance appraisals give employees feedback on performance, identify their developmental needs, and influence promotion, demotion, termination, selection and placement decisions.

6-4c Measuring Performance

Ideally, actual performance matches measured performance, but this is actually seldom the case. Since operational performance generates more quantifiable data, it is easier to measure than managerial performance. Recent research measuring motivation for task performance has found that wording and context may influence the validity of direct self-reports.[51] Accuracy of self-performance evaluations is also important. The more accurately individuals evaluate their performance on a task, the better their performance will be on a subsequent task.[52]

Performance appraisal systems should improve the accuracy of measured performance and increase its parity with actual performance. The extent of their agreement is called the *true assessment*, as Figure 6.3

FIGURE 6.3   ACTUAL AND MEASURED PERFORMANCE

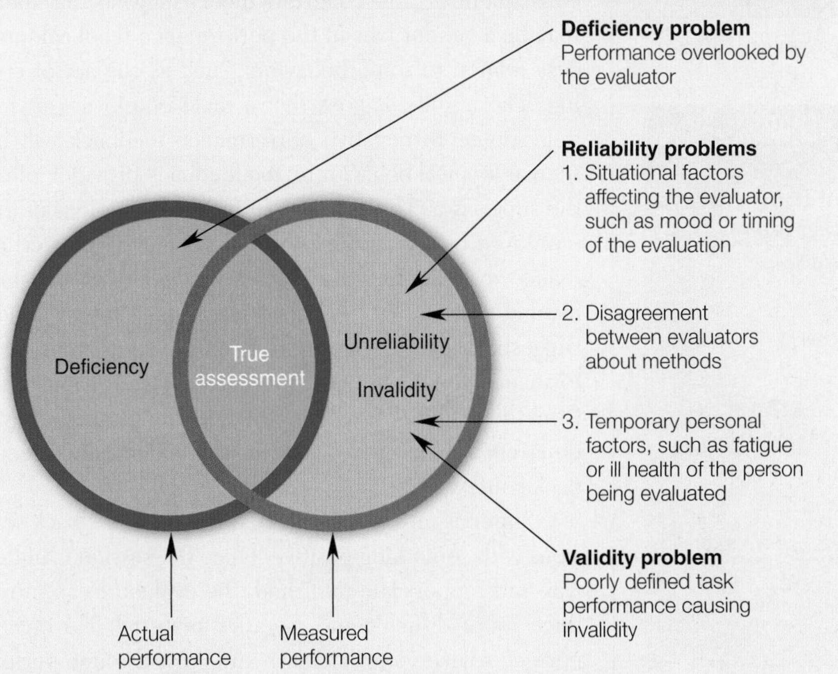

Deficiency problem
Performance overlooked by the evaluator

Reliability problems
1. Situational factors affecting the evaluator, such as mood or timing of the evaluation

2. Disagreement between evaluators about methods

3. Temporary personal factors, such as fatigue or ill health of the person being evaluated

Validity problem
Poorly defined task performance causing invalidity

Deficiency — True assessment — Unreliability — Invalidity

Actual performance   Measured performance

SOURCE: Table from *The Air Officer's Guide*, 6th ed. Copyright © 1952 Stackpole Books. Used with permission.

performance management
A process of defining, measuring, appraising, providing feedback on, and improving performance.

performance appraisal   The evaluation of a person's performance.

shows. Performance measurement problems such as deficiency, unreliability, and invalidity contribute to inaccuracy. *Deficiency* occurs when important aspects of a person's actual performance are overlooked. Unreliability results from poor-quality performance measures. *Invalidity* stems from inaccurate definition of the expected job performance.

Table 6.3, a sample of officer effectiveness reports from a nineteenth-century infantry company, demonstrates the bias of early performance appraisals. Even contemporary executive appraisals have a dark side, arousing the defenses of managers and executives. Addressing emotions and defenses is important to the effectiveness of appraisal sessions.[53] Some performance review systems lead to forced rankings of employees, which may be controversial or counterproductive. Although a recent study found that supervisors were reluctant to give negative feedback overall, they were more likely to emphasize social factors when describing the performance of ethnic minorities.[54]

Many performance-monitoring systems use modern electronic technology to measure the performance of vehicle operators, computer technicians, and customer service representatives. For example, such systems might record the rate or the total number of keystrokes for a computer technician.

Sometimes employees are unaware that their performance is being measured. What constitutes inappropriate electronic monitoring of an employee? The ethics of monitoring performance differ by culture. For example, firms in the United States and Sweden generally respect individual privacy more than those in Japan or China.

TABLE 6.3	OFFICER EFFECTIVENESS REPORTS, CIRCA 1813

Alexander Brown, Lt. Col., Comdg.—A good-natured man.

Clark Crowell, 1st Major—A good man, but no officer.

Jess B. Wordsworth, 2nd Major—An excellent officer.

Captain Shaw—A man of whom all unite in speaking ill. A knave despised by all.

Captain Thomas Lord—Indifferent, but promises well.

Captain Rockwell—An officer of capacity, but imprudent and a man of violent passions.

1st Lt. Jas. Kearns—Merely good, nothing promising.

1st Lt. Robert Cross—Willing enough, has much to learn, with small capacity.

2nd Lt. Stewart Berry—An ignorant unoffending fellow.

Ensign North—A good young man who does well.

SOURCE: J. C. Benton, The Air Officer's Guide, 6th ed. (Mechanicsburg, Penn.: Stackpole Books 1952). Copyright © 1952 Stackpole Books. Used with Permission.

Goal setting and MBO are results-oriented performance appraisal methods that do not necessarily rely on modern technology. Like performance-monitoring systems, they focus on observable, verifiable results, instead of subjective, judgmental performance dimensions. Goals established during planning serve as the standard for measuring subsequent performance. However, managers who adhere rigidly to a results-oriented approach risk overlooking performance opportunities.

6-5 PERFORMANCE FEEDBACK

Feedback sessions create stress for both supervisors and employees. Early research at General Electric found, not surprisingly, that employees responded constructively to positive feedback but often responded defensively to critical or negative feedback. In response to negative feedback, they shifted responsibility for the problem, denied it outright, or provided a wide range of excuses.[55] In a study of 499 Chinese supervisor–subordinate pairs, supervisors responded positively to employees who sought performance feedback if their motive was performance enhancement or improvement but not so positively if the employee's motive was to influence how their supervisor perceived them.[56]

Employee responses to negative feedback may be consequential. Role congruity theory suggests that there may be a gender bias in the performance feedback process related to some behaviors, such as the act of crying. The argument goes that a male employees crying in response to negative performance feedback will be seen as atypical behavior by the feedback provider, often the supervisor. This result then biases evaluations of the employee on a number of dimensions, such as performance evaluations, assessments of leadership capability, and written recommendations. In fact, the evidence suggests that men who cry in response to negative performance feedback will experience biased evaluations from the feedback provider.[57] Hence, the message "boys, don't cry" has positive value in the performance feedback context.

Supervisors should start performance feedback sessions with something positive. Once the session is under way and rapport is established, the evaluator can introduce more difficult and negative material. No one is perfect, so everyone can learn and grow through performance feedback and review sessions. Critical feedback is the basis for improvement. Managers should be aware, however, that although specific feedback can improve initial performance, it may also undermine the learning needed for later, more independent performance.[58]

6-5a 360-Degree Feedback

Many organizations use **360-degree feedback**, which is based on multiple sources of information, to improve the accuracy of performance appraisals. Evidence suggests that including self-evaluations in this process makes evaluation interviews more satisfying, more constructive, and less defensive.[59] Some dislike the fact that self-evaluations often conflict with supervisory evaluations.[60] However, these disagreements are part of the full picture of the person's performance. The 360-degree feedback method provides a well-rounded view of performance from superiors, peers, followers, and customers.[61]

As an illustration of the benefits of a 360-degree feedback evaluation, consider a mid-level civilian executive working in a large military organization. The executive is positive, compliant, and deferential toward superiors but largely indifferent toward peers. With followers, he is tough and demanding, bordering on abusive. Without each of these perspectives, the executive's performance cannot be accurately assessed.

Adding a systematic coaching component can improve 360-degree feedback.[62] By focusing on enhanced self-awareness and behavioral management, feedback coaching improves performance, satisfaction, and commitment, and reduces turnover. Separating the performance feedback component from the management development component also improves the 360-degree method.[63] The feedback component contains quantitative feedback and performance measures, while the management development component emphasizes qualitative feedback and competencies for development.

6-5b Developing People and Enhancing Careers

Good performance appraisal systems develop people and enhance careers. They should explore individual growth needs and future performance. However, in order to coach and develop employees successfully, the supervisor must establish mutual trust. This means she must be vulnerable and open to challenge from the subordinate while maintaining responsibility for the subordinate's best interests.[64] Good supervisors are skilled, empathetic listeners who encourage employees to discuss their aspirations.[65]

Employees must also take active responsibility for future development and growth. This might mean challenging the supervisor's ideas about future development and expressing their own goals. Passive, compliant employees cannot accept responsibility for themselves or achieve full emotional development.

Individual responsibility is a key characteristic of the culture of the steel manufacturer Gerdau Ameristeel. The company joke is that the company manages by "adultry" (pun intended). Gerdau Ameristeel treats people like adults and expects adult behavior from them.

6-5c Key Characteristics of an Effective Appraisal System

Effective performance appraisal systems have five key characteristics: validity, reliability, responsiveness, flexibility, and equitability. *Validity* means capturing multiple dimensions of a person's job performance. *Reliability* means collecting evaluations from multiple sources and at different times throughout the evaluation period. *Responsiveness* means allowing the person being evaluated to have some input. *Flexibility* means staying open to modification based on new information such as federal requirements. *Equitability* means evaluating fairly against established criteria, regardless of individual differences. High-quality performance appraisals with these characteristics have a positive effect on employee participation in voluntary informal learning activities.[66]

FedEx has incorporated a novel and challenging approach to evaluation in its blueprint for service quality. All managers at FedEx are evaluated by their employees through a survey-feedback-action system. Employees, in turn, evaluate their managers using a five-point scale on twenty-nine standard statements and ten local option ones. Low ratings suggest problem areas requiring management attention. One year the survey revealed that employees thought upper management was not paying attention to ideas and suggestions from people at their level. In response, CEO Fred Smith developed a biweekly employee newsletter to correct the problem.

360-degree feedback A process of self-evaluation and evaluations by a manager, peers, direct reports, and possibly customers.

6-6 REWARDING PERFORMANCE

Performance appraisals can provide input for reward decisions. If companies celebrate teamwork, values, and customer focus, they must reward behaviors demonstrating these ideas. Despite their importance, reward decisions are among the most difficult and complicated decisions managers make. There is abundant research documenting a gender pay gap, with women earning less than men, all else being equal. However, the "all else being equal" caveat does not always hold. Theory and research evidence show that high-potential women are more valuable for achieving organizational diversity goals than high-potential men, thus challenging the assumption that the gender pay gap uniformly disadvantages women.[68] High-potential women are those with the abilities needed to reach the upper echelons of organizations. Their advantage over high-potential men ends up reversing the gender pay gap and enables them to receive a pay premium. While pay and rewards for performance have value, so too do trust, fun, and meaningful work. In fact, some compensation professionals have advanced the idea of Total Rewards that include extrinsic rewards like compensation and benefits as well as intrinsic ones like work-life benefits, performance and recognition, and career-development opportunities.

Reward and punishment decisions affect entire organizations, not just the people receiving the consequence. Reward allocation involves sequential decisions about which people to reward, how to reward them, and when to reward them. These decisions shape all employees' behavior, either directly or through vicarious learning, especially when new programs are implemented. People watch what happens to peers who make mistakes and adjust their own behavior accordingly.

> Reward and punishment decisions affect entire organizations, not just the people receiving the consequence.

6-6a Individual versus Team Reward Systems

While motivation and reward systems outside the United States are often group focused, many U.S. organizations use systems that are focused on rewarding employees as individuals.[69] These systems foster independent behavior and encourage creativity, problem solving, and distinctive contributions to the organization. Different types of employees may prefer different rewards. For example, adventure seekers may prefer travel awards, while nesters prefer days off.[70]

Individual reward systems directly affect individual behavior and encourage competition within a work team.[71] Too much competition, however, may create a dysfunctional work environment. At the Western Company of North America (now part of BJ Services Company), individual success in the MBO program was tied too tightly to rewards, and individual managers became divisively competitive. Some managers took last-minute interdepartmental financial actions to meet their objectives. By doing so, they caused other managers to miss their objectives. These actions raise ethical questions about how far individual managers should go in serving their own self-interest at the expense of their peers.

Team reward systems solve the problems caused by individual competitive behavior in that they encourage cooperation, joint efforts, and the sharing of information and expertise. The collectivist orientations of Japanese and Chinese cultures position the individual as an element of the team, not as a separate individual.

Some organizations have experimented with individual and group alternative reward systems. At the individual level, these include skill-based and pay-for-knowledge systems that emphasize skills or knowledge possessed by an employee beyond the requirements for the basic job. At the group level, gain–sharing plans emphasize collective cost reduction by allowing workers to share in the gains achieved by reducing production costs. In such plans, everyone shares equally in the collective gain. Avnet, Inc. found that collective profit sharing improved performance. The most effective incentives are those that celebrate the group's accomplishments collectively rather than those that single out individuals.[72]

6-6b The Power of Earning

Both individual and team reward systems can shape productive behavior, so effective performance management boosts both individual and team achievements in an organization. Performance management and reward systems assume a demonstrable connection between performance and rewards; that is, organizations get the performance they reward, not the performance they say they want.[73]

When there is no apparent link between performance and rewards, people may begin to believe they are entitled to rewards regardless of their performance. The notion of entitlement at work counteracts the *power of earning*.[74] People who believe they are entitled to rewards without earning them are not motivated to behave constructively. Merit raises in some organizations, for example, have come to be viewed as entitlements, thus reducing their positive value in the organizational reward system. Entitlement engenders passive, irresponsible behavior, whereas earning engenders active, responsible behavior. The power of earning rests on a direct link between performance and rewards. Managers play a critical role in helping to establish this link by establishing performance goals, providing employees with feedback and assistance toward goal completion, evaluating their performance, then recommending rewards based on performance. These "contingent reward leadership" behaviors strengthen the line-of-sight that helps employees more clearly see the connection between the pay they receive and their performance of established goals.[75]

Managers must identify the cause of an employee's poor performance and develop a plan for improvement.

6-7 CORRECTING POOR PERFORMANCE

Often a challenge for supervisors, correcting poor performance can be conceived as a three-step process. First, supervisors must identify the cause or primary responsibility for the poor performance. Second, if the primary responsibility is the employee's (and not the organization's) supervisors must determine the source of the personal problem. Third, they must develop a plan for correcting the poor performance.

A number of problems trigger poor performance. These include poorly designed work systems, poor selection processes, inadequate training and skills development, lack of personal motivation, and personal problems intruding on the work environment. Not all poor performance is self-motivated, though; some is induced by the work system. Therefore, a good diagnosis should precede corrective action, and work systems should be the first factor considered. It may be that an employee is subject to a work design or selection system that keeps him from exhibiting good performance.

If the poor performance can't be attributed to work design or organizational process problems, then supervisors should examine the employee. The problem may lie in (1) some aspect of the person's relationship to the organization or supervisor, (2) some area of the employee's personal life, or (3) a training or developmental deficiency. In the latter two cases, poor performance can be treated as a symptom rather than as a motivated consequence. In such cases, identifying financial problems, family difficulties, or health disorders may help the employee solve problems before they become too extensive.

Poor performance may also stem from an employee's displaced anger or conflict with the organization or supervisor. In such cases, the employee may be unaware of the internal reactions causing the problem. Such angry motivations can generate sabotage, work slowdowns, and work stoppages. The supervisor might be attributing the cause of the

FIGURE 6.4 | INFORMATIONAL CUES AND ATTRIBUTIONS

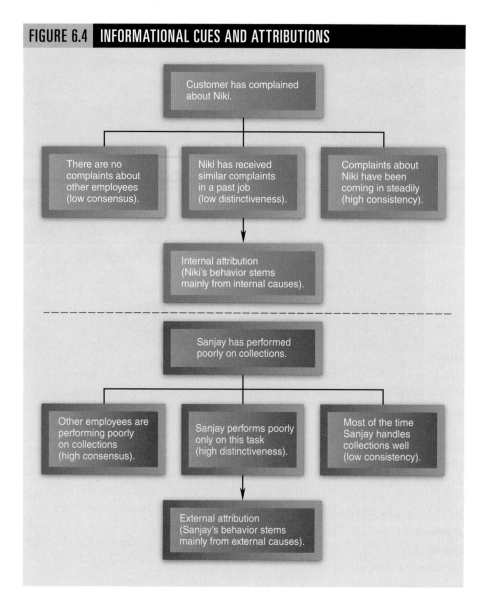

concerning employees' behavior and performance.[76] The attributions may not always be accurate. Supervisors and employees who share perceptions and attitudes tend to evaluate each other highly.[77] Those who do not share perceptions and attitudes are more likely to blame each other for performance problems.

Kelley's attribution theory proposes that individuals make attributions based on information gathered in the form of three informational cues: consensus, distinctiveness, and consistency.[78] **Consensus** is an informational cue indicating the extent to which peers in the same situation behave in a similar fashion. **Distinctiveness** is a cue indicating the degree to which an individual behaves the same way in other situations. **Consistency** is a cue indicating the frequency of behavior over time. We form attributions based on whether these cues are low or high.

Certain combinations of cues suggest an internal attribution, while other combinations suggest that the cause of the poor performance is external. Suppose you have received several complaints from customers regarding one of your customer service representatives, Niki. You have not received complaints about your other service representatives (low consensus). Reviewing Niki's records, you find that she also received customer complaints during her previous job as a sales clerk (low distinctiveness). The complaints have been coming in steadily for three months (high consistency). In this case, you would most likely make an internal attribution and conclude that the complaints must stem from Niki's behavior. The combination of low consensus, low distinctiveness, and high consistency suggests internal attributions.

Other combinations of these cues, however, point to external attributions. High consensus, high distinctiveness, and low consistency, for example, produce external attributions. Suppose one of your employees, Sanjay, is

problem to the employee while the employee is attributing it to the supervisor or organization. Supervisors must treat the poor performance as a symptom with a deeper cause and resolve the underlying anger or conflict.

6-7a Performance and Kelley's Attribution Theory

Recall from Chapter 3 that humans want to know why people behave the way they do. The same is true for managers. According to Harold Kelley's *attribution theory*, managers make attributions, or inferences,

consensus An informational cue indicating the extent to which peers in the same situation behave in a similar fashion.

distinctiveness An informational cue indicating the degree to which an individual behaves the same way in other situations.

consistency An informational cue indicating the frequency of behavior over time.

performing poorly on collecting overdue accounts. You find that the behavior is widespread within your work team (high consensus) and that Sanjay is performing poorly only on this aspect of the job (high distinctiveness), and that most of the time he handles this aspect of the job well (low consistency). You will probably decide that something about the work situation caused the poor performance.

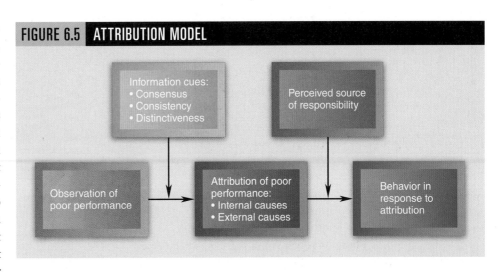

FIGURE 6.5 ATTRIBUTION MODEL

On the basis of the informational cues, the supervisor makes either an internal (personal) attribution or an external (situational) attribution. Internal attributions might include low effort, lack of commitment, or lack of ability. External attributions are outside the employee's control and might include equipment failure or unrealistic goals. These examples are illustrated visually in Figure 6.4. Be warned, however, that the process of determining the cause of a behavior is not always as simple and clear-cut as these examples suggest, because biases sometimes interfere.

Figure 6.5 presents an attribution model of supervisors' responses to poor performance. Supervisors may choose from a wide range of responses. They can, for example, express personal concern, reprimand the employee, or provide training. Supervisors who attribute the cause of poor performance to a person (an internal cause) will respond more harshly than supervisors who blame the work situation (an external cause). Supervisors should avoid both common attribution errors discussed in Chapter 3: the fundamental attribution error and the self-serving bias.

6-7b Coaching, Counseling, and Mentoring

Supervisors and coworkers are often more effective guides than formally as-signed mentors from higher up in the organizational hierarchy.[79] Consequently, they have important coaching, counseling, and mentoring responsibilities to their subordinates. Success in the mentoring relationship depends on openness and trust.[80] This relationship may help address performance-based deficiencies or personal problems.[81] In either case, supervisors can play a helpful role in employee problem-solving activities without accepting responsibility for the employees' problems. They may refer the employee to trained professionals.

Coaching and counseling are among the career and psychosocial functions of a mentoring relationship.[82] **Mentoring** is a work relationship that encourages development and career enhancement for people moving through the career cycle. Research has found a positive relationship between supervisory mentoring and OCBs. Employees who receive mentoring from their immediate supervisors are more likely to engage in individually-focused OCBs (OCB-Is). OCB-Is are those helping behaviors that directly benefit co-workers as opposed to those that benefit the organization as a whole.[83] Mentor relationships typically go through four phases: initiation, cultivation, separation, and redefinition. Mentoring offers protégés many career benefits.[84] The relationship can significantly enhance the early development of a newcomer and the midcareer development of an experienced employee. Some companies, such as IBM, offer mentoring at all levels of employment.[85] Peer relationships can also enhance career development.[86] Executive coaching is increasingly used to outsource the business mentoring functions. Informational, collegial, and special peers aid the individual's development by sharing information, career strategies, job-related feedback, emotional support, and friendship.

mentoring A work relationship that encourages development and career enhancement for people moving through the career cycle.

How Am I Doing?

Regardless of age, gender, and other individual differences, people desire feedback on how they are doing. The amount and the timing of the feedback may vary by individual, but the need for feedback never goes away. Stacia Sherman Garr of Deloitte's Bersin human resources consulting division suggests, "We need to have more frequent conversations about what goals are and where employees should be going." That is coaching work. Eighty percent of large companies, including Accenture, G.E., Goldman Sachs, IBM, and Morgan Stanley, are overhauling (or planning to overhaul) the ways they appraise their workforces. Because the ops tempo and rate of change in business is now so fast, annual performance reviews can be moot by the time they are completed. The goal is to enhance the timeliness of performance feedback and performance reviews, merging into a near constant feedback stream that enables employees to make micro-adjustments in their performance and work process, rather than finding out at the end of a long cycle that they have been doing the wrong thing or working toward the wrong goal. So, how am I doing? is a great question and segue for a coaching opportunity.

SOURCE: H.C., "How Am I Doing?" *Fortune*, 1 Mar. 2017, 34.

STUDY TOOLS 6

LOCATED AT BACK OF THE TEXTBOOK

☐ Rip out chapter review card

LOCATED AT WWW.CENGAGE.COM/LOGIN

☐ Gain unique perspectives on key concepts with new Concept Clip videos in the e-book

☐ Review key term flashcards and create your own

☐ Increase your comprehension with online homework and quizzes

7 | Stress and Well-Being at Work

LEARNING OBJECTIVES

7-1 Define stress, distress, and strain.

7-2 Compare four different approaches to stress.

7-3 Explain the psychophysiology of the stress response.

7-4 Identify work and nonwork causes of stress.

7-5 Describe the consequences of stress.

7-6 Discuss individual factors that influence a person's response to stress and strain.

7-7 Identify the stages and elements of preventive stress management for individuals and organizations.

After finishing this chapter go to **PAGE 122** for **STUDY TOOLS**

7-1 WHAT IS STRESS?

Stress and well-being are and have been concerns for organizations for more than 100 years.[1] Competitive pressures cause stress and tension for workers and managers alike. Some organizations have full-time psychologists on staff to provide expert counseling to sustain world-class performance. The Hot Trend (page 106) exemplifies this in the world of fine-dining. What exactly is stress? Several key terms help answer that question. **Stress**, or the *stress response*, can be described as the unconscious preparation to fight or flee that a person experiences when faced with any demand.[2] A **stressor**, or demand, is a person or event that triggers the stress response. While stress is a neutral concept, it carries a negative connotation for some people, as though it should be avoided. This is unfortunate because stress is a great asset

stress The unconscious preparation to fight or flee that a person experiences when faced with any demand.

stressor The person or event that triggers the stress response.

Image Source/Getty Images

in managing legitimate emergencies and achieving peak performance. **Distress**, or **strain**, refers to the adverse psychological, physical, behavioral, and organizational consequences that may occur as a result of stressful events.

 7-2 ## FOUR APPROACHES TO STRESS

The *stress response* was discovered by Walter B. Cannon, a medical physiologist, early in the twentieth century.[3] Later, however, researchers defined stress differently than Cannon did, so we will review four different approaches to define stress: the homeostatic/medical, cognitive appraisal, person–environment fit, and psychoanalytic approaches. These four approaches to stress will give you a more complete understanding of what stress really is.

7-2a The Homeostatic/Medical Approach

When Walter B. Cannon first developed the concept of stress, he called it the *emergency response* or the *militaristic response*, arguing that it was rooted in "the fighting

> **Stress is a great asset in managing legitimate emergencies and achieving peak performance.**

emotions." His early writings showed emotions such as fear and rage cause the *fight-or-flight* response.[4] In Cannon's *homeostatic/medical approach*, stress

distress The adverse psychological, physical, behavioral, and organizational consequences that may arise as a result of stressful events.

strain Distress.

occurs when deep emotions or environmental demands upset an individual's natural steady-state balance, what he calls **homeostasis**.[5] Cannon believed the body was designed with natural defense mechanisms to keep it in homeostasis. He was especially interested in the role of the sympathetic nervous system in activating a person under stressful conditions.

7-2b The Cognitive Appraisal Approach

Richard Lazarus was more concerned with the psychology of stress, emphasizing the psychological and cognitive aspects of the stress response in his *cognitive appraisal approach*.[6] Like Cannon, Lazarus saw stress as a result of a person–environment interaction, yet he emphasized the individual's cognitive appraisal in classifying persons or events as stressful or not. When appraising stressful workplace events, an important distinction can be made between "hindrance" and "threat" stressors. Whereas hindrance stressors tend to block goal achievement, threat stressors pose immediate personal harm or loss.[7] Individuals differ in their appraisals of events and people. Perception and cognitive appraisal are important processes in determining what is stressful. One study found higher instances of major depression when job demands were objectively assessed.[8] Another study found culture-specific differences in the perception of job stress between China and the United States.[9] American employees reported lack of control as a source of stress, while Chinese employees reported job evaluations as a significant source. In addition to cognitive appraisal, Lazarus introduced the ideas of problem-focused and emotion-focused coping. The former emphasizes managing the stressor, while the latter emphasizes managing the response. Whether individuals use problem- or emotion-focused coping strategies depends on motivation. For example, students planning and preparing for exams would more likely use problem-focused coping.[10] Those who evaluate themselves positively and consider themselves capable and in control of their own lives tend to favor emotion-focused coping when faced with stressors.[11]

7-2c The Person–Environment Fit Approach

Robert Kahn was concerned with the social psychology of stress, so his *person–environment fit* approach emphasized the idea that confusing and conflicting expectations of a person in a social role create stress for that person.[12] He extended the approach to consider a person's fit in the environment. A good person–environment fit occurs when one's skills and abilities match a clearly defined, consistent set of role expectations. Stress occurs when the role expectations are confusing and/or conflict with one's skills and abilities. After a period of this type of stress, one can expect to experience symptoms of strain such as depression.

7-2d The Psychoanalytic Approach

Freudian psychoanalytic theory can help us understand the role of unconscious personality factors as causes of stress within a person.[13] Applying this *psychoanalytic* approach, Harry Levinson argued that two elements of the personality interact to cause stress. The first element is the **ego-ideal**—the embodiment of a person's perfect self. The second element is the **self-image**—how the person really sees herself, both positively and negatively. Although not sharply defined, the ego-ideal encompasses admirable attributes of parental personalities, desired and/or imaginable qualities, and the absence of any negative or distasteful qualities. Stress results from the discrepancy between the idealized self (ego-ideal) and the real self-image; the greater the discrepancy, the more stress a person experiences.

homeostasis A steady state of bodily functioning and equilibrium.

ego-ideal The embodiment of a person's perfect self.

self-image How a person sees himself or herself, both positively and negatively.

7-3 THE STRESS RESPONSE

Whether activated by an ego-ideal/self-image discrepancy, a poorly defined social role, a cognitive appraisal suggesting threat, or a lack of balance, the resulting stress response is characterized by a predictable sequence of mind and body events. The stress response begins with the release of chemical messengers, primarily adrenaline, into the bloodstream. These messengers activate the sympathetic nervous system and the endocrine (hormone) system. These two systems work together to trigger four mind–body changes that prepare the person for fight or flight. (Refer to "The Psychophysiology of Stress" in Section 7-7.)

As the body responds, the person shifts from a neutral posture to an offensive posture. The stress response can be very effective in preparing a person to handle legitimate emergencies through peak performance. Thus, it is neither inherently bad nor necessarily destructive. Perceptions of interactional injustice in the workplace can trigger the physiological stress response, with high levels of cortisol being released into the bloodstream of individuals who perceive they are being treated unfairly.[14]

7-4 SOURCES OF WORK STRESS

Work stress is caused by factors in the work environment as well as by nonwork (external) pressures that spill over into the workplace. The two major categories of sources of both types of work stress are shown in Table 7.1. An example of an external pressure is when a working mother or father is called at work to come pick up a sick child from day care. Job insecurity can be a pervasive source of work stress. Job insecurity can trigger employee responses that are very costly for organizations, such as workplace deviance and developing intentions to leave.[15] The reasoning behind these dysfunctional behaviors is that employees morally disengage. A positive relationship with leadership and the supervisor can help mitigate against these dysfunctional employee responses.

7-4a Work Demands

The four major categories of on-the-job work demands that trigger stress for employees in organizations are task demands, role demands, interpersonal demands, and physical demands. Table 7.1 does not present an exhaustive list of work demands but rather aims to show major causes of work stress in each of the four major domains of the work environment.

TABLE 7.1	WORK AND NONWORK DEMANDS	
WORK DEMANDS		
Task Demands		**Role Demands**
Change		Role conflict:
Lack of control		Interrole
Career progress		Intrarole
New technologies		Person–role
Temporal pressure		Role ambiguity
Interpersonal Demands		**Physical Demands**
Emotional toxins		Extreme environments
Sexual harassment		Strenuous activities
Poor leadership		Hazardous substances
		Global travel
NONWORK DEMANDS		
Home Demands		**Personal Demands**
Family expectations		
Child-rearing/day care arrangements		Civic and volunteer work
Parental care		Traumatic events

TASK DEMANDS Dramatic changes at work lead to uncertainty in a person's daily tasks and activities, provoking on-the-job pressure and stress. Globalization and large-scale business trends lead to change, as do smaller-scale shifts in company policy. In recent years, the global economic recession has led many companies to make stressful changes, such as downsizing. At least 20 million jobs were lost by the end of 2009 due to the crisis.[16] Even during periods of growth, when hundreds of thousands of jobs are created every month, there may be significant numbers of jobs lost within certain sectors of the U.S. economy. For those who do not lose their jobs, underemployment, monotony, and boredom may be problematic.

Technological innovation creates change and uncertainty for many employees, requiring additional training, education, and skill development. New technologies create both career stress and so-called technostress for those who wonder if smart machines will replace them.[17] Although they enhance the organization's productive capacity, new technologies may be viewed as the enemy by workers who must ultimately learn to use them. This creates a real dilemma for management. Intended to make work easier and more convenient, information technology may have the paradoxical effect of incurring stress rather than relieving it.

Effects of Stress on the Body

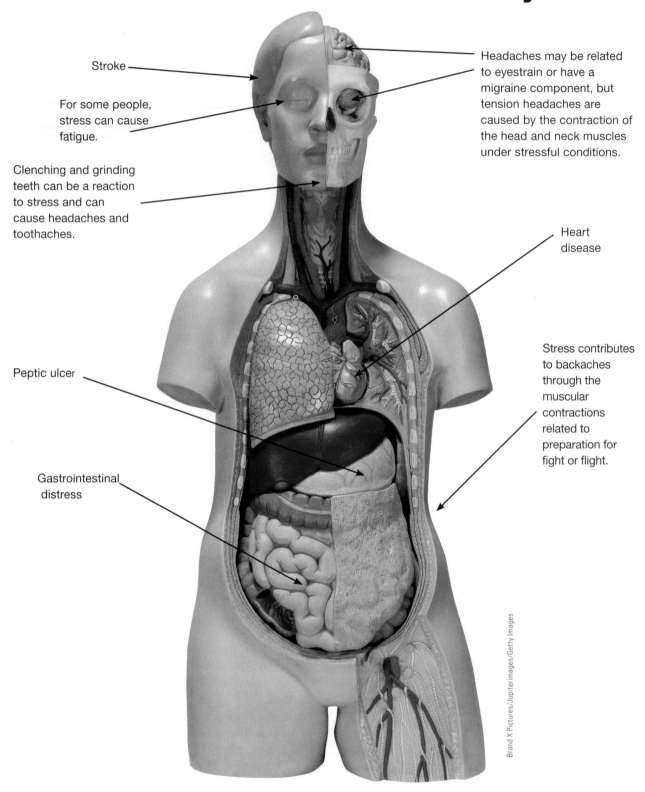

Stroke

For some people, stress can cause fatigue.

Clenching and grinding teeth can be a reaction to stress and can cause headaches and toothaches.

Headaches may be related to eyestrain or have a migraine component, but tension headaches are caused by the contraction of the head and neck muscles under stressful conditions.

Heart disease

Stress contributes to backaches through the muscular contractions related to preparation for fight or flight.

Peptic ulcer

Gastrointestinal distress

Brand X Pictures/Jupiterimages/Getty Images

Lack of control is another major task-related source of stress, especially in positions that are difficult and psychologically demanding. The lack of control may be caused by the inability to

- influence the timing of tasks and activities;
- select tools or methods for accomplishing the work;
- make decisions that influence work outcomes; or
- exercise direct action to affect the work outcomes.

Concerns over career progress and time pressures (or work overload) are two additional task demands triggering stress at work. Career stress has occurred in many organizations over the past two decades as middle-manager ranks have been thinned by mergers, acquisitions, and downsizing.[18] Leaner organizations, unfortunately, mean overload for the retained employees. Fewer people doing the same amount of work or more creates time pressure, a leading cause of stress often associated with work overload. Time pressure may also result from poor time-management skills. But not all task demands are negative. Challenge stressors that promote personal growth and achievement are positively related to job satisfaction and organizational commitment.[19]

ROLE DEMANDS The social–psychological demands of the work environment may be every bit as stressful as task demands. Role stress may be particularly harmful to the job satisfaction and affective commitment of newcomers to the organization.[20] People encounter two major categories of role stress at work: role conflict and role ambiguity.[21] *Role conflict* results from inconsistent or incompatible expectations. The conflict may be an inter-role, intrarole, or person–role conflict.

Interrole conflict is caused by opposing expectations related to two separate roles assumed by the same individual, such as employee and parent. For example, the employee with a major sales presentation due on Monday and a sick child at home Sunday night is likely to experience interrole conflict. Work–family conflicts such as these can lead individuals to withdrawal behaviors.[22] High levels of strain may also lead to increased work–family conflicts for women and men.[23] *Intrarole conflict* is caused by opposing expectations related to a single role. For example, the manager who presses employees for both very fast and high-quality work may be viewed at some point as creating a conflict for employees.

Ethics violations are likely to cause *person–role conflicts*. Employees expected to behave in ways that violate personal values, beliefs, or principles experience this type of conflict. Person–role conflicts and ethics violations create a sense of divided loyalty for an employee.

New technologies create both career stress and so-called technostress for those who wonder if smart machines will replace them.

For example, if a distributor tells an organic farmer to cut costs by using a synthetic pesticide, the farmer may find that his personal beliefs are compromised by his role as a producer. Organizations with high ethical standards, such as Johnson & Johnson, are less likely to create ethical conflicts for employees.

The second major cause of role stress is *role ambiguity*, which is the confusion a person experiences in relation to the expectations of others. Role ambiguity may be caused by misunderstanding what is expected, not knowing how to do it, or not knowing the result of failure to do it. For example, a new magazine employee asked to copyedit a manuscript may experience confusion because she mistakes copyediting for proofreading, she doesn't know what formatting style to use, or she doesn't know what will happen if she misses her deadline.

A twenty-one-nation study examined middle managers' experiences in role conflict, role ambiguity, and role overload. The results indicated that role stress varies more by country than it does by demographic and organizational factors. For example, non-Western managers experience less role ambiguity and more role overload than do their Western counterparts.[24] Another study, this time of 2,273 Norwegian employees, found that role conflict, role ambiguity, and conflict with coworkers increased under laissez-faire leadership, suggesting that a hands-off leadership style is destructive.[25] On the other hand, a study of U.S. military personnel found that when role clarity was high in a supportive work group, psychological strain was low.[26]

INTERPERSONAL DEMANDS *Emotional toxins*, such as sexual harassment and poor leadership in the organization, are examples of interpersonal demands, often generated at work by abrasive personalities.[27] Employees' ability to recharge and replace physical and psychological resources depleted during the work day is necessary for well-being. This recovery of resources often takes place once employees leave the workplace. Though considered less severe than other forms of interpersonal demands, workplace incivility experienced one day often remains with the individual and negatively affects the employee's ability to detach from the work and replenish resources needed for the next work day.[28] Another consequence of interpersonal demands can be *emotional dissonance*, which can spread through a work environment and cause a range of disturbances and stress.[29] Organizations are increasingly less tolerant of sexual harassment, a gender-related interpersonal demand that creates a stressful working environment for both the person being harassed and for others. The vast majority of sexual harassment is directed at women in the workplace and is a chronic yet preventable problem.[30]

Poor organizational leadership and demanding managerial styles are leading causes of work stress for employees. But much depends on an employee's individual characteristics. Employees who feel secure under strong, directive leadership may be anxious under an open, self-directed style of management. Those comfortable with participative leaders may feel restrained by a directive style. In every case, however, trust is an important characteristic of the leader–follower interpersonal relationship, so a threat to a worker's reputation with his supervisor may be especially stressful.[31] Functional diversity in project groups also causes difficulty in the establishment of trusting relationships. Lack of trust increases job stress, which in turn leads to lower cohesiveness within the group.[32]

PHYSICAL DEMANDS Extreme environments, strenuous activities, hazardous substances, and global travel

Office work has physical hazards, such as eye-strain, neck stiffness, and lower back pain.

create physical demands for people at work. One cross-cultural study that examined the effects of ambient temperature on role stress concluded that uncomfortable temperatures diminish human well-being, leading to the development of the term *sweatshop* for inhumane working conditions.[33] The unique physical demands of work are often occupation-specific, such as the gravitational forces on military pilots flying high-performance fighters or jet lag and loss of sleep for globetrotting CEOs. Despite the fact that there are many positive aspects to business travel, the associated demands are increasingly recognized as sources of stress.[34]

Office work has its physical hazards as well. Noisy, crowded offices, such as those of some stock brokerages, can prove stressful, and even harmful. Working with a computer can also be stressful, especially if the ergonomic design of the workstation is not correct. Eyestrain, neck stiffness, and arm and wrist problems may result. Office designs that use partitions rather than full walls may create stress by offering little privacy and little protection from interruptions. *Stress audits* provide companies with detailed assessments of possible workplace stressors. Identification and alleviation of overlooked stress factors can save a company money and boost productivity.

7-4b Nonwork Demands

Nonwork demands are stressful, too, and can carry over into the work environment. *Nonwork demands* may broadly be identified as impositions from an individual's personal life environment (home) and self-imposed restrictions.

HOME DEMANDS The wide array of home and family arrangements in contemporary American society has created great diversity in the arena of home demands. Traditional and nontraditional families may experience demands that create role conflicts or overloads that are difficult to manage. For example, the loss of good day care for children may be especially stressful for dual-career and single-parent families.[35] The tension between work and family may lead to a real struggle for balance in life. This struggle led Rocky Rhodes, cofounder of Silicon Graphics, to establish four priorities for his life: God, family, exercise, and work.[36] These priorities helped him reallocate his time for better balance in his life. Moreover, as a result of the maturing of the American population, an increasing number of people face the added demand of parental care. Even when a person dedicates herself to reducing stress by integrating opposing social and work-related roles into a balanced, "whole" identity, the process is not an easy one.[37]

PERSONAL DEMANDS Self-imposed personal demands are the second major category of nonwork demands identified in Table 7.1 **workaholism** a form of addiction, may be the most notable of these stressinducing demands.[38] Some of the early warning signs of workaholism include over-commitment to work, inability to enjoy vacations and respites from work, preoccupation with work problems when away from the workplace, and insistence on working at home over weekends.

Another type of personal demand comes from civic activities, volunteer work, and organizational commitments to religious or public service organizations. These demands become more or less stressful depending on their compatibility with work and family life, and their capacity to provide alternative satisfactions for the individual. Finally, traumatic events, such as the devastating earthquake and tsunami in Japan in March 2011, are stressful for people who experience them.[39] Not all traumatic events are as catastrophic as natural disasters, of course, but job loss, failed exams, and romantic break-ups are all traumatic and may lead to distress if not addressed and resolved.

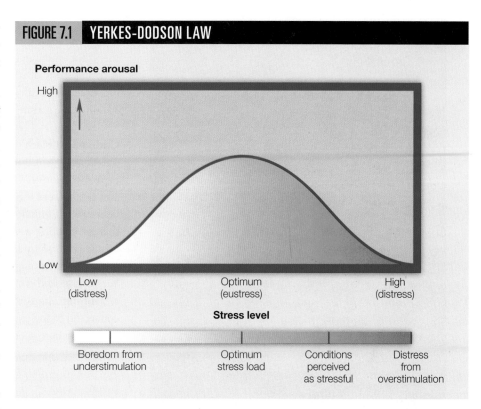

FIGURE 7.1 | YERKES-DODSON LAW

 7-5 THE CONSEQUENCES OF STRESS

Stress may be positive or negative. Positive stress can create a healthy, thriving work environment, while negative stress, or distress, can erode morale and performance.

7-5a Positive Stress

Some managers and executives thrive under pressure because they practice what world-class athletes already know—that bringing mind, body, and spirit to peak condition requires recovering energy, which is as important as expending energy.[40] Hence, world-class athletes and managers get high marks on any stress test because they use stress-induced energy in positive, healthy, and productive ways. The consequences of healthy, normal stress (*eustress*; see Chapter 5) include a number of performance and health benefits.[41] An organization striving for high-quality products and services needs a healthy workforce to support the effort. Eustress is a characteristic of healthy people; distress is not.

The *Yerkes-Dodson law*, shown in Figure 7.1, indicates that stress leads to improved performance up to an optimum point.[42] Beyond that point, stress has a detrimental effect on performance. Therefore, healthy amounts of stress are desirable to improve performance by arousing a person to action. The greatest performance benefits from stress are achieved in the midrange of the Yerkes-Dodson curve, and after that, as Joseph McGrath has suggested, increasing difficulty of the task is probably what causes performance to decline.[43] Thus, the stress response invokes heightened strength and physical force for limited periods of exertion. This is how stress provides a basis for peak performance in athletic competition, and it can do the same for any type of job performance. In addition, psychological well-being reduces stress and thereby contributes positively to job performance.[44]

Specific stressful activities, including aerobic exercise, weight training, and flexibility training, improve health and enhance a person's ability to manage stressful demands or situations. Cannon argued that the stress response better prepares soldiers for combat.[45] In the outdoors, in survival or combat situations, stress

workaholism An imbalanced preoccupation with work at the expense of home and personal life satisfaction.

It is theorized that the stress response better prepares soldiers for the experience of combat.

provides one with the necessary energy boost to manage the situation successfully.

The various individual and organizational forms of distress often associated with the word *stress* are the result of prolonged activation of the stress response, mismanagement of the energy induced by the response, or unique vulnerabilities in a person. We next examine the forms of individual distress and then the forms of organizational distress.

7-5b Individual Distress

An extreme preoccupation with work may result in acute individual distress. In its most extreme form, individual distress can lead to a phenomenon described by the Japanese word *karoshi*, or death by overwork.[46] Work-related psychological disorders are among the ten leading health disorders and diseases in the United States, according to the National Institute for Occupational Safety and Health.[47] The most common symptoms of psychological distress are depression, burnout, and psychosomatic disorders—physical ailments with psychological origins. These psychological distresses usually lead to *emotional exhaustion*, a form

of psychological fatigue caused by energy depletion.[48] Emotional exhaustion may also be caused by the requirement for sustained emotional expression on the job.[49] A recent study of 257 Australian police officers found that emotional exhaustion at work had the potential to spill over to home life, causing work–family conflict.[50]

Burnout is a psychological response to job stress that Christina Maslach characterizes along three dimensions: emotional exhaustion, depersonalization, and reduced perceptions of personal accomplishment. Emotional exhaustion is at the heart of the burnout experience. The conventional belief is that emotional drain leads to reduced job performance, creating a direct link between burnout and performance. A study by the National Institute questions this assumption and suggests that the influence of motivation has been overlooked in understanding the burnout–performance relationship. Its authors believe that motivation is directly connected to the psychological processes of voluntary goal-directed action, specifically its arousal, direction, intensity, and persistence. Because motivation is considered a direct antecedent of performance, this study suggests that motivation mediates the burnout–performance relationship. Hence, their model is burnout-motivation-performance.[51]

Burnout is not the same as *rust-out*, which is a form of psychological distress caused by a lack of challenge, inspiration, and/or opportunity on the job.[52] For example, a fast-food line cook who has flipped burgers at minimum wage for three years may experience rust-out for all the previously mentioned reasons, resulting in apathy, resentment, and diminished performance.

A number of medical illnesses have a stress-related component.[53] The most significant are heart disease, strokes, backaches, peptic ulcers, and headaches. Ford Motor Company found that cardiovascular diseases, the leading cause of death in the United States since 1910, constituted only 1.5% of the medical incidents among 800 salaried employees at its headquarters but accounted for 29% of the reported medical costs.[54]

Behavioral problems are another form of individual distress. These problems include workplace aggression, insomnia, substance abuse, and accidents. Workplace aggression may be triggered by perceptions of injustice in the workplace.[55] Interpersonal conflicts can be a form of nonphysical aggression. Insomnia is a nonaggressive behavioral problem that does have harmful effects on work outcomes such as job satisfaction, interpersonal deviance, and self-control.[56] The use of Internet-based cognitive behavior therapy has been found to be a partial solution to mitigate the harmful effect of insomnia.

Substance abuse ranges from legal behaviors such as alcohol abuse, excessive smoking, and the overuse of

Is It Burnout or Depression?

A significant challenge in studying burnout is distinguishing it from depression, especially clinical depression. Managers and peers are not in the best position to make an accurate diagnosis. While relentlessly stressful work environments, especially where people have limited control, can produce the exhaustion, cynicism, and inefficiency of burnout, this does not mean someone is hopelessly depressed. However, a clinical depression can be made worse by burnout-provoking conditions. Those who experience burnout can work to recover through mindful effort and healthy interpersonal connections. Alternatively, depression calls for professional help, especially given the concomitant risk of suicide. For those uncertain if it is burnout or depression, ask for a professional assessment.

SOURCE: M. Valcour and C. Dierickx, "Beating Burnout," *Harvard Business Review*, January–February 2017, p. 19

prescription drugs to illegal behaviors such as heroin and cocaine use. The abuse of certain substances, such as tobacco and heroin, can lead to addiction—a physical and/or psychological dependency. Abuse and addiction are behavioral problems that can impair job performance and often lead to significant individual distress.

Accidents, both on and off the job, are still another behavioral form of distress that can sometimes be traced to work-related stressors. For example, an unresolved problem at work may preoccupy or distract an employee, causing an accident either at the office or on the road. These three forms of individual distress—psychological disorders, medical illnesses, and behavioral problems—cause a burden of personal suffering. They also cause a collective burden of suffering reflected in organizational distress.

7-5c Organizational Distress

Studies performed at the University of Michigan on *organizational stress* identified a variety of indirect costs of mismanaged stress for an organization, such as low morale, dissatisfaction, breakdowns in communication, and disruption of working relationships. The direct costs of organizational distress include the high cost of turnover, the often hidden costs of absenteeism, and poor performance on the job.[57] Research suggests that even positive performance stereotypes can have an adverse effect on organizational health.[58] Three major costs of organizational distress are participation problems, performance decrements, and compensation awards.

Participation problems include absenteeism, tardiness, strikes and work stoppages, and turnover. In the case of absenteeism, the organization may compensate by hiring temporary personnel who take the place of the absentee, possibly elevating personnel costs. When considering turnover, a distinction should be made between dysfunctional and functional turnover. *Dysfunctional turnover* occurs when an organization loses a valuable employee. Replacement costs, including recruiting and retraining, range from five to seven months of the individual monthly salary. *Functional turnover*, in contrast, benefits the organization by creating opportunities for new members, new ideas, and fresh approaches. Functional turnover occurs when an organization loses an employee who has little or no value to the organization; thus the loss of that employee is considered a positive result. The up-or-out promotion policy for members of some organizations is designed to create functional turnover.

Performance decrements are the costs resulting from poor quality or low quantity of production, grievances, and unscheduled machine downtime and repair. As in the case of medical illness, stress is not the only causal agent in these performance decrements. Stress does play a role, however, whether the poor quality or low quantity of production is motivated by distressed employees or by an unconscious response to stress on the job. Some employees in California have the option of taking a "stress leave" rather than filing a grievance against the boss.

Compensation awards are the organizational costs resulting from

participation problem A cost associated with absenteeism, tardiness, strikes and work stoppages, and turnover.

performance decrement A cost resulting from poor quality or low quantity of production, grievances, and unscheduled machine downtime and repair.

compensation award An organizational cost resulting from court awards for job distress.

court awards for job distress.[59] In a federal lawsuit against Allstate, Frank Deus claimed that the company created a high-strain job for him that resulted in incapacitating depression.[60] A jury awarded him a $1.5 million judgment that was later overturned. Job stress–related claims have skyrocketed and threaten to bankrupt the workers' compensation system in some states, although claims and costs are down in other states.[61] Employers need not panic because fair procedures go a long way toward avoiding legal liability, and legal rulings are setting realistic limits on employers' obligations.[62]

7-6 INDIVIDUAL DIFFERENCES IN THE STRESS–STRAIN RELATIONSHIP

Individual differences play a central role in the stress–strain relationship. The *weak organ hypothesis* in medicine, also known as the *Achilles' heel phenomenon*, suggests that a person breaks down at her weakest point. Individual differences, such as gender and Type A behavior pattern, enhance vulnerability to strain under stressful conditions. Other individual differences, such as personality hardiness and self-reliance, reduce vulnerability to strain under stressful conditions. One study of personality and emotional performance found that individuals high on extraversion experienced elevated heart rates when asked to express personality-incongruent emotions such as anger and that neuroticism was more generally associated with increased heart rate and poor performance.[63] Extraversion and neuroticism thus seem to affect the stress–strain relationship.

7-6a Gender Effects

While prevailing stereotypes suggest that women are the weaker sex, the truth is that the life expectancy for American women is almost six years longer than for American men. The weaker sex stereotype is further challenged by research in public accounting, which finds that female public accountants have no higher turnover rates than males even though they report more stress.[64] Moreover, research finds that women's behavioral responses to stress are not only different from men's responses but that they are also strengths in women rather than weaknesses.[65]

Some literature suggests that there are differences in the stressors to which the two sexes are subject.[66] For example, sexual harassment is a gender-related source of stress for many working women. Men sometimes experience sexual harassment as well, though, and are more likely than women to abuse alcohol as a coping mechanism. This may be because harassment is not a normative occurrence for men.[67]

There is substantive evidence that vulnerabilities constitute the important differences between the sexes.[68] Males are more vulnerable at an earlier age to fatal health problems such as cardiovascular disorders, whereas women report more nonfatal but long-term and disabling health problems. Although we can conclude that gender indeed creates a differential vulnerability between the two sexes, it may actually be more important to examine the differences *among* women or *among* men.

7-6b Type A Behavior Pattern

Type A behavior pattern is a combination of personality and behavioral characteristics that include competitiveness, time urgency, social status insecurity, aggression, hostility, and a quest for achievements. Type A behavior pattern is also labeled *coronary-prone behavior* because it is linked with coronary heart disease.[69] There are two primary hypotheses concerning which part of the Type A behavior pattern is lethal. One suggests that the problem is time urgency, while the other suggests that it is hostility and aggression. The weight of evidence suggests that hostility and aggression, not time urgency, are the lethal agents.[70]

The alternative to the Type A behavior pattern is the Type B behavior pattern. People with Type B personalities are relatively free of Type A behaviors and characteristics. Type B people are less coronary prone, but if they do have a heart attack, they do not appear to recover as well as those with Type A personalities.

Type A behavior can be modified. The first step is for Type A people to recognize that they are prone to the Type A pattern and possibly to spend time with Type B individuals. Type B people often recognize Type A behavior and can help Type A individuals judge situations realistically. Type A individuals can also pace themselves, manage their time well, and try not to do multiple things at once. Focusing only on the task at hand and its completion rather than worrying about other tasks can help Type A individuals cope more effectively.

Dima Sobko/Shutterstock.com

Type A behavior pattern
A complex of personality and behavioral characteristics, including competitiveness, time urgency, social status insecurity, aggression, hostility, and a quest for achievements.

7-6c Personality Hardiness

People who have hardy personalities resist strain reactions when subjected to stressful events more effectively than do people who are not hardy.[71] The components of **personality hardiness** are commitment, control, and challenge. Commitment is an engagement with one's environment that leads to the experience of activities as interesting and enjoyable. Employees with high levels of commitment are less likely to leave the organization or experience promotion-related stress.[72] Control is an ability to influence the processes and outcomes of events that lead to the experience of activities as personal choices. Challenge is the conception of change as a stimulus to personal development, which leads to the welcome experience of new activities.

The hardy personality appears to use these three components actively to engage in transformational coping when faced with stressful events.[73] **Transformational coping** is the active process of modifying one's perception of an event in order to reduce stress. This is accomplished by viewing the event in broader terms, by altering the course and outcome through action, and/or by achieving greater understanding of the process. The alternative to transformational coping is *regressive coping*, characterized by a passive avoidance of events and decreased interaction with the environment. Regressive coping may lead to short-term stress reduction at the cost of healthy, long-term life adjustment.

Hardy	Not Hardy
Commitment	Alienation
Control	Powerlessness
Challenge	Threat

7-6d Self-Reliance

There is increasing evidence that social relationships have an important impact on health and life expectancy.[74] **Self-reliance**, a healthy, secure interdependent pattern of behavior, is a personality attribute strongly related to social relationships. The concept of self-reliance was originally based on *attachment theory*, a psychological approach to normal human development that identifies three distinct patterns of attachment.[75] Research suggests that these patterns become behavioral strategies during adulthood in professional as well as personal relationships.[76] A secure pattern of attachment and *interdependent* behavior results in self-reliance. The connection between self-reliance and the word *interdependent* may appear paradoxical because a person appears independent while maintaining a host of supportive attachments.[77] But self-reliant people respond

iStock.com/Maica

to stressful, threatening situations by reaching out to others appropriately. Indeed, self-reliance is a flexible, responsive strategy of forming and maintaining multiple, diverse relationships. Self-reliant people are confident, enthusiastic, and persistent in facing challenges. Their flexibility allows them to form healthy partner relationships that buffer work-related stress.[78]

Interpersonal attachment is emotional and psychological connectedness to another person. In contrast, the two insecure patterns of attachment are counterdependence and overdependence. **Counterdependence** is an unhealthy, insecure pattern of behavior that leads to separation in relationships with other people. When faced with stressful and threatening situations, counterdependent people withdraw. Counterdependence may be characterized as a rigid, dismissing denial of the need for other people in difficult and stressful times. Counterdependent people exhibit a fearless, aggressive, and active response to challenges, but they are not truly self-reliant.

Overdependence is also an unhealthy, insecure pattern of behavior. Overdependent people respond to stressful and threatening situations by clinging to other people in any way possible. Overdependence

personality hardiness A personality characterized by commitment, control, and challenge and, hence, resistant to distress.

transformational coping A way of managing stressful events by changing them into less subjectively stressful events.

self-reliance A healthy, secure, interdependent pattern of behavior related to how people form and maintain supportive attachments with others.

counterdependence An unhealthy, insecure pattern of behavior that leads to separation in relationships with other people.

overdependence An unhealthy, insecure pattern of behavior that leads to preoccupied attempts to achieve security through relationships.

FIGURE 7.2 **A FRAMEWORK FOR PREVENTIVE STRESS MANAGEMENT**

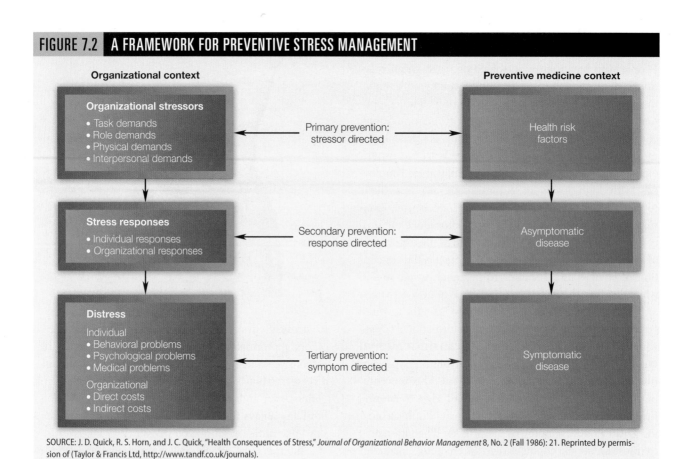

SOURCE: J. D. Quick, R. S. Horn, and J. C. Quick, "Health Consequences of Stress," *Journal of Organizational Behavior Management* 8, No. 2 (Fall 1986): 21. Reprinted by permission of (Taylor & Francis Ltd, http://www.tandf.co.uk/journals).

may be characterized as a desperate, preoccupied attempt to achieve a sense of security through relationships. Overdependent people exhibit an active but disorganized and anxious response to challenges. This quality prevents a person from being able to organize and maintain healthy relationships; therefore, it creates distress. Interestingly, both counterdependence and overdependence can be exhibited by military personnel who are experiencing adjustment difficulties during the first thirty days of basic training.[79] The recruits who have the most difficulty adjusting to new jobs demonstrate severe overdependence. They often find it difficult to function on their own during training.

preventive stress management An organizational philosophy according to which people and organizations should take joint responsibility for promoting health and preventing distress and strain.

primary prevention The stage in preventive stress management designed to reduce, modify, or eliminate the demand or stressor causing stress.

secondary prevention The stage in preventive stress management designed to alter or modify the individual's or the organization's response to a demand or stressor.

tertiary prevention The stage in preventive stress management designed to heal individual or organizational symptoms of distress and strain.

7-7 PREVENTIVE STRESS MANAGEMENT

Stress is an inevitable part of work and personal life. **Preventive stress management** is an organizational philosophy according to which people and organizations should take joint responsibility for promoting health and preventing distress and strain. This philosophy is rooted in public health practices first used in preventive medicine. A framework for understanding preventive stress management is presented in Figure 7.2, which includes three stages of prevention that apply in a preventive medicine context as well as an organizational context.

Primary prevention is intended to reduce, modify, or eliminate the stress-causing demand or stressor. The idea behind primary prevention is to eliminate or alleviate the source of a problem. True organizational stress prevention is largely primary in nature because it reduces the demands the organization places on the employee. **Secondary prevention** is intended to modify the individual's or the organization's response to a demand or stressor. Employees must learn to manage the inevitable, unalterable work stressors and demands to avert distress and strain while improving health and well-being. **Tertiary prevention** is intended to heal individual or

The Psychophysiology of Stress

In preparing to fight or flee, the body:

1. redirects blood to the brain and large-muscle groups;

2. increases alertness through improved vision, hearing, and other sensory processes;

3. releases glucose (blood sugar) and fatty acids into the bloodstream to sustain the body during the stressful event; and

4. suppresses the immune system as well as restorative and emergent processes (such as digestion).

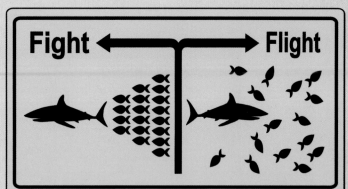

organizational symptoms of distress and strain. The symptoms may range from early warning signs (such as headaches or absenteeism) to more severe forms of distress (such as hypertension, work stoppages, and strikes). An innovative approach used by the data recovery company DriveSavers bolsters treatment and prevention with a full-time grief counselor.[80] The stages of prevention can be applied to organizational prevention, individual prevention, and comprehensive health promotion.

7-7a Organizational Stress Prevention

Some organizations maintain low-stress, healthy environments, while others cultivate high-stress environments that may place their employees' health at risk. The experience of organizational justice and fairness is emerging as one contextual factor that leads to a positive, low-stress work environment.[81] One comprehensive approach to organizational health and preventive stress management was pioneered in the U.S. Air Force by Colonel Joyce Adkins, who developed an Organizational Health Center (OHC) with the Air Force Materiel Command.[82] The OHC's goal is to keep workers happy, healthy, and on the job while increasing efficiency and productivity to their highest levels. This goal is achieved by focusing on workplace stressors, organizational and individual forms of distress, and managerial and individual strategies for preventive stress management. Adkins's comprehensive, organizational health approach addresses primary, secondary, and tertiary prevention. Most organizational prevention, however, is primary prevention, including job redesign, goal setting, role negotiation, and career management.

Two organizational stress prevention methods—team building and social support at work—are secondary prevention. We discuss team building in Chapter 9, but we should note here that under stress, team structure may influence team effectiveness. Specifically, teams experiencing quantitative demands are more effective when more tightly structured, while teams experiencing qualitative demands are more effective when more loosely structured.[83] Finally, companies such as Kraft Foods (a subsidiary of Altria Group, Inc.) and Hardee's Food Systems (part of CKE Restaurants, Inc.) have developed specific violence prevention programs to combat the rise in workplace violence. Violence in organizations is a category of dysfunctional behaviors that is often motivated by stressful events and whose negative consequences need to be prevented.[84] Ethical decision-making may also be affected by worker anxiety. Studies have shown that anxiety increases threat perception, which in turn often leads individuals to focus narrowly on their own self-interests rather than ethical principles.[85]

JOB REDESIGN The job strain model illustrated in Figure 7.3 suggests that the combination of stringent demands and restricted control leads to a high-strain job. A major goal in job redesign should be to increase worker control. In many cases, this reduces distress and strain without reducing productivity. The direct costs of organizational distress include the high cost of turnover, the often hidden costs of absenteeism, and poor performance on the job.

Increasing worker control is a strategy of preventive stress management that can be accomplished in a number of ways, the most common being to increase job decision latitude. Increased latitude might include

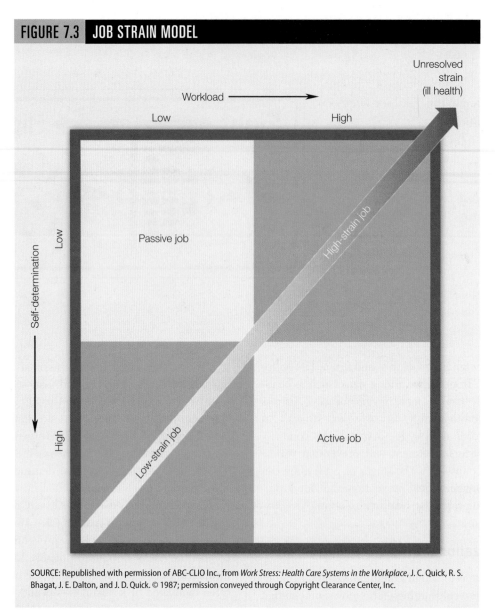

FIGURE 7.3 JOB STRAIN MODEL

Unresolved strain (ill health)

Workload →
Low   High

Self-determination
Low
High

Passive job

High-strain job

Low-strain job

Active job

SOURCE: Republished with permission of ABC-CLIO Inc., from *Work Stress: Health Care Systems in the Workplace*, J. C. Quick, R. S. Bhagat, J. E. Dalton, and J. D. Quick. © 1987; permission conveyed through Copyright Clearance Center, Inc.

greater authority over the sequencing of work activities, the timing of work schedules, the selection and sequencing of work tools, or the selection of work teams. A second objective of job redesign should be to reduce uncertainty and increase predictability in the workplace.

GOAL SETTING Preventive stress management can also be achieved through goal-setting activities. These activities are designed to increase task motivation while reducing role conflict and ambiguity. Goal setting focuses a person's attention while directing energy into a productive channel. Implicit in much of the goal-setting literature is the assumption that people participate in determining their work goals.

ROLE NEGOTIATION The organizational development technique of role negotiation has value as a stress-management method because it allows individuals to modify their work roles.[86] Role negotiation begins with the definition of a focal role within the organizational context. The person in the focal role identifies the expectations understood for the role, and organizational supervisors specify their own expectations of the person in the focal role. A negotiation of integrated role expectation follows. In the process of such negotiation, points of confusion and conflict become opportunities for clarification and resolution. The final result of the role negotiation process should be a clear, well-defined focal role with which the incumbent and organizational members are all comfortable.

SOCIAL SUPPORT SYSTEMS Team building is one way to develop supportive social relationships in the workplace. However, team building is primarily task oriented, not socioemotional, in nature. Although employees may receive much of their socio-emotional support

Surprise Your Employees with a Break

LeBron James (#23) took a game break sitting on the bench during the Eastern Conference Finals of the 2015 NBA Playoffs when his Cleveland Cavaliers were playing the Atlanta Hawks in Atlanta. The game break was not a disengaged time-out for James. Rather, he was studying his opponents' game strategy on an iPad. One Harvard study found that this type of break is exactly what can increase employees' productivity and give them a psychological reboot in the process. Routine or scheduled breaks are programmed time-outs predicated on strategic disengagement from work.  Returning to work from routine breaks requires some effort in psychological reengagement. Alternatively, surprise work breaks redirect employee attention without fully disengaging them from the work flow. Surprise work breaks might include a brainstorming session related to a work challenge or a teaching session focused on a new work-related skill. Employees do not have to be completely disengaged to benefit from a work break. Go ahead, surprise them!

SOURCE: D. Kleinman, "Surprising Your Employees with a Break Could Boost Their Productivity," *Forbes*, 27 Jan. 2017, p. 1.

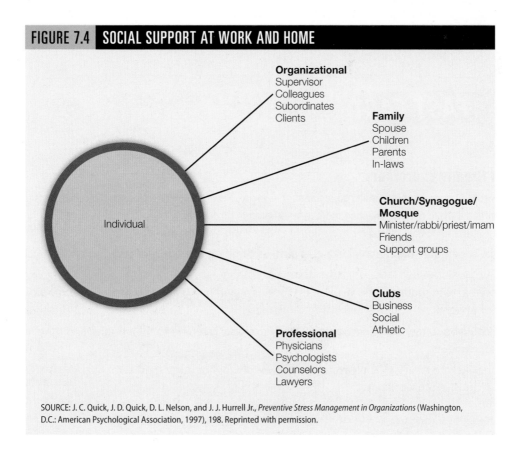

FIGURE 7.4	SOCIAL SUPPORT AT WORK AND HOME

Organizational
Supervisor
Colleagues
Subordinates
Clients

Family
Spouse
Children
Parents
In-laws

Church/Synagogue/Mosque
Minister/rabbi/priest/imam
Friends
Support groups

Clubs
Business
Social
Athletic

Professional
Physicians
Psychologists
Counselors
Lawyers

Individual

SOURCE: J. C. Quick, J. D. Quick, D. L. Nelson, and J. J. Hurrell Jr., *Preventive Stress Management in Organizations* (Washington, D.C.: American Psychological Association, 1997), 198. Reprinted with permission.

from personal relationships outside the workplace, some socioemotional support within the workplace is also necessary for psychological well-being.

Social support systems can be enhanced through the work environment in a number of ways. Implementing support systems that help employees identify with the company may buffer the negative effects of workplace stressors and improve employees' ability to adjust.[87] Interpersonal communication is the key to unlocking social support for preventive stress management.[88] Figure 7.4 identifies key elements in a person's work and nonwork social support system. These relationships provide emotional caring, information, evaluative feedback, modeling, and instrumental support.

7-7b Individual Prevention

Clinical research shows that individuals may use a number of self-directed interventions to help prevent distress and enhance positive well-being.[89] Such individual prevention can be of a primary, secondary, or tertiary nature. The *primary prevention* activities we discuss are learned optimism, time management, and leisure time activities. The *secondary prevention* activities we discuss are physical exercise, relaxation, and diet. The *tertiary prevention* activities we discuss are opening up and professional help.

POSITIVE THINKING The power of *positive thinking* too often goes unappreciated. When one cultivates an optimistic frame of mind, bad life events are bathed in a positive light, preventing future and healing past distress.[90] An optimistic style of thought must be practiced habitually in order to be effective. It is usually learned over time, though some are predisposed to it. *Pessimism* is an alternative style of thought that focuses on the negative. It can lead to depression, health problems, and low levels of achievement. By contrast, positive thinking enhances physical health and achievement and decreases susceptibility to depression.

Positive thinking does not mean ignoring stressors and challenges. It means viewing them through a different lens. Optimistic people avoid distress by framing the difficult times in their lives as temporary, limited in scope, and often unavoidable. They face adversity with hope, and take credit for the good events in their lives, which they see as more pervasive and generalized. Optimists are also more motivated and more likely to use proactive coping skills to achieve goals and pursue development opportunities.[91] *Learned optimism* begins with identifying pessimistic thoughts and then distracting oneself from these thoughts or disputing them with evidence and alternative thoughts. Psychological capital (PsyCap) is an evidence-based positive

FAST FACT

5 Secrets of Steady Exercisers

The data show that 21 percent of U.S. adults do get enough exercise. How do they do it? The evidence suggests that these adults have five common traits and habits enabling them to be fit through physical activity.

They exercise at the same time most days, averaging five hours a week of exercise.

> Active people widen their definition of exercise, such as climbing five floors of stairs rather than using the elevator.

> They have pre-exercise routines with visual cues, such as a gym bag ready to go to work or running clothes and shoes laid out at home.

> They are flexible about how long and vigorously they exercise, listening to their bodies and other commitments in making adjustments.

> They are more likely to exercise for pleasure than for weight loss or other long-term health goals. So, fitness activities that are also fun work best.

SOURCE: R. Bachman, "Fitness: Five Secrets of Steady Exercisers," Wall Street Journal, 22 May 2017, p. A1534.

approach that extends from positive psychology and positive organizational behavior (POB). The positive psychological resources that make up PsyCap include **h**ope, **e**fficacy, **r**esilience and **o**ptimism, or the HERO within. A review suggests that PsyCap has scientific, evidence-based rigor and practical relevance.[92]

TIME MANAGEMENT Temporal pressure is one of the major sources of stress, as listed in Table 7.1. It applies to people both at work and in school. Symptoms of poor time management include constant rushing, missed deadlines, work overload, the sense of being overwhelmed, insufficient rest time, and indecision. Effective time managers employ the macro-level *GP³ method* of time management.[93] The GP³ method is to (1) set *goals* that are challenging yet attainable; (2) *prioritize* these goals in terms of their relative importance; (3) *plan* for goal attainment through specific tasks, activities, scheduling, and delegation; and (4) *praise* oneself for specific achievements along the way. Setting concrete goals and prioritizing these goals are the most important first steps in time-management skills, ensuring that the most important work and study activities receive enough time and attention. This system of time management enables a person to track his success over time and goes a long way toward reducing unnecessary stress and confusion.

LEISURE TIME ACTIVITIES People with a high need for achievement are often characterized by an unremitting urge to strive for excellence. Leisure time provides employees an opportunity for rest and recovery from strenuous activities at home and work. When asked what they do with their leisure time, many individuals say that they clean the house or mow the lawn. These activities are fine, as long as the individual gets the stress-reducing benefit of pleasure from them. Some say our work ethic is a cultural barrier to pleasure. We work longer hours, and two-income families are the norm. Leisure is increasingly a luxury among working people. The key to the effective use of leisure time is enjoyment. Leisure time can be used for spontaneity, joy, and connection with others in our lives. Although vacations can be a relief from job burnout, they may incur fade-out effects.[94] Hence, leisure time and vacations must be periodic, recurring activities.

PHYSICAL EXERCISE Different types of physical exercise are important secondary stress prevention activities for individuals. Colleges and universities often implement physical exercise through physical education classes, while military organizations implement it through fitness standards and regulated training. Kenneth Cooper, among others, has long advocated aerobic exercise to improve a person's responsiveness to stressful activities.[95] Research at the Aerobics Center in Dallas has found that aerobically fit people (1) have lower levels of adrenaline in their blood at rest; (2) have a slower, stronger heart beat; and (3) recover from stressful events more quickly.

Flexibility training is an important type of exercise because muscular contractions are associated with the stress response. One component of the stress response is the contraction of the flexor muscles, which prepares a person to fight or flee. Flexibility training enables a person to stretch and relax these muscles to prevent the accumulation of unnecessary muscular tension.[96] In addition, flexibility exercises help maintain joint mobility, increase strength, and play an important role in the prevention of injury.

RELAXATION TRAINING Herbert Benson was one of the first people to identify the relaxation response as the natural counterresponse to stress.[97] In studying Western and Eastern peoples, Benson found that Jews and Christians have elicited this response through their time-honored traditions of prayer, whereas those with backgrounds in Eastern religions have elicited it through meditation. The relaxation response does not require a theological or religious component, however. Reading, massage, and secular yoga practice can all elicit the relaxation response. If you have an unwinding ritual, you may already elicit the relaxation response regularly.

DIET Diet may play an indirect role in stress and stress management. Large amounts of sugar in one's diet can stimulate the stress response, and foods high in cholesterol can adversely affect blood chemistry. Good dietary practices contribute to overall health. In his nonsurgical, nonpharmacological approach to reversing heart disease, Dean Ornish proposes a very stringent "reversal diet" for individuals with identifiable blockage of the arteries.[98] He recommends a somewhat less stringent "prevention diet" as one of four methods for opening up the arteries of healthy individuals. Another element in his program is an emotional one—openness in relationships with other people.

OPENING UP Traumatic, distress-inducing events are an unfortunate fact of life. One of the most therapeutic responses to such events is to confide in other people.[99] Discussing difficult experiences with another person is not always easy, but mental and physical heath improves through self-disclosure. Confessions need not be made in person, or to another person at all. Writing in a private diary and posting anonymously on the Internet are also therapeutic. In a study comparing those who wrote once a week about traumatic events with those

> Mental and physical health improves through self-disclosure.

who wrote about nontraumatic events, significant health benefits and reduced absenteeism were found in the first group.[100] Whatever form it takes, the process of opening up and confessing appears to counter the detrimental effects of stress.

PROFESSIONAL HELP Confession and opening up may occur in professional healing relationships. Psychological counseling, career counseling, physical therapy, medical treatment, surgical intervention, and other therapeutic techniques are available to people who need help. *Employee assistance programs (EAPs)* may be very helpful in referring employees to appropriate caregivers. Even soldiers who experience battle stress reactions severe enough to take them out of action can experience healing through EAPs and then participate in subsequent combat missions.[101] The early detection of distress and strain reactions, coupled with prompt professional treatment, can be instrumental in averting permanent physical and psychological damage, such as posttraumatic stress disorder.

7-7c Comprehensive Health Promotion

Whereas organizational stress prevention programs are aimed at eliminating health risks at work, wellness, and well-being approaches aim at enhancing a "strong and resistant host" in the case of individuals, organizations, and their communities.[102] Physical fitness and exercise programs characterize corporate health promotion programs in the United States and Canada.[103] A health and wellness survey of accredited medical schools in the United States, Canada, and Puerto Rico found that these programs place significant emphasis on physical well-being and minor emphasis on spiritual well-being.[104] A new approach to comprehensive health promotion places emphasis on the organization and *organizational wellness*.[105] Still, social and cognitive processes are key considerations in the successful implementation of stress prevention programs.[106]

Johnson & Johnson developed a comprehensive health promotion program with a wide array of educational modules for individuals and groups. Each of these educational modules addresses a specific topic, such as Type A behavior, stress, diet (through cooperative activities with the American Heart Association), and risk assessment (through regular health evaluations for participants). Upon implementation of this health promotion program, Johnson & Johnson found that the health status of employees improved, even if they didn't participate in the program.

STUDY TOOLS 7

LOCATED AT BACK OF THE TEXTBOOK
☐ Rip out chapter review card

LOCATED AT WWW.CENGAGE.COM/LOGIN
☐ Gain unique perspectives on key concepts with new Concept Clip videos in the e-book
☐ Review key term flashcards and create your own
☐ Increase your comprehension with online homework and quizzes

8 | Communication

LEARNING OBJECTIVES

8-1 Describe the interpersonal communication process and the role of listening in the process.

8-2 Describe the five communication skills of effective supervisors.

8-3 Explain five communication barriers and the gateways through them.

8-4 Distinguish between civility and incivility, and defensive and nondefensive communication.

8-5 Explain the impact of nonverbal communication.

8-6 Explain positive, healthy communication.

8-7 Identify how new communication technologies and social media affect the communication process.

After finishing this chapter go to **PAGE 141** for **STUDY TOOLS**

Klaus Vedfelt/Taxi/Getty Images

8-1 INTERPERSONAL COMMUNICATION

Communication evokes a shared, or common, meaning in another person. **Interpersonal communication** occurs between two or more people in an organization. It is central to health and well-being, both at home and on the job. Reading, listening, managing and interpreting information, and serving clients are among the interpersonal communication skills identified by the Department of Labor as necessary for success in the workplace.[1] In Chapter 7, we noted that interpersonal communication is the key to unlocking social support for preventive stress management.[2] It is also important in building and sustaining human relationships at work. Recent advances in information technology and data management cannot replace interpersonal

communication The evoking of a shared or common meaning in another person.

interpersonal communication Communication between two or more people in an organization.

communication. Figure 8.1 illustrates the key elements of interpersonal communication: the communicator, the receiver, the perceptual screens, and the message.

8-1a An Interpersonal Communication Model

The **communicator** is the person sending the message. The **receiver** is the person accepting the message. **Perceptual screens** are the windows through which we interact. The communicator's and the receiver's respective perceptual screens influence the quality, accuracy, and clarity of the message. They can allow the message to transmit smoothly, or they can cause static and distortion. Perceptual screens are built upon the sender's and receiver's individual attributes, such as age, gender, values, beliefs, past experiences, cultural influences, and individual needs. The degree to which these screens are open significantly influences both sent and received messages.

The **message** contains the thoughts and feelings that the communicator intends to evoke in the receiver. The message has two primary components. The *thought*, or conceptual component, of the message (its content) is contained in the words, ideas, symbols, and concepts chosen to relay the message. The *feeling*, or emotional component, of the message (its

communicator The person sending a message.

receiver The person accepting a message.

perceptual screen A window through which one interacts with others. It influences the quality, accuracy, and clarity of the communication.

message The thoughts and feelings that the communicator is attempting to evoke in the receiver.

affect) is contained in the intensity, demeanor, and gestures of the communicator. The emotional component of the message adds overtones of joy, anger, fear, or pain to the conceptual component. This addition often enriches and clarifies the message.

Feedback may or may not be activated in communication. It occurs when the receiver provides the communicator with a response to the message. More broadly, feedback occurs when information is fed back to the sender that completes two-way communication.

The **language** of the message is important. *Language* is a broad term denoting the words, their pronunciations, and the methods of combining them used and understood by a group of people. Culture and situation dictate the specific language utilized in a message.

Data are the uninterpreted, unanalyzed elements of a message. **Information** is data with meaning to the person who interprets or analyzes them. Since messages are conveyed through a *medium*, such as a telephone or face-to-face discussion, they differ in **richness** according to the ability of that medium to transmit meaning to a receiver.[3] Despite the popularity of text messaging as a communication medium, e-mail remains the preferred method of workplace communication. A recent survey found that workers are almost three times as likely to send an e-mail to a colleague rather than a text message to communicate work-related as well as non-work-related information.[4] Table 8.1 compares different media with regard to data capacity and richness. Such attributes of communication media affect how influence-seeking behavior is generated and perceived in organizations.[5]

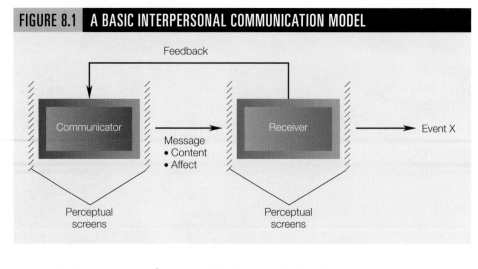

FIGURE 8.1 **A BASIC INTERPERSONAL COMMUNICATION MODEL**

feedback Information fed back that completes two-way communication.

language The words, their pronunciations, and the methods of combining them used and understood by a group of people.

data Uninterpreted and unanalyzed elements of a message.

information Data that have been interpreted, analyzed, and have meaning to some user.

richness The ability of a medium to convey meaning to a receiver.

employee voice behavior communication of suggestions, concerns, information about problems, or work-related opinions to effect constructive changes in the workplace.

reflective listening Carefully listening to message and immediately repeating it back to the speaker.

8-1b Employee Voice Behavior

Employees may communicate and give voice through their behavior. **Employee voice behavior** refers to the behavior that proactively challenges the status quo and makes constructive changes in the workplace. Research shows that core employee self-evaluations can influence voice behavior, especially when moderated by personal control and approach motivation, especially when procedural justice is perceived to be high.[6] While some aspects of the status quo may be good, other aspects need to be challenged and constructively changed. Employee voice behavior may lead to difficult conversations, as seen in the accompanying feature.

8-1c Reflective Listening

One skill essential for being successful in difficult conversations and enacting voice behavior in the workplace is good listening. **Reflective listening** is the skill of carefully listening to a message and immediately repeating it back to the speaker. This technique helps the communicator clarify the intended message and correct inaccuracies or misunderstandings. Reflective listening emphasizes the role of the receiver, or audience, in interpersonal communication. Reflective listening better enables the listener to comprehend the communicator's meaning, reduce perceptual distortions, and overcome interpersonal barriers that lead to communication failures. Especially useful in problem solving, reflective listening can be learned in a short time. Given its positive effects on behavior and emotion in the corporate environment, reflective listening is a valuable skill to possess.[7]

Reflective listening can be characterized as personal, feeling oriented, and responsive.[8] First, it emphasizes the *personal* elements of the communication process. The reflective listener demonstrates empathy and

Challenging the Status Quo May Lead to Difficult Conversations

Employees who do not like conflict or who dread discord may find it natural to avoid, or delay, a challenging and difficult conversation. This may both hurt relationships and have other negative outcomes, such as the failure to achieve constructive change in the workplace. To succeed in difficult conversations may mean reframing one's thoughts. Think curiosity and respect; don't think about popularity or being liked. Refocus attention on hearing what the other person is saying, thinking less about what you are saying. Be direct and to the point; do not put it off. Finally, expect a positive outcome. An optimistic expectation can help keep the communication constructive. Challenging the status quo and achieving constructive change may mean a pathway through difficult conversations. Be prepared!

M-SUR/Shutterstock.com

SOURCE: J. Garfinkle, "How to Have Difficult Conversations When You Don't Like Conflict," *Harvard Business Review*, March 24, 2017.

concern for the communicator as a person, not an object. Second, reflective listening emphasizes the *feelings* communicated in the message—the receiver must pay special attention to the feeling component as she repeats the message. Third, reflective listening emphasizes a rational and considerate *response*. Receivers should distinguish their own feelings and thoughts from those of the speaker. In other words, the conversation's focus must remain at all times on the ideas and emotions of the speaker in order for the receiver to effectively respond to them. Empathy and emotional self-control are key emotional competencies in good reflective listening.

Reflective listening necessitates four levels of verbal response: affirming contact, paraphrasing expressed thoughts and feelings, clarifying implicit thoughts and feelings, and reflecting core feelings not fully expressed. Nonverbal behaviors, such as eye contact and silence, are also important in reflective listening. Each of these responses can be illustrated through an example: the interaction between a software engineer, who has just discovered a major problem in a large information system she is building for a difficult customer, and her supervisor.

AFFIRMING CONTACT The receiver (in this case, the supervisor of the software engineer) affirms contact with the communicator (the software engineer) by making periodic statements such as "I see," "Okay," and "Yes, I understand." The purpose of an affirmation response is to communicate attentiveness, not necessarily agreement. Affirming contact is especially reassuring to a speaker

in the early stages of expression, and even more so when there may be some associated anxiety or discomfort. As the problem is more fully explored and expressed, it is increasingly important for the receiver to employ other reflective responses.

PARAPHRASING THE EXPRESSED After an appropriate length of time, the receiver (the supervisor in our example) might paraphrase the expressed thoughts and feelings of the speaker (the engineer). Paraphrasing is useful because it tells the speaker what the receiver heard and what the receiver's thoughts and feelings are about what he heard. This verbal response enables the

TABLE 8.1	COMMUNICATION MEDIA: INFORMATION RICHNESS AND DATA CAPACITY	
Medium	**Information Richness**	**Data Capacity**
Face-to-face discussion	Highest	Lowest
Telephone	High	Low
Electronic mail	Moderate	Moderate
Blog	Moderate	Moderate
Individualized letter	Moderate	Moderate
Personalized note or memo	Moderate	Moderate
Formal written report	Low	High
Flyer or bulletin	Low	High
Formal numeric report	Lowest	Highest

SOURCE: Adapted from E. A. Gerloff, "Information Richness: A New Approach to Managerial Behavior and Organizational Design," by R. L. Daft and R. H. Lengel in *Research in Organizational Behavior* 6 (1984): 191–233. Reprinted by permission of JAI Press Inc.

speaker and receiver to build greater empathy, openness, and acceptance into their relationship while ensuring the accuracy of the communication process.

In the case of the software engineer, the supervisor may find paraphrasing the engineer's message particularly useful for both of them in developing a clearer understanding of the system problem. He might say, "I can tell that you're very upset about this problem. Even though you're not quite sure how it happened, it sounds like you have a few good leads." It is difficult to solve a problem until it is clearly understood.

CLARIFYING THE IMPLICIT People often communicate *implicit* thoughts and feelings—that is, thoughts and feelings that are not clearly or fully expressed—along with their explicitly expressed message. The receiver may or may not assume that this implicit component of the message is within the awareness of the speaker. For example, the software engineer may be anxious about how to approach a difficult customer with the system problem. This may be implicit in her discussion with her supervisor because of a previous discussion about this customer. If her feelings of anxiety are not expressed, the supervisor may want to clarify them. He might say, "You seem particularly stressed . . . were you worried about the client's reaction?" This would help the engineer shift the focus of her attention from the main problem, which is in the software, to the important issue of discussing the matter with the customer.

REFLECTING CORE FEELINGS Next, the receiver should look beyond the speaker's explicit and implicit messages to understand the speaker's *core feelings*, the speaker's deepest and most important emotions, beliefs, and values. If the software engineer had not been aware of any anxiety in her relationship with the difficult customer, her supervisor's ability to sense the tension and bring it to the engineer's awareness would exemplify the reflection of core feelings. Emotional intelligence is especially important here.

However, the receiver runs a risk of overreaching if a secure, empathetic relationship with the speaker has not already been established or if strongly repressed feelings are reflected back. Even if the receiver is correct, the speaker may not want those feelings brought to her awareness. Therefore, it is important to exercise caution and care in reflecting core feelings to a speaker.

SILENCE Long periods of silence may cause discomfort or embarrassment, but a certain amount of silence can help both speaker and listener in reflective listening. From the speaker's perspective, silence may be useful in moments of thought or confusion about how to express difficult ideas or feelings. The

software engineer may need some patient silence from her supervisor as she thinks through what to say next. Listeners can use brief periods of silence to sort their own thoughts and feelings from those of the speaker. In the case of the software engineer's supervisor, any personal feelings toward the difficult customer should not intrude on the engineer's immediate problem. Silence provides time to identify and isolate the listener's personal responses and exclude them from the dialogue.

EYE CONTACT Eye contact is a nonverbal behavior that may promote openness in communication between two people. During a dialog, the absence of appropriate eye contact tends to close communication. However, the presence of inappropriate eye contact can also hinder a relationship. Cultural and individual differences influence what constitutes appropriate and inappropriate eye contact. For example, direct eye contact initiated by women and children is discouraged in India. In fact, too much direct eye contact, regardless of the individual or culture, can have an intimidating effect.

Moderate direct eye contact communicates openness and affirmation without causing either speaker or listener to feel intimidated. Periodic aversion of the eyes allows for a sense of privacy and control, even in intense interpersonal communication. The software engineer and the supervisor make eye contact throughout their discussion, though each looks away periodically to ease the tension of intimacy.

Tyler Olson/123RF

Law enforcement, firefighters, and military personnel rely on abbreviated one-way communication in emergency situations.

ONE-WAY VERSUS TWO-WAY COMMUNICATION Reflective listening encourages **two-way communication**, an interactive form of communication in which there is an exchange of thoughts, feelings, or both, and through which shared meaning often occurs. Problem solving and decision-making are often examples of two-way communication. **One-way communication** occurs when a person sends a message to another person and no feedback, questions, or interaction follows. Giving instructions and giving directions are examples of one-way communication.

One-way communication tends to be efficient, although how efficient it is depends on the amount and complexity of information communicated and the medium chosen. Even though it is faster than two-way communication, one-way communication is often less accurate. This is especially true for complex tasks that require clarification for completion. When time and accuracy are both important to the successful completion of a task and two-way communication is not an option (such as in combat or emergency situations), extensive training prior to execution enhances accuracy and efficiency.[9] Firefighters and military combat personnel engage extensively in such training to minimize the need for communication during emergencies. These highly trained professionals rely on abbreviated one-way communication as shorthand for more complex information. However, this communication works only within the range of situations for which the professionals are specifically trained.

It is difficult to draw generalizations about individual preference for one-way or two-way communication. Communicators with a stronger need for feedback or who are comfortable with conflict or confusing questions may find two-way communication more satisfying. By contrast, receivers who believe that a message is straightforward may be satisfied with one-way communication and be impatient with lengthy two-way communication.

8-2 COMMUNICATION SKILLS FOR EFFECTIVE MANAGERS

Interpersonal communication is a critical foundation for effective performance and individual well-being in organizations. Power is intertwined in the language of communication between managers and their employees.[10] This power dynamic is especially critical when leaders are articulating an organizational vision and attempting to achieve buy-in from employees.[11] One large study of managers in a variety of industries found that those with the most effective work units engaged in routine communication with their employees, whereas the managers with the highest promotion rates engaged in networking activities with superiors.[12] A study of banking managers found that higher performing managers were more effective, less apprehensive communicators than lower performing managers.[13] Oral communication and managerial cooperation are important contextual performance skills that have positive effects on the psychosocial quality of the work environment.[14]

Research on manager–employee communication identifies five communication skills that distinguish good supervisors from bad ones.[15] A good supervisor is an expressive speaker, an empathetic listener, a persuasive leader, a sensitive person, and an informative manager. Some supervisors are effective without possessing all of these skills, however, and some organizations value one or two skills over the others. But because dyadic relationships are at the core of much organization-based communication, possessing all five skills makes a supervisor that much more effective in communicating to employees.[16]

8-2a Expressiveness

Effective supervisors express their thoughts, ideas, and feelings openly and aren't afraid to voice opinions in meetings. They tend toward extroversion. Supervisors who are not talkative or who tend toward introversion may at times leave their employees wondering what they're thinking about certain issues. Supervisors who speak out let the people they work with know where they stand, what they believe, and how they feel.

8-2b Empathy and Sensitivity

In addition to being expressive speakers, good supervisors are willing, empathetic, reflective listeners. Empathetic listeners are able to hear the emotional dimensions of the messages people send them, as well as the content of the ideas and issues. Good supervisors are approachable and willing to

> **two-way communication**
> An interactive form of communication in which there is an exchange of thoughts, feelings, or both.
>
> **one-way communication**
> Communication in which a person sends a message to another person and no feedback, questions, or interaction follows.

> Good supervisors keep their employees well informed by appropriately and selectively disseminating information.

listen to suggestions and complaints. In a recent study of physicians, those with higher perceptions of control were more open in their communication, and patients found them more empathetic.[17] Good supervisors are emotionally intelligent.

Good supervisors are also sensitive to the feelings, self-images, and psychological defenses of their employees. They know how and when to communicate with employees to maximize psychological health. For example, employees' accomplishments, honors, and achievements should be announced in public, while criticism should be delivered in private. The best supervisors are sensitive to the self-esteem of others.

8-2c Persuasiveness

All supervisors must exercise power and influence in organizations if they want to ensure high performance and achieve positive results. Effective supervisors tend to be persuasive leaders, distinguished by their use of persuasive language to influence others. They are not deceitful or autocratic; they encourage results earnestly instead of manipulating others.

Of course, sometimes emergencies and high-risk situations necessitate the abandonment of sensitive and subtle persuasion. In cases such as a fire at an oil rig or a life-threatening trauma in an emergency room, a supervisor must be direct and assertive.

8-2d Informative Managing Style

Finally, good supervisors keep their employees well informed by appropriately and selectively disseminating information. Failing to effectively filter information may lead to either information overload or a lack of sufficient information for task accomplishment. Good supervisors give advance notice of organizational changes and explain the rationale for organizational policies. Good supervisors are also transparent, communicating openly and honestly with employees. Such transparency leads to increased trust among employees, which, in turn, results in increased employee engagement.[18]

A person may become a good supervisor even in the absence of one of these communication skills. For example, a manager with special talents in planning, organizing, or decision-making may compensate for a shortcoming in expressiveness or sensitivity. No matter their perceived skill level or effectiveness, when supervisors and employees engage in open communication and forward planning, they have a greater number of agreements about the employee's performance and behavior.[19]

8-3 BARRIERS AND GATEWAYS TO COMMUNICATION

Barriers to communication are factors that distort, disrupt, or even halt successful communication. They may be temporary and easily resolved or long-lasting and deeply rooted. Roughly 20 percent of all such barriers to communication can be prevented or solved by communicationpolicy guidelines.[20] **Gateways to communication** are the openings that break down communication barriers. Awareness and recognition of communication barriers are the first steps in opening the gateways. Obvious barriers are physical separation (employees in different geographic locations or buildings) and status differences (related to the organizational hierarchy). One apparent gateway for the separation of geographically dispersed teams is to improve the frequency of face-to-face interaction. Geographically dispersed teams can also increase their performance by targeting their use of information and communication technologies (ICTs) to address specific coordination needs. For example, if teams are responsible for performing nonroutine tasks, their performance can be enhanced by using ICTs to provide task knowledge.[21] Not so obvious are the barriers caused by gender differences, cultural diversity, and language.

8-3a Gender Differences

Communication barriers can be attributed in part to differences in conversational styles.[22] When individuals of different economic backgrounds converse, the receiver's understanding may not be the same as the speaker's meaning. In a similar vein, men and women tend

barriers to communication Factors that distort, disrupt, or even halt successful communication.

gateways to communication Openings that break down communication barriers.

to have different conversational styles. For example, women often prefer to converse face to face, whereas men are comfortable conversing while sitting side by side, concentrating on a focal point in front of them. Hence, conversational differences may result in a barrier of communication between men and women. Male–female conversation is really cross-cultural communication. In a work context, one study found that female employees sent less information to their supervisors and experienced less information overload than did male employees.[23]

An important gateway through the gender barrier is the development of an awareness and appreciation of gender-specific differences in conversational style. These differences can enrich organizational communication and empower professional relationships.[24] A second gateway is to actively seek clarification of the person's meaning rather than freely interpreting meaning from one's own frame of reference.

8-3b Cultural Diversity

Culturally influenced values and patterns of behavior can be very confusing barriers to communication. Significant differences in work-related values exist among people in the United States versus those in Germany, the United Kingdom, Japan, and other nations.[25] These differences in value impact motivation, leadership, and teamwork in work organizations.[26] Habitual patterns of interaction can obstruct communication in any given culture. For example, the German culture places greater value

on authority and hierarchical differences than does the United States. It is therefore more difficult for German workers to engage in open communication with their supervisors than it is for U.S. workers.[27]

When a person from one culture views people from another culture through the lens of a stereotype, she discounts the individual differences that exist within that foreign culture. For example, a stereotype of Americans common throughout Asia is that they are aggressive and arrogant, and thus insensitive and unapproachable. Stereotypes of Asians common throughout America are that they are studious, subservient, and assimilative. Individuals who depend on the accuracy of cultural stereotypes may unknowingly create barriers in communicating with people from other cultures.

One gateway through the barrier of diversity is increasing cultural awareness and sensitivity. Part of that knowledge is paying attention to message context when communicating cross-culturally. Whereas Westerners are categorized as being low-context communicators who emphasize message content, Easterners, such as Japanese, Korean, and Chinese, are categorized as high-context communicators who focus more on the context of the message rather than the explicit content.[28] Further, companies can provide seminars for expatriate managers as part of their training for overseas assignments. Bernard Isautier, president and CEO of Sunningdale Berkshire, believes that understanding and communication are two keys to harmonious workplace diversity, an essential ingredient for success in international markets.[29] A second gateway is developing or acquiring a guide for understanding and interacting with members of other cultures. For example, Irish pubs, the Spanish bullfight, and American football are consensually derived metaphors for culturally specific conversational styles that can enable those outside the culture to understand members within.

8-3c Language

Language can be another barrier to communication. Growing numbers of businesspeople are bilingual or multilingual, but even subtle distinctions in dialects within the same language can be barriers. For example, the word *chemist* means a molecular scientist in the United States and a drugstore worker in Great Britain. Language barriers are created across disciplines and professional boundaries by technical terminology. Although acronyms and professional jargon may be very useful tools of communication within a discipline, they may serve only to confuse and derail any attempt at clear understanding by those unfamiliar with the profession. When doing business, it's best to use simple, direct, declarative language. One should speak in brief sentences and employ terms or words already used by one's audience. As much as possible, one should speak in the language of the listener. Above all else, one should not use jargon or technical language except with those who are already familiar with it.

8-4 CIVILITY AND INCIVILITY

While **incivility** can create a barrier between people and jar people's emotions, **civility** may be a gateway to communication that smoothes troubled waters at work. Workplace incivility is low-intensity deviant workplace behavior with an ambiguous intent to harm. A review of the literature suggests that there are three types of incivility: experienced, witnessed, and instigated.[30] There are, however, some instances in which incivility can have positive effects when it is strategically used. In this section, we examine the full range of consequences of incivility and the blessings of civility. In addition, we examine defensive and nondefensive communication that may spring from civil and uncivil communication behavior.

incivility Discourteous communication and rude behavior that are disrespectful, hurtful, or injurious.

civility Communication and behavior that respect the integrity and dignity of the individual.

8-4a Consequences of Incivility

Workplace incivility can jar the emotions and cause a range of adverse outcomes both in the workplace and at home. Discourteousness, rudeness, impatience, and lack of respect are very common forms of incivility. The consequences of incivility depend on its source. Research suggests that vulnerability to the negative effects of workplace civility may also depend on ethnicity and cultural values.[31] Much incivility originates with superiors and those in powerful positions within the organization. This type of incivility is often tolerated even though it leads to a decline in satisfaction with the supervisor. Coworkers may display incivility too. As we would expect, someone subject to coworker incivility experiences less satisfaction with the coworker and that may generalize to all coworkers. In fact, observing incivility at work may destroy perceptions of professional conduct and cause the observer concern about whether he or other coworkers will receive similar treatment.[32] In addition, coworker incivility can trigger the perception of being treated unfairly at work and may even lead to depression. So the emotional and psychological adverse effects of coworker incivility are quite real along with additional costs from unfair treatment and depression. Understanding the dynamics of workplace incivility can enable incivility change with positive secondary effects in reducing burnout and turnout cognitions.[33] These positive effects may vary across time and individuals.

Before rushing to judgment that all incivility is destructive, we need to point out that there is a place in the workplace for what may appear uncivil. Take, for example, swearing. Annoyance swearing is a problem because of the emotional jarring and stressful impact on others, often disrupting social support within a team as well as the team's well-being. Social swearing, on the other hand, can be a stress release for an individual provided the language is not aimed at someone else. It may even be something in which others can empathize and vicariously share while building relationships and camaraderie.

> Civility should not be confused with the avoidance of difficult or complicated workplace issues, which must be confronted and addressed.

8-4b Blessings of Civility

The blessings of civility are found in its gracious and positive nature. Civil communication and behavior carry the potential to avoid hurt feelings, prevent harm and damage to working relationships, and contribute to well-being in the workplace. There are several ways to create a more civil workplace: bring difficult issues out in the open, write things down before speaking, set enforcement guidelines for incivility, and be consistent in enforcing those guidelines. Civility ensures respect for the integrity and dignity of every member of the workplace.

8-4c Defensive and Nondefensive Communication

In the workplace, defensive language creates barriers between people, whereas nondefensive communication helps to open and deepen relationships.[34] **Defensive communication** includes aggressive, malevolent messages as well as passive, withdrawn messages. **Nondefensive communication** is assertive, direct, and powerful. Though it can be misinterpreted as aggressiveness, assertiveness is indeed nondefensive. Corporations today are increasingly engaged in situations such as courtroom battles and media exchanges that are fertile ground for defensive communication yet benefit greatly from nondefensive language and emotionally intelligent communication.

Defensive communication leads to a wide range of problems, including injured feelings, communication barriers, alienation in working relationships, destructive and retaliatory behaviors, nonproductive efforts, and problem-solving failures. Defensive reactions such as counterattack and sheepish withdrawal derail communication. These responses tend to lend heat, not light, to the process of communication. Defensive communication often evokes still more defensive communication.

Nondefensive communication, in contrast, provides a positive and productive basis for asserting and defending oneself against aggression without further damaging the communication process. An assertive, nondefensive style restores order, balance, and effectiveness in working relationships. Further discussion of nondefensive communication and defensive communication in the workplace follows.

8-4d Defensive Communication at Work

The two basic patterns of defensiveness are dominant defensiveness and subordinate defensiveness. Subordinate defensiveness is characterized by passive or submissive behavior. The psychological attitude of the subordinately defensive person is "You are right, and I am wrong." People with low self-esteem may be prone to this form of defensive behavior, as may people at lower organizational levels. Individuals who are subordinately defensive do not adequately assert their thoughts and feelings. Their input is likely to be lost, even if it is critical to organizational performance.[35] Passive-aggressive behavior is a form of defensiveness that begins as subordinate defensiveness and ends up as dominant defensiveness. It is behavior that appears very passive, though it actually masks underlying aggression and hostility.

In contrast, dominant defensiveness is characterized by overtly aggressive and domineering behavior. It is offensive in nature, sometimes culminating in verbal or physical harassment. The psychological attitude of the dominantly defensive person is "I am right, and you are wrong." People who are egotistical or overcompensating for low self-esteem may exhibit this pattern of behavior, as may people in higher-level positions within the organizational hierarchy.

8-4e Defensive Tactics

Defensive tactics are subversive actions that employ defensive communication. Unfortunately, these tactics are common in many work organizations. Until defensiveness and defensive tactics are recognized for what they are at an organizational level, it is difficult to address them or respond to them in nondefensive ways. In many cases, defensive tactics raise ethical dilemmas for victims and their supervisors. At what point does simple defensiveness become unethical behavior? Consider the following defensive tactics.

Power plays are tactics used to control and manipulate others. Restricting the choices of employees, enforcing either/or conditions, intentionally ignoring or insulting others, bullying, and displaying overt aggression are all power plays. The underlying dynamic in power plays is that of domination and control. The aggressor attempts to gain the upper hand in the relationship by making the victim feel inferior and thus vulnerable to control.

Labeling is often used to portray another person as abnormal or deficient. Medical and legal labels are often used out of context for this purpose. The words *paranoid*, *retarded*, and *insane* have specific,

defensive communication Messages that are aggressive, malevolent, passive, or withdrawn.

nondefensive communication Messages that are assertive, direct, and powerful.

An individual who consistently communicates nondefensively may be characterized as centered, assertive, controlled, informative, realistic, and honest.

clinical meanings that are discarded in defensive labeling. Similar to labeling is publicly raising doubts about a person's abilities, values, sexual orientation, or other personal aspects. This tactic breeds confusion and uncertainty, though it tends to lack the specificity and clarity of labeling.

Disseminating misleading information, a form of deception, is the selective presentation of information intentionally designed to produce an inaccurate impression in the listener's mind. This obfuscated information can be used to scapegoat, or pass the buck, which shifts responsibility for an error or problem to the wrong person. If information cannot be altered, defensive individuals may simply blame others for their own wrongdoing.

Finally, *hostile jokes* are a passive-aggressive defensive tactic. Because a jocular framing is used to mask aggressive and even overtly mean sentiments, hostile jokes often go uncited. They should not be confused with good humor, which is both therapeutic and nondefensive. Jokes made at the expense of others are destructive to self-esteem and workplace communication.

8-4f Nondefensive Communication

Nondefensive communication is a healthy alternative to defensive communication in working relationships. An individual who consistently communicates nondefensively may be characterized as centered, assertive, controlled, informative, realistic, and honest. Nondefensive communication is powerful because the speaker exhibits self-control and self-possession without rejecting the listener. It should be self-affirming without being self-aggrandizing—a sometimes difficult balance to maintain.

nonverbal communication
All elements of communication that do not involve words or language.

Converting defensive patterns of communication to nondefensive ones builds relationships at work. Behaviors that build relationships simultaneously reduce adverse responses, such as blame and anger, when negative events occur at work.[36]

To strengthen nondefensive patterns, the subordinately defensive person must learn to be more assertive. One way to do this is to report what one intends to do and invite confirmation instead of asking for permission to do something. Another way is to stop using self-deprecating phrases such as "I'm just following orders." One should drop the *just* and thereby convert the message into a self-assertive, declarative statement.

To strengthen nondefensive patterns, the dominantly defensive person must learn to be less aggressive. This may be especially difficult because it requires overcoming the sense of certitude. Those who are working to overcome dominant defensiveness should be particularly sensitive to feedback from others about their behavior. To change this behavior, one can stop giving and denying permission. Instead, one should give others free rein (except in situations where permission is essential to clearance or the security of the task). Alternatively, instead of becoming inappropriately angry, one should provide information about the adverse consequences of a particular course of action.

8-5 NONVERBAL COMMUNICATION

Whereas defensive and nondefensive communication focus on the language used in delivering a message, most of the meaning in a message is nonverbal or behavioral. Rudeness is an example of low-intensity negative behavior that may communicate an ambiguous message but more importantly be contagious in organizations.[37] Mindfulness of both the verbal and nonverbal elements of communication are therefore important. **Nonverbal communication** includes all elements of communication that do not involve words or language such as gestures and the use of space.[38] The four basic types of nonverbal communication that managers need to understand are proxemics, kinesics, facial and eye behavior, and paralanguage. Managers also need to understand that nonverbal communication is influenced by both psychological and physiological processes.[39]

The interpretation of nonverbal communication is specific to the context of the interaction and the actors.

Keeping the Tables Turning without Rushing Guests

Jean-Marie Guyon/123RF

Restaurants are more successful when they keep things moving, including their guests. However, they do not want their clientele to feel rushed or "on the clock." Therefore, restaurants rely on a range of nonverbal communication out front to keep things moving, including how they organize tables and lay out the dining areas while ensuring that critical communication between managers, servers, and cooks is high fidelity if behind-the-scenes. Opting for at least some communal tables in the dining area will speed up the flow of customers as will backless stools at the bar. Ensuring the food is served to guests sitting at high-demand spots in the restaurant helps move them along too. The initial drink order can serve as a litmus test of when a party might leave, so restaurants will take note of this nonverbal behavior.

Not all of the important communication in restaurants is verbal, just watch.

SOURCE: A. Dizik, "How Restaurants Stick to Their Schedules," *Wall Street Journal*, 22 Feb. 2017.

That is, the particular meaning of any nonverbal cue relies on its sender, receiver, and the environment in which the cue occurs. For example, some federal and state judges attempt to curb nonverbal communication in the courtroom. Though it may mean nothing outside the courtroom, some nonverbal behavior may unfairly influence jurors' decisions if displayed during a trial. Beyond the contextual element, nonverbal behavior is also culturally bound. (Recall from Chapter 2 the difference in meaning the "thumbs-up" sign has in Australia versus the United States.)

8-5a Proxemics

The study of an individual's perception and use of space, including territorial space, is called **proxemics**.[40] **Territorial space** refers to bands of concentric space radiating outward from the body. These bands are commonly known as *comfort zones*. Figure 8.2 illustrates the four zones of territorial space common to U.S. culture.

Territorial space varies greatly around the world. Both the sizes of comfort zones and their acceptable modes of interaction are culturally defined. And people often become uncomfortable when operating in territorial spaces different from those with which they are familiar.

According to leading proxemics researcher Edward Hall, Americans working in the Middle East tend to back away to a comfortable distance when conversing with Arabs because Arabs' comfortable conversation distance is closer than that of Americans. As a result, Arabs sometimes perceive Americans as cold and aloof. One Arab wondered, "What's the matter? Does he find me somehow offensive?"[41] The circumference of personal space tends to be larger in cultures with cool climates, such as the United States, Great Britain, and northern Europe, and smaller in cultures with warm climates, such as southern Europe, the Caribbean, India, and South America.[42]

Our relationships shape our use of territorial space. For example, we hold hands with or put an arm around significant others to pull them into *intimate space*. Conversely, we can use territorial space to shape our interactions. A four-foot-wide desk pushes business interactions into the *social distance* zone. Not comfortable with that definition of space, one SBC manager met with her seven first-line supervisors crowded around her four-foot desk, putting them elbow to elbow with each other. As a result of being placed in one another's intimate space, they appeared to act more like friends and frequently talked about their children, favorite television shows, and other personal concerns. When the manager moved the staff meetings to a larger room and thus relocated the supervisors into each others' social distance zones, the personal exchanges ceased, and they acted more like business associates again.

Seating dynamics, another aspect of proxemics, is the art of seating people in certain positions according to their purpose in communication. Figure 8.3

proxemics The study of an individual's perception and use of space.

territorial space Bands of concentric space radiating outward from the body.

FIGURE 8.2 | ZONES OF TERRITORIAL SPACE IN U.S. CULTURE

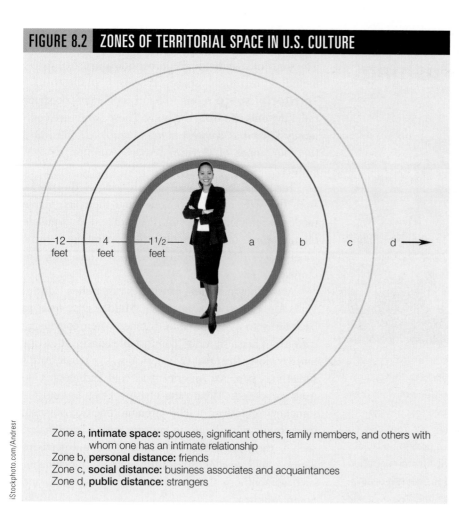

-12- -4- -1½- a b c d →
feet feet feet

iStockphoto.com/Andresr

Zone a, **intimate space:** spouses, significant others, family members, and others with whom one has an intimate relationship
Zone b, **personal distance:** friends
Zone c, **social distance:** business associates and acquaintances
Zone d, **public distance:** strangers

depicts some common seating dynamics. To encourage cooperation, one should seat the adjoining party beside oneself, facing the same direction. To facilitate direct and open communication, one should seat the other party across a corner of one's desk or in another place where he will be at right angles. This allows for more honest disclosure. To take a competitive stand with someone, one must position the person directly across from oneself. Suppose a manager holds a meeting around a conference table, and two of the attendees are disrupting the meeting by chatting loudly. Where should they be seated? If the manager places the two disruptive attendees on either side of herself, the talking should be stifled (unless one is so bold as to lean in front of the manager to keep chatting).

8-5b Kinesics

Kinesics is the study of body movement and posture.[43] Like proxemics, kinesics is bound to culture. With this in mind, we can interpret some common U.S. gestures. Rubbing one's hands

kinesics The study of body movement and posture.

together while inhaling sharply indicates anticipation. Stress is indicated by balled fists, clenched teeth, hand wringing, and rubbing the temples. Nervousness may be indicated by drumming fingers, pacing, or jingling coins in one's pocket. Kinesics also includes insulting gestures like giving someone "the finger."

8-5c Facial and Eye Behavior

The face is a rich source of nonverbal communication. Facial expression and eye behavior are used to communicate an emotional state, reveal behavioral intentions, and cue the receiver. It may even give unintended clues to emotions the sender is trying to hide.[44] Unintended facial movements can undermine the illusion of truthfulness, especially in stressful situations.[45]

Culture, environment, and specific actors must be taken into consideration when interpreting smiles, frowns, raised eyebrows, and other expressions. One study of Japanese and U.S. students illustrated the point. The students were shown a stress-inducing film, and their facial expressions were videotaped. When alone, the students had almost identical expressions. When in the presence of others, however, the Japanese students masked their facial expressions of unpleasant feelings much better than the American students did.[46]

As mentioned earlier, eye contact can enhance reflective listening. Along with smiling, eye contact is an easy way to express honesty and positive emotion.[47] However, eye contact must be understood in a cultural context. A direct gaze indicates dedication, truthfulness, and forthrightness in the United States. The eyes not only communicate to another person, they are the pathways for receiving significant messages. What is seen cannot be unseen, which may be very troubling in traumatic contexts. However, seeing war traumas is not universally injurious psychologically. A person's organizational context can give meaning to what is seen, therefore determining in

FIGURE 8.3 SEATING DYNAMICS

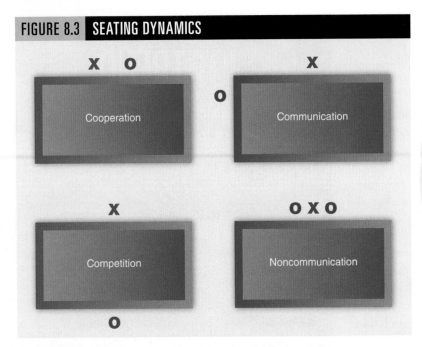

part whether the outcome is psychological growth or psychological injury.[48]

8-5d Paralanguage

Paralanguage consists of variations in speech, such as pitch, loudness, tempo, tone, duration, laughing, and crying.[49] People make assumptions about the communicator by deciphering paralanguage cues. A female's high-pitched, breathy voice may lead coworkers to stereotype her as a "dumb blonde." Rapid, loud speech may be taken as a sign of nervousness or anger. Interruptions such as "mmm" and "okay" may be used to speed up the speaker so that the receiver can get in a few words. Clucking of the tongue and the tsk-tsk sound are used to shame someone. All these cues relate to how something is said.

8-6 POSITIVE, HEALTHY COMMUNICATION

The absence of heartfelt communication in relationships leads to loneliness and social isolation. This condition has been labeled **communicative disease** by James Lynch.[50] Communicative disease has adverse effects on the heart and cardiovascular system and can ultimately lead to premature death. According to Lynch, the only cure for communicative disease is to reengage in thoughtful, heartwarming conversation with friends and loved ones. Yet, even though feelings may be more important

to the communication process than cognition, a stable balance between the two is integral. This balance between head and heart is achieved when a person displays positive emotional competence and can maintain a healthy internal conversation between his thoughts and emotions.

Positive, healthy communication is an important aspect of *working together*—that is, cooperating to reach a shared goal—in both the interpersonal and intrapersonal settings.[51] Such communication requires trust and truthfulness. However, it does not exclude honest competition within the workplace, which in fact is consistent with the concept of working together. Sincere, well-managed competition can bring out the best in all those involved.

Healthy communication is at the core of personal integrity and managerial success, as is evident in the lives of most successful executives, including those in the executive branch of the U.S. government.[52] President Ronald Reagan was nicknamed "the great communicator" for his ability to connect with the American people. He conveyed strong ethical character, personal integrity, and simplicity in his communication. Reagan exemplified Lynch's concept of heartfelt communication because his language in speeches and interviews seemed to stem from core values and sincere aspirations. Communication from the heart is communication anchored in personal integrity and ethical character.

Personal integrity is a product of emotional competence and a stable balance of head and heart, as mentioned earlier. Psychologist Karol Wasylyshyn has shown that one method of developing personal integrity is to coach an executive in developing her capacity to talk through challenging issues, both personally and professionally.[53] James Campbell Quick and Marilyn Macik-Frey developed a similar coaching program that works to cultivate executives' inner selves through deep, interpersonal communication.[54] This executive coaching model relies on what Lynch might call a "healing dialogue" between executive and coach. In addition to improving interpersonal communication between executives and employees, this model can enhance positive, healthy communication in a wider range of human relationships.

communicative disease
Loneliness and social isolation resulting from the absence of heartfelt communication in relationships.

8-7 COMMUNICATING THROUGH NEW TECHNOLOGIES AND SOCIAL MEDIA

Nonverbal behaviors can be important in establishing trust in working relationships, but modern technologies may challenge our ability to maintain that trust. Too much emphasis on technology tools in communication may have an adverse impact on rich interpersonal communication and relationships. On the positive side, lawyers and legal consultants use Facebook and Twitter to do background checks on potential jurors.[55] Facebook's Mark Zuckerberg wants the thirteen-year-old social network to play a larger role in tackling issues including terrorism, disease, and climate change.[56] Finally, information technology can encourage or discourage moral dialogue, and these types of conversations are central to addressing ethical issues at work.

8-7a Written Communication

Even though many organizations are working toward paperless offices and paperless interfaces with their customers, written communication is far from dead—many types of written communication are still necessary to business. Manuals and reports are generally the longest forms of written communication found in the office. Policy manuals are important in organizations because they establish guidelines for decision-making and codes of conduct. Operations and procedures manuals explain how to perform various tasks and resolve problems that may occur at work. Reports, such as annual company finance reports, may summarize the results of a committee's or department's work or provide information on progress toward certain objectives.

Letters and memorandums (memos) are briefer than manuals and reports and are more frequently used in larger organizations. Letters are used to communicate formally with individuals and businesses outside the organization. They vary substantially in length and topic. Memos are also used for formal, internal communication within an organization. They are sometimes used as historical records of specific events or occurrences that individuals within the organization can refer back to later.

The shortest kind of written communication is the form, which may be used to collect information inside or outside the organization.

HOT TREND

Donald Trump Tweets, Hard to Read

Donald Trump's use of tweets and social media upended previous presidential communication protocols and created significant challenges for a range of those attempting to interpret his message. This is especially true on Wall Street when presidential communication and behavior may have significant financial consequences. For example, when President Eisenhower was reported to have a heart attack, the stock market dropped 25 percent in a day. (It did recover, as did the president.) In the case of President Trump, traders have a difficult time knowing how to translate a Trump tweet into a buy or sell. In addition, big bank restrictions on social media placed some at a significant timing disadvantage in the market. Therefore, firms lifted the social media ban to give traders greater access to market-moving information, not just to Trump's tweets. In financial markets, there is real value in having access to the timeliest information, and social media may provide that timeliness.

SOURCE: C. Dieterich, B. Eisen, C. Dulane, and T. Demos, "How to Trade a Donald Trump Tweet," *Wall Street Journal*, 14 Jan. 2017.

8-7b Communication Technologies

Computer-mediated communication influences virtually all behavior in the work environment. E-mail, voice mail, instant messaging, and facsimile (fax) machines have been common in the business world for more than a decade. Recently, large information databases have become relatively commonplace. These databases provide a tremendous amount of information at the push of a button. An example of an information database is the electronic card catalog system used in university libraries throughout the world. These systems, sometimes linked with each other to form massive networks of data, store information about books' and journals' contents, distributions, and availability.

The newest technology to impact the work environment is the smartphone, which is nearly as ubiquitous at work as standard cell phones are in our personal lives. Smartphones combine the capabilities of advanced cell phones with computer-like applications and connectivity. Examples include the Apple iPhone, Samsung

2nix Studio/Shutterstock.com

of online communication can therefore depreciate the richness of personal interaction. Studies show that using these technologies may increase one's likelihood to flame—that is, to make rude, needlessly argumentative or obscene comments by means of computer-mediated communication.[57] Employees' interpersonal skills such as tact and graciousness subside online, and managers tend to be more blunt when using electronic media. People who normally participate in discussions quietly and politely may become more intimate, impolite, or uninhibited when they communicate using computer conferencing or electronic mail.[58]

Another effect of computer-mediated communication is that the nonverbal cues we rely on to decipher a message are absent. Gesturing, touching, facial expressions, and eye contact are not possible, so the emotional aspect of the message is difficult to discern. Even in teleconferencing, where users can see each others' faces, it is often difficult to perceive nonverbal cues.[59] Clues to power such as organizational position and departmental membership may not be available, so the social context of the exchange is often altered.

Communication via technology also changes group dynamics by equalizing participation. As a result, charismatic or higher-status members may lose some power.[60] Studies of group decision-making have shown that computer-mediated groups took longer to reach consensus than face-to-face groups. In addition, they were less cooperative, more uninhibited, and there was less influence from any one dominant person. Another study found that ICTs, especially e-mail and e-meetings, reduce tension caused by intercultural communication.[61] Groups that communicate via computer seem to experience a breakdown of social and organizational barriers.

The potential for information overload is particularly great when individuals are first introduced to new communication technologies. Both the sheer volume of information available and its speed of delivery are staggering. An individual can easily become overwhelmed by information and must learn to be selective about its access.

Galaxy devices, and the Google Pixel. The smartphone's introduction was particularly transformative for sales jobs involving travel. While they are widely used, not all reactions to smartphones are positive. For example, one oil producer did not want his daily commute disturbed by outside interference; he used driving as a time for thought and relaxation. Some estimates suggest that using a phone while driving is as risky as driving while under the influence of alcohol. For this reason, some states have outlawed cell phone talking or texting while driving a motor vehicle.

8-7c How Do Communication Technologies Affect Behavior?

Information communication technology (ICT) is an extensive category of new developments in interpersonal communication that allow fast, even immediate, access to information. E-mail, teleconferencing, and Wi-Fi are all classified as ICT. It can facilitate the instant exchange of information in minutes or seconds across geographic boundaries and time zones. With adequate ICT implementation, schedules and office hours become irrelevant in that considerations of time and distance that once beleaguered international and intranational business become far less important in the exchange. Given its impact on the way business is done, ICT has a significant influence on people's behavior.

Computer-mediated communication is impersonal in nature. Instant messaging, e-mail, and other forms

information communication technology (ICT) An extensive category of new developments in interpersonal communication that allow fast, even immediate, access to information.

New technologies encourage multitasking.

While modern ICT may make work easier and increase employees' productivity, it can also prove precarious for managers. In the wake of mobile e-mail, instant messaging, and texting, managers are more accessible to coworkers, subordinates, and the boss today than they've ever been. Researchers coined the term *workplace telepressure* to describe the pressure employees feel when they perceive asynchronous communication methods as having the same requirements for response time as synchronous communication methods have. Typically, sending an e-mail will give individuals flexibility and additional time to respond, unlike communicating face-to-face. Face-to-face communications require an immediate response. Viewing ICTs as having the same properties as face-to-face communication may cause employees to prioritize these communication methods similarly, making it more difficult for employees to disengage.[62]

Further, many new technologies encourage *polyphasic activity*, or multitasking (i.e., doing more than one thing at a time). Managers can simultaneously make phone calls, send instant messages, and work on memos. Polyphasic activity has its advantages in terms of getting more done—but only up to a point. Paying attention to more than one thing at a time splits a person's attention and may reduce effectiveness at individual tasks. At its extreme, focusing on multiple tasks can become a destructive habit, making it psychologically difficult for a person to let go of work.

Finally, new technologies may make people less patient with face-to-face communication. The speed of electronic media may lead to expectations of acceleration in all forms of communication. However, if they spend too much time communicating online, individuals may come to miss social interaction with others, and may find their social needs unmet.

Communicating via computer often means the end of small talk. In the name of speed, amenity is sacrificed for efficiency. Managers can use new technologies more efficiently and effectively by keeping in mind the suggestions presented in Table 8.2.

TABLE 8.2 — CHANNEL ETIQUETTE

Facebook	Twitter	YouTube	LinkedIn
> Take sensitive queries into a private sphere online or offline > Remember all wall posts are public; don't write anything there that is not for wider consumption. > Ensure that all updates are frequent and relevant but not too frequent. > Use language relevant to the channel and to the target demographics > Show appreciation, and acknowledge positive comments > Follow up and respond to any feedback.	> Begin with an introduction if used for outreach or active engagement > Develop a tone of voice and personality > Keep requests for re-tweets to a minimum. > Keep tweets as short and sweet as possible (less than 140 characters) > Avoid pure self-promotion. Twitter is a knowledge-sharing and conversation channel.	> Develop a thick skin. Many comments are not constructive, so do not take such comments to heart or argue; defensive reactions only fan the flames. > Use video replies because these can be powerful and a good way to spread a message > Acknowledge comments, and thank those who are being positive about a brand.	> Join groups and contribute information about relevant experience.. > Answer questions, and contribute to share pages and communities.. > Avoid asking for references unless the person is someone already known or if the company has genuinely delivered great service. > Support unsolicited contacts with a full explanation of who is contacting and why; don't assume that contacts will view the underlying profile.

STUDY TOOLS 8

LOCATED AT BACK OF THE TEXTBOOK

☐ Rip Out Chapter Review Card

LOCATED AT WWW.CENGAGE.COM/LOGIN

☐ Gain unique perspectives on key concepts with new Concept Clip videos in the e-book

☐ Review key term flashcards and create your own

☐ Increase your comprehension with online homework and quizzes

9 | Work Teams and Groups

LEARNING OBJECTIVES

9-1 Define group and work team.

9-2 Explain the benefits organizations and individuals derive from working in teams.

9-3 Identify the factors that influence group behavior.

9-4 Describe how groups form and develop.

9-5 Explain how task and maintenance functions influence group performance.

9-6 Discuss the factors that influence group effectiveness.

9-7 Describe how empowerment relates to self-managed teams.

9-8 Explain the importance of upper echelons and top management teams.

After finishing this chapter go to **PAGE 158** for **STUDY TOOLS**

9-1 GROUPS AND WORK TEAMS

A **group** is formed when two or more people have common interests, objectives, and continuing interaction. A **work team** is a group of people with complementary skills who are committed to a common mission. The early work group research focused on individuals within teams or on individual versus work team comparisons while more recent research in the past few decades focuses on the work team itself.[1] Groups emphasize individual leadership, personal accountability, and exclusive work products. Work teams emphasize shared leadership, mutual accountability, and collective work products.

Work teams are task-oriented groups, though in some organizations the word *team* has a negative connotation for union members. Work teams make valuable contributions to the organization and are important to the need satisfaction of members.

Several kinds of work teams exist. Some are like baseball teams in that members have set responsibilities, others are like football teams in that members have coordinated action, and still others are like doubles tennis teams in that members have primary yet flexible

Morsa Images/Digital Vision/Getty Images

responsibilities. Another analogy for work teams is that some operate like groundskeeping crews in that all members work synergistically toward a single goal.[2] All work teams need to attend to knowledge-based processes and interactions as well as contextual factors if they are to improvise effectively, such as in R&D environments.[3]

Teams and groups do not all work face-to-face. Advanced computer and telecommunications technologies enable organizations to be more flexible through the use of *virtual teams*.[4] Organizations use virtual teams to access expertise and the best employees around the world. Whether traditional or virtual, groups and teams continue to play a vital role in organizational behavior and performance at work.

9-2 WHY WORK TEAMS?

Teams are very useful in performing work that is complicated, fragmented, and/or more voluminous than one person can handle. Harold Geneen, while chairman of ITT, said, "If I had enough arms and legs and time, I'd do it all myself." Obviously, no one person in an organization can do everything by himself, not only because of

> **Work teams emphasize shared leadership, mutual accountability, and collective work products.**

the limitations of arms, legs, and time, but also expertise, knowledge, and other resources. However, individual limitations can be overcome through teamwork and collaboration. World-class U.S. corporations, such as Motorola Inc., are increasingly deploying work teams in their global affiliates to meet the competition and gain advantage.[5] Motorola's "Be Cool" team in the Philippines has a family atmosphere (and may even begin a meeting with a prayer) yet is committed to improving individual and team performance.

group Two or more people with common interests, objectives, and continuing interaction.

work team A group of people with complementary skills who are committed to a common mission, performance goals, and approach for which they hold themselves mutually accountable.

Integrated involvement in the workplace results in enjoyment of work and being valued for one's skills and abilities.

9-2a Benefits to Organizations

Teams make the most significant contributions to organizations when members can put aside individual interests in favor of unity. This joint action is called **teamwork**. Complex, collaborative work tasks and activities tend to require considerable amounts of teamwork. When knowledge, talent, and abilities are dispersed across numerous workers and require an integrated effort for task accomplishment, teamwork is often the only solution.

A recent movement toward team-oriented work environments has championed empowerment through collaboration rather than self-reliance and competition. Teams with experience working together may produce valuable innovations, and individual contributions within teams are valuable as well.[6] Larry Hirschhorn labeled this structure "the new team environment," founded on a significantly more empowered workforce in the industrial sectors of the American economy. (See Table 9.1 for a comparison of new and old environments.) In this new environment, teams must bring together members with different specialties and knowledge to work on complex problems. The ability to do so improves team performance and psychological well-being.[7]

9-2b Social Benefits to Individuals

On an individual level, team or group members derive benefits from the collective experience of teamwork. These individual benefits are best organized into two categories. One set of benefits accrues from achieving psychological intimacy, while the other comes from achieving integrated involvement.[8]

Psychological intimacy is emotional and psychological closeness to other team or group members. It results in feelings of affection and warmth, unconditional positive regard, opportunity for expression, security and emotional support, and nurturing. Failure to achieve psychological intimacy may result in feelings of emotional isolation and loneliness. This can be especially problematic for chief executives, who sometimes report experiencing loneliness at the top. However, although psychological intimacy is valuable for emotional health and well-being, it need not necessarily be achieved in the work setting. Many executives satisfy their need for intimacy with a rich home life.

Integrated involvement is closeness achieved through tasks and activities. It results in enjoyment of work, social identity and self-definition, being valued for one's skills and abilities, opportunities for power and influence, conditional positive regard, and support for one's beliefs and values. Failure to achieve integrated involvement may result in social isolation. Whereas psychological intimacy is based more in emotion, integrated involvement is based in behavior and activity. Integrated involvement contributes to social psychological health and well-being.

teamwork Joint action by a team of people in which individual interests are subordinated to team unity.

psychological intimacy Emotional and psychological closeness to other team or group members.

integrated involvement Closeness achieved through tasks and activities.

TABLE 9.1	NEW TEAM ENVIRONMENT VERSUS OLD WORK ENVIRONMENT	
New Team Environment	**Old Work Environment**
Person comes up with initiatives.	Person follows orders.
Team has considerable authority to chart its own steps.	Team depends on the manager to chart its course.
Members form a team because people learn to collaborate in the face of their emerging right to think for themselves. People both rock the boat and work together.	Members were a team because people conformed to direction set by the manager. No one rocked the boat.
People cooperate by using their thoughts and feelings. They link up through direct talk.	People cooperated by suppressing their thoughts and feelings. They wanted to get along.

SOURCE: L. Hirschhorn, *Managing in the New Team Environment: Skills, Tools, and Methods* (San Jose: Authors Choice Press). © 2002. Reprinted with permission.

9-3 GROUP BEHAVIOR

Group behavior has been a subject of interest in social psychology for a long time, and many different aspects of group behavior have been studied over the years. We now look at four of those aspects: norms of behavior, group cohesion, social loafing, and loss of individuality. Group behavior topics related to decision-making, such as polarization and groupthink, are addressed in Chapter 10.

9-3a Norms of Behavior

The standards that a work group uses to evaluate the behavior of its members are its **norms of behavior**. These norms may be written or unwritten, verbalized or not verbalized, implicit or explicit. As long as individual members of the group understand them, the norms can be effective in influencing behavior. They may specify what members of a group should do (such as a specified dress code) or not do (such as executives not behaving arrogantly with employees).

Norms may exist in any aspect of work group life. They may evolve informally or unconsciously, or they may arise in response to specific challenges, such as firefighters' disciplined behavior in responding to a three-alarm fire in a manner that protects the group.[9] *Morality norms* are more important than *competence norms* when it comes to making decisions about improving the status of one's work group.[10] *Performance norms* are among the most important group norms from the organization's perspective. Even when group members work in isolation on creative projects, they display conformity to group norms.[11] Group norms of cooperative behavior within a team can lead to members working for mutual benefit, which in turn facilitates team performance.[12] On the other hand, verbal expressions of negativity can be detrimental to team performance and a violation of group norms.[13] Organizational culture and corporate codes of ethics, such as Johnson & Johnson's credo (recall Figure 2.3), reflect behavioral norms expected within work groups. Finally, norms that create awareness of and help regulate emotions are critical to groups' effectiveness.[14]

9-3b Group Cohesion

The interpersonal glue that makes the members of a group stick together is **group cohesion**. Group cohesion can enhance job satisfaction for members and improve organizational productivity.[15] Highly cohesive groups are able to manage their membership better than work groups low in cohesion. In one study of 381 banking teams in Hong Kong and the United States, increased job complexity and task autonomy led to increased group cohesiveness, which translated into better performance.[16] A recent study found that when there is a fit between the group's values and those of the organization, groups will report more cohesion and exhibit higher levels of organizational citizenship behavior (OCB).[17] In addition to improved performance, highly cohesive groups can lead to the maintenance of close relationships among the members. We will discuss group cohesion in further detail when we examine the common characteristics of well-developed groups.

9-3c Social Loafing

Social loafing occurs when one group member comes to rely on the efforts of other group members and fails to contribute her own time, effort, thoughts, or other resources to a group.[18] This may create a real drag on the group's efforts and achievements. Some scholars argue that social loafing, also known as *free riding*, is a rational response to feelings of inequity or situations in which individual efforts are hard to observe. Team member personality factors may mitigate the negative effects of social loafing on team performance. Team members who possess high levels of conscientiousness and agreeableness tend to compensate for social loafers so that team performance is not reduced.[19] However, social loafing shortchanges the group, which loses potentially valuable resources possessed by individual members.[20]

One method for countering social loafing is a member self-evaluation system. If members must formally review their contributions to the group, they are less likely to loaf. Identifying individual contributions to the group product also counters loafing. If each group member is responsible for a specific input, an individual's failure to contribute will be noticed by everyone.

9-3d Loss of Individuality

Social loafing may be detrimental to group achievement, but it does not have the potentially explosive effects of. **Loss of individuality** is a social process through which group members lose self-awareness and its accompanying senses of accountability, inhibition, and responsibility for individual behavior.[21]

norms of behavior The standards that a work group uses to evaluate the behavior of its members.

group cohesion The interpersonal glue that makes members of a group stick together.

Social loafing The failure of a group member to contribute personal time, effort, thoughts, or other resources to the group.

loss of individuality A social process in which individualgroup members lose self-awareness and its accompanying sense of accountability, inhibition, and responsibility for individual behavior.

People may engage in morally reprehensible acts and even violent behavior as committed members of their group or organization when their individuality is lost. Loss of individuality was one of several contributing factors to the riot that destroyed sections of Los Angeles following the Rodney King verdict in April 1992. Yet loss of individuality is not always negative or destructive. The loosening of normal ego control mechanisms in the individual sometimes leads to prosocial behavior and even heroic acts in dangerous situations.[22]

9-4 GROUP FORMATION AND DEVELOPMENT

After its formation, a group goes through predictable. According to one group development model, a group addresses three issues: interpersonal issues, task issues, and authority issues.[23] The *interpersonal issues* include matters of trust, personal comfort, and security. Trust, in particular, is a key issue for any company in its working relationships. The *task issues* include the mission or purpose of the group, the methods the group employs, and the outcomes expected of the group. The *authority issues* include decisions about who is in charge, how power and influence are managed, and who has the right to tell whom to do what. This section addresses group formation, each stage of group development, and the characteristics of a mature group.

9-4a Group Formation

Formal and informal groups coalesce in organizations for different reasons. Formal groups are sometimes called *official* or *assigned* groups, and informal groups may be called *unofficial* or *emergent* groups. Formal groups such as project task forces, boards of directors, and temporary committees come together to perform specific tasks. An example of a formal group was the task force assembled by the University of Texas at Arlington to design the Goolsby Leadership Academy. Chaired by the associate dean of business, the task force was composed of seven members with diverse academic expertise and business experience. The task force established a five-year plan to inaugurate the select undergraduate program, which cultivates advanced leadership skills in its Goolsby Fellows and Associates.

Informal groups evolve in the work setting to gratify a variety of member needs not met by formal groups. For example, organizational members' inclusion and affirmation needs might be satisfied through informal athletic or specialized interest groups. Athletic teams representing a department, unit, or company may achieve semiofficial status, such as the AT&T National Running Team that uses the corporate logo on its race shirts.

Diversity is an important consideration in the formation of groups, as it can enhance performance and lead to new ways of thinking. Team members will defer more often to members with task-related diversity, such as education and tenure, for their expertise and perceived contributions to task performance.[24] One study of gender diversity among U.S. workers found that men and women in gender-balanced groups had higher job satisfaction than those in homogeneous groups.[25] Organizations have been challenged to blend culturally and linguistically diverse peoples into effective work groups since America's founding. This task was especially demanding during the early years of the 1900s, when waves of immigrant workers arrived from numerous European nations.

In addition to ethnic, gender, and cultural diversity, there is interpersonal diversity, which may be indicated by different needs for inclusion, control of people and events, and affirmation from others. Successful interpersonal relationships are made stronger when group members are emotionally intelligent.

9-4b Stages of Group Development

All groups go through stages of development, some more successfully than others. Mature groups are able to work through the interpersonal, task, and authority issues inevitable at the highest echelons of the business world. The path to maturity does not always go smoothly, however. Immature groups often experience personality clashes and other fault lines (i.e., potential breaking points within the group) at various stages of development.[26]

Bruce Tuckman's five-stage model of group development proposes that team behavior progresses through

10.2 Million Internal Messages Cannot Be Wrong

Whether newcomers will become part of the team can be hard to predict. So a team of California researchers used a novel approach to predict whether newcomers would adjust or exit a midsized technology firm. The team reviewed 10.2 million internal messages of 601 employees between 2009 and 2014. The new hires who assimilated used language skills similar to established employees. There were 64 language style categories considered, including curses, expressions of positive emotion, and use of concrete imagery. Fired recruits failed to accommodate their colleagues linguistically from the beginning. Quitters experienced decreased linguistic fit midway through their tenure. To becomes part of the team, it appears one needs to talk the talk of the members.

SOURCES J. S. Lublin, "The Telltale Sign a New Hire Isn't Fitting In," *Wall Street Journal*, 10 Jan. 2017.

five stages: forming, storming, norming, performing, and adjourning.[27] These stages and their properties are illustrated in Figure 9.1.

Dependence on guidance and direction is the defining characteristic of the *forming* stage. At this point, team members are unclear about individual roles and responsibilities and tend to rely heavily on the leader to answer questions about the team's purpose, objectives, and external relationships. Moving from this stage requires that team members feel they are part of the team. During this time, it may also be beneficial for leaders to encourage team members to get to know each other on an interpersonal level before focusing on task performance.[28]

Team members compete for position in the *storming* stage. As the name suggests, this is a period of considerable conflict as power struggles, cliques, and factions within the group begin to surface. Clarity of purpose increases, but uncertainties still exist. This is also the stage in which members assess one another with regard to trustworthiness, emotional comfort, and evaluative acceptance. The group leader's coaching style is key during this stage of development, as team members may challenge her. The supervisor's ability to control her own emotions is important during this phase.

Agreement and consensus are characteristic of team members in the *norming* stage. It is during this period that roles and responsibilities become clear and are accepted. The group's focus will turn from interpersonal relations to decision-making and task accomplishment. Insignificant decisions may be delegated to individuals or small teams, while larger decisions will be discussed and decided by the entire group. The group may address questions of authority, such as the necessity of a primary spokesperson and the delegation of roles within the group. Wallace Supply Company, an industrial distributor of pipes, valves, and fittings, found employee teams particularly valuable in raising and answering questions of authority.[29] The teams concluded that leadership ought to be facilitative and that certain responsibilities could be delegated to teams themselves.

As a team moves into the *performing* stage, it becomes more strategically aware of its mission and purpose. In this stage of development, the group has successfully worked through interpersonal, task, and authority issues and can stand on its own with little interference from the leader. Disagreements are resolved positively with necessary changes to structure and processes attended to by the team. A mature group is able to control its members through the judicious application of positive and negative sanctions based on the evaluation

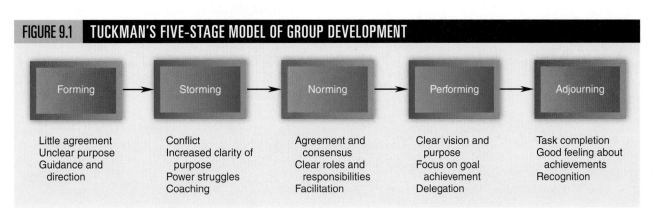

FIGURE 9.1   TUCKMAN'S FIVE-STAGE MODEL OF GROUP DEVELOPMENT

Forming	Storming	Norming	Performing	Adjourning
Little agreement Unclear purpose Guidance and direction	Conflict Increased clarity of purpose Power struggles Coaching	Agreement and consensus Clear roles and responsibilities Facilitation	Clear vision and purpose Focus on goal achievement Delegation	Task completion Good feeling about achievements Recognition

of specific behaviors. Recent research shows that evaluation biases stemming from liking someone operate in face-to-face groups but not in electronic groups, such as virtual teams.[30] Members at this stage do not need to be instructed but may ask for assistance from the leader in regard to personal or interpersonal development.

The final stage of group development is the *adjourning* stage. When the task is completed, everyone on the team can move on to new and different things. Team members retain a sense of accomplishment and feel good knowing that their purpose was fulfilled. The leader's role at this point is primarily to recognize the group's achievements. But unless the group is a task force or other informal team, most groups in organizations remain at the performing stage and do not disband as the adjourning stage suggests.

9-4c Punctuated Equilibrium Model

Though it is still highly cited in team and group research, Tuckman's model may be unrealistic from an organizational perspective. Research has shown that many teams experience relational conflicts at different times and in different contexts. Connie Gersick proposes that groups do not necessarily progress linearly from one step to another in a predetermined sequence but alternate between periods of inertia with little visible progress toward goal achievement. Progress is punctuated by bursts of energy as work groups develop. It is in these bursts that the majority of work is accomplished.[31] For example, a task force given nine months to complete a task may use the first four months to choose its norms, explore contextual issues, and determine how it will communicate. The final five months would then be dedicated to executing the task itself.

9-4d Characteristics of a Mature Group

A mature group has four characteristics: a clear purpose and mission, well-understood norms and standards of conduct, a high level of group cohesion, and a flexible status structure.

PURPOSE AND MISSION The group's purpose and mission may be assigned (as in the example of the Goolsby Leadership Academy task force) or emerge from within the group (as in the example of the AT&T National Running Team). In the case of an assigned mission, the group may embrace the mission as stated or reexamine, revise, or question it. The importance of mission is exemplified by IBM's Process Quality Management, which requires that a process team of no more than twelve people develop a clear understanding of the group's mission as the first step in the process.[32] The IBM approach demands that all members agree to go in the same direction. The mission statement is converted into a specific agenda, clear goals, and a set of critical success factors. Stating the purpose and mission in the form of specific goals enhances productivity and performance far more effectively than individual goal setting.[33]

BEHAVIORAL NORMS *Behavioral norms*, which evolve over time, are well-understood standards of behavior within a group.[34] They are benchmarks against which team members are evaluated by other team members. For example, team altruism is the result of norms established as a result of one or more individual team members engaging in altruistic behaviors, often with different motivations ranging from prosocial to impression management.[35] Although some norms become written rules, such as an attendance policy or an ethical code, other norms remain informal, such as dress codes and norms about after-hours socializing. Additionally, behavioral norms may evolve around performance and productivity.[36] For example, productivity norms

Shifting Norms from Competition to Collaboration

Star-driven work environments such as existed at Dana-Farber Cancer Institute often rest on competitive norms. Shifting norms of behavior is difficult and challenging. Shifting to a collaborative teamwork set of norms goes against the grain of specialists and experts. However, teamwork demands collaboration and cooperation. Dana-Farber created a sense of urgency and facilitated buy-in for the norm change by engaging the faculty stars in the strategic planning process for the entire institute. This drove a common purpose and mission, which then helped underpin the norm of collaboration. Smart collaboration was reinforced by giving the stars the quantitative evidence that collaboration works. In addition, they changed their stars' behavior by tweaking systems and structures that support the desired norms. Finally, providing stars with collaborative skills further embedded the new norm of collaboration. Shifting norms may be challenging, but it is doable.

SOURCE: H. K. Gardner, "Getting Your Stars to Collaborate," *Harvard Business Review*, January–February 2017, pp. 100–108.

can influence the performance of sports teams in office leagues as well as in the professional realm.[37]

A group's productivity norm may or may not be consistent with the organization's productivity standards. A high-performance team sets productivity standards above organizational expectations, average teams set productivity standards consistent with organizational expectations, and noncompliant or counterproductive teams set productivity standards below organizational expectations, sometimes with the intent of damaging the organization or creating change. Usually, however, behavioral norms affect organizational culture in a beneficial way for all.

GROUP COHESION Group cohesion enables a group to exercise effective control over its members in relation to its behavioral norms and standards. Mature teams have the capacity to share the deep acting strategies employed by individual team members, resulting in members behaving more similarly when expressing emotions.[38] Among the threats to a group's cohesion are goal conflict, unpleasant experiences, and domination of a subgroup. Groups with low levels of cohesion have greater difficulty exercising control over their members and enforcing their standards of behavior; hence, they are more vulnerable to such threats. Specifically, work-related tensions and anxieties decrease in highly cohesive teams and increase in teams low in cohesion, as depicted in Figure 9.2. This relationship suggests that cohesion has a calming effect on team members.

In addition, actual productivity was found to vary significantly less in highly

Prestigious groups such as the U.S. Navy Blue Angels are highly cohesive.

FIGURE 9.2 COHESIVENESS AND WORK-RELATED TENSION*

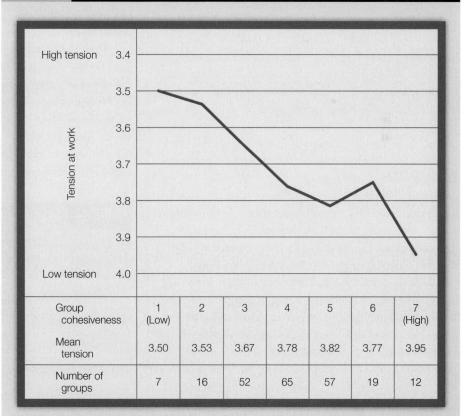

Group cohesiveness	1 (Low)	2	3	4	5	6	7 (High)
Mean tension	3.50	3.53	3.67	3.78	3.82	3.77	3.95
Number of groups	7	16	52	65	57	19	12

Note: Product–moment correlation is 0.28, and critical ratio is 4.20; the group cohesion–tension relationship is highly significant at the .001 level.

*The measure of tension at work is based on group mean response to the question "Does your work ever make you feel 'jumpy' or nervous?" A low numerical score represents relatively high tension.

SOURCE: S. E. Seashore, *Group Cohesiveness in the Industrial Work Group*, 1954. Research conducted by Stanley E. Seashore at the Institute for Social Research, University of Michigan. Reprinted by permission.

cohesive teams, making them much more predictable. The actual productivity levels, though, were primarily determined by the productivity norms within each work group. Thus, highly cohesive groups with high production standards were very productive, but highly cohesive groups with low productivity standards were unproductive despite their high level of cohesion. Nevertheless, no matter what the productivity was, member satisfaction, commitment, and communication were greater in highly cohesive groups.

Group cohesion is influenced by a number of factors, most notably time, size, the prestige of the team, external pressure, and internal competition. Usually cohesion evolves gradually throughout group development. In other words, the more time a group spends together, the more cohesive it will be. Also, smaller groups—those of five or seven members, for example—tend to be more cohesive than those of more than twenty-five, although cohesion does not decline much with size after forty or more members.

Prestige or social status may enhance a group's cohesion as well. More prestigious groups, such as the U.S. Air Force Thunderbirds or the U.S. Navy Blue Angels, are highly cohesive. However, even groups of very low prestige may be highly cohesive as a result of other factors tending toward cohesion, such as the aforementioned factors of longer time together and smaller group size. Finally, external pressure and internal competition are two other factors influencing group cohesion. Although the mechanics' union, pilots, and other internal constituencies at Eastern Airlines had various differences of opinion, they all pulled together in a cohesive fashion in resisting Frank Lorenzo when he came in to reshape the airline before its demise. Whereas external pressures tend to enhance it, internal competition usually decreases cohesion within a team. One study found that company-imposed pressure disrupted group cohesion by increasing internal competition and reducing cooperative interpersonal activity.[39]

STATUS STRUCTURE Status structure is the set of authority and task relations among a group's members. It may be hierarchical or egalitarian, depending on the group. Successful resolution of the authority issue within a team results in a well-understood status structure of leader–follower relationships. Where leadership problems arise, it is important to find solutions and build team leader effectiveness.[40] Although groups usually have just one leader, teams tend to share leadership. For example, one person may be the team's taskmaster, who sets the agenda, initiates much of the work activity, and ensures that the team meets its deadlines. Another team member may take a leadership role in maintaining effective interpersonal relationships in the group. Hence, shared leadership is very feasible in teams. An effective status structure results in role interrelatedness among group members.[41] Bill Perez and Bill Wrigley have promoted interrelatedness through a tag-team style of cooperation in leadership that has served the Wm. Wrigley Jr. Company well.

status structure The set of authority and task relations among a group's members.

task function An activity directly related to the effective completion of a team's work.

9-5 TASK AND MAINTENANCE FUNCTIONS

An effective group or team carries out various task functions to perform its work successfully and various maintenance functions to ensure member satisfaction and a sense of team spirit.[42] Teams that successfully fulfill these functions afford their members the potential for the social benefits of psychological intimacy and integrated involvement we discussed at the beginning of the chapter. Table 9.2 presents nine task and nine maintenance functions in teams or groups.

Task functions are those activities directly related to the effective completion of the team's work. For example, the task of initiating activity involves suggesting ideas, defining problems, and proposing approaches and/or solutions to problems. The task of seeking information involves asking for ideas, suggestions, information, or facts. A study of security analysts found that the quality of colleagues' work helped to improve and maintain the quality of individual

TABLE 9.2	TASK AND MAINTENANCE FUNCTIONS IN TEAMS OR GROUPS	
Task Functions	**Maintenance Functions**
Initiating activities	Supporting others
Seeking information	Following others' leads
Giving information	Gatekeeping communication
Elaborating concepts	Setting standards
Coordinating activities	Expressing member feelings
Summarizing ideas	Testing group decisions
Testing ideas	Consensus testing
Evaluating effectiveness	Harmonizing conflict
Diagnosing problems	Reducing tension

Humor and joking behavior have been found to enhance social relationships in work groups.

member performance.[43] Effective teams have members who fulfill various task functions as they are required.

Different task functions vary in importance throughout the life cycle of a group. For example, during the engineering test periods for new technologies, the engineering team needs members who focus on testing the practical applications of suggestions and those who diagnose problems and suggest solutions. The effective use of task functions leads to the success of the group. In one case, the successful initiation and coordination of an emergency room team's activities by the senior resident saved the life of a knife wound victim.[44] The victim was stabbed one-quarter inch below the heart, and the team acted quickly to stem the bleeding, begin intravenous fluids, and monitor the victim's vital signs. A recent study found that team member familiarity increases team performance up to a point by reducing team coordination errors (TCEs). Too much team familiarity may lead to increased TCEs as teams begin to rely on habitual routines and implicit coordination rather than explicit coordination methods. The relationship between team familiarity and the occurrence of TCEs is moderated by leader experience.[45]

Maintenance functions are those activities essential to the effective, satisfying interpersonal relationships within a group or team. Following another group member's lead may be as important as being a leader. Communication gatekeepers within a group ensure balanced contributions from all members. Because task activities build tension within teams or groups, tension-reduction activities are important to drain off negative or destructive feelings. In a study of twenty-five work groups over a five-year period, humor and joking behavior were found to enhance the social relationships in the groups.[46] The researchers concluded that performance improvements in the twenty-five groups indirectly resulted from improved relationships attributable to the humor and joking behaviors. Maintenance functions enhance togetherness, cooperation, and teamwork, enabling members to achieve psychological intimacy while furthering the success of the team. Emotional competencies such as empathy self-control are beneficial for maintaining group relationships. Jody Grant's supportive attitude and comfortable demeanor as chair and CEO of Texas Capital Bancshares enabled him to build a vibrant bank in the aftermath of the great Texas banking crash. Grant was respected for his expertise *and* his ability to build relationships. Both task and maintenance functions are important for successful groups and teams.

9-6 FACTORS THAT INFLUENCE GROUP EFFECTIVENESS

Work team effectiveness in the new team environment requires management's attention to both work team structure and work team process.[47] In addition to how the team is structured and what the team does, diversity and creativity are emerging as two areas with significant impact on team performance.

9-6a Work Team Structure

Work team structure issues include goals and objectives, operating guidelines, performance measures, and role specification. A work team's goals and objectives specify what must be achieved, while the operating guidelines set the organizational boundaries and decision-making limits within which the team must function. The goal-setting process discussed in Chapter 6 applies to work teams, too. In addition to these two structural elements, the work team needs to know what performance measures are being used to assess its task accomplishment. For example, a medical emergency team's performance measures might include the success rate in saving critically injured patients and

> **maintenance function** An activity essential to effective, satisfying interpersonal relationships within a team or group.

the average number of hours a patient is in the emergency room before being transferred to a hospital bed.

Finally, work team structure requires a clearly specified set of roles for the executives and managers who oversee the work of the team, for the work team leaders who exercise influence over team members, and for team members. These role specifications should include information about required role behaviors, such as decision-making and task performance, as well as restrictions or limits on role behaviors, such as the limitations on managerial interventions in work team activities and decision-making. Expectations as well as experience may be especially important for newcomer role performance in work teams.[48]

9-6b Work Team Process

Work team process is the second important dimension of effectiveness. Two of the important process issues in work teams are the managing of cooperative behaviors and the managing of competitive behaviors. Both sets of behaviors are helpful in task accomplishment, and they should be viewed as complementary. *Cooperative teamwork skills* include open communication, trust, personal integrity, positive interdependence, and mutual support. On the other hand, *positive competitive teamwork skills* include the ability to enjoy competition, play fair, and be a good winner or loser; to have access to information for monitoring where the team and members are in the competition; and not to overgeneralize or exaggerate the results of any specific competition. In a study of reward structures in seventy-five four-member teams, competitive rewards enhanced speed of performance, while cooperative rewards enhanced accuracy of performance.[49]

Work team process issues have be-come more complex in the global workplace, where teams are composed of members from many cultures and backgrounds. This complexity is increased by the presence of virtual work teams operating on the global landscape. In addition to the process issues of cooperation, competition, and diversity, three other process issues are related to topics we discuss elsewhere in the text. These are empowerment, which is discussed in the next major section of this chapter; team decision-making, which is discussed in Chapter 10; and conflict management and resolution, which are discussed in Chapter 13.

9-6c Diversity

Diversity also plays a large role in how effective work groups and teams are. Diversity in a group is healthy, and members may contribute to the collective effort through one of four basic styles: the contributor, the collaborator, the communicator, or the challenger.[50] The *contributor* is data driven, supplies necessary information, and adheres to high performance standards. The *collaborator* sees the big picture and is able to keep a constant focus on the mission and urge other members to join efforts for mission accomplishment. The *communicator* listens well, facilitates the group's process, and humanizes the collective effort. The *challenger* is the devil's advocate who questions everything from the group's mission, purpose, and methods to its ethics. Members may exhibit one or more of these four basic styles over a period of time. In addition, an effective group must have an *integrator*, especially when the group is a cross-functional one, where different perspectives carry the seeds of conflict.[51] However, cross-functional teams are not necessarily a problem. Effectively managing cross-functional teams of artists, designers, printers, and financial experts enabled Hallmark Cards to cut its new product development time in half.[52]

DISSIMILARITY Recent research in diversity has focused on the effect of dissimilarity within a team. This issue is often studied in relation to social identity theory and self-categorization theory. Since creativity concerns new ideas, some amount of dissimilarity is necessary within a team in order for creativity, novelty, and innovation to blossom. Although creativity is discussed in some detail in Chapter 10, we address it briefly here in the context of teams.

We defined diversity in Chapter 1 in terms of individual differences. Recent relational demography research finds that demographic dissimilarity influences employees' absenteeism, commitment, turnover intentions, beliefs, work group relationships, self-esteem, and OCB.[53] Thus, dissimilarity may have positive or negative effects in teams and on team members. Racial dissimilarity may also impact the extent to which team members communicate with each other and develop a sense of group identity.[54] While value dissimilarity may be positively related to task and relationship conflict, it is negatively related to team involvement.[55] This fact highlights the importance of managing dissimilarity in teams, being open to diversity, and turning conflicts about ideas into positive outcomes.

Functional background is one way to look at dissimilarity in teams. One study of 262 professionals in thirty-seven cross-functional teams found that promoting social identification with functional background helped individuals perform better as team members.[56] Another study of multifunctional management teams in a *Fortune* 100 company found that functional background predicted team involvement.[57] Finally, in a slightly different study of 129 members on twenty multidisciplinary project teams,

Diversity in a group is healthy.

informational dissimilarity had no adverse effects when there was member task and goal congruence.[58]

STRUCTURAL DIVERSITY Structural diversity concerns the number of *structural holes*, or disconnections between members, within a work team. One research study examined structural diversity and performance of nineteen teams in a wood-products company. The investigators were interested in demographic diversity among team members as well as the structural diversity, or presence of structural holes, in the teams. Neither race nor gender was a demographic factor that influenced the proportion of structural holes within the teams. However, age diversity significantly improved structural integrity. Hence, greater variance in age within a team leads to more member-to-member connections and fewer member-to-member disconnections.

Are disconnections of team members good or bad for the team? What are the consequences of having more or fewer structural holes between team members? Teams with few structural holes may have problems with creativity, while teams with a high proportion of structural holes may have difficulty coordinating. These observations led the researchers to conclude that there is a curvilinear relationship between structural diversity, or structural integrity, and team performance. The teams with moderate structural diversity achieve the best performance. This research is important because it points out that managers should look at the overall structure and network of relationships within their work teams in addition to the individual characteristics of team members in attempting to achieve the best performance from these teams.[59]

9-6d Creativity

Creativity is often thought of in an individual context rather than a team context. However, there is such a thing as team creativity. In a study of fifty-four research and development teams, team creativity scores were explained by aggregation processes across both people and time.[60] Finding creative solutions to workplace problems may require teamwork, collaboration, and a set of seven practices for effectively reframing the problem, as seen in the accompanying Hot Trend.

Some think that the deck is stacked against teams as agents of creativity. Leigh Thompson, a management and organizations professor at Northwestern University, thinks differently and suggests that team creativity and divergent thinking can be enhanced through greater diversity in teams, electronic brainstorming, training facilitators, membership change in teams, and building a playground.[61] Human capital diversity in teams can be a source of team social capital, which has the potential to enhance the level of team creativity through increased access to a variety of individuals with varying knowledge

Creative Solutions for Problems Using Seven Practices

Even for a team, some workplace problems seem intractable and difficult. The way to creatively solve these problems may be through reframing the problem. Here are seven practices that can be used to find creative solutions after reframing the problem. (1) Establish legitimacy with the team to show that you know what you are talking about. (2). Bring outsiders into the discussion who disrupt established thinking. (3) Get people's definitions in writing. (4) Ask what's missing. (5) Consider multiple categories. (6) Analyze positive exceptions. (7) Question the objective. The purpose of reframing the problem is to enable team members to come at the problem in new and fresh ways.

SOURCE: T. Wedell-Wedellsborg, "Are You Solving the Right Problems?" *Harvard Business Review*, January–February 2017, pp. 76–83.

and experiences.[62] These practices can overcome social loafing, conformity, and downward norm setting in teams and organizations. Team members might exercise care in timing the insertion of their novel ideas into the team process so as to maximize the positive impact and benefits.[63]

9-7 EMPOWERMENT AND SELF-MANAGED TEAMS

To be successful, teams require a culture of empowerment in the organization in which they are implemented. This is especially true of *self-managed teams*, discussed shortly, which are designed to take on responsibilities and address issues traditionally reserved for management.

As an individual attribute, empowering leadership positively affects employee psychological empowerment, thus reducing employee cynicism and time theft, when the quality of the relationship with the boss is a good one.[64] As an organizational culture attribute, empowerment encourages participation, an essential ingredient for teamwork.[65] *Quality action teams (QATs)* at FedEx are the primary *quality improvement process (QIP)* technique used by the company to engage management and hourly employees in four- to ten-member problem-solving teams.[66] The teams are empowered to act and solve problems as specific as

charting the best route from the Phoenix airport to the local distribution center or as global as making major software enhancements to the online package-tracking system.

Empowerment may give employees the power of a lightning strike, but empowered employees must be properly focused through careful planning and preparation before they strike.[67]

To be successful, teams require a culture of empowerment in the organization in which they are implemented. Not all companies empower employees, as seen in the boxed feature on this page.

9-7a Empowerment Skills

Empowerment through employee self-management is an alternative to empowerment through teamwork.[68] Whether through self-management or teamwork, empowerment requires the development of certain skills if it is to be enacted effectively.

Competence skills are the first set of skills required for empowerment. Mastery and experience in one's chosen discipline and profession provide an essential foundation for empowerment. New employees and trainees should experience only limited empowerment until they demonstrate the capacity to accept more responsibility.

Empowerment also requires certain *process skills*. The most critical process skills include negotiating skills,

Challenging the Company May Disempower Workers

Employers who experience labor disputes with groups of workers are increasingly requiring each employee to submit to individual arbitration. This has placed two federal laws in conflict: the National Labor Relations Act and the Federal Arbitration Act. The former allows workers to take collective action for mutual aid and protection. In other words, the Labor Act empowers employees to act in their collective best interests when they experience a dispute with the company. The Arbitration Act disempowers employees by denying them mutual aid and protection. The lower courts in the United States are divided on whether arbitration clauses are enforceable in a labor context. Therefore, the Supreme Court is taking several cases that will help resolve the inherent conflict in the federal acts. The power between management and labor is in the balance.

SOURCE: B. Kendall and J. Bravin, "Supreme Court to Decide Whether Employers Can Prohibit Groups of Workers from Suing," *Wall Street Journal,* 13 Jan. 2017.

Scott Maxwell LuMaxArt/Shutterstock.com

especially with allies, opponents, and adversaries.[69] Allies are the easiest people to negotiate with because they agree with you about the team's mission and you can trust their actions and behavior. Opponents require a different negotiating strategy; although you can predict their actions and behavior, they do not agree with your concept of the team's mission. Adversaries are dangerous, difficult people to negotiate with because you cannot predict their actions or behaviors and they do not agree with your concept of the team's mission.

A third set of empowerment skills involves the development of *cooperative and helping behaviors*.[70] Cooperative people engage in encouraging, helpful behavior to maximize the gains for everyone on the team. The alternative orientations to cooperation are competitive, individualistic, and egalitarian approaches. *Competitive people* are motivated to maximize their personal gains regardless of the expense to other people. This motivation can be very counterproductive to the team. *Individualistic people* are motivated to act autonomously, though not necessarily to maximize their personal gains. They are less prone to contribute to the efforts of the team. *Egalitarian people* are motivated to equalize the outcomes for each team member, which may or may not be beneficial to the team's well-being. Paradoxically, the team members who need the most help often get the least help because helping behaviors often target the most expert team members, a dynamic that actually compromises overall team performance.[71]

Communication skills are a final set of essential empowerment skills.[72] These skills include self-expression skills and skills in reflective listening. Empowerment cannot occur in a team unless members are able to express themselves in emotionally intelligent ways as well as listen carefully to one another.

9-7b Self-Managed Teams

Self-managed teams, also called *self-directed teams* or *autonomous work groups*, are teams that make decisions that were once reserved for managers. Self-managed teams are one way to implement empowerment in organizations. Even though self-managed teams are self-directed, that fact does not negate the influence of managers. In fact, managers have an important role in providing leadership and influence.[73] There is strong support for the use of soft-influence tactics in managers' communication with self-directed teams, which yields more positive results.[74]

A one-year study of self-managed teams suggests that they have a positive impact on employee attitudes but not on absenteeism or turnover.[75] Evaluative research is helpful in achieving a better understanding of this relatively

> **self-managed team** A team that makes decisions that were once reserved for managers.

new way of approaching teamwork and the design of work. Such research helps establish expectations for self-managed teams. Nevertheless, there are risks, such as groupthink in self-managed teams, that must be prevented or managed if the team is to achieve full development and function.[76]

It is noteworthy that one evaluation of empowerment, teams, and *Total Quality Management (TQM)* programs found that companies associated with these popular management techniques did not have higher economic performance.[77] Other evaluations of self-managed teams are more positive. Southwest Industries, a high-technology aerospace manufacturing firm, embarked on a major internal reorganization in the early 1990s that included the creation of self-managed teams to fit its high-technology production process. Southwest's team approach resulted in a 30 percent increase in shipments, a 30 percent decrease in lead time, a 40 percent decrease in total inventory, a decrease in machinery downtime, and almost a one-third decrease in production costs.[78] An overall positive history has resulted in U.S.-based multinational corporations increasingly using self-managed teams in their global operations.

9-8 UPPER ECHELONS: TEAMS AT THE TOP

Self-managed teams at the top of the organization—top-level executive teams—are referred to as **upper echelons**. Organizations are often a reflection of these upper echelons.[79] *Upper echelon theory* argues that the background

upper echelon A top-level executive team in an organization.

characteristics of the top management team can predict organizational characteristics and set standards for values, competence, ethics, and unique characteristics throughout the organization. In addition, the distributed cognition and transactive memory systems in top teams affect the ability of the organization to be both explorative with regard to the future and exploitive of present opportunities.[80] The ability to exert power and influence throughout the entire organization makes the top management team a key to the organization's success. This ability may be compromised if the top team sends mixed signals about teamwork and if executive pay systems foster competition, politics, and individualism.[81]

For example, when Lee Iacocca became CEO at the Chrysler Corporation, his top management team was assembled to bring about strategic realignment within the corporation by building on Chrysler's historical engineering strength. The dramatic success of Chrysler during the early 1980s was followed by struggle and accommodation during the late 1980s. This raises the question of how long a CEO and the top management team can sustain organizational success.

Hambrick and Fukutomi addressed this question by examining the dynamic relationship between a CEO's tenure and the success of the organization.[82] They found five *seasons* in a CEO's tenure: (1) response to a mandate, (2) experimentation, (3) selection of an enduring theme, (4) convergence, and (5) dysfunction. A summary of each season is shown in Table 9.3. All else being equal, the seasons model has significant implications for organizational performance. Specifically, organizational performance increases during a CEO's tenure to a peak, after which performance declines. This relationship is depicted in Figure 9.3. The peak has been found to come at about seven years—somewhere in the middle of the executive's seasons. As indicated by the dotted lines in the figure, the peak may be extended, depending on several factors, such as diversity in the executive's support team.

9-8a Diversity at the Top

From an organizational health standpoint, diversity and depth in the top management team enhance the CEO's well-being.[83] From a performance standpoint, the CEO's top management team can influence the timing of the performance peak, the degree of dysfunction during the closing season of the CEO's tenure, and the rate of decline in organizational performance. Thus, diversity and heterogeneity in the top management team help sustain high levels of organizational performance at the peak and help maintain the CEO's vitality. A study of 207

TABLE 9.3	THE FIVE SEASONS OF A CEO'S TENURE				
	1	2	3	4	5
Critical CEO Characteristics	**Response to Mandate**	**Experimentation**	**Selection of an Enduring Theme**	**Convergence**	**Dysfunction**
COMMITMENT TO A PARADIGM	Moderately strong	Could be strong or weak	Moderately strong	Strong; increasing	Very strong
TASK KNOWLEDGE	Low but rapidly increasing	Moderate; somewhat increasing	High; slightly increasing	High; slightly increasing	High; slightly increasing
INFORMATION DIVERSITY	Many sources; unfiltered	Many sources but increasingly unfiltered	Fewer sources; moderately filtered	Few sources; highly filtered	Very few sources; highly filtered
TASK INTEREST	High	High	Moderately high	Moderately high but diminishing	Moderately low and diminishing
POWER	Low; increasing	Moderate; increasing	Moderate; increasing	Strong; increasing	Very strong; increasing

SOURCE: D. Hambrick and G. D. S. Fukutomi, "The Seasons of a CEO's Tenure," *Academy of Management Review* (1991): 729. Permission conveyed through Copyright Clearance Center, Inc.

U.S. firms in eleven industries found that functional diversity of top management teams had a positive effect on firm performance as the proportion of leaders in the same location increased.[84]

The presence of a so-called wild turkey in the top management team can be a particularly positive force. The wild turkey is a devil's advocate who challenges the thinking of the CEO and other top executives and provides a counterpoint during debates. If not shouted down or inhibited, the wild turkey helps the CEO and the team sustain peak performance and retard the CEO's dysfunction and decline. For example, former Secretary of State Colin Powell enhanced President George W. Bush's administration by exercising an independent voice. Often taking a more moderate position on policy issues than either the secretary of defense or the vice president, Powell brought variance and value to President Bush's administration.

Leaders must develop communication strategies to bring together team members who are functionally, intellectually, demographically, and temperamentally diverse

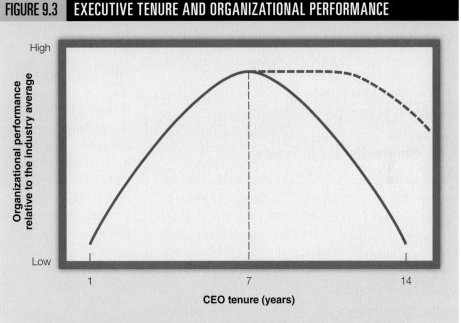

FIGURE 9.3 EXECUTIVE TENURE AND ORGANIZATIONAL PERFORMANCE

SOURCE: D. Hambrick, "The Seasons of an Executive's Tenure," keynote address, the Sixth Annual Texas Conference on Organizations, Lago Vista, Texas, April 1991.

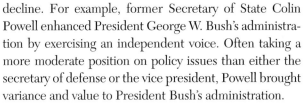

Most organizations report benefits from increased diversity.

so that they can act in ways that complement one another. It is out of dissimilarity that strength is developed, and it is out of similarity that connections are built. Therefore, top management should strive for a balance of dissimilarity and similarity within work teams. Keeping top teams working together requires attention to multiple concurrent pay structures to avoid undesired top-team turnover.[85]

We conclude that the leadership, composition, and dynamics of the top management team have an important influence on the organization's performance, leading, in some cases, to a change from having only one CEO to having more than one. While more common in Europe than in the United States, a historical U.S. example of a co-CEO arrangement includes a three-member team created by Walter Wriston while he was chairman at Citicorp (now part of Citigroup).

9-8b Multicultural Top Teams

Homogeneous groups, in which all members share similar backgrounds, are giving way to *token groups*, in which all but one member come from the same background; *bicultural groups*, in which two or more members represent each of two distinct cultures; and *multicultural groups*,

in which members represent three or more ethnic backgrounds.[86] On the negative side, diversity within a group may increase the uncertainty, complexity, and inherent confusion in group processes, making it more difficult for the group to achieve its full productivity.[87] On the positive side, most organizations report benefits from increased diversity, such as Merck, which attributes its long-term success to its leadership model that promotes diversity. Former chair, President, and CEO Ray Gilmartin values diversity in Merck's top management team because he believes that it sparks innovation when employees with different perspectives work together to offer solutions. Diversities of age and educational specialization within top management teams were found in other studies to have a positive effect on team performance, especially when members needed to participate in cognitive tasks.[88] One study found that the PERFORMANCE of top management teams was greatly increased when the CEO had numerous shared experiences with executives from other companies and cultures.[89] The advantages of culturally diverse groups appear to include the generation of more and better ideas while limiting the risk of groupthink, to be discussed in Chapter 10.

> The wild turkey is a devil's advocate who challenges the thinking of the CEO and provides a counterpoint during debates.

Mike Neale/Shutterstock.com

STUDY TOOLS 9

LOCATED AT BACK OF THE TEXTBOOK
- ☐ Rip out chapter review card

LOCATED AT WWW.CENGAGE.COM/LOGIN
- ☐ Gain unique perspectives on key concepts with new Concept Clip videos in the e-book
- ☐ Review key term flashcards and create your own
- ☐ Increase your comprehension with online homework and quizzes

ORGB
ONLINE

PREPARE FOR TESTS ON
THE STUDYBOARD!

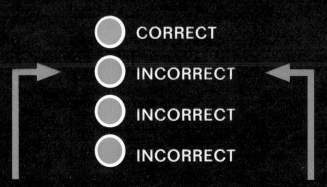

○ CORRECT
○ INCORRECT
○ INCORRECT
○ INCORRECT

**Personalize Quizzes
from Your StudyBits**

**Take Practice
Quizzes by Chapter**

CHAPTER QUIZZES
▶ Chapter 1
Chapter 2
Chapter 3
Chapter 4

4LTR
PRESS

Access ORGB ONLINE at www.cengagebrain.com

10 | Decision Making by Individuals and Groups

LEARNING OBJECTIVES

10-1 Identify the steps in the decision-making process.

10-2 Describe various models of decision making.

10-3 Discuss the individual influences that affect decision making.

10-4 Explain how groups make decisions.

10-5 Describe the role culture plays in decision making.

10-6 Explain how organizations can improve the quality of decisions through participation.

Morsa Images/DigitalVision/Getty Images

After finishing this chapter go to **PAGE 178** for **STUDY TOOLS**

10-1 THE DECISION-MAKING PROCESS

Decision making is a critical activity in the lives of managers. The decisions a manager faces can range from very simple, routine matters for which the manager has an established decision rule (**programmed decisions**) to new and complex decisions that require creative solutions (**nonprogrammed decisions**).[1] Scheduling lunch hours for one's work group, for example, is a programmed decision. The manager performs this programmed decision activity daily, using an established procedure with the same clear goal in mind each time. In contrast, decisions like buying out another company are nonprogrammed, providing a unique, unstructured situation and requiring considerable judgment. Regardless of the type of

programmed decision A simple, routine matter for which a manager has an established decision rule.

nonprogrammed decision A new, complex decision that requires a creative solution.

decision made, it is helpful to understand as much as possible about how individuals and groups make decisions.

Decision making is a process involving a series of steps, as shown in Figure 10.1. The first step is recognizing the problem; that is, the manager realizes that a decision must be made. Identifying the real problem is important; otherwise, the manager may be reacting to symptoms rather than dealing with the root cause of the problem. Next, a manager must identify the objective of the decision. In other words, the manager must determine what is to be accomplished by the decision. The third step in the decision-making process is gathering information relevant to the problem. The manager must accumulate sufficient information about why the problem occurred. This involves conducting a thorough diagnosis of the situation and going on a fact-finding mission.

The fourth step is listing and evaluating alternative courses of action. During this step, a thorough "what-if" analysis should be conducted to determine

> The first step is recognizing the problem; that is, the manager realizes that a decision must be made.

the various factors that could influence the outcome. It is important to generate a wide range of options and creative solutions in order to be able to move on to the next step. Next, the manager selects the alternative that best meets the decision objective. If the problem has been diagnosed correctly and sufficient alternatives have been identified, this step is much easier. After the solution is implemented, the situation must then be monitored to see whether the decision met its

Zingerman's Deli Grows but Stays Local

The owners of Ann Arbor, Michigan–based Zingerman's Deli had a lot of success in their first ten years and faced a decision on how to grow. Should they franchise? They decided against franchising because they would lose control and, more importantly, what they loved about their business was the local relationships they developed. Instead, they took a long look at what they were good at: fresh bread, so they started a bakehouse; coffee, so they created a coffee-roasting company; ice cream and cheese, so a creamery was started; great food, so they started a dine-in restaurant. And finally, they had great customer service, so they started a training module for independent businesses in the area. The result of the decision to stay local is nine separate local businesses, each with its own partnership. The partners meet weekly to make decisions. Staying local has worked for Zingerman's, with 550 jobs created in Ann Arbor and sales of $40 million per year.

Opportunities for expansion are always presenting themselves, and the founders struggle with the decision. There are opportunities to open Zingerman's cafes in prime airport locations. Is it feasible to keep Zingerman's quality and uniqueness in an airport store? So far, the founders are split on the decision.

SOURCES: www.zingermansdeli.com; M. F. Dunbar, "Interview with Michael Shuman," *Conscious Company* 1 (2015): 45–47; B. Burlingham, "Decades Later, the Owners of Ann Arbor's Iconic Zingerman's Are Still at Odds Over Expansion," *Forbes,* November 8, 2016, accessed at https://www.forbes.com/sites/boburlingham/2016/10/20/what-price-growth/#5d1fedc832e8

FIGURE 10.1 — THE DECISION-MAKING PROCESS

Recognize the problem and the need for a decision.

↓

Identify the objective of the decision.

↓

Gather and evaluate data and diagnose the situation.

↓

List and evaluate alternatives.

↓

Select the best course of action.

↓

Implement the decision.

↓

Gather feedback.

↓

Follow up.

---

objective. Consistent monitoring and periodic feedback are essential parts of the follow-up process.

Decision making can be stressful. Managers must make decisions with significant risk and uncertainty, and often without all of the necessary information. They must trust and rely on others in their decision-making process, yet they are ultimately responsible for the final decision. Sometimes decisions are painful and involve exiting businesses, firing people, and admitting wrong.

Blue Man Group has a history of making effective decisions. Its theatrical productions blend comedy, music, and multimedia in a unique brand of entertainment. It has grown wildly famous and successful by making sound business choices, even though none of the founders has any formal training in music, acting, or business. The group has turned down offers to sell credit cards, soft drinks, breath mints, and paint, all related to the color blue. With each new opportunity, the three founders use the same evaluation: "Okay, that's all good and well, that's a nice thought—but is it Blue Man?" The group has also completed a detailed 132-page operating manual, a task many businesses never complete. Finally, the founders make decisions by unanimous agreement.[2]

> **effective decision** A timely decision that meets a desired objective and is acceptable to those individuals affected by it.

10-2 MODELS AND LIMITS OF DECISION MAKING

The success of any organization depends on managers' abilities to make **effective decisions**. An effective decision is timely, is acceptable to the individuals affected by it, and meets the desired objective.[3] This section describes three models of decision making: the rational model, the bounded rationality model, and the Z model. The section will conclude with a discussion of the limits of decision-making techniques.

10-2a Rational Model

Rationality refers to a logical, step-by-step approach to decision making with a thorough analysis of alternatives and their consequences. The *rational model* of decision making comes from classic economic theory and assumes the following:

1. The outcome will be completely rational.
2. The decision maker has a consistent system of preferences, which is used to choose the best alternative.
3. The decision maker is aware of all the possible alternatives.
4. The decision maker can calculate the probability of success for each alternative.[4]

In the rational model, the decision maker strives to *optimize*, that is, to select the best possible alternative.

Given the assumptions of the rational model, it is unrealistic. There are time constraints and limits to human knowledge and information-processing capabilities. In addition, a manager's preferences and needs change often. The rational model is thus an ideal that managers strive for in making decisions, and it captures the way a decision should be made, but it does not reflect the reality of managerial decision making.[5]

10-2b Bounded Rationality Model

Recognizing the deficiencies of the rational model, Herbert Simon suggested that there are limits on how rational a decision maker can actually be. His decision theory, the *bounded rationality model*, earned a

Managers often sacrifice because of time constraints.

Nobel Prize in economics in 1978. Simon's theory rests on the idea that there are constraints that force a decision maker to be less than completely rational. The bounded rationality model has four assumptions:

1. Managers select the first alternative that is satisfactory.
2. Managers recognize that their conception of the world is simple.
3. Managers are comfortable making decisions without determining all the alternatives.
4. Managers make decisions by rules of thumb, or heuristics.

Bounded rationality assumes that managers **satisfice**; that is, they select the first alternative that is "good enough," because the costs of optimizing in terms of time and effort are too great.[6] Further, the theory assumes that managers develop shortcuts, called **heuristics**, to make decisions in order to save mental activity. Heuristics are rules of thumb that allow managers to make decisions based on what has worked in past experiences.

Does the bounded rationality model portray the managerial decision process more realistically? Research indicates that it does. One of the reasons managers face limits to their rationality is that they must make decisions under risk and time pressure. The situation they find themselves in is highly uncertain, and the probability of success is not known.

Herbert Simon felt his theory would be incomplete until the role of emotion in decision making was understood, and researchers are beginning to untangle the complex role that emotion plays in the process.[7]

10-2c Z Model

Isabel Briggs Myers, co-creator of the Myers-Briggs

rationality A logical, step-by-step approach to decision making, with a thorough analysis of alternatives and their consequences.

bounded rationality A theory that suggests that there are limits to how rational a decision maker can actually be.

satisfice To select the first alternative that is "good enough," because the costs in time and effort are too great to optimize.

heuristics Shortcuts in decision making that save mental activity.

Type Indicator, also developed the *Z problem-solving model*, which capitalizes on the strengths of the four separate preferences (Sensing, Intuiting, Thinking, and Feeling). By using the Z problem-solving model, managers can use both their preferences and nonpreferences to make decisions more effectively. The Z model is presented in Figure 10.2. According to this model, good problem solving has four steps:

1. *Examine the facts and details.* Use Sensing to gather information about the problem.

2. *Generate alternatives.* Use Intuiting to develop possibilities.

3. *Analyze the alternatives objectively.* Use Thinking to logically determine the effects of each alternative.

FIGURE 10.2 | THE Z PROBLEM-SOLVING MODEL

Look at the facts and details.
- What are the facts?
- Be specific and realistic.
- List all relevant details.
- Be clear.

Sensing → Intuition

What alternatives do the facts suggest?
- Let your imagination run wild.
- Brainstorm.
- Consider various solutions.

Can it be analyzed objectively?
- Consider the consequences of each alternative.
- If you were not involved, what would you suggest?
- What is the cause and effect of each action?

Thinking → Feeling

What impact will it have on those involved?
- Is it something you can live with?
- How do you feel about the action?
- What hunches do you have about others' reactions?

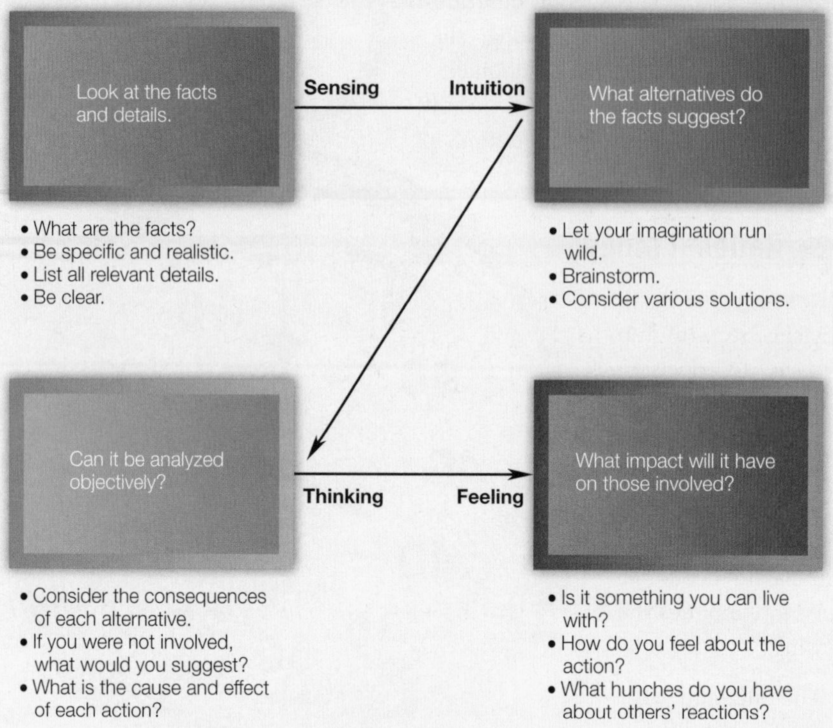

SOURCE: From *Type Talk at Work* by Otto Kroeger and Janet Theusen, copyright © 1992 by Janet Theusen and Otto Kroeger. Used by permission of Delacorte Press, an imprint of The Random House Publishing Group, a division of Random House, Inc.

4. *Weigh the impact.* Use Feeling to determine how the people involved will be affected.

Using the Z model can help an individual develop his nonpreferences. Another way to use the Z model is to rely on others to perform nonpreferred activities. For example, an individual who is an NF (Intuition-Feeling person) might want to turn to a trusted NT (Intuition-Thinking person) for help in analyzing alternatives objectively.

10-2d Escalation of Commitment

Each decision-making model carries its own unique limits. There is, however, one limitation that they all share: the decision maker's unwillingness to abandon a bad decision. Continuing to support a failing course of action is known as **escalation of commitment**.[8] In situations characterized by escalation of commitment, individuals who make decisions that turn out to be poor choices tend to hold fast to those choices, even when substantial costs are incurred.[9] An example of escalation is the price wars that often occur between airlines. The airlines reduce their prices in response to competitors until at a certain stage both airlines are in no-win situations. They continue to compete despite the heavy losses they incur. The desire to win is a motivation to continue to escalate, and each airline continues to reduce prices (lose money) based on the belief that the other airline will pull out of the price war.

Another example of escalation of commitment is the Drug Abuse Resistance Education Program (D.A.R.E.). Despite growing scientific evidence that the program does not produce reductions in drug use among young people, it continues to receive billions of dollars in donations and taxpayer funds.[10]

Why does escalation of commitment occur? One explanation is offered by cognitive dissonance theory, as we discussed in Chapter 4. This theory assumes that people dislike inconsistency and that when it exists among their attitudes or between their attitudes and behavior, they strive to reduce the dissonance.[11] Other reasons why people may hang on to a losing course of action are optimism and control. Some people are overly optimistic and overestimate the likelihood that positive things will happen to them. Other people operate under an illusion of control—that they have special skills to control the future that other people don't have.[12] Some individuals "throw good money

escalation of commitment The tendency to continue to support a failing course of action.

FAST FACT

The Time You Take to Make a Decision Signals Doubt

People make assumptions about the time others take to make a decision. For example, in the blind auditions on the television show *The Voice*, any of four coaches hit a buzzer and turn their chair to show interest in a singer. The singer then picks among those who turned to choose a coach—a risky decision. A study showed that coaches who were first to turn their chair were more frequently chosen by contestants, and those who turned last were much less likely to be chosen. So contestants tended to choose the coach who signaled the most confidence and avoided the coach who signaled the most doubt. Interestingly, a survival analysis showed that the contestants who chose the coach who turned first were eliminated early in the competition.

SOURCES: P. P. Van de Calseyde, G. Keren, and M. Zeelenberg, "Decision Time as Information in Judgment and Choice," *Organizational Behavior and Human Decision Processes* 125 (2014): 113–122. A. M. Evans and P. P. van de Calseyde, "The Effects of Observed Decision Time on Expectations of Extremity and Cooperation," *Journal of Experimental Social Psychology*, 68 (2017): 50–59.

after bad." They think, "Well, I've invested this much … what's a few dollars more?" The closer a project is to completion, the more likely escalation is to occur.[13]

Hanging on to a poor decision can be costly to organizations. While many foreign automakers saw promise in the *green movement* and shifted their development toward hybrid vehicles in 2002, General Motors stuck with a cost-cutting strategy that streamlined its operations and focused on production of SUVs and trucks. Between 2005 and 2008 GM lost $82 billion, and even these losses did not change the ailing company's strategy.[14] In 2009 CEO Rick Wagoner finally attempted to de-escalate, announcing that GM's focus on SUVs and trucks was no longer a viable strategy. It was too late, however, and despite a multibillion-dollar loan from the U.S. government, GM declared bankruptcy.

Recent research on de-escalation found that individuals with higher self-esteem and those who are given an opportunity to affirm an important value are more likely to deescalate.[15] Organizations can use this information to deal with escalation of commitment in several ways. One method of reducing escalation is to split the responsibility for project decisions by allowing different individuals to make decisions at different project stages. Mindfulness meditation, which enhances present-moment awareness, reduces the tendency to think in terms of sunk-costs. Just a brief fifteen-minute breath meditation may help reduce escalation of commitment.[16] Still another suggestion is to provide individuals with a graceful exit from poor decisions so that their images are not threatened. There can be a reward of some type for those who admit to poor decisions

before escalating their commitment to them or having groups make an initial investment decision. This way participants in group decision making may experience a diffusion of responsibility for the failed decision rather than feeling personally responsible; thus, they can pull out of a bad decision without threatening their image.[17]

We have seen that there are limits to how rational a manager can be in making decisions. On reason is that most managerial decisions involve considerable risk, and individuals react differently to risk situations, a subject we address in the next section.

 10-3 ## INDIVIDUAL INFLUENCES ON DECISION MAKING

No decision is made in a vacuum. In many ways, decisions reflect the people who make them, so it is appropriate to examine the individual influences on decision making: comfort with risk, **cognitive style**, personality, intuition, and creativity.

10-3a Risk and the Manager

Many decisions involve some element of risk. For managers, decisions regarding hiring, promotions, delegation, acquisitions and mergers, overseas expansions, and new product development

> **cognitive style** An individual's preferred method for gathering information and evaluating alternatives.

alphaspirit/Shutterstock.com

are among many that make risk a part of the job. As individuals, managers, of course, differ in terms of their willingness to take risks—that is, their degree of **risk aversion**. Some choose options that entail fewer risks, preferring familiarity and certainty, while others are *risk takers* and will accept greater potential for loss in decisions as well as tolerating greater uncertainty. Those prone to making risky decisions are more likely to take the lead in group discussions.[18]

Research indicates that women are more risk averse than men and that older, more experienced managers are more risk averse than younger managers. There is also some evidence that successful managers take more risks than unsuccessful managers.[19] However, the tendency to take risks or avoid them is only part of behavior toward risk. Risk taking is influenced not only by an individual's tendency but also by organizational factors. In commercial banks, loan decisions that require the assessment of risk are made every day.

Upper-level managers face a tough task in managing risk-taking behavior. By discouraging lower-level managers from taking risks, they may stifle creativity and innovation. If upper-level managers are going to encourage risk taking, however, they must allow employees to fail without fear of punishment. One way to accomplish this is

risk aversion The tendency to choose options that entail fewer risks and less uncertainty.

intuition A fast, positive force in decision making that is utilized at a level below consciousness and involves learned patterns of information.

to consider failure as "enlightened trial and error."[20] The key is establishing a consistent attitude toward risk within the organization.

Obviously, when individuals take risks, losses may occur. Suppose an oil producer thinks there is an opportunity to uncover oil by reentering an old drilling site. She gathers a group of investors and shows them the logs, and they chip in to finance the venture. The reentry is drilled to a certain depth, and nothing is found. Convinced they did not drill deep enough, the producer goes back to the investors and requests additional financial backing to continue drilling. The investors consent, and she drills deeper, only to find nothing. She approaches the investors, and after lengthy discussion, they agree to provide more money to drill deeper. Why do decision makers sometimes throw good money after bad? Why do they continue to provide resources to what looks like a losing venture?

10-3b Personality, Attitudes, and Values

In addition to all of the individual differences variables (discussed in Chapters 3 and 4)—personality characteristics, attitudes, and values—managers must use both their logic and their creativity to make effective decisions. Most of us are more comfortable using either logic or creativity, and we show that preference in everyday decision making.

Our brains have two lateral halves (Figure 10.3). The right side is the center for creative functions, while the left side is the center for logic, detail, and planning. There are advantages to both kinds of thinking, so the ideal situation is to be brain-lateralized, that is, be able to use either logic or creativity or both, depending on the situation.[21] There are ways to develop the side of the brain that you use less often. To develop your right side, or creative side, you can ask what-if questions, engage in play, and follow your intuition. To develop the left side, you can set goals for completing tasks and work to attain those goals. For managers, it is important to see the big picture, craft a vision, and plan strategically, all of which require right-brain skills. But it is equally important to be able to understand day-to-day operations and flowchart work processes, which are left-hemisphere brain skills.

Two particular individual influences that can enhance decision-making effectiveness will be highlighted next: intuition and creativity.

10-3c Intuition

There is evidence that managers often use their **intuition** to make decisions.[22] Henry Mintzberg, in his work on managerial roles, found that in many cases managers do not

FIGURE 10.3 FUNCTIONS OF THE LEFT AND RIGHT BRAIN HEMISPHERES

Two Brains,
Two Cognitive Styles

Left hemisphere	Right hemisphere
Verbal	Nonverbal, visuospatial
Sequential, temporal, digital	Simultaneous, spatial, analogical
Logical, analytic	Gestalt, synthetic
Rational	Intuitive
Western thought	Eastern thought

SOURCE: Based on ideas from S. P. Springer and G. Deutsch, *Left Brain, Right Brain* (New York: W. H. Freeman and Company, 1993), 272.

appear to use a systematic, step-by-step approach to decision making. Rather, Mintzberg argued, managers make judgments based on "hunches."[23] Daniel Isenberg studied the way senior managers make decisions and found that intuition was used extensively, especially as a mechanism to evaluate decisions made more rationally.[24] Robert Beck studied the way managers at Bank of America made decisions about the future direction of the company following the deregulation of the banking industry. Beck described their use of intuition as an antidote to analysis paralysis, or the tendency to analyze decisions rather than developing innovative solutions.[25]

Dr. Gary Klein, a renowned cognitive psychologist, has written a book on the power of intuition. Dr. Klein and colleagues insist that skilled decision makers rely on patterns of learned information in making quick and efficient decisions. In a series of studies conducted with the U.S. Navy, firefighters, and the U.S. Army, they found that decision makers normally rely on intuition in unfamiliar, challenging situations. These decisions were superior to those made after careful evaluation of information and potential alternatives.[26]

Just what is intuition? In Jungian theory, intuiting (N) is a preferred method used for gathering data. This is only one way that the concept of intuition has been applied to managerial decision making, but it is perhaps

the most widely researched form of the concept of intuition. There are, however, many definitions of *intuition* in the managerial literature. Chester Barnard, one of the early influential management researchers, argued that intuition's main attributes were speed and the inability of the decision maker to determine how the decision was made.[27] Other researchers have contended that intuition occurs at an unconscious level and that this is why the decision maker cannot verbalize how the decision was made.[28]

Intuition has been variously described as follows:

- The ability to know or recognize quickly and readily the possibilities of a situation.[29]

- Smooth automatic performance of learned behavior sequences.[30]

- Simple analyses frozen into habit and into the capacity for rapid response through recognition.[31]

These definitions share some common assumptions. First, there seems to be a notion that intuition is fast. Second, intuition is used at a level below consciousness. Third, there seems to be agreement that intuition involves learned patterns of information. Fourth, intuition appears to be a positive force in decision making.

The use of intuition may lead to more ethical decisions as intuition allows an individual to take on another's role with ease, and role taking is a fundamental part of developing moral reasoning. You may recall from Chapter 4 the role of cognitive moral development in ethical decision making. One study found a strong link between cognitive moral development and intuition. The development of new perspectives through intuition leads to higher moral growth, and thus to more ethical decisions.[32]

One question that arises is whether managers can be taught to use their intuition. Weston Agor, who has conducted workshops on developing intuitive skills in managers, has attained positive results in organizations such as the city government of Phoenix and entertainment powerhouse Walt Disney Enterprises. After giving intuition tests to more than 10,000 executives, he has concluded that in most cases, higher management positions are held by individuals with higher levels of intuition. But, just as the brain needs both hemispheres to work, Agor cautions that organizations need both analytical and intuitive minds to function at their peak. Lee Iacocca, in his autobiography, spends pages extolling intuition: "To a certain extent, I've always operated by gut feeling."[33] Agor suggests relaxation techniques, using images to guide the mind, and taking creative pauses before making a decision.[34] A review of the research on intuition suggests that, although intuition itself cannot be taught, managers can be trained to rely more fully on the promptings of their intuition.[35]

Intuition, with its many definitions, is an elusive concept. Some researchers view so-called rational methods as preferable to intuition, yet satisfaction with a rational decision is usually determined by how the decision feels intuitively.[36] Intuition appears to have a positive effect on managerial decision making, but it is not without controversy. Some writers argue that intuition has its place and that instincts should be trusted, but not as a substitute for reason. With new technologies, managers can analyze a lot more information in a lot less time, making the rational method less time-consuming than it once was.[37]

10-3d Creativity

In some ways, creativity is as elusive a concept as intuition. (We know it when we encounter it and when we feel its absence.) Even though creativity is highly individual, it is also collective. Personal creativity plays a role in the decisions made in organizations every day. For our purposes in this text, we can define **creativity** as a process influenced by individual and organizational factors that results in the production of novel and useful ideas, products, or both.[38]

The four stages of the creative process are preparation, incubation, illumination, and verification.[39] *Preparation* means seeking out new experiences and opportunities to learn because creativity grows from a base of knowledge. *Incubation* is a process of reflective thought and is often conducted subconsciously. During incubation, the individual engages in other pursuits while the mind considers the problem and works on it. *Illumination* occurs when the individual senses an insight for solving the problem. Finally, *verification* is conducted to determine if the solution or idea is valid.

creativity A process influenced by individual and organizational factors that results in the production of novel and useful ideas, products, or both.

Illumination is essential to the creative process.

Verification is accomplished by thinking through the implications of the decision, presenting the idea to another person, or trying out the decision. Momentary quieting of the brain through relaxation can increase coherence, or the ability of different parts of the brain to work together.[40] Both individual and organizational influences affect the creative process.

INDIVIDUAL INFLUENCES Several individual variables are related to creativity. One group of factors involves the cognitive processes that creative individuals tend to use. One such cognitive process is *divergent thinking*, meaning the individual's ability to generate several potential solutions to a problem.[41] In addition, associational abilities and the use of imagery are associated with creativity.[42] Unconscious processes such as dreams are also essential cognitive processes related to creative thinking.[43]

Personality factors have also been related to creativity in studies of individuals from several different occupations. These characteristics include intellectual and artistic values, breadth of interests, high energy, concern with achievement, independence of judgment, intuition, self-confidence, and a creative self-image.[44] Tolerance of ambiguity, intrinsic motivation, risk taking, and a desire for recognition are associated with creativity as well.[45] Not surprisingly, people who have a high level of motivation are more creative, since they are more likely to try to think of different ways to get things done. Also, people who are able to see and understand others' perspectives are more creative since they have skills at seeing situations from more than one viewpoint.[46]

There is evidence that people who are in a good mood are more creative.[47] Positive affect is related to creativity in work teams because being in a positive mood allows team members to explore new ways of thinking.[48] Positive emotions enhance creativity by broadening one's cognitive patterns and resources. These positive emotions initiate thoughts and actions that are novel and unscripted.[49] Moreover, it is a cyclical process: thinking positively makes us more creative, and being more creative makes us think positively.

The phase of creativity you're in at work can affect time spent with your spouse or partner at home in the evening. During the first three stages discussed earlier, preparation, incubation, and illumination, individuals spent less time with their spouses in the evenings. In the final phase, verification, individuals spent more time with their spouses or partners. Creative behavior at work may spill over and affect relationships at home.[50]

ORGANIZATIONAL INFLUENCES The organizational environment in which people work can either support creativity or impede creative efforts. Creativity killers include focusing on how work is going to be evaluated, being closely monitored while you are working, and competing with other people in win–lose situations. In contrast, creativity facilitators include feelings of autonomy, being part of a team with diverse skills, and having creative supervisors and coworkers.[51] High-quality, supportive relationships with supervisors are related to creativity.[52] Plus, high-quality, cohesive social networks can

> People who have a high level of motivation are more creative, since they are more likely to try to think of different ways to get things done.

have a positive impact on creative decision making. Such social networks encourage creative decision making by facilitating shared *sense-making* of relevant information and *consensus building*.[53] In addition, flexible organizational structures and participative decision making have been associated with creativity.

An organization can present impediments to creativity by means of internal political problems, harsh criticism of new ideas, destructive internal competition, and avoidance of risk.[54] Even the physical environment can hamper creativity. Companies like Oticon, a Danish hearing aid manufacturer, and Ethicon Endo-Surgery, a division of Johnson & Johnson, use open-plan offices that eliminate walls and cubicles so that employees can interact more frequently. When people mix, ideas mix as well.[55] Organizations can therefore enhance individuals' creative decision making by providing a supportive environment, participative decision making, and a flexible structure.

INDIVIDUAL–ORGANIZATION FIT Research has indicated that creative performance is highest when there is a match, or fit, between the individual and organizational influences on creativity. When individuals who desire to be creative are matched with an organization that values creative ideas, the result is more creative performance.[56]

A common mistaken assumption regarding creativity is that either you have it or you do not. Research refutes this myth and has shown that individuals can be trained to be more creative.[57] The Disney Institute, for example, features a wide range of programs offered to companies, and one of their best sellers is creativity training. Part of creativity training involves learning to open up *mental locks* that keep us from generating creative alternatives to a decision or problem. Following are some mental locks that diminish creativity:

- Searching for the "right" answer
- Trying to be logical
- Following the rules

AT&T's Foundry for Connected Health in Houston

Slyworks Photography

AT&T Foundries came from the idea of planting a seed of innovation as a place where startups, developers, and other innovators can come together in a mix of technology, design, and expertise to solve big problems. The idea is to get more successful innovations to market faster through fast-paced, collaborative environments.

The AT&T Foundry for Connected Health at Texas Medical Center's Innovation Institute Campus focuses on digital healthcare innovations. It features three digital test environments: home monitoring after a patient is released, nurse station remote access to patient data in real time, and connected hospital environments. The dedicated space will allow doctors, nurses, and patients to work alongside technicians, insurance experts, and others to provide real-world feedback on how AT&T can help solve the challenges of digital healthcare.

Connecting caregivers with patients through wireless monitoring will help provide faster, more effective data transmission both inside and out of medical centers. Wirelessly connecting devices such as glucose monitors and even wheelchairs helps ensure that a patient recovers well after leaving the hospital.

SOURCE: http://about.att.com/innovationblog/houston_foundry; L. Lorenzetti, "AT&T Just Announced a Major New Healthcare Venture," *Fortune*, January 5, 2016, accessed at http://fortune.com/2016/01/05/att-connected-health/.

- Avoiding ambiguity
- Striving for practicality
- Being afraid to look foolish
- Avoiding problems outside our own expertise
- Fearing failure
- Believing we are not really creative
- Not making play a part of work[58]

Note that many of these mental locks stem from values within organizations.

Organizations can facilitate creative decision making in many ways. Rewarding creativity, allowing employees to fail, making work more fun, and providing creativity training are a few suggestions. Another way companies can encourage creativity is by exposing employees to new ideas through job rotation. As employees move through different jobs, they can be exposed to different information, projects, and teams, either within or outside the company. Finally, managers can encourage employees to surround themselves with stimuli that they have found to enhance their creative processes. These may be music, artwork, books, or anything else that encourages creative thinking.[59]

We have seen that both individual and organizational factors can produce creativity. Leaders can play key roles in modeling creative behavior. One of the most critical skills that determines leader performance is creative thinking.[60] Sir Richard Branson, founder and chair of the U.K.-based Virgin Group, believes that if you do not use your employees' creative potential, you are doomed to failure. At Virgin Group, the culture encourages risk taking and rewards innovation rather than following rules and regulations. Branson says an employee should be able to have an idea in the morning and implement it that afternoon.

Culture also affects creativity. Tight cultures are those with strong social norms and strong sanctions for violating the norms. Pakistan, Norway, and Malaysia are culturally tight. Loose cultures are less predictable and lack clear norms and enforcement of behavior. Hungary, Brazil, and Australia are looser cultures. Individuals from loose cultures are more likely to take on and succeed in foreign, unfamiliar creative tasks than individuals from tight cultures. However, tight cultures are more successful with innovation within their own cultures.[61]

Helga Esteb/Shutterstock.com

Sir Richard Branson believes that letting employees be creative is vital to success.

10-4 THE GROUP DECISION-MAKING PROCESS

Managers use groups to make decisions for several reasons. One is **synergy**, which occurs when group members stimulate new solutions to problems through the process of mutual influence and encouragement within the group. Another reason for using a group is to gain commitment to a decision. Groups also bring more knowledge and experience to the problem-solving situation.

Group decisions can sometimes be predicted by comparing the views of the initial group members with the final group decision. These simple relationships are known as **social decision schemes**. One social decision scheme is the *majority-wins rule*, in which the group supports whatever position is taken by the majority of its members. Another scheme, the *truth-wins rule*, predicts that the correct decision will emerge as an increasing number of members realize its appropriateness. The *two-thirds-majority rule* means that the decision favored by two-thirds or more of the members is supported. Finally, the *first-shift rule* states that members support a decision represented by the first shift in opinion shown by a member.

Research indicates that these social decision schemes can predict a group decision as much as 80% of the time.[62] Current research is aimed at discovering which rules are used in particular types of tasks. For example, studies indicate that the majority-wins rule is used most often in judgment tasks (i.e., when the decision is a matter of

synergy A positive force that occurs in groups when group members are stimulated to produce new solutions to problems through the process of mutual influence and encouragement within the group.

social decision schemes Simple rules used to determine final group decisions.

preference or opinion), whereas the truth-wins rule predicts decisions best when the task is an intellective one (i.e., when the decision has a correct answer).[63]

10-4a Advantages and Disadvantages of Group Decision Making

Group decision making has advantages and disadvantages. The advantages of group decision making include (1) more knowledge and information through the pooling of group member resources, (2) increased acceptance of and commitment to the decision because the members had a voice in it, and (3) greater understanding of the decision because members were involved in the various stages of the decision process. The disadvantages of group decision making include (1) pressure within the group to conform and fit in, (2) domination of the group by one forceful member or a dominant clique who may ramrod the decision, and (3) the amount of time required because a group makes decisions more slowly than an individual.[64]

Given these advantages and disadvantages, should decisions be made by an individual or a group? Substantial empirical research indicates that effectively making that determination depends on the type of task involved. For judgment tasks requiring an estimate or a prediction, groups are usually superior to individuals because of the breadth of experience that multiple individuals bring to the problem.[65] On tasks that have a correct solution, other studies have indicated that the most competent individual outperforms the group.[66] This finding has been called into question, however. Much of the previous research on groups was conducted in the laboratory, where group members interacted only for short periods of time. Researchers wanted to know how a longer group experience would affect decisions. Their study showed that groups who worked together for longer periods of time outperformed the most competent member 70% of the time. As groups gained experience, the best members became less important to the group's success.[67] This study demonstrated that experience in the group is an important variable to consider when evaluating the individual versus group decision-making question.

Given the emphasis on teams in the workplace, many managers believe that groups produce better decisions than individuals, yet the evidence is mixed. More research needs to be conducted in organizational settings to help answer this question.

10-4b Limits of Group Decision Making

There are two potential liabilities in group decision making: groupthink and group polarization.

GROUPTHINK One liability of a cohesive group is its tendency to develop the dysfunctional process of **groupthink**. Irving Janis, the originator of this concept, describes groupthink as "a deterioration of mental efficiency, reality testing, and moral judgment" resulting from pressures within the group.[68] One of the conditions that leads to the development of groupthink is high cohesiveness. Cohesive groups tend to favor solidarity because members identify strongly with the group.[69] High-ranking teams that make decisions without outside help are especially prone to groupthink because they are likely to have shared mental models; that is, they are more likely to think alike.[70] Homogeneous groups (ones with little to no diversity among members) are more likely to suffer from groupthink.[71]

Two other conditions that encourage groupthink are (1) having to make a highly consequential decision and (2) time constraints.[72] A highly consequential decision is one that will have a great impact on the group members and on outside parties. Time restraints may cause group members to rush through the decision-making process. Both conditions can influence members to desire concurrence in decisions so much that they fail to evaluate one another's suggestions critically. A group suffering from groupthink shows recognizable symptoms. Table 10.1 presents these symptoms and makes suggestions on how to avoid groupthink.

An incident cited as a prime example of groupthink is the 1986 space shuttle *Challenger* disaster, in which the shuttle exploded, killing all seven crew members. A presidential commission concluded that flawed decision making was the primary cause of the accident. In 2003, the shuttle *Columbia* exploded over Texas upon reentering the earth's atmosphere, killing all seven crew members. Within days of the *Columbia* disaster, questions began to surface about the decision-making process that led flight engineers to assume that damage caused to the shuttle upon take-off was minor and to continue the mission. The subsequent investigation of the disaster led observers to note that NASA's decision-making process appeared just as flawed in 2003 as it was in 1986, exhibiting all the classic symptoms of groupthink. The final accident report blamed the NASA culture that downplayed risk and suppressed dissent for the decision.[73]

Consequences of groupthink include an incomplete survey of alternatives, failure to evaluate the risks of the preferred course of action, biased information processing, and a failure to work out contingency plans. Consequences like these can be devastating in medicine, where artificial intelligence (AI) is used more and more for diagnostic assistance,

> **groupthink** A deterioration of mental efficiency, reality testing, and moral judgment resulting from pressures within the group.

TABLE 10.1 SYMPTOMS OF GROUPTHINK AND HOW TO PREVENT IT

Symptoms of Groupthink

> *Illusions of invulnerability.* Group members feel that they are above criticism. This symptom leads to excessive optimism and risk taking.
> *Illusions of group morality.* Group members feel they are moral in their actions and therefore above reproach. This symptom leads the group to ignore the ethical implications of their decisions.
> *Illusions of unanimity.* Group members believe there is unanimous agreement on the decisions. Silence is misconstrued as consent.
> *Rationalization.* Group members concoct explanations for their decisions to make them appear rational and correct. The results are that other alternatives are not considered, and there is an unwillingness to reconsider the group's assumptions.
> *Stereotyping the enemy.* Competitors are stereotyped as evil or stupid. This leads the group to underestimate its opposition.
> *Self-censorship.* Members do not express their doubts or concerns about the course of action. This prevents critical analysis of the decisions.
> *Peer pressure.* Any members who express doubts or concerns are pressured by other group members who question their loyalty.
> *Mindguards.* Some members take it upon themselves to protect the group from negative feedback. Group members are thus shielded from information that might lead them to question their actions.

Guidelines for Preventing Groupthink

> Ask each group member to assume the role of the critical evaluator who actively voices objections or doubts.
> Have the leader avoid stating his or her position on the issue prior to the group decision.
> Create several groups that work on the decision simultaneously.
> Bring in outside experts to evaluate the group process.
> Appoint a devil's advocate to question the group's course of action consistently.
> Evaluate the competition carefully, posing as many different motivations and intentions as possible.
> Once consensus is reached, encourage the group to rethink its position by reexamining the alternatives.

SOURCE: From Breckler/Wiggins/Olson. *Social Psychology Alive!*, 1E. © 2008 Nelson Education Ltd. Reproduced by permission. www.cengage.com/permissions

therapy critiquing, and image interpretation. Advances in AI are narrowing the gap with human intelligence, emphasizing creativity, empathy, and judgment. If AI can include positive human decision-making attributes, it may also fall prey to negative human decision processes such as groupthink, which in the case of AI is called "loopthink." AI is limited by the biases and assumptions of its programming and may exclude moral principles such as human dignity and ethical reasoning. One avenue for preventing loopthink would be to program AI in medicine to be more self-critical and self-correcting, along the lines of ways of preventing groupthink in humans.[74]

Table 10.1 presents Janis's guidelines for avoiding groupthink. Many of these suggestions center around ensuring that decisions are evaluated completely, with opportunities for discussion from all group members. This strategy encourages members to evaluate one another's ideas critically. Groups that are educated about the value of diversity tend to perform better as a result. Less successful are groups that are homogenous and not educated about the value of diversity.[75]

Janis has used the groupthink framework to conduct historical analyses of several political and military fiascoes, including the Bay of Pigs invasion, the Vietnam War, and Watergate. One review of the decision situation in the *Challenger* incident proposed that two variables, time and leadership style, are important to include.[76]

When a decision must be made quickly, there is more potential for groupthink. Leadership style can either promote groupthink (if the leader makes his or her opinion known up front) or avoid groupthink (if the leader encourages open and frank discussion).

There are few empirical studies of groupthink, and most of these involved students in a laboratory setting. More applied research may be seen in the future, however, as a questionnaire has been developed to measure the constructs associated with groupthink.[77] Janis's work on groupthink has led to several interdisciplinary efforts at understanding policy decisions.[78] The work underscores the need to examine multiple explanations for failed decisions. Teams that experience cognitive (task-based) conflict are found to make better decisions than teams that experience affective (emotion-based) conflict. As such, one prescription for managers has been to encourage cognitive conflict while minimizing affective conflict. However, these two forms of conflict can also occur together and more research is needed on how one can be encouraged while minimizing the other.[79]

GROUP POLARIZATION Another group phenomenon was discovered by a graduate student. His study showed that groups and individuals within the group made riskier decisions and accepted greater levels of risk following a group discussion of the issue. Subsequent studies uncovered another shift—toward caution. Thus,

Crowdthink: Making a Mockery of Ideas

Crowdsourcing, or using IT to outsource ideas in an open call, has resulted in several successes, such as for Glassdoor and Shock Top beer. Sometimes, though, crowdsourcing can backfire. The Name Our Ship campaign from the Natural Environment Research Council (NERC) in the UK asked Brits to submit names for a new research vessel in the form of RRS (Name). The press release gave regal names like *Falcon* and *Endeavor* as suggestions.

Crowdsourcing yielded four names that were most popular: (1) RRS *Boaty McBoatface*, (2) RRS *Henry Worsely*, (3) *David Attenborough*, and (4) *It's Bloody Cold Here*. Other funny suggestions included RRS *I Like Big Boats and I Cannot Lie*. The campaign was so popular that the website was shut down temporarily due to the high traffic. The final decision was left to the council, which selected RRS *Sir David Attenborough* as the vessel's name. *Boaty McBoatface*, however, lives on as the name of the ship's remotely operated sub-sea vehicle.

This crowdsourcing experience is an example of *crowdthink*, when crowds react to crowdsourcing campaigns by making a mockery of them. Sometimes crowdsourcing backfires, fails, or is not taken seriously by the crowd.

SOURCE: M. Wilson, K. Robson, and E. Botha, "Crowdsourcing in a Time of Empowered Stakeholders: Lessons from Crowdsourcing Campaigns," *Business Horizons* (2017), accessed at http://www.sciencedirect.com/science/article/pii/S0007681316301318.

---

group discussion produced shifts both toward more risky positions and toward more cautious positions.[80] Further research revealed that individual group member attitudes simply became more extreme following group discussion. Individuals who were initially against an issue became more radically opposed, and individuals who were in favor of the issue became more strongly supportive following discussion. These shifts came to be known as **group polarization**.[81]

The tendency toward polarization has important implications for group decision making. Groups whose initial views lean a certain way can be expected to adopt more extreme views following interaction between members. Several ideas have been proposed to explain why group polarization occurs. One explanation is the *social comparison approach*. Prior to group discussion, individuals believe they hold better views than the other members. During group discussion, they see that their views are not so far from average, so they shift to more extreme positions.[82] A second explanation is the *persuasive arguments view*. It contends that group discussion reinforces the initial views of the members, so they take a more extreme position.[83] Both explanations are supported by research. It may be that both processes, along with others, cause the group to develop more polarized attitudes.

In sum, group polarization leads groups to adopt extreme attitudes. In some cases, this can be disastrous. For instance, if individuals are leaning toward a dangerous decision, they are likely to support it more strongly following discussion. A recent study found that after discussing hiring decisions as a group, employers were less accurate in their ratings and were more susceptible both to contrast effects and halo effects.[84]

Both groupthink and group polarization are potential liabilities of group decision making, but several techniques can be used to help prevent or control these two liabilities.

10-4c Techniques for Group Decision Making

Once a manager has determined that a group decision approach should be used, he can determine the technique that is best suited to the decision situation. Seven techniques will be briefly summarized: brainstorming, nominal group technique, devil's advocacy, dialectical inquiry, quality circles and quality teams, and self-managed teams.

BRAINSTORMING Brainstorming is a good technique for generating alternatives. The idea behind **brainstorming** is to generate as many ideas as possible, suspending evaluation until all of the ideas have been suggested. Participants are encouraged to build on the suggestions of others, and imagination is emphasized.

> **group polarization** The tendency for group discussion to produce shifts toward more extreme attitudes among members.

> **brainstorming** A technique for generating as many ideas as possible on a given subject while suspending evaluation until all the ideas have been suggested.

The BP oil spill, captured in the movie *Deepwater Horizon*, may have been the product of groupthink. Numerous investigations explored the causes of the explosion and record-setting oil spill, citing overconfidence, pressure on whistleblowers, and illusions of control as contributing factors.

U S Coast Guard phot/AGE Fotostock

Evidence suggests, however, that group brainstorming is less effective than a comparable number of individuals working alone. This may be because in groups, participants engage in discussions that can make them lose their focus.

To overcome the production blocking of group brainstorming, electronic brainstorming was developed. In this technique, group members use computers to simultaneously produce as many ideas as possible during a short period of time.[85] Studies show that electronic brainstorming is slightly more effective than traditional brainstorming. One of the limitations of electronic brainstorming is that people may spend more time generating their own ideas rather than looking at the ideas of others. This limitation can be overcome if participants are told in advance that others in the brainstorming group are creative. This entices them to pay attention to others' ideas and can improve the quality and quantity of ideas produced in electronic brainstorming.[86]

NOMINAL GROUP TECHNIQUE A structured approach to decision making that focuses on generating alternatives and choosing one is called **nominal group technique (NGT)**, which involves the following discrete steps:

1. Individuals silently list their ideas.

2. Ideas are written on a chart one at a time until all ideas are listed.

3. Discussion is permitted but only to clarify the ideas. No criticism is allowed.

4. A written vote is taken.

NGT is a good technique to use when group members fear criticism from others.[87]

DEVIL'S ADVOCACY In the **devil's advocacy** decision method, a group or individual is given the role of critic. This devil's advocate has the task of coming up with the potential problems of a proposed decision. By identifying potential pitfalls in advance, organizations can often avoid costly mistakes in decision making.[88] As we discussed in Chapter 9, a devil's advocate who challenges the CEO and top management team can help sustain the vitality and performance of the upper echelon.

DIALECTICAL INQUIRY Dialectical inquiry is essentially a debate between two opposing sets of recommendations. Although it sets up a conflict, it is a constructive approach because it brings out the benefits and limitations of both sets of ideas.[89] However, when using this technique, it is important to guard against a win–lose attitude and to concentrate on reaching the most effective solution for all concerned. Research has shown that the way a decision is framed (i.e., win–win versus win–lose) is very important. A decision's outcome could be viewed as a gain or a loss depending on the way the decision is framed.[90]

10-4d Factors in Selecting the Appropriate Technique

Before choosing a group decision-making technique, the manager should carefully evaluate the group members and the decision situation. Only then can the best method for accomplishing the objectives of the group decision-making process be selected. If the goal is generating a large number of alternatives, for example, brainstorming would be a good choice. If group members are reluctant to contribute ideas, the nominal group technique would be appropriate. The need for expert input would be best facilitated by the Delphi technique, which uses a panel of experts. To guard against groupthink, devil's advocacy or dialectical inquiry would be effective. Decisions that concern quality or production would benefit from the advice of quality circles or the empowered decisions of quality teams. Moreover, recent

nominal group technique (NGT) A structured approach to group decision making that focuses on generating alternatives and choosing one.

devil's advocacy A technique for preventing groupthink in which a group or individual is given the role of critic during decision making.

dialectical inquiry A debate between two opposing sets of recommendations.

research results suggest that if individuals within a team are made accountable for the process of decision making (rather than the end decision itself), then such teams are more likely to gather diverse information, share information, and eventually make better decisions.[91] Finally, a manager who wants to provide total empowerment to a group should consider self-managed teams.

10-4e Special Decision-Making Groups

Even though in organizations many types of groups make collective decisions, quality-oriented groups and self-managed teams have higher levels of involvement and authority in group decision making.

QUALITY CIRCLES AND QUALITY TEAMS A **quality circle** is a small group of employees who work voluntarily on company time, typically one hour per week, to address work-related problems such as quality control, cost reduction, production planning and techniques, and even product design. Quality circles also extend participative decision making into teams. Managers often listen to recommendations from quality circles and implement the suggestions. Involvement in the decision-making process is the primary reward.

Quality circles are not empowered to implement their own recommendations. They operate in parallel fashion to the organization's structure, and they rely on voluntary participation.[92] In Japan, quality circles have been integrated into the organization instead of being added on. This may be one reason for Japan's success with this technique. In contrast, the U.S. experience is not as positive. It has been estimated that 60 to 75% of the quality circles in U.S. firms have failed. Reasons for the failures have included a lack of top management support and a lack of problem-solving skills among quality circle members.[93]

Quality teams, in contrast, are included in total quality management and other quality improvement efforts as part of a change in the organization's structure. Quality teams are generated from the top down and are empowered to act on their own recommendations. Whereas quality circles emphasize the generation of ideas, quality teams make data-based decisions about improving product and service quality. Various decision-making techniques are employed in quality teams. Brainstorming, flowcharts, and cause-and-effect diagrams help pinpoint problems that affect quality.

Quality circles and quality teams are methods for using groups in the decision-making process. Self-managed teams take the concept of participation one step further.

SELF-MANAGED TEAMS Another group decision-making method is the use of self-managed teams, discussed in Chapter 9. The decision-making activities of self-managed teams are more broadly focused than those of quality circles and quality teams. Self-managed teams make many of the decisions that were once reserved for managers, such as work scheduling, job assignments, and staffing.

Many organizations have claimed success with self-managed teams. At Northern Telecom (now Nortel Networks), revenues rose 63%, and sales increased 26% following the implementation of self-managed teams.[94] Research evidence shows that self-managed teams can lead to higher productivity, lower turnover among employees, and flatter organization structure.[95]

Self-managed teams, like any cohesive group, can fall victim to groupthink. The key to stimulating innovation and better problem solving in these groups is welcoming dissent among members. Dissent breaks down complacency and sets in motion a process that results in better decisions. Team members must know that dissent is permissible so that they won't fear embarrassment or ridicule.[96]

10-5 DIVERSITY AND CULTURE IN DECISION MAKING

Styles of decision making vary greatly among cultures. Many of the dimensions proposed by Hofstede that were presented in Chapter 2 affect decision making. Uncertainty avoidance, for example, can affect the way people view decisions. In the United States, a culture with low uncertainty avoidance, decisions are seen as opportunities for change. In contrast, cultures such as those of Indonesia and Malaysia attempt to accept situations as they are rather than try to change them.[97] Power distance also affects decision making. In more hierarchical cultures, such as India, top-level managers make nearly all decisions. In countries with low power distance, lower-level employees make many decisions. The Swedish culture exemplifies this type.

The individualist/collectivist dimension has implications for decision

> **quality circle** A small group of employees who work voluntarily on company time, typically one hour per week, to address work-related problems such as quality control, cost reduction, production planning and techniques, and even product design.
>
> **quality team** A team that is part of an organization's structure and is empowered to act on its decisions regarding product and service quality.

dpa picture alliance/Alamy Stock Photo

Facebook's VP of engineering Regina Dugan believes that putting together a diverse group of perspectives is essential for creativity.

making. Japan, with its collectivist culture, favors group decisions. The United States has a more difficult time with group decisions because it is an individualistic culture. Time orientation affects the frame of reference of the decision. In China, with its long-term view, decisions are made with the future in mind. In the United States, many decisions are made considering only the short term.

The masculine/feminine dimension can be compared to the Jungian thinking/feeling preferences for decision making. Masculine cultures, as in many Latin American countries, value quick, assertive decisions. Feminine cultures, as in many Scandinavian countries, value decisions that reflect concern for others.

Recent research examining the effects of cultural

participative decision making Decision making in which individuals who are affected by decisions influence the making of those decisions.

diversity on decision making has found that when individuals in a group are racially dissimilar, they engage in more open information sharing, encourage dissenting perspectives, and arrive at better decisions than racially similar groups.[98] Other kinds of diversity, such as functional background, have been studied as well. Top management teams that have members who come from a variety of functional backgrounds (e.g., marketing, accounting, information systems) engage in greater debate in decision making than top management teams in which the members come from similar backgrounds. This diversity results in better financial performance for the firm.[99] To capitalize on diversity in decision-making, leaders may need to deal with inherent biases. One such bias is toward nonnative accents. Often, individuals will choose new companies, products, or employees based on accents and are more favorable toward accents that are similar to their own. Biases like this have serious implications for companies engaging in global business, and managers can provide training to reduce biases and stereotypes regarding accents different from one's own.[100]

10-6 PARTICIPATION IN DECISION MAKING

Effective management of people can improve a company's economic performance. Firms that capitalize on this fact share several common practices. Chief among them is participation of employees in decision making.[101] Many companies do this through highly empowered self-managed teams. Even in situations where formal teams are not feasible, decision authority can be handed down to frontline employees who have the knowledge and skills to make a difference. At Hampton Inn hotels, for example, guest services personnel are empowered to do whatever is necessary to make guests happy—without consulting their superiors.

10-6a The Effects of Participation

Participative decision making occurs when individuals who are affected by decisions influence the making of those decisions. Participation buffers employees from the negative experiences of organizational politics.[102] Participation in decisions such as how technology is developed has also been found to affect employee's attitudes toward the technology and how they use it.[103] In addition, participative management has been found to increase employee creativity, job satisfaction, and productivity.[104] GE Capital is one company that believes in participation. Each year it holds so-called dreaming sessions, in which employees from all levels of the company attend strategy and budget meetings to discuss where the company is heading.

As our economy becomes increasingly based on knowledge work and as new technologies make it easier for decentralized decision makers to connect, participative decision making will undoubtedly increase.[105] Consider the city and county of San Francisco, a combined city/county government organization. Needing to adopt a single messaging system to meet the requirements of more than 20,000 employees, it faced a huge challenge in getting all the users to provide input into the decision. Technology helped craft a system that balanced the needs of all the groups involved, and IT planners developed a twenty-eight-page spreadsheet to pull together the needs and desires of all sixty departments into a focused decision matrix. Within two years, 90 percent of the users had agreed on and moved to a single system, reducing costs and complexity.[106]

10-6b Foundations for Participation and Empowerment

What conditions must be in place in order for participative decision making to work? The organizational

> If participative decision making is to work, employees must be able to comprehend how it provides a personal benefit to them.

foundations include a supportive organizational culture and a team-oriented work design. A supportive work environment is essential because of the uncertainty within the organization. Lower-level organizational members must be able to make decisions and take action on them. As operational employees are encouraged to take part in making decisions, however, fear, anxiety, or even terror can be created among middle managers in the organization.[107] Thus, senior leadership must create an organizational culture that is supportive and reassuring for these middle managers as the power dynamics of the system change.

A second organizational foundation for participative decision making concerns the design of work. A team-oriented work design is a key organizational foundation because it leads to broader tasks and a

Ben Bloom/Stone/Getty Images

greater sense of responsibility. For example, Volvo builds cars using a team-oriented work design in which each person does many different tasks; therefore, each person retains direct responsibility for the finished product.[108] These work designs create a context for effective participation.

The three individual prerequisites for participative decision making are

1. the capability to become psychologically involved in participative activities,

2. the motivation to act autonomously, and

3. the capacity to see the relevance of participation for one's own well-being.[109]

First, people must be psychologically equipped to become involved in participative activities if they are to be effective team members. Not all people are so predisposed. For example, Germany has an authoritarian tradition that runs counter to participative decision making at the individual and group levels. As a result, General Motors encountered significant difficulties implementing quality circles in its German plants because workers expected to be directed by supervisors, not to engage in participative problem solving. New initiatives to establish supervisory/worker boards in German corporations are intended to change this authoritarian tradition.

The second individual prerequisite is the motivation to act autonomously. People with dependent personalities are predisposed to be told what to do and to rely on external motivation rather than internal, intrinsic motivation.[110] These dependent people are not often effective contributors to decision making.

Finally, if participative decision making is to work, employees must be able to comprehend how it provides a personal benefit to them. The personal payoff for the individual need not be short term. It may be a long-term benefit that results in workers receiving greater rewards through enhanced organizational profitability.

10-6c What Level of Participation?

Participative decision making is complex, and one of the things managers must understand is that employees can be involved in some, or all, of the stages of the decision-making process. For example, employees could be variously involved in identifying problems, generating alternatives, selecting solutions, planning implementations, or evaluating results. Research shows that greater involvement in all five of these stages has a cumulative effect. Employees who are involved in all five processes have higher satisfaction and performance levels. And, all decision processes are not created equal. If employees can't be provided with full participation in all stages, they should be involved in the stages that seem to have the highest payoffs: generating alternatives, planning implementations, and evaluating results.[111] Styles of participation in decision making may need to change as the company grows or as its culture changes.

11 | Power and Political Behavior

LEARNING OBJECTIVES

11-1 Describe the concept of power.

11-2 Identify forms and sources of power in organizations.

11-3 Describe the role of ethics in using power.

11-4 Identify symbols of power and powerlessness in organizations.

11-5 Define organizational politics and understand the role of political skill and major influence tactics.

11-6 Identify ways to manage political behavior in organizations.

After finishing this chapter go to **PAGE 196** for **STUDY TOOLS**

11-1 THE CONCEPT OF POWER

Power is the ability to influence another person. As an exchange relationship, it occurs in transactions between an agent and a target. The agent is the person using the power, and the target is the recipient of the attempt to use power.[1] Because power is an ability, individuals can learn to use it effectively, employing either influence or authority or both. **Influence** is the process of affecting the thoughts, behavior, and feelings of another person. **Authority** is the right to influence another person.[2] It is important to understand the subtle differences among these terms. For instance, a manager may have authority but no power. She may have the right, by virtue of her position as boss, to tell someone what to do. But she may not have the skill or ability to influence other people.

power The ability to influence another person.

influence The process of affecting the thoughts, behavior, and feelings of another person.

authority The right to influence another person.

REDPIXEL.PL/Shutterstock.com

In a relationship between the agent and the target, there are many influence attempts that the target will consider legitimate. Working forty hours per week, greeting customers, solving problems, and collecting bills are actions that, when requested by the manager, are considered legitimate by a customer service representative. Requests such as these fall within the employee's **zone of indifference**—the range in which attempts to influence the employee are perceived as legitimate and are acted on without a great deal of thought.[3] The employee accepts that the manager has the authority to request such behaviors and complies with the requests. Some requests, however, fall outside the zone of indifference, so there the manager must work to enlarge the employee's zone of indifference. Enlarging the zone is accomplished with power (an ability) rather than with authority (a right).

Suppose the manager asks an employee to purchase a birthday gift for the manager's wife or to overcharge a customer for a service call. The employee may think that the manager has no right to ask these things. These requests fall outside the zone of indifference. They're viewed as extraordinary, and the manager has to operate from outside the authority base to induce the employee

> # Individuals have many forms of power to use in their work settings.

to fulfil them. In some cases, no power base is enough to induce the employee to comply, especially if the employee considers the behaviors requested by the manager to be unethical.

11-2 FORMS AND SOURCES OF POWER IN ORGANIZATIONS

Individuals have many forms of power to use in their work settings. Some of them are interpersonal, that is, used in interactions with

zone of indifference The range in which attempts to influence a person will be perceived as legitimate and will be acted on without a great deal of thought.

Fast Fact: Gender Diversity on Boards Benefits Everyone

Catalyst conducted a global census of women's share of board seats in stock market index companies across twenty countries. A sample of their findings by country and percentage of board seats held by women:

> Norway, 46.7%

> France, 34%

> Australia, 23.4%

> Canada, 21.6%

> Germany, 22%*

> United States, 19.9%

> India, 9.5%

> South Korea, 4.1%

> Japan, 3.5%

Having women on corporate boards is associated with better financial performance, increased innovation, and a stronger talent pipeline. A gender-balanced board of directors is linked with better corporate social performance, which benefits business and society through stronger, more sustainable enterprises.

*Germany's new law that women hold 30% of top board seats went into effect in January 2016.

SOURCE: catalyst.org, "Women on Boards Globally," January 4, 2017, accessed at http://www.catalyst.org/knowledge/women-corporate-boards-globally# footnote20_7m7dqj9.

---

reward power Power based on an agent's ability to control rewards that a target wants.

coercive power Power that is based on an agent's ability to cause an unpleasant experience for a target.

legitimate power Power that is based on position and mutual agreement; agent and target agree that the agent has the right to influence the target.

referent power An elusive power that is based on interpersonal attraction.

expert power The power that exists when an agent has specialized knowledge or skills that the target needs.

others. One of the earliest and most influential theories of power comes from John French and Bertram Raven, who tried to determine both the forms and the sources of power managers use to influence other people.

11-2a Interpersonal Forms of Power

French and Raven identified five forms of interpersonal power that managers use: reward, coercive, legitimate, referent, and expert power.[4]

Reward power is power based on an agent's ability to control rewards that a target wants, such as salary increases, bonuses, and promotions. Reward power can lead to better performance, but only as long as the employee sees a clear and strong link between performance and rewards. To use reward power effectively, then, the manager should be explicit about the behavior being rewarded and should make the connection clear between the behavior and the reward.

Coercive power is power that is based on an agent's ability to cause the target to have an unpleasant experience. To coerce someone into doing something means to force the person to do it, often with threats of punishment. Managers using coercive power may verbally abuse employees or withhold support from them.

Legitimate power, which is similar to authority, is power that is based on position and mutual agreement. The agent and target agree that the agent has the right to influence the target. Just because a manager thinks he has the right to influence his employees doesn't mean that he will have legitimate power in their eyes. For legitimate power to be effective, the employees must also believe the manager has the right to tell them what to do. For example, in Native American societies, the chief has legitimate power because tribe members believe in his right to influence the decisions in their lives.

Referent power is an elusive power that is based on interpersonal attraction. The agent has referent power over the target because the target identifies with or wants to be like the agent. Charismatic individuals are often thought to have referent power. Interestingly, the agent need not be superior to the target in any way. People who use referent power well are most often individualistic and respected by the target.

Expert power is the power that exists when an agent has specialized knowledge or skills that the target needs. For expert power to work, three conditions must be in place. First, the target must trust that the expertise given is accurate. Second, the knowledge involved must be relevant and useful to the target. Third, the target's perception of the agent as an expert is crucial. Using easy-to-understand language signals the target that the expert has an appreciation for real-world concerns and increases the target's trust in the expert.[5]

Which type of interpersonal power is most effective? Research has focused on this question since French and Raven introduced their five forms of power. Some of the results are surprising. Reward power and coercive power have similar effects.[6] Both lead to compliance. That is, employees will do what the manager asks them to, at least temporarily, if the manager offers a reward or threatens them with punishment. Reliance on these sources of power is dangerous, however, because it may require the manager to be physically present and watchful in order to apply rewards or punishment when the behavior occurs. Constant surveillance creates an uncomfortable situation for managers and employees and eventually results in a dependency relationship: employees will not work unless the manager is present.

Legitimate power also leads to compliance. When told "Do this because I'm your boss," most employees will comply. However, the use of legitimate power has not been linked to organizational effectiveness or to employee satisfaction.[7] In organizations where managers rely heavily on legitimate power, organizational goals are not necessarily met.

Referent power is linked with organizational effectiveness. It is the most dangerous power, however, because it can be too extensive and intensive in altering the behavior of others. Charismatic leaders need an accompanying sense of responsibility for others. Actor Michael J. Fox puts referent power to good use. Diagnosed with Parkinson's disease in 1991, he has written three books, done voiceover work in films, and continued his acting on television. He created the Michael J. Fox Foundation, which focuses on finding a cure for Parkinson's.

Expert power has been called the power of the future.[8] Of the five forms of power, it has the strongest relationship with performance and satisfaction. It is through expert power that vital skills, abilities, and knowledge are passed on within the organization. Employees internalize what they observe and learn from managers they perceive to be experts.

The results on the effectiveness of these five forms of power pose a challenge in organizations. The least effective power bases—legitimate, reward, and coercive—are the ones most likely to be used by managers.[9] Managers inherit these power bases as part of the position when they take a supervisory job. In contrast, the most effective power bases—referent and expert—are ones that must be developed and strengthened through interpersonal relationships with employees. Indra Nooyi, CEO of

Pepsi, has both referent and expert power. Her expertise lies not only in leading the company and exceeding analyst's expectations, but also in her emotional intelligence. Nooyi wrote the parents of each of her direct reports so that they would know they had succeeded as a parent, thanking them for the gift of their children. She believes leaders should work hard to bond the employees to the company and to win hearts as well as minds.[10] Expert power and social networks help CEOs influence their top management teams in ways that are profitable for the firm.

Indra Nooyi has referent and expert power as a leader.

Dario Pignatelli/Bloomberg/Getty Images

11-2b Intergroup Sources of Power

Groups or teams within an organization can also use power from several sources. One source of intergroup power is control of *critical resources*.[11] When one group controls an important resource that another group desires, the first group holds power. Controlling resources needed by another group allows the power-holding group to influence the actions of the less powerful group. This process can continue in an upward spiral. Groups seen as powerful tend to be given more resources from top management.[12]

Groups also have power to the extent that they control **strategic contingencies**—activities that other groups depend on in order to complete their tasks.[13] The dean's office, for example, may control the number of faculty positions to be filled in each department of a college. The departmental hiring plans are thus contingent on approval from the dean's office. In this case, the dean's office controls the strategic contingency of faculty hiring, and thus has power.

Three factors can give a group control over a strategic contingency.[14] One is the *ability to cope with uncertainty*. If a group can help another group deal with uncertainty, it has power. One group that has gained power in recent years in most organizations is the legal department. Faced with increasing government regulations and fears

strategic contingencies Activities that other groups depend on in order to complete their tasks.

of litigation, many other departments seek guidance from the legal department.

Another factor that can give a group control power is a *high degree of centrality* within the organization. If a group's functioning is important to the organization's success, it has high centrality. The sales force in a computer firm, for example, has power because of its immediate effect on the firm's operations and because other groups (accounting and servicing groups, for example) depend on its activities.

The third factor that can give a group power is *nonsubstitutability*—the extent to which a group performs a function that is indispensable to an organization. A team of computer specialists may be powerful because of its expertise with a system. It may have specialized experience that another team cannot provide.

The strategic contingencies model thus shows that groups hold power over other groups when they can reduce uncertainty, when their functioning is central to the organization's success, and when the group's activities are difficult to replace.[15] The key to all three of these factors, as you can see, is dependency. When one group controls something that another group needs, it creates a dependent relationship—and gives one group power over the other.

TABLE 11.1	GUIDELINES FOR THE ETHICAL USE OF POWER
Form of Power	**Guidelines for Use**
Reward power	Verify compliance. Make feasible, reasonable requests. Make only ethical requests. Offer rewards desired by subordinates. Offer only credible rewards.
Coercive power	Inform subordinates of rules and penalties. Warn before punishing. Administer punishment consistently and uniformly. Understand the situation before acting. Maintain credibility. Fit punishment to the infraction. Punish in private.
Legitimate power	Be cordial and polite. Be confident. Be clear and follow up to verify understanding. Make sure request is appropriate. Explain reasons for request. Follow proper channels. Exercise power consistently. Enforce compliance. Be sensitive to subordinates' concerns.
Referent power	Treat subordinates fairly. Defend subordinates' interests. Be sensitive to subordinates' needs and feelings. Select subordinates similar to oneself. Engage in role modeling.
Expert power	Maintain credibility. Act confident and decisive. Keep informed. Recognize employee concerns. Avoid threatening subordinates' self-esteem.

SOURCE: G. A. Yuki, *Leadership in Organizations*, 1st ed., © 1981. Reprinted by permission of Pearson Education, Inc., Upper Saddle River, N.J.

11-3 USING POWER ETHICALLY

Managers can work at developing all five forms of power for future use. The key to using them well is to use them ethically, as Table 11.1 shows. Coercive power, for example, requires careful administration if it is to be used in an ethical manner. Employees should be informed of the rules in advance, and any punishment should be used consistently, uniformly, and privately. The key to using all five types of interpersonal power ethically is to be sensitive to employees' concerns and to communicate well.

To French and Raven's five power sources we can add a source that is very important in today's organizations. **Information power** is access to and control over important information. Consider, for example, the CEO's administrative assistant. He has information about the CEO's schedule that people need if they are going to get in to see the CEO. Central to the idea of information power is the person's position within the communication networks in the organization, both formal and informal. Also important is the idea of *framing*, which is the "spin" that managers put on information. Managers not only pass information on to subordinates, they also interpret this information and influence the subordinates' perceptions of it. Information power may flow upward from subordinates to managers as well as downward from managers to subordinates. For instance, in manufacturing plants, database operators often control information about plant metrics and shipping performance that is vital to managerial decision making. Information power can also flow laterally. Salespeople convey information from the outside environment (their customers) that is essential for marketing efforts.

information power Access to and control over important information.

Using Personal Power to Create Social Power: The Giving Pledge

According to Oxfam, the antipoverty group, eight men now hold as much wealth as the world's poorest 3.6 billion people. Collectively, their worth is $426 billion: Michael Bloomberg, Warren Buffett, Bill Gates, Jeff Bezos, Amancio Ortega, Larry Ellison, Carlos Slim, and Mark Zuckerberg. Income inequality is a big source of power differentials, and you could view amassing wealth as an accumulation of personal power.

Some of these wealth holders are turning personal power into social power by joining The Giving Pledge, a campaign to inspire the wealthy people in the world to donate half of their net worth to philanthropy, either during their lifetime or after their deaths. Bill Gates, Warren Buffett, Larry Ellison, Michael Bloomberg, and Mark Zuckerberg have all joined The Giving Pledge. Founded by Bill and Melinda Gates and Warren Buffett, the goal of the organization is to address society's most pressing problems, from alleviating poverty to healthcare and education.

Bill and Melinda Gates and Warren Buffett

SOURCES: https://www.oxfam.org/sites/www.oxfam.org/files/file_attachments/bp-economy-for-99-percent-160117-en.pdf; L. Lorenzetti, "17 More Billionaires Join Buffett and Gates' Giving Pledge This Year," *Fortune*, June 1 (2016), accessed at http://fortune.com/2016/06/01/giving-pledge-new-members-2016/.

Determining whether a power-related behavior is ethical is complicated. One helpful method for establishing criteria in this respect is to ask three questions[16]:

1. *Does the behavior produce a good outcome for people both inside and outside the organization?* This question represents the criterion of *utilitarian outcomes*. The behavior should result in the greatest good for the greatest number of people. If the power-related behavior serves only the individual's self-interest and fails to help the organization reach its goals, it is considered unethical. A salesperson might be tempted to deeply discount a product in order to make a sale that would win a contest. Doing so would be in her self-interest but would not benefit the organization.

2. *Does the behavior respect the rights of all parties?* This question emphasizes the criterion of *individual rights*. Free speech, privacy, and due process are individual rights that are to be respected, and power-related behaviors that violate these rights are considered unethical.

3. *Does the behavior treat all parties equitably and fairly?* This question represents the criterion of *distributive justice*. Power-related behavior that treats one party arbitrarily or benefits one party at the expense of another is unethical. Granting a day of vacation to one employee in a busy week in which coworkers must struggle to cover for him might be considered unethical.

To be considered ethical, power-related behavior must meet all three criteria. If the behavior fails to meet the criteria, then alternative actions should be considered.

Unfortunately, most power-related behaviors are not easy to analyze. Conflicts may exist among the criteria; for example, a behavior may maximize the greatest good for the greatest number of people but may not treat all parties equitably. Individual rights may need to be sacrificed for the good of the organization. A CEO may need to be removed from power for the organization to be saved. Still, these criteria can be used on a case-by-case basis to sort through the complex ethical issues surrounding the use of power. The ethical use of power is one of the hottest topics in the current business arena due to the abuse of power by top executives such as Bernie Madoff, who was convicted of running a $50 billion Ponzi scheme that financially ruined people and businesses around the world.

11-3a Positive versus Negative Power

We turn now to a theory of power that takes a strong stand on the "right" versus "wrong" kind of power to use in organizations. David McClelland has spent a great deal of his career studying the need for power and the ways managers use power. As was discussed in Chapter 5, he believes that there are two distinct faces of power, one negative and one positive.[17] The negative face of power is **personal power**—power used for personal gain. Managers who use personal power are commonly described as "powerhungry." Sexual harassment is an abuse of personal power. One of Uber's top executives was asked to resign after others learned he was accused of sexual harassment at his former employer, Google. Amit Singhal did not disclose the allegations when he was hired. Uber is now facing an internal investigation into alleged sexual harassment after a former engineer blogged about problems within Uber's culture. People who approach relationships with an exchange orientation often use personal power to ensure that they get at least their fair share—and often more—in the relationship. They are most interested in their own needs and interests. One way to encourage ethical behavior in organizations is to encourage *principled dissent*. This term refers to valid criticism that can benefit the organization rather than mere complaints about working conditions. Much like whistle-blowers, who can serve as checks on powerful people within the organization, dissenters can pinpoint wrongdoings, encourage employee voice in key issues, and create a climate conducive to the ethical use of power.[18]

Individuals who rely on personal power at its extreme might be considered *Machiavellian*—willing to do whatever it takes to get one's own way. Niccolo Machiavelli was an Italian statesman during the sixteenth century who wrote *The Prince*, a guide for acquiring and using power.[19] Among his methods for using power was manipulating others, believing that it was better to be feared than loved. Machiavellians (or high Machs) are willing to manipulate others for personal gain and are unconcerned with others' opinions or welfare.

The positive face of power is **social power**—power used to create motivation or to accomplish group goals. McClelland clearly favors the use of social power by managers. People who approach relationships with a communal orientation focus on the needs and interests of others. In other words, they rely on social power.[20] McClelland has found that managers who use power successfully have four power-oriented characteristics:

1. *Belief in the authority system.* They believe that the institution is important and that its authority system is valid. They are comfortable influencing and being influenced. The source of their power is the authority system of which they are a part.

2. *Preference for work and discipline.* They like their work and are very orderly. They have a basic value preference for the Protestant work ethic, believing that work is good for a person over and beyond its income-producing value.

3. *Altruism.* They publicly put the company and its needs before their own needs. They are able to do this because they see their own well-being as integrally tied to the company's well-being.

4. *Belief in justice.* They believe justice is to be sought above all else. People should receive that to which they are entitled and that which they earn.

McClelland takes a definite stand on the proper use of power by managers. When power is used for the good of the group, rather than for individual gain, it is positive.

SYMBOLS OF POWER

Organization charts show who has authority, but they do not reveal much about who has power. Two very different ideas about the symbols of power come from Rosabeth Moss Kanter and Michael Korda.

11-4a Kanter's Symbols of Power

Kanter offers a scholarly approach to determining who has power and who feels powerless, providing several characteristics of powerful people in organizations[21]:

1. *Ability to intercede for someone in trouble.* An individual who can pull someone out of a jam has power.

2. *Ability to get placements for favored employees.* Getting a key promotion for an employee is a sign of power.

3. *Exceeding budget limitations.* A manager who can go above budget limits without being reprimanded has power.

4. *Procuring above-average raises for employees.* One faculty member reported that her department head distributed 10 percent raises to the most productive faculty members although the budget allowed for only 4 percent increases. "I don't know how he did it; he must have pull," she said.

5. *Getting items on the agenda at meetings.* If a manager can raise issues for action at meetings, it's a sign of power.

personal power Power used for personal gain.

social power Power used to create motivation or to accomplish group goals.

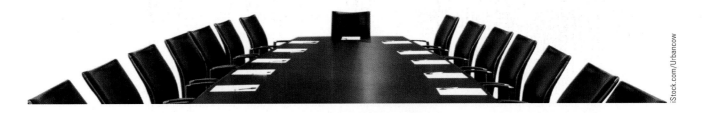

6. *Access to early information.* Having information before anyone else does is a signal that a manager is plugged into key sources.

7. *Having top managers seek out their opinion.* When top managers have a problem, they may ask for advice from lower-level managers. The managers they turn to have power.

A theme that runs through Kanter's list is doing things for others—for people in trouble, for employees, for bosses. There is an active, other-directed element in her symbols of power. You can use Kanter's symbols of power to identify powerful people in organizations. They can be particularly useful in finding a mentor who can effectively use power.

11-4b Kanter's Symbols of Powerlessness

Kanter also wrote about symptoms of **powerlessness**—a lack of power—in managers at different levels of the organization. First-line supervisors, for example, often display three symptoms of powerlessness: overly close supervision, inflexible adherence to the rules, and a tendency to do the job themselves rather than training their employees to do it. Staff professionals such as accountants and lawyers display different symptoms of powerlessness. When they feel powerless, they tend to resist change and try to protect their turf. Top executives can also feel powerless. They show symptoms such as focusing on budget cutting, punishing others, and using dictatorial, top-down communication. Acting in certain ways can lead employees to believe that a manager is powerless. By making *external attributions* (blaming others or circumstances) for negative events, a manager looks as if she has no power.[22]

11-4c Korda's Symbols of Power

Michael Korda offers a semiserious look at some tangible symbols of power: office furnishings, time power, and standing by.[23] Furniture is not just physically useful; it also conveys a message about power. Locked file cabinets are signs that the manager has important and confidential information in the office. A rectangular (rather than round) conference table enables the most

> By identifying powerful people and learning from their modeled behavior, you can learn the keys to power use in the organization.

important person to sit at the head of the table. The size of one's desk may convey the amount of power, too, as most executives prefer large, expensive desks.

Time power means using clocks and watches as power symbols. Korda says that the biggest compliment a busy executive can pay a visitor is to remove his watch and place it facedown on the desk, thereby communicating "my time is yours." He also notes that the less powerful the executive, the more intricate the watch. Moreover, managers who are really secure in their power wear no watch at all, since they believe nothing important can happen without them. A full calendar is also proof of power. Personal planners are left open on the desk to display busy schedules.

Standing by is a game in which people are obliged to keep their cell phones, pagers, and so forth with them at all times so executives can reach them. The idea is that the more you can impose your schedule on other people, the more power you have. In fact, Korda defines *power* as follows: there are more people who inconvenience themselves on your behalf than there are people on whose behalf you would inconvenience yourself. Closely tied to this is the ability to make others perform simple tasks for you, such as getting your coffee or fetching the mail.

While Kanter's symbols focus on the ability to help others, Korda's symbols focus on status—a person's relative standing in a group based on prestige and having other people defer to him.[24] By identifying powerful people and learning from their modeled behavior, you can learn the keys to power use in the organization.

> **powerlessness** A lack of power.

11-5 POLITICAL BEHAVIOR IN ORGANIZATIONS

Like the word *power*, the phrase *politics in organizations* may conjure up negative images. However, **organizational politics** is not necessarily negative; it is the use of power and influence in organizations. Because organizations are arenas in which people have competing interests, effective managers must reconcile competing interests. Organizational politics are central to managing. As people try to acquire power and expand their power base, they use various tactics and strategies. Some are sanctioned (acceptable to the organization); others are not. **Political behavior** refers to actions not officially sanctioned by an organization that are taken to influence others in order to meet one's personal goals.[25] Sometimes personal goals are aligned with team or organizational goals, and they can be achieved in support of others' interests. But other times personal goals and the interests of others collide, and individuals pursue politics at the expense of others' interests.[26]

Politics is a controversial topic among managers. Some managers take a favorable view of political behavior; others see it as detrimental to the organization. Some workers who perceive their workplace as highly political actually find the use of political tactics more satisfying and report greater job satisfaction when they engage in political behavior. Some people may therefore thrive in political environments, while others may find office politics distasteful and stressful.[27] It's important to remember, however, that political behavior is not inherently constructive or destructive.[28]

Most people are also amazingly good at recognizing political behavior at all levels of the firm. Employees are not only keenly aware of political behavior at their level but can also spot political behavior at both their supervisor's level and the topmost levels of the organization.[29]

Many organizational conditions encourage political activity. Among them are unclear goals, autocratic decision making, ambiguous lines of authority, scarce resources, and uncertainty.[30] Moreover, even supposedly objective activities may involve politics. One such activity is the performance appraisal process. A study of sixty executives who had extensive experience in employee evaluation indicated that political considerations were nearly always part of the performance appraisal process.[31]

The effects of political behavior in organizations can be quite negative when the political behavior is strategically undertaken to maximize self-interest. If people within the organization are competitively pursuing selfish ends, they're unlikely to be attentive to the concerns of others. As a consequence, the workplace can seem less helpful, more threatening, and more unpredictable. When people focus on their own concerns rather than on organizational goals, we see the negative face of power described earlier by David McClelland as personal power. And when employees view the organization's political climate as extreme, they experience more anxiety, tension, fatigue, and burnout. They are also dissatisfied with their jobs and are more likely to leave.[32]

However, not all political behavior is destructive. Though positive political behavior still involves self-interest, when it is aligned with organizational goals, the self-interest is perceived positively by employees. Political behavior is also viewed positively when it is seen as the only means by which to accomplish something. Job satisfaction and satisfaction with coworkers and supervisors is affected by any kind of political behavior.[33]

11-5a Influence Tactics

Influence is the process of affecting the thoughts, behavior, or feelings of another person. That other person could be the boss (upward influence), an employee (downward influence), or a coworker (lateral influence). There are eight basic types of influence tactics. They are listed and described in Table 11.2.[34] Research has shown that the four tactics used most frequently are consultation, rational persuasion, inspirational appeals, and ingratiation. Upward appeals and coalition tactics are used moderately. Exchange tactics are used least often.

Influence tactics are used for *impression management*, which was described in Chapter 3. In impression management, individuals use influence tactics to control others' impressions of them. One way in which people engage in impression management is through image building. The interview is a prime example of image building being used by all parties. Job candidates are trying to create favorable impressions with the interviewer through firm handshakes, strong eye contact, and confident posture. Similarly, interviewers are trying to make a good impression with the candidates by displaying warmth, referring to the candidates by name, and portraying themselves as similar to the candidates.[35]

organizational politics The use of power and influence in organizations.

political behavior Actions not officially sanctioned by an organization that are taken to influence others in order to meet one's personal goals.

TABLE 11.2 INFLUENCE TACTICS USED IN ORGANIZATIONS

Tactics	Description	Examples
Pressure	The person uses demands, threats, or intimidation to convince you to comply with a request or to support a proposal.	"If you don't do this, you're fired. You have until 5:00 to change your mind, or I'm going without you."
Upward appeals	The person seeks to persuade you that the request is approved by higher management or appeals to higher management for assistance in gaining your compliance with the request.	"I'm reporting you to my boss. My boss supports this idea."
Exchange	The person makes an explicit or implicit promise that you will receive rewards or tangible benefits if you comply with a request or support a proposal or reminds you of a prior favor to be reciprocated.	"You owe me a favor. I'll take you to lunch if you'll support me on this."
Coalition	The person seeks the aid of others to persuade you to do something or uses the support of others as an argument for you to agree also.	"All the other supervisors agree with me. I'll ask you in front of the whole committee."
Ingratiation	The person seeks to get you in a good mood or to think favorably of him or her before asking you to do something.	"Only you can do this job right. I can always count on you, so I have another request."
Rational persuasion	The person uses logical arguments and factual evidence to persuade you that a proposal or request is viable and likely to result in the attainment of task objectives.	"This new procedure will save us $150,000 in overhead. It makes sense to hire John; he has the most experience."
Inspirational appeals	The person makes an emotional request or proposal that arouses enthusiasm by appealing to your values and ideals or by increasing your confidence that you can do it.	"Being environmentally conscious is the right thing. Getting that account will be tough, but I know you can do it."
Consultation	The person seeks your participation in making a decision or planning how to implement a proposed policy, strategy, or change.	"This new attendance plan is controversial. How can we make it more acceptable? What do you think we can do to make our workers less fearful of the new robots on the production line?"

SOURCE: First two columns from G. Yukl and C. M. Falbe, "Influence Tactics and Objectives in Upward, Downward, and Lateral Influence Attempts," Journal of Applied Psychology 75 (1990): 132–140. Copyright © 1990 by the American Psychological Association. Reprinted with permission.

Ingratiation is an example of one tactic often used for impression management. Ingratiation can take many forms, including flattery, opinion conformity, and subservient behavior. *Exchange* is another influence tactic that may be used for impression management. Offering to do favors for someone in an effort to create a favorable impression is an exchange tactic.

Which influence tactics are most effective? It depends on the target of the influence attempt and the objective. Individuals use different tactics for different purposes, and they use different tactics for different people. Influence attempts with subordinates, for example, usually involve assigning tasks or changing behavior. With peers, the objective is often to request help. With superiors, influence attempts are often made to request approval, resources, political support, or personal benefits. *Rational persuasion* and *coalition tactics* are used most often to get support

from peers and superiors to change company policy. *Consultation* and *inspirational appeals* are particularly effective for gaining support and resources for a new project.[36] Overall, the most effective tactic in terms of achieving objectives is rational persuasion. *Pressure* is the least effective tactic.

Influence tactics are often used on bosses to get them to evaluate employees more favorably or to give the employees a promotion. Two tactics—rational persuasion and ingratiation—appear to work effectively in this way. Employees who use these tactics receive higher performance evaluations than employees who don't.[37] When supervisors believe an employee's motive for doing favors for the boss is simply to be a good citizen, they are likely to reward that employee. However, when the motive is seen as "brownnosing" (ingratiation), supervisors respond negatively.[38] And, as it becomes more obvious that the employee has something

Influencing Sustainability and Climate Change at Eileen Fisher

Fashion designer Eileen Fisher takes responsibility for sustainable design. "It's massive, the mess we're making. As designers, we became more aware of our responsibility to take care of the planet and not do any harm." Part of her commitment is Green Eileen, which allows customers to mail in unwanted clothing from her line and receive $5, and the knowledge that the garments will be put to good use. She's hoping to make a dent in the fashion industry's waste—84 percent of unwanted clothing ends up in landfills.

Eileen Fisher is a natural fiber-based company, using cotton, linen from flax, and wool from grass-fed sheep, so climate change is a real threat to the business. The issue of climate change really hit home when the company headquarters was flooded during Hurricane Sandy. Eileen Fisher joined CEOs from Gap, H&M, and other apparel firms at the Paris climate talks, asking world leaders to take meaningful action. Combining personal responsibility with the use of influence, the designer encourages others to think of business as a bridge to positive change in the world.

SOURCES: L. Rose, "Eileen Fisher Is Growing Her Business by Reducing Its Environmental Impact," *Fast Company*, November 13 (2016), accessed at https://www.fastcompany.com/3065315/the-fast-company-innovation-festival/eileen-fisher-is-growing-her-business-by-reducing-its-e; D. Brodwin, "Eileen Fisher: Making the Point," *Conscious Company*, 10 (2016): 31.

to gain by impressing the boss, the likelihood that ingratiation will succeed decreases. So, how does one use ingratiation effectively?

Results from a study conducted among supervisors and subordinates of a large state agency indicate that subordinates with higher scores on political skill used ingratiation regularly and received higher performance ratings, whereas individuals with lower scores on political skill who used ingratiation frequently received lower performance ratings.[39]

Managers and other people with high social status and power are often the most difficult to ingratiate successfully. One technique for success is to reflect on genuine positive feelings such as admiration for the high-status colleague, which translates into ingratiation that feels more genuine to the receiver and less like a blatant attempt to gain favors.[40]

CEOs are often the targets of ingratiation attempts such as flattery or opinion conformity, and they often respond to these attempts with positive affect toward the ingratiator. Falling for ingratiation often, though, can backfire. Top managers who feel they need to use ingratiation with their CEO can become resentful. The resentment can escalate into social undermining of the CEO with important other people such as journalists who are writing about the company.[41]

There is evidence that men and women view politics and influence attempts differently. Men tend to view political behavior more favorably than do women. When both men and women witness political behavior, they view it more positively if the agent is of their gender and the target is of the opposite gender.[42] Some women executives may view politics with distaste, and may expect to be recognized and promoted solely on the merit of their work. A lack of awareness of organizational politics is a barrier that holds women back in terms of moving into senior executive ranks.[43] Moreover, women may have fewer opportunities to develop political skills because of a lack of mentors and role models and because they are often excluded from informal networks.[44]

Different cultures prefer different influence tactics at work. One study found that American managers dealing with a tardy employee tended to rely on pressure tactics such as, "If you don't start reporting on time for work, I will have no choice but to start docking your pay." In contrast, Japanese managers relied on influence tactics that either appealed to the employee's sense of duty ("It is your duty as a responsible employee of this company to begin work on time.") or emphasized a consultative approach ("Is there anything I can do to help you overcome the problems that are preventing you from coming to work on time?").[45]

Influence can also stem from the way a person's personality fits into his work environment. A recent study found that extraverts have more influence in team-oriented work environments, whereas conscientious employees have more influence in environments where individuals work alone on technical tasks.[46]

It is important to note that influence tactics do have some positive effects. When investors form coalitions and put pressure on firms to increase their research and development efforts, it works.[47] However, some influence tactics, including pressure, coalition building, and exchange, can have strong ethical implications. There is a fine line between being an impression manager and being seen as a manipulator.

How can a manager use influence tactics well? First, a manager can develop and maintain open lines of communication in all directions: horizontally, vertically, and laterally. Then, the manager can treat the targets

HOT TREND

Saying You're Sorry May Not Work If You're in a Powerful Position

Leaders make mistakes, just like everyone, and often they have to express remorse for the mistakes and ask for forgiveness. Former Lululemon CEO Chip Wilson's fat-shaming comments prompted him to issue what some saw as an insincere apology and led to the alienation of customers. The company's yoga pants were garnering complaints for being too sheer and for the fabric pilling. Wilson claimed that "some women's bodies just don't actually work" in yoga pants. He later stepped down.

Research shows that apologies can often work in terms of generating forgiveness. They are least likely to be effective, though, when given from a high-power person to a low-power person. The reason: low-power people tend to interpret the apology from high-power people in a cynical way. In contrast to the perceived insincerity of the Lululemon CEO's apology, even the most sincere apologies offered by a high-power person may be met with cynicism and disbelief.

SOURCE: X. Zheng, M. van Dijke, J. Leunissen, and D. de Cremer, "When Saying Sorry May Not Help: Transgressor Power Moderates the Effect of an Apology on Forgiveness in the Workplace," *Human Relations*, 69 (2016): 1287–1313.

of influence attempts—whether managers, employees, or peers—with basic respect. Finally, the manager can understand that influence relationships are reciprocal—they are two-way relationships. As long as the influence attempts are directed toward organizational goals, the process of influence can be advantageous to all involved.

11-5b Political Skill

Researchers at Florida State University have generated an impressive body of research on political skill.[48] They have found that political skill is a distinct interpersonal attribute that is important for managerial success. Researchers suggest therefore that political skill should be considered in hiring and promotion decisions. Leaders' political skills have a positive effect on team performance, trust for the leader, and support for the leader.[49] Furthermore, political skill buffers the negative effects of stressors such as role conflict in work settings. This set of research findings points to the importance of developing political skill for managerial success.[50]

So what exactly is **political skill**? It is the ability to get things done through positive interpersonal relationships outside the formal organization. Politically skilled individuals have the ability to accurately understand others and use this knowledge to influence others in order to meet personal or organizational goals. Political skill is made up of four key dimensions: social astuteness, interpersonal influence, networking ability, and sincerity.

Social astuteness refers to the accurate perception and evaluation of social situations. Socially astute individuals manage social situations in ways that present them in the most favorable light. *Interpersonal influence* refers to a subtle and influential personal style that is effective in getting things done. Individuals with interpersonal influence are very flexible in adapting their behavior to differing targets of influence or differing contexts in order to achieve one's goals. *Networking ability* is an individual's capacity to develop and retain diverse and extensive social networks. Individuals with political skills can thrive in the challenging central position of a network in which colleagues turn to you for information. Finally, *sincerity* refers to an individual's ability to portray forthrightness and authenticity in all of his or her dealings. Individuals who have behavioral integrity inspire more confidence and trust, making them more

> **political skill** The ability to get things done through favorable interpersonal relationships outside formally prescribed organizational mechanisms.

successful in influencing others.[51] These four dimensions of political skill can each be learned.

High self-monitors and politically savvy individuals score higher on an index of political skill. Individuals who are emotionally intelligent are better able to develop political skills at work.[52] Recruiting new members to the organization is important, and political skill can make a better recruiter. Even in college football, the recruiter's political skill, combined with the head coach's winning record, leads to more success in recruiting NCAA football players.[53] Individuals who have political skill have been shown to be more likely to engage in organizational citizenship behaviors, have more total promotions, have higher perceived career success, and greater life satisfaction.[54]

11-6 MANAGING POLITICAL BEHAVIOR IN ORGANIZATIONS

Politics cannot and should not be eliminated from organizations. Managers should, however, take a proactive stance and manage the political behavior that inevitably occurs.[55] The first step in managing political behavior is to recognize it. Some behaviors to watch for include networking, finding key players to support initiatives, making friends with powerful people, bending the rules, and self-promoting. Lesser-used tactics include misinformation, spreading rumors, and blackmailing.[56]

To diffuse these behaviors, open communication is an important tool. Uncertainty tends to increase political behavior, and communication that reduces uncertainty is important. One way to open communication is to clarify the sanctioned and nonsanctioned political behaviors in the organization. For example, managers may want to encourage social power as opposed to personal power.[57]

Another key is to clarify expectations regarding performance. This can be accomplished through the use of specific, quantifiable goals and through the establishment of a clear connection between goal accomplishment and rewards.[58] Participative management is yet another key. Often, people engage in political behavior when they feel excluded from decision-making processes in the organization. By including them, managers will encourage

positive input and eliminate behind-the-scenes maneuvering. Also, encouraging cooperation among work groups is helpful in managing political behavior. Managers can instill a unity of purpose among work teams by rewarding cooperative behavior and by implementing activities that emphasize the integration of team efforts toward common goals.[59]

Managing scarce resources well is also important. An obvious solution to the problem of scarce resources is to increase the resource pool, but few managers have this luxury. However, clarifying the resource allocation process and making the connection between performance and resources explicit can discourage dysfunctional political behavior. Providing a supportive organizational climate allows employees to discuss controversial issues promptly and openly, thus preventing an issue from festering and potentially causing friction among employees.[60]

Managing political behavior at work is important, since the perception of dysfunctional political behavior can lead to job dissatisfaction.[61] When employees perceive that there are dominant interest groups or cliques at work, they are less satisfied with pay and promotions. When they believe that the organization's reward practices are influenced by who you know rather than how well you perform, they are less satisfied.[62] Furthermore,

when employees believe that their coworkers are exhibiting increased political behavior, they are less satisfied with their coworkers. Open communication, clear expectations about performance and rewards, participative decision-making practices, work group cooperation, effective management of scarce resources, and a supportive organizational climate can help managers prevent the negative consequences of political behavior.

11-6a Managing Up: Managing the Boss

One of the least discussed aspects of power and politics is the relationship between you and your boss. This is a crucial relationship because your boss is your most important link with the rest of the organization.[63] The employee–boss relationship is one of mutual dependence; you depend on your boss to give you performance feedback, provide resources, and supply critical information. Your boss depends on you for performance, information, and support. Because it's a mutual relationship, you should take an active role in managing it. Too often, the management of this relationship is left to the boss; but if the relationship doesn't meet the employee's needs, chances are the employee hasn't taken the responsibility to manage it proactively.

Table 11.3 shows the basic steps to take in managing your relationship with your boss. The first step is to try to understand as much as you can about your boss. What are her goals and objectives? What kind of pressures does she face in the job? Many individuals naively expect the boss to be perfect and are disappointed when they find that this is not the case. What are the boss's strengths, weaknesses, and blind spots? Because this is an emotionally charged relationship, it is difficult to be objective; but this is a critical step in forging an effective working relationship. What is the boss's preferred work style? Does she prefer everything in writing or hate detail? Does the boss prefer that you make appointments or is dropping in acceptable? The point is to gather as much information about your boss as you can and to try to put yourself in her shoes.

The second step in managing this important relationship is to assess yourself and your own needs much in the same way you analyzed your boss's. What are your strengths, weaknesses, and blind spots? What is your work style? How do you normally relate to authority figures? Some of us have tendencies toward counterdependence; that is, we rebel against the boss as an authority and view him as a hindrance to our performance. Or, in contrast, we might take an overdependent stance, passively accepting the employee–boss relationship and treating the boss as an all-wise, protective parent. What is your tendency? Knowing how you react to authority figures can help you understand your interactions with your boss.

Once you have done a careful self-analysis and tried to understand your boss, the next step is to work to develop an effective relationship. Both parties' needs and styles must be accommodated. A fundraiser for a large volunteer organization related a story about a new boss, describing him as cold, aloof, unorganized, and inept. She made repeated attempts to meet with him and clarify expectations, and his usual reply was that he didn't have the time. Frustrated, she almost looked for a new job. "I just can't reach him!" was her refrain. Then she stepped back to consider her boss's and her own styles. Being an Intuitive-Feeling type of person, she prefers constant feedback and reinforcement from others. Her boss, an Intuitive-Thinker type, works comfortably without feedback from others and has a tendency to fail to praise or reward others. She sat down with him and cautiously discussed the differences in their needs. This discussion became the basis for working out a comfortable relationship. "I still don't like him, but I understand him better," she said.

TABLE 11.3 MANAGING YOUR RELATIONSHIP WITH YOUR BOSS

Make sure you understand your boss and her context, including:

Her goals and objectives.

The pressures on her.

Her strengths, weaknesses, and blind spots.

Her preferred work style.

Assess yourself and your needs, including:

Your own strengths and weaknesses.

Your personal style.

Your predisposition toward dependence on authority figures.

Develop and maintain a relationship that:

Fits both your boss's and your own needs and styles.

Is characterized by mutual expectations.

Keeps your boss informed.

Is based on dependability and honesty.

Selectively uses your boss's time and resources.

SOURCE: Reprinted by permission of *Harvard Business Review*. From "Managing Your Boss," by J. J. Gabarro and J. P. Kotter (May–June 1993): 155.

> The driving idea of empowerment is that the individuals closest to the work and to the customers should make the decisions and that this makes the best use of employees' skills and talents.

Another aspect of managing the relationship involves working out mutual expectations. One key activity is to develop a plan for work objectives and have the boss agree to it.[64] It is important to do things right, but it is also important to do the right things. Neither party to the relationship is a mind reader, so clarifying the goals is a crucial step. Keeping the boss informed is also a priority. No one likes to be caught off guard.

The employee–boss relationship must be based on dependability and honesty. This means giving and receiving positive and negative feedback. Most of us are reluctant to give any feedback to the boss, but positive feedback is welcomed at the top. Negative feedback, while tougher to initiate, can clear the air. If given in a problem-solving format, it can even bring about a closer relationship.[65]

Finally, remember that your boss is on the same team you are. The golden rule is to make your boss look good because you expect the boss to do the same for you.

11-6b Sharing Power: Empowerment

As modern organizations grow flatter, eliminating layers of management, empowerment becomes more and more important. Jay Conger defines **empowerment** as "creating conditions for heightened motivation through the development of a strong sense of personal self-efficacy."[66] This means sharing power in such a way that individuals learn to believe in their ability to do the job. The driving idea of empowerment is that the individuals closest to the work and to the customers should make the decisions and that this makes the best use of employees' skills and talents. You can empower yourself by developing your sense of self-efficacy.

empowerment Sharing power in such a way that individuals learn to believe in their ability to do the job.

Four dimensions comprise the essence of empowerment: meaning, competence, self-determination, and impact.[67] *Meaning* is a fit between the work role and the employee's values and beliefs. It is the engine of empowerment through which employees become energized about their jobs. If employees' hearts are not in their work, they cannot feel empowered. *Competence* is the belief that one has the ability to do the job well. Without competence, employees will feel inadequate and lack a sense of empowerment. *Self-determination* is having control over the way one does work. Employees who feel they're just following orders from the boss cannot feel empowered. *Impact* is the belief that one's job makes a difference within the organization. Without a sense of contributing to a goal, employees cannot feel empowered. Effective empowerment results in employees with better job performance, strong organizational commitment, and lower levels of job stress. One way to make individuals feel more empowered is to empower their work units or teams. Individuals who work in empowered groups feel more psychologically empowered, and this enhances both individual and team performance.[68]

Empowerment is easy to advocate for but difficult to put into practice. Conger offers some guidelines on how leaders can empower others in the organization. First, managers should express confidence in employees and set high performance expectations. Positive expectations can go a long way toward enabling good performance, as the Pygmalion effect shows (Chapter 3). Second, managers should create opportunities for employees to participate in decision making. This means participation in the forms of both voice and choice. Employees should not just be asked to contribute their opinions about an issue; they should also have a vote in the decision that is made. One method for increasing participation is using *self-managed teams*, which, as discussed in Chapter 9, are the ultimate in empowered teams because they take on decisions and activities that traditionally belong to managers.

Third, managers should remove bureaucratic constraints that stifle autonomy. Often, companies have antiquated rules and policies that prevent employees from managing themselves. An example is a collection agency, where a manager's signature was once required to approve long-term payment arrangements for delinquent customers. Collectors, who spoke directly with customers, were the best judges of whether the payment arrangements were workable, and having to consult a manager made them feel closely supervised and powerless. The rule was dropped, and collections increased. Fourth, managers should set inspirational or meaningful goals. When individuals feel they "own" a goal, they are more willing to take personal responsibility for it.

Empowerment is a matter of degree. Jobs can be thought of in two dimensions: job content and job context. *Job content* consists of the tasks and procedures necessary for doing a particular job. *Job context* is broader. It is the reason the organization needs the job and includes the way the job fits into the organization's mission, goals, and objectives. These two dimensions are depicted in Figure 11.1, the employee empowerment grid.

Both axes of the grid contain the major steps in the decision-making process. As shown on the horizontal axis, decision-making authority over job content increases in terms of greater involvement in the decision-making process. Similarly, the vertical axis shows that authority over job context increases with greater involvement in that decision-making process. Combining job content and job context authority in this way produces five points that vary in terms of the degree of empowerment.[69]

No Discretion (point A) represents the traditional, assembly-line job—highly routine and repetitive with no decision-making power. Recall from Chapter 7 that if these jobs have a demanding pace and if workers have no discretion, distress will result.

Task Setting (point B) is the essence of most empowerment programs in organizations today. In this case, the worker is empowered to make decisions about the best way to get the job done but has no decision responsibility for the job context.

Participatory Empowerment (point C) represents a situation that is typical of autonomous work groups that have some decision-making power over both job content and job context. Their involvement is in identifying problems, developing alternatives, and evaluating alternatives, but the actual choice of alternatives is often beyond their power. Participatory empowerment can lead to job satisfaction and productivity.

Mission Defining (point D) is an unusual case of empowerment and is seldom seen. Here, employees have power over job context but not job content. An example would be a unionized team that is asked to decide whether their jobs could be better done by an outside vendor. Deciding to outsource would dramatically affect the mission of the company but would not

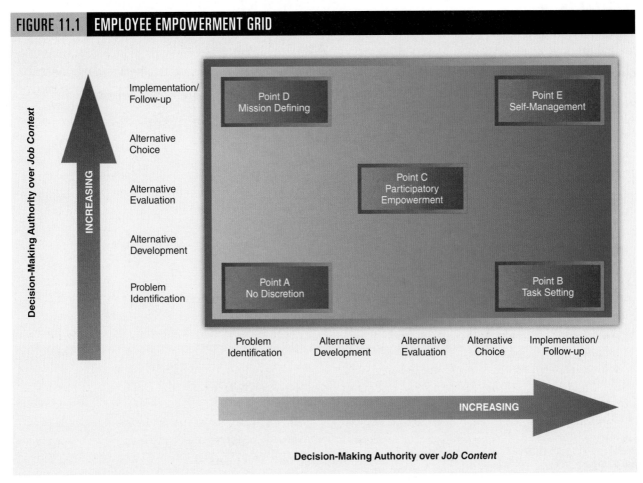

FIGURE 11.1 | EMPLOYEE EMPOWERMENT GRID

affect job content, which is specified in the union contract. Assuring these employees of continued employment regardless of their decision would be necessary for this case of empowerment.

Self-Management (point E) represents total decision-making control over both job content and job context. It is the ultimate expression of trust. One example is TXI Chaparral Steel (part of Texas Industries), where employees redesign their own jobs to add value to the organization.

Empowerment should begin with job content and proceed to job context. Because the workforce is so diverse, managers should recognize that some employees are more ready for empowerment than others. Hence, managers must diagnose situations and determine the degree of empowerment to extend to employees. Managers can also empower entire teams of employees with appropriate interventions. When they do empower a team, individuals learn more and they are more committed to their teams.[70] Empowered individuals are also valuable to organizations because they are more motivated, satisfied, and creative.[71]

Unfortunately, the empowerment process carries with it a risk of failure. When you delegate responsibility and authority, you must be prepared to allow employees to fail, and failure is not something most managers tolerate well. Although the airline industry gets criticized for poor customer service, Southwest Airlines has maintained its loyal following for fifty years by providing excellent service through empowering employees. Southwest empowers employees to bend the rules if they believe it's in the customer's best interest. The result is employees who go the extra mile to make customers happy, because it's within their power to do so.[72]

STUDY TOOLS 11

LOCATED AT BACK OF THE TEXTBOOK

☐ Rip out chapter review card

LOCATED AT WWW.CENGAGE.COM/LOGIN

☐ Gain unique perspectives on key concepts with new Concept Clip videos in the e-book

☐ Review key term flashcards and create your own

☐ Increase your comprehension with online homework and quizzes

12 | Leadership and Followership

LEARNING OBJECTIVES

12-1 Discuss the differences between leadership and management and between leaders and managers.

12-2 Explain the role of trait theory in describing leaders.

12-3 Describe the role of foundational behavioral research in the development of leadership theories.

12-4 Describe and compare the four contingency theories of leadership.

12-5 Discuss the recent developments in leadership theory of leader–member exchange and inspirational leadership.

12-6 Discuss how issues of emotional intelligence, trust, gender, and servant leadership are informing today's leadership models.

12-7 Define followership and identify different types of followers.

12-8 Synthesize historical leadership research into key guidelines for leaders.

Brian Jackson/123RF

After finishing this chapter go to **PAGE 216** for **STUDY TOOLS**

Leadership in organizations is the process of guiding and directing the behavior of people in the work environment. In the first section, we discuss the ways that leadership differs from *management*. **Formal leadership** is officially sanctioned leadership based on the authority of a formal position. **Informal leadership** is unofficial leadership accorded to a person by other members of the organization. Though one of the most researched topics in organizational behavior, leadership remains one of the least understood social processes in organizations.

leadership The process of guiding and directing the behavior of people in the work environment.

formal leadership Officially sanctioned leadership based on the authority of a formal position.

informal leadership Unofficial leadership accorded to a person by other members of the organization.

12-1 LEADERSHIP VERSUS MANAGEMENT

John Kotter describes leadership and management as two distinct yet complementary systems of action in organizations.[1] Specifically, he believes that effective leadership produces useful change in organizations while good management controls complexity in the organization and its environment.

The *management process* involves (1) planning and budgeting, (2) organizing and staffing, and (3) controlling and problem solving. Done effectively, the management process reduces uncertainty and stabilizes an organization. Alfred P. Sloan's integration and stabilization of General Motors after its early years of growth are an example of good management. In contrast, the *leadership process* involves (1) setting a direction for the organization; (2) aligning people with

Healthy organizations need both effective leadership and good management.

that direction through communication; and (3) motivating people to action, partly through empowerment and partly through basic need gratification. The leadership process creates uncertainty and change in an organization. Effective leaders not only control the future of the organization but also act as enablers of change in organizations. They disturb existing patterns of behaviors, promote novel ideas, and help organizational members make sense of the change process.[2] Sheryl Sandberg, chief operating officer of Facebook, knows about creating change. Since joining the company in 2007, she has helped lead the company to great success by creating an advertising platform that's attracted the world's largest brands.[3]

TABLE 12.1 LEADERS AND MANAGERS

Personality Dimension	Manager	Leader
Attitudes toward goals	Has an impersonal, passive, functional attitude; believes goals rise out of necessity and reality	Has a personal and active attitude; believes goals arise from desire and imagination
Conceptions of work	Views work as an enabling process that combines people, ideas, and things; seeks moderate risk through coordination and balance	Looks for fresh approaches to old problems; seeks high-risk positions, especially with high payoffs
Relationships with others	Avoids solitary work activity, preferring to work with others; avoids close, intense relationships; avoids conflict	Is comfortable in solitary work activity; encourages close, intense working relationships; is not conflict averse
Sense of self	Is once born; makes a straightforward life adjustment; accepts life as it is	Is twice born; engages in a struggle for a sense of order in life; questions life

SOURCE: Reprinted by permission of *Harvard Business Review*. From "Managers and Leaders: Are They Different?" by A. Zaleznik (January 2004).

the other. Leaders and managers differ along four separate dimensions of personality: attitudes toward goals, conceptions of work, relationships with other people, and sense of self. The differences between these two personality types are summarized in Table 12.1.

It has been proposed that some people are *strategic leaders* who combine the stability of managers with the visionary abilities of leaders in a synergistic way. PepsiCo's CEO Indra Nooyi shifted the company's strategy toward healthier options, and it has paid off. Less than 25 percent of sales come from soda, and the emphasis now is on water and noncarbonated beverages, along with Frito-Lay and Quaker products.[5]

Effective leaders, like Sheryl Sandberg of Facebook, act as enablers of change.

Krista Kennell/Shutterstock.com

Abraham Zaleznik proposes that leaders have distinct personalities that stand in contrast to the personalities of managers.[4] Therefore, although both leaders and managers make valuable contributions to an organization, their contributions are different. Whereas **leaders** agitate for change and new approaches, **managers** advocate stability and the status quo. As a result, there is a dynamic tension between leaders and managers that makes it difficult for each to understand

leaders An advocate for change and new approaches to problems.

managers An advocate for stability and the status quo.

12-2 EARLY TRAIT THEORIES

The first studies of leadership attempted to identify what physical attributes, personality characteristics, and abilities distinguished leaders from other members of a group.[6] The physical attributes that were considered were height, weight, physique, energy, health, appearance, and age. Although this line of research yielded some interesting findings, it provided insufficient evidence for concluding that leaders can be distinguished on the basis of physical attributes.

Leader *personality* characteristics that have been examined include originality, adaptability, introversion–extroversion, dominance, self-confidence, integrity, conviction, mood optimism, and emotional control. There is some evidence that leaders may be more adaptable and self-confident than the average group member. With regard to leader *abilities*, attention has been devoted to such constructs as social skills, intelligence, scholarship, speech fluency, cooperativeness, and insight. In this area, there is some evidence that leaders are more intelligent, verbal, and cooperative and have a higher level of scholarship than the average group member.

Narcissistic CEOs, Big Signatures

Does a large signature mean the CEO is a narcissist? A recent study indicates that it may. Researchers compared the signatures of 605 CEOs of U.S. companies from annual reports and proxy filings. They then analyzed the size of the signatures using a custom software program and found that the large signatures predicted overinvestment, lower sales growth, and lower ROA. Despite lower financial performance, CEOs with large signatures enjoyed higher compensation but shorter tenures.

Narcissistic leaders' egotism and conceit lead them to inflated views of their own performance, but their self-assessments are not in line with the reality of their performance. They often belittle others and ignore feedback about their behavior. And narcissism is on the rise, making it more likely that you may encounter narcissists in the workplace. The best strategy may be to try and avoid working for one.

pio3/Shutterstock.com

SOURCE: C. Ham, N. Seybert, and S. Wang, "Narcissism Is a Bad Sign: CEO Signature Size, Investment, and Performance" (March 22, 2016). UNC Kenan-Flagler Research Paper No. 2013-1, accessed at http://ssrn.com/abstract=2144419; P. Korkki, "Bosses Who Love Themselves," *New York Times*, March 7, 2015, accessed at http://www.nytimes.com/2015/03/08/business/the-perils-of-narcissists-in-the-workplace.html?_r=0. M. J. C. Guedes, "Mirror, Mirror on the Wall, Am I the Greatest Performer of All? Narcissism and Self-Reported and Objective *Performance*," *Personality and Individual Differences*, 108 (2017): 182–185.

Nonetheless, these findings are neither strong nor uniform. For each attribute or trait claimed to distinguish leaders from followers, there were always at least one or two studies with contradictory findings. For some, the trait theories are invalid, though interesting and intuitively of some relevance. It is generally agreed that the trait theories have had very limited success in being able to identify universal, distinguishing attributes of leaders.

12-3 BEHAVIORAL THEORIES

Behavioral theories emerged as a response to the deficiencies of the trait theories. Trait theories attempted to tell us what leaders were like but didn't address how leaders behaved. Three research studies built the foundations of many modern leadership theories: the Lewin, Lippitt, and White studies; the Ohio State studies; and the Michigan studies.

12-3a Foundational Behavioral Research

The earliest research on leadership style, conducted by Kurt Lewin and his students, identified three basic styles: autocratic, democratic, and laissez-faire.[7] A leader uses one of these three basic styles when approaching a group of followers in a leadership situation. The specific situation is not an important consideration because the leader's style does not vary with the situation. The leader with an **autocratic style** uses strong, directive actions to control the rules, regulations, activities, and relationships in the work environment. Followers have little discretionary influence over the nature of the work, its accomplishment, or other aspects of the work environment. The leader with a **democratic style** uses interaction and collaboration with followers to direct work and the work environment. Followers have a high degree of discretionary influence, although the leader has ultimate authority and responsibility. The leader with a **laissez-faire style** entails a hands-off approach. A laissez-faire

autocratic style A style of leadership in which the leader uses strong, directive actions to control the rules, regulations, activities, and relationships in the work environment.

democratic style A style of leadership in which the leader uses interaction and collaboration with followers to direct the work and work environment.

laissez-faire style A style of leadership in which the leader has a hands-off approach.

Forgiveness for Leaders Is Hard to Come By

Leaders sometimes must apologize for their own or their company's mistakes. Former Uber CEO Travis Kalanick apologized to employees after a video emerged of him yelling at one of his drivers in San Francisco. He also apologized publicly for Uber's cultural failings after several sexual harassment and discrimination claims emerged. Kalanick was forced to resign in August 2017, although he remains on the board of directors.

Research indicates that Uber employees may not forgive him. Apologies from people in positions of power, especially those who influence pay and promotions and can tell employees what to do, are met with cynicism. Employees tend to be skeptical of the leader's words and motives. High power may be associated with hidden agendas and exploitation of others. And, the content of the apology doesn't seem to make a difference. The power dynamics between leaders and employees make forgiveness of leaders a tough prospect.

SOURCE: X. Zheng, M. Van Dijke, J. M. Leunissen, and D. De Cremer, "When Saying Sorry May Not Help: Transgressor Power Moderates the Effect of an Apology on Forgiveness in the Workplace," *Human Relations,* 69 (2016): 1387–1418.

leader abdicates the authority and responsibility of the position, and this style often results in chaos. Laissez-faire leadership also causes role ambiguity for followers because the leader fails to clearly define goals, responsibilities, and outcomes. It leads to higher interpersonal conflict at work.[8]

The leadership research program at The Ohio State University also measured specific leader behaviors. The initial results suggested that there were two important underlying dimensions of leader behaviors—initiating structure and consideration.[9] **Initiating structure** is leader behavior aimed at defining and organizing work relationships and roles, as well as establishing clear patterns of organization, communication, and ways of getting things done. **Consideration** is leader behavior aimed at nurturing friendly, warm working relationships, as well as encouraging mutual trust and interpersonal respect within the work unit. These two leader behaviors are independent of each other; that is, a leader may be high on both, low on both, or high on one and low on the other.[10]

Finally, studies conducted at the University of Michigan suggest that the leader's style has very important implications for the emotional atmosphere of the work environment and, therefore, for the followers who work under that leader. Two styles of leadership were identified: production oriented and employee oriented.[11]

A *production-oriented style* leads to a work environment where the focus is on getting things done. The leader in this environment uses direct, close supervision or many written and unwritten rules and regulations to control behavior.

In contrast, an *employee-oriented leadership* style leads to a work environment that focuses on relationships. The leader exhibits less direct, or less close, supervision and establishes fewer written or unwritten rules and regulations for behavior. Employee-oriented leaders display concern for people and their needs.

Taken together, these three groups of studies (the Lewin studies, the Ohio State studies, and the Michigan studies) form the building blocks of many recent leadership theories. What the studies have in common is that two basic leadership styles were identified, with one focusing on *tasks* (autocratic, production oriented, initiating structure) and one focusing on *people* (democratic, employee oriented, consideration).

12-3b The Leadership Grid: A Contemporary Extension

Robert Blake and Jane Mouton's **Leadership Grid**, originally called the Managerial Grid, was developed with a focus on attitudes.[12] The two underlying dimensions of the grid are labeled Concern for Results and

initiating structure Leader behavior aimed at defining and organizing work relationships and roles, as well as establishing clear patterns of organization, communication, and ways of getting things done.

consideration Leader behavior aimed at nurturing friendly, warm working relationships as well as encouraging mutual trust and interpersonal respect within the work unit.

leadership grid An approach to understanding a leader's or manager's concern for results (production) and concern for people.

Concern for People. These two attitudinal dimensions are independent of each other, and, in different combinations, they form various leadership styles. Blake and Mouton originally identified five distinct managerial styles, and further development of the grid has led to the seven distinct leadership styles shown in Figure 12.1.

The **organization man manager (5,5)** is a middle-of-the-road leader who has a medium concern for people and production. This leader attempts to balance a concern for people and production without a commitment to either.

organization man manager (5,5) A middle-of-the-road leader.

FIGURE 12.1 THE LEADERSHIP GRID

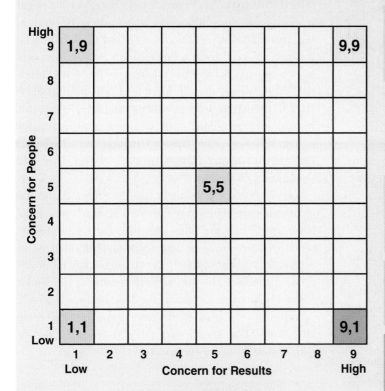

1,9 Country Club Management:
Thoughtful attention to the needs of the people for satisfying relationships leads to a comfortable, friendly organization atmosphere and work tempo.

9,9 Team Management:
Work accomplishment is from committed people; interdependence through a "common stake" in organization purpose leads to relationships of trust and respect.

5,5 Middle-of-the-Road Management:
Adequate organization performance is possible through balancing the necessity to get work out while maintaining morale of people at a satisfactory level.

1,1 Impoverished Management:
Exertion of minimum effort to get required work done is appropriate to sustain organization membership.

9,1 Authority-Compliance Management:
Efficiency in operations results from arranging conditions of work in such a way that human elements interfere to a minimum degree.

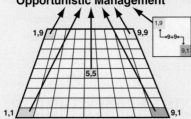

Opportunistic Management

In Opportunistic Management, people adapt and shift to any grid style needed to gain the maximum advantage. Performance occurs according to a system of selfish gain. Effort is given only for an advantage for personal gain.

9+9: Paternalism/Maternalism Management:
Reward and approval are bestowed to people in return for loyalty and obedience; failure to comply leads to punishment.

SOURCE: B. Dumaine, "Buffett's Mr. Fix-It," *Fortune* (August 16, 2010): 78–86; M. M. Rose, "NetJets Returns to Profit in the First Quarter," *The Columbus Dispatch* (April 22, 2010), http://www.dispatch.com/live/content/business/stories/2010/04/22/netjets-returns-to-profit-in-first-quarter.html, accessed August 22, 2010.

S'Well CEO Sarah Kauss has a mission to rid the world of plastic bottles. Her success has led her to commit $800,000 to provide clean water to the world's most vulnerable communities by partnering with UNICEF.

The **authority-compliance manager (9,1)** has great concern for production and little concern for people. This leader desires tight control in order to get tasks done efficiently and considers creativity and human relations unnecessary. Authority-compliance managers may become so focused on running an efficient organization that they actually use tactics such as bullying. Some authority-compliance managers may intimidate, verbally and mentally attack, and otherwise mistreat subordinates. This form of abuse is quite common, with one in six U.S. workers reporting that they have been bullied by a manager.[13] The inverse position is the **country club manager (1,9)**, who has great concern for people and little

concern for production, attempts to avoid conflict, and seeks to be well liked. This leader's goal is to keep people happy through good interpersonal relations, which are more important to her than the task. (This style is not a sound human relations approach but rather a soft Theory X approach.)

The **team manager (9,9)** builds a highly productive team of committed people. This leader works to motivate employees to reach their highest levels of accomplishment, is flexible, is responsive to change, and understands the need for change. The **impoverished manager (1,1)** exerts just enough effort to get by. This leader has little concern for people or production, avoids taking sides, and stays out of conflicts; he is often referred to as a laissez-faire leader. Two new leadership styles have been added to these five original leadership styles within the grid. The **paternalistic father-knows-best manager (9+9)** promises reward for compliance and threatens punishment for noncompliance. The **opportunistic what's-in-it-for-me manager (Opp)** uses whichever style will maximize self-benefit.

It's important to highlight that the grid evaluates the *team manager* (9,9) as the very best style of managerial behavior. This is the basis on which the grid has been used for team building and leadership training in an organization's development. As an organizational development method, the grid aims to transform the leader in the organization to lead in the "one best way," which, according to the grid, is the team approach. The team style is one that combines optimal concern for people with optimal concern for results.

SAME BASIC IDEA, VERY DIFFERENT MANIFESTATION	
Ohio State	**Blake-Mouton**
Descriptive	Normative
Nonevaluative	Prescriptive
No attitude	Attitudinal overtones

12-4 CONTINGENCY THEORIES

Contingency theories involve the belief that leadership style must be appropriate for the particular situation. By their nature, contingency theories are if-then theories: If the situation is x, then the appropriate leadership behavior is y. We examine four such theories, including Fiedler's contingency theory, path–goal theory, normative decision theory, and situational leadership theory.

---

authority-compliance manager (9,1) A leader who emphasizes efficient production.

country club manager (1,9) A leader who has great concern for people and little concern for production, attempts to avoid conflict, and seeks to be well liked.

team manager (9,9) A leader who builds a highly productive team of committed people.

impoverished manager (1,1) A leader who exerts just enough effort to get by.

paternalistic father-knows-best manager (9+9) A leader who promises reward and threatens punishment.

opportunistic what's-in-it-for-me manager (Opp) A leader who uses whichever style will maximize self-benefit.

12-4a Fiedler's Contingency Theory

Fiedler's contingency theory of leadership proposes that the fit between the leader's need structure and the favorableness of the leader's situation determines the team's effectiveness in work accomplishment. This theory assumes that leaders are either task oriented or relationship oriented, depending upon how the leaders obtain their primary need gratification.[14] Task-oriented leaders are primarily gratified by accomplishing tasks and getting work done. Relationship-oriented leaders are primarily gratified by developing good, comfortable interpersonal relationships. Accordingly, the effectiveness of both types of leaders depends on the favorableness of their situation. The theory classifies the favorableness of the leader's situation according to the leader's position power, the structure of the team's task, and the quality of the leader–follower relationships.

THE LEAST PREFERRED COWORKER Fiedler classifies leaders using the Least Preferred Coworker (LPC) Scale, a projective technique in which a leader is asked to choose the person he least prefers to work with (the **least preferred coworker**, or **LPC**).[15] The leader is asked to describe this LPC using sixteen eight-point bipolar adjective sets. Two of these bipolar adjective sets follow (the leader marks the one most descriptive of the LPC):

Efficient : : : : : : : : : Inefficient
Cheerful : : : : : : : : : Gloomy

Leaders who describe their LPC in positive terms (i.e., pleasant, efficient, cheerful, and so on) are classified as high LPC, or relationship-oriented, leaders. Those who describe their LPC in negative terms (i.e., unpleasant, inefficient, gloomy, and so on) are classified as low LPC, or task-oriented, leaders.

The LPC score is a controversial element in contingency theory.[16] It has been critiqued conceptually and methodologically because it is a projective technique with low measurement reliability.

SITUATIONAL FAVORABLENESS The leader's situation has three dimensions: task structure, position power, and leader–member relations. Based on these three dimensions, the situation is either favorable or unfavorable for the leader. **Task structure** refers to the degree of clarity, or ambiguity, in the work activities assigned to the group. **Position power** refers to the authority associated with the leader's formal position in the organization.

Leader–member relations, the quality of interpersonal relationships among a leader and the group

> Recent research has shown that relationship-oriented leaders encourage team learning and innovation, which helps products get to market faster.

members, is measured by the *Group-Atmosphere Scale*, composed of nine eight-point bipolar adjective sets. Two of these bipolar adjective sets follow:

Friendly : : : : : : : : Unfriendly
Accepting : : : : : : : : Rejecting

A favorable leadership situation, according to Fiedler, is one with a structured task for the work group, strong position power for the leader, and good leader–member relations. In contrast, an unfavorable leadership situation is one with an unstructured task, weak position power for the leader, and moderately poor leader–member relations. Between these two extremes, the leadership situation has varying degrees of moderate favorableness for the leader.

	Favorable Moderate	Unfavorable
Task structure	Structured	Unstructured
Position power	Strong	Weak
Leader–member relations	Good	Poor

LEADERSHIP EFFECTIVENESS The contingency theory suggests that low LPC and high LPC leaders are both effective if placed in the right situation.[17] Specifically, low LPC (task-oriented) leaders are most effective in either very favorable or very unfavorable leadership situations. In contrast, high LPC (relationship-oriented) leaders are most effective in situations of intermediate favorableness. Figure 12.2 shows the nature of these

least preferred coworker LPC The person a leader has least preferred to work with.

task structure The degree of clarity, or ambiguity, in the work activities assigned to the group.

position power The authority associated with the leader's formal position in the organization.

leader–member relations The quality of interpersonal relationships among a leader and the group members.

FIGURE 12.2 LEADERSHIP EFFECTIVENESS IN THE CONTINGENCY THEORY

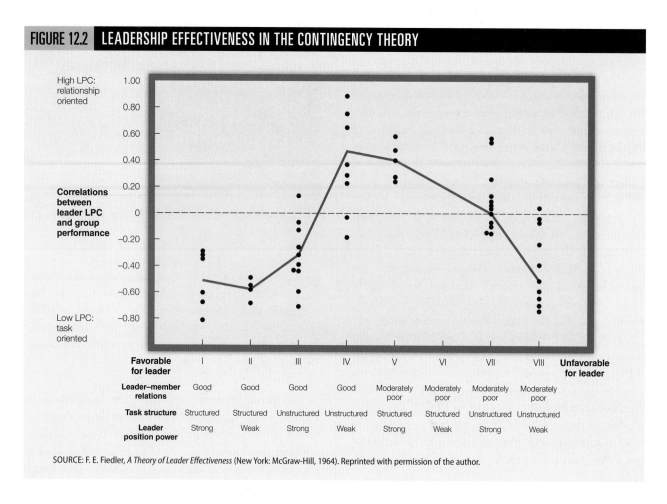

Favorable for leader: I (Favorable) ... VIII (Unfavorable for leader)

	I	II	III	IV	V	VI	VII	VIII
Leader–member relations	Good	Good	Good	Good	Moderately poor	Moderately poor	Moderately poor	Moderately poor
Task structure	Structured	Structured	Unstructured	Unstructured	Structured	Structured	Unstructured	Unstructured
Leader position power	Strong	Weak	Strong	Weak	Strong	Weak	Strong	Weak

SOURCE: F. E. Fiedler, *A Theory of Leader Effectiveness* (New York: McGraw-Hill, 1964). Reprinted with permission of the author.

relationships and suggests that leadership effectiveness is determined by the degree of fit between the leader and the situation. Recent research has shown that relationship-oriented leaders encourage team learning and innovation, which helps products get to market faster. This means that most relationship-oriented leaders perform well in leading new product development teams. In short, the right team leader can help get new products out the door faster, while a mismatch between the leader and the situation can have the opposite effect.[18]

What, then, is to be done if there is a misfit? What happens when a low LPC leader is in a moderately favorable situation or when a high LPC leader is in a highly favorable or highly unfavorable situation? It is unlikely that the leader can be changed, according to the theory, because the leader's need structure is an enduring trait that is hard to change. Fiedler recommends that the situation be changed to fit the leader's style.[19] A moderately favorable situation would be reengineered to be more favorable and therefore more suitable for the low LPC leader. A highly favorable or highly unfavorable situation would be changed to one that is moderately favorable and more suitable for the high LPC leader.

12-4b Path–Goal Theory

Robert House developed a path–goal theory of leader effectiveness based on an expectancy theory of motivation.[20] From the perspective of path–goal theory, the basic role of the leader is to clear the follower's path to the goal. The leader uses the most appropriate of four leader behavior styles to help followers clarify the paths that lead them to work and personal goals. The key concepts in the theory are shown in Figure 12.3.

A leader selects from the four leader behavior styles, shown in Figure 12.3, the one that is most helpful to followers at a given time. The directive style is used when the leader must give specific guidance about work tasks, schedule work, and let followers know what is expected. The *supportive style* is used when the leader needs to express concern for followers' well-being and social status. The *participative style* is used when the leader must engage in joint decision-making activities with followers. The *achievement-oriented style* is used when the leader must set challenging goals for followers and show strong confidence in those followers.

In selecting the appropriate leader behavior style, the leader must consider both the followers and the

FIGURE 12.3   THE PATH—GOAL THEORY OF LEADERSHIP

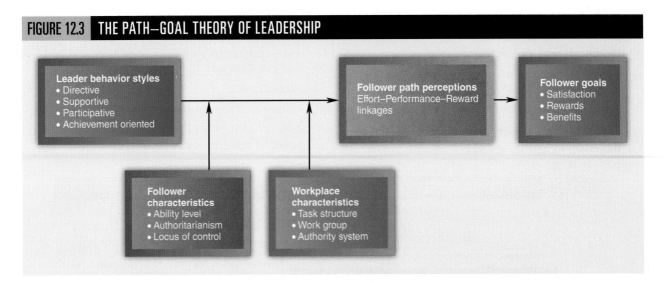

work environment. A number of characteristics are included in Figure 12.3. Let us consider two scenarios. In scenario one, the followers are inexperienced and are working on an ambiguous, unstructured task. The leader in this situation might best use a directive style. In scenario two, the followers are highly trained professionals, and the task is difficult but achievable. The leader in this situation might best use an achievement-oriented style.

In path–goal theory, the leader always chooses the leader behavior style that helps followers achieve their goals. The theory assumes that leaders adapt their behavior and style to fit the characteristics of the followers and the environment in which they work. Actual tests of the path–goal theory and its propositions provide conflicting evidence.[21] The path–goal theory does have intuitive appeal and reinforces the idea that the appropriate leadership style depends on both the work situation and the followers. Research is focusing on which style

works best in specific situations. For example, in small organizations, leaders who used visionary, transactional, and empowering behaviors, while avoiding autocratic behaviors, were most successful.[22]

12-4c Vroom-Yetton-Jago Normative Decision Model

Victor Vroom, Phillip Yetton, and Arthur Jago developed and refined the normative decision model, which helps leaders and managers determine the appropriate level of employee participation in decision making. The model recognizes the benefits of authoritative, democratic, and consultive styles of leader behavior.[23] Five forms of decision making are described in the model:

1. *Decide.* The manager makes the decision alone and either announces it or "sells" it to the group.

Mark Zuckerberg of Facebook: Would I Want to Work for This Person?

Facebook CEO Mark Zuckerberg thinks that hiring top talent is important. He has a rule of thumb for hiring individuals that takes the way we traditionally think about hiring and turns it upside down. Most managers may think, "Do I want this person working for me?" Instead, Zuckerberg says, "I would only hire someone to work directly for me if I would work for that person." He cites Sheryl Sandberg, Facebook's COO, as one of his successful hires and a person he would enjoy reporting to. His hiring strategy works. Facebook is a social media powerhouse worth $350 billion.

SOURCES: A. Lashinsky, "The Unexpected Management Genius of Facebook's Mark Zuckerberg," *Fortune*, November 10, 2016, accessed at http://fortune.com/facebook-mark-zuckerberg-business/; J. Bercovici, "Mark Zuckerberg's Foolproof Rule for Hiring," *Inc.*, March 4, 2015, accessed at http://www.inc.com/jeff-bercovici/mark-zuckerberg-hiring-rule.html.

2. *Consult individually*. The manager pre-sents the problem to the group members individually, gets their input, and then makes the decision.
3. *Consult group*. The manager presents the problem to the group members in a meeting, gets their input, and then makes the decision.
4. *Facilitate*. The manager presents the problem to the group in a meeting and acts as a facilitator,

defining the problem and the boundaries that surround the decision. The manager's ideas are not given more weight than any other group member's ideas. The objective is concurrence.

5. *Delegate*. The manager permits the group to make the decision within prescribed limits, providing needed resources and encouragement.[24]

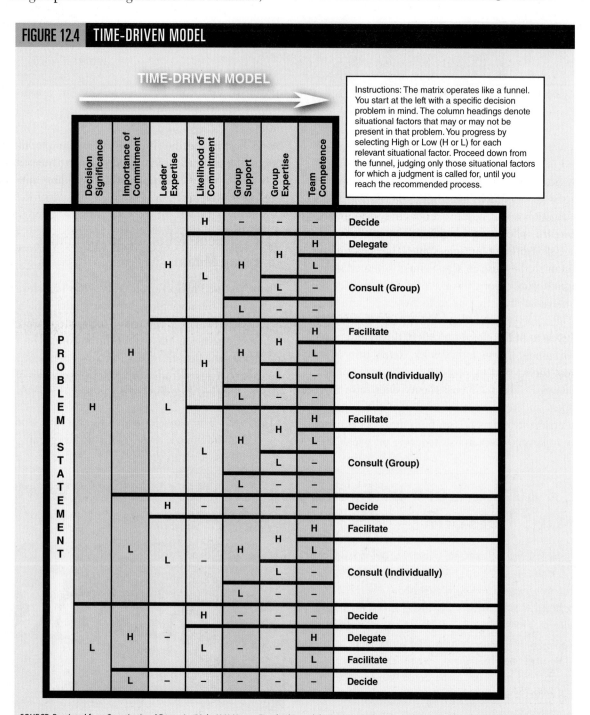

| FIGURE 12.4 | TIME-DRIVEN MODEL |

Instructions: The matrix operates like a funnel. You start at the left with a specific decision problem in mind. The column headings denote situational factors that may or may not be present in that problem. You progress by selecting High or Low (H or L) for each relevant situational factor. Proceed down from the funnel, judging only those situational factors for which a judgment is called for, until you reach the recommended process.

Decision Significance	Importance of Commitment	Leader Expertise	Likelihood of Commitment	Group Support	Group Expertise	Team Competence	
H	H			H	–	–	–	Decide
		H	L	H	H	H	Delegate
						L	
					L	–	Consult (Group)
				L	–	–	
		H	L	H	H	H	Facilitate
						L	
					L	–	Consult (Individually)
				L	–	–	
		L	L	H	H	H	Facilitate
						L	
					L	–	Consult (Group)
				L	–	–	
	L	H	–	–	–	–	Decide
		L	L	H	H	H	Facilitate
						L	
					L	–	Consult (Individually)
				L	–	–	
L	H	–	H	–	–	–	Decide
			L	–	–	H	Delegate
						L	Facilitate
	L	–	–	–	–	–	Decide

SOURCE: Reprinted from Organizational Dynamics 28, by V. H. Vroom, "Leadership and the Decision-Making Process," pp. 82–94 (Spring 2000) with permission from Elsevier.

The key to the normative decision model is that a manager should use the decision method most appropriate for a given decision situation. The manager arrives at the proper method by working through matrices like the one in Figure 12.4. The factors across the top of the model (decision significance, commitment, leader expertise, and so on) are the situational factors in the normative decision model. This matrix is for decisions that must be made under time pressure, but other matrices are also available. For example, there is a different matrix managers can use when their objective is to develop subordinates' decision-making skills. Although the model offers very explicit predictions as well as prescriptions for leaders, its utility is limited to the leader decision-making tasks.

12-4d The Situational Leadership® Model

The Situational Leadership model, developed by Paul Hersey and Kenneth Blanchard, suggests that the leader's behavior should be adjusted to the maturity level of the followers.[25] The model employs two dimensions of leader behavior as used in the Ohio State studies; one dimension is task oriented, and the other is relationship oriented. Follower maturity is categorized into four levels, as shown in Figure 12.5. Follower readiness is determined by the follower's ability and willingness to complete a specific task. Readiness can therefore be low or high depending on the particular task. In addition, readiness varies within a single person according to the task. One person may be willing and able to satisfy simple requests from customers (high readiness) but less able or willing to give highly technical advice to customers (low readiness). It is important that the leader be able to evaluate the readiness level of each follower for each task. The four styles of leader behavior associated with the four readiness levels are depicted in Figure 12.5.

According to the Situational Leadership model, a leader should use a *telling style* (S1) when a follower is unable and unwilling to do a certain task. This style involves providing instructions and closely monitoring performance. As such, the telling style involves considerable task behavior and low relationship behavior. When a follower is unable but willing and confident to do a task, the leader can use the *selling style* (S2), in which there is high task behavior and high relationship behavior. In this case, the leader explains decisions and provides opportunities for the employee to seek clarification or help. Sometimes a follower will be able to complete a task but

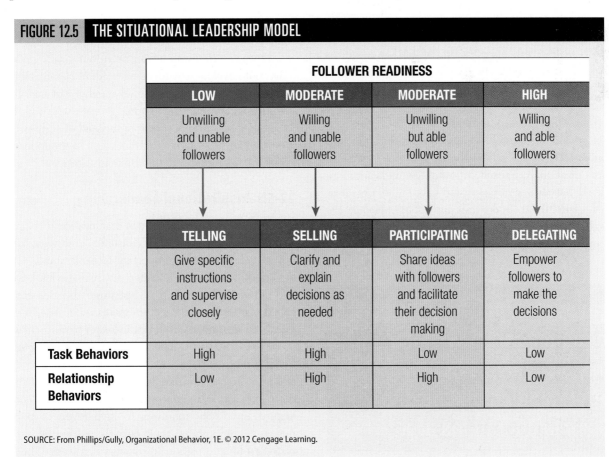

FIGURE 12.5 THE SITUATIONAL LEADERSHIP MODEL

FOLLOWER READINESS			
LOW	**MODERATE**	**MODERATE**	**HIGH**
Unwilling and unable followers	Willing and unable followers	Unwilling but able followers	Willing and able followers

	TELLING	**SELLING**	**PARTICIPATING**	**DELEGATING**
	Give specific instructions and supervise closely	Clarify and explain decisions as needed	Share ideas with followers and facilitate their decision making	Empower followers to make the decisions
Task Behaviors	High	High	Low	Low
Relationship Behaviors	Low	High	High	Low

SOURCE: From Phillips/Gully, Organizational Behavior, 1E. © 2012 Cengage Learning.

may seem unwilling or insecure about doing so. In these cases, a *participating style* (S3) is warranted, which involves high relationship but low task behavior. The leader here encourages the follower to participate in decision making. Finally, for tasks in which a follower is able and willing, the leader is able to use a *delegating style* (S4), characterized by low task behavior and low relationship behavior. In this case, follower readiness is high, and low levels of leader involvement (task or relationship) are needed.

One key limitation of the situational leadership model is the absence of central hypotheses that could be tested and would therefore make it a more valid, reliable theory of leadership.[26] However, the theory has intuitive appeal and is widely used for training and development in corporations. In addition, the theory focuses attention on follower maturity as an important determinant of the leadership process.

 ## 12-5 RECENT LEADERSHIP THEORIES

Many newer developments in leadership theory merit discussion here, specifically, leader–member exchange theory and inspirational leadership, which includes transformational, charismatic, and authentic styles.

12-5a Leader–Member Exchange

Leader–member exchange theory, or *LMX*, recognizes that leaders may form different relationships with followers. The basic idea behind LMX is that leaders form two groups of followers: in-groups and out-groups. *In-group members* tend to be similar to the leader and are given greater responsibilities, more rewards, and more attention. They work within the leader's inner circle of communication. As a result, in-group members are more satisfied, have lower turnover, and have higher organizational commitment. In contrast, *out-group members* are outside the circle and receive less attention and fewer rewards. They are managed by formal rules and policies.[27]

Employees who enjoy more frequent contact with the boss also have a better understanding of what the boss's expectations are.

Research on LMX is supportive. In-group members are more likely to engage in organizational citizenship behavior, while out-group members are more likely to retaliate against the organization.[28] And the type of stress varies according to the group. In-group members' stress comes from the additional responsibilities placed on them by the leader, whereas out-group members' stress comes from being left out of the communication network.[29] One surprising finding is that more frequent communication with the boss may either help or hurt a worker's performance ratings, depending on whether the worker is in the in-group or the out-group. Among the in-group, more frequent communication generally leads to higher performance ratings, while members of the out-group who communicate more often with the superior tend to receive lower performance ratings.[30]

In-group members feel more empowered, and this contributes to their higher performance. Empowerment also keeps in-group members healthier by buffering them from emotional exhaustion and depression.[31]

In-group members may also be more creative. When employees have a positive relationship with their supervisor, it increases their confidence and self-efficacy, which in turn increase creativity. Followers view communication from leaders differently, and it seems to depend on whether the leader is viewed as "one of us," as shown in neuroscience studies. Followers processed the same statements differently depending on whether the leader was an in-group leader or an out-group leader.[32] This could explain why former President Barack Obama was considered an inspirational speaker but may have found it challenging to inspire people who saw him as associated with an out-group instead of an in-group. Neuroscientific studies show that when in-group leaders speak for "us," followers find them inspirational.[33]

12-5b Inspirational Leadership

Leadership is an exciting area of organizational behavior, one in which new research is constantly emerging. Three new developments are important to understand. These are transformational leadership, charismatic leadership, and authentic leadership. These three theories can be called *inspirational leadership theories* because in each one, followers are inspired by the leader to perform well.

TRANSFORMATIONAL LEADERSHIP *Transactional leaders*, you will recall, are those who use rewards and punishment to strike deals with followers and shape their behavior. In contrast, *transformational leaders* inspire and excite followers to high levels of performance.[34] They rely on their personal attributes instead of their official position to manage followers. There is some evidence that transformational leadership can be learned.[35] Transformational leadership consists of the following four subdimensions: charisma, individualized consideration, inspirational motivation, and intellectual stimulation. We describe *charisma* in detail shortly. *Individualized consideration* refers to how much concern the leader displays for each follower's individual needs and acts as a coach or a mentor. *Inspirational motivation* is the extent to which the leader is able to articulate a vision that is appealing to followers.[36]

Transformational leadership has been shown to increase firm performance. U.S. corporations increasingly operate in a global economy, so there is a greater demand for leaders who can practice transformational leadership by converting their visions into reality and by inspiring followers to perform "above and beyond the call of duty."[37] Howard Schultz, founder and chair of Starbucks Coffee, is the transformational leader and visionary heart of Starbucks. After two stints as CEO, Schultz will remain as executive chair and turns his attention to building Starbucks' new premium Roasteries and high-end Reserve coffee.[38]

Transformational leadership is very important for individual followers as well. Transformational leadership that is focused on individuals increases task performance and initiative. Employees who work for a transformational leader are more satisfied, motivated, and perform better than those who do not.[39] Leaders can be both transformational and transactional.[40] However, whereas transformational leadership adds to the effects of transactional leadership, even exceptional transactional leadership cannot substitute for transformational leadership.[41] Questions have been raised about whether transformational leadership is effective with Millennials. Because Millennials are individualistic and see work as less central to their lives, transformational leadership may be less effective at motivating them to put the company's needs first. The inspirational nature of transformational leadership and intrinsic rewards may not be effective for Millennials, who are more interested in extrinsic rewards such as rapid recognition and advancement.[42]

CHARISMATIC LEADERSHIP Steve Jobs, the pioneer behind Apple, had an uncanny ability to create a vision and convince others to become part of it. Jobs's unique ability was so powerful that Apple employees coined a term in the 1980s for it—the *reality-distortion field*. This expression is used to describe the persuasive ability and peculiar charisma of managers like Steve Jobs. His reality-distortion field allowed Jobs to convince even skeptics that his plans were worth supporting, no matter how unworkable they may appear. Those close to charismatic managers become passionately committed to possibly insane projects

Howard Shultz transformed Starbucks from a single specialty coffee bar into one of the most widely known brands in the world. Now he's turning his attention to Starbucks' Roasteries (pictured) and high-end Reserve Coffees.

without regard to the practicality of their implementation or competitive forces in the marketplace.[43]

Charismatic leadership results when a leader uses the force of personal abilities and talents to have profound and extraordinary effects on followers.[44] Charismatic leadership falls to those who are chosen (are born with the "gift" of charisma) or who cultivate that gift. Some say charismatic leaders are born, and others say they are taught.

Charismatic leadership carries with it not only great potential for high levels of achievement and performance on the part of followers but also shadowy risks of destructive courses of action that might harm followers or other people.[45] The ugly face of charisma is revealed in the personalized power motivations of Adolf Hitler in Nazi Germany and David Koresh of the Branch Davidian cult in Waco, Texas. Both men led their followers into struggle, conflict, and death. The brighter face of charisma is revealed in the socialized power motivations of former presidents Bill Clinton and Ronald Reagan. While worlds apart in terms of their political beliefs, were actually quite similar in their use of personal charisma to inspire followers and motivate them to pursue a specific vision. In each case, followers perceived the leader as imbued with a unique vision for America and unique abilities to lead the country there.

Charisma is in the eye of the beholder and relies on the emotional connection between leaders and followers. Both men and

charismatic leadership
A leader's use of personal abilities and talents to have profound and extraordinary effects on followers.

women can be perceived as charismatic leaders, and social networks may affect how each gender is perceived in terms of charisma. Men are seen as more charismatic leaders when their work team network is centralized around one individual. Women leaders are seen as charismatic when their work team network involves many connections among different people.[46]

AUTHENTIC LEADERSHIP Recently, a new form of leadership has started to garner attention thanks to the ethical scandals rocking the business environment. In response to concerns about the potential negative side of inspirational forms of leadership, researchers have called for authentic leadership, which includes transformational, charismatic, or transactional leadership as the situation might demand but only in accordance with the leader's conscious and well-developed sense of values.[47] Because authentic leaders act in ways that are consistent with their value systems, they have a highly evolved sense of moral right and wrong. Authentic leaders are self-aware, confident, optimistic, and resilient. They have a deep sense of self and act as role models to others by conveying what they believe and stand for.[48]

Authentic leaders arouse and motivate followers to higher levels of performance by building a workforce characterized by high levels of hope, optimism, resiliency, and self-efficacy.[49] Followers also experience more positive emotions and trust as a result of the authentic leader's transparency and the collective caring climate engendered by such a leader. Researchers contend that this is the kind of leadership embodied by Gandhi, Nelson Mandela, and others like them throughout history. Only time and solid management research will tell if this approach can yield results for organizational leadership.

One recent development in the identification of authentic leaders stems from the arena of emotions. Emotions act as checks on the ugly side of charisma and also provide certain cues to followers. For example, a leader who espouses benevolence (as a value) and does not display compassion (an emotion) might not be very authentic in followers' eyes.[50] Similarly, a leader who displays compassion when announcing a layoff may be seen by followers as more morally worthy and held in high regard.[51]

Authentic leadership produces authentic followers. When employees see a leader display genuine emotion, they are more likely to feel like they are free to be themselves at work.[52] Authentic leaders also encourage followers to report wrongdoing in the organization. Followers of authentic leaders engage in internal whistle-blowing because they work in a climate of psychological safety, modeled by the authentic leader.[53] Authentic leadership can be learned. Becoming an authentic leader requires two processes, one social and one intrapersonal. The social process is the development of authentic relationships, and the intrapersonal process is gaining self-awareness and self-management skills.[54]

12-6 EMERGING ISSUES IN LEADERSHIP

Along with the recent developments in theory, some exciting issues have emerged of which leaders should be aware. These include emotional intelligence, trust, women leaders, and servant leadership.

12-6a Emotional Intelligence

It has been suggested that effective leaders possess emotional intelligence, which is the ability to recognize and manage emotion in oneself and in others. In fact, some researchers argue that emotional intelligence is more important for effective leadership than either IQ or technical skills.[55] Emotional intelligence is made up of several competencies, including self-awareness, empathy, adaptability, and self-confidence. While most people gain emotional intelligence as they age, not everyone starts with an equal amount. Fortunately, emotional intelligence can be learned. With honest feedback from coworkers and ongoing guidance, almost any leader can improve emotional intelligence, and with it, the ability to lead in times of adversity.[56]

Emotional intelligence affects the way leaders make decisions. Under high stress, leaders with higher emotional

If employees trust their leaders, they will buy in more readily.

I Believe I Can Fly/Shutterstock.com

intelligence tend to keep their cool and make better decisions, while leaders with low emotional intelligence make poor decisions and lose their effectiveness.[57] When Joe Torre was manager of the New York Yankees, he got the most out of his team, worked for a notoriously tough boss, and kept his cool. As manager of the Los Angeles Dodgers, he was still a model of emotional intelligence: compassionate, calm under stress, and a great motivator. He advocates "managing against the cycle," which means staying calm when situations are tough, but turning up the heat on players when things are going well.[58]

12-6b Trust

Trust, the willingness to be vulnerable to the actions of another, is an essential element in leadership.[59] Trust implies that followers believe that their leader will act with the followers' welfare in mind. Trustworthiness is also one of the competencies in emotional intelligence. Among top management team members, trust facilitates strategy implementation. That means that if team members trust each other, they have a better chance of getting buy-in from employees on the direction of the company.[60] And if employees trust their leaders, they will buy in more readily.

Trust in top business leaders may be at an all-time low given the highly publicized failures of many CEOs. Rick Wagoner, CEO of General Motors from 2000 to 2009, lost more money than any CEO in history, yet he continued to express confidence in his company and his strategy. He was fired by the government just before GM went bankrupt.[61] In the midst of the biggest oil spill in history, BP CEO Tony Hayward suggested that the environmental impact of the spill would be "very, very modest" and later complained to reporters that he would like his life back. As people around the Gulf region scrambled for their livelihoods, Hayward took a day off to go yacht racing.

Effective leaders understand both *whom* to trust and *how* to trust. At one extreme, leaders often make the mistake of trusting only a close circle of advisors, listening only to them and gradually cutting themselves off from dissenting opinions. At the opposite extreme, lone-wolf leaders may trust nobody, leading to preventable mistakes. Wise leaders carefully evaluate both the competence and the position of those they trust, seeking out a variety of opinions and input.[62]

12-6c Gender and Leadership

An important, emergent leadership question is whether women and men lead differently. Historical stereotypes persist, and people characterize successful managers as having more male-oriented attributes than

> Evidence shows that women tend to use a more people-oriented style that is inclusive and empowering. Women managers excel in positions that demand strong interpersonal skills.

female-oriented attributes.[63] Although legitimate gender differences may exist, the same leadership traits may be interpreted differently in a man and a woman because of stereotypes. The real issue should be leader behaviors that are not bound by gender stereotypes.

Early evidence shows that women tend to use a more people-oriented style that is inclusive and empowering. Women managers excel in positions that demand strong interpersonal skills.[64] Even though more and more women are assuming positions of leadership in organizations, interestingly, much of what we know about leadership is based on studies that were conducted on men. We need to know more about the ways women lead.

Recent research looks at the phenomenon of the *glass cliff* (as opposed to the *glass ceiling* effect discussed in Chapter 2). The *glass cliff* represents a trend in organizations wherein more women are placed in difficult leadership situations. Women perceive these assignments as necessary to accept due to the difficulty of attaining leadership positions and lack of alternate opportunities combined with male in-group favoritism. On the other hand, men perceive that women are better suited to difficult leadership positions because women are better decision makers.[65]

12-6d Servant Leadership

Robert Greenleaf, director of management research at AT&T for many years, believed that leaders should serve employees, customers, and the community, and his essays are the basis for today's view of *servant leadership*. His personal and professional philosophy was that leaders lead by serving others. Other tenets of servant leadership are that work exists for the person as much as the person exists for work and that servant leaders try to find out the will of the group and lead based on that. Servant leadership leads to higher team

Companies with Female CEOs Outperform Those Led by Men

As more women rise to the rank of CEO, the natural question arises as to whether companies led by female or male CEOs fare better. Researchers at Quantopian did a study of the Fortune 100 and found that companies led by females produced equity returns 226 percent better than the S&P 500.

NG Images/Alamy Stock Photo

One of the CEOs who performed well is Marillyn Hewson, CEO of Lockheed Martin, the world's biggest defense contractor. Under her leadership, the company has produced record profits, and its stock price has more than doubled. Her strategy has included the purchase of helicopter company Sikorsky and expansion into overseas markets.

It's not just having a woman CEO that makes a difference. Another global study found that going from having no women in corporate leadership (CEO, Board of Directors, other C-Suite positions) to a 30 percent female share of leaders increases firm profitability by 15 percent.

SOURCES: P. Wechsler, "Women-Led Companies Perform Three Times Better Than the S&P 500," *Fortune*, March 3, 2015, accessed at http://fortune.com/2015/03/03/women-led-companies-perform-three-times-better-than-the-sp-500/; M. Noland and T. Moran, "Study: Firms with More Women in the C-Suite Are More Profitable," *Harvard Business Review*, February 8, 2016, accessed at https://hbr.org/2016/02/study-firms-with-more-women-in-the-c-suite-are-more-profitable; "The World's 100 Most Powerful Women," *Forbes* (2016), accessed at https://www.forbes.com/power-women/#/tab:overall_page:3.

performance and increased organizational citizenship behaviors in the organization.[66] Servant leaders consider themselves stewards who regard leadership as a trust and desire to leave the organization in better shape for future generations.[67] Although Greenleaf's writings were completed thirty years ago, many have now been published and are becoming more popular.

12-6e Abusive Supervision

Research has investigated not only what makes leaders effective but also negative leadership behaviors. The most common include sexual harassment, physical violence, angry outbursts, public ridicule, taking credit for employees' successes, and scapegoating employees.[68] *Abusive supervision*, as these behaviors are called, is estimated to affect about 13 percent of U.S. workers and leads to many negative consequences. Abused workers report diminished well-being along with increased deviance behavior, problem drinking, psychological distress, and emotional exhaustion.[69] In addition, abusive supervision increases absenteeism and reduces productivity. In fact, the cost of abusive supervision to U.S. corporations has been estimated at $23.8 billion.[70] It is not clear why supervisors abuse others. Some research suggests that injustice experienced by supervisors increases the likelihood that they will, in turn,

followership The process of being guided and directed by a leader in the work environment.

abuse others. Other studies suggest that abuse stems from the failure of managers to control themselves and handle stress.[71] One type of stress that leads to abusive supervision is family-work conflict. Supervisors who experience high levels of conflict between family and work display more abusive behaviors toward direct reports.[72]

12-7 FOLLOWERSHIP

In contrast to leadership, the topic of **followership** has not been extensively researched. Much of the leadership literature suggests that leader and follower roles are highly differentiated. The traditional view casts followers as passive, whereas a more contemporary view casts the follower role as an active one with potential for leadership.[73] The follower role has alternatively been cast as one of self-leadership in which the follower assumes responsibility for influencing his own performance.[74] This approach emphasizes the follower's individual responsibility and self-control. Self-led followers perform tasks that are naturally motivating and also do work that must be done but is not naturally motivating. Self-leadership enables followers to be disciplined and effective, essential first steps if one is to become a leader. Organizational programs such as empowerment and self-managed work teams may be used to further activate the follower role.[75]

12-7a Types of Followers

Contemporary work environments are ones in which followers recognize their interdependence with leaders and learn to challenge them while at the same time respecting the leaders' authority.[76] Effective followers are active, responsible, autonomous in their behavior, and critical in their thinking without being insubordinate or disrespectful—in essence, they are highly engaged at work.

Effective followers and four other types of followers are identified based on two dimensions: (1) activity versus passivity and (2) independent, critical thinking versus dependent, uncritical thinking.[77] Figure 12.6 shows these follower types.

Alienated followers think independently and critically, yet are very passive in their behavior. As a result, they become psychologically and emotionally distanced from their leaders. These alienated followers are potentially disruptive and a threat to the health of the organization. *Sheep* are followers who do not think independently or critically and are passive in their behavior. *Yes people* are followers who do not think independently or critically, yet are very active in their behavior. They uncritically reinforce the thinking and ideas of their leaders with enthusiasm, never questioning or challenging the wisdom of the leaders' ideas and proposals. Yes people are the most dangerous to a leader because they are the most likely to give a false positive reaction and give no warning of potential pitfalls. *Survivors* (see the center of the figure) are the least disruptive and the lowest-risk followers in an organization. They perpetually sample the wind, and their motto is "better safe than sorry."

Effective followers are the most valuable to a leader and an organization because of their active contributions. Effective followers share four essential qualities. First, they practice self-management and self-responsibility. A leader can delegate to an effective follower without anxiety about the outcome. Second, they are committed both to the organization and a purpose, principle, or person outside themselves. Effective followers are not self-centered or self-aggrandizing. Third,

FIGURE 12.6 FIVE TYPES OF FOLLOWERS

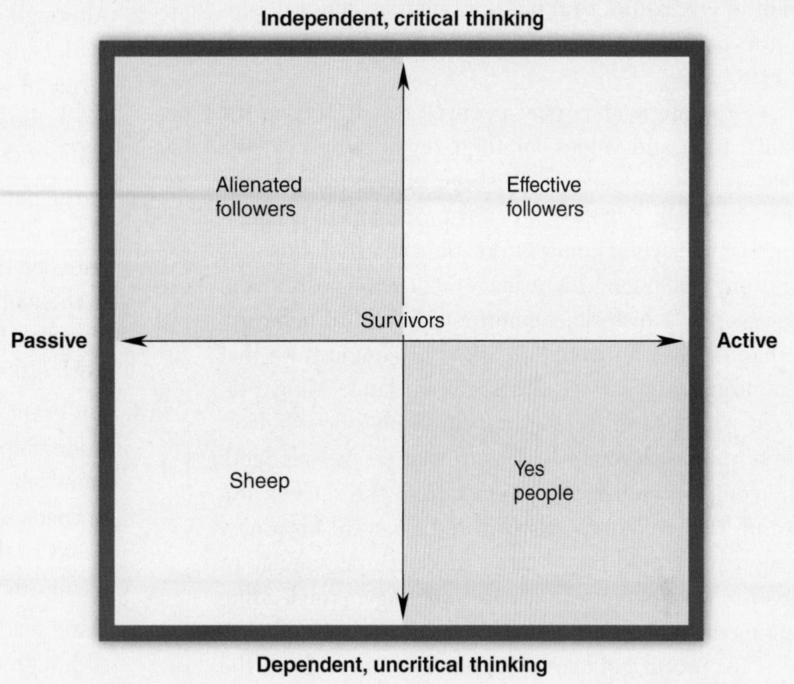

SOURCE: Reprinted by permission of Harvard Business Review. From "In Praise of Followers" by R. E. Kelley (November–December 1988, p. 145. Copyright © 1988 by Harvard Business School Publishing Corporation; all rights reserved.

effective followers invest in their own competence and professionalism and focus their energy for maximum impact. Effective followers look for challenges and ways in which to add to their talents or abilities. Fourth, they are courageous, honest, and credible. Companies can support such qualities among followers by providing training in mindfulness.[78]

Effective followers might be thought of as self-leaders who do not require close supervision. The notion of *self-leadership*, or *superleadership*, blurs the distinction between leaders and followers. Caring leaders are often able to encourage the development of self-leadership in their employees, creating effective, dynamic followers.

12-8 GUIDELINES FOR LEADERSHIP

Leadership is a key to influencing organizational behavior and achieving organizational effectiveness. When artifacts are eliminated, studies of leadership succession show a moderately strong leader influence on organizational performance.[79] With this said, it is important to recognize that other factors also influence organizational performance. These include environmental factors (such as general economic conditions) and technological factors (such as efficiency).

Corporate leaders play a central role in setting the ethical tone and values for their organizations. While many corporate leaders talk about ethics, many never have to actually risk the firm's fortune on an ethical decision. In 1976, when James Burke, then head of Johnson & Johnson, challenged his management team to reaffirm the company's historic commitment to ethical behavior, he had no idea he would be asked to demonstrate that commitment in action. But six years later, when poisoned packages of Tylenol appeared on store shelves, Burke did not hesitate to act on what he had pledged. The company pulled the product from the shelves at a cost of $100 million. It also offered a reward for a new design that would revamp the product's packaging. In the end, Tylenol recovered and is once again the leading pain medication in the United States.

Five useful guidelines appear to emerge from the extensive leadership research of the past sixty years:

1. Leaders and organizations should appreciate the unique attributes, predispositions, and talents of each leader. No two leaders are the same, and there is value in this diversity.

2. Although there appears to be no single best style of leadership, there are organizational preferences in terms of style. Leaders should be chosen who challenge the organizational culture, when necessary, without destroying it.

3. Participative, considerate leader behaviors that demonstrate a concern for people appear to enhance the health and well-being of followers in the work environment. This does not imply, however, that a leader must ignore the team's work tasks.

4. Different leadership situations call for different leadership talents and behaviors. Leaders must know when to give advice, when to counsel, when to coach, and when to mentor.[80] To meet the needs of their followers, they must be good diagnosticians.

5. Good leaders are likely to be good followers. Although there are distinctions between their social roles, the attributes and behaviors of leaders and followers may not be as distinct as is sometimes thought.

STUDY TOOLS 12

LOCATED AT BACK OF THE TEXTBOOK
☐ Rip out chapter review card

LOCATED AT WWW.CENGAGE.COM/LOGIN
☐ Gain unique perspectives on key concepts with new Concept Clip videos in the e-book
☐ Review key term flashcards and create your own
☐ Increase your comprehension with online homework and quizzes

13 | Conflict and Negotiation

rrecrutt/Getty Images

LEARNING OBJECTIVES

13-1 Describe the nature of conflicts in organizations.

13-2 Explain the role structural and personal factors play in causing conflict in organizations.

13-3 Discuss the nature of group conflict in organizations.

13-4 Describe the factors that influence conflict between individuals in organizations.

13-5 Describe effective and ineffective techniques for managing conflict.

13-6 Identify five styles of conflict management.

After finishing this chapter go to **PAGE 235** for **STUDY TOOLS**

13-1 THE NATURE OF CONFLICTS IN ORGANIZATIONS

All of us have experienced conflict of various types, yet we probably fail to recognize the variety of conflicts that occur in organizations. *Conflict* is defined as any situation in which incompatible goals, attitudes, emotions, or behaviors lead to disagreement or opposition between two or more parties.[1] Today organizations may face greater potential for conflict than ever before in history. The marketplace, with its increasing competition and globalization, magnifies differences among people in terms of personality, values, attitudes, perceptions, languages, cultures, and national backgrounds.[2] With the increasing diversity of the workforce comes the potential for incompatibility and conflict.

13-1a Importance of Conflict Management Skills for the Manager

Estimates show that managers spend about 21 percent of their time, or one day every week, dealing with conflict.[3] Not surprisingly, then, conflict management skills are a major predictor of managerial success.[4] A critical indicator of a manager's ability to manage conflict is his or her *emotional intelligence (EI)*, which is the power to control one's emotions and perceive emotions in others, adapt to change, and manage adversity. (Conflict management skills may be more a reflection of EI than of IQ.) People who lack emotional intelligence, especially empathy, or the ability to see life from another person's perspective, are more likely to be causes of conflict than managers of conflict. Management development programs that focus on EI competencies such as impulse control can help with conflict management skills.[5]

13-1b Functional versus Dysfunctional Conflict

Not all conflict is bad. In fact, some types of conflict encourage new solutions to problems and enhance creativity in the organization. In these cases, managers will

Estimates show that managers spend about 21% of their time, or one day every week, dealing with conflict.

want to encourage the conflicts. Thus, the key to conflict management is to stimulate functional conflict and prevent or resolve dysfunctional conflict. The difficulty, however, is distinguishing between dysfunctional and functional conflicts. The consequences of conflict can be positive or negative, as shown in Table 13.1.

Functional conflict is a healthy, constructive disagreement between two or more people. New ideas, learning, and growth among individuals can result from functional conflict. Such conflict is constructive conflict; individuals can develop a better awareness of themselves and others through it. In addition, functional conflict can improve working relationships

> **functional conflict** A healthy, constructive disagreement between two or more people.

DreamBox Learning CEO Encourages "Benevolent Friction"

The Haitian side of Jessie Woolley-Wilson's family, as she remembers, argued loudly and a lot at the dinner table. The conversations might be about the economy or what was happening in different countries. When the extended family gathered, cultural differences were bridged and relationships were built.

As CEO of DreamBox Learning, she turned that memory into "benevolent friction," the idea that conflict can be a positive force. It was a tough sell with her colleagues until she explained that a diamond cannot be made without enough pressure exerted on the carbon. Translated: Ideas should be given tough but respectful scrutiny, and every person has important ideas to contribute. Her recommendation? Be hard on ideas but soft on people.

In a startup like DreamBox, benevolent friction is essential. The company provides adaptive online learning systems for children, and it relies on positive conflict for innovation.

LifetimeStock/Shutterstock.com

SOURCE: http://www.dreambox.com; A. Bryant, "Jessie Woolley-Wilson on Creating Benevolent Friction at Work," *The New York Times*, accessed at https://nyti.ms/2nCTZdy.

TABLE 13.1   CONSEQUENCES OF CONFLICT

Positive Consequences	Negative Consequences
> Leads to new ideas	> Diverts energy from work
> Stimulates creativity	> Threatens psychological well-being
> Motivates change	> Wastes resources
> Promotes organizational vitality	> Creates a negative climate
> Helps individuals and groups establish identities	> Breaks down group cohesion
> Serves as a safety valve to indicate problems	> Can increase hostility and aggressive behaviors

because when two parties work through disagreements, they feel they have accomplished something together. By releasing tensions and solving problems in working together this way, they experience improved morale.[6] Functional conflict can lead to innovation and positive change for the organization.[7] Because it tends to encourage creativity among individuals, this positive form of conflict often translates into increased productivity.[8] A key to recognizing functional conflict is that it is often cognitive in origin; that is, it arises from someone challenging old policies or thinking of new ways to approach problems. In fact, managers should work to stimulate this type of conflict when they suspect their group is suffering from groupthink.[9]

Dysfunctional conflict is an unhealthy, destructive disagreement between two or more people. Its danger is that it takes the focus away from the work to be done and places it on the conflict itself and the parties involved. Excessive conflict drains energy that could be used more productively. A key to recognizing a dysfunctional conflict is that its origin is often emotional or behavioral. For example, disagreements that involve personalized anger and resentment directed at specific individuals rather than specific ideas are dysfunctional.[10] Individuals involved in dysfunctional conflict tend to act before thinking, and they often rely on threats, deception, and verbal abuse to communicate. Moreover, dysfunctional conflict can often lead to aggressive acts or retaliation directed at supervisors, peers, subordinates, or even service providers.[11] In dysfunctional conflict, losses to both parties may exceed any potential gain from the conflict.

13-1c Diagnosing Conflict

Diagnosing conflict as functional or dysfunctional is not easy. The manager must look at the issue, the context of the conflict, and the parties involved. Once the manager has diagnosed the type of conflict, he or she can either

dysfunctional conflict An unhealthy, destructive disagreement between two or more people.

work to resolve it (if it is dysfunctional) or to stimulate it (if it is functional).

It is easy to make mistakes in diagnosing conflicts. Sometimes task conflict, which is functional, can be misattributed as being personal, and dysfunctional conflict can follow. Developing trust within the work group can keep this misattribution from occurring.[12] A study of group effectiveness found that decision-making groups made up of friends were able to engage more openly in disagreement than groups made up of strangers, allowing the friends' groups to make more effective decisions. Relationship conflict, in contrast with task conflict, is more likely to become dysfunctional, especially if it persists over time. Prolonged, unresolved relationship conflict depletes employees' energy, and they become burned out. Burned-out employees perform poorly and may want to leave the organization to get away from the dysfunctional conflict.[13]

13-2 CAUSES OF CONFLICT IN ORGANIZATIONS

Conflict is pervasive in organizations. To manage it effectively, managers should understand its many sources. These can be classified into two broad categories: *structural factors*, which stem from the nature of the organization and the way in which work is organized, and *personal factors*, which arise from differences among individuals. Figure 13.1 summarizes the causes of conflict within each category.

13-2a Structural Factors

The causes of conflict related to the organization's structure include specialization, interdependence, common resources, goal differences, authority relationships, status inconsistencies, and jurisdictional ambiguities.

SPECIALIZATION When jobs are highly specialized, employees become experts at certain tasks. For example, one software company has one specialist for databases, one for statistical packages, and another for expert systems. Highly specialized jobs can lead to conflict because people have little awareness of the tasks that others perform.

A classic conflict of specialization often occurs between salespeople and engineers. Engineers are technical specialists responsible for product design and quality. Salespeople are marketing experts and liaisons with customers. Salespeople are often accused of making delivery promises to customers that engineers cannot keep because the sales force lacks the technical knowledge necessary to develop realistic delivery deadlines.

INTERDEPENDENCE Work that is interdependent requires groups or individuals to depend on one another to accomplish goals.[14] Depending on other people to get work done is fine when the process works smoothly. When there is a problem, however, it becomes very easy to blame the other party, and conflict escalates. In a garment manufacturing plant, for example, when the fabric cutters get behind in their work, the workers who sew the garments are delayed as well. Considerable frustration may result when the workers at the sewing machines feel their efforts are being blocked by the cutters' slow pace and their pay is affected because they are paid piece-rate.

COMMON RESOURCES Anytime multiple parties must share resources, there is potential for conflict.[15] This potential is enhanced when the shared resources become scarce. For example, managers often share administrative support. Not uncommonly,

FIGURE 13.1   CAUSES OF CONFLICT IN ORGANIZATIONS

Structural Factors
• Specialization
• Interdependence
• Common resources
• Goal differences
• Authority relationships
• Status inconsistencies
• Jurisdictional ambiguities

Conflict

Personal Factors
• Skills and abilities
• Personalities
• Perceptions
• Values and ethics
• Emotions
• Communication barriers
• Cultural differences

Tsurukame Design/Shutterstock.com

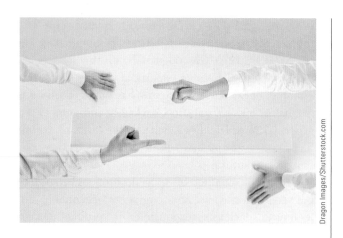

one administrative assistant supports ten or more managers, each of whom believes his or her work is most important. This puts pressure on the administrative assistant and leads to potential conflicts in prioritizing and scheduling work.

GOAL DIFFERENCES When work groups have different goals, these goals may be incompatible. For example, in one cable television company, the salesperson's goal was to sell as many new installations as possible. This created problems for the service department because its goal was timely installations. With increasing sales, the service department's workload became backed up, and orders were delayed. Often these types of conflicts occur because individuals do not have knowledge of another department's objectives.

AUTHORITY RELATIONSHIPS A traditional boss–employee relationship is hierarchical in nature, with a boss who is superior to the employee. For many employees, such a relationship is not a comfortable one; they don't like another person having the right to tell them what to do. Some people resent authority more than others, and obviously this creates conflicts. In addition, some bosses are more autocratic than others, compounding the potential for conflict in the relationship. As organizations move toward the team approach and empowerment, there should be less potential for conflict from authority relationships.

STATUS INCONSISTENCIES Some organizations have a strong status difference between management and nonmanagement workers. Managers may enjoy privileges—such as flexible schedules, reserved parking spaces, and longer lunch hours—that are not available to nonmanagement employees and that may result in resentment and conflict.

jurisdictional ambiguity The presence of unclear lines of responsibility within an organization.

JURISDICTIONAL AMBIGUITIES Have you ever called a company with a problem and had your call transferred through several different people and departments? This situation illustrates **jurisdictional ambiguity**, that is, unclear lines of responsibility within an organization.[16] The classic situation here involves the hardware/software dilemma. You call the company that made your computer, and it informs you that the problem is caused by the software. You call the software division, and it tells you it's the hardware….

13-2b Personal Factors

Not all conflicts arise out of structural factors in the organization. Some conflicts arise out of differences among individuals. The causes of conflict that arise from individual differences include skills and abilities, personalities, perceptions, values and ethics, emotions, communication barriers, and cultural differences.

SKILLS AND ABILITIES Diversity in skills and abilities may be positive for the organization, but it also holds potential for conflict, especially when jobs are interdependent. Experienced, competent workers may find it difficult to work alongside new and unskilled recruits. Workers can become resentful when their new boss, fresh from college, knows a lot about managing people but is unfamiliar with the technology with which they are working.

PERSONALITIES Individuals do not leave their personalities at the doorstep when they enter the workplace. Personality conflicts are thus realities in organizations. It is naïve to expect that you will like all of your coworkers, just as it is naïve to expect that they will all like you.

One personality trait that many people find difficult to deal with is abrasiveness.[17] An abrasive person ignores the interpersonal aspects of work and the feelings of colleagues. These types of people are often achievement oriented and hardworking, but their perfectionist, critical style can leave others feeling unimportant. The working style of abrasive individuals causes stress and strain for those around them.[18]

PERCEPTIONS Differences in perception can also lead to conflict. For example, managers and workers may not have a shared perception of what motivates people. In this case, the reward system can create conflicts if managers provide what they *think* employees want rather than what they actually want.

VALUES AND ETHICS Differences in values and ethics can be sources of disagreement. Older workers, for example, value company loyalty and probably would not take a sick day when they were not really ill. Younger

Personality conflicts are realities in organizations; it is naive to expect that you will like all of your coworkers or to expect that they will all like you.

workers, valuing mobility, like the concept of "mental health days," or calling in sick to get away from work. This may not be true for all workers, but it illustrates that differences in values can lead to conflict.

Most people have their own sets of values and ethics, although the extent to which they apply these ethics in the workplace varies. Some people have strong desires for approval from others and will work to meet others' ethical standards. Others are relatively unconcerned about approval from others and strongly apply their own ethical standards. Still others operate seemingly without regard to ethics or values.[19] When conflicts about values or ethics do arise, heated disagreement is common because of the personal nature of the differences.

EMOTIONS Conflict is by nature an emotional interaction, and the emotions of the parties involved in conflict play a pivotal role in how they perceive any type of negotiation and therefore how they respond to one another.[20] In fact, emotions are now considered critical elements of negotiation and must be included in an examination of the process and how it unfolds.[21] When negotiators begin to act based on emotions rather than on cognitions, they become much more likely to reach an impasse.[22]

COMMUNICATION BARRIERS Communication barriers such as physical separation and language can create distortions in messages, and these can lead to conflict. Another communication barrier is value judgment, in which a listener assigns worth to a message before it is received. For example, suppose a team member is a chronic complainer. When this individual enters the manager's office, the manager is likely to devalue the message before it is even delivered. Conflict can then emerge.

CULTURAL DIFFERENCES Although cultural differences are assets in organizations, sometimes they can be sources of conflict. Often, these conflicts stem from a lack of understanding of another culture. In one MBA class, for example, Indian students were horrified when American students challenged the professor. Meanwhile, the American students thought the students from India were too passive. Subsequent discussions revealed

HOT TREND

More Conflict Among Women at Work? No!

Popular press coverage of women at work and the conflicts they have among themselves shows a negative slant. Queen bee syndrome, token woman syndrome, and female competition for top spots paint a picture of women having more conflict with other women than other types of workplace conflict. Is this really the case?

Researchers challenged the notion that women at work are more likely to have conflict with each other. Instead, they proposed that conflict between women is more likely to be seen as more problematic by third parties. Other people tend to focus more on female same-sex conflict and highlight its occurrence. This leads to the misperception that women have more dysfunctional conflict with other women at work.

When third parties stereotype women working together as more conflict-prone, it deflects attention away from the real barriers to advancement that women face at work.

SOURCE: L. D. Sheppard and K. Aquino, "Sisters at Arms: A Theory of Female Same-Sex Conflict and Its Problematization in Organizations," *Journal of Management*, 43 (2017): 691–715.

Empathy Can Help Promote Forgiveness at Work

When we are slighted or harmed at work, most of us think the damage was intentional, which is not always the case. Workers who commit the offense often feel guilty and want forgiveness for their behavior. This disconnect creates a lot of workplace conflict. One way to help deescalate the tension is to have the victim empathize with the transgressor. This can help the victim understand that in some cases, the wrongdoing was not intentional and that the transgressor wants forgiveness. By encouraging empathy and forgiveness, some workplace conflicts can be resolved.

Of course, this is not effective when the transgressor doesn't believe he or she has done anything wrong. For empathy and forgiveness to work, both parties need to have a mutual understanding of the wrongdoing.

SOURCE: G. S. Adams and M. E. Inesi, "Impediments to Forgiveness: Victim and Transgressor Attributions of Intent and Guilt," *Journal of Personality and Social Psychology*, 111 (2016): 866–881.

that professors in India expect to be treated deferentially and with great respect. While students might challenge an idea vigorously, they would rarely challenge the professor. Diversity training that emphasizes education on cultural differences can make great strides in preventing misunderstandings.

13-3 FORMS OF GROUP CONFLICT IN ORGANIZATIONS

Conflict in an organization can take on any of several different forms that can mainly be sorted into two core groups: conflicts that occur at the group level and conflicts that occur at the individual level. Conflicts at each level can be further classified as either *inter* or *intra*. It is important to note that the prefix *inter* means "between," whereas the prefix *intra* means "within." Conflict at the group level can occur between organizations (interorganizational), between groups (intergroup), or within a group (intragroup).

13-3a Interorganizational Conflict

Conflict that occurs between two or more organizations is called **interorganizational conflict**. Competition can heighten interorganizational conflict. Corporate takeovers, mergers, and acquisitions can also produce interorganizational conflict. What about the interorganizational conflict between the National Football League's

interorganizational conflict Conflict that occurs between two or more organizations.

intergroup conflict Conflict that occurs between groups or teams in an organization.

players unions and team owners, which was often characterized as a battle between millionaires and billionaires? The players regularly go on strike to extract more of the profits from the owners, while the owners cry that they are not making a dime.

13-3b Intergroup Conflict

When conflict occurs between groups or teams, it is known as **intergroup conflict**. Conflict between groups can have positive effects within each group, such as increased group cohesiveness, increased focus on tasks, and increased loyalty to the group. There are, however, negative consequences as well. Groups in conflict tend to develop an us-against-them mentality whereby each sees the other team as the enemy, becomes more hostile, and decreases its communication with the other group. Groups are even more competitive and less cooperative than individuals. The inevitable outcome is that one group gains and the other group loses.[23]

Competition between groups must be managed carefully so that it does not escalate into dysfunctional conflict. Research has shown that when multiple groups compete for a goal that only one group can achieve, negative consequences such as territoriality, aggression, and prejudice toward other groups can result.[24] Commitment also plays a role in intergroup conflict. When employees are more committed to their own groups or teams than to the organization as a whole, dysfunctional conflict handling strategies are likely to result. To prevent this, managers should encourage both team commitment and organizational commitment among employees.[25] In addition, managers should encourage social interactions across groups so that trust can be developed. Trust allows individuals to exchange ideas and resources with members of other groups and results in innovation when members of different groups cooperate.[26]

13-3c Intragroup Conflict

Conflict that occurs within groups or teams is called **intragroup conflict**. Some conflict within a group is functional, since it can help prevent groupthink, as discussed in Chapter 10.

Even virtual teams are not immune to conflict. The nuances and subtleties of face-to-face communication are often lacking in these teams, and misunderstandings can result. Face-to-face and telephone interactions early on can eliminate later conflicts and allow virtual teams to move on to use electronic communication because trust has been developed. When top management teams make strategic decisions, conflicts within the team frequently arise because so much is at stake. If a crisis occurs, however, intragroup conflicts may be superseded by the need for urgent decisions and collaboration among the team members.[27]

INDIVIDUAL CONFLICT IN ORGANIZATIONS

As with groups, conflict can occur between individuals (interpersonal) or within a single individual (intrapersonal).

13-4a Types of Intrapersonal Conflict

When conflict occurs within an individual, it is called **intrapersonal conflict**. There are several types of intrapersonal conflict, including interrole, intrarole, and person–role conflicts. A *role* is a set of expectations placed on an individual by others.[28] The person occupying the focal role is the *role incumbent*, and the individuals who place expectations on the person are *role senders*. Figure 13.2 depicts a set of role relationships.

Interrole conflict occurs when a person experiences conflict among the multiple roles in his or her life. One interrole conflict

> **intragroup conflict** Conflict that occurs within groups or teams.
>
> **intrapersonal conflict** Conflict that occurs within an individual.
>
> **interrole conflict** A person's experience of conflict among the multiple roles in his or her life.

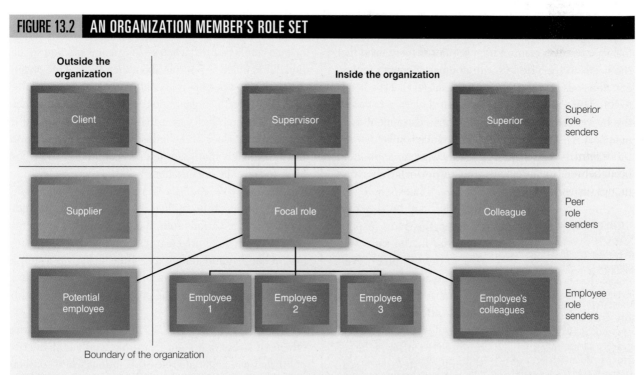

FIGURE 13.2   AN ORGANIZATION MEMBER'S ROLE SET

SOURCE: J. C. Quick, J. D. Quick, D. L. Nelson, and J. J. Hurrell Jr., *Preventive Stress Management in Organizations* (Washington, DC: American Psychological Association, 1997). Copyright © 1997 by the American Psychological Association. Reprinted with permission.

that many employees experience is *work–home conflict*, in which their role as worker clashes with their role as spouse or parent.[29] Work–home conflict can arise from time constraints, strain, and having responsibilities for people in the workplace and at home.[30] This type of conflict has become even more common with the rise of work-at-home professionals and telecommuting, in which the home becomes the office and the boundary between work and family life is blurred.[31] Ambitious and highly involved employees use office communications (e.g., texting, e-mail, and so on) nights and weekends. After-hours communication usage is associated with increased work–life conflict as reported by the employee and a significant other.[32] Work–home conflict reduces personal well-being, decreases organizational citizenship behavior, and increases stress. People also tend to drink more alcohol on days they experience work–home conflict.[33] Work-home conflicts make it difficult to concentrate at work, and job performance suffers.[34]

Intrarole conflict is conflict within a single role. It often arises when a person receives conflicting messages from role senders about how to perform a certain role. Suppose a manager receives counsel from her department head that she needs to socialize less with nonmanagement employees. She is also told by her project manager that she needs to be a better team member and that she can accomplish this by socializing more with other nonmanagement team members. This situation is one of intrarole conflict.

Person–role conflict occurs when an individual in a particular role is expected to perform behaviors that clash with his personal values.[35] Salespeople, for example, may be required to offer the most expensive item in the sales line first to the customer, even when it is apparent that the customer does not want or cannot afford it. A computer salesperson may be required to offer a large, elaborate system to a student he knows is on a tight budget. This may conflict with the salesperson's values, and he may experience person–role conflict.

Intrapersonal conflicts can have positive consequences. Often, professional responsibilities clash with deeply held values. A budget shortfall may force you to lay off a loyal, hardworking employee. Your daughter may have a piano recital on the same day your largest client is scheduled to be in town visiting the office. In such conflicts, we often have to choose between right and right; that is, there's no wrong response, only one that is better than the other. These decisions pose what may be thought of as *defining moments* that challenge individuals to choose between two or more things in which they believe.[36] Character is formed in defining moments because they cause individuals to shape their identities. They help people crystallize their values and serve as opportunities for personal growth.

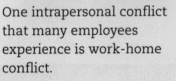

One intrapersonal conflict that many employees experience is work-home conflict.

Gene Chutka/E+/Getty Images

13-4b Managing Intrapersonal Conflict

Intrapersonal conflict can be managed with careful self-analysis and diagnosis of the situation. Three actions in particular can help prevent or resolve intrapersonal conflicts. First, when seeking a new job, you should find out as much as possible about the values of the organization.[37] Many person–role conflicts center around differences between the organization's values and the individual's values. Research has shown that when there is a good fit between the values of the individual and the organization, the individual is more satisfied and committed and is less likely to leave the organization.[38]

Second, *role analysis* is a good tool for managing intrarole or interrole conflicts.[39] In role analysis, the individual asks the various role senders what they expect of him. The outcomes are clearer work roles and the reduction of conflict and ambiguity.[40] Role analysis is a simple tool that clarifies the expectations of both parties in a relationship and reduces the potential for conflict within a role or between roles.

Third, political skills can help buffer the negative effects of stress that stem from role conflicts. Effective politicians can negotiate role expectations when conflicts occur. All these forms of conflict can be managed. An understanding of the many forms is a first step.

intrarole conflict Conflict that occurs within a single role, such as when a person receives conflicting messages from role senders about how to perform a certain role.

person–role conflict Conflict that occurs when an individual in a particular role is expected to perform behaviors that clash with his or her personal values.

Passenger Gets Concussion; United Airlines' Reputation Takes a Hit

Airlines routinely overbook flights and offer rewards to passengers to give up their seats. When that doesn't work, they may involuntarily bump passengers. In one case, a United Airlines passenger was asked to leave the plane and he refused, saying he was a doctor and needed to see patients the next day. Security was called and dragged the innocent passenger from the plane, eventually taking him on a stretcher because he was bleeding from the violent altercation. His injuries included broken teeth, a broken nose, and a concussion. Worldwide outrage followed when other passengers' video footage of the conflict was released.

United Airlines' CEO Oscar Munoz issued multiple apologies, calling the incident a mistake of epic proportions. United settled with the injured passenger and vowed to reduce (not eliminate) overbooking. This very public conflict ignited a debate about poor customer service in the airline industry. United Airlines faced severe backlash from the public.

JOSHUA LOTT/Getty Images

Reverend Jesse Jackson stages a protest against United Airlines at Chicago's O'Hare International Airport in 2017 in response to airport police officers physically removing passenger Dr. David Dao from his seat and dragging him off the airplane.

SOURCES: D. Temin, "How United Became the World's Most Hated Airline in a Day," *Forbes*, April 11, 2017, accessed at https://www.forbes.com/sites/daviatemin/2017/04/11/how-united-became-the-worlds-most-hated-airline-in-one-day/#6d24c30c61f2.

13-4c Managing Interpersonal Conflict

Conflict that occurs between two or more individuals, or **interpersonal conflict**, can arise from many individual differences, including personalities, attitudes, values, and perceptions. To manage interpersonal conflict, it is helpful to understand power networks in organizations and defense mechanisms exhibited by individuals when they are in conflict situations.

POWER NETWORKS According to W.F.G. Mastenbroek, individuals in organizations are organized into three basic types of power networks.[41] Based on these power relationships, certain kinds of conflict tend to emerge. Figure 13.3 illustrates three basic kinds of power relationships in organizations. The first relationship is *equal versus equal*, in which there is a horizontal balance of power among the parties. An example of this type of relationship would be a conflict between individuals from two different project teams. The behavioral tendency is toward *suboptimization*; that is, the focus is on a win–lose approach to problems, and each party tries to maximize its power at the expense of the other party. Conflict within this type of network can lead to depression, low self-esteem, and other distress symptoms. Interventions such as improving coordination between the parties and working toward common interests can help manage these conflicts.

The second power network is *high versus low*, or a powerful party versus a less powerful party. Conflicts that emerge here take the basic form of the powerful individuals trying to control others, with the less powerful people trying to become more autonomous. Conflict in this network can lead to job dissatisfaction, low organizational commitment, and turnover.[42] Organizations typically respond to these conflicts by tightening the rules. However, the more successful ways of managing these conflicts are to try a different style of leadership, such as a coaching and counseling style, or to change the structure to a more decentralized one.

The third power network is *high versus middle versus low*. This power network illustrates the classic conflicts felt by middle managers. Two particular conflicts are evident for middle managers: *role conflict*, in which conflicting expectations are placed on the manager from bosses and employees, and *role ambiguity*, in which the expectations of

interpersonal conflict Conflict that occurs between two or more individuals.

FIGURE 13.3 **POWER RELATIONSHIPS IN ORGANIZATIONS**

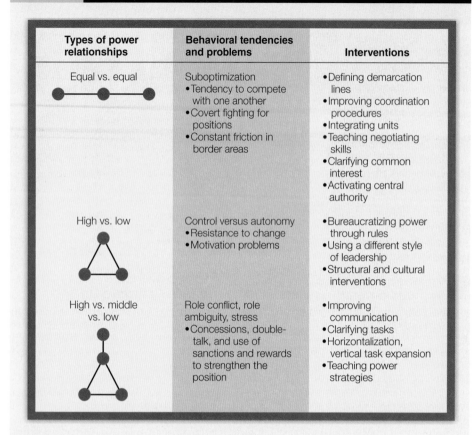

Types of power relationships	Behavioral tendencies and problems	Interventions
Equal vs. equal	Suboptimization • Tendency to compete with one another • Covert fighting for positions • Constant friction in border areas	• Defining demarcation lines • Improving coordination procedures • Integrating units • Teaching negotiating skills • Clarifying common interest • Activating central authority
High vs. low	Control versus autonomy • Resistance to change • Motivation problems	• Bureaucratizing power through rules • Using a different style of leadership • Structural and cultural interventions
High vs. middle vs. low	Role conflict, role ambiguity, stress • Concessions, double-talk, and use of sanctions and rewards to strengthen the position	• Improving communication • Clarifying tasks • Horizontalization, vertical task expansion • Teaching power strategies

SOURCE: W. F. G. Mastenbroek, *Conflict Management and Organization Development* (New York: Wiley, 1987). Copyright John Wiley & Sons Limited. Reproduced with permission.

the boss are unclear. Improved communication among all parties can reduce role conflict and ambiguity. In addition, middle managers can benefit from training in positive ways to influence others.

Knowing the typical kinds of conflicts that arise in various kinds of relationships can help a manager diagnose conflicts and devise appropriate ways to manage them.

13-4d Defense Mechanisms

When individuals are involved in conflict with another human being, frustration often results.[43] Conflicts can often arise within the context of a performance appraisal session. Most people do not react well to negative feedback, as was illustrated in a classic study in which more than 50 percent of employees reacted defensively when given criticism about their work.[44]

When individuals are frustrated, as they often are in interpersonal conflict, they respond by exhibiting *defense mechanisms*.[45] Aggressive mechanisms, such as fixation, displacement, and negativism, are aimed at attacking the source of the conflict. In **fixation**, an individual fixates on the conflict, or keeps up a dysfunctional behavior that obviously will not solve the conflict. An example of fixation occurred in a university where a faculty member became embroiled in a battle with the dean because the faculty member felt he had not received a large enough salary increase. He persisted in writing angry letters to the dean, whose hands were tied because of a low budget allocation to the college. Another aggressive defense mechanism is **displacement**, which means directing anger toward someone who is not the source of the conflict. For example, a manager may respond harshly to an employee after a telephone confrontation with an angry customer. **Negativism** is an aggressive mechanism in which a person responds with pessimism to any attempt at solving a problem. Negativism is illustrated by a manager who, when appointed to a committee on which she did not want to serve, made negative comments throughout the meeting.

Compromise mechanisms, such as compensation, identification, and ratiaonalization, are used by individuals to make the best of a conflict situation. **Compensation** is a compromise mechanism in which an individual attempts to make up for a negative situation by devoting himself to another pursuit with increased vigor. Compensation can be seen when a person makes up for a bad relationship at home by spending

fixation An aggressive mechanism in which an individual keeps up a dysfunctional behavior that obviously will not solve the conflict.

displacement An aggressive mechanism in which an individual directs his or her anger toward someone who is not the source of the conflict.

negativism An aggressive mechanism in which a person responds with pessimism to any attempt at solving a problem.

compensation A compromise mechanism in which an individual attempts to make up for a negative situation by devoting himself or herself to another pursuit with increased vigor.

Withdrawal mechanisms are exhibited when frustrated individuals try to flee from a conflict.

more time at the office. **Identification** is a compromise mechanism whereby an individual patterns her behavior after another's. One supervisor at a construction firm, not wanting to acknowledge consciously that she was not likely to be promoted, mimicked the behavior of her boss, even going so far as to buy a car just like the boss's. **Rationalization** is trying to justify one's behavior by constructing bogus reasons for it. Employees may rationalize unethical behavior like padding their expense accounts with the argument that "everyone else does it."

Withdrawal mechanisms are exhibited when frustrated individuals try to flee from a conflict using either physical or psychological means. Flight, conversion, and fantasy are examples of withdrawal mechanisms. Physically escaping a conflict is **flight**. An employee taking a day off after a blowup with the boss is an example. **Withdrawal** may take the form of emotionally leaving a conflict, such as exhibiting an "I don't care anymore" attitude. **Conversion** is a process whereby emotional conflicts become expressed in physical symptoms. Most of us have experienced the conversion reaction of a headache following an emotional exchange with another person. **Fantasy** is a withdrawal mechanism that provides an escape from a conflict through daydreaming. In the Internet age, fantasy as an escape mechanism has found new meaning. A study conducted by International Data Corporation (IDC) showed that 30 to 40 percent of all Internet surfing in the office is nonwork-related and that more than 70 percent of companies have had sex sites accessed from their networks, suggesting that employees' minds aren't always focused on their jobs.[46]

When employees exhibit withdrawal mechanisms, they often pretend to agree with their bosses or coworkers in order to avoid facing an immediate conflict. Many employees fake a positive response this way because the firm informally rewards agreement and punishes dissent. The long-term consequence of withdrawal and faking a positive response is emotional distress for the employee.[47]

Knowledge of these defense mechanisms can be extremely beneficial to a manager. By understanding the ways in which people typically react to interpersonal conflict, managers can be prepared for employees' reactions and help them uncover their feelings about a conflict.

13-5 CONFLICT MANAGEMENT STRATEGIES AND TECHNIQUES

The overall approach (or strategy) you use in a conflict is important in determining whether the conflict will have a positive or negative outcome. Overall strategies to deal with conflict can be classified as competitive versus cooperative strategies. Table 13.2 depicts the two strategies and four different conflict scenarios. The *competitive strategy* is founded on assumptions of win–lose and entails dishonest communication, mistrust, and a rigid position from both parties.[48] The *cooperative strategy* is founded on different assumptions: the potential for win–win outcomes, honest communication, trust, openness to risk and vulnerability, and the notion that the whole may be greater than the sum of the parts.

To illustrate the importance of the overall strategy, consider the case of two groups competing for scarce resources. Suppose budget cuts have to be made at an insurance company. The claims manager argues that the sales training staff should be cut because agents are fully trained. The sales training manager argues that claims personnel should be cut because the company is processing fewer

identification A compromise mechanism whereby an individual patterns his or her behavior after another's.

rationalization A compromise mechanism characterized by trying to justify one's behavior by constructing bogus reasons for it.

flight/withdrawal A withdrawal mechanism that entails physically escaping (flight) or psychologically escaping (withdrawal) a conflict.

conversion A withdrawal mechanism in which emotional conflicts are expressed in physical symptoms.

fantasy A withdrawal mechanism that provides an escape from a conflict through daydreaming.

TABLE 13.2 WIN–LOSE VERSUS WIN–WIN STRATEGIES

Strategy	Department A	Department B	Organization
Competitive	Lose	Lose	Lose
	Lose	Win	Lose
	Win	Lose	Lose
Cooperative	Win 2	Win 2	Win

claims. This could turn into a dysfunctional brawl, with both sides refusing to give ground. The result would be a win–lose, lose–win, or lose–lose scenario. Personnel cuts could be made in one department or the other, or in both departments. In all three cases, the organization winds up in a losing position with the competitive approach.

Even in such intense conflicts as those over scarce resources, a win–win strategy can lead to an overall win for the organization. In fact, conflicts over scarce resources can be productive if the parties have cooperative goals—a strategy that seeks a winning solution for both parties. To achieve a win–win outcome, the conflict must be approached with open-minded discussion of opposing views. Through open-minded discussion, both parties integrate views and create new solutions that facilitate productivity and strengthen their relationship; the result is feelings of unity rather than separation.[49]

In the example of the conflict between the claims manager and sales training manager, open-minded discussion might reveal that there are ways to achieve budget cuts without cutting personnel. Sales support might surrender part of its travel budget, and claims might cut overtime. This represents a win–win situation for the company. The budget has been reduced, and relationships between the two departments have been preserved. Both parties have given up something (note the "Win–" in Table 13.2), but the conflict has been resolved with a positive outcome.

You can see the importance of the broad strategy used to approach a conflict. We now move from broad strategies to more specific techniques.

nonaction Doing nothing in hopes that a conflict will disappear.

secrecy Attempting to hide a conflict or an issue that has the potential to create conflict.

administrative orbiting Delaying action on a conflict by buying time.

due process nonaction A procedure set up to address conflicts that is so costly, time-consuming, or personally risky that no one will use it.

character assassination An attempt to label or discredit an opponent.

Effective conflict management techniques include appealing to superordinate goals, expanding resources, changing personnel, changing structure, and confronting and negotiating.

13-5a Ineffective Techniques

There are many specific techniques for dealing with conflict. Before turning to techniques that work, it should be recognized that some actions commonly taken in organizations to deal with conflict are not effective.[50]

Nonaction is doing nothing in hopes that the conflict will disappear. Generally, this is not a good technique because most conflicts do not go away, and the individuals involved in the conflict react with frustration. **Secrecy**, attempting to hide a conflict or an issue that has the potential to create conflict, only creates suspicion. An example is an organizational policy of pay secrecy. In some organizations, discussion of salary is grounds for dismissal. When this is the case, employees suspect that the company has something to hide. **Administrative orbiting** is delaying action on a conflict by buying time, usually by telling the individuals involved that the problem is being worked on or that the boss is still thinking about the issue. Like nonaction, this technique leads to frustration and resentment.

Due process nonaction is a procedure set up to address conflicts that is so costly, time-consuming, or personally risky that no one will use it. Some companies' sexual harassment policies are examples of this technique. To file a sexual harassment complaint, the accuser must complete detailed paperwork, has to go through appropriate channels, and may be branded a troublemaker. Thus, the company has a procedure for handling complaints (due process), but no one uses it (nonaction).

Character assassination is an attempt to label or discredit an opponent. Character assassination can backfire and make the individual who uses it appear dishonest and cruel. It often leads to name-calling and accusations by both parties, who both end up losers in the eyes of those who witness the conflict. In 2010, Dana Holgorsen was hired as the head football coach at West Virginia University. The only problem was that the school already had a head coach, Bill Stewart. Holgorsen was hired to serve as an assistant for a year under Stewart and then replace him. This arrangement angered Stewart, who contacted journalists to "dig up dirt" on Holgorsen so that he could use it for character assassination. When this became public knowledge, Stewart resigned from his position.[51]

13-5b Effective Techniques

Fortunately, there are effective conflict management techniques. These include appealing to superordinate goals, expanding resources, changing personnel, changing structure, and confronting and negotiating.

SUPERORDINATE GOALS An organizational goal that is more important to both parties in a conflict than their individual or group goals is a **superordinate goal**.[52] Superordinate goals cannot be achieved by an individual or by one group alone. The achievement of these goals requires cooperation by both parties. One effective technique for resolving conflict is to appeal to this superordinate goal—in effect, to focus the parties on a larger issue on which they both agree. This helps them realize their similarities rather than their differences.

In the conflict between service representatives and cable television installers that was discussed earlier, appealing to a superordinate goal would be an effective technique for resolving the conflict. Both departments can agree that superior customer service is a goal worthy of pursuit and that this goal cannot be achieved unless cables are installed properly and in a timely manner, and customer complaints are handled effectively. Quality service requires that both departments cooperate to achieve the goal.

EXPANDING RESOURCES One conflict resolution technique is so simple that it may be overlooked. If the conflict's source is common or scarce resources, providing more resources may be a solution. Of course, managers working with tight budgets may not have the luxury of obtaining additional resources. Nevertheless, it is a technique to be considered. In the example of shared administrative support presented earlier in this chapter, one solution to the conflict among managers over administrative support would be to hire more administrative assistants.

CHANGING PERSONNEL In some cases, long-running severe conflict may be traced to a specific individual. For example, managers with lower levels of emotional intelligence demonstrate more negative work attitudes, exhibit less altruistic behavior, and produce more negative work outcomes. A chronically disgruntled manager who exhibits low emotional intelligence might not only frustrate his employees but also impede his department's performance. In such cases, transferring or firing an individual could be the best solution, but only after due process.[53]

CHANGING STRUCTURE Another way to resolve a conflict is to change the structure of the organization. One way of accomplishing this is to create an integrator role. An *integrator* is a liaison between groups with very different interests. In severe conflicts, it may be best

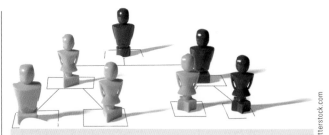

Changing the structure of an organization is one way to resolve conflict.

Greg Brave/Shutterstock.com

that the integrator be a neutral third party.[54] Creating the integrator role is a way of opening dialogue between groups that have difficulty communicating.

Using *cross-functional teams* is another way of changing the organization's structure to manage conflict. In the old methods of designing new products in organizations, many departments had to contribute, and delays resulted from difficulties in coordinating the activities of the various departments. Using a cross-functional team made up of members from different departments improves coordination and reduces delays by allowing many activities to be performed at the same time rather than sequentially.[55] The team approach allows members from different departments to work together and reduces the potential for conflict. However, recent research also suggests that such functional diversity can lead to slower informational processing in teams due to differences in members' perceptions of what might be required to achieve group goals. When putting together cross-functional teams, organizations should emphasize superordinate goals and train team members on resolving conflict. One such training technique could involve educating individual members in other functional areas so that everyone on the team can have a shared language.[56] In teamwork, it is helpful to break up a big task so that it becomes a collection of smaller, less complex tasks and to have smaller teams work on the smaller tasks. This helps to reduce conflict, and organizations can potentially improve the performance of the overall team by improving the outcomes in each subteam.[57]

CONFRONTING AND NEGOTIATING Some conflicts require confrontation and negotiation between the parties. Both of these strategies require skill on the part of the negotiator and careful planning before engaging in negotiations. The process of negotiating involves an open discussion of problem solutions,

superordinate goal An organizational goal that is more important to both parties in a conflict than their individual or group goals.

and the outcome often is an exchange in which both parties work toward a mutually beneficial solution.

Negotiation is a joint process of finding a mutually acceptable solution to a complex conflict. There are two major negotiating approaches: distributive bargaining and integrative negotiation.[58] **Distributive bargaining** is an approach in which the goals of one party are in direct conflict with the goals of the other party. Resources are limited, and each party wants to maximize its share of the resources (get its piece of the pie). It is a competitive, or win–lose, approach to negotiations. Sometimes distributive bargaining causes negotiators to focus so much on their differences that they ignore their common ground. In these cases, distributive bargaining can become counterproductive. The reality is, however, that some situations are distributive in nature, particularly when the parties are interdependent. If a negotiator wants to maximize the value of a single deal and is not worried about maintaining a good relationship with the other party, distributive bargaining may be an option.

In contrast, **integrative negotiation** is an approach in which the parties' goals are not seen as mutually exclusive, but the focus is on both sides achieving their objectives. Integrative negotiation focuses on the merits of the issues and is a win–win approach. (How can we make the pie bigger?) For integrative negotiation to be successful, certain preconditions must be present. These include having a common goal, faith in one's own problem-solving abilities, a belief in the validity of the other party's position, motivation to work together, mutual trust, and clear communication. It also helps if both parties are good at perspective taking, which is the ability to see the other person's point of view.[59]

Cultural differences play a role in negotiation styles. For example, negotiation strategies differ among dignity cultures (e.g., the United States), face cultures (China), and honor cultures (Qatar). In dignity cultures, people derive their self-worth intrinsically and see each individual as having inherent self-worth. Independence and choosing one's own goals are valued. In face cultures, people derive their self-worth from social interactions. A premium is placed on saving face, showing humility, and preserving social harmony. In honor cultures, people are tough in protecting self and family, but polite and warm in social interactions depending on the context. Researchers have shown that individuals from face and honor cultures use more competitive negotiation strategies than individuals from dignity cultures when negotiating a new business relationship. The finding that honor cultures produce more competitive negotiation styles is not surprising, but the finding that face cultures such as China use competitive styles is interesting. It is a reminder that not all face cultures are alike. In China, reform policies have placed more emphasis on competition, which may lead to tougher negotiation styles. This may not be the case in other face cultures such as Korea or Japan, and this is a reminder that we shouldn't assume that negotiators in a particular cultural prototype (dignity, face, or honor) share the same negotiation behavior. Even among prototypes there may be subtle differences.[60]

Gender may also play a role in negotiation. There appears to be no evidence that men are better negotiators than women or vice versa. It depends on the context of the negotiation. Men achieve better economic outcomes when negotiating for themselves. In contrast, women achieve better outcomes when they are negotiating on behalf of another individual. Often, women lack experience when it comes to negotiating and can benefit from training in negotiation skills.[61]

distributive bargaining A negotiation approach in which the goals of the parties are in conflict, and each party seeks to maximize its resources.

integrative negotiation A negotiation approach in which the parties' goals are not seen as mutually exclusive, but the focus is on both sides achieving their objectives.

13-6 CONFLICT MANAGEMENT STYLES

Managers have at their disposal a variety of conflict management styles: avoiding, accommodating, competing, compromising, and collaborating. One way of classifying styles of conflict management is to examine the styles' *assertiveness* (the extent to which you want your goals met) and *cooperativeness* (the extent to which you want to see the other party's concerns met).[62] Figure 13.4

FIGURE 13.4 | CONFLICT MANAGEMENT STYLES

SOURCE: K. W. Thomas, "Conflict and Conflict Management," in M. D. Dunnette, *Handbook of Industrial and Organizational Psychology* (Chicago: Rand McNally, 1976), 900. Used with permission of M. D. Dunnette.

graphs the five conflict management styles using these two dimensions. Table 13.3 lists appropriate situations for using each conflict management style.

13-6a Avoiding

Avoiding is a style low on both assertiveness and cooperativeness. Avoiding is a deliberate decision to take no action on a conflict or to stay out of a conflict situation. In recent times, Airbus, a European manufacturer of aircraft, has faced massive intraorganizational conflict stemming from major expansions that included French, German, Spanish, and British subsidiaries within the same parent company. Power struggles among executives combined with massive changes in organizational structure are believed to have led to this conflict. Airbus seems to be adopting the avoidance strategy in an effort to let these conflicts subside on their own.[63] Some relationship conflicts, such as those involving political norms and personal tastes, may distract team members from their tasks, in which case, avoiding may be an appropriate strategy.[64] When the parties are angry and need time to cool down, it may be best to use avoidance. There is a potential danger in using an avoiding style too often, however. Research shows that overuse of this style results in negative

evaluations from others in the workplace.[65]

13-6b Accommodating

A style in which you are concerned that the other party's goals be met but relatively unconcerned with getting your own way is called accommodating. It is cooperative but unassertive. Appropriate situations for accommodating include times when you find you are wrong, when you want to let the other party have his way so that that individual will owe you similar treatment later, or when the relationship is important. Overreliance on accommodating has its dangers. Managers who constantly defer to others may find that others lose respect for them. In addition, accommodating managers may become frustrated because their own needs are never met, and they may lose self-esteem.[66] Research has also shown that individuals will overestimate the importance of the relationship and accommodate at the expense of actual outcomes. Research has shown that two females involved in conflict or negotiation overuse accommodation more than two males involved in similar situations.[67]

13-6c Competing

Competing is a style that is very assertive and uncooperative. You want to satisfy your own interests and are willing to do so at the other party's expense. In an emergency or in situations where you know you are right, it may be appropriate to put your foot down. Greenpeace has long used an aggressive strategy to force corporations to respond to environmental issues. One of its notable efforts was to influence toymaker LEGO to quit doing business with oil giant Shell because of Shell's drilling in the Arctic. Millions of people joined in to sign petitions, hold protests in LEGO costumes, and tell Shell to stop exploiting the melting Arctic for more oil. LEGO responded by not renewing its contract with Shell (for Shell-branded LEGO toys sold at gas stations).[68] This is one of many ways Greenpeace uses active resistance in conflicts. Relying solely on competing strategies is

TABLE 13.3 USES OF FIVE STYLES OF CONFLICT MANAGEMENT

Conflict-Handling Style	Appropriate Situation
Competing	When quick, decisive action is vital (e.g., emergencies). On important issues for which unpopular actions need implementing (e.g., cost cutting, enforcing unpopular rules, discipline). On issues vital to company welfare when you know you are right. Against people who take advantage of noncompetitive behavior.
Collaborating	To find an integrative solution when both sets of concerns are too important to be compromised. When your objective is to learn. To merge insights from people with different perspectives. To gain commitment by incorporating concerns into a consensus. To work through feelings that have interfered with a relationship.
Compromising	When goals are important but not worth the effort or potential disruption of more assertive modes. When opponents with equal power are committed to mutually exclusive goals. To achieve temporary settlements to complex issues. To arrive at expedient solutions under time pressure. As a backup when collaboration or competition is unsuccessful.
Avoiding	When an issue is trivial or more important issues are pressing. When you perceive no chance of satisfying your concerns. When potential disruption outweighs the benefits of resolution. To let people cool down and regain perspective. When gathering information supersedes immediate decision. When others can resolve the conflict more effectively. When issues seem tangential or symptomatic of other issues.
Accommodating	When you find you are wrong—to allow a better position to be heard, to learn, and to show your reasonableness. When issues are more important to others than to yourself—to satisfy others and maintain cooperation. To build social credits for later issues. To minimize loss when you are outmatched and losing. When harmony and stability are especially important. To allow employees to develop by learning from mistakes.

SOURCE: K. W. Thomas, "Toward Multidimensional Values in Teaching: The Example of Conflict Behaviors," *Academy of Management Review*, 2 (1977): 309–325. Reproduced by permission of the publisher via Copyright Clearance Center, Inc.

dangerous, though. Managers who do so may become reluctant to admit when they are wrong and may find themselves surrounded by people who are afraid to disagree with them. As noted earlier, task conflict and relationship conflict could occur together in team settings, although task conflict is seen as functional and relationship conflict as dysfunctional for the team. In a recent study, dyads of participants were exposed to task-based conflict. One of the two members of the dyads was trained on using either the competing conflict-handling style or the collaborative style. Results indicated that the competing style led to the most relationship conflict, whereas the collaborative style led to the least relationship conflict.[69]

13-6d Compromising

The compromising style is intermediate in both assertiveness and cooperativeness because each party must give up something to reach a solution to the conflict. Compromises are often made in the final hours of union–management negotiations, when time is of the essence. Compromise may be an effective backup style when efforts toward collaboration are not successful.[70]

It is important to recognize that compromises are not optimal solutions. Compromise means partially surrendering one's position for the sake of coming to terms. For this reason, people often inflate their demands when they begin a compromise. A problem with compromise

Greenpeace activists at a Shell station in Chile demand that LEGO remove Shell logos from its toys because of Shell's oil search in the Arctic.

MARTIN BERNETTI/Getty Images

and arriving at a solution that is satisfactory to both parties. Situations where collaboration may be effective include times when both parties need to be committed to a final solution or when a combination of different perspectives can be formed into a solution. Long-term collaboration leads to improved relationships and effective performance.[71] Teams that use collaboration effectively view conflict as a mutual problem that needs common consideration to achieve resolution. Understanding this, team members have confidence that other members will work toward mutually beneficial solutions and ultimately generate diverse ideas to facilitate team performance.[72]

is that the solutions reached may only be temporary, and often compromises do nothing to improve relationships between the parties in the conflict.

13-6e Collaborating

A win–win style that is high on both assertiveness and cooperativeness is known as collaborating. Working toward it involves an open and thorough discussion of the conflict

Research on the five styles of conflict management indicates that although most managers favor a certain style, they have the capacity to change styles as the situation demands.[73] When supervisors are a third party to a conflict, using collaboration rather than competing or accommodating, and intervening early in the conflict, minimizes anxiety and bullying among team members.[74]

14 | Jobs and the Design of Work

LEARNING OBJECTIVES

14-1 Differentiate between job and work.

14-2 Discuss the traditional approaches to job design.

14-3 Identify and describe alternative approaches to job design.

14-4 Identify and describe contemporary issues facing organizations in the design of work.

After finishing this chapter go to **PAGE 251 for STUDY TOOLS**

14-1 WORK IN ORGANIZATIONS

A **job** can be defined as a set of specified work and task activities that engage an individual in an organization. A job is not the same as an organizational position or a career. *Organizational position* identifies a job in relation to other parts of the organization; *career* refers to a sequence of job experiences over time. A job is also not the same as *work*, at least not in relation to an organization. **Work**, which can be defined as mental or physical activity that has productive results, is organized into jobs. Thus, a *job* is composed of a set of specific tasks, each of which is an assigned piece of *work* to be done in a specific time period.

job A set of specified work and task activities that engage an individual in an organization.

work Mental or physical activity that has productive results.

Work is one important reason organizations exist. Plus, work is an especially important human endeavor because through work, people become securely attached to reality and securely connected in human relationships. Applied psychology has played an instrumental role in work design research for a century,

dating back to 1917.[1] The research has spanned the design of work systems and the study of work groups as well as the study of job design and job redesign. Jobs and the design of work are the key subjects of Chapter 14. Chapter 15 focuses on the larger issue of organizational design. Together, these two chapters emphasize the set of task and authority relationships in organizations through which people get work done.

14-1a The Meaning of Work

The **meaning of work** differs by person, by culture, by country, and by profession. It is not uncommon for contemporary workers to describe their work and careers as a calling, a sense of fulfilling life's purpose.[2] In an increasingly global workplace, it is important to understand and appreciate differences among individuals and cultures with regard to the meaning of work. One study found six patterns people follow in defining *work*, and these help explain the cultural differences in people's motivation to work.[3]

- *Pattern A* people define *work* as an activity in which value comes from performance and for which a person is accountable. It is generally self-directed and devoid of negative affect.

> For all people, work is organized into jobs, and jobs fit into the larger structure of an organization.

- *Pattern B* people define *work* as an activity that provides a person with positive personal affect and identity. Work contributes to society and is not unpleasant.

- *Pattern C* people define *work* as an activity from which profit accrues to others by its performance and that may be done in various settings other than a working place. Work is usually physically strenuous and somewhat compulsive.

- *Pattern D* people define *work* as primarily a physical activity a person must do that is directed by others and generally performed in a working place. Work is

meaning of work The way a person interprets and understands the value of work as part of life.

usually devoid of positive affect and is unpleasantly connected to performance.

- *Pattern E* people define *work* as a physically and mentally strenuous activity. It is generally unpleasant and devoid of positive affect.

- *Pattern F* people define *work* as an activity constrained to specific time periods that does not bring positive affect through its performance.

These six patterns were studied in six different countries: Belgium, Germany, Israel, Japan, the Netherlands, and the United States. Table 14.1 summarizes the percentage of workers in each country who defined work according to each of the six patterns. An examination of the table shows that a small percentage of workers in all six countries used either Pattern E or Pattern F to define *work*. Furthermore, there are significant differences among countries in how *work* is defined. In the Netherlands, *work* is defined most positively and with the most balanced personal and collective reasons for doing it. *Work* is defined least positively and with the most collective reason for doing it in Germany and Japan. Belgium, Israel, and

the United States represent a middle position between these two poles.

In another international study, 5,550 people across ten occupational groups in twenty different countries completed the *Work Value Scales (WVS)*.[4] The WVS is composed of thirteen items measuring various aspects of the work environment, such as responsibility and job security. The study found two common basic work dimensions across cultures: *work content*, measured by items such as "the amount of responsibility on the job," and *job context*, measured by items such as "the policies of my company." This finding suggests that people in many cultures distinguish between the nature of the work itself and elements of the context in which work is done. The idea of two work dimensions supports Herzberg's two-factor theory of motivation (see Chapter 5) and his job enrichment method discussed later in this chapter. Although the meaning of *work* differs among countries, new theorizing about crafting a job also suggests that individual employees can alter work meaning and work identity by changing task and relationship configurations in their work.[5]

14-1b Jobs in Organizations

Task and authority relationships define an organization's structure. Jobs, being the basic building blocks of this task–authority structure, are considered the micro-structural element to which employees most directly relate. Jobs are usually designed to complement and support other jobs in the organization. A new trend is flexible jobs that are a better fit for the emerging agile workforce. These new flexible jobs have less rigidity and less structure than did many of the manufacturing jobs of earlier eras in U.S. work life. The Hot Trend discusses some of the data about the rising agile workforce and flexible jobs.

Jobs in organizations are interdependent and designed to make a contribution to the organization's overall mission and goals. For salespeople to be successful, the production people must be effective. For production people to be effective, the material department must be effective. These interdependencies require careful planning and design so that all of the pieces of work fit together into a

TABLE 14.1	**WORK DEFINITION PATTERNS BY NATION**					
	PATTERN[a]					
SAMPLE	**A**	**B**	**C**	**D**	**E**	**F**
Total Sample ($N \times 4{,}950$)	11%	28%	18%	22%	11%	12%
NATION						
Belgium	8%	40%	13%	19%	11%	9%
Germany	8%	26%	13%	28%	11%	14%
Israel	4%	22%	33%	23%	9%	9%
Japan	21%	11%	13%	29%	10%	17%
The Netherlands	15%	43%	12%	11%	9%	9%
United States	8%	30%	19%	19%	12%	11%

Note: $X^2 = 680.98$ (25 degrees of freedom). $P < 0.0001$ Significance level.

[a]In Pattern A, work is valued for its performance. The person is accountable and generally self-directed. In Pattern B, work provides a person with positive affect and identity. It contributes to society. In Pattern C, work provides profit to others by its performance. It is physical and not confined to a working place. In Pattern D, work is a required physical activity directed by others and generally unpleasant. In Pattern E, work is physically and mentally strenuous. It is generally unpleasant. In Pattern F, work is constrained to specific time periods. It does not bring positive affect through performance.

SOURCE: From G. W. England and I. Harper, "How Working Is Defined: National Contexts and Demographic and Organizational Role Influences," *Journal of Organizational Behavior,* 11 (1990): 253–266. This material is used by permission of John Wiley & Sons, Inc.

whole. Suppose an envelope salesperson wants to take an order for 1 million envelopes from John Hancock Financial Services. He must coordinate that order with the production department to establish an achievable delivery date. Failure to incorporate this interdependence into his planning could create conflict, resulting in late delivery to John Hancock.

The central concerns of this chapter are designing work and structuring jobs to prevent such problems and to ensure employee well-being. Inflexible jobs that are rigidly structured have an adverse effect, as they cause stress to employees and limit their career growth. In contrast, so-called smart jobs stimulate learning and growth and thus serve as building blocks for a person's career.[6]

The larger issues in the design of organizations are the competing processes of differentiation and integration (see Chapter 15). *Differentiation* is the process of subdividing and departmentalizing the work of an organization. Jobs result from differentiation, which is necessary because no one can do it all (contrary to the famous statement made by Harold Geneen, former chair of ITT: "If I had enough arms and legs and time, I'd do it all myself"). Even small organizations must divide work so that each person is able to accomplish a manageable piece of the whole. At the same time that the organization divides up the work, however, it must also integrate those pieces back into a whole. *Integration* is the process of connecting jobs and departments into a coordinated, cohesive whole. For example, if the envelope salesperson coordinates his order from John Hancock with the production manager, the company will meet the customer's expectations because integration will have occurred.

14-2 TRADITIONAL APPROACHES TO JOB DESIGN

Failure to differentiate, integrate, or both may result in badly designed jobs, which in turn cause a variety of performance problems in organizations. Good job design helps avoid these problems, improves productivity, and enhances employee well-being. Approaches to job design that were developed during the twentieth century are job enlargement/job rotation, job enrichment, and the job characteristics theory. Each approach offers unique benefits to the organization, the employee, or both, but each also has limitations and drawbacks. Furthermore, an unthinking reliance on a traditional approach can be a serious problem in any company. The later job design approaches were developed to overcome the limitations of traditional job design approaches. For example, job enlargement was intended to overcome the problem of boredom associated with scientific management's narrowly defined approach to jobs.

14-2a Scientific Management

Scientific management, an approach to work design first advocated by Frederick Taylor, emphasizes work simplification. **Work simplification** is the standardization and the narrow, explicit specification of task activities for workers.[7] Jobs designed through scientific management have a limited number of tasks, and each task is scientifically designed so that the worker is not required to think or deliberate. According to Taylor, the role of management and the

> **work simplification** The standardization and the narrow, explicit specification of task activities for workers.

Work simplification can give an employee a renewed sense of confidence in his or her work.

industrial engineer is to calibrate and define each task carefully. The role of the worker is to execute the task. Elements of scientific management, such as time and motion studies, differential piece-rate systems of pay, and the scientific selection of workers, all focus on the efficient use of labor to the economic benefit of the corporation.

14-2b Job Enlargement/Job Rotation

Job enlargement is a method of job design that increases the number of activities in a job to overcome the boredom of overspecialized work. It is a traditional approach to solving not only the problem of boredom but also the difficulty of coordinating work.[8] **Job rotation**, a variation of job enlargement, exposes a worker to a variety of specialized job tasks over time. Both of these approaches came into being to solve the perceived problems of overspecialization that arose from lack of variety. In other words, jobs designed by scientific management were too narrow and limited in the number of tasks and activities assigned to each worker. The lack of variety led to understimulation and underutilization of the worker.

job enlargement A method of job design that increases the number of activities in a job to overcome the boredom of overspecialized work.

job rotation A variation of job enlargement in which workers are exposed to a variety of specialized jobs over time.

cross-training A variation of job enlargement in which workers are trained in different specialized tasks or activities.

Variety can be increased by adding to a worker's activities by means of job enlargement or by giving a worker different activities by means of job rotation. For example, job enlargement for a lathe operator in a steel plant might include selecting the steel pieces to be turned and performing all of the maintenance work on the lathe in addition to running it. As an example of job rotation, an employee at a small bank might take new accounts one day, serve as a cashier another day, and process loan applications on a third day.

One of the first studies of the problem of repetitive work was conducted at IBM after World War II. The company implemented a job enlargement program during the war and evaluated the effort after six years.[9] The two most important results were a significant increase in product quality and a reduction in idle time, both for people and for machines. Less obvious and measurable benefits were enhanced worker status and improved manager–worker communication. The IBM concluded that job enlargement countered the problems of work specialization. A contemporary study in a Swedish electronics assembly plant used physiological measures of muscle tension.[10] Job enlargement had a positive effect on mechanical exposure variability.

A later study examined the effects of mass production jobs on assembly line workers in the automotive industry.[11] Mass production jobs have six characteristics: mechanically controlled work pace, repetitiveness, minimum skill requirements, predetermined tools and techniques, minute division of the production process, and a requirement for surface mental attention rather than thoughtful concentration. The researchers conducted 180 private interviews with assembly line workers and found generally positive attitudes toward pay, security, and supervision. They concluded that job enlargement and job rotation would improve other job aspects, such as repetition and a mechanical work pace.

Job rotation and **cross-training** programs are variations of job enlargement. Pharmaceutical company Eli Lilly has found that job rotation can be a proactive means for enhancing work experiences for career development and can have tangible benefits for employees in the form of salary increases and promotions.[12] In cross-training, workers are trained in different specialized tasks or activities of different jobs. While job rotation may be common practice for high-potential employees, they should remain in a position long enough to see the consequences of their decisions.[13]

All three kinds of programs—job enlargement, job rotation, and cross-training horizontally—enlarge jobs; that is, the number and variety of an employee's tasks and activities are increased. Graphic Controls Corporation (now a subsidiary of Tyco International) used cross-training to develop a flexible workforce that enabled the company to maintain high levels of production.[14] The predictions are that global productivity will rise over the next 50 years. The Fast Fact discusses how this will likely occur. Engaged workers are often productive workers, but over focus does have its limitations. Therefore, it is important that employees be able to disengage from one task before moving on to another to achieve high levels of performance.[15]

14-2c Job Enrichment

Job enrichment is designing or redesigning a job by incorporating motivational factors into it. Whereas job enlargement increases the number of job activities through horizontal loading, job enrichment increases the amount of job responsibility through vertical loading. Both approaches to job design are intended, in part, to increase job satisfaction for employees. A study to test whether job satisfaction results from characteristics of the job or of the person found that an interactionist approach is most accurate and that job redesign can contribute to increased job satisfaction for some employees. Another two-year study found that intrinsic job satisfaction and job perceptions are reciprocally related to each other.[16]

Jobs Change and Workers Adapt

While some suggest that robots and automation are getting ready to take over jobs people are working in today, the fact is that only 5 percent of all occupations are at risk of being completely automated. While jobs will not disappear, they will change dramatically. A study of 800 occupations and 2,000 job tasks predicts that 50 percent of workers' current tasks could be automated by the year 2055 using current technology. The result will not be mass unemployment but rather an annual increase in global productivity by 0.8 to 1.4 percent annually. While four in 10 workers are unsure of the skills they will need to stay professionally relevant, already 50 percent of the workforce is high skilled. Some countries, such as Switzerland, are at the top of the global continuum of countries developing a future-ready workforce. Workers will feel pressure to adapt, retrain, and upgrade their skills. If they do those things, they will be ready for the jobs of the future.

SOURCE: L. Weber, "Three New Predictions for Automation and Jobs," *Wall Street Journal*, 17 Jan. 2017.

Job enrichment builds on Herzberg's two-factor theory of motivation, which distinguished between motivational and hygiene factors for people at work. Whereas job enlargement recommends increasing and varying the number of activities a person does, job enrichment recommends increasing the recognition, responsibility, and opportunity for achievement. For example, enlarging the lathe operator's job means adding maintenance activities, and enriching the job means having the operator meet with customers who buy the products.

Herzberg believed that only certain jobs should be enriched and that the first step is to select the jobs appropriate for job enrichment.[17] He recognized that some people prefer simple jobs. Once jobs are selected for enrichment, management should brainstorm about possible changes, revise the list to include only specific changes related to motivational factors, and screen out generalities and suggestions that would simply increase activities or numbers of tasks. Those whose jobs are to be enriched should not participate in this process, as doing so would present a conflict of interest.

A seven-year implementation study of job enrichment at AT&T found that approach beneficial.[18] Job enrichment required a big change in management style, and AT&T found that it could not ignore hygiene factors in the work environment just because it was enriching existing jobs. Although the AT&T experience with job enrichment was positive, a critical review of job enrichment did not find that to be the case generally.[19] One problem with job enrichment as a strategy for work design is that it is based on an oversimplified motivational theory. Another problem is the lack of consideration for individual differences among employees. Job enrichment, like scientific management's work specialization and job enlargement/job rotation, is a universal approach to the design of work and thus does not differentiate among individuals. Many chief marketing officers (CMOs) appear to believe they do not have enriched jobs, as discussed in the feature box.

14-2d Job Characteristics Theory

The job characteristics theory, which was initiated during the mid-1960s, is a traditional approach to the design of work that makes a significant departure from the three earlier approaches. It emphasizes the interaction between the individual and specific attributes of the job; therefore, it is a person–job fit model rather than a universal job design model. It originated in a research study of 470 workers in forty-seven

> **job enrichment** Designing or redesigning a job by incorporating motivational factors into it.

Even C-Level Executives May Not Have Enriched Jobs

Rawpixel.com/Shutterstock.com

Enriched jobs are characterized by responsibility, authority, and opportunity for achievement. New chief marketing officers (CMOs) often think that is what they are in for, based on the job description, their experience, and their conversations with recruiters and CEOs. Once in the job, the CMOs may find the job was poorly designed, not enabling them to maximize their skill set. Seventy-four percent of CMOs do not believe their jobs allow them to maximize their impact on the business. Their frustration is reflected in high turnover rates at the C-Level. Fifty-seven percent of CMOs have been in their positions three years or less; their average tenure is 4.1 years. This compares to 8 years for CEOs, 5.1 years for CFOs, 5 years for CHROs, and 4.3 years for CIOs. Just getting to the C-Level does not guarantee an enriched job, nor job satisfaction.

SOURCE: K. A. Whitler and N. Morgan, "Why CMOs Never Last," *Harvard Business Review*, July–Aug. 2017.

Job Characteristics Model
A framework for understanding person–job fit through the interaction of core job dimensions with critical psychological states within a person.

Job Diagnostic Survey (JDS) The survey instrument designed to measure the elements in the Job Characteristics Model.

different jobs across eleven industries.[20] The study measured and classified relevant task characteristics for these forty-seven jobs and found four core job characteristics: job variety, autonomy, responsibility, and interpersonal interaction. The study also found that core job characteristics did not affect all workers in the same way. A person's values, religious beliefs, and ethnic background influenced how the worker responded to the job. Specifically, workers with rural values and workers with strong religious beliefs preferred jobs high in core characteristics, and workers with urban values and those with weaker religious beliefs preferred jobs low in core characteristics. Another study tested the effect of job and work characteristics on employee turnover intentions and found that employees consider both when deciding to leave a company.[21]

Richard Hackman and his colleagues modified the original model by including three critical psychological states of the individual and refining the measurement of core job characteristics. The result is the **Job Characteristics Model** shown in Figure 14.1.[22] The **Job Diagnostic Survey (JDS)**, the most commonly used job design measure, was developed to diagnose jobs by measuring the five core job characteristics and three critical psychological states shown in the model. The core job characteristics stimulate the critical psychological states in the manner shown in Figure 14.1. This results in varying personal and work outcomes, as identified in the figure. A new proposal to modify the job characteristics model suggests that psychological ownership is an important factor in job design.[23]

Hackman and his colleagues say that the five core job characteristics interact to determine an overall *Motivating Potential Score (MPS)* for a specific job. The MPS indicates a job's potential for motivating incumbents. An individual's MPS is determined by the following equation:

$$MPS = \frac{\left[\begin{array}{c}\text{Skill}\\\text{variety}\end{array}\right] + \left[\begin{array}{c}\text{Task}\\\text{identity}\end{array}\right] + \left[\begin{array}{c}\text{Task}\\\text{significance}\end{array}\right]}{3} [\text{Autonomy}] \times [\text{Feedback}]$$

The Job Characteristics Model includes *growth need strength* (the desire to grow and fully develop one's abilities) as a moderator. People with high growth need strength respond favorably to jobs with high MPSs, and individuals with low growth need strength respond less favorably to such jobs. The job characteristics theory further suggests that core job dimensions stimulate three critical psychological states according to the relationships specified in the model. These critical psychological states are defined as follows:

1. *Experienced meaningfulness of the work*, or the degree to which the employee experiences the job as one that is generally meaningful, valuable, and worthwhile.

2. *Experienced responsibility for work outcomes*, or the degree to which the employee feels personally accountable and responsible for the results of the work he or she does.

3. *Knowledge of results*, or the degree to which the employee knows and understands, on a continuous basis, how effectively he or she is performing the job.

In one early study, Hackman and Oldham administered the JDS to 658 employees working on sixty-two different jobs in seven business organizations.[24] The JDS was useful for job redesign efforts through one or more

FIGURE 14.1   THE JOB CHARACTERISTICS MODEL

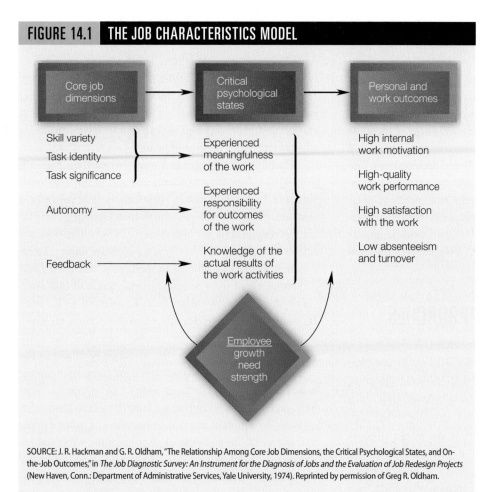

SOURCE: J. R. Hackman and G. R. Oldham, "The Relationship Among Core Job Dimensions, the Critical Psychological States, and On-the-Job Outcomes," in *The Job Diagnostic Survey: An Instrument for the Diagnosis of Jobs and the Evaluation of Job Redesign Projects* (New Haven, Conn.: Department of Administrative Services, Yale University, 1974). Reprinted by permission of Greg R. Oldham.

of five implementing concepts: (1) combining tasks into larger jobs, (2) forming natural work teams to increase task identity and task significance, (3) establishing relationships with customers, (4) loading jobs vertically with more responsibility, and/or (5) opening feedback channels for the job incumbent. For example, if an automotive mechanic received little feedback on the quality of repair work performed, one redesign strategy would be to solicit customer feedback one month after each repair.

A recent sequence of two studies conducted in Egypt aimed to disaggregate *work autonomy*, an important component in job design theory.[25] Study 1 included 534 employees in two Egyptian organizations. Study 2 involved 120 managers in four organizations. The results indicated that separate work method, work schedule, and work criteria autonomy were three separate facets of work autonomy.

An alternative to the Job Characteristics Model is the *Job Characteristics Inventory (JCI)* developed by Henry Sims and Andrew Szilagyi.[26] The JCI primarily measures core job characteristics. It is not as comprehensive as the JDS because it does not incorporate

critical psychological states, personal and work outcomes, or employee needs. The JCI does give some consideration to structural and individual variables that affect the relationship between core job characteristics and the individual.[27] One comparative analysis of the JCI and JDS found similarities in the measures and in the models' predictions.[28] The comparative analysis also found two differences. First, the variety scales in the two models appear to have different effects on performance. Second, the autonomy scales in the two models appear to have different effects on employee satisfaction. Overall, the JCI and JDS both support the usefulness of a person–job fit approach to the design of work over the earlier, universal theories.

ENGAGEMENT Psychological conditions related to job design features are a particular concern of the Job Characteristics Model.[29] One study of more than 200 managers and employees in a Midwestern insurance company found that meaningfulness, safety, and availability were three important psychological conditions that affected employees' **engagement** in their jobs and work roles. The extent to which employees are engaged in their jobs has an impact on workplace behaviors. Employees who identify with supervisor goals are less likely to engage in counterproductive behaviors in the workplace, and this relationship operates through employee engagement. The degree to which work engagement functions as a bridge between goal congruence and deviant behaviors depends on the emotional intelligence of employees. Employees with highly developed emotional intelligence skills will be more likely to respond positively to goal congruence.[30] Gallup's Q12 survey was used to improve engagement for a clinical nutrition group at St. Mary's/Duluth Clinic Health System with successful results.[31] Despite its

engagement The expression of oneself as one performs in work or other roles.

importance to company success, however, only one-third of employees in a recent study reported that they were engaged in their work.[32]

Full engagement requires the strategic management of one's energy in response to the environment.[33] Being fully engaged in one's work role and job can be highly appropriate and yet demand energy, time, and effort. To achieve balance and afford opportunity for recovery, there is a commensurate need to strategically and appropriately disengage from one's job and work role on a periodic basis. The effective management of energy in response to one's job and work role leads to both high performance and personal renewal. Thus, while the design of work is important, the human spirit's response to job characteristics and work design features is equally important.

 ## 14-3 ALTERNATIVE APPROACHES TO JOB DESIGN

Because each of the traditional job design approaches has limitations, several alternative approaches have emerged over the past couple of decades. This section examines four alternatives that are in the process of being tried and tested. First, it examines the social information-processing model. Second, it reviews ergonomics and the interdisciplinary framework of Michael Campion and Paul Thayer. Their framework builds on traditional job design approaches. Third, this section examines the international perspectives of the Japanese, Germans, and Scandinavians. Finally, it focuses on the health and well-being aspects of work design. Healthy work enables individuals to adapt, function well, and balance work with private life activities.[34] An emerging fifth approach to the design of work through teams and autonomous work groups was addressed in Chapter 9.

14-3a Social Information Processing

The traditional approaches to the design of work emphasize objective core job characteristics. In contrast, the social information-processing (SIP) model emphasizes the interpersonal aspects of work design. Specifically, the SIP model says that what others tell us about our jobs is important.[35] The SIP model has four basic premises about the work environment.[36]

social information-processing (SIP) model A model that suggests that the important job factors depend in part on what others tell a person about the job.

ergonomics The science of adapting work and working conditions to the employee or worker.

First, other people provide cues we use to understand the work environment. Second, other people help us judge what is important in our jobs. Third, other people tell us how they see our jobs. Fourth, other people's positive and negative feedback helps us understand our feelings about our jobs. This is very consistent with the dynamic model of the job design process that views it as a social one involving job-holders, supervisors, and peers.[37]

People's perceptions and reactions to their jobs are shaped by information from other people in the work environment.[38] In other words, what others believe about a person's job may be important to understanding the person's perceptions of, and reactions to, the job. This does not mean that objective job characteristics are unimportant; rather, it means that others can modify the way these characteristics affect us. For example, one study of task complexity found that the objective complexity of a task must be distinguished from the subjective task complexity experienced by the employee.[39] Although objective task complexity may be a motivator, the presence of others in the work environment, social interaction, or even daydreaming may be important additional sources of motivation. The SIP model makes an important contribution to the design of work by emphasizing the importance of other people and the social context of work. For example, relational job design may motivate employees to take prosocial action and make a positive difference in other people's lives.[40] In addition, the relational aspects of the work environment may be more important than objective core job characteristics. Therefore, the subjective feedback of other people about how difficult a particular task is may be more important to a person's motivation to perform than an objective estimate of the task's difficulty.

14-3b Ergonomics and Interdisciplinary Framework

Michael Campion and Paul Thayer used **ergonomics** based on engineering, biology, and psychology to develop an interdisciplinary framework for the design

Akespyker/Shutterstock.com

TABLE 14.2 SUMMARY OF OUTCOMES FROM VARIOUS JOB DESIGN APPROACHES

Job Design Approach (Discipline)	Positive Outcomes	Negative Outcomes
Mechanistic Approach (mechanical engineering)	Decreased training time Higher personnel utilization levels Lower likelihood of error Less chance of mental overload Lower stress levels	Lower job satisfaction Lower motivation Higher absenteeism
Motivational Approach (industrial psychology)	Higher job satisfaction Higher motivation Greater job involvement Higher job performance Lower absenteeism	Increased training time Lower personnel utilization levels Greater chance of errors Greater chance of mental overload and stress
Biological Approach (biology)	Less physical effort Less physical fatigue Fewer health complaints Fewer medical incidents Lower absenteeism Higher job satisfaction	Higher financial costs because of changes in equipment or job environment
Perceptual Motor Approach (experimental psychology)	Lower likelihood of error Lower likelihood of accidents Less chance of mental stress Decreased training time Higher personnel utilization levels	Lower job satisfaction Lower motivation

SOURCE: Reprinted from *Organizational Dynamics,* 15(3), Michael A. Campion, Paul W. Thayer, "Job Design: Approaches, Outcomes, and Trade-Offs," Winter/1987. Copyright © 1987, with permission from Elsevier.

of work. Actually, they say that four approaches—the mechanistic, motivational, biological, and perceptual/motor approaches—are necessary because no one approach can solve all performance problems caused by poorly designed jobs. Table 14.2 describes the benefits and limitations of each approach; we will take a closer look at the biological and perceptual/motor approaches below. One ergonomics study of eighty-seven administrative municipal employees found lower levels of upper body pain along with other positive outcomes thanks to the workstation redesign.[41]

The interdisciplinary framework allows the job designer or manager to consider trade-offs and alternatives among the approaches based on desired outcomes. If a manager finds poor performance a problem, for example, the manager should analyze the job to ensure a design aimed at improving performance. The interdisciplinary framework is important because badly designed jobs cause far more performance problems than managers realize.[42]

The *biological approach* to job design emphasizes the person's interaction with physical aspects of the work environment and is concerned with the amount of physical exertion, such as lifting and muscular effort, required by the position. For example, an analysis of medical claims at TXI's Chaparral Steel Company identified lower back pain as the most common physical problem experienced by steel workers and managers alike. As a result, the company instituted an education and exercise program under expert guidance to improve employees' lower back care. Program graduates received back cushions for their chairs with "Chaparral Steel Company" embossed on them.[43]

The *perceptual/motor approach* to job design also emphasizes the person's interaction with physical aspects of the work environment and is based on engineering that considers human factors such as strength or coordination, ergonomics, and experimental psychology. It places an important emphasis on human interaction with computers, information, and other operational systems. This approach addresses how people mentally process information acquired from the physical work environment through perceptual and motor skills. The approach emphasizes perception and fine motor skills as opposed to the gross motor skills and muscle strength emphasized in the *mechanistic approach*. The perceptual/motor approach is more likely to be relevant to operational and technical work, such as keyboard operations and data entry jobs, which may tax a person's concentration and attention, than to managerial, administrative, and custodial jobs, which are less likely to strain concentration and attention.

One study using the interdisciplinary framework to improve jobs evaluated 377 clerical, 80 managerial, and 90 analytical positions.[44] The jobs were improved by combining tasks and adding ancillary duties. The improved jobs provided greater motivation for the incumbents and were better from a perceptual/motor standpoint. The jobs were poorly designed from a mechanical engineering standpoint, however, and they were unaffected from a biological standpoint. Again, the interdisciplinary framework considers trade-offs and alternatives when evaluating job redesign efforts. Table 14.2 presents a summary of the positive and negative outcomes of redesign.

14-3c International Perspectives on the Design of Work

Each culture has a unique way of understanding and designing work.[45] As organizations become more global and international, an appreciation of the perspectives of others is increasingly important. A study of 2,359 call centers in sixteen countries found that an organization's management strategy and operational context influences variation in work design.[46] The Japanese, Germans, and Scandinavians in particular have distinctive perspectives on the design and organization of work.[47] Each of these cultures has a perspective forged within its unique cultural and economic system, and each is distinct from the approaches used in North America.

THE JAPANESE APPROACH The Japanese began harnessing their productive energies during the 1950s by drawing on the product quality ideas of W. Edwards Deming.[48] In addition, the central government became actively involved in the economic resurgence of Japan, and it encouraged companies to conquer industries rather than to maximize profits.[49] Such an industrial policy, built on the Japanese cultural ethic of collectivism, has implications for how work is done. Whereas Frederick Taylor and his successors in the United States emphasized the job of an individual worker, the Japanese system emphasizes the strategic level and encourages collective and cooperative working arrangements.[50]

Also, the Japanese emphasize performance, accountability, and other- or self-directedness in defining work, whereas Americans emphasize the positive affect, personal identity, and social benefits of work.

Japanese success with lean production has drawn the attention of managers. **Lean production** methods are similar to the production concept of **sociotechnical systems (STS)**, although there are some differences.[51] In particular,

lean production Using committed employees with ever expanding responsibilities to achieve zero waste and 100% good product, delivered on time, every time.

sociotechnical systems (STS) Giving equal attention to technical and social considerations in job design.

technocentric Placing technology and engineering at the center of job design decisions.

anthropocentric Placing human considerations at the center of job design decisions.

> A study of 2,359 call centers in sixteen countries found that an organization's management strategy and operational context influences variation in work design.

STS gives greater emphasis to (1) teamwork and self-managed and autonomous work groups, (2) the ongoing nature of the design process, and (3) human values in the work process. The approaches are similar, however, in that both differ from Taylor's scientific management and both emphasize job variety, feedback to work groups and teams, support of human resources, and control of production variance close to the point of origin. One three-year evaluation of lean teams, assembly lines, and workflow formalization as lean production practices conducted in Australia found that employees in all lean production groups were negatively affected, with the assembly line employees experiencing the worst effects.[52]

THE GERMAN APPROACH The German approach to work has been shaped by Germany's unique educational system, cultural values, and economic system. The Germans are a highly educated and well-organized people. For example, their educational system has a multitrack design with technical and university alternatives. The German economic system puts a strong emphasis on free enterprise, private property rights, and management–labor cooperation. A comparison of voluntary and mandated management–labor cooperation in Germany found that productivity was superior under voluntary cooperation.[53] The Germans value hierarchy and authority relationships and, as a result, are generally disciplined.[54] Germany's workers are highly unionized, and their discipline and efficiency have enabled Germany to be highly productive while its workers labor substantially fewer hours than do Americans.

The traditional German approach to work design was **technocentric**, an approach that placed technology and engineering at the center of job design decisions. Also, German industrial engineers have a more **anthropocentric** approach, which places human considerations at the center of job design decisions. The former approach uses a natural scientific process in the design of work, whereas the latter relies on a more humanistic process, as shown in Figure 14.2. In the anthropocentric

Is Your Office Watching You?

Journalists at the British newspaper *Telegraph* found little black boxes installed under their desks in 2016. The newspaper claimed they were installed to monitor energy expenditure by sensing whether someone was in the workspace, or not. The National Union of Journalists thought otherwise, complaining about what appeared to be Big Brother–style surveillance of people on the job. Technology sensors are now more James Bond–like in their unobtrusiveness in the workplace. When people are on the job and in their workspaces, they may not even notice a variety of sensors because the technology is so advanced. They may be dime-sized devices in light fixtures that detect motion, daylight, and energy usage. Legally, U.S. businesses have the right to technologically monitor the workplace however they choose, with the exception of the bathroom. Surveillance in those rooms is off limits. On the positive side, some employees find comfort if they are working late at night knowing that the company has an eye on the workspace. Some employers even have sensing devices that employees wear around. Sensors and surveillance devices put a whole new meaning on people at the center of the workplace.

SOURCE: R. Greenfield, "Sensory Overload," *Bloomberg Businessweek*, Feb. 20–Mar. 5, 2017, p. 82.

approach, work is evaluated using the criteria of practicability and worker satisfaction at the individual level and the criteria of endurability and acceptability at the group level. Figure 14.2 also identifies problem areas and disciplines concerned with each aspect of the work design. Can technology in the workplace be overdone? The above feature discusses this possibility.

THE SCANDINAVIAN APPROACH The Scandinavian cultural values and economic system stand in contrast to the German system. The social democratic tradition in Scandinavia has emphasized social concern rather than industrial efficiency. Accordingly, the Scandinavians place great emphasis on a work design model that encourages a high degree of worker control and good social support systems for workers.[55] Lennart Levi believes that circumstantial and inferential scientific evidence provides a sufficiently strong basis for legislative and policy actions for redesigns aimed at enhancing worker well-being. An example of such an action for promoting good working environments and occupational health was

Swedish Government Bill 1976/77:149, which stated, "Work should be safe both physically and mentally *but also* provide opportunities for involvement, job satisfaction, and personal development." In 1991, the Swedish Parliament set up the Swedish Working Life Fund to fund research, intervention programs, and demonstration projects in work design. For example, a study of

FIGURE 14.2 HIERARCHICAL MODEL OF CRITERIA FOR THE EVALUATION OF HUMAN WORK

Scientific approaches of labor sciences	Levels of evaluation of human work	Problem areas and assignment to disciplines
View from natural science	Practicability	Technical, anthropometric, and psychophysical problems (ergonomics)
	Endurability	Technical, physiological, and medical problems (ergonomics and occupational health)
Primarily oriented to individuals — Primarily oriented to groups	Acceptability	Economical and sociological problems (occupational psychology and sociology, personnel management)
View from cultural studies	Satisfaction	Sociopsychological and economic problems (occupational psychology and sociology, personnel management)

SOURCE: H. Luczak, "'Good Work' Design: An Ergonomic, Industrial Engineering Perspective," in J. C. Quick, L. R. Murphy, and J. J. Hurrell, eds., *Stress and Well-Being at Work* (Washington, D.C.: American Psychological Association, 1997). Copyright © 1997 by the American Psychological Association. Reprinted with permission.

Stockholm police on shift schedules found that going from a daily, counterclockwise rotation to a clockwise rotation was more compatible with human biology and resulted in improved sleep, less fatigue, lower systolic blood pressure, and lower blood levels of triglycerides and glucose.[56] Hence, the work redesign improved the police officers' health.

14-3d Work Design and Well-Being

An international group of scholars, including American social scientists, is concerned about designing work and jobs that are both healthy and productive.[57] For example, the effort-reward imbalance model emphasizes the adverse effects of demands and obligations when the work exceed the rewards provided, such as salary, esteem, and security.[58] Health and well-being accompany the restoration of balance. The job demands-resources (JD-R) model is a second imbalance model that emphasizes the strain and well-being effects of the imbalance.[59] Frank Landy believes that organizations should redesign jobs to increase worker control and reduce worker uncertainty, while at the same time managing conflict and task/job demands. In instances where organizations allow employees to craft their own jobs by adjusting task demands or resources, it is important to realize the potential negative effects of job crafting practices on the workloads of other coworkers.[60]

In addition to these effects of work and job design on well-being, there are also direct effects of sleep on well-being.[61] Actually, the well-being concern with sleep is when individuals fail to get enough sleep, or sleep deprivation. Sleep disorders can increase cardiovascular disease risk along with less server medical and psychological problems. Shift work is one place where work and sleep have interactive effects on well-being. Beyond the individual adverse well-being effects of sleep deprivation, there can be spillover effects into the workplace, influencing emotions, perceptions of work, as well as workplace (and even non-worksite) injuries and accidents. On the positive side, achieving sufficient and restful sleep carries well-being benefits that

TABLE 14.3 ADJUSTING WORK DESIGN PARAMETERS		
Increase control by:	**Reduce uncertainty by:**	**Manage conflict through:**
> Giving workers the opportunity to control several aspects of the work and the workplace	> Providing employees with timely and complete information needed for their work	> Participative decision making
> Designing machines and tasks with optimal response times and/or ranges	> Making clear and unambiguous work assignments	> Supportive supervisory styles
> Implementing performance-monitoring systems as a source of relevant feedback to workers	> Improving communication at shift change time	> Having sufficient resources available to meet work demands, thus preventing conflict
	> Increasing employee access to information sources	

may have positive spillover effects into the workplace. See Table 14.3 for more information on increasing control, reducing uncertainty, and managing conflict.

14-4 CONTEMPORARY ISSUES IN THE DESIGN OF WORK

A number of contemporary issues related to specific aspects of the design of work have an effect on increasing numbers of employees. Rather than addressing job design or worker well-being in a comprehensive way, these issues—telecommuting, alternative work patterns, technostress, and skill development—address one or another aspect of a job. One study found that employees stay motivated when their work is relationally designed to provide opportunities for respectful contact with those critical to their work.[62] Telecommuting and alternative work patterns such as job sharing can increase employee flexibility. Flexible work arrangements have also been linked to increased employee retention in developing countries. For example, one study of Malaysian banking employees found that allowing workers to participate in flexible work arrangements increased the likelihood that they would remain in their jobs once minimum salary requirements had been met.[63] Companies use job sharing, flextime, and other approaches to the design of work as ways to manage a growing business while contributing to a better balance of work and family life for employees.

14-4a Telecommuting

Telecommuting, as noted in Chapter 2, is when employees work at home or in other locations geographically separate from their company's main location. An estimated 28 million Americans telecommute. Telecommuting may entail working in a combination of home, satellite office, and main office locations. This flexible arrangement is designed to achieve a better fit between the needs of the individual employee and the organization's task demands. A recent study found that telecommuting had positive benefits on task performance primarily through increased employee perceptions of autonomy.[64]

Telecommuting has been around since the 1970s but was slower to catch on than some expected.[65] This was due to confusion and scheduling errors.[66] Actually, with a greater emphasis on managing the work rather than the worker, managers can enhance control, effectively decentralize, and even encourage teamwork through telecommuting. A number of companies, such as AT&T in Phoenix and Verizon Communications, have programs in telecommuting for a wide range of employees. These flexible arrangements help some companies respond to changing demographics and a shrinking labor pool. The Travelers Group (now part of Citigroup) was one of the first companies to try telecommuting and was considered an industry leader in the practice. Because of its confidence in its employees, Travelers reaped significant rewards from telecommuting, including higher productivity, reduced absenteeism, expanded opportunities for workers with disabilities, and an increased ability to attract and retain talent.[67]

Pacific Bell (now part of AT&T) tried telecommuting on a large scale.[68] In 1990, Pacific Bell had 1,500 managers who telecommuted. For example, an information systems designer might work at home four days a week and spend one day a week at the main office location in meetings, work exchanges, and coordination with others. Of 3,000 Pacific Bell managers responding to a mail survey, 87 percent. said telecommuting would reduce employee stress, 70 Percent said it would increase job satisfaction while reducing absenteeism, and 64 percent said it would increase productivity.

However, telecommuting is neither a cure-all nor a universally feasible alternative. A recent study showed that the employees who were most satisfied with telecommuting were those who were comfortable with technology and had more experience within the organization.[69] Many telecommuters feel a sense of social isolation. Some executives are concerned that while telecommuters are more productive, their lack of visibility may hold back their careers. Furthermore, not all forms of work are amenable to telecommuting. For example, firefighters and police officers must be at their duty stations to be successful in their work. Employees for whom telecommuting is not a viable option within a company may feel jealous of those able to telecommute.

14-4b Alternative Work Patterns

Job sharing is an alternative work pattern in which more than one person occupies a single job. As an alternative to telecommuting and a way of addressing demographic and labor pool concerns, job sharing is found throughout a wide range of managerial and professional jobs as well as production and service jobs. It is not common among senior executives.

The *four-day workweek* is a second type of alternative work schedule. Information systems personnel at the United Services Automobile Association (USAA) in San Antonio, Texas, work four ten-hour days and enjoy a three-day weekend. This arrangement provides the benefit of more time for those who want to balance work and family life through weekend travel. However, the longer workdays may be a drawback for employees with many family or social activities on weekday evenings. Hence, the four-day workweek has both benefits and limitations.

In **flextime**, a third alternative work pattern, employees set their own daily work schedules. Companies in highly concentrated urban areas, such as Houston, Los Angeles, and New York City, may allow employees to set their own daily work schedules

AT&T has a telecommuting plan in place for a number of its employees.

Rob Wilson/Shutterstock.com

> **job sharing** An alternative work pattern in which more than one person occupies a single job.
>
> **flextime** An alternative work pattern that enables employees to set their own daily work schedules.

Employees who are the most satisfied with telecommuting are those who are comfortable with technology and have more experience within an organization.

as long as they start their eight hours at any thirty-minute interval between 6:00 A.M. and 9:00 A.M. This arrangement is designed to ease traffic and commuting pressures. It is also responsive to individual biorhythms, allowing early risers to go to work early and nighthawks to work late. Even in companies without formal programs, flextime may be an individual option arranged between supervisor and subordinate. For example, a first-line supervisor who wants to complete a college degree may negotiate a work schedule accommodating both job requirements and course schedules.

Flextime is best used in moderation. The evidence suggests that occasional flextime use has unequivocal positive benefits while chronic flextime use undermines the completion of work goals, which is counterproductive.[70] Although flextime can also lead to reduced absenteeism, on the cautionary side, one study found that a woman on a flexible work schedule was perceived to have less job–career dedication and less advancement motivation, though no less ability.[71]

14-4c Technology at Work

New technologies and electronic commerce are here to stay and are changing the face of work environments, dramatically in some cases. For instance, increased technology can blur the lines between work and home. A common practice for many employers is to provide employees with company-sponsored cell phones. Whether the daily use of cell phones outside normal work hours leads to work-home interference depends on perceived supervisor expectations and employee engagement.[72] Many government jobs are expected to change, and even disappear, with the advent of e-government using the Internet. The concept involves work being where people are, rather than people moving to where the work is. New technologies make connectivity, collaboration, and communication easy. Critical voice mails and messages can be delivered to and from the central office, a client's office, the airport, the car, or home. Wireless Internet access and online meeting software such as WebEx make it possible for employees to participate in meetings anywhere, any time.

As a force for change, new technology is a double-edged sword that can be used to improve job performance or to create stress. On the positive side, modern technologies are helping to revolutionize the way jobs are designed and the way work gets done. The **virtual office** is a mobile platform of computer, telecommunication, and information technology and services that allows mobile workforce members to conduct business virtually anywhere, anytime. While virtual offices have benefits, they may also lead to a lack of social connection or to **technostress**, which is stress caused by new and advancing technologies, most often information technologies, in the workplace.[73] For example, the widespread use of web forums or blogs as a source for rumors of layoffs may cause feelings of uncertainty and anxiety (technostress). However, the same electronic bulletin boards can be an important source of information and thus reduce uncertainty for workers.

New information technologies enable organizations to monitor employee work performance, even when the employee is not aware of the monitoring.[74] These new technologies also allow organizations to tie pay to performance because performance is electronically monitored.[75] Three guidelines can help make electronic workplace monitoring, especially of performance, less stressful: First, workers should participate in the introduction of the monitoring system. Second, performance standards should be seen as fair. Third, performance records should be used to improve performance, not to punish the performer. In the extreme, new technologies that allow for virtual work in remote locations take employees beyond such monitoring.[76]

virtual office A mobile platform of computer, telecommunication, information technology and services.

technostress The stress caused by new and advancing technologies in the workplace.

14-4d Skill Development

Problems in work system design are often seen as the source of frustration for those dealing with technostress.[77] However, system and technical problems are not the only sources of technostress in new information technologies. Some experts see a growing gap between the skills demanded by new technologies and the skills possessed by employees in jobs using these technologies.[78] Although technical skills are important and are emphasized in many training programs, the largest sector of the economy is actually service-oriented, and service jobs require interpersonal skills. Managers also need a wide range of nontechnical skills to be effective in their work.[79] Therefore, any discussion of jobs and the design of work must recognize the importance of incumbent skills and abilities to meet the demands of the work. Organizations must consider the talents and skills of their employees when they engage in job design efforts. The two issues of employee skill development and job design are interrelated. The knowledge and information requirements for jobs of the future are especially high.

STUDY TOOLS 14

LOCATED AT BACK OF THE TEXTBOOK

☐ Rip out chapter review card

LOCATED AT WWW.CENGAGE.COM/LOGIN

☐ Gain unique perspectives on key concepts with new Concept Clip videos in the e-book

☐ Review key term flashcards and create your own

☐ Increase your comprehension with online homework and quizzes

15 | Organizational Design and Structure

LEARNING OBJECTIVES

15-1 Define differentiation and integration as organizational design processes.

15-2 Discuss the basic design dimensions managers must consider in structuring an organization.

15-3 Describe five structural configurations for organizations.

15-4 Describe four contextual variables that influence organizational structure.

15-5 Explain the forces reshaping organizations.

15-6 Identify and describe emerging organizational structures.

15-7 Identify factors that can adversely affect organizational structure.

janews/Shutterstock.com

After finishing this chapter go to **PAGE 271** for **STUDY TOOLS**

Strategic management is the process of formulating and implementing an organization's major goals in a competitive environment.[1] The Fast Fact on page 255 discusses the challenges of strategic management in this age of superabundant capital. **Organizational design** is the process of constructing and adjusting an organization's structure to achieve its business strategy and goals.

The design process begins with the organization's goals. These goals are broken into tasks, or pieces of work, as the basis for jobs, as discussed in Chapter 14. Jobs are grouped into departments, and departments are linked to form the **organizational structure**.

organizational design
The process of constructing and adjusting an organization's structure to achieve its business strategy and goals.

organizational structure The linking of departments and jobs within an organization.

KEY ORGANIZATIONAL DESIGN PROCESSES

Differentiation, which will be defined in more detail shortly, can be described as the design process of breaking organizational goals into tasks. *Integration*, also defined in more detail shortly, can then be considered the design process of linking the tasks together to form a structure that supports goal accomplishment. These two processes are the keys to successful organizational design. The organizational structure is designed to prevent chaos through an orderly set of reporting relationships and communication channels. Understanding the key design processes and organizational structure helps a person understand the larger working environment and may prevent confusion in the organization.

The *organization chart* is the most visible representation of the organization's structure and underlying components. Figure 15.1 is the organizational chart for the World Trade Organization. Most organizations have a series of organization charts showing reporting relationships throughout the system. The underlying components are (1) formal lines of authority and

> ## Differentiation and integration are the keys to successful organizational design.

responsibility (the organizational structure designates reporting relationships by the way jobs and departments are grouped) and (2) formal systems of communication, coordination, and integration (the organizational structure designates the expected patterns of formal interaction among employees).[2]

15-1a Differentiation

Differentiation occurs in organizations, especially large ones, to structure the work into manageable units. Differentiation ensures that all essential organizational tasks are assigned to one or more jobs and that the tasks receive

> **differentiation** The process of deciding how to divide the work in an organization.

FIGURE 15.1 | ORGANIZATION

WTO structure

All WTO members may participate in all councils, committees, etc., except Appellate Body, Dispute Settlement panels, Textiles Monitoring Body, and plurilateral committees.

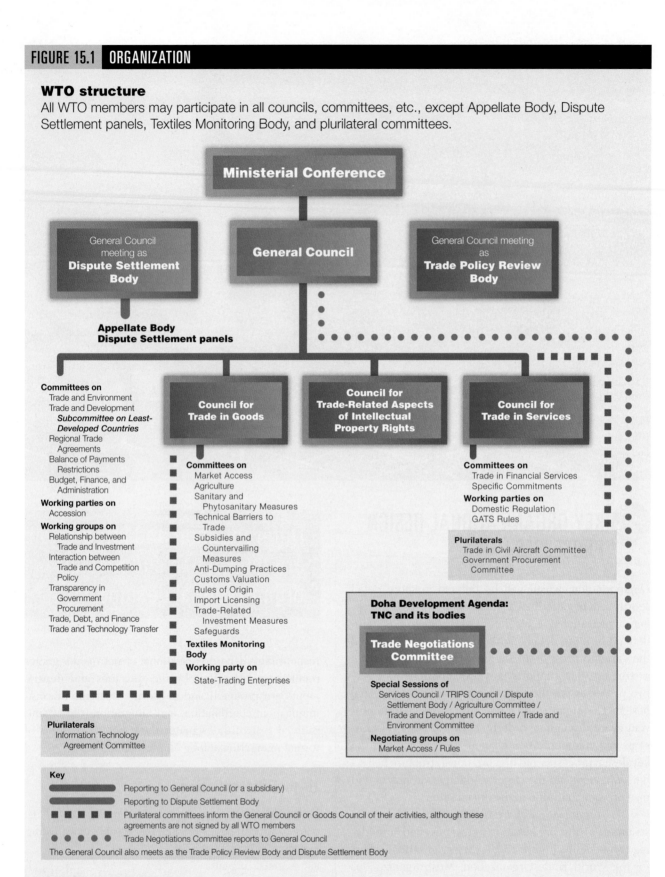

SOURCE: WTO Organization Chart, http://www.wto.org/english/thewto_e/whatis_e/tif_e/org2_e.htm.

Strategy in the Age of Superabundant Capital

In the current age, capital is abundant and cheap for organizations. Corporate capital is growing faster than GDP. This has important implications for corporate strategy, organization design, and organization structures. In the new capital environment, organizations should consider fewer big bets and pursue numerous small, varied growth opportunities. Companies need organization structures that support this small ball business game. In this new age, companies need to embrace the risk of failure as necessary for success. In addition, human capital is the truly scarce resource, which again has important implications for the design and structure of the organization. The organization design and structure must support the strategy of the firm. Creating structures and processes that enable their workforces to unleash and support the human talent within is crucial to the success of the firm.

SOURCE: M. Mankins, K. Harris, and D. Harding, "Strategy in the Age of Superabundant Capital," *Harvard Business Review*, March–April 2017, pp. 66–75.

the attention they need. Many dimensions of differentiation have been considered in organizations. Lawrence and Lorsch found four dimensions of differentiation in one study: (1) manager's goal orientation, (2) time orientation, (3) interpersonal orientation, and (4) formality of structure.[3] Three different forms of differentiation are horizontal, vertical, and spatial.

HORIZONTAL DIFFERENTIATION Horizontal differentiation is the degree of differentiation between organizational subunits and is based on employees' specialized knowledge, education, or training. For example, two university professors who teach specialized subjects in different academic departments are subject to horizontal differentiation. Horizontal differentiation increases with specialization and departmentalization.

Specialization refers to the particular grouping of activities performed by an individual.[4] The degree of specialization, or the division of labor, in the organization gives an indication of how much training is needed for various jobs, what the scope of various jobs is, and what individual characteristics are needed for job holders. Specialization can lead to the development of a specialized vocabulary, as well as other behavioral norms. As the two college professors specialize in their subjects, abbreviations or acronyms take on unique meanings. For example, OB means "organizational behavior" to a professor of management but "obstetrics" to a professor of medicine.

Usually, the more specialized the jobs within an organization, the more departments are differentiated within that organization (in other words, the greater is the *departmentalization*). Departmentalization can be by function, product, service, client, geography, process, or some combination of these. A large organization may departmentalize its structure using some or all of these methods at different levels of the organization. For example, the U.S. Army Reserve changed its departmentalization first from divisional to an operational strategic reserve and then to an operational force structure.[5]

VERTICAL DIFFERENTIATION Vertical differentiation is the difference in authority and responsibility in the organizational hierarchy. Vertical differentiation occurs, for example, between a chief executive and a maintenance supervisor. Tall, narrow organizations have greater vertical differentiation, and flat, wide organizations have less vertical differentiation. The height of the organization is also influenced by level of horizontal differentiation and span of control. The *span of control* refers to and defines the number of subordinates a manager can and should supervise.[6]

Tall structures—those with narrow spans of control—tend to be characterized by closer supervision and tighter controls. In addition, the communication becomes more burdensome, since directives and information must be passed through more layers. The banking industry has often had tall structures. *Flat structures*—those with wider spans of control—have simpler communication chains and reduced promotion opportunities due to fewer levels of management. Sears is an example of an organization that has gone to a flat structure. With the loss of more than a million middle management positions, many organizations are now flatter. The degree of vertical differentiation affects organizational effectiveness, but there is no strong evidence that flatter or taller organizations are better.[7]

SPATIAL DIFFERENTIATION Spatial differentiation is the geographic dispersion of an organization's offices, plants, and personnel. A salesperson who works in New York for a company based in Portland experiences spatial differentiation. An increase in the number of locations increases the complexity of organizational design because of spatial differentiation but may be necessary for organizational goal achievement or organizational protection. For example, if an organization wants to expand into a different country, it may be best to form a separate subsidiary that is partially owned and managed by citizens of that country. Few U.S. citizens think of Shell Oil Company as being a subsidiary of Royal Dutch/Shell Group, a company whose international headquarters is in the Netherlands. International organizations have the challenge of dealing with cross-cultural issues that impact the work-life interface of their employees, such as differences in public policies and attitudes toward gender equality.[8]

IMPLICATIONS OF DIFFERENTIATION Horizontal, vertical, and spatial differentiation indicate the amount of width, height, and breadth an organizational structure needs. Just because an organization is highly differentiated along one of these dimensions does not mean it must be highly differentiated along the others. The university environment, for example, is generally characterized by great horizontal differentiation but relatively little vertical and spatial differentiation. By contrast, a company such as Coca-Cola is characterized by a great deal of all three types of differentiation.

The more structurally differentiated an organization is, the

more complex it is.[9] *Complexity* refers to the number of activities, subunits, or subsystems within the organization. Lawrence and Lorsch suggest that an organization's complexity should mirror the complexity of its environment. As the complexity of an organization increases, its need for mechanisms to link and coordinate the differentiated parts also increases. If these links do not exist, the departments or differentiated parts of the organization can lose sight of the organization's larger mission, and the organization runs the risk of chaos. Chaos is not inevitable, however, as research suggests that environmental complexity may be viewed as a "puzzle" that, if understood correctly, increases competence and increases organizational learning.[10]

15-1b Integration

To be effective, organizations must design and build linkage and coordination mechanisms. This process of coordinating the different parts of the organization is known as **integration**. Integration mechanisms are designed to achieve unity among individuals and groups in various jobs, departments, and divisions in the accomplishment of organizational goals and tasks.[11] Effective integration helps keep the organization in a state of *dynamic equilibrium*, a condition in which all the parts of the organization are interrelated and balanced.

Integration The process of coordinating the different parts of an organization.

Songquan Deng/Shutterstock.com

To integrate activities up and down the organizational chain of command, a variety of structural devices can be used to achieve *vertical linkages*. These devices include hierarchical referral, rules and procedures, plans and schedules, positions added to the structure of the organization, and management information systems.[12] On an organization chart, the vertical lines indicate these vertical linkages, showing the lines of hierarchical referral up and down the organization. When employees do not know how to solve a problem, they can refer it upward for consideration and resolution. Work that needs to be assigned is usually delegated downward.

Rules and procedures, as well as plans and schedules, provide standing information for employees without direct communication. These vertical integrators, such as an employee handbook, communicate to employees standard information, or information that they can understand on their own. Such integrators allow managers to have wider spans of control because they do not have to inform each employee of what is expected and when it is expected. Vertical integrators encourage managers to use *management by exception*—to make decisions when employees bring problems up the hierarchy. Military organizations depend heavily on vertical linkages, having a well-defined chain of command. Certain duties are expected to be carried out, and proper paperwork is to be in place. In times of crisis, however, much more information is processed, and the proper paperwork becomes secondary to getting the job done. Vertical linkages help individuals understand their roles in the organization, especially in times of crisis.

Adding positions to the hierarchy is used as a vertical integrator when a manager becomes overloaded by hierarchical referral or problems arise in the chain of command. Positions such as "assistant to" may be added, or another level may be added. Such additions often reflect an organization's growth and increasing complexity. This action tends to reduce the span of control, thus allowing more communication and closer supervision.

Generally, the taller the organization, the more vertical integration mechanisms are needed. This is because the chains of command and communication are longer. Additional length requires more linkages to minimize the potential for misunderstandings and miscommunications.

Military organizations have a well-defined chain of command and depend heavily on vertical linkages.

NEstudio/Shutterstock.com

Horizontal integration mechanisms provide the communication and coordination that are necessary for links across jobs and departments in the organization. The need for horizontal integration mechanisms increases as the complexity of the organization increases. These linkages are built into the design of the organization by including liaison roles, task forces, integrator positions, and teams.

A *liaison role* is created when a person in one department or area of the organization has the responsibility for coordinating with another department (e.g., a liaison between the engineering and production departments). *Task forces* are temporary committees composed of representatives from multiple departments who assemble to address a specific problem affecting these departments.[13]

A stronger device for integration is to develop a person or department designed to be an *integrator*. In most organizations, the integrator has a good deal of responsibility but not much authority. Such an individual must have the ability to get people together to resolve differences within the perspective of organizational goals.[14]

The strongest method of horizontal integration is through *teams*. Horizontal teams cut across existing lines of organizational structure to create new entities that make organizational decisions. An example of this may occur in product development with the formation of a team that includes marketing, research, design, and production personnel. Ford used such a cross-functional team to develop the Taurus automobile, which was designed to restore the company's market share in the United States. The information exchanged by such a product development team should lead to a product that is acceptable to a wider range of organizational groups, as well as to customers.[15]

The use of these linkage mechanisms varies from organization to organization, as well as within areas of the same organization. In general, the flatter the organization, the more necessary are horizontal integration mechanisms.

15-2 BASIC DESIGN DIMENSIONS

Differentiation, then, is the process of dividing work in the organization, and integration is the process of coordinating work in the organization. From a structural perspective, every manager and organization looks for the best combination of differentiation and integration for accomplishing the goals of the organization. There are many ways to approach this process. One way is to establish a desired level of each structural dimension on a high-to-low continuum and then develop a structure that meets the desired configuration. These structural dimensions include the following:

1. **Formalization**. The degree to which an employee's role is defined by formal documentation (procedures, job descriptions, manuals, and regulations).

2. **Centralization**. The extent to which decision-making authority has been delegated to lower levels of an organization. An organization is centralized if the decisions are made at the top of the organization and decentralized if decision-making is pushed down to lower levels in the organization.

3. **Specialization**. The degree to which organizational tasks are subdivided into separate jobs. The division of labor and the degree to which formal job descriptions spell out job requirements indicate the level of specialization in the organization.

4. **Standardization**. The extent to which work activities are described and performed routinely in the same way. Highly standardized organizations have little variation in the defining of jobs.

5. **Complexity**. The number of activities within the organization and the amount of differentiation needed within the organization.

6. **Hierarchy of authority**. The degree of vertical differentiation through reporting relationships and the span of control within the structure of the organization.[16]

An organization that is high in formalization, centralization, specialization, standardization, and complexity and has a tall hierarchy of authority is said to be highly *bureaucratic*. Bureaucracies are not inherently bad; however, they are often tainted by abuse and red tape. There are cases, however, where centralized structures can be beneficial. For example, one study found that a more centralized structure is effective for increased job satisfaction when perceptions of interactional and procedural justice are present.[17] study of 1,000 U.S. firms found that centralized firms had the highest levels of research investments and owned more patents per R&D dollars.[18]

An organization that is on the opposite end of each of these continua is very flexible and loose. Control is very hard to implement and maintain in such an organization, but at certain times such a structure is appropriate. The research and development departments in many organizations are often more flexible than other departments in order to stimulate creativity. Flexibility may be a key in **business model innovation**, which is discussed in the accompanying Hot Trend.

Another approach to the process of accomplishing organizational goals is to describe what is and is not important to the success of the organization rather than worry about specific characteristics. Henry Mintzberg argued that the following questions can guide managers in designing formal structures that fit each organization's unique set of circumstances:

1. How many tasks should a given position in the organization contain, and how specialized should each task be?

2. How standardized should the work content of each position be?

3. What skills, abilities, knowledge, and training should be required for each position?

4. What should be the basis for the grouping of positions within the organization into units, departments, divisions, and so on?

formalization The degree to which the organization has official rules, regulations, and procedures.

centralization The degree to which decisions are made at the top of the organization.

specialization The degree to which jobs are narrowly defined and depend on unique expertise.

standardization The degree to which work activities are accomplished in a routine fashion.

complexity The degree to which many different types of activities occur in the organization.

hierarchy of authority The degree of vertical differentiation across levels of management.

business model innovation The innovative processes and rationale for how an organization creates, delivers, and captures value.

5. How large should each unit be, and what should the span of control be (i.e., how many individuals should report to each manager)?

6. How much standardization should be required in the output of each position?

7. What mechanisms should be established to help individuals in different positions and units adjust to the needs of other individuals?

8. How centralized or decentralized should decision-making power be in the chain of authority? Should most of the decisions be made at the top of the organization (centralized) or be made down in the chain of authority (decentralized)?[19]

The manager who can answer these questions has a good understanding of how the organization should implement the basic structural dimensions. These basic design dimensions act in combination with one another and are not entirely independent characteristics of an organization.

15-3 FIVE STRUCTURAL CONFIGURATIONS

Differentiation, integration, and the basic design dimensions combine to yield various structural configurations. Very early organization structures were often either based on product or function. The *matrix organization* structure merged these two ways of organizing.[20] Mintzberg moved beyond these early approaches and proposed five structural configurations: the simple structure, the machine bureaucracy, the professional bureaucracy, the divisionalized form, and the adhocracy.[21] Table 15.1 shows

TABLE 15.1 FIVE STRUCTURAL CONFIGURATIONS OF ORGANIZATIONS

Structural Configuration	Prime Coordinating Mechanism	Key Part of Organization	Type of Decentralization
Simple structure	Direct supervision	Upper echelon	Centralization
Machine bureaucracy	Standardization of work processes	Technical staff	Limited horizontal decentralization
Professional bureaucracy	Standardization of skills	Operating level	Vertical and horizontal decentralization
Divisionalized form	Standardization of outputs	Middle level	Limited vertical decentralization
Adhocracy	Mutual adjustment	Support staff	Selective decentralization

SOURCE: Mintzberg, Henry, *Structuring of Organizations*, 1st Edition, © 1979. Reprinted by permission of Pearson Education, Inc., Upper Saddle River, N.J.

the prime coordinating mechanism, the key part of the organization, and the type of decentralization for each of these structural configurations. The five basic parts of the organization, for Mintzberg, are the upper echelon, or strategic apex; the middle level, or middle line; the operating core, where work is accomplished; the technical staff, or technostructure; and the support staff. Figure 15.2 depicts these five basic parts with a small strategic apex, connected by a flaring middle line to a large, flat operating core. Each configuration affects people in the organization somewhat differently, and all organizational structures should support the firm's strategic goals.

15-3a Simple Structure

The **simple structure** is a centralized form of organization that emphasizes a small technical and support staff, strong centralization of decision-making in the upper echelon, and a minimal middle level. This structure has a minimum of vertical differentiation of authority and minimal formalization. It achieves coordination through direct supervision, often by the chief executive in the upper echelon. An example of a simple structure is a small, independent landscape practice in which one or two landscape architects supervise the vast majority of work with no middle-level managers.

15-3b Machine Bureaucracy

The **machine bureaucracy** is a moderately decentralized form of organization that emphasizes a support staff differentiated from the line operations of the organization, limited horizontal decentralization of decision-making, and a well-defined hierarchy of authority. The technical staff is powerful in a machine bureaucracy. There is strong formalization through policies, procedures, rules, and regulations. Coordination is achieved through the standardization of work processes. An example of a machine bureaucracy is an automobile assembly plant with routinized operating tasks. The strength of the machine bureaucracy is efficiency of operation in

simple structure A centralized form of organization that emphasizes a small technical and support staff, strong centralization of decision-making in the upper echelon, and a minimal middle level.

machine bureaucracy A moderately decentralized form of organization that emphasizes support staff differentiated from the line operations of the organization, limited horizontal decentralization of decision-making, and a well-defined hierarchy of authority.

FIGURE 15.2 **MINTZBERG'S FIVE BASIC PARTS OF AN ORGANIZATION**

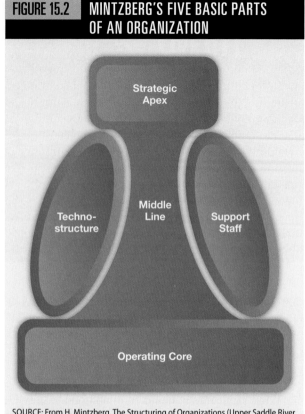

SOURCE: From H. Mintzberg, The Structuring of Organizations (Upper Saddle River, N.J.: Pearson, 1979): 20. Reprinted by permission of Pearson Education, Inc., Upper Saddle River, N.J.

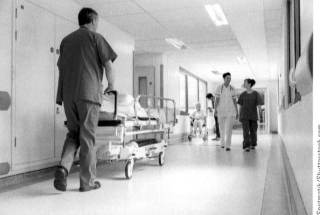

Hospitals exemplify professional bureaucracies; the expertise of doctors, nurses, and technicians is emphasized as the operating core of the organization.

stable, unchanging environments. The weakness of the machine bureaucracy is its slow responsiveness to external changes and to individual employee preferences and ideas.

15-3c Professional Bureaucracy

The **professional bureaucracy** is a decentralized form of organization that emphasizes the expertise of the professionals in the operating core of the organization. The technical and support staffs serve the professionals. There is both vertical and horizontal differentiation in the professional bureaucracy. Coordination is achieved through the standardization of the professionals' skills. Examples of organizations, where professional bureaucracies can be found, are hospitals and universities. The doctors, nurses, and professors are given wide latitude to pursue their work based on professional training and indoctrination through professional training programs. Large accounting firms may also fall into the category of professional bureaucracies.

15-3d Divisionalized Form

The **divisionalized form** is a loosely coupled, composite structural configuration composed of divisions, each of which may have its own structural configuration.[22] Each division is designed to respond to the market in which it operates. There is vertical decentralization from the upper echelon to the middle of the organization, and the middle level of management is the key part of the organization. This form of organization may have one division that is a machine bureaucracy, one that is an *adhocracy* (discussed next), and one that is a simple structure. The divisionalized organization uses standardization of outputs as its coordinating mechanism.

15-3e Adhocracy

The **adhocracy** is a selectively decentralized form of organization that emphasizes the support staff and mutual adjustment among people. It is designed to fuse interdisciplinary experts into smoothly functioning ad hoc project teams. Liaison devices are the primary mechanism for integrating the project teams through a process of mutual adjustment. There is a high degree of horizontal specialization based on formal training and expertise. Selective decentralization of the project teams occurs within the adhocracy. An example of this form of organization is the National Aeronautics and Space Administration (NASA), which is composed of many talented experts who work in small teams on a wide range of projects related to America's space agenda. New high-technology businesses also often select an adhocracy design.

> Competitive pressures in many industries led to outsourcing, labeled one of the greatest shifts in organization structure in a century.

15-4 CONTEXTUAL VARIABLES

The basic design dimensions and the resulting structural configurations play out in the context of the organization's internal and external environments. Four **contextual variables** influence the success of an organization's design: size, technology, environment, and strategy and goals. These variables provide a manager with key considerations for the right organizational design, although they do not determine the structure. Competitive pressures in many industries led to *outsourcing*, labeled one of the greatest shifts in organization structure in a century.[23] The maturity of capital markets may be an instrumental contextual factor for organizations as they engage in restructuring and resizing, especially following economic shocks in the environment.[24]

15-4a Size

The total number of employees is the appropriate definition of size when discussing the design of organizational structure. This is logical because people and their interactions are the building blocks of structure. Other measures, such as net assets, production rates, and total sales, are usually highly correlated with the total number of employees. However, these may not reflect the actual number of interpersonal relationships that are necessary to effectively structure an organization.

Although there is some argument over the

professional bureaucracy A decentralized form of organization that emphasizes the expertise of the professionals in the operating core of the organization.

divisionalized form A loosely coupled, composite structural configuration composed of divisions, each of which may have its own structural configuration.

adhocracy A selectively decentralized form of organization that emphasizes the support staff and mutual adjustment among people.

contextual variables A set of four characteristics that influence the success of an organization's design: size, technology, environment, and strategy and goals.

degree of influence that size has on organizational structure, there is no argument that it does influence design options. In one study, Meyer found the size of the organization to be the most important of all variables influencing the organization's structure and design, whereas other researchers argue that the decision to expand the organization's business causes an increase in size as the structure is adjusted to accommodate the planned growth.[25] Downsizing is a planned strategy to reduce the size of an organization, and it is often accompanied by related restructuring and revitalization activities.[26] Researchers predicted and found that firms experienced the most significant post-downsizing performance improvements when they downsized their workforces on either a large or small scale. Intermediate downsizing led to the least positive performance improvements.[27]

How much influence size exerts on the organization's structure is not as important as the relationship between size and the design dimensions of structure. In other words, when exploring structural alternatives, the manager needs to know certain facts about designing structures for large versus small organizations. For example, formalization, specialization, and standardization all tend to be greater in larger organizations because they are necessary to control activities within the organization. Larger organizations are more likely to use documentation, rules, written policies and procedures, and detailed job descriptions than to rely on personal observation by the manager. McDonald's has several volumes of manuals that describe how to make all its products, how to greet customers, how to maintain facilities, and so on. This level of standardization, formalization, and specialization helps McDonald's maintain the same quality of product no matter where a restaurant is located. In contrast, at a small, locally owned café, your hamburger and French fries may taste a little different every time you visit—evidence of a lack of standardization.

Formalization and specialization also help large and growing organizations decentralize decision-making. For example, when Australian management consulting firm Nous Group's staff grew from 20 employees in the early 2000s to 150 employees in 2014, the organization pushed decision-making down to lower-level managers and to other personnel according to their job descriptions, policies, standard operating procedures, and norms.[28] Because of the complexity and number of decisions in a large organization, formalization and specialization are used to set parameters for decision-making at lower levels. Can you imagine the chaos if the president of the United States, commander-in-chief of all military forces, had to make operational-level decisions in the war on terrorism? By decentralizing decision-making, a large organization adds horizontal and vertical complexity, but not necessarily spatial complexity. However, it is more common for a large organization to have more geographic dispersion. For example, the San Diego County Government in California created a regionalized structure to decentralize decision- making, share common resources and competencies, and meet its unique client needs.[29]

Hierarchy of authority is another dimension of design related to complexity. As size increases, complexity increases; thus, more levels are added to the hierarchy of authority. This keeps the span of control from getting too large. However, there is a balancing force because formalization and specialization are added. The more formalized, standardized, and specialized the roles within the organization, the wider the span of control can be.

15-4b Technology

An organization's technology is an important contextual variable in determining the organization's structure.[30]

HOT TREND

Digital Technologies Impact Organizations and Senior Leadership

Spending on digital technology in the United States alone is expected to reach $732 billion in 2019, growing at a compound annual rate of 16 percent. Worldwide forecast is to reach $2.1 trillion in digital technology spending. The effects of these significant expenditures on digital technology are on organizational models and senior leadership. More traditional business models and organizational structures must give way to ones built around technology and IT. The technology changes demand changes in management practices that support the evolution. Examples of large organizations being impacted include insurer Liberty Mutual and consumer-products giant Procter & Gamble Company. Evolving technologies are pushing CIOs into broader senior leadership in organizations. Digital technology will continue to shape organizational design and senior leadership.

SOURCE: A. Loten and J. Simons, "Leadership Evolves Amid Tech Changes," *Wall Street Journal*, 3 Jan. 2017.

Technology is defined as the tools, techniques, and actions used by an organization to transform inputs into outputs.[31] The inputs of the organization include human resources, machines, materials, information, and money. The outputs are the products and services that the organization offers to the external environment. Determining the relationship between technology and structure is complicated because different departments may employ very different technologies. As organizations become larger, there is greater variation in technologies across units in the organization. Joan Woodward, Charles Perrow, and James Thompson developed ways to understand traditional organizational technologies. Modern and digital technologies are shaping organizations in new ways as seen in the Hot Trend on the previous page.

Woodward introduced one of the best-known classification schemes for technology, identifying three types: unit, mass, or process production. *Unit technology* is small-batch manufacturing technology and, sometimes, made-to-order production. Examples include the arms manufacturer Smith & Wesson and the production of fine furniture. *Mass technology* is large-batch manufacturing technology. Examples include automotive assembly lines and latex glove production. *Process production* is a continuous-production process. Examples include oil refining and beer making. Woodward classified unit technology as the least complex, mass technology as more complex, and process technology as the most complex. The more complex the organization's technology, the more complex the administrative component or structure of the organization needs to be.

Perrow proposed an alternative to Woodward's scheme based on two variables: task variability and problem analyzability. *Task variability* considers the number of exceptions encountered in doing the tasks within a job. *Problem analyzability* examines the types of search procedures followed to find ways to respond to task exceptions. For example, for some exceptions encountered while doing a task, the appropriate response is easy to find. If you are driving down a street and see a sign that says, "Detour—Bridge Out," it is very easy to respond to the task variability, so analyzability is low (i.e., limited analysis is needed). By contrast, when Thomas Edison was designing the first electric light bulb, the problem analyzability was very high for his task.

Perrow went on further to identify the four key aspects of structure that could be modified to technology: (1) the amount of discretion that an individual can exercise to complete a task, (2) the power of groups to control the unit's goals and strategies, (3) the level of interdependence among groups, and (4) the extent to which organizational units coordinate work using either feedback or planning.

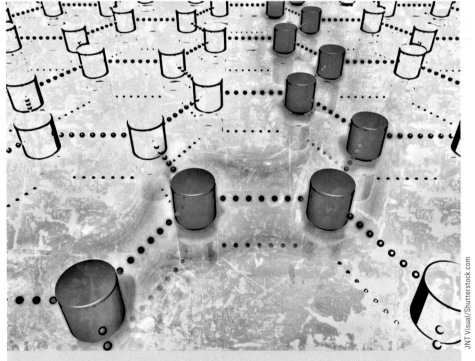

Technological interdependence is the degree of interrelatedness of an organization's technological elements.

JNT Visual/Shutterstock.com

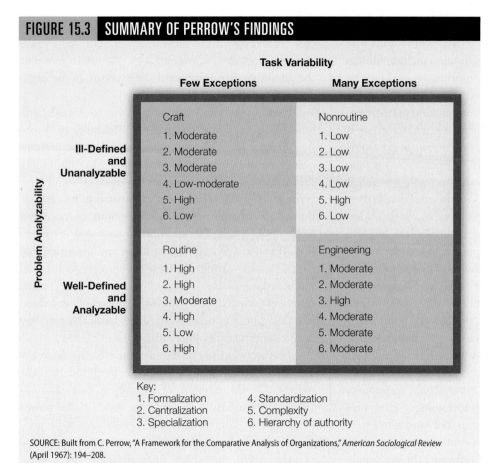

FIGURE 15.3 — SUMMARY OF PERROW'S FINDINGS

Task Variability

	Few Exceptions	Many Exceptions
Ill-Defined and Unanalyzable (Problem Analyzability)	**Craft** 1. Moderate 2. Moderate 3. Moderate 4. Low-moderate 5. High 6. Low	**Nonroutine** 1. Low 2. Low 3. Low 4. Low 5. High 6. Low
Well-Defined and Analyzable	**Routine** 1. High 2. High 3. Moderate 4. High 5. Low 6. High	**Engineering** 1. Moderate 2. Moderate 3. High 4. Moderate 5. Moderate 6. Moderate

Key:
1. Formalization
2. Centralization
3. Specialization
4. Standardization
5. Complexity
6. Hierarchy of authority

SOURCE: Built from C. Perrow, "A Framework for the Comparative Analysis of Organizations," *American Sociological Review* (April 1967): 194–208.

The more routine and repetitive the tasks of the organization, the higher the degree of formalization that is possible, the more centralized, specialized, and standardized the organization can be, and the more hierarchical levels with wider spans of control that are possible.

15-4c Environment

The third contextual variable for organizational design is **environment**. The environment of an organization is most easily defined as anything outside the boundaries of that organization. Different aspects of the environment have varying degrees of influence on the organization's structure. In one study of 318 CEOs between 1996 and 2000, strategic decision speed was found to moderate the relationship between the environment, the structure of an organization, and performance.[34] The general environment includes all conditions that might have an impact on the organization, such as economic factors, political considerations, ecological changes, sociocultural demands, and governmental regulation. Governmental complexity can impact firms' corporate social responsibility (CSR) reporting as seen in the accompanying feature.

TASK ENVIRONMENT When aspects of the general environment become more focused in areas of direct interest to the organization, those aspects become part of the **task environment**, or specific environment. The task environment is that part of the environment that is directly relevant to the organization. Typically, this level of environment includes stakeholders such as unions, customers, suppliers, competitors, government regulatory agencies, and trade associations. The *domain* of the organization refers to the area the organization claims for itself with respect to how it fits into its relevant environments. The domain is particularly important because it is defined by the organization, and it influences how the organization perceives and acts within its environments.[35] For example, Walmart and Neiman Marcus both sell clothing, but their domains are very different.

Figure 15.3 summarizes Perrow's findings about types of technology and basic design dimensions.[32]

Thompson offered yet another view of technology and its relationship to organizational design. This view is based on the concept of **technological interdependence**, which is the degree of interrelatedness of the organization's various technological elements, and the pattern of an organization's work flows. Thompson's research suggests that greater technological interdependence leads to greater organizational complexity and that the problems of greater complexity may be offset by decentralized decision making.[33]

The research of these three early scholars on the influence of technology on organizational design can be combined into one integrating concept—*routineness* in the process of changing inputs into outputs in an organization. This routineness has a very strong relationship with organizational structure.

technological interdependence The degree of interrelatedness of the organization's various technological elements.

environment Anything outside the boundaries of an organization.

task environment The part of the environment that is directly relevant to the organization.

Impact of Institutional Complexity and Conflicting Demands

While governmental regulations and guidelines in an organization's environment are acknowledged as influencing corporate social responsibility (CSR), less attention has been given to conflicting state demands. In a 2008 to 2011 study of publicly listed firms in China, attention was given to the conflicting demands from the central government and local governments. While local provincial governments place high priority on short-term GDP growth, the central government's expectation CSR reporting creates tension and conflict for companies. This was especially a problem for firms whose characteristics made them vulnerable to increased scrutiny by both local and central governmental institutions. The study found that many firms did respond with early adoption of CSR reporting but that the quality of the reports was low.

SOURCES: X. R. Luo, D. Wang, and J. Zhang, "Whose Call to Answer: Institutional Complexity and Firms' CSR Reporting," *Academy of Management Journal*, 60, JCQ: 2017, pp. 321–344.

The organization's perceptions of its environment and the actual environment may not be the same. The environment that the manager perceives is the environment that the organization responds to and organizes for.[36] Therefore, two organizations may be in relatively the same environment from an objective standpoint, but if the managers perceive differences, the organizations may enact very different structures to deal with this same environment. For example, one company may decentralize and use monetary incentives for managers that lead it to be competitively aggressive, while another company may centralize and use incentives for managers that lead it to be less intense in its rivalry.[37]

ENVIRONMENTAL UNCERTAINTY Environmental uncertainty is the amount and rate of change in the organization's environment. The perceived level of environmental uncertainty is the environmental variable that most influences organizational design. The level of environmental uncertainty can also impact the degree to which internal practices are standardized to match multinational firm policies and practices. For instance, customization of HRM practices in high uncertainty environments led to increased financial performance and customer satisfaction.[38] Some organizations have relatively static environments with little uncertainty, whereas others are so dynamic that no one is sure what tomorrow may bring. Binney & Smith, for example, has made basically the same product for more than fifty years with very few changes in the product design or packaging. The environment for its Crayola products is relatively static. In fact, customers rebelled when the company tried to get rid of some old colors and add new ones. In contrast, in the last two decades, competitors in the airline industry have encountered deregulation, mergers, bankruptcies, changes in cost and price structures, changes in customer and employee demographics, and changes in global competition. In such uncertain conditions, fast-response organizations must use expertise coordination practices to ensure that distributed expertise is managed and applied in a timely manner.[39]

The amount of uncertainty in the environment influences the structural dimensions. Burns and Stalker labeled two structural extremes that are appropriate for the extremes of environmental uncertainty: **mechanistic structure** and **organic structure**.[40] The mechanistic and organic structures occupy opposite ends of a continuum of organizational design possibilities. Although the general premise of environmental uncertainty and structural dimensions has been upheld by research, the organization must make adjustments for the realities of its perceived environment when designing its structure.[41] Some research suggests that the type of structure, either mechanistic or organic, depends on a manager's level of organizational design experience and formal training.[42]

---

environmental uncertainty
The amount and rate of change in the organization's environment.

mechanistic structure
An organizational design that emphasizes structured activities, specialized tasks, and centralized decision-making.

organic structure An organizational design that emphasizes teamwork, open communication, and decentralized decision-making.

If the organization's environment is uncertain, dynamic, and complex and resources are scarce, the manager needs an organic structure that is better able to adapt to its environment. Managerial risk taking is a critical aspect of strategic management and must often be taken under conditions of environmental uncertainty. Despite the uncertainty, managers must take risks to improve competitive advantage and performance.[43]

15-4d Strategy and Goals

Strategies and goals are the fourth contextual variable that influences how the design dimensions of structure should be enacted. Strategies and goals provide legitimacy to the organization, as well as employee direction, decision guidelines, and criteria for performance.[44] In addition, strategies and goals help the organization fit into its environment.

For example, when Apple introduced its line of personal computers to the market, its strategies were very innovative. The structure of the organization was relatively flat and very informal. Apple had Friday afternoon beer and popcorn discussion sessions, and eccentric behavior was easily accepted. As the personal computer market became more competitive, however, the structure of Apple changed to help it differentiate its products and to help control costs. The innovative strategies and structures devised by Steve Jobs, one of Apple's founders, were no longer appropriate. So the board of directors recruited John Scully, a marketing expert from PepsiCo, to help Apple better compete in the market it had created. In 1996 and 1997, Apple reinvented itself again and brought back Jobs to try to restore its innovative edge. After his return, Apple became a major player in the digital music market with its introduction of several models of the iPod and the iPhone.

Limitations exist, however, on the extent to which strategies and goals influence structure. Because the structure of the organization includes the formal information-processing channels in the organization, it stands to reason that the need to change strategies might not be communicated throughout the organization without going through those formal channels. In such a case, the organization's structure influences its strategic choice. Changing the organization's structure might not unlock value but instead drive up costs and difficulties. Therefore, strategic success may hinge on choosing an organization design that works reasonably well, then fine-tuning the structure through a strategic system.[45]

The link between strategy and structure extends to acquisitions. Different acquisition strategies, whether unrelated, vertical, or related, will require different levels of centralization and integration. Acculturation processes will also depend on the type of acquisition strategy the organization implements.[46]

The inefficiency of the structure to perceive environmental changes can even lead to organizational failure. In the airline industry, several carriers failed to adjust quickly enough to deregulation and the highly competitive marketplace. Only those airlines that were generally viewed as lean structures with good information-processing systems have flourished in the turbulent years since deregulation. Examples of how different design dimensions can affect the strategic decision process are listed in Table 15.2.

TABLE 15.2 EXAMPLES OF HOW STRUCTURE AFFECTS THE STRATEGIC DECISION PROCESS

Formalization

As the level of formalization increases, so does the probability of the following:
1. The strategic decision process will become reactive to crisis rather than proactive through opportunities.
2. Strategic moves will be incremental and precise.
3. Differentiation in the organization will not be balanced with integrative mechanisms.
4. Only environmental crises that are in areas monitored by the formal organizational systems will be acted upon.

Centralization

As the level of centralization increases, so does the probability of the following:
1. The strategic decision process will be initiated by only a few dominant individuals.
2. The decision process will be goal-oriented and rational.
3. The strategic process will be constrained by the limitations of top managers.

Complexity

As the level of complexity increases, so does the probability of the following:
1. The strategic decision process will become more politicized.
2. The organization will find it more difficult to recognize environmental opportunities and threats.
3. The constraints on good decision processes will be multiplied by the limitations of each individual within the organization.

SOURCE: Republished with permission of Academy of Management, from "The Strategic Decision Process and Organizational Structure" (Table), J. Fredrickson, *Academy of Management Review* (1986): 284; permission conveyed through Copyright Clearance Center, Inc.

The four contextual variables—size, technology, environment, and strategy and goals—combine to influence the design process. However, the existing structure of the organization influences how the organization interprets and reacts to information about each of the variables. Each of the contextual variables has management researchers who claim that it is the most important variable in determining the best structural design. Because of the difficulty in studying the interactions of the four contextual dimensions and the complexity of organizational structures, the argument about which variable is most important continues.

What is apparent is that there must be some level of fit between the structure and the contextual dimensions of the organization. The better the fit, the more likely the organization will achieve its short-run goals. In addition, the better the fit, the more likely the organization will process information and design appropriate organizational roles for long-term prosperity, as indicated in Figure 15.4. Some design elements are theorized to fit better during different phases of firm operations. For instance, existing firms engaged in entrepreneurial activities have traditionally favored decentralization and formalization only during opportunity discovery. Recent research suggests that these design elements may also facilitate entrepreneurship during opportunity realization.[47]

15-5 FORCES RESHAPING ORGANIZATIONS

Managers and researchers traditionally examine organizational design and structure within the framework of basic design dimensions and contextual variables. In recent decades, though, several forces reshaping organizations are causing managers to go beyond the traditional frameworks to examine ways to make organizations more responsive to customer needs. Some of these forces include shorter organizational life cycles, globalization, and rapid changes in information technology, and high-performance work systems. These four forces increase the demands for organizations to change and adapt in design and structure. Thus to retain their health and vitality, organizations must function as open systems that are responsive to their task environment.[48]

15-5a Life Cycles in Organizations

Organizations are dynamic entities. As such, they ebb and flow through different stages. Usually, researchers think

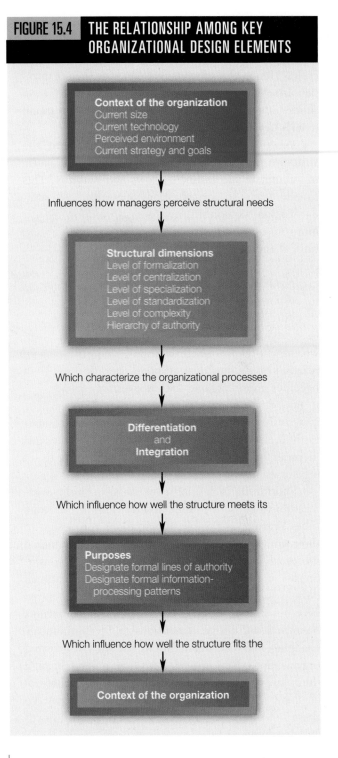

FIGURE 15.4 THE RELATIONSHIP AMONG KEY ORGANIZATIONAL DESIGN ELEMENTS

Context of the organization
Current size
Current technology
Perceived environment
Current strategy and goals

Influences how managers perceive structural needs

Structural dimensions
Level of formalization
Level of centralization
Level of specialization
Level of standardization
Level of complexity
Hierarchy of authority

Which characterize the organizational processes

Differentiation and Integration

Which influence how well the structure meets its

Purposes
Designate formal lines of authority
Designate formal information-processing patterns

Which influence how well the structure fits the

Context of the organization

of these stages as **organizational life cycles**. The whole organization has a life cycle that begins at birth, moves through growth and maturity to a stage of decline, and possibly experiences revival.[49]

Organizational subunits may have very similar life

organizational life cycle
The differing stages of an organization's life from birth to death.

cycles. Because of changes in technology and product design, many organizational subunits, especially those that are product based, are experiencing shorter life cycles. Hence, the subunits that compose the organization are changing more rapidly than in the past. These shorter life cycles enable the organization to respond quickly to external demands and changes.

When a new organization or subunit is born, the structure is organic and informal. If the organization or subunit is successful, it grows and matures. This usually leads to formalization, specialization, standardization, complexity, and a more mechanistic structure. If the environment changes, however, the organization must be able to respond. A mechanistic structure is not able to respond to a dynamic environment as well as an organic one. If the organization or subunit does respond, it becomes more organic and revives; if not, it declines and possibly dies. New research suggests that it may be wise to temporarily cycle through mechanistic and organic designs in order to meet the often conflicting demands of organizations.[50]

Shorter life cycles put more pressure on the organization to be both flexible and efficient at the same time. Further, as flexible organizations use design to their competitive advantage, discrete organizational life cycles may give way to a kaleidoscope of continuously emerging, efficiency-seeking organizational designs.[51] The manager's challenge in this context becomes one of creating congruency among various organizational design dimensions to fit continuously changing markets and locations. Many fast-growing organizations face critical transition points through their life cycles that present growth and structural challenges. The organization should attempt to resolve these before moving on to the next phase of growth and development.[52]

15-5b Globalization

Another force that is reshaping organizations is the process of globalization, in which organizations operate worldwide rather than in just one country or region. One potential problem with globalization is that corporations can become pitted against sovereign nations when

Likee68/Shutterstock.com

rules and laws conflict across national borders. Also, globalization makes spatial differentiation even more of a reality for organizations. Besides the obvious geographic differences, there may be deep cultural and value-system differences between the various countries that an organization operates in. This adds another type of complexity to the structural design process and necessitates the creation of integrating mechanisms so that people are able to understand and interpret one another, as well as coordinate with one another.

The choice of structure for managing an international business is generally based on choices concerning the following three factors:

1. *The level of vertical differentiation.* A hierarchy of authority must be created that clarifies the responsibilities of both domestic and foreign managers.

2. *The level of horizontal differentiation.* Foreign and domestic operations should be grouped in such a way that the company effectively serves the needs of all customers.

3. *The degree of formalization, specialization, standardization, and centralization.* The global structure must allow decisions to be made in the most appropriate area of the organization. However, controls must be in place that reflect the strategies and goals of the parent firm.[53]

15-5c Changes in Information-Processing Technologies

Many of the changes in information-processing technologies have allowed organizations to move into new product and market areas more quickly. However, just as shorter life cycles and globalization have caused new concerns for designing organizational structures, so has the increased availability of advanced information-processing technologies. New business technologies are increasingly changing and shaping future business processes, initiatives, and organizational designs.[54]

Organizational structures are already feeling the impact of advanced information-processing technologies. More integration and coordination are evident because managers worldwide can be connected through computerized networks. The basic design dimensions have also been affected as follows:

1. The hierarchy of authority has been flattened.
2. The basis of centralization has been changed. Now managers can use technology to acquire more information and make more decisions, or they can use technology to push information and decision-making lower in the hierarchy and thus decrease centralization.
3. Less specialization and standardization are needed because people using advanced information-processing technologies have more sophisticated jobs that require a broader understanding of how the organization gets work done.[55]

Advances in information processing are leading to knowledge-based organizations that incorporate virtual enterprising, dynamic teaming, and knowledge networking.[56]

15-5d High-Performance Work Systems

High-performance work systems (HPWS) are a group of separate but integrated human resource (HR) practices that aim to increase employee efficiency and organizational productivity.[57] The HR practices in HPWS include selection, training, performance appraisal, and compensation. HPWS have effects on organizational design and structure through the alignment of HR functions with the firm's strategic goals to boost organizational performance. This is a process of dynamic fit. One of the key questions concerns whether there is a causal connection between HPWS and organizational performance. Research shows that past HPWS positively contributes to later productivity, but there is evidence that the reverse is also true.[58] That is, organizational productivity has effects on HPWS, making the relationship a reciprocal one, suggesting that HR practices and performance both shape the organization over time.

TABLE 15.3	STRUCTURAL ROLES OF MANAGERS TODAY VERSUS MANAGERS OF THE FUTURE
Roles of Managers Today	1. Strictly adhering to boss–employee relationships. 2. Getting things done by giving orders. 3. Carrying messages up and down the hierarchy. 4. Performing a prescribed set of tasks according to a job description. 5. Having a narrow functional focus. 6. Going through channels, one by one by one. 7. Controlling subordinates.
Roles of Future Managers	1. Having hierarchical relationships subordinated to functional and peer relationships. 2. Getting things done by negotiating. 3. Solving problems and making decisions. 4. Creating the job by developing entrepreneurial projects. 5. Having broad cross-functional collaboration. 6. Emphasizing speed and flexibility. 7. Coaching their workers.

SOURCE: T. R. Horton and P. C. Reid (1991). "What Fate for Middle Managers?" *Management Review,* 80(1), 22. © 1991. Thomas R. Horton. American Management Association, New York. All rights reserved.

15-6 EMERGING ORGANIZATIONAL STRUCTURES

The demands placed on managers and on process capabilities in turn place demands on structures. Consequently, the emphasis in organizations is shifting to organizing around processes (see Table 15.3). For example, Procter & Gamble increased its level of innovation by creating teams dedicated to conducting market research, developing technology, creating business plans, and testing assumptions for specific projects.[59] This process orientation emerges from the combination of three streams of applied organizational design: high-performance, self-managed teams; managing processes rather than functions; and the evolution of information technology. Information technology and advanced communication systems have in turn led to *internetworking*. In a study of 469 firms, deeply internetworked firms were found to be more focused and specialized, less hierarchical, and more engaged in external partnering.[60] Three emerging organizational structures associated with these changes are network organizations, virtual organizations, and the

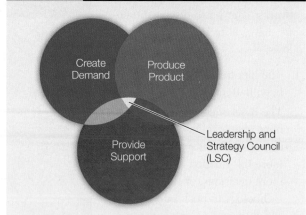

FIGURE 15.5 HARLEY-DAVIDSON'S CIRCLE ORGANIZATION

Create Demand

Produce Product

Provide Support

Leadership and Strategy Council (LSC)

SOURCE: Reprinted by permission of Harvard Business School Press from R. Teerlink and L. Ozley, *More Than a Motorcycle: The Leadership Journey at Harley-Davidson* (Boston, Mass.: Harvard Business School Press, 2000): 139. Copyright © 2000 by the Harvard Business School Publishing Corporation; all rights reserved.

circle organization. Virtuality in organizations is often broken down into four interlocking components: geographic dispersion, electronic interdependence, dynamic structure, and national diversity.[61]

Network organizations are weblike structures that contract some or all of their operating functions to other organizations and then coordinate their activities through managers and other employees at their headquarters. Information technology is the basis for building the weblike structure of the network organization and business unit managers that are essential to the success of these systems. This type of organization has arisen in the age of electronic commerce and brought into practice transaction-cost economics, interorganizational collaborations, and strategic alliances. Network organizations can be global in scope.[62]

Virtual organizations are temporary network organizations consisting of independent enterprises. Many dot-coms are virtual organizations designed to come together swiftly to exploit an apparent market opportunity. They may function much like a theatrical troupe that comes together for a "performance."[63] Trust—a complex phenomenon involving ethics, morals, emotions, values, and natural attitudes—can be particularly challenging for virtual organizations. However, trust and trustworthiness are important connective issues in virtual environments. Three key ingredients for the development of trust in virtual organizations are (1) technology that can communicate emotion; (2) a sharing of values, vision, and organizational identity; and (3) a high standard of ethics.[64]

The *circle organization* is a third emerging structure, crafted by Harley-Davidson in its drive to achieve teamwork without teams.[65] The three organizational parts, shown in Figure 15.5, are those that (1) create demand, (2) produce product, and (3) provide support. As the figure indicates, these three parts are linked by the *leadership and strategy council (LSC)*. The circle organization is a more open system than most and an organic structure

for customer responsiveness. One innovation in this organizational scheme is the so-called circle coach, who possesses acute communication, listening, and influencing skills so as to be highly respected by circle members and the company's president.

15-7 FACTORS THAT CAN ADVERSELY AFFECT STRUCTURE

This chapter has identified the purposes of structure, the processes of organizational design, and the dimensions and contexts that must be considered in structure. In addition, it has looked at forces and trends in organizational design. Two cautionary notes are important for the student of organizational behavior. First, an organizational structure may be weak or deficient if it is out of alignment with its contextual variables, in which case one or more of the following four symptoms appears:

- Decision-making is delayed because the hierarchy is overloaded and too much information is being funneled through one or two channels.

- Decision-making is of poor quality because information linkages are not providing the correct information to the right person in the right format.

- The organization does not respond innovatively to a changing environment, especially when coordinated effort is lacking across departments.

- A great deal of conflict is evident as some departments work against one another rather than for the strategies and goals of the organization as a whole; the structure is often at fault.

Second, the personality of the chief executive may adversely affect the structure of the organization.[66] Managers' personal, cognitive biases and political ideologies may affect their good judgment and decision-making.[67] Five dysfunctional combinations of personality and organization have been identified: the paranoid, the depressive, the dramatic, the compulsive, and the schizoid.[68] Each of these personality–organization constellations can create problems for the people who work in the organization. For example, in a paranoid constellation, people are suspicious of each other, hence distrust in working relationships may interfere with effective communication and task accomplishment. In a depressive constellation, people feel depressed and inhibited in their work activities, which can lead to low levels of productivity and task accomplishment.

STUDY TOOLS 15

LOCATED AT BACK OF THE TEXTBOOK

☐ Rip out chapter review card

LOCATED AT WWW.CENGAGE.COM/LOGIN

☐ Gain unique perspectives on key concepts with new Concept Clip videos in the e-book

☐ Review key term flashcards and create your own

☐ Increase your comprehension with online homework and quizzes

16 | Organizational Culture

Bloomberg/Getty Images

LEARNING OBJECTIVES

16-1 Identify the three levels of organizational culture and evaluate the roles they play in an organization.

16-2 Evaluate the four functions of organizational culture within an organization.

16-3 Explain the relationship between organizational culture and performance.

16-4 Describe five ways leaders reinforce organizational culture.

16-5 Describe the three stages of organizational socialization and the ways culture is communicated in each step.

16-6 Discuss how managers assess their organization's culture.

16-7 Explain actions managers can take to change organizational culture.

16-8 Identify the challenges organizations face developing positive, cohesive cultures.

After finishing this chapter go to **PAGE 288** for **STUDY TOOLS**

The concept of organizational culture has its roots in cultural anthropology. Just as there are cultures in larger human society, there are cultures within organizations. Like societal cultures, they are shared, communicated through symbols, and passed down from generation to generation of employees.

The concept of cultures in organizations was alluded to as early as the Hawthorne studies, which described work group culture. The topic came into its own during the early 1970s, when managers and researchers began to search for keys to survival for organizations in a competitive and turbulent environment. Then, in the early 1980s, several books on corporate culture were published, including Terry Deal and Allan Kennedy's *Corporate Cultures*,[1] William Ouchi's *Theory Z*,[2] and Thomas Peters and Robert Waterman's *In Search of Excellence*.[3] These books found wide audiences, and research began in earnest on the elusive topic of organizational cultures. Executives indicated that these cultures were real and could be managed.[4]

16-1 LEVELS OF ORGANIZATIONAL CULTURE

Many definitions of *organizational culture* have been proposed. Most of them agree that there are several levels of culture and that these levels differ in terms of their visibility and their ability to be changed. Culture has been viewed both as what defines the values of the organization and as a toolkit as to how to behave in an organization. As such, culture influences outcomes that an organization desires to achieve, as well as the processes necessary to achieve those outcomes.[5] The definition adopted in this

chapter is that **organizational (corporate) culture** is a pattern of basic assumptions that are considered valid and that are taught to new members as the way to perceive, think, and feel in the organization.[6]

In his comprehensive book on organizational culture and leadership, Edgar Schein suggests that organizational culture has three levels. His view of culture is presented in Figure 16.1. The levels range from visible *artifacts* and creations to testable *values* to invisible and even preconscious basic *assumptions*. To achieve a complete understanding of an organization's culture, all three levels must be studied.

16-1a Artifacts

Symbols of culture in the physical and social work environments are called **artifacts**. They are the most visible and accessible level of culture. The key to understanding culture through artifacts lies in figuring out their meanings. Artifacts are also the most frequently studied manifestation of organizational culture, perhaps because of their accessibility. Examples of the artifacts of culture include

> Organizational cultures are shared, communicated through symbols, and passed down from generation to generation of employees.

personal enactment, ceremonies and rites, stories, rituals, and symbols.[7]

The corporate culture of Google is apparent in the offices of Google headquarters located in Mountain View, California. The lobby is replete with lava lamps, pianos, and

organizational (corporate) culture A pattern of basic assumptions that are considered valid and that are taught to new members as the way to perceive, think, and feel in the organization.

artifacts Symbols of culture in the physical and social work environments.

FIGURE 16.1 LEVELS OF ORGANIZATIONAL CULTURE

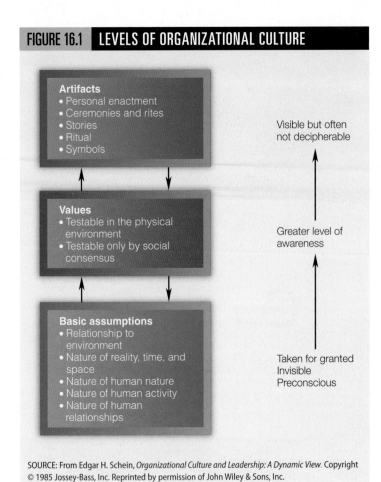

Artifacts
- Personal enactment
- Ceremonies and rites
- Stories
- Ritual
- Symbols

Visible but often not decipherable

Values
- Testable in the physical environment
- Testable only by social consensus

Greater level of awareness

Basic assumptions
- Relationship to environment
- Nature of reality, time, and space
- Nature of human nature
- Nature of human activity
- Nature of human relationships

Taken for granted
Invisible
Preconscious

SOURCE: From Edgar H. Schein, *Organizational Culture and Leadership: A Dynamic View.* Copyright © 1985 Jossey-Bass, Inc. Reprinted by permission of John Wiley & Sons, Inc.

displays of live searches on the Google search engine from around the world. The hallways house bikes and exercise machines, while office spaces are laid back, with couches and dogs who follow their owners to work.[8] The artifacts at Google reinforce the notion that the company cares about employees and wants them to be creative and comfortable.

PERSONAL ENACTMENT Culture can be understood, in part, through an examination of the behavior of organization members. When this behavior reflects the organization's values, it is called *personal enactment*. In particular, personal enactment by the top managers provides insight into the organization's values. When Charles Sharf became CEO at Visa, the credit card company had a reputation among merchants for being difficult to work with. Recognizing that the payment world is much more competitive, Sharf eliminated 50 percent of the cumbersome rulebook for merchants. He kept the original 1,538-page rulebook as a doorstop in his office. Stepping down after his four-year tenure, the metrics Sharf achieved show that his approach was a great success. Visa's stock rose 130 percent and income climbed 26 percent while he was CEO.[8]

Eskimo Joe's, a restaurant chain based in Stillwater, Oklahoma, and one of the largest T-shirt sellers in the United States, could probably have become a national franchise years ago. But founder Stan Clark, who began as co-owner of the once tiny bar, says his intent is to become better, not bigger. Clark still meets personally with new hires for the restaurant's serving staff, ensuring that they receive a firm grounding in his philosophy of food and fun.[9]

Modeled behavior is a powerful learning tool for employees, as Bandura's social learning theory demonstrated.[10] As we saw in Chapter 5, individuals learn vicariously by observing others' behavior and patterning their own behavior similarly. In this way, culture can be an important leadership tool. Managerial behavior can clarify what is important and coordinate the work of employees, in effect negating the need for close supervision.[11]

CEREMONIES AND RITES Relatively elaborate sets of activities that are repeatedly enacted on important occasions are known as organizational ceremonies and rites.[12] These occasions provide opportunities to reward and recognize employees whose behavior is congruent with the values of the company. Ceremonies and rites send a message that individuals who both espouse and exhibit corporate values are heroes to be admired.

The ceremonies also bond organization members together. Southwestern Bell (now AT&T) emphasized the importance of management training to the company.

Warren Buffett is known for hosting celebrations that appear more as rock concerts than ceremonies for his annual shareholders meeting.

TABLE 16.1 SIX RITES IN ORGANIZATIONS

Rite	Role	Example
1. *Rites of passage*	Show that an individual's status has changed	Retirement dinners
2. *Rites of enhancement*	Reinforce the achievement of individuals	Awarding certificates to sales contest winners
3. *Rites of renewal*	Emphasize change in the organization and commitment to learning and growth	Opening a new corporate training center
4. *Rites of integration*	Unite diverse groups or teams within the organization and renew commitment to the larger organization	Company functions such as annual picnics
5. *Rites of conflict reduction*	Dealing with conflicts or disagreements that arise naturally in organizations	Grievance hearings and the negotiation of union contracts
6. *Rites of degradation*	Used to visibly punish persons who fail to adhere to values and norms of behavior	Publicly replacing a CEO for unethical conduct or for failure to achieve organizational goals

Training classes were kicked off by a high-ranking executive (a rite of renewal), and completion of the classes was signaled by a graduation ceremony (a rite of passage). Six kinds of rites in organizations have been identified, as shown in Table 16.1.[13]

Berkshire Hathaway, Inc., is an Omaha-based company that owns and operates a number of insurance firms and several other subsidiaries. Chair and CEO Warren Buffett is known for his business acumen and for ensuring good returns on shareholder investments. Berkshire's annual shareholder meeting is a ceremony of celebration and appears more like a major rock music festival than a corporate meeting. Each meeting starts with a short film poking fun at the CEO and his cantankerous sidekick, Charlie Munger. Attendees watch the short film eagerly to see who will make cameo appearances and were recently rewarded with an appearance by the cast from *Breaking Bad*. Others who have made cameos include Arnold Schwarzenegger, Donald Trump, and the women of *Desperate Housewives*. One year Jimmy Buffett sang "Margaritaville" at the meeting, with some of the lyrics changed to "wasting away in Berkshire-Hathaway-a-ville!" Bill Gates, who is on the board of directors, often makes it to the meeting and has been seen playing ping-pong with Warren Buffett. More than 40,000 shareholders, employees, and Buffett relatives attend the star-studded event annually.[14]

STORIES Some researchers have argued that the most effective way to reinforce organizational values is through stories.[15] As they are retold, stories give meaning and identity to organizations and are especially helpful in orienting new employees. Part of the strength of organizational stories is that the listeners are left to draw their own conclusions—a powerful communication tool.[16]

Some corporate stories even transcend cultural and political boundaries. Visit the website of Walmart China, and you will read the true story of Jeff, a pharmacist in Harrison, Arkansas, a small town deep in the Ozarks. When Jeff received an early morning weekend call telling him that a diabetic patient needed insulin, he quickly opened his pharmacy and filled the prescription.[17] While Arkansas and Beijing are worlds apart, stories such as this one help transfer Walmart's corporate "personality" to its new Asian associates. Research by Joanne Martin and her colleagues has indicated that certain themes appear in stories across different types of organizations[18]:

1. *Stories about the boss.* These stories may reflect whether the boss is "human" or how the boss reacts to mistakes.

2. *Stories about getting fired.* Events leading to employee firings are recounted.

3. *Stories about how the company deals with employees who have to relocate.* These stories relate to the company's actions toward employees who have to move—whether the company is helpful and takes family and other personal concerns into account.

4. *Stories about whether lower-level employees can rise to the top.* Often these stories describe a person who started out at the bottom and eventually became the CEO. QuikTrip is well known for promoting from within, one reason it has been voted one of *Fortune*'s 100 Best Companies to Work For seven years running. In fact, two-thirds of QuikTrip's top 100 managers started at entry-level positions in the organization.[19]

5. *Stories about how the company deals with crisis situations.* These stories show how the company overcomes obstacles. Employees at SAS, a software company in North Carolina, love to tell stories of how the company has never once laid off an employee, even during the global recession. Such stories illustrate that even during financial crisis, SAS cares more about employees than about the bottom line.[20]

6. *Stories about how status considerations work when rules are broken.* When Tom Watson, Sr., was the CEO of IBM, he was once confronted by a security guard because he was not wearing an ID badge.

These are the themes that can emerge when stories are passed down. The information from these stories serves to guide the behavior of organization members.

To be effective cultural tools, however, stories must be credible. You can't tell a story about your flat corporate hierarchy and then have reserved parking spaces for managers. Stories that aren't backed by reality can lead to cynicism and mistrust.

Effective stories are not only motivational; they can also reinforce culture and create renewed energy. Storytelling reinforces the culture at Southwest Airlines and reminds employees of their purpose in interactions with customers. Southwest's internal corporate videos are full of stories about employees who go above and beyond to serve customers. In one video, a Southwest customer and her family took her husband to the airport for a six-month deployment in Kuwait. A customer service agent saw the family and asked whether they wanted to go to the departure gate with the soldier. Then, at the departure gate, another employee asked whether the family would like to go onto the plane with him. As passengers cheered, the soldier's children were able to give him one last hug. Stories about employees engaging in behavior consistent with company values motivate other employees to do the same.[21]

RITUALS Everyday, repetitive, organizational practices are rituals. They are usually unwritten, but they send a clear message about "the way we do things around here." While some companies insist that people address each other by their titles and surnames to reinforce a professional image, others prefer that employees operate on a first-name basis—from the top manager on down. Hewlett-Packard values open communication, so its employees address one another by first names only.

Mark Zuckerberg, the founder of Facebook, used to end company meetings with a ritual—pumping his fist into the air and leading employees in a chant of "Domination!" He later replaced this ritual by quoting movie lines aimed at reminding employees that they are engaged in something greater and more meaningful than making money.[22] As everyday practices, rituals reinforce the organizational culture. Insiders who commonly practice the rituals may be unaware of their subtle influence, but outsiders recognize it easily.

SYMBOLS Symbols communicate organizational culture through unspoken messages. They are representative of organizational identity and membership to employees. Some Nike employees proudly display tattoos of the Nike swoosh above their ankles. Symbols are used to build solidarity in the organizational culture.[23]

Personal enactment, rites and ceremonies, stories, rituals, and symbols serve to reinforce the values that are the next level of culture.

16-1b Values

Values are the second, deeper, level of culture. They reflect a person's inherent beliefs of what should or should not be. Values are often consciously articulated, both in conversation and in a company's mission statement or annual report. However, there may be a difference between a company's **espoused values** (what the members say they value) and its **enacted values** (values reflected in the way the members actually behave).[24] Clif Bar, the energy bar maker, states its values clearly and calls them their Five Aspirations. The company recognizes that enacting these values is an ongoing journey. The five values are sustaining their business, brands, people, community, and planet. Clif Bar believes the values are like spokes in a wheel, keeping the company in balance.[25]

espoused values What members of an organization say they value.

enacted values Values reflected in the way individuals actually behave.

How a firm promotes and publicizes its values may also affect how workers feel about their jobs and themselves. A study of 180 managers evaluated their employers' effectiveness in communicating concern for employees' welfare. Managers in organizations that consistently communicated concern for workers' well-being and that focused on treating employees fairly reported feeling better about themselves and their role in the organization.[26] The lesson? *Treat* employees like valuable team members, and they are more likely to *feel* like valuable team members.

Some organizational cultures are characterized by values that support healthy lifestyle behaviors. When the workplace culture values workers' health and psychological needs, there is enhanced potential for high performance and improved well-being.[27] Clif Bar, the energy bar maker, even has a twenty-two-foot rock-climbing wall in its corporate office.

Source: Clif Bar & Company

Actress Gina Rodriguez partnered with Luna nutrition bars to support women's equality and Equal Pay Day in 2017.

16-1c Assumptions

Assumptions are the deeply held beliefs that guide behavior and tell members of an organization how to perceive situations and people. At the deepest and most fundamental level of an organization's culture, according to Edgar Schein, they are the essence of culture. Assumptions are so strongly held that a member behaving in a fashion that would violate them is unthinkable. Another characteristic of assumptions is that they are often unconscious. Organization members may not be aware of their assumptions and may be reluctant or unable to discuss them or change them.

While unconscious assumptions often guide a firm's actions and decisions, some companies are quite explicit in their assumptions about employees. Some companies operate under the assumption that work/life balance creates more satisfied and productive companies, and capSpire is a company that makes this explicit. capSpire is a global consulting and technology solutions company that has an unlimited vacation policy. They were awarded the national Alfred P. Sloan Award for their use of creative ideas to promote quality family lives and productive careers.[28]

16-2 FUNCTIONS OF ORGANIZATIONAL CULTURE

In an organization, culture serves four basic functions. First, culture provides a sense of identity to members and increases their commitment to the organization.[29] When employees internalize the values of the company, they find their work intrinsically rewarding and identify with their fellow workers. As a result, motivation is enhanced, and employees are more committed.[30]

Second, culture provides a way for employees to interpret the meaning of organizational events.[31] Leaders can use organizational symbols such as corporate logos to help employees understand the changing nature of their organizational identity. Sometimes symbols should remain the same to ensure that some things stay constant despite changing conditions. Other times symbols may have to change to reflect the new culture in the organization.

Third, culture reinforces the values of the organization.

And, fourth, culture serves as a control

> **assumptions** Deeply held beliefs that guide behavior and tell members of an organization how to perceive situations and people.

mechanism for shaping behavior. Norms that guide behavior are part of culture. Thus, if the norm the company wants to promote is teamwork, then its culture must reinforce that norm. The company's culture must be characterized by open communication, cooperation between teams, and integration of teams.[32] Some norms involve how to show emotion in acceptable or preferred ways. Firefighters, for example, engage in extremely dangerous work. They often have to suppress their emotions and they experience high levels of work-family conflict. When the fire stations where they work have cultures that are jovial and loving, firefighters take fewer unnecessary risks and cope better with their jobs.

16-3 THE RELATIONSHIP OF CULTURE TO PERFORMANCE

The effects of organizational culture are hotly debated by organizational behaviorists and researchers. It seems that although managers attest strongly to the positive effects of culture in organizations, it is difficult to quantify these effects. John Kotter and James Heskett have reviewed three theories about the relationship between organizational culture and performance and the evidence that either supports or refutes these theories.[34] The three are the strong-culture perspective, the fit perspective, and the adaptation perspective.

16-3a The Strong-Culture Perspective

The strong-culture perspective states that organizations with strong cultures perform better than other organizations.[35] A **strong culture** is an organizational culture with a consensus on the values that drive the company and with an intensity that is recognizable even to outsiders. Thus, a strong culture is deeply held and widely shared. It is also highly resistant to change. A good example is IBM, which has a strong culture of conservatism, workforce loyalty, and emphasis on customer service.

Strong cultures are thought to facilitate performance for three reasons. First, these cultures are characterized by goal alignment; that is, all employees share common goals. Second, strong cultures create a high level of motivation because of the values shared by the members. Third, strong cultures provide control without the oppressive effects of a bureaucracy.

Two perplexing questions about the strong-culture perspective are (1) what can be said about

strong culture An organizational culture with a consensus on the values that drive the company and with an intensity that is recognizable even to outsiders.

evidence showing that strong economic performance can create strong cultures, rather than the reverse, and (2) what if the strong culture leads the firm down the wrong path? Sears, for example, is an organization with a strong culture, but since the 1980s, it focused inward, ignoring competition and consumer preferences and damaging its performance.[36]

TABLE 16.2	ADAPTIVE VERSUS NONADAPTIVE ORGANIZATIONAL CULTURES	
	Adaptive Organizational Cultures	**Nonadaptive Organizational Cultures**
Core values	Most managers care deeply about customers, stockholders, and employees. They also strongly value people and processes that can create useful change (e.g., leadership up and down the management hierarchy).	Most managers care mainly about themselves, their immediate work group, or some product (or technology) associated with that work group. They value the orderly and risk-reducing management process much more highly than leadership initiatives.
Common behavior	Managers pay close attention to all their constituencies, especially customers, and initiate change when needed to serve their legitimate interests, even if that entails taking some risks.	Managers tend to behave somewhat insularly, politically, and bureaucratically. As a result, they do not change their strategies quickly to adjust to or take advantage of changes in their business environments.

SOURCE: Reprinted with the permission of The Free Press, a Division of Simon & Schuster, Adult Publishing Group, from *Corporate Culture and Performance* by John P. Kotter and James L. Heskett. Copyright © 1992 by Kotter Associates, Inc. and James L. Heskett. All rights reserved.

16-3b The Fit Perspective

The fit perspective argues that a culture is good only if it fits the industry or the firm's strategy. For example, a culture that values a traditional hierarchical structure and stability would not work well in the computer manufacturing industry, which demands fast response and a lean, flat organization. Three particular industry characteristics may affect culture: the competitive environment, customer requirements, and societal expectations.[37]

A study of twelve large U.S. firms indicated that cultures consistent with industry conditions help managers make better decisions. It also indicated that cultures need not change as long as the industry doesn't change. If the industry does change, however, many cultures change too slowly to avoid negative effects on firms' performance.[38]

The fit perspective is useful in explaining short-term performance but not long-term performance. It also indicates that it is difficult to change culture quickly, especially if the culture is widely shared and deeply held. But it doesn't explain how firms can adapt to environmental change.

16-3c The Adaptation Perspective

The third theory about culture and performance is the adaptation perspective. Its theme is that only cultures that help organizations adapt to environmental change are associated with excellent performance. An **adaptive culture** is a culture that encourages confidence and risk taking among employees,[39] has leadership that produces change,[40] and focuses on the changing needs of customers. To test the adaptation perspective, Kotter and Heskett interviewed industry analysts about the cultures of twenty-two firms. The contrast between adaptive cultures and nonadaptive cultures was striking. The results of the study are summarized in Table 16.2.

Adaptive cultures facilitate change to meet the needs of three groups of constituents: stockholders, customers, and employees. Nonadaptive cultures are characterized by cautious management that tries to protect its own interests. Adaptive firms showed significantly better long-term economic performance in Kotter and Heskett's study. When strong cultures focus intensely on adaptability, they can perform better financially.[41] Given that high-performing cultures are adaptive ones, it is important to know how managers can develop adaptive cultures.

> **adaptive culture** An organizational culture that encourages confidence and risk taking among employees, has leadership that produces change, and focuses on the changing needs of customers.

16-4 THE LEADER'S ROLE IN SHAPING AND REINFORCING CULTURE

According to Edgar Schein, leaders play crucial roles in shaping and reinforcing culture.[42] The five most important elements in managing culture are (1) what leaders pay attention to, (2) how leaders react to crises, (3) how leaders behave, (4) how leaders allocate rewards, and (5) how leaders hire and fire individuals.

16-4a What Leaders Pay Attention To

Leaders in an organization communicate their priorities, values, and beliefs through the themes that consistently emerge from their focus. These themes are reflected in what they notice, comment on, measure, and control. If leaders are consistent in their focus, employees receive clear signals about what is important in the organization. If, however, leaders are inconsistent, employees spend a lot of time trying to decipher and find meaning in the inconsistent signals.

16-4b How Leaders React to Crises

The way leaders deal with crises communicates a powerful message about culture. Emotions are heightened during a crisis, and learning is intense. Difficult economic times present crises for many companies and illustrate their different values. Some organizations avoid laying off workers at all costs. Others, despite their claim that employees are important, quickly institute major layoffs at the first signal of an economic downturn. Employees may perceive that the company shows its true colors in a crisis and thus pay careful attention to the reactions of their leaders.

16-4c How Leaders Behave

Through role modeling, teaching, and coaching, leaders reinforce the values that support the organizational culture. Employees often emulate leaders' behavior and look to the leaders for cues to appropriate behavior. Many companies encourage employees to be more entrepreneurial, using more initiative and innovation. A study showed that if managers want employees to be more entrepreneurial, they must demonstrate such behaviors themselves.[43] This is the case with any cultural value. Employees observe the behavior of leaders to find out what the organization values.

16-4d How Leaders Allocate Rewards

To ensure that values are accepted, leaders should reward behavior that is consistent with the values. Some companies, for example, may claim that they use a pay-for-performance system that distributes rewards on the basis of performance. When the time comes for raises, however, the increases are awarded according to length of service with the company. Imagine the feelings of a high-performing newcomer who receives only a tiny raise after hearing company leaders espouse the value of rewarding individual performance.

Some companies may claim to value teamwork. They form cross-functional teams and empower these teams to make important decisions. However, when performance is appraised, the criteria for rating employees focus on individual performance. This sends a confusing signal to employees about the company's culture: Is individual performance valued, or is teamwork the key?

16-4e How Leaders Hire and Fire Individuals

A powerful way that leaders reinforce culture is through the selection of newcomers to the organization. With the advent of electronic recruitment practices, applicant

perceptions of organizational culture are shaped by what the organization advertises on its recruitment website. Typical perception-shaping mechanisms are organizational values, policies, awards, and goals.[44] Just as newcomers learn culture from perusing corporate websites, leaders shape and communicate culture by the way they hire employees. Many CEOs have a set of questions they like to use in interviews. Mitch Rothschild is CEO of Vitals, a website that connects patients and doctors. Vitals is a small company that prides itself on moving quickly, so Rothschild wants to get a sense of whether a candidate is comfortable with change. The question "What percentage of your life do you control?" helps him understand whether the candidate believes he or she can make change happen. Rothschild is looking for a high number because at Vitals there is a need for rapid change.[45]

The way a company fires an employee and the rationale behind the firing also communicates the culture. Some companies deal with poor performers by trying to find a place within the organization where they can perform better and make a contribution. Other companies seem to operate under the philosophy that those who cannot perform are out quickly.

The reasons for terminations may not be directly communicated to other employees, but curiosity leads to speculation. Suppose an employee caught in the act of unethical behavior is simply reprimanded, with no other penalty, even though such behavior is clearly against the organization's values. Other employees may view this as a failure to reinforce the values within the organization.

In summary, leaders play a critical role in shaping and reinforcing organizational culture. Managers need to create a positive culture through what they pay attention to, how they react to crises, how they behave, the way they allocate rewards, and how they hire and fire employees. Transformational leaders create a more adaptive culture, which in turn increases business unit performance.[46]

16-5 ORGANIZATIONAL SOCIALIZATION

We have seen that leaders play key roles in shaping an organization's culture. Another process that perpetuates culture is the way it is passed on from generation to generation of employees. Newcomers learn the culture through **organizational socialization**—the process by which newcomers are transformed from outsiders to participating, effective members of the organization.[47] As we saw earlier, cultural socialization begins with the careful selection of newcomers who are likely to reinforce the organizational culture.[48] Once selected, newcomers pass through the stressful socialization process.

16-5a The Stages of the Socialization Process

The organizational socialization process is generally described as having three stages: anticipatory socialization, encounter, and change and acquisition. Figure 16.2 pre-sents a model of the process and the key concerns at each stage of it.[49] It also describes the outcomes of the process, which will be discussed in the next section of the chapter.

ANTICIPATORY SOCIALIZATION The first stage of the socialization process, **anticipatory socialization**, encompasses all of the learning that takes place prior to the newcomer's first day on the job, including the newcomer's expectations. The two key concerns at this stage are realism and congruence.

Realism is the degree to which a newcomer holds realistic expectations about the job and organization. One thing newcomers should receive information about during entry into the organization is the culture. Information about values at this stage can help newcomers begin to construct a scheme for interpreting their organizational experiences. Later, a deeper understanding of the organization's culture will be possible through time and experience in the organization.

When organizations give realistic job previews that not only highlight major stressors but also teach various coping strategies to deal with them, newcomers feel less stressed and report higher levels of adjustment six and nine months postentry.[50]

> **organizational socialization** The process by which newcomers are transformed from outsiders to participating, effective members of the organization.
>
> **anticipatory socialization** The first socialization stage, which encompasses all of the learning that takes place prior to the newcomer's first day on the job.

FIGURE 16.2 THE ORGANIZATIONAL SOCIALIZATION PROCESS: STAGES AND OUTCOMES

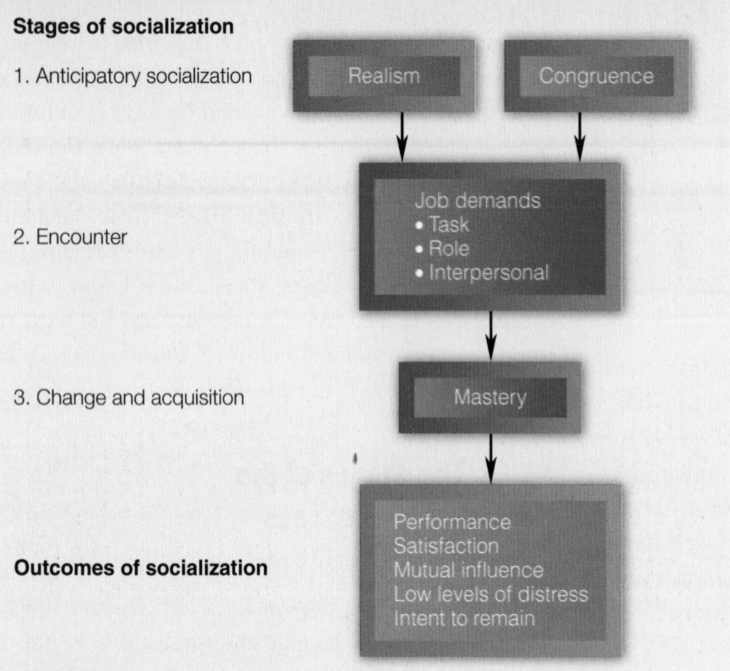

Stages of socialization

1. Anticipatory socialization

Realism   Congruence

2. Encounter

Job demands
• Task
• Role
• Interpersonal

3. Change and acquisition

Mastery

Outcomes of socialization

Performance
Satisfaction
Mutual influence
Low levels of distress
Intent to remain

SOURCE: Reprinted from *Organizational Dynamics*, Autumn 1989, "An Ethical Weather Report: Assessing the Organization's Ethical Climate" by John B. Cullen et al. Copyright © 1989, with permission from Elsevier Science.

There are two types of *congruence* between an individual and an organization: congruence between the individual's abilities and the demands of the job, and the fit between the individual's values and the organization's values. Organizations disseminate information about their values through their web pages, annual reports, and recruitment brochures. *Value congruence* is particularly important for organizational culture. It is also important in terms of newcomer adjustment. Newcomers whose values match the company's values are more satisfied with their new jobs, adjust more quickly, and say they intend to remain with the firm longer.[51] Newcomers will cope better throughout the socialization experience if they believe the organization has fulfilled its promises and met the newcomer's expectations.[52]

ENCOUNTER The second stage of socialization, **encounter**, is when newcomers learn the tasks associated with the job, clarify their roles, and establish new relationships at work. This stage commences on the first day at work and is thought to encompass the first six to nine months on the new job. Newcomers face task demands, role demands, and interpersonal demands during this period.

Task demands involve the actual work performed. Learning to perform tasks is related to the organization's culture. In some organizations, where creativity is valued, newcomers are given considerable latitude to experiment with new ways to do their job. In others, newcomers are expected to learn the established procedures for their tasks. Early experiences with trying to master task demands can affect employees' entire careers. Auditors, for example, are often forced to choose between being thorough and being fast in completing their work. By pressuring auditors in this way, firms often set themselves up for problems later, when these pressures may lead auditors to make less-than-ethical decisions.

Role demands involve the expectations placed on newcomers. Newcomers may not know exactly what is expected of them (role ambiguity) or may receive conflicting expectations from other individuals (role conflict). The way newcomers approach these demands depends in part on the culture of the organization. Are newcomers expected to operate with considerable uncertainty, or is the manager expected to clarify the newcomers' roles? Some cultures even put newcomers through considerable stress in the socialization process, including humility-inducing experiences, so newcomers will be more open to accepting the firm's values and norms. Long hours, tiring travel schedules, and an overload of work are examples of some socialization practices.

Interpersonal demands arise from relationships at work. Politics, leadership style, and group pressure are interpersonal demands. All of them reflect the values and assumptions that operate within the organization. Most organizations have basic assumptions about the nature of human relationships. For example, the Korean *chaebol* LG Group strongly values harmony in relationships and in society, and its decision-making policy emphasizes unanimity.

In the encounter stage, the expectations formed in anticipatory socialization may clash with the realities of the job. It is a time of facing the task, role, and interpersonal demands of the new job.

encounter The second socialization stage, in which newcomers learn the tasks associated with the job, clarify their roles, and establish new relationships at work.

CHANGE AND ACQUISITION In the third and final stage of socialization, **change and acquisition**, newcomers begin to master the demands of the job. They become proficient at managing their tasks, clarifying and negotiating their roles, and engaging in relationships at work. The time when the socialization process is completed varies widely depending on the individual, the job, and the organization. The end of the process is signaled by newcomers being considered by themselves and others as organizational insiders.

16-5b Outcomes of Socialization

Newcomers who are successfully socialized should exhibit good performance, high job satisfaction, and the intention to stay with the organization. In addition, they should exhibit low levels of distress symptoms.[53] A high level of organizational commitment is also a mark of successful socialization.[54] This commitment is facilitated throughout the socialization process by the communication of values that newcomers can buy into. Successful socialization is also signaled by mutual influence; that is, the newcomers have made adjustments in the job and organization to accommodate their knowledge and personalities. Newcomers are expected to leave their mark on the organization and not be completely conforming.

When socialization is effective, newcomers understand and adopt the organization's values and norms. This ensures that the company's culture, including its central values, survives. Newcomers adopt the company's norms and values more quickly when they receive positive support from organizational insiders. Sometimes this is accomplished through informal social gatherings.[56]

Socialization is not just the responsibility of the organization and the manager but of the employees as well. Newcomers who are more curious and adaptable adjust to their new jobs more effectively, leading to better performance.[57] Additionally, newcomers who have proactive personalities adjust more effectively to the organization because they are more likely to seek out the information they need to become socialized.[58]

16-6 ASSESSING ORGANIZATIONAL CULTURE

Although some organizational scientists argue for assessing organizational culture with quantitative methods, others say that organizational culture must be assessed with qualitative methods.[59] Quantitative methods, such as questionnaires, are valuable because of their precision, comparability, and objectivity.

> **Newcomers who are successfully socialized should exhibit good performance, high job satisfaction, and the intention to stay with the organization.**

Qualitative methods, such as interviews and observations, are valuable because of their detail, descriptiveness, and uniqueness.

Two widely used quantitative assessment instruments are the Organizational Culture Inventory (OCI) and the Kilmann–Saxton Culture-Gap Survey. Both assess the behavioral norms of organizational cultures, as opposed to the artifacts, values, or assumptions of the organization.

16-6a Organizational Culture Inventory

The OCI focuses on behaviors that help employees fit into the organization and meet the expectations of coworkers. Using Maslow's motivational need hierarchy as its basis, it measures twelve cultural styles. The two underlying dimensions of the OCI are task/people and security/satisfaction. There are four satisfaction cultural styles and eight security cultural styles.

A self-report instrument, the OCI contains 120 questions. It provides an individual assessment of culture and may be aggregated to the work group and to the organizational level.[60] It has been used in firms throughout North America, Western Europe, New Zealand, and Thailand, as well as in U.S. military units, the Federal Aviation Administration, and nonprofit organizations.

16-6b Kilmann–Saxton Culture-Gap Survey

The Kilmann–Saxton Culture-Gap Survey focuses on what actually happens and on the expectations of others in the organization.[61] Its two underlying dimensions are (1) technical/human orientation and (2) short-term versus long-term time. With these two dimensions, the actual operating norms and the ideal norms in four areas are assessed. The areas are *task support* (short-term

change and acquisition
The third socialization stage, in which the newcomer begins to master the demands of the job.

Levi Strauss and Co.'s Culture of Employee Wellness and Supplier Well-Being

Levi Strauss and Co. has long focused on employee wellness at its headquarters in San Francisco. They subsidize gym memberships for employees and serve fresh, organic foods in their company cafeteria. They offer in-house wellness programs and incentives to lose weight, quit smoking, and exercise. Now, the company is taking its case for well-being to suppliers.

Beyond the "do no harm" labor standards, Levi wants to help workers thrive around the world. The efforts start with focus groups in a particular location to understand what challenges workers are facing. In a Turkish factory, for example, women were missing work at least once a month. It turns out that their work schedules didn't allow them to run errands that were only possible on workdays, so schedules were changed, and stress was reduced. In Bangladesh, programs include training on money management and free doctor consultations for workers' family members. In Cambodia, health programs focus on nutrition and hygiene, seeking to prevent waterborne diseases. By 2025, Levi's goal is to implement its Worker Well-Being initiative with all strategic suppliers around the world, reaching 300,000 workers. The company makes its Worker Well-Being tools and resources publicly available and is challenging other businesses with global supply chains to work with suppliers to focus on helping workers thrive.

BUSINESS RETURN:

BANGLADESH More women returned after maternity leave

EGYPT Women's health education reduced absenteeism and turnover rates

HAITI Financial empowerment led to improved workplace satisfaction

INDIA Increased aware: services, inclu family plannii

Source: Levi Strauss and Co

SOURCE: A. Peters, "How Levi's Is Building Well-Being Programs Where They Matter Most: In Its Factories," *Fast Company*, October 13, 2016, accessed at https://www.fastcompany.com/3064477/how-levis-is-building-well-being-programs-where-they-matter-most-in-its-factories; http://www.levistrauss.com/sustainability/people/#apparel-workers.

technical norms), *task innovation* (long-term technical norms), *social relationships* (short-term human orientation norms), and *personal freedom* (long-term human orientation norms). Significant gaps in any of the four areas are used as a point of departure for cultural change to improve performance, job satisfaction, and morale.

Like the OCI, the Gap Survey, as a self-report instrument, provides an individual assessment of culture and may be aggregated to the work group. It has been used in firms throughout the United States and in not-for-profit organizations.

16-6c Triangulation

A study of a rehabilitation center in a 400-bed hospital incorporated **triangulation**—the use of multiple methods to measure organizational culture—to improve inclusiveness and accuracy in measuring the organizational culture.[62] Triangulation has been used by anthropologists, sociologists, and other behavioral scientists to study organizational culture. Its name comes from the navigational technique of using multiple reference points to locate an object. In the rehabilitation center study, the three methods used to triangulate on the culture were (1) obtrusive observations by eight trained observers, which provided an outsider perspective; (2) self-administered questionnaires, which provided quantitative insider information; and (3) personal interviews with the center's staff, which provided qualitative contextual information.

The study showed that each of the three methods made unique contributions to the discovery of the rehabilitation center's culture. The complete picture could not have been drawn with just a single technique. Triangulation can lead to a better understanding of the phenomenon of culture and is the best approach to assessing organizational culture.

16-7 CHANGING ORGANIZATIONAL CULTURE

With rapid environmental changes such as globalization, workforce diversity, and technological innovation, the fundamental assumptions and basic values that drive the organization may need to be altered.

triangulation The use of multiple methods to measure organizational culture.

Changing an organization's culture is feasible but difficult.[63] One reason for the difficulty is that assumptions—the deepest level of culture—are often unconscious. As such, they are often resistant to confrontation and debate. Another reason for difficulty is that culture is deeply ingrained and behavioral norms and rewards are well learned.[64] In a sense, employees must unlearn the old norms before they can learn new ones. Managers who want to change the culture should look first to the ways culture is maintained. Research among hospitals found that change was welcomed in private hospitals with a collaborative culture whereas it was met with opposition in public hospitals with an autocratic culture.[65]

A model for cultural change that summarizes the interventions managers can use is presented in Figure 16.3. In this model, the numbers represent the steps managers can take. There are two basic approaches to changing the existing culture: (1) helping current members buy into a new set of values (steps 1, 2, and 3) or (2) adding newcomers and socializing them into the organization while removing current members as appropriate (steps 4 and 5).[66]

The first step is to change behavior in the organization. Even if behavior does change, however, this change is not sufficient for cultural change to occur. Behavior is an artifact (level 1) of culture. Individuals may change their behavior but not the values that drive it. They may rationalize, "I'm only doing this because my manager wants me to."

Therefore, managers must use step 2, which is to examine the justifications for the changed behavior. Are employees buying into the new set of values, or are they just complying?

The third step, cultural communication, is extremely important. All of the artifacts (personal enactment, stories, rites and ceremonies, rituals, and symbols) must send a consistent message about the new values and beliefs. It is crucial that the communication be credible; that is, managers must live the new values and not just talk about them. Leaders should pay attention to the informal social networks more so than structural positions in leading organizational change. These informal network communication channels combined with employees' values, and beliefs that managers are highly committed to the change effort, can go a long way in making the change a success.[67]

The two remaining steps (4 and 5) involve shaping the workforce to fit the intended culture. First, the

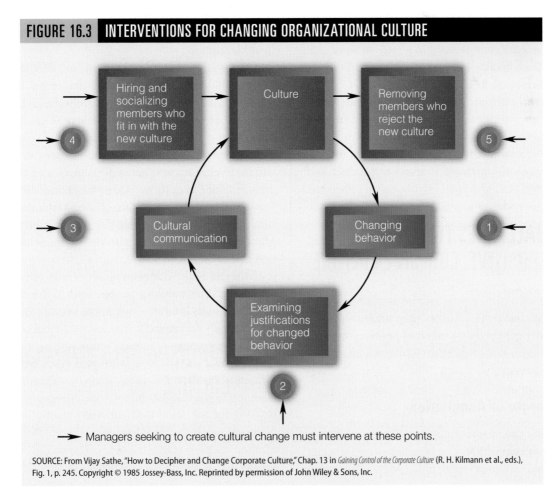

FIGURE 16.3 INTERVENTIONS FOR CHANGING ORGANIZATIONAL CULTURE

Hiring and socializing members who fit in with the new culture

Culture

Removing members who reject the new culture

4

5

Cultural communication

Changing behavior

3

1

Examining justifications for changed behavior

2

➤ Managers seeking to create cultural change must intervene at these points.

SOURCE: From Vijay Sathe, "How to Decipher and Change Corporate Culture," Chap. 13 in *Gaining Control of the Corporate Culture* (R. H. Kilmann et al., eds.), Fig. 1, p. 245. Copyright © 1985 Jossey-Bass, Inc. Reprinted by permission of John Wiley & Sons, Inc.

organization can revise its selection strategies to more accurately reflect the new culture. Second, the organization can identify individuals who resist the cultural change or who are no longer comfortable with the values in the organization. Reshaping the workforce should not involve a ruthless pursuit of nonconforming employees; it should be a gradual and subtle change that takes considerable time. Changing personnel in the organization is a lengthy process; it cannot be done effectively in a short period of time without considerable problems.

George W. Bailey/Shutterstock.com

Evaluating the success of cultural change may be best done by looking at behavior. Cultural change can be assumed to be successful if the behavior is intrinsically motivated—that is, on "automatic pilot." If the new behavior were to persist even if rewards were not present, and if the employees have internalized the new value system, then the behavior is probably intrinsically motivated. If employees automatically respond to a crisis in ways consistent with the corporate culture, then the cultural change effort can be deemed successful.

Given the current business environment, managers may want to focus on three particular cultural modifications: (1) support for a global view of business, (2) reinforcement of ethical behavior, and (3) empowerment of employees to excel in product and service quality.

16-8 CHALLENGES TO DEVELOPING A POSITIVE, COHESIVE CULTURE

Developing an organizational culture is challenging in its own right, but certain factors pose additional challenges to managers in their pursuit of positive, cohesive cultures: mergers and acquisitions, globalization, ethics, and empowerment and quality.

16-8a Merger or Acquisition

One particular situation that may require cultural change is a merger or acquisition. The blending of two distinct organizational cultures may prove difficult despite

Terry Putman/Shutterstock.com

good-faith efforts. The merger of H. J. Heinz and Kraft Foods combined two companies that are each more than 100 years old, selling the most familiar brands of ketchup, hot dogs, pickles, mustard, and other packaged foods. Following the completion of that merger, the new Kraft Heinz continued as a competitive, cost-cutting culture. The company then made a bid to acquire and merge with Unilever, but the deal unraveled because of a clash of corporate cultures. Anglo-Dutch company Unilever's culture is global and purpose driven, whereas Kraft Heinz's culture is more U.S.-centric and efficiency driven. The question is whether a new culture will emerge that can be responsive to changing consumer tastes, as people move away from packaged foods to less processed, healthier options.

Mergers that involve both organizational culture and national culture present many challenges. Sweden's Volvo Construction Equipment acquired South Korea's Samsung Heavy Industry's construction division, and employees from both firms encountered challenges. They expressed concerns about differences in the two corporate cultures and national cultures and how "we" are different from "them." Complaints arose about why "they" did not understand "us." Careful attention to cultural differences and thoughtful post-acquisition integration efforts are necessary to help manage acculturation stress.[68]

Alterations in culture may also be required when an organization employs people from different countries. Research indicates that some organizational cultures actually enhance differences in national cultures.[69] One study compared foreign employees working in a multinational organization with employees working in different organizations within their own countries. The assumption was that the employees from various countries working for the same multinational organization would be more similar than employees working in diverse organizations in their native countries. The results were surprising in that there were significantly greater differences among the employees of the multinational than among managers working for different companies within their native countries. In the multinational, Swedes became more Swedish, Americans became more American, and so forth. It appears that employees enhance their national culture traditions even when working within a single organizational culture.[70] This is more likely to occur when diversity is moderate. When diversity is very high, employees are more likely to develop a shared identity in the organization's culture instead of relying on their own national culture.[71]

16-8b Developing a Global Organizational Culture

The values that drive the organizational culture should support a global view of the company and its efforts. Management should embody the shared values and reward employees who support the global view. Finally, the values should be consistent over time. Consistent values give an organization a unifying theme that competitors may be unable to emulate.[72] Because global corporations suffer from the conflicting pressures of centralization and decentralization, an overarching corporate culture that integrates the decentralized subsidiaries in locations around the world can be an asset in the increasingly competitive global marketplace.

16-8c Developing an Ethical Organizational Culture

The culture of an organization can have profound effects on the ethical behavior of organization members.[73] Organizations in which supervisors and top managers act as role models of ethical behavior and create an openness to discuss ethical issues have fewer incidents of unethical behavior.[74] When a company's culture promotes ethical norms, individuals behave accordingly. Managers can encourage ethical behavior by being good role models for employees. They can institute the philosophy that ethical behavior makes good business sense and puts the company in congruence with the larger values of society. Managers can also communicate that rationalizations for unethical behavior are not tolerated.

Employees who work in high-trust cultures enjoy their jobs more, are more aligned with their companies' purpose and values, and treat each other better because they have more empathy for each other.[75] Creating and nurturing a high-trust culture can pay off in higher productivity and more ethical behavior among employees.

A behavior that might be considered unethical is cyberloafing, or using the Internet for personal business at work while pretending to do legitimate work, and it can cost millions of dollars in lost productivity. Companies

Can Sterling Jewelers Develop a More Ethical Culture?

Jewelry giant Sterling, parent company of Zales, Jared's, and Kay Jewelers, has faced allegations of a culture of sexual harassment, gender bias, and discrimination in several civil suits. Its culture is described in class-action arbitration cases as one of sexual aggression and abuses of power, where women were paid substantially less than men. More than 250 male and female employees gave statements describing the abusive culture. Some of the allegations included forcing female subordinates into sex in exchange for better jobs, pay raises, or protection from punishment.

The abusive culture arose, ironically, in a company where 68 percent of its store managers are women. Whether Sterling can change its culture, and how, are open questions. Meanwhile, the damage has been done both to the employees and to the company. Sterling's share price dropped to half its 2015 high following the allegations and negative press.

Ken Wolter/Shutterstock.com

SOURCE: D. Harwell, "Hundreds Allege Sex Harassment, Discrimination at Kay and Jared Jewelry Company," *The Washington Post, Business*, February 27 (2017), accessed at https://www.washingtonpost.com/business/economy/hundreds-allege-sex-harassment-discrimination-at-kay-and-jared-jewelry-company/2017/02/27/8dcc9574-f6b7-11e6-bf01-d47f8cf9b643_story.html?utm_term=.c11da7c37ae6; R. Adams, "Sterling Jewelers Settles Charges of Bias Against Female Workers," *New York Times*, May 5 (2017), accessed at https://www.nytimes.com/2017/05/05/business/sterling-jewelers-settles-bias-case.html?_r=0.

have tried all sorts of tactics to manage cyberloafing, including forbidding personal Internet use and turning off employees' Internet access. One way to discourage cyberloafing is to promote an ethical corporate culture. This method works especially well in adhocracies, which are flexible, adaptable cultures with a lack of formal structure (as opposed to bureaucracies).[76]

16-8d Developing an Inclusive Culture

Throughout this book, we have seen that successful organizations promote cultures that value diversity and encourage inclusion. Leader behavior drives an inclusive culture more strongly than policy statements.[77] There are several concrete steps leaders can take to promote an inclusive workplace:

Ensure diversity in every meeting. Diverse views lead to diverse ideas.

Be a role model of inclusive behavior.

Adopt a "no tolerance" position for disrespectful behavior of any kind.

Take quick action to eliminate even subtle behaviors that lead to disrespect.[78]

Software company SAP has earned recognition for promoting gender diversity in an industry that is male-dominated. To gauge their efforts, SAP underwent an independent audit that examined compensation policies, accommodations for flexible work, corporate culture, and recruiting and promotion policies.[79] The company's goal is to have at least 25 percent of its leadership positions filled by women. SAP carefully revised its recruiting practices to ensure gender-neutral language in job postings, hoping to recruit more diverse executive talent.

The Human Rights Campaign foundation publishes a Corporate Equality Index annually that rates how companies promote inclusion for LGBT employees. Some of the companies earning a perfect score are Ford, Bank of America, J. P. Morgan Chase, Chevron, and Wells Fargo.[80] Eliminating LGBT discrimination makes a company more competitive by helping it attract and retain top talent, win business from discerning consumers, and capitalize on LGBT employees' knowledge to drive innovation.

AT&T consistently earns praise for its history of diversity and inclusion. At AT&T every voice matters, and the company supports 12 Employee Resource Groups and 9 Employee Networks, with memberships surpassing 122 thousand employees.[81] The groups provide support, mentoring, education, and advocacy to cultural populations, veterans, female employees, the disabled, young professionals, LGBT community, and others. AT&T also embeds inclusion in its overall business strategy.

STUDY TOOLS 16

LOCATED AT BACK OF THE TEXTBOOK

☐ Rip Out Chapter Review Card

LOCATED AT WWW.CENGAGE.COM/LOGIN

☐ Gain unique perspectives on key concepts with new Concept Clip videos in the e-book

☐ Review key term flashcards and create your own

☐ Increase your comprehension with online homework and quizzes

17 | Career Management

LEARNING OBJECTIVES

17-1 Explain occupational and organizational choice decisions.

17-2 Identify foundations for a successful career.

17-3 Explain the career stage model.

17-4 Explain the major tasks facing individuals in the establishment stage of the career stage model.

17-5 Identify the issues confronting individuals in the advancement stage of the career stage model.

17-6 Describe how individuals can navigate the challenges of the maintenance stage of the career stage model.

17-7 Explain how individuals withdraw from the workforce.

17-8 Explain how career anchors help form a career identity.

After finishing this chapter go to **PAGE 308** for **STUDY TOOLS**

A **career** is a pattern of work-related experiences that spans the course of a person's life.[1] The two elements in a career are the objective element and the subjective element.[2] The *objective element* of the career is the observable, concrete environment. For example, you can manage a career by getting training to improve your skills. In contrast, the *subjective element* involves your perception of the situation. Rather than getting training (an objective element), you might change your aspirations (a subjective element). Thus, both objective events and the individual's perception of those events are important in defining a career.

career The pattern of work-related experiences that spans the course of a person's life.

career management A lifelong process of learning about self, jobs, and organizations; setting personal career goals; developing strategies for achieving the goals; and revising the goals based on work and life experiences.

Career management is a lifelong process of learning about self, jobs, and organizations, setting personal career goals, developing strategies for achieving the goals, and revising the goals based on work and life experiences.[3] Whose responsibility is career management? It is tempting to place the responsibility solely on individuals, but it is also the organization's duty to form partnerships with

individuals in managing their careers. Careers are made up of exchanges between individuals and organizations; in other words, give-and-take is a part of the relationship between an organization and an individual when a career is involved.

Whether we approach it as managers or as employees, career management is an integral activity in our lives. It is important to understand careers for three reasons:

1. If we know what to look forward to over the course of our careers, we can take a proactive approach to planning and managing them.

2. As managers, we need to understand the experiences of our employees and colleagues as they pass through the various stages of careers over their life spans.

3. Career management is good business. It makes good financial sense to have highly trained employees keep up with their fields so that organizations can protect valuable investments in human resources.

> Whether we approach it as managers or as employees, career management is an integral activity in our lives.

17-1 OCCUPATIONAL AND ORGANIZATIONAL CHOICE DECISIONS

The time of the fast track to the top of the hierarchical organization is past. Also gone is the idea of lifetime employment in a single organization. Today's environment demands leaner organizations, and the paternalistic attitude that organizations should take care of employees no longer exists. Individuals now take on

TABLE 17.1 THE NEW VERSUS OLD CAREER PARADIGMS

New Career Paradigm	Old Career Paradigm
Discrete exchange means: > explicit exchange of specified rewards in return for task performance > basing job rewards on the current market value of the work being performed > engaging in disclosure and renegotiation on both sides as the employment relationship unfolds > exercising flexibility as each party's interests and market circumstances change	**The mutual loyalty contract meant:** > implicit trading of employee compliance in return for job security > allowing job rewards to be routinely deferred into the future > leaving the mutual loyalty assumptions as a political barrier to renegotiation > assuming employment and career opportunities are standardized and prescribed by the firm
Occupational excellence means: > performance of current jobs in return for developing new occupational expertise > employees identifying with and focusing on what is happening in their adopted occupation > emphasizing occupational skill development over the local demands of any particular firm > getting training in anticipation of future job opportunities; having training lead jobs	**The one-employer focus meant:** > relying on the firm to specify jobs and their associated occupational skill base > employees identifying with and focusing on what is happening in their particular firm > forgoing technical or functional development in favor of firm-specific learning > doing the job first to be entitled to new training: making training follow jobs
Organizational empowerment means: > strategic positioning is dispersed to separate business units > everyone is responsible for adding value and improving competitiveness > business units are free to cultivate their own markets > new enterprise, spinoffs, and alliance building are broadly encouraged	**The top-down firm meant:** > strategic direction is subordinated to "corporate headquarters" > competitiveness and added value are the responsibility of corporate experts > business unit marketing depends on the corporate agenda > independent enterprise is discouraged, and likely to be viewed as disloyalty
Project allegiance means: > shared employer and employee commitment to the overarching goal of the project > a successful outcome of the project is more important than holding the project team together > financial and reputational rewards stem directly from project outcomes > upon project completion, organization and reporting arrangements are broken up	**Corporate allegiance meant:** > project goals are subordinated to corporate policy and organizational constraints > being loyal to the work group can be more important than the project itself > financial and reputational rewards stem from being a "good soldier" regardless of results > social relationships within corporate boundaries are actively encouraged

more responsibility for managing their own careers. So the concept of the career is undergoing a paradigm shift, as shown in Table 17.1. The old career is giving way to a new career characterized by discrete exchange, occupational excellence, organizational empowerment, and project allegiance.[4] Moreover, one recent study found that both individuals and organizations are actively involved in the management of the new career of employees. As such, the new career involves a type of participatory management technique on the part of the individual, but the organization responds to each individual's needs and thus is more flexible in its career development programs.[5]

Discrete exchange occurs when an organization gains productivity while a person gains work experience. It is a short-term arrangement that recognizes that job skills

change in value and that renegotiation of the relationship must occur as conditions change. This idea contrasts sharply with the mutual loyalty contract of the old career paradigm in which employee loyalty was exchanged for job security.

Occupational excellence means continuously honing skills that can be marketed across organizations. The individual identifies more with the occupation ("I am an engineer") than the organization ("I am an IBMer"). In contrast, the old one-employer focus meant that training was company specific and not meant to prepare the person for future job opportunities. A research study that focused on ethnographic data (interviews and stories) was conducted among software engineers in three European firms and two U.S. firms. The study showed that software engineers did not have much regard for their immediate supervisors, the organization, or formal dress codes. The only thing they did believe in was occupational excellence so that they could be better at what they do. In this regard, the authors of the study note that software engineers represent a unique group in terms of career development and that they fit well within the model of the "new career."[6]

Organizational empowerment means that power flows down to business units and in turn to employees. Employees are expected to add value and help the organization remain competitive by being innovative and creative. The old top-down approach meant that control and strategizing were done only by the top managers, and individual initiative could even be viewed as disloyalty or disrespect.

Project allegiance means that both individuals and organizations are committed to the successful completion of a project. The firm's gain is the project outcome; the individual's gain is experience and shared success. Upon project completion, the project team breaks up as individuals move on to new projects. Under the old paradigm, *corporate allegiance* was paramount, not project allegiance. The needs of projects were overshadowed by corporate policies and procedures. Work groups were long term, and keeping the group together was often a more important goal than project completion.

17-1a Preparing for the World of Work

When viewed from one perspective, you might say that we spend our youth preparing for the world of work. Educational and personal life experiences help an individual develop the skills and maturity needed to enter a career. Preparation for work is a developmental process that gradually unfolds over time.[7] As the time approaches for beginning a career, individuals face two difficult decisions: occupational choice and organizational choice.

17-1b Occupational Choice

In choosing an occupation, individuals assess their needs, values, abilities, and preferences and attempt to match them with an occupation that provides a fit. Personality plays a role in the selection of occupation. John Holland's theory of occupational choice contends that there are six types of personalities and that each personality is characterized by a set of interests and values.[8]

Holland also states that occupations can be classified using this typology. For example, realistic occupations include mechanic, restaurant server, and mechanical engineer. Artistic occupations include architect, voice coach,

and interior designer. Investigative occupations include physicist, surgeon, and economist. Real estate agent, human resource manager, and lawyer are enterprising occupations. Social occupations include counselor, social worker, and member of the clergy. Conventional occupations include word processor, accountant, and data entry operator. Holland's typology has been used to predict career choices with a variety of international participants, including Australians, Germans, Indians, Mexicans, New Zealanders, Pakistanis, South Africans, and Taiwanese.[9]

An assumption that drives Holland's theory is that people choose occupations that match their personalities. People who fit Holland's social types are those who prefer jobs that are highly interpersonal in nature. They may see careers in physical and math sciences, for example, as not affording the opportunity for interpersonal relationships.[10] Therefore, to fulfill the desire for interpersonal work, they may gravitate toward jobs in customer service.

Although personality is a major influence on occupational choice, it is not the only influence. There are a host of other influences, including social class, parents' occupations, economic conditions, and geography.[11] Once a choice of occupation has been made, another major decision individuals face is the choice of organizations. Individuals are often attracted to organizations whose mission matches their passions and values.

17-1c Organizational Choice and Entry

There are several theories of how individuals choose organizations, ranging from theories that postulate very logical and rational choice processes to those that offer seemingly irrational processes. *Expectancy theory*, discussed in Chapter 5, can be applied to organizational choice.[12] According to expectancy theory, individuals choose organizations that maximize positive outcomes and avoid negative outcomes. Job candidates calculate the probability that an organization will provide a certain outcome and then compare the probabilities across organizations.

Other theories propose that people select organizations in a much less rational fashion. Job candidates

> Organizational empowerment means that power flows down to business units and in turn to employees.

may *satisfice*, that is, select the first organization that meets one or two important criteria and then justify their choice by distorting their perceptions.[13] The method of selecting an organization varies greatly among individuals and may reflect a combination of the expectancy theory and theories that postulate less rational approaches.

Entry into an organization is further complicated by the conflicts that occur between individuals and organizations during the process. Figure 17.1 illustrates these potential conflicts. The arrows in the figure illustrate four types of conflicts that can occur as individuals choose organizations and organizations choose individuals. The first two conflicts (1 and 2) occur between individuals and organizations. The first is a conflict between the organization's effort to attract candidates and the individual's choice of an organization. The individual needs complete and accurate information to make a good choice, but the organization may not provide it. Since the organization is trying to attract a large number of qualified candidates, it presents itself in an overly attractive way.

The second conflict is between the individual's attempt to attract several organizations and the organization's need to select the best candidate. Individuals want good offers, so they do not disclose their faults. They describe their preferred job in terms of the organization's opening instead of describing a job they would really prefer.

The third and fourth conflicts are internal to the two parties. The third is a conflict between the organization's desire to recruit a large pool of qualified applicants and the organization's need to select and retain the best candidate. In recruiting, organizations tend to give only positive information, and this sometimes results in mismatches between the individual and the organization. The fourth conflict is internal to the individual; it concerns his or her need to make a good choice from among more than one desirable job offer. This situation can occur when individuals present themselves as overly attractive and consequently receive more job offers than they would have otherwise received, some of which might be a poor fit in terms of their skills and career goals.[14]

The organizational choice and entry process is very complex due to the nature of these conflicts. Partial responsibility for preventing these conflicts rests with the individual. Individuals should conduct thorough research of the organization through published reports and industry analyses. In addition, they should conduct a careful self-analysis and be as honest as possible with organizations to ensure a good match. The job interview process can be stressful, but also fun if it is engaged properly. Of course, the organization bears part of the responsibility for avoiding a mismatch by conducting an effective job interview.

REALISTIC JOB PREVIEWS The conflicts just discussed may result in unrealistic expectations on the part of the candidate. People entering the world of work may expect, for example, that they will receive explicit directions from their boss, only to find that they are left with ambiguity about how to do the job. They may expect that promotions will be based on performance but find that promotions are based mainly on political considerations. Some new hires also expect to be given managerial responsibilities right away, but they rarely are.

Giving potential employees a realistic picture of the job they are applying for is known as a **realistic job preview (RJP)**. When candidates are given both positive and negative information, they can make more effective job choices. Traditional recruiting practices often produce unrealistically high expectations, which produce low job satisfaction, whereas RJPs tend to create expectations that are much closer to reality and thus encourage many candidates to withdraw from further consideration.[15]

Time Warner Cable gives applicants RJPs through videos on its website. In the videos, current Time

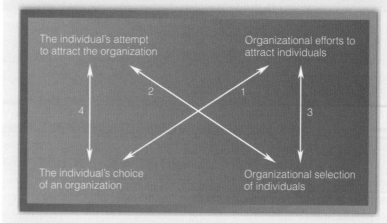

FIGURE 17.1 CONFLICTS DURING ORGANIZATIONAL ENTRY

The individual's attempt to attract the organization

Organizational efforts to attract individuals

The individual's choice of an organization

Organizational selection of individuals

SOURCE: Figure in L. W. Porter, E. E. Lawler III, and J. R. Hackman, *Behavior in Organizations*, New York: McGraw-Hill, Inc., 1975, p. 134. Reproduced with permission of The McGraw-Hill Companies.

realistic job preview (RJP)
Both positive and negative information given to potential employees about the job they are applying for, thereby giving them a realistic picture of the job.

Warner employees discuss the nature of their jobs and the skills necessary for dealing with the challenges and frustrations that are involved with various jobs within the company.[16] Alcoa, a global leader in metals technology, engineering, and manufacturing, posts RJP information on its website about what it's like to be an entry-level employee at the company, and also provides a self-assessment of job fit so that candidates can decide whether to go forward with the next steps of the recruiting process. The Texas Department of Aging and Disability Services website shows videos of actual direct-support workers on the job, describing the rewards and challenges of working with people who have developmental disabilities.[17] Other companies' websites use photo and video tours of their offices and locations, videos of meetings, and testimonials from current employees about what it's like to work there.

RJPs can also be thought of as inoculation against disappointment. If new recruits know what to expect in the new job, they can prepare for the experience. Newcomers who are not given RJPs may find that their jobs don't measure up to their expectations. They may then believe that their employer was deceitful in the hiring process, become unhappy and mishandle job demands, and ultimately leave the organization.[18]

Job candidates who receive RJPs view the organization as honest and also have a greater ability to cope with the demands of the job.[19] RJPs perform another important function: uncertainty reduction.[20] Knowing what to expect, both good and bad, gives a newcomer a sense of control that is important to job satisfaction and performance.

With today's emphasis on ethics, organizations need to do all they can to be seen as operating consistently and honestly. Realistic job previews are one way in which companies can provide ethically required information. Ultimately, RJPs result in more effective matches, lower turnover, and higher organizational commitment and job satisfaction.[21] There is much to gain in providing realistic job information. The U.S. Army hopes to increase its recruitment and retention for Officer Candidate School by using a realistic job preview. By helping potential candidates understand what they will encounter in OCS, the Army looks to establish trust and honesty, reduce role ambiguity, and promote realistic expectations.[22]

In summary, the needs and goals of individuals and organizations can clash during entry into an organization. To avoid potential mismatches, individuals should conduct a careful self-analysis and provide accurate information about themselves to potential employers. They also need to ask appropriate questions. While applicants often focus on asking questions about organizational rewards

Barbara Corcoran on Interviewing

Entrepreneur Barbara Corcoran built and grew her agency, the Corcoran Group, to become New York's largest real estate company. You may have seen her as a judge on the TV show *Shark Tank*.

As a successful businessperson, she has definite opinions on hiring people. Resumes, she believes, can be misleading, and she never looks at one until after interviewing the applicant. Corcoran says that reading the resume beforehand limits the interview to small talk focused only on the resume. She looks for "the light in the person" to spot the good in them. Some of her favorite questions include: "What do you like?" "Tell me about your mom." "What's your hobby?" "Tell me about your family."

By asking these questions, Corcoran is trying to determine whether the candidate is a happy person. Energy and a positive attitude are critical to success in the workplace, and she believes just one unhappy employee out of 30 employees can bring a workplace down. Who does she love to fire? Complainers!

Kathy Hutchins/Shutterstock.com

SOURCES: A. Bryant, "Barbara Corcoran on the Power of a Positive Attitude," *The New York Times*, June 2, 2017, accessed at https://www.nytimes.com/2017/06/02/business/barbara-corcoran-shark-tank.html?_r=0; B. Mikel, "Barbara Corcoran Swears by 1 Interview Question to Weed Out Complainers," Inc., June 6, 2017, accessed at https://www.nytimes.com/2017/06/02/business/barbara-corcoran-shark-tank.html?_r=0.

and not employee contributions, they should seek both in obtaining a realistic job preview.[23] Organizations should present realistic job previews to show candidates both the positive and negative aspects of the job, along with the potential career paths available to the employee.

17-2 FOUNDATIONS FOR A SUCCESSFUL CAREER

In addition to planning and preparation, building a career takes attention and self-examination. One way you can build a successful career is by becoming your own career coach. Another is by developing your emotional intelligence, which is an important attribute if you want to climb the corporate ladder.

17-2a Becoming Your Own Career Coach

The best way to stay employed is to see yourself as being in business for yourself, even if you work for someone else. Know what skills you can package for other employers and what you can do to ensure that your skills are state of the art. Organizations need employees who have acquired multiple skills and are adept at more than one job. Employers want employees who have demonstrated competence in dealing with change.[24] To be successful, think of organizational change not as a disruption to your work but instead as the central focus of your work. You will also need to develop self-reliance, as discussed in Chapter 7, to deal effectively with the stress of change. Self-reliant individuals take an interdependent approach to relationships and are comfortable both giving and receiving support from others.

The people who will be most successful in the new career paradigm are individuals who are flexible, team oriented (rather than hierarchical), energized by change, and tolerant of ambiguity. Those who will become frustrated in the new career paradigm are individuals who are rigid in their thinking and learning styles and who have high needs for control. A commitment to continuous, lifelong learning will prevent you from becoming a professional dinosaur.[25] An intentional and purposeful commitment to taking charge of your professional life will be necessary in managing the new career.

Behaving in an ethical manner, standing by your values, and building a professional image of integrity are also very important. Major corporations such as Google conduct extensive reference checks on their applicants— not just with the references supplied in the application, but also with friends of such references. Behaving ethically is not just a benefit to your job application, since an ethical foundation can also help you withstand pressures

Olivier Le Moal/Shutterstock.com

that might endanger your career. One study suggests that executives succumb to the temptation of fraud because they feel pressure to keep up with inflated expectations and changes in cultural norms, short-term versus long-term orientations, the composition of the board of directors, and senior leadership in the organization.[26]

17-2b Emotional Intelligence and Career Success

Almost 40 percent of new managers fail within the first eighteen months on the job. What are the reasons for the failure? Newly hired managers flame out because they fail to build good relationships with peers and subordinates, are confused about what their bosses expect, lack internal political skills, or are unable to achieve the two or three most important objectives of the new job.[27] You'll note that these failures are all due to a lack of interpersonal skills.

In Chapter 13, we introduced the concept of *emotional intelligence (EI)* as an important determinant of conflict management skills. Daniel Goleman argues that emotional intelligence is a constellation of the qualities that mark a star performer at work. These attributes include self-awareness, self-control, trustworthiness, confidence, and empathy, among others. Goleman's belief is that emotional competencies are twice as important to people's success today as raw intelligence or technical know-how. He also argues that the further up the corporate ranks you go, the more important emotional intelligence becomes.[28] Employers, either consciously or unconsciously, look for emotional intelligence during the hiring process. And emotional intelligence applies across careers. EI predicts success in medical school and success as a doctor. Physicians who show interpersonal sensitivity and effective communication skills improve therapeutic outcomes for their patients.[29] Neither gender seems to have cornered the market on EI. Both men and women who can demonstrate high levels of EI are seen as particularly gifted and may be promoted more rapidly.[30]

Emotional intelligence is important to career success in many cultures. A recent study in Australia found that high levels of emotional intelligence are associated with job success. EI improves one's ability to work with other team members and to provide high-quality customer service, and workers with high EI are more likely to take steps to develop their skills. Several U.S. studies have confirmed that high emotional intelligence is an important attribute for the upwardly mobile worker.[31]

The good news is that emotional intelligence can be developed and does tend to improve throughout life. Accordingly, some companies are providing training in emotional intelligence competencies. When American Express began sending managers through an emotional competence training program, it found that trained managers outperformed those who lacked this training. In the year after completing the course, managers trained in emotional competence grew their businesses by an average of 18.1 percent compared to 16.2 percent for those businesses whose managers were untrained.[32]

17-3 THE CAREER STAGE MODEL

A common way of understanding careers is viewing them as a series of stages through which individuals pass during their working lives.[33] Figure 17.2 presents the career stage model, which will form the basis for our discussion in the remainder of this chapter.[34] The career stage model shows that individuals pass through four stages in their careers: establishment, advancement, maintenance, and withdrawal. It is important to note that the age ranges shown are approximations; that is, the timing of the career transitions varies greatly among individuals.

Establishment is the first stage of a person's career. The activities that occur in this stage center around learning the job and fitting into the organization and occupation. **Advancement** is a high achievement-oriented stage in which people focus on increasing their competence. The **maintenance** stage finds the individual trying to maintain productivity while evaluating progress toward career goals. The **withdrawal** stage involves contemplation of retirement or possible career change.

Along the horizontal axis in Figure 17.2 are the corresponding life stages for each career stage. These life stages are based on the pioneering research on adult development conducted by Levinson and his colleagues. Levinson conducted extensive biographical interviews to trace the life stages of men and women. He interpreted his research in two books, *The Seasons of a Man's Life* and *The Seasons of a Woman's Life*.[35] Levinson's life stages are characterized by an alternating pattern of stability and transition.[36] Throughout the discussion

establishment The first stage of a person's career in which the person learns the job and begins to fit into the organization and occupation.

advancement The second, high achievement-oriented career stage in which people focus on increasing their competence.

maintenance The third stage in an individual's career in which the individual tries to maintain productivity while evaluating progress toward career goals.

withdrawal The final stage in an individual's career in which the individual contemplates retirement or possible career changes.

Kindness at KIND Healthy Snacks

littleny/Shutterstock.com

KIND's CEO Daniel Lubetsky has based his career on building bridges between people and creating opportunities for kindness to flourish. KIND bars are the fastest growing snack bar in the world, and the company has doubled its revenue each year. KIND's mission is to make the world a little kinder, one act at a time. #kindawesome is a program created to recognize and reward acts of kindness. Through the website https://www.howkindofyou.com, users can spot a random act of kindness and send the person a #kindawesome card electronically. The card awards the recipient a KIND bar and another #kindawesome card to pass on to another recipient—a way of paying kindness forward.

Lubetsky believes that empathy and kindness should not be confused with weakness. Being kind takes strength and confidence. He believes it's important to listen to other people and seek to understand. The socially conscious CEO has established the KIND Foundation, which awarded $1.1 million in grants to seven individuals who are transforming their communities through kindness.

SOURCES: https://www.kindsnacks.com; R. Zurer, "Forget Fear," *Conscious Company*, January/February 2017: 64–65.

FIGURE 17.2 THE CAREER STAGE MODEL

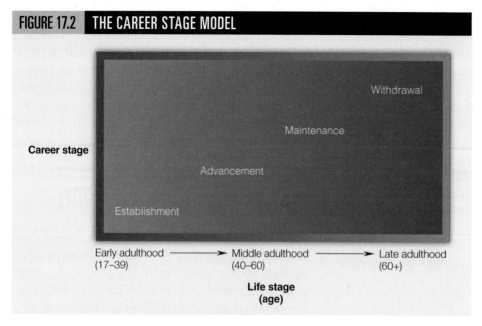

Career stage

Withdrawal

Maintenance

Advancement

Establishment

Early adulthood → Middle adulthood → Late adulthood
(17–39)   (40–60)   (60+)

Life stage (age)

of career stages that follows, we weave in the transitions of Levinson's life stages. Work and personal life are inseparable, and to understand a person's career experiences, we must also examine the unfolding of the person's personal experiences.

You can see that adult development provides unique challenges for the individual and that there may be considerable overlap between the stages. Now let us examine each career stage in detail.

17-4 THE ESTABLISHMENT STAGE

During the establishment stage, the individual begins a career as a newcomer to the organization. This is a period of great dependence on others, as the individual is learning about the job and the organization. The establishment stage usually occurs during the beginning of the early adulthood years (ages eighteen to twenty-five). During this time, Levinson notes, an important personal life transition into adulthood occurs: the individual begins to separate from his or her parents and becomes less emotionally and financially dependent on them. Following this period is a fairly stable time of exploring the adult role and settling down.

The transition from school to work is a part of the establishment stage. Many graduates find the transition to be a memorable experience. The following description was provided by a new graduate who went to work at a large public utility:

> We all tried to one-up each other about jobs we had just accepted ... bragging that we had the highest salary, the best management training program, the most desirable coworkers, the most upward mobility ... and believed we were destined to become future corporate leaders.... Every Friday after work we met for happy hour to visit and relate the events of the week. It is interesting to look at how the mood of those happy hours changed over the first few months ... at first, we jockeyed for position in terms of telling stories about how great these new jobs were, or how weird our bosses were.... Gradually, things quieted down at happy hour. The mood went from "Wow, isn't this great" to "What in the world have we gotten ourselves into?" There began to be general agreement that business wasn't all it was cracked up to be.[37]

Establishment is thus a time of big transitions in both personal and work life. At work, three major tasks face the newcomer: negotiating effective psychological contracts, managing the stress of socialization, and making a transition from organizational outsider to organizational insider.

17-4a Psychological Contracts

A **psychological contract** is an implicit agreement between the individual and the organization that specifies what each is expected to give and receive in the relationship.[38] Individuals expect to receive salary, status, advancement opportunities, and challenging work to meet their needs. Organizations expect to receive time, energy, talents, and loyalty in order to meet their goals. Working out the psychological contract with the organization begins with entry, but the contract is modified as the individual proceeds through the career.

Psychological contracts also exist between individuals.[39] During the establishment stage, newcomers form attachment relationships with many people in the organization. This process of working out effective psychological contracts within each relationship is important.

psychological contract
An implicit agreement between an individual and an organization that specifies what each is expected to give and receive in the relationship.

Key Areas Where New Managers Struggle

The Center for Creative Leadership trains leaders and conducts research on what contributes to leader success and failure. Part of their findings include four key areas that first-time managers struggle to master:

> **Communication.** Be aware of not only verbal but especially nonverbal communication and the subtle messages that you're sending.

> **Influence.** Understand that each individual needs a different style of influence, and adapt.

> **Leading teams.** Take the time to get to know your team members individually, and build strong relationships.

> **Development of others.** Give frequent feedback and look for assignments that "stretch" team members.

SOURCE: W. Gentry (2016), *Be The Boss Everyone Wants to Work For*, with the Center for Creative Leadership. Berrett-Koehler: Oakland, CA.

Newcomers need social support in many forms and from many sources. Table 17.2 shows the type of psychological contracts, in the form of social support, that newcomers may work out with key insiders in the organization.

One common newcomer concern, for example, is whose behavior to watch for cues to appropriate behavior. Senior colleagues can provide modeling support by displaying behavior that the newcomer can emulate. Newcomers also depend on colleagues for information they need. If newcomers encounter conflicts with coworkers, they can still succeed by building strong relationships with their immediate supervisors.[40] Broken or breached psychological contracts can have detrimental outcomes. When a breach occurs, employees might experience negative emotional reactions that can lead to loss of trust, reduced job satisfaction, lower commitment to the organization, and higher turnover.[41]

17-5 THE ADVANCEMENT STAGE

The advancement stage is a period when many individuals strive for achievement. They seek greater responsibility and authority and strive for upward mobility. Usually

TABLE 17.2 NEWCOMER–INSIDER PSYCHOLOGICAL CONTRACTS FOR SOCIAL SUPPORT			
Type of Support	**Function of Supportive Attachments**	**Newcomer Concern**	**Examples of Insider Response/Action**
Protection from stressors	Direct assistance in terms of resources, time, labor, or environmental modification	What are the major risks/threats in this environment?	*Supervisor* cues newcomer to risks/threats.
Informational	Provision of information necessary for managing demands	What do I need to know to get things done?	*Mentor* provides advice on informal political climate in organization.
Evaluative	Feedback on both personal and professional role performances	How am I doing?	*Supervisor* provides day-to-day performance feedback during first week on new job.
Modeling	Evidence of behavioral standards provided through modeled behavior	Whom do I follow?	Newcomer is apprenticed to *senior colleague*.
Emotional	Empathy, esteem, caring, or love	Do I matter? Who cares if I'm here or not?	*Other newcomers* empathize with and encourage individual when reality shock sets in.

SOURCE: Table from D. L. Nelson, J. C. Quick, and J. R. Joplin, "Psychological Contracting and Newcomer Socialization: An Attachment Theory Foundation," from *Journal of Social Behavior and Personality*, 6 (1991): 65.

around age thirty, an important life transition occurs, leading people to reassess their goals and make changes in their career dreams.[42] The transition at age thirty is followed by a period of stability during which the individual tries to find a role in adult society and wants to succeed in the career. During this stage, several issues are important: exploring career paths, finding a mentor, working out dual-career partnerships, and managing conflicts between work and personal life.

17-5a Career Paths and Career Ladders

Career paths are sequences of job experiences along which employees move during their careers.[43] At the advancement stage, individuals examine their career dreams and the paths they must follow to achieve those dreams. For example, suppose a person's dream is to become a top executive in the pharmaceutical industry. She majors in chemistry in college and takes a job with a nationally recognized firm. After she has adjusted to her job as a quality control chemist, she reevaluates her plan and decides that further education is necessary. Now she plans to pursue an MBA degree part time, hoping to gain expertise in management. From there, she hopes to be promoted to a supervisory position within her current firm. If this does not occur within five years, she will consider moving to a different pharmaceutical company. An alternate route would be to try to transfer to a sales position, from which she might advance into management.

The career paths of many women have moved from working in large organizations to starting their own businesses. Currently, there are 9.1 million women-owned firms in the United States. From 1997 to 2014, the number of woman-owned firms grew at 1.5 times the national average. What is the motivation for this exodus to entrepreneurship? The main reasons are to seek additional challenge and self-fulfillment and to have more self-determination and freedom.[44]

A **career ladder** is a structured series of job positions through which an individual progresses in an organization. For example, at Southwestern Bell, it is customary to move through a series of alternating line and staff supervisory assignments to advance toward upper management. Supervisors in customer service might be assigned next to the training staff and then rotate back as line supervisors in network services to gain experience in different departments.

Some companies use the traditional concept of career ladders to help employees advance in their careers. Other organizations take a more contemporary approach to career advancement. Sony, for instance, encourages creativity from its engineers by using nontraditional career paths in which people have the freedom to move on to interesting and challenging job assignments without notifying their supervisors. If they join a new project team, their current boss is expected to let them move on. This self-promotion philosophy at Sony is seen as a key to high levels of innovation and creative new product designs.

There has been heightened interest in international assignments in response to globalization and global staffing issues. One problem in this regard has been that most expatriate assignments are not successful. Therefore, organizations have been facing the challenge of properly training and preparing individuals for such assignments. One proposed solution is alternative international work assignments such as commuter work assignments, virtual assignments, short-term assignments, and so on, which can be used to help individuals gain international work experience in preparation for higher levels in the organization.[45]

Another approach used by some companies to develop skills is the idea of a *career lattice*—an approach to building competencies by moving laterally through different departments in the organization or by moving through different projects. Top management support for the career lattice is essential because in traditional terms an employee who has made several lateral moves might not be viewed with favor. However, the career lattice approach is an effective way to develop an array of skills to ensure one's employability.[46]

17-5b Finding a Mentor

Exploring career paths is one important activity in advancement. Another crucial activity during advancement is finding a mentor. A **mentor** is an individual who provides guidance, coaching, counseling, and friendship to a protégé. Mentors are important to career success because they perform both career and psychosocial functions.[47]

The *career functions* provided by a mentor include sponsorship, facilitating exposure and visibility, coaching, and protection. *Sponsorship* means actively

career path A sequence of job experiences that an employee moves along during his or her career.

career ladder A structured series of job positions through which an individual progresses in an organization.

mentor An individual who provides guidance, coaching, counseling, and friendship to a protégé.

helping the individual get job experiences and promotions. *Facilitating exposure and visibility* means providing opportunities for the protégé to develop relationships with key figures in the organization in order to advance. *Coaching* involves providing advice in both career and job performance. *Protection* is provided by shielding the protégé from potentially damaging experiences. Career functions are particularly important to the protégé's future success. One study found that the amount of career coaching received by protégés was related to more promotions and to higher salaries four years later.[48]

The mentor also performs *psychosocial functions*: role modeling, acceptance and confirmation, counseling, and friendship. *Role modeling* occurs when the mentor displays behavior for the protégé to emulate. Such modeling facilitates social learning. *Acceptance and confirmation* are important to both the mentor and protégé. When the protégé feels accepted by the mentor, it fosters a sense of pride. Likewise, positive regard and appreciation from the junior colleague provide a sense of satisfaction for the mentor. *Counseling* by a mentor helps the protégé explore personal issues that arise and require assistance. *Friendship* is another psychosocial function that benefits both mentor and protégé alike.

In effective mentoring relationships, there is regular contact between mentor and protégé that has clearly specified purposes. Mentoring should be consistent with the corporate culture and the organization's goals. Both mentors and protégés alike should be trained in ways to manage the relationship. Mentors should be held accountable and rewarded for their role. They should be perceived (accurately) by protégés as having considerable influence within the organization.[49] While it may be tempting to go after the "top dog" as your mentor, personality compatibility is also an important factor in the success or failure of a mentoring relationship. Thus, mentors who are similar to their protégés in terms of personality traits such as extraversion, and whose expectations are largely met by the relationship, are more likely to show interest in continuing the arrangement.[50]

At IBM, mentoring isn't optional; it's an important performance metric, and senior managers are evaluated on specific mentoring goals. From their first day on the job, employees are told that they are expected to have a mentor and given help on getting a mentor and contracting with a mentor. Senior managers are evaluated on the development of their mentees and their own effectiveness as mentors. IBM has goals

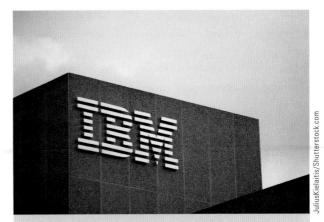

JuliusKielaitis/Shutterstock.com

At IBM, mentoring isn't optional; it's an important performance metric, and senior managers are evaluated on specific mentoring goals.

around cross-cultural and cross-gender mentoring as well.[51]

Mentoring programs are also effective ways of addressing the challenge of workforce diversity. The mentoring process, however, presents unique problems—including the availability of mentors, issues of language and acculturation, and cultural sensitivity—for minority groups such as Hispanic Americans. Negative stereotypes can limit minority members' access to mentoring relationships and the benefits associated with mentoring.[52] To address this problem, companies need to take steps to facilitate access to mentors for minority employees.

Mentoring programs may be informal or formal. *Informal mentoring programs* identify pools of mentors and protégés, provide training in the development of effective mentoring and diversity issues, and then provide informal opportunities for the development of mentoring relationships. *Network groups* are another avenue for mentoring. These groups help

In effective mentoring relationships, there is regular contact between mentor and protégé that has clearly specified purposes.

Corporate Citizenship Report › Safety, health and the workplace › ☑

Diversity and inclusion

ExxonMobil's emphasis on diversity and inclusion is evidenced by its support of many employee networks.

members identify with a few others who are like them within an organization, build relationships with them, and build social support. Network groups enhance the chance that minorities will find mentors.[53] ExxonMobil's emphasis on diversity and inclusion is evidenced by its support of many employee networks. The networks provide professional development programs, mentor new employees, and engage in community service. Some of the networks at ExxonMobil are the Black Employee Success Team (BEST), Inclusion and Diversity of Employees (PRIDE), and Women's Interest Network (WIN).[54]

Some companies have *formal mentoring programs*. At PricewaterhouseCoopers (PwC) each intern is assigned both a peer mentor to help with day-to-day questions and an experienced mentor to help with larger issues such as career path development. As an international firm, PwC also employs similar methods overseas. In PwC's Czech Republic operations, a team of two mentors—one of whom is called a "counselor"—fills the same guidance role as the two mentors generally fill for U.S. employees.[55]

Mentoring has had a strong impact in shaping the identities of the Big Four accounting firms. In one study, every partner who was interviewed reported having at least one mentor who played a critical role in his or her attainment of the partnership and beyond. These protégés' work identities were shaped through mentoring, and their work goals, language, and even lifestyles reflected the imperatives of the Big Four firm for which they worked.[56] Protégés were schooled on partners' "hot buttons" (what not to talk about), what to wear, to "tuck in the tie," and not to "cut the grass" without wearing a shirt.

In companies without formal mentoring programs, junior employees are often left to negotiate their own mentoring relationships. The barriers to finding a mentor under these circumstances include lack of access to mentors, fear of initiating a mentoring relationship, and fear that supervisors or coworkers might not approve of the mentoring relationship. Individuals may also be afraid to initiate a mentoring relationship because it might be misconstrued as a sexual advance by the potential mentor or by others. Potential mentors may fear this misinterpretation as well. Some are therefore unwilling to develop a relationship because of their own or the protégé's gender. Women report more of these barriers than men, and individuals who lack previous experience report more barriers to finding a mentor.[57]

There are other gender differences found in mentoring relationships. Male protégés report receiving less psychological support than female protégés. Additionally, male mentors report giving more career development support, whereas female mentors report giving more psychological support.[58] Mentoring can be particularly important for women in male-dominated professions. In these environments, women who have male mentors have higher levels of compensation and career progress satisfaction than those without a male mentor.[59] Organizations can encourage junior workers to approach mentors by providing opportunities for them to interact with senior colleagues. The immediate supervisor is not always the best mentor for an individual, so exposure to other senior workers is important. Seminars, multilevel teams, and social events can serve as vehicles for bringing together potential mentors and protégés.

Mentoring relationships go through a series of phases: initiation, cultivation, separation, and redefinition. There is no fixed time length for each phase because each relationship is unique. The *initiation* phase is when the mentoring relationship begins to take on significance for both the mentor and the protégé. In the *cultivation* phase the relationship becomes more meaningful, and the protégé shows rapid progress because of the career support and psychosocial support provided by the mentor. Protégés influence mentors as well. In the *separation* phase the protégé feels the need to assert independence and work more autonomously. Separation can be voluntary, or it can result from an involuntary change (the protégé or mentor may be promoted or transferred). The separation phase can be difficult if it is resisted, either by the mentor (who is reluctant to let go of the relationship) or by the protégé (who resents the mentor's withdrawal of support). Moreover, separation may result from a conflict that disrupts the mentoring relationship rather than proceeding smoothly and naturally.

The *redefinition* phase occurs if separation has been successful. In this phase, the relationship takes on a new identity as the two parties consider each other colleagues or friends. The mentor feels pride in the protégé, and the protégé develops a deeper appreciation for the support from the mentor.

Why are mentors so important? Aside from the support they provide, research shows that mentors are important to the protégé's future success. For example, studies have demonstrated that individuals with mentors have higher promotion rates and higher incomes than individuals who do not have mentors.[60] Professionals who have mentors earn between $5,600 and $22,000 more per year than those who do not.[61] Individuals with mentors are also better decision makers.[62] Mentors can also help protégés make the transition into leadership positions. In addition to an individual being promoted into leadership position, the team members grant leadership; it's a two-way process. Team members are more likely to accept leaders who are older. Younger individuals, seen as less prototypical leaders, are not automatically accepted and granted status. Mentors can provide advice on how to navigate this challenge.[63]

17-5c Dual-Career Partnerships

During the advancement stage, many individuals face another transition. They settle into a relationship with a life partner. This lifestyle transition requires adjustment in many respects—learning to live with another person, being concerned with someone besides yourself, dealing with an extended family, and many other demands. The partnership can be particularly stressful if both members are career oriented.

The two-career lifestyle has increased in recent years due in part to the need for two incomes to maintain a preferred standard of living. **Dual-career partnerships** are relationships in which both people have important career roles. This type of partnership can be mutually beneficial, but it can also be stressful. Often these stresses center around stereotypes that providing income is a man's responsibility and taking care of the home is the woman's domain. Thus, men who adhere to traditional gender beliefs may be threatened when the wife's income exceeds their own. However, working women's satisfaction with their marriage is affected by how much the husband helps with child care. Beliefs about who should do what in the partnership complicate the dual-career issue.

One stressor in a dual-career partnership is time pressure. When both partners work outside the home, there may be a time crunch in fitting in work, family, and leisure time.[64] Demonstrating gender equality at home benefits the next generation in their work lives. When fathers do an equal share of housework, daughters are less likely to limit their career aspirations to female-stereotyped jobs.[65] Another issue to work out is whose career takes precedence. For example, what happens if one partner is transferred to another city? Must the other partner make a move that might threaten his or her own career in order to be with the partner who was transferred? And who, if anyone, will stay home and take care of a new baby?

Working out a dual-career partnership takes careful planning and consistent communication between the partners. Each partner must serve as a source of social support for the other. In addition, couples may need to turn to other family members, friends, and professionals for support.

17-5d Work–Home Conflicts

An issue related to dual-career partnerships that is faced throughout the career cycle but often first encountered in the advancement phase is the conflict between work and personal life. Such conflict negatively affects an individual's overall quality of life and may even lead to emotional exhaustion. Dealing with customer complaints all day, failed sales calls, or missed deadlines can magnify negative events at home, and vice versa.[66]

Responsibilities at home will likely clash at times with responsibilities at work, so these conflicts must be planned for. Suppose a child gets sick at school. Who will pick up the child and stay home with him? Couples must work together to resolve these conflicts.[67] Work-home conflicts can mean taking out work-related frustrations on family. When individuals feel undermined at work, they sleep poorly, have less patience, and vent their anger at home. One way to interrupt this pattern is to exercise, which helps people control their behavior.[68] Sleep is also important for staying healthy at work and at home. After a good night's sleep, people are more positive at work and at home, have more positive interactions with colleagues, and are more engaged at work.[69]

Work–home conflicts are particular problems for working women. Women have been quicker to share

> **dual-career partnership**
> A relationship in which both people have important career roles.

When working women experience work–home conflict, their performance may decline, and they suffer more strain.

the provider role than men have been to share responsibilities at home.[70] When working women experience work–home conflict, their performance declines, and they suffer more strain. Work–home conflict is a broad topic. It can be narrowed further into work–family conflict, in which work interferes with family, or family–work conflict, in which family or home life interferes with work.[71] Individuals who believe that men and women should share work and home lives equally experience more guilt from work–home conflict than traditionalists, who tend to feel more guilt when home life interferes with work.[72] Cultural differences arise in these types of conflicts. One study showed that while Americans experience more family–work conflict, Chinese experience more work–family conflict.[73] For example, women in management positions in China were very positive about future advancements and carried a strong belief in their ability to succeed. This, in turn, caused them to reevaluate their personal and professional identities. Such an identity transformation is marked by happiness associated with career advancement, even though many women foresaw emotional costs with such career advancement. This study indicated that female Chinese managers experience work–family conflict in part because the Chinese culture emphasizes close social ties and *guanxi*.[74]

flexible work schedule
A work schedule that allows employees discretion in order to accommodate personal concerns.

eldercare Assistance in caring for elderly parents and/or other elderly relatives.

WAYS TO MANAGE WORK–HOME CONFLICT To help individuals deal with work–home conflict, companies like Ernst & Young offer **flexible work schedules**, programs that give employees the freedom to set their own hours so that they can attend to personal issues.[75] *Telecommuting* breaks down barriers of time and space by allowing people to work no matter where they are. At Cisco Systems, employees who telecommuted experienced higher productivity, work-life flexibility, and job satisfaction. Furthermore, they reported saving a combined $10.3 million in fuel costs, while the company saved $277 million per year in time and productivity costs.

Company-sponsored child care is another way to help. Companies with on-site day-care centers include Johnson & Johnson, Perdue Farms, and Campbell Soup. Mitchell Gold + Bob Williams, an award-winning furniture maker, believes that treating people right must come first. Its 2,700-square-foot on-site day-care center is education-based rather than activity-based and operates at break-even rates to make it more accessible.[76] Whereas large companies may offer corporate day care, small companies can also assist their workers by providing referral services for locating the type of child care the workers need. For smaller organizations, this is a cost-effective alternative. At the very least, companies can be sensitive to work–home conflicts and handle them on a case-by-case basis with flexibility and concern.

A program of increasing interest that organizations can provide is **eldercare**. Often workers find themselves part of the so-called sandwich generation. They are expected to care for both their children and their elderly parents. In many countries, the need for eldercare is expected to increase dramatically over the next decade.[77] Inclusion in this extremely stressful role is reported more often by women than men.[78] The impact of caring for an aging loved one is often underestimated—17 percent of those who provide such care eventually quit their jobs due to time constraints, and another 15 percent cut back their work hours.[79] Caring for an elderly dependent at home not only creates work–home conflicts for an employee but also takes a toll on the employee's own well-being and performance at work. This is most often the case if the organization is not one that provides a supportive climate for discussion of eldercare issues.[80] Harvard University has taken steps to help its faculty and staff dealing with eldercare issues by contracting with Parents in a Pinch, Inc., a firm that specializes in nanny services and also offers eldercare. Fannie Mae's comprehensive approach to eldercare began in 1999.

Harvard University has partnered with Parents in a Pinch to provide eldercare services for its employees who may have family in need.

The company, which has more than 6,000 employees, offers an Elderkit planner, reimbursement for emergency backup care, and sessions with a professional eldercare consultant to assist with options for elderly parents.[81]

John Beatrice is one of a growing number of men making work fit their family rather than trying to fit family around career. John remembers his father working most of the night so he could be at John's athletic events during the day, and John wants the same for his family. So while job sharing, flexible scheduling, and telecommuting have traditionally been viewed as meeting the needs of working mothers, John and other men are increasingly taking advantage of such opportunities. In John's case, flexible work hours at Ernst & Young allow him to spend part of his mornings and afternoons coaching a high school hockey team. In John's assessment, flexible work hours actually lead him to work more hours than he would otherwise, and he's happier about doing it. Not surprisingly, John's employer also benefits from the arrangement. After nineteen years, John is more loyal than ever and still loves what he does.[82]

Alternative work arrangements such as flextime, compressed workweeks, work-at-home arrangements, part-time hours, job sharing, and leave options can help employees manage work–home conflicts. Managers must not let their biases get in the way of these benefits. Top managers may be less willing to grant alternative work arrangements to men than to women, to supervisors than to subordinates, and to employees caring for

HOT TREND

Busyness as a Lifestyle? Is There a Trophy for That?

In times past, enjoying leisure time was a status symbol and a sign of success. Now things are different. The refrain "I'm so busy" is a humblebrag indicating that one's time is scarce, valuable, and not to be wasted. Studies indicate that when we perceive others as busy, we infer that they have high social status and are wealthier.

The glorification of "busy" seems to be a distinctly American phenomenon. Italians, for example, equate working more hours with lower, not higher, social status. Americans, in contrast, seldom take all the vacation they've earned, and they may have trouble relaxing when they do go on vacation.

Is this a good trend? It is worth noting that the Chinese character for busyness has two parts, one for "killing" and one for "heart." Also noteworthy are the research findings that the more we try to multitask, the less productive we are. And busyness equals more stress and less attention to the needs of others.

SOURCES: S. Bellezza, N. Paharia, and A. Keinan, "Conspicuous Consumption of Time: When Busyness and Lack of Leisure Time Become a Status Symbol," *Journal of Consumer Research*, 44 (2017): 118–138.

elderly parents rather than children, but it is important that family-friendly policies be applied fairly.[83]

17-6 THE MAINTENANCE STAGE

Maintenance may be a misnomer for this career stage because some people continue to grow in their careers, although the growth is usually not at the rate it was earlier. A career crisis at midlife may accompany the midlife transition. A senior product manager at Borden found himself in such a crisis and described it this way: "When I was in college, I had thought in terms of being president of a company…. But at Borden I felt used and cornered. Most of the guys in the next two rungs above me had either an MBA or fifteen to twenty years of experience in the food business. My long-term plans stalled."[84]

Some individuals who reach a career crisis are burned out, and a month's vacation will help, according to Carolyn Smith Paschal, who owns an executive search firm. She recommends that companies give employees in this stage sabbaticals instead of bonuses. This would help rejuvenate them. Some individuals, on the other hand, reach the maintenance stage with a sense of achievement and contentment, feeling no need to strive for further upward mobility. Whether the maintenance stage is a time of crisis or contentment, however, there are two issues to grapple with: sustaining performance and becoming a mentor.

17-6a Sustaining Performance

Remaining productive is a key concern for individuals in the maintenance stage. This becomes challenging when one reaches a **career plateau**, a point where the probability of moving further up the hierarchy is low. Some people handle career plateauing fairly well, but others may become frustrated, bored, and dissatisfied with their jobs. To keep employees productive, organizations can provide challenges and opportunities for learning. *Lateral moves* are one option. Another option is to involve the employee in *project teams* that provide new tasks and skill development. The key is keeping the work stimulating and involving. Individuals at this stage also need continued affirmation of their value to the organization. They need to know that their contributions are significant and appreciated.[85]

17-6b Becoming a Mentor

During maintenance, individuals can make a contribution by sharing their wealth of knowledge and experience with others. Opportunities to be mentors to new employees can keep senior workers motivated and involved in the organization. It is important for organizations to reward mentors for the time and energy they expend. Some employees adapt naturally to the mentor role, but others may need training on how to coach and counsel junior workers.

Maintenance is a time of transition, like all career stages. It can be managed by individuals who know what to expect and plan to remain productive, as well as by organizations that focus on maximizing employee involvement in work. According to Levinson, during the latter part of the maintenance stage, another life transition occurs. The so-called age-fifty transition is another time of reevaluating the dream and working further on the issues

career plateau A point in an individual's career at which the probability of moving farther up the hierarchy is low.

raised in the midlife transition. Following the age-fifty transition is a fairly stable period. During this time, individuals begin to plan seriously for withdrawing from their careers.

17-7 THE WITHDRAWAL STAGE

The withdrawal stage usually occurs later in life and signals that a long period of continuous employment will soon come to a close. Older workers may face discrimination and stereotyping. They are often viewed by others as less productive, more resistant to change, and less motivated. However, older workers are one of the most undervalued groups in the workforce. They can provide continuity in the midst of change and can serve as mentors and role models to younger generations of employees.

Discrimination against older workers is prohibited under the Age Discrimination in Employment Act (go to eeoc.gov/policy/adea.html to read the provisions of this 1967 act). Organizations should strive to create a culture that values older workers' contributions. With their level of experience, strong work ethic, and loyalty, these workers have much to contribute. In fact, older workers have lower rates of tardiness and absenteeism, are more safety conscious, and are more satisfied with their jobs than are younger workers.[86]

17-7a Planning for Change

The decision to retire is an individual one, but the need for planning is universal. A retired sales executive from Boise Cascade said that the best advice is to "plan no unplanned retirement."[87] This means carefully planning not only the transition but also the activities you will be involved in once the transition is made. All options should be open for consideration. One recent trend is to work as a temporary top-level executive. The qualities of a good temporary executive include substantial high-level management experience, financial security that allows the executive to choose only assignments that really interest her, and a willingness to relocate.[88] Some individuals at the withdrawal stage find this an attractive option.

Planning for retirement should include not only financial planning but also a plan for psychologically withdrawing from work. The pursuit of hobbies and travel, volunteer work, or more time with extended

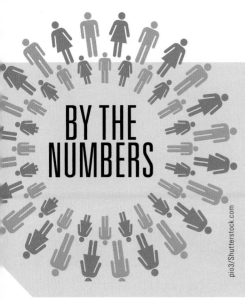
family can all be part of the plan. The key is to plan early and carefully, as well as to anticipate the transition with a positive attitude and a full slate of desirable activities.

17-7b Retirement

There are several retirement trends right now, ranging from early retirement to phased retirement to never retiring. Some adults are choosing a combination of these options, leaving their first career for some time off before reentering the workforce either part time or full time doing something they enjoy. For more and more Americans, the idea of a retirement spent sitting beside the swimming pool sounds, for lack of a better word, boring. Factors that influence the decision of when to retire include company policy, financial considerations, family support or pressure, health, and opportunities for other productive activities.

During the withdrawal stage, the individual faces a major life transition that Levinson refers to as the *late adulthood transition* (ages sixty to sixty-five). One's own mortality becomes a major concern, and the loss of family members and friends becomes more frequent. The person works to achieve a sense of integrity in life; that is, the person works to find the encompassing meaning and value in life.

Retirement need not be a complete cessation of work. Many alternative work arrangements can be considered, and many companies offer flexibility in these options. **Phased retirement** is a popular option for retirement-age workers who want to gradually reduce their hours and/or responsibilities. There are many forms of phased retirement, including reduced workdays or workweeks, job sharing, and consulting and mentoring arrangements. Many organizations cannot afford the loss of large numbers of experienced employees at once. The average retirement age in the United States is 62, and it has been slowly increasing. In fact, Americans who are still working say they expect to work until age 66. This may reflect better health and longer life spans, changes in employer-sponsored retirement plans, or lifestyle choices to simply work longer.[89] Many individuals do not fully retire, but engage in **bridge employment**, which is employment that takes place after a person retires from a full-time position but before the person's permanent withdrawal from the workforce. Bridge employment is related to retirement satisfaction and overall life satisfaction.[90]

Some companies are helping employees transition to retirement in innovative ways. For example, retired individuals can continue their affiliation with the organization by serving as mentors to employees who are embarking on retirement planning or other career transitions. This helps diminish the fear of loss some people have about retirement because the retiree has an option to serve as a mentor or consultant to the organization.

Lawrence Livermore National Labs (LLNL) employs some of the best research minds in the world. And when these

phased retirement
An arrangement that allows employees to reduce their hours and/or responsibilities in order to ease into retirement.

bridge employment
Employment that takes place after a person retires from a full-time position but before the person's permanent withdrawal from the workforce.

great minds retire from full-time work, they have numerous opportunities to continue contributing. LLNL's retiree program website lists a wide variety of requests, ranging from guiding tours and making phone calls to providing guidance on current research and helping researchers make contact with other researchers.[91] Programs like this one help LLNL avoid the typical knowledge drain that takes place when seasoned veteran employees retire.

Now that you understand the career stage model, you can begin to conduct your own career planning. It is never too early to start.

17-8 CAREER ANCHORS

Much of an individual's self-concept rests upon a career. Over the course of the career, **career anchors** are developed—self-perceived talents, motives, and values that guide an individual's career decisions.[92] Edgar Schein developed the concept of career anchors based on a twelve-year study of MBA graduates from the Massachusetts Institute of Technology (MIT). Schein found great diversity in the graduates' career histories but great similarities in the way they explained the career decisions they had made.[93] From extensive interviews with the graduates, Schein developed the five career anchors. He analyzed 44 MBA students as they started their careers out of graduate school, and he found that these students tended to be driven by one of five things: (1) Managerial competence; (2) Technical-functional competence; (3) Security; (4) Creativity; and (5) Autonomy and independence. Schein called these motivators "career anchors" and suggested that the career anchor that was most important to a person

career anchors A network of self-perceived talents, motives, and values that guide an individual's career decisions.

Bridge employment takes place after a person retires from full-time work but before a permanent withdrawal from the workforce.

Minerva Studio/Shutterstock.com

would shape that person's career. In other words, if the managerial competence anchor was most important to you, you would seek out jobs that allowed you to rise up in an organization, while if your primary career anchor was technical-functional competence, you would try to become good at a particular type of work (for example, accounting) without being driven by the need to be a manager. In Schein's later research, he noted that there were eight career anchors: the five mentioned above, plus (6) Sense of service; (7) Pure challenge; and (8) Freedom to organize oneself around one's private life.

Career anchors emerge over time and may be modified by work or life experiences. The importance of knowing your career anchor is that it can help you find a match between you and an organization. For example, individuals with creativity as an anchor may find themselves stifled in bureaucratic organizations. Textbook sales may not be the place for an individual with a security anchor because of the frequent travel and seasonal nature of the business.

STUDY TOOLS 17

LOCATED AT BACK OF THE TEXTBOOK
☐ Rip out chapter review card

LOCATED AT WWW.CENGAGE.COM/LOGIN
☐ Gain unique perspectives on key concepts with new Concept Clip videos in the e-book
☐ Review key term flashcards and create your own
☐ Increase your comprehension with online homework and quizzes

18 | Managing Change

LEARNING OBJECTIVES

18-1 Identify the major external and internal forces for change in organizations.

18-2 Describe how different types of change vary in scope.

18-3 Discuss methods organizations can use to manage resistance to change.

18-4 Explain Lewin's organizational change model.

18-5 Explain how companies determine the need to conduct an organization development intervention.

18-6 Discuss the major group-focused techniques for organization development intervention.

18-7 Discuss the major individual-focused techniques for organization development intervention.

After finishing this chapter go to **PAGE 327** for **STUDY TOOLS**

18-1 FORCES FOR CHANGE IN ORGANIZATIONS

Change has become the norm in most organizations. Many American companies have experienced plant closings, failures, mergers and acquisitions, and downsizing. *Adaptiveness, flexibility,* and *responsiveness* are characteristics of organizations that will succeed in meeting the competitive challenges that businesses face.[1] In the past, organizations could succeed by claiming excellence in one area—quality, reliability, or cost, for example—but this is not the case today. The current environment demands excellence in all areas and vigilant leaders. A recent survey of CEOs who were facing crises found that 50 percent of them said they believed problems arrived "suddenly" and that they had not prepared adequately for them. More than 10 percent said they were, in fact, the last to know about problems.[2]

As we saw in Chapter 1, change is what's on managers' minds. The pursuit of organizational effectiveness through downsizing, restructuring, reengineering, productivity management, cycle-time reduction, and other efforts is paramount. Organizations are in a state of tremendous turmoil and transition, and all members are affected. Continued downsizings may have left firms leaner but not necessarily richer. Though downsizing can increase shareholder value by better aligning costs with revenues, firms may suffer from public criticism for their actions. Laying off employees may be accompanied by increases in CEO pay and stock options, linking the misery of employees with the financial success of owners and management.[3]

Organizations must also deal with ethical, environmental, and other social issues. Competition is fierce, and companies can no longer afford to rest on their laurels. Understanding this situation, American Airlines has developed a series of programs to constantly reevaluate and change its operating methods to prevent the company from stagnating. General Electric holds off-site WorkOut sessions with groups of managers and employees, with the goal of making GE a faster, less complex

> **Organizations are in a state of tremendous turmoil and transition, and all members are affected.**

organization that can respond effectively to change. In the WorkOut sessions, employees recommend specific changes, explain why they are needed, and propose ways the changes can be implemented. Top management must make an immediate response: an approval, a disapproval (with an explanation), or a request for more information. The GE WorkOut sessions eliminate the barriers that keep employees from contributing to change.

There are two basic forms of change in organizations. **Planned change** results from a deliberate

> **planned change** Change resulting from a deliberate decision to alter the organization.

> The workforce will be more culturally diverse as a result of globalization and changing U.S. demographics, such as the dramatic rise in the participation of Hispanic Americans.

decision to alter the organization. For example, companies that wish to move from a traditional hierarchical structure to one that facilitates self-managed teams must use a proactive, carefully orchestrated approach. **Unplanned change** is imposed on the organization and is often unforeseen. Changes in government regulations and changes in the economy are two examples. Responsiveness to unplanned change requires tremendous flexibility and adaptability on the part of organizations. Managers must be prepared to handle both planned and unplanned forms of change in organizations.

Forces for change can come from many sources. Some of these are external, arising from outside the company, whereas others are internal, arising from sources within the organization.

18-1a External Forces

The four major managerial challenges described throughout the book are major external forces for change: globalization, workforce diversity, technological change, and managing ethical behavior.

GLOBALIZATION The power players in the global market are the organizations that can capitalize on emerging markets throughout the world. The prime example is China, which has become the second largest economy in the world. Western firms like Nestlé, Procter & Gamble, and Kentucky Fried Chicken are all trying to pick up market share in China. Companies that understand what makes Chinese culture unique are finding success while others, who ignore these elements, are not. Home Depot, for example, has struggled in China because it did not understand that most Chinese people do not have places to store tools and typ-

unplanned change
Change that is imposed on the organization and is often unforeseen.

ically hire people to work on their homes rather than doing it themselves. In addition to differences in consumers, companies must negotiate different legal requirements, as the Chinese government is still writing the rule of business.[4] Because global business implicitly involves multiple governments and legal systems, it carries unique risks not found by firms competing within a single nation.

The United States is but one nation in the drive to open new markets. Japan and Germany are responding to global competition in sufficient ways, and the emergence of the European Union as a powerful trading group will have a profound impact on world markets. By joining with their European neighbors, companies in smaller countries will begin to make major progress in world markets, thus increasing the fierce competition that already exists.

These changes, among others, have led companies to rethink the borders of their markets and to encourage their employees to think globally. Jack Welch, former CEO of GE, was among the first to call for a *borderless company*, in which there are no mental distinctions between domestic and foreign operations or between managers and employees.[5] GE has locations in 160 countries across the globe and has become a truly multinational corporation. The thought that drives the borderless company is that barriers interfere with people working together and should be removed. Globalizing an organization means rethinking the most efficient ways to use resources, disseminate and gather information, and develop people. It requires not only structural changes but also changes in the minds of employees. You may think of Costco, the big box retailer, solely as a North American company. But in reality, Costco has more than 500 outlets in the United States, Canada, Mexico, Britain, South Korea, and Japan. Its expansion into Australia has been a big success, with plans to open more stores. Although Wal-Mart has considered expansion into Australia, so far it has no presence there, which bodes well for Costco.[6]

WORKFORCE DIVERSITY Related to globalization is the challenge of workforce diversity. As we have seen throughout this book, workforce diversity is a powerful force for change in organizations. Women's participation in the workforce has climbed steadily, and the proportion of women with college degrees has quadrupled since 1970.[7] Women earn more than half of bachelor's degrees, master's degrees, and doctorates. Currently, the U.S. labor force is 47 percent female.[8] Second, the workforce will be increasingly more culturally diverse as a result of globalization and changing U.S. demographics such as the dramatic rise in the participation of Hispanic Americans. Third, as the workforce ages, there will be fewer young workers and more older workers.

Warby Parker—A Brand Made on the Internet

The popular eyewear brand Warby Parker started on the Internet, and the company's success has looked easy. But according to co-CEOs Dave Gilboa and Neil Blumenthal, it is actually painstaking and deliberate. They

have produced disruptive change in the eyewear industry by being carefully focused on execution and brand. By designing and making their own frames, sold to consumers on the Internet for as little as $95, they have taken a bite out of the luxury eyewear business. Warby Parker has moved into the retail market by opening 70 million stores. They rigorously test their customers' experiences—it's how they learned to install full-length mirrors in their stores instead of the small ones eyewear stores usually use. The company has also opened its first optical lab. Instead of sending glasses to third parties to install the lenses, the company will streamline the experience by doing it themselves, meaning customers get faster delivery. And, for each pair of glasses sold, the company partners with nonprofits to distribute a pair to someone in need. Warby Parker is a company that has changed the way consumers think about buying eyewear.

SOURCES: https://news.fastcompany.com/warby-parker-opens-its-first-optical-lab-streamlining-its-operations-4028556; https://www.warbyparker.com/history.

The global workforce is also diversifying.[9] Following a high-profile bribery scandal (during which many top executives resigned), Siemens, the 160-year-old German technology and equipment firm, moved to represent better the diversity of its customers. Siemens hired a chief diversity officer who has since launched several programs focusing on mentoring and increasing diversity in the company's previously all-male managerial ranks. The percentage of women in management at Siemens globally has nearly doubled since 2002 to 15.6.[10]

TECHNOLOGICAL CHANGE Rapid technological innovation is another force for change in organizations, and those who fail to keep pace can quickly fall behind. Technology has enabled the mobile payment market to become competitive. The major players in the market, Google Wallet, PayPal, and Apple Pay, are hoping that consumers will ditch their wallets in favor of cell phones. But retailers are less excited about investing in the technologies.[11] Merchants will have to install new technologies to take advantage of mobile pay, and consumers worry about cyber theft and payment hacks. Apple Pay, the newest of the players, is building its list of participating merchants; however, its use is limited to the newest iPhones (6 or 6 Plus) and leaves out consumers who have earlier versions.

Credit cards underwent a similar change recently. Magnetic strip cards were replaced with EMV cards, which have a chip that reduces the possibility of fraud. Merchants had to replace their existing credit card terminals with new ones, which made mobile pay businesses happy because the new terminals also accommodated mobile pay applications.[12]

Technological innovations bring about profound change within organizations because the innovation process promotes associated changes in work relationships and organizational structures.[13] The team approach adopted by many organizations leads to flatter structures, decentralized decision making, and more open communication between leaders and team members.

MANAGING ETHICAL BEHAVIOR Recent scandals have brought ethical behavior in organizations to the forefront of public consciousness. Ethical issues, however, are not always public and monumental. Employees face ethical dilemmas in their daily work lives. The need to manage daily ethical behavior has brought about several changes in organizations, most centering around the idea that an organization must create a culture that encourages ethical behavior.

Can Wells Fargo Change Its (Un)Ethical Culture?

Wells Fargo has faced a rash of scandals involving ethics. First, its retail bankers created more than two million fake bank and credit-card accounts, resulting in a $185 million fine and costing CEO John Stumpf his job. The company's culture was a pressure cooker and bonuses were based on new accounts opened. The transgression delivered a strong hit to the bank's reputation, and 5,300 employees were terminated as a result of the scandal.

Next, Wells Fargo was sued for changing borrowers' mortgage agreements without their consent. Although the intent of the changes might have been to help bankrupt borrowers, the moves were fishy. The bank lowered borrowers' monthly payments but also extended the years on the loans, meaning the total interest increased, without the consent of the borrower or the bankruptcy courts. The company is denying the charges.

The sad irony is that Wells Fargo espouses the value of an ethical culture. Terminating employees may not be enough; the company may have to dig much deeper into its culture and change it, if it can be changed. After regulators imposed stiff fines on the company, Wells Fargo adopted a

jetcityimage/Getty Images

Is Wells Fargo stuck in the mud because of its ethical scandals?

new advertising campaign, "Wells Fargo Re-established 2018." Time will tell whether the company can change its culture and salvage its reputation.

SOURCES: C. Cancialosi, "Wells Fargo and the True Cost of Culture Gone Wrong," *Forbes*, September 15 (2016), accessed at https://www.forbes.com/sites/chriscancialosi/2016/09/15/wells-fargo-and-the-true-cost-of-culture-gone-wrong/2/#10c4d1af42ec; A. Currie, "Oops, Wells Fargo Did It Again," *New York Times*, June 15 (2017), accessed at https://www.nytimes.com/2017/06/15/business/dealbook/wells-fargo-mortgage-home-loan.html?_r=0. J.B. Stewart, "Punishing Wells Fargo: Just Deserts, or Beating a Dead Horse?" The New York Times, April 19 (2018).

All public companies issue annual financial reports; Gap Inc. has gone a step further by issuing an annual ethical report. The clothing industry is almost synonymous with the use of sweatshops, but what sets Gap apart is its candid admission that none of its 3,000 suppliers fully complies with the firm's ethical code of conduct. Rather than retreat from these problems, Gap chose to work with its suppliers to improve conditions overseas. The Vendor Engagement & Monitoring team at Gap Inc. includes more than thirty people located in twelve countries, monitoring working conditions in the factories that do not participate in the Better Work Program.[14] The annual report includes extensive descriptions of workers' activities, including which factories were monitored, violations that were found, and which factories are no longer used by Gap because of the violations. It also addresses media reports critical of Gap and its operations.

Gap tries to improve worker conditions by providing training and encouraging suppliers to develop their own conduct codes. For example, in China it has encouraged lunchtime sessions in which workers are advised of their rights. While most facilities respond positively to these efforts, some don't, and Gap pulled its business from 136 factories it concluded were not going to improve. It also terminated contracts with two factories that had verified use of child labor. Gap's approach to overseas labor offers a model for other garment firms.[15]

Society expects organizations to maintain ethical behavior both internally and in relationships with other organizations, as well as with customers, the environment, and society. These expectations may be informal, or they may come in the form of increased regulation. In addition to the pressure from societal expectations, legal developments, changing stakeholder expectations, and shifting consumer demands can also lead to change.[16] And some companies change simply because others are changing.[17] Other powerful forces for change originate from within the organization.

18-1b Internal Forces

Pressures for change that originate inside the organization are generally recognizable by symptoms such as declining effectiveness. A company that experiences its third quarterly loss within a fiscal year undoubtedly experiences a pressure for change. Some companies react by instituting layoffs and massive cost-cutting programs, whereas others look at the bigger picture, view the loss as symptomatic of an underlying problem, and seek out its cause.

A crisis may also stimulate change in an organization. Strikes or walkouts may lead management to change the wage structure. The resignation of a key decision maker may cause the company to rethink the composition of its management team and its role in the organization.

Changes in employee expectations can trigger change in organizations as well. A company that hires a group of young newcomers may find that their expectations are very different from those of older workers. One reason for changed expectations is that the workforce is more educated than ever before. Although this has its advantages, workers with more education demand more of employers. Furthermore, today's workers are concerned with career and family balance issues, such as dependent care. And the many sources of workforce diversity hold potential for a host of other differing expectations among employees.

Still another pressure is a change in the work climate that produces a workforce that is lethargic, unmotivated, and dissatisfied. Such symptoms are common in organizations that have experienced layoffs. Workers who have escaped a layoff may grieve for those who have lost their jobs and may find it difficult to continue to be productive. They may fear that they will be laid off as well, and many feel insecure in their jobs.

Transformational change occurred when Orville and Wilbur Wright gave up their bicycle business to concentrate on building flying transportation.

 THE SCOPE OF CHANGE

Change can be of a relatively small scope, such as a modification in a work procedure (an **incremental change**). Such changes are a fine-tuning of the organization. For example, Intel and other chip producers must continually upgrade their manufacturing equipment just to stay competitive. Intel's conversion of an Arizona fab (a chip-making plant) from older to newer technology cost $3 billion.[18] While radical change is more exciting and interesting to discuss, most organizational change—and therefore most research on organizational change—has focused on evolutionary (incremental) rather than revolutionary change.[19] Change can also be on a larger scale, such as the restructuring of an organization (a **strategic change**).[20] In strategic change, the organization moves from an old state to a known new state during a controlled period of time. Sometimes strategic changes work; sometimes they don't. YouTube was a startup that was acquired by Google for $1.65 billion, and Google altered YouTube's strategy by going after premium content providers such as ABC, NBC, and CBS. In addition, a partner program was launched that allowed popular users to share in the advertising revenue their videos generated. This change in strategy has not worked, however. Although it now has one billion viewers, YouTube has yet to become profitable. Some say that a new strategy is needed that focuses on attracting a broader audience beyond young people.[21]

The most massive scope of change is **transformational change**, in which the organization moves to a radically different, and sometimes unknown, future state.[22] In transformational change, the organization's mission, culture, goals, structure, and leadership may all change dramatically.[23] Just over a century ago, two successful bicycle makers decided to leave the safety of their business to devote time to building and selling an amazing new invention—the airplane—which transformed travel, warfare, and communications around the world. The Wright brothers transformed not only their bike business but the whole world! Of all the tasks a leader undertakes, many say that changing the form and nature of the organization itself may be the most difficult, an observation supported by research.[24]

incremental change
Change of a relatively small scope, such as making small improvements.

strategic change Change of a larger scale, such as organizational restructuring.

transformational change Change in which the organization moves to a radically different, and sometimes unknown, future state.

One of the toughest decisions faced by leaders is the proper pace of change. Some scholars argue that rapid change is more likely to succeed than slower change because it creates momentum,[25] while others argue that these short, sharp changes are actually rare and not experienced by most firms.[26] Still others observe that change in a large organization may occur incrementally in some parts of the firm and quickly in others.[27] In summary, researchers agree that the pace of change is important, but they can't quite agree on which pace of change is most beneficial.

One thing that both researchers and managers alike can agree on is the increasing volatility, interconnection, and uncertainty in business. These changes demand that leaders understand what it takes to lead in a fast-paced and ever-changing world. Complexity leadership means leading both people and organizations so that they handle complex changes with adaptability and resilience.[28]

18-2a The Change Agent's Role

The individual or group that introduces and manages change in an organization is known as the **change agent**. Change agents can be internal, such as managers or employees who are appointed to oversee the change process. In her book *The Change Masters*, Rosabeth Moss Kanter notes that at companies like Hewlett-Packard and Polaroid, managers and employees alike are developing the needed skills to produce change and innovation in the organization.[29]

Internal change agents have certain advantages in managing the change process. First, they know the organization's history, its political system, and its culture. Then, because they must live with the results of their change efforts, internal change agents are likely to be very careful about managing change. There are disadvantages, however, to using internal change agents. They may be associated with certain factions within the organization, be accused of favoritism, or be too close to the situation to have an objective view of what needs to be done.

Change leaders within organizations tend to be young, between twenty-five and forty. A high number of change leaders are women. Also, change agents are more flexible than ordinary general managers and much more people oriented. Using a balance of technical and interpersonal skills, they are tough decision makers who focus on performance results. Plus, they know how to energize people and get them aligned in the same direction. In addition, they

have the ability to operate in more than one leadership style and can shift from a team mode to command and control, depending on the situation. Finally, change agents are comfortable with uncertainty.[30]

If change is large scale or strategic in nature, it may require a team of leaders with a variety of skills, expertise, and influence that can work together harmoniously.[31]

External change agents bring an outsider's objective view to the organization. They may be preferred by employees because of their impartiality. External change agents face certain problems, however. Not only is their knowledge of the organization's history limited, but they may also be viewed with suspicion by organization members. External change agents have more power in directing changes if employees perceive them as being trustworthy, possessing important expertise, having a track record that establishes credibility, and being similar to them.[32]

Different change agent competencies are required at different stages of the change process. Leadership, communication, training, and participation have varying levels of impact as the change proceeds, meaning change agents must be flexible in how they work through the different phases of the process.[33] Effective change leaders build strong relationships within their leadership team, between the team and organizational members, and between the team and key environmental players. Maintaining all three relationships simultaneously is quite difficult, so successful leaders are continually coupling and uncoupling with the different groups as the change process proceeds. Adaptability is a key skill for both internal and external change leaders.[34]

18-3 RESISTANCE TO CHANGE

People often resist change in a rational response based on self-interest. However, there are countless other reasons people resist change. Many of these center around the notion of *reactance*—that is, a negative reaction that occurs when individuals feel that their personal freedom is threatened.[35] Let us take a look at some expressions of reactance and then at some ways of dealing with it.

18-3a Major Reasons People Resist Change

Common reasons people resist change include fear of the unknown, fear of loss, fear of failure, fear of disruption of interpersonal relationships, personality factors, politics, and cultural assumptions and values.

change agent
The individual or group that undertakes the task of introducing and managing a change in an organization.

"My profession has probably been transformed again just since we started this session."

FEAR OF THE UNKNOWN Change often brings with it substantial uncertainty. Employees facing a technological change may resist the change simply because it introduces ambiguity into what was once a comfortable situation for them.

FEAR OF LOSS Some employees may fear losing their jobs with impending change, especially when an advanced technology like robotics is introduced. Employees may also fear losing their status because of change.[36] Computer systems experts, for example, may feel that their expertise will be less appreciated when a more user-friendly networked information system is installed. Another common fear is that changes may diminish the positive qualities the individual enjoys in the job. Computerizing the customer service positions at Southwestern Bell (now part of SBC Communications), for example, threatened the autonomy that representatives previously enjoyed.

FEAR OF FAILURE Some employees fear changes because they fear their own failure as a result of those changes. They may question their competence to deal with changes that might mean increased workloads or increased task difficulty. They may also fear that performance expectations will be elevated following the change and that they might not measure up.[37]

Resistance can also stem from the fear that change will not really take place. In other words, there can be fear of failure on the part of the organization, not the individual. In one large library that was undergoing a major automation effort, employees were doubtful that the vendor could deliver the state-of-the-art system that was promised. In this case, the implementation never became a reality; the employees' fears were well founded.[38]

FEAR OF DISRUPTION OF INTERPERSONAL RELATIONSHIPS Employees may resist change that threatens to limit meaningful interpersonal relationships on the job. Librarians facing the automation effort feared that once the computerized system was implemented, they would not be able to interact as they did when they had to go to another floor of the library to get help finding a resource.

PERSONALITY Individuals with an internal locus of control, high growth needs, strong motivation, and a positive outlook are more likely to embrace changes at work.[39] Personality conflicts may impact workers' acceptance of change. A change agent who appears insensitive to employees' concerns and feelings may meet considerable resistance from those who feel that their needs are not being taken into account.

POLITICS Organizational change may also shift the existing balance of power in the organization. Individuals or groups empowered under the current arrangement may be threatened with losing these political advantages in the advent of change.

CULTURAL ASSUMPTIONS AND VALUES Sometimes cultural assumptions and values can be impediments to change, particularly if the assumptions underlying the change are alien to employees. Other times, employees might interpret strategic change initiatives from the standpoint of the organization's value system and ideologies of the management team. In fact, research indicates that employees pay attention to the informal sense-making process prevalent in organizations and leading top-down change initiatives to fail.[40] This form of resistance can be very difficult to overcome because some cultural assumptions are unconscious. As discussed in Chapter 2, some cultures tend to avoid uncertainty. In Mexican and Greek cultures, for example, change that creates a great deal of uncertainty may be met with great resistance.

We have described several sources of resistance to change, but the reasons for resistance are as diverse as the workforce itself and vary with different individuals and organizations. The challenge for managers is introducing change in a positive manner and managing employee resistance.

18-3b Managing Resistance and Developing Resilience

The traditional view of managing resistance to change was to treat it as something to be overcome, and many organizational attempts to reduce the resistance have only served to intensify it. The contemporary view holds that resistance is simply a form of feedback and that this feedback can be used very productively to manage the change process. When individuals, teams, or organizations are not ready for change, it is an opportunity to gather important diagnostic information that can be used to identify weaknesses in the organization's approach to change and to improve the process.[41] In this view, the idea is to manage resistance by planning for it and being ready with a variety of strategies for using the resistance as feedback and helping employees negotiate the transition. Three key strategies for managing resistance to change are communication, participation, and empathy and support.[42]

Communication about impending change is essential if employees are to adjust effectively.[43] The details and, equally important, the rationale of the change should be provided. Accurate and timely information can help prevent unfounded fears and potentially damaging rumors from developing. Conversely, delaying announcements and withholding information can serve to fuel the rumor mill. Open communication in a culture of trust is a key ingredient for successful change.[44] Managers should pay attention to the informal communication networks in an organization because they can serve as power channels for disseminating change-related information.[45] Educating employees on new work procedures and other potential consequences of change is helpful. In addition, both mentors and mentees derive benefits from going

One key strategy for managing resistance to change is open communication.

through the process of organizational change together. Mentees are assisted by mentors who help them make sense of the change, and mentors experience satisfaction in having helped the mentee through the change process. Another key ingredient that can help employees adjust to change is a supervisor whom they can trust. When employees trust their supervisors, it serves as a social support mechanism, and they are more committed to the organization even if they feel they can't control the change process.[46]

There is substantial research support underscoring the importance of *participation* in the change process. Employees must be engaged and involved in order for change to work—as supported by the notion "That which we create, we support." Participation helps employees become involved in the change and establishes a feeling of ownership in the process. Mergers and acquisitions are widely prevalent in the current business environment.

Another strategy for managing resistance is to provide *empathy and support* to employees who have trouble dealing with the change. Active listening is an excellent tool for identifying the reasons behind resistance and for uncovering fears. An expression of concerns about the change can provide important feedback that managers can use to improve the change process. Emotional support and encouragement can help an employee deal with the anxiety that is a natural response to change. Employees who experience severe reactions to change can benefit from talking with a counselor. Some companies provide counseling through their employee assistance plans.

Promoting resilience among employees helps them stay healthy and productive during times of change. Resilience is the ability to use positive skills to remain steady and focused when encountering challenges and adversities. Stressful work environments are health risks, and employees who feel appreciated and supported at work are more resilient. Resilience has a protective effect on sleep, stress, burnout, depression, and productivity during times of change. Many companies offer resilience training because of these benefits.[47] Among the companies that use resilience training are Aetna, IBM, and Goldman Sachs.

18-4 LEWIN'S MODEL FOR MANAGING CHANGE

Kurt Lewin developed a model of the change process that has stood the test of time and continues to influence the way organizations manage planned change.

FIGURE 18.1   FORCE FIELD ANALYSIS OF A DECISION TO ENGAGE IN EXERCISE

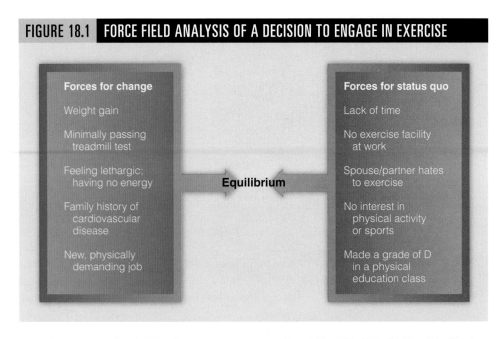

Forces for change

Weight gain

Minimally passing treadmill test

Feeling lethargic; having no energy

Family history of cardiovascular disease

New, physically demanding job

Equilibrium

Forces for status quo

Lack of time

No exercise facility at work

Spouse/partner hates to exercise

No interest in physical activity or sports

Made a grade of D in a physical education class

FIGURE 18.2   LEWIN'S CHANGE MODEL

Unfreezing

Reducing forces for status quo

Moving

Developing new attitudes, values, and behaviors

Refreezing

Reinforcing new attitudes, values, and behaviors

Lewin's model is based on the idea of *force field analysis*.[48] Figure 18.1 shows a force field analysis of a decision to engage in exercise behavior. This model contends that a person's behavior is the product of two opposing forces: one force pushes toward preserving the status quo, and the other force pushes for change. When the two opposing forces are approximately equal, current behavior is maintained. For behavioral change to occur, the forces maintaining the status quo must be overcome. This can be accomplished by increasing the forces for change, by weakening the forces for the status quo, or by a combination of these actions.

Lewin's change model is a three-step process, as shown in Figure 18.2. The process begins with **unfreezing**, which is a crucial first hurdle in the change process. Unfreezing involves encouraging individuals to discard old behaviors by shaking up the equilibrium state that maintains the status quo. Change management literature has long advocated that certain individuals have personalities that make them more resistant to change. However, recent research indicates that only a small portion of a study's respondents

(23 percent) displayed consistency in their reactions to three different kinds of change: structural, technological, and office relocation. The majority of respondents (77 percent) reacted differently to these different kinds of change, suggesting that reactions to change might be more situationally driven than was previously thought.[49] Organizations often accomplish unfreezing by eliminating the rewards for current behavior and showing that current behavior is not valued. In essence, individuals surrender by allowing the boundaries of their status quo to be opened in preparation for change.[50]

The second step in the change process is **moving**. In the moving stage, new attitudes, values, and behaviors are substituted for old ones. Organizations accomplish moving by initiating new options and explaining the rationale for the change, as well as by providing training to help employees develop the new skills they need. Employees should be given the overarching vision for the change so that they can establish their roles within the new organizational structure and processes.[51]

Refreezing is the final step in the change process. In this step, new attitudes, values, and behaviors are established as the new status quo. The new ways of operating are cemented in and reinforced. Managers should ensure that the organizational culture and formal

unfreezing The first step in Lewin's change model, in which individuals are encouraged to discard old behaviors by shaking up the equilibrium state that maintains the status quo.

moving The second step in Lewin's change model, in which new attitudes, values, and behaviors are substituted for old ones.

refreezing The final step in Lewin's change model, in which new attitudes, values, and behaviors are established as the new status quo.

Amazon Keeps Changing

Jeff Bezos founded Amazon on the promise of continuous innovation. Prime, the $119 per year membership option, has grown substantially. Dash buttons let customers reorder household products with a touch. A focus on logistics means that high-tech robots power its latest fulfillment centers. The company is also experimenting with retail—Amazon Go is smartphone-integrated buying, with no lines and no cashiers. Instead, customers walk in, take what they need, and walk out, and their Amazon accounts are billed automatically.

Amazon's acquisition of Whole Foods could mean lower prices and automation similar to that used at Amazon Go. Whole Foods' reputation as a great place to work, with fair pay and a great culture, and sustainable sourcing may clash with the intense, demanding culture

of Amazon. This latest change promises to shake up the U.S. grocery industry.

SOURCES: K. Lightbody, "How Amazon Is Infiltrating the Physical World," *Fast Company*, February 13 (2017), accessed at https://www.fastcompany.com/3067456/most-innovative-companies/amazon-gets-physical; F. Manjoo, "In Whole Foods, Bezos Gets a Sustainably Sourced Guinea Pig," *New York Times*, June 17 (2017), accessed at https://www.nytimes.com/2017/06/17/technology/whole-foods-amazon-jeff-bezos.html.

reward systems encourage the new behaviors. Changes in the reward structure may be needed to ensure that the organization is not rewarding the old behaviors and merely hoping for the new behaviors. A study by Exxon Research and Engineering showed that framing and displaying a mission statement in managers' offices may eventually change the behavior of 2 percent of the managers. In contrast, changing managers' evaluation and reward systems will change the behavior of 55 percent of the managers almost overnight.[52]

The approach used by Monsanto to increase opportunities for women within the company is an illustration of how to use Lewin's model effectively. First, Monsanto emphasized unfreezing by helping employees debunk negative stereotypes about women in business. This also helped overcome resistance to change. Second, Monsanto moved employees' attitudes and behaviors through diversity training in which differences were emphasized as positive, and supervisors learned ways of training and developing female employees. Third, Monsanto changed its reward system so that managers were evaluated and paid according to how they coached and promoted women, which helped refreeze the new attitudes and behaviors.

One frequently overlooked issue is whether or not the change is consistent with the company's deeply held core values. Value consistency is critical to making a change stick. Organizations whose members perceive the changes to be consistent with the firm's values adopt the changes much more easily and fully. Conversely, organizations whose members' values conflict with the changes may display "superficial conformity," in which members pay lip service to the changes but ultimately revert to their old behaviors.[53]

18-5 DETERMINING THE NEED FOR ORGANIZATION DEVELOPMENT INTERVENTIONS

Related to change is the subject of *organization development*, a method that consists of various programs for making organizations more effective. **Organization development (OD)** is defined as a systematic approach to organizational improvement that applies behavioral science theory and research in order to increase individual and organizational well-being and effectiveness.[54] This definition implies certain characteristics. First,

organization development (OD)
A systematic approach to organizational improvement that applies behavioral science theory and research in order to increase individual and organizational well-being and effectiveness.

FIGURE 18.3 **THE ORGANIZATION DEVELOPMENT CYCLE**

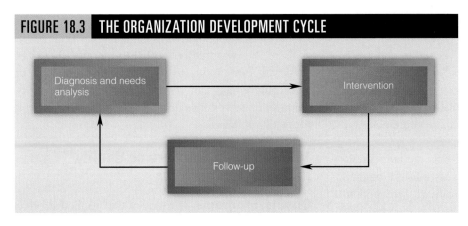

can begin. The first part of the diagnosis involves achieving an understanding of the organization's history. In the second part, the organization as a whole is analyzed to obtain data about its structure and processes. In the third part, interpretive data about attitudes, relationships, and current organizational functioning are gathered. In the fourth part of the diagnosis, the data are analyzed and conclusions are reached. In each stage of the diagnosis, the data can be gathered using a variety of methods, including observation, interviews, questionnaires, and archival records.

A *needs analysis* is another crucial step in managing change. This is an analysis of the skills and competencies that employees must have to achieve the goals of the change. A needs analysis is essential because interventions such as training programs must target these skills and competencies.

Hundreds of alternative OD intervention methods exist. One way of classifying these methods is by the target of change, which can be the organization, groups within the organization, or individuals.

as a systematic approach to planned change, OD is a structured cycle of diagnosing organizational problems and opportunities and then applying expertise to them. Second, OD is grounded in solid research and theory. It involves the application of behavioral science knowledge to the challenges that organizations face. Third, OD recognizes the reciprocal relationship between individuals and organizations. It acknowledges that for organizations to change, individuals must change. Finally, OD is goal oriented. It is a process that seeks to improve both individual and organizational well-being and effectiveness.

Prior to deciding on a method of intervention, managers must carefully diagnose the problem they are attempting to address. Diagnosis and needs analysis is a critical first step in any OD intervention. Following this, an intervention method is chosen and applied. Finally, a thorough follow-up of the OD process is conducted. Figure 18.3 presents the OD cycle, a continuous process of moving the organization and its employees toward effective functioning.

18-5a **Diagnosis and Needs Analysis**

Before any intervention is planned, a thorough organizational diagnosis should be conducted. Diagnosis is an essential first step for any organization development intervention.[55] The term *diagnosis* comes from two Greek words, *dial* (through) and *gnosis* (knowledge). Thus, the diagnosis should pinpoint specific problems and areas in need of improvement. Six areas to examine carefully are the organization's purpose, structure, reward system, support systems, relationships, and leadership.[56]

Harry Levinson's diagnostic approach asserts that the process should begin by identifying where the pain (the problem) in the organization is, what it is like, how long it has been happening, and what has already been done about it.[57] Then a four-part, comprehensive diagnosis

GROUP-FOCUSED TECHNIQUES FOR OD INTERVENTION

Some OD intervention methods emphasize changing the organization itself or changing the work groups within the organization rather than targeting the employees as individuals. Intervention methods in this category include survey feedback, management by objectives, product and service quality programs, team building, and process consultation.

18-6a **Survey Feedback**

Survey feedback is a widely used intervention method whereby employee attitudes are solicited using a questionnaire. Once the data are collected, they are analyzed and fed back to the employees to diagnose problems and plan other interventions. Survey feedback is often used as an exploratory tool and then is combined with some other

> **survey feedback** A widely used intervention method whereby employee attitudes are solicited using a questionnaire.

intervention. The effectiveness of survey feedback in actually improving outcomes (e.g., absenteeism or productivity) increases substantially when this method is combined with other interventions.[58] Furthermore, the effectiveness of this technique is contingent upon trust between management and subordinates, and this can be reinforced through the anonymity and confidentiality of survey responses.

For survey feedback to be an effective method, certain guidelines should be used. Employees must be assured that their responses to the questionnaire will be confidential and anonymous. Feedback should be reported in a group format. Employees must be able to trust that negative repercussions will not result from their responses. Employees should be informed of the purpose of the survey. Failing to do this can set up unrealistic expectations about the changes that might come from the surveys.

In addition, management must be prepared to follow up on the survey results. If some things cannot be changed, the rationale (e.g., prohibitive cost) must be explained to the employees. Without appropriate follow-through, employees will not take the survey process seriously the next time.

18-6b Management by Objectives

As an organization-wide technique, **management by objectives (MBO)** involves joint goal setting between employees and managers. The MBO process includes the setting of initial objectives, periodic progress reviews, and problem solving to remove any obstacles to goal achievement.[59] All these steps are joint efforts between managers and employees.

MBO is a valuable intervention because it meets three needs. First, it clarifies what is expected of employees. This reduces role conflict and ambiguity. Second, MBO provides knowledge of results, an essential ingredient in effective job performance. Finally, MBO provides an opportunity for coaching and counseling by the manager. The problem-solving approach encourages open communication and discussion of obstacles to goal achievement.[60]

Companies that have used MBO successfully include the former Tenneco, Mobil (now part of ExxonMobil), and General Electric. The success of MBO in effecting organizational results hinges on the linking of individual goals to the goals of the organization.[61] MBO programs should be used with caution, however. An excessive emphasis on goal achievement can result in cutthroat competition among employees, falsification of results, and striving for results at any cost.

18-6c Product and Service Quality Programs

Quality programs—programs that embed product and service quality excellence in the organizational culture—are assuming key roles in the organization development efforts of many companies. The success or failure of a service company may hinge on the quality of customer service it provides.[62] Even manufacturing companies need high-quality customer service in addition to high-quality products. Toyota Motor Corporation constantly finds ways to integrate cutting-edge technological innovations with the growing pains of global expansion. The famed Toyota Way of doing business is focused on two key principles: continuous improvement focused on innovation and respect for people.[63]

18-6d Team Building

Team building programs can improve the effectiveness of work groups. Usually they begin with a diagnostic process through which team members identify problems and continue with the team planning actions to resolve those problems. The OD practitioner in team building serves as a facilitator, and the work itself is completed by team members.[64]

Team building is a very popular OD method. A survey of *Fortune* 500 companies indicated that human resource managers considered team building the most successful OD technique.[65] Managers are particularly interested in building teams that can learn. To build *learning teams*, members must be encouraged to seek feedback, discuss errors, reflect on successes and failures, and experiment with new ways of performing. Mistakes should be analyzed for ways to improve, and a climate of mutual support should be developed. Leaders of learning teams are good coaches who promote a climate of psychological safety so that team members feel comfortable discussing problems.[66]

One popular technique for team building is the use of outdoor challenges. Teambuilding, Inc. uses rowing as a team-building exercise. It enlisted the services of an Olympic gold medalist, Dan Lyons, to design a seminar focused

management by objectives (MBO) An organization-wide intervention technique that involves joint goal setting between employees and managers.

quality program A program that embeds product and service quality excellence in the organizational culture.

team building An intervention designed to improve the effectiveness of a work group.

A popular method for team building is the use of outdoor challenges.

on team building using rowing as the central organizing theme. This activity encourages participants to practice leadership, communication, goal setting, conflict management, and motivation. GE Healthcare, ING Direct, and Wyeth Corporate Communications have all used this technique for their team-building programs as well.[67] One of TeamBonding's culinary challenges takes advantage of the popularity of food trucks. In the Food Truck Challenge, teams design the façade of their tabletop food trucks, along with a logo for their aprons.[68] They create recipes, prepare their signature dishes, and market their creations from one of three cuisines: Southwest, All-American, or Tailgater. A panel of judges does a taste test, and then the teams are evaluated on best taste, best presentation, and culinary champion. The objective of the Food Truck Challenge is to improve teamwork through the power of play.

Team building is particularly challenging in virtual teams, in which members rarely if ever meet face-to-face. Normal processes such as conflict management, decision making, and communication of emotions are challenges with which virtual teams may need help. It takes time in virtual teams to build relationships, and interventions that help build trust among the geographically dispersed team members are valuable. Topics such as intercultural teamwork are helpful, and new members of virtual teams can especially benefit from teambuilding training.[69]

18-6e Process Consultation

Pioneered by Edgar Schein, **process consultation** is an OD method that helps managers and employees improve the processes that are used in organizations.[70] The processes most often targeted are communication, conflict resolution, decision making, group interaction, and leadership.

One of the distinguishing features of process consultation is that an outside consultant is used. The role of the consultant is to help employees help themselves. In this way, the ownership of a successful outcome rests with the employees.[71] The consultant guides the organization members in examining the processes in the organization and in refining them. The steps in process consultation are entering the organization, defining the relationship, choosing an approach, gathering data and diagnosing problems, intervening, and gradually leaving the organization.

Process consultation is an interactive technique between employees and an outside consultant, so it is seldom used as a sole OD method. Most often it is used in combination with other OD interventions.

All the preceding OD methods focus on changing the organization or the work group, whereas the following OD methods are aimed at individual change.

INDIVIDUAL-FOCUSED TECHNIQUES FOR OD INTERVENTION

OD efforts that are targeted at individuals include skills training, leadership training and development, executive coaching, role negotiation, job redesign, health promotion programs, and career planning.

18-7a Skills Training

The key question addressed by **skills training** is, "What knowledge, skills, and abilities are necessary to do this job effectively?" Skills training is accomplished either in formal

process consultation An OD method that helps managers and employees improve the processes that are used in organizations.

skills training Increasing the job knowledge, skills, and abilities that are necessary to do a job effectively.

Companies like General Mills are including mindfulness training in their leadership development programs.

classroom settings or on the job. The challenge is integrating skills training into OD in today's rapidly changing organizational environments. The job knowledge in most positions requires continual updates to keep pace with rapid change.

Companies such as Google and Genentech are supplementing their traditional skills training with training in mindfulness skills. At Dow Chemical Company, researchers wondered whether mindfulness skills taught online would have as much impact as mindfulness skills taught in a classroom setting. A group of employees participated in an online mindfulness course, and they were compared to a group of employees who were wait-listed for the training. The employees from the mindfulness online intervention reported decreased stress, better resilience and vigor, more work engagement, and higher overall well-being than those who had not yet completed the training.[72]

18-7b Leadership Training and Development

Companies invest millions of dollars in **leadership training and development**, a term that encompasses a variety of techniques that are designed to enhance individuals' leadership skills. One popular technique is to send future leaders to off-site training classes. Research shows that this type of education experience can have some impact, but participants' enthusiastic return to work may be short-lived due to

leadership training and development A variety of techniques that are designed to enhance individuals' leadership skills.

executive coaching A technique in which managers or executives are paired with a coach in a partnership to help them perform more efficiently.

the challenges and realities of work life. Classroom learning alone thus has a limited effect on leadership skills.

Some leadership training and development programs combine classroom learning with on-the-job experiences. One way of accomplishing development is through the use of *action learning*, a technique that was pioneered in Europe. In action learning, leaders take on unfamiliar problems or familiar problems in unfamiliar settings. The leaders work on the problems and meet weekly in small groups made up of individuals from different organizations. The outcome of action learning is that leaders learn about themselves through the challenges of their comrades. Other techniques that provide action learning for participants are simulation, business games, role-playing, and case studies.[73]

Eli Lilly has an action-learning program that pulls together eighteen future company leaders and gives them a strategic business issue to resolve. For six weeks, the trainees meet with experts, best-practices organizations, and customers, and then present their recommendations to top brass. One action-learning team was charged with coming up with an e-business strategy; their plan was so good that executives immediately implemented it. At Eli Lilly and other firms, action-learning programs provide developmental experiences for leaders and result in useful initiatives for the company.[74]

Companies such as General Mills and Apple are including mindfulness training in their leadership development programs. Google has long done so and integrates mindfulness with emotional intelligence in its training. Mindfulness training benefits the leaders themselves in terms of lower stress, more empathy, and improved well-being. Mindfulness training also has spillover effects for the leaders' employees. When leaders are more mindful, their employees have better job satisfaction and performance, along with improved well-being.[75]

Leadership training and development is an ongoing process that takes considerable time and effort. There are no quick fixes. At IBM, managers are held accountable for leadership development. In fact, IBM's managers will not be considered for promotion into senior executive positions unless they have a record of developing leaders. Top management must be committed to the process of leadership training and development if it wants to create a pipeline of high-potential employees to fill leadership positions.

18-7c Executive Coaching

Executive coaching is a technique in which managers or executives are paired with a coach in a partnership to help the executive perform more efficiently. Although

Keys to Wellness Program Success

Holistic wellness programs such as those at Facebook, Valero Energy, General Mills, and Target focus on the five pillars of well-being: career, social, financial, physical, and community. To maximize the impact of a corporate wellness effort, there are several keys:

- Design an internal marketing campaign and create internal buzz.
- Lead with the benefits, not the activities—increased productivity, resilience, and health.
- Provide an appealing physical space.
- Give explicit permission to use time out of the workday for wellness.
- Make it optional; give employees the power to choose.

Some companies are even moving wellness programs out of human resources and into their sustainability departments, emphasizing that human capital is just as important to sustain as the environment is.

Source: N. Klemp, "Rethinking Wellness at Work," *Conscious Company*, January/February (2017): 41–45.

coaching is usually done in a one-on-one manner, it is sometimes attempted in groups. The popularity of executive coaching has increased dramatically in recent years. The International Coach Federation, a group that trains and accredits executive coaches, doubled its membership in just two years of existence to 7,000 members in thirty-five countries.

Coaching is typically a special investment in top-level managers. Coaches provide another set of eyes and ears and help executives see beyond their own blinders. They elicit solutions and ideas from the client rather than making suggestions. Thus they develop and enhance the talents and capabilities within the client. Many coaching arrangements focus on developing the emotional intelligence of the client executive and may use a 360-degree assessment in which the executive, her boss, peers, subordinates, and even family members rate the executive's emotional competencies.[76] This information is then fed back to the executive, and along with the coach, a development plan is put in place.

Good coaches form strong connections with clients, exhibit professionalism, and deliver forthright, candid feedback. The top reasons executives seek out coaches are to make personal behavior changes, enhance their effectiveness, and foster stronger relationships. Does executive coaching pay off? Evidence suggests that successful coaching can result in sustained changes in executives' behavior, increased self-awareness and understanding, and more effective leadership competencies.[77] In one study, for example, executives who worked with executive coaches were more likely to set specific goals, ask for feedback from their supervisors, and were rated as better performers by their supervisors and subordinates when compared to executives who simply received feedback from surveys.[78] Effective coaching relationships depend on a professional, experienced coach, an executive who is motivated to learn and change, and a good fit between the two.

18-7d Role Negotiation

Individuals who work together sometimes have differing expectations of one another within the working relationship. **Role negotiation** is a technique whereby individuals meet and clarify their psychological contract, that is, their expectations of each other. The outcome of role negotiation is a better understanding between the two parties. When both parties have a mutual agreement on expectations, there is less ambiguity in the process of working together.

18-7e Job Redesign

As an OD intervention method, **job redesign** alters jobs to improve the fit between individual skills and the demands of the job. Chapter 14 outlined several approaches to job design. Many of these methods are used as OD techniques for realigning task demands and individual capabilities or for redesigning jobs to fit new techniques or organizational structures better.

Ford Motor Company has redesigned virtually all of its manufacturing jobs, shifting workers from individual to team-based roles in which they have greater control of their work and can take the initiative to improve products and production techniques. Ford began trying this technique more than a decade ago and found that it not only improved employee job satisfaction but also productivity and product quality.

Another form of job redesign is telecommuting. Companies including American Express, AT&T, and Merrill Lynch have significant numbers of

role negotiation A technique whereby individuals meet and clarify their psychological contract.

job redesign An OD intervention method that alters jobs to improve the fit between individual skills and the demands of the job.

Green Mountain Coffee Roasters offers yoga, meditation and physical therapy programs to reduce stress for their employees.

employees who work this way. During times of change, employees often initiate job redesign efforts themselves. Some request flexible work arrangements such as telecommuting. Others request additional resources to meet their increased workloads, and some ask for additional job challenges to ensure their job survival if they feel their jobs are threatened. Engaging employees in job redesign efforts helps protect their well-being during stressful changes.[79]

18-7f Wellness Programs

As organizations have become increasingly concerned with the costs of stress in the workplace, wellness programs have become a part of larger OD efforts. In Chapter 7, we examined stress and strain at work. To relieve stress and strain, companies such as Levi Strauss and Co., Motley Fool, Chesapeake Energy Co., and Johnson & Johnson have successfully integrated wellness programs into their organizations.

Wellness programs may include on-site fitness centers, smoking cessation and weight-loss programs, nutritional counseling, lunch and healthy snacks, yoga, and massage therapy, along with other options. One health risk that is of increasing concern is lack of sleep. Poor sleep quality and/or lack of sleep increases multiple health risks for employees and affects productivity at work. Companies that invest in employee well-being do so to preserve the health of their employees, and also to reap the benefits of lower healthcare spending, higher productivity, and improved recruiting and retention of employees.[80]

The American Psychological Association recognizes companies for innovative programs that support psychologically healthy work environments. Past winners Green Mountain Coffee Roasters has yoga, meditation, and physical therapy programs to reduce work-related stress and injury. It pays for 90 percent of healthcare costs of its full-time employees. Furthermore, it reimburses each employee up to $400 per year for participation in wellness programs, health club memberships, or smoking cessation programs.[81]

Although companies have long recognized the importance of maintenance on their machinery, many are only recently learning that their human assets need maintenance as well, and they are supplying that need in the form of employee wellness and health promotion activities. These programs focus on helping employees manage their stress and prevent health problems.

18-7g Career Planning

Matching an individual's career aspirations with the opportunities in the organization is career planning. This proactive approach to career management is often part of an organization's development efforts although it is a joint responsibility of organizations and individuals. Certainly career-planning activities benefit both the organization and its individuals. Through counseling sessions, employees identify their skills and skill deficiencies. The organization then can plan its training and development efforts based on this information. In addition, the process can be used to identify and nurture talented employees for potential promotion.

To sum up, managers can choose from a host of organization development techniques to facilitate organizational change. Large-scale changes in organizations require the use of multiple techniques. For example, implementing

> As organizations have become increasingly concerned with the costs of stress in the workplace, health promotion programs have become a part of larger OD efforts.

a new technology like robotics may require simultaneous changes in the structure of the organization, the configuration of work groups, and individual attitudes.

Since organization development is designed to help organizations manage change, it is important to evaluate the effectiveness of these efforts. The success of any OD intervention depends on a host of factors, including the technique used, the competence of the change agent, the organization's readiness for change, and top management commitment. No single method of OD is effective in every instance. Instead, multiple-method OD approaches are recommended because they allow organizations to capitalize on the benefits of several approaches.

Efforts to evaluate OD effects have focused on outcomes such as productivity. One review of more than 200 interventions indicated that worker productivity improved in 87 percent of the cases.[82] We can conclude that when properly applied and managed, organization development programs have positive effects on performance.[83]

STUDY TOOLS 18

LOCATED AT BACK OF THE TEXTBOOK

☐ Rip out chapter review card

LOCATED AT WWW.CENGAGE.COM/LOGIN

☐ Gain unique perspectives on key concepts with new Concept Clip videos in the e-book

☐ Review key term flashcards and create your own

☐ Increase your comprehension with online homework and quizzes

1

1. H. Schwartz, "The Clockwork or the Snakepit: An Essay on the Meaning of Teaching Organizational Behavior," *Organizational Behavior Teaching Review* 11, No. 2 (1987): 19–26.

2. P. Schilpzand, I. E. Depater, and A. Erez, "Workplace Incivility: A Review of the Literature and Agenda for Future Research," *Journal of Organizational Behavior*, early view published Online October 28, 2014.

3. Rath and Strong Management Consultants, "Creating an Energized Organization," http://www.rathstrong.com/whitepaper_creatingenergized.htm, accessed June 27, 2008.

4. H. G. Barkem, J. A. C. Baum, and E. A. Mannix, "Management Challenges in a New Time," *Academy of Management Journal* 45 (2002): 916–930.

5. K. Lewin, "Field Theory in Social Science: Selected Theoretical Papers" (edited by Dorin Cartwright) (New York: Harper, 1951).

6. N. Schmitt, ed., Industrial/Organizational Section in *Encyclopedia of Psychology* (Washington, D.C.: American Psychological Association, and New York: Oxford University Press, 2000).

7. R. E. Poyhart, N. Schmitt, and N. T. Tippins, "Solving the Supreme Problem: 100 years of selection and recruitment at the Journal of Applied Psychology," *Journal of Applied Psychology*, 102 (2017): 291–304.

8. R. Lopopolo, "Development of the Professional Role Behaviors Survey (PROBES)," *Physical Therapy* 81 (July 2001): 1317–1327.

9. F. W. Taylor, *The Principles of Scientific Management* (New York: Norton, 1911).

10. E. A. Locke and G. P. Latham, *A Theory of Goal Setting and Task Performance* (Englewood Cliffs, N.J.: Prentice-Hall, 1990).

11. A. L. Wilkins and W. G. Ouchi, "Efficient Cultures: Exploring the Relationship between Culture and Organizational Performance," *Administrative Science Quarterly* 28 (1983): 468–481.

12. M. F. R. Kets de Vries and D. Miller, "Personality, Culture, and Organization," *Academy of Management Review* 11 (1986): 266–279.

13. H. Schwartz, *Narcissistic Process and Corporate Decay: The Theory of the Organizational Ideal* (New York: NYU Press, 1990).

14. J. G. March and H. A. Simon, *Organizations* (New York: Wiley, 1958).

15. H. B. Elkind, *Preventive Management: Mental Hygiene in Industry* (New York: B. C. Forbes, 1931).

16. J. C. Quick, "Occupational Health Psychology: Historical Roots and Future Directions," *Health Psychology* 18 (1999): 82–88.

17. R. Eby and D. Mahone, "How to Use Ergonomics as a Loss Control Tool," *Risk Management* (March 1, 1991).

18. "Workplace Initiative Reduces Headaches, Neck and Shoulder Pain," *Occupational Health and Safety* (June 10, 2008), http://www.ohsonline.com/articles/64148.

19. B. M. Staw, L. E. Sandelands, and J. E. Dutton, "Threat-Rigidity Effects in Organizational Behavior: A Multilevel Analysis," *Administrative Science Quarterly* 26 (1981): 501–524.

20. D. Kirkpatrick, "The Net Makes It All Easier—Including Exporting U.S. Jobs," *Fortune* (May 26, 2003): 146.

21. C. Crosby, "Quest for Talent Is Driving Evolution in Outsourcing," *Banking Wire* (June 25, 2008): 59.

22. E. V. Brown, Vice President of Global Business Development, Alberto Culver, Inc., "Commencement Address—College of Business Administration, the University of Texas at Arlington" (December 2003).

23. T. Reay, K. Golden-Biddle, and K. Germann, "Legitimizing a New Role: Small Wins and Microprocesses of Change," *Academy of Management Journal* 49 (2006): 977–998.

23a. H. A. Haveman, N. Jia, J. Shi, and Y. Wang, "The Dynamics of Political Embeddedness in China," *Administrative Science Quarterly* 62 (2017): 67–104.

24. R. L. A. Sterba, "The Organization and Management of the Temple Corporations in Ancient Mesopotamia," *Academy of Management Review* 1 (1976): 16–26; S. P. Dorsey, *Early English Churches in America* (New York: Oxford University Press, 1952).

25. Sir I. Moncreiffe of That Ilk, *The Highland Clans: The Dynastic Origins, Chiefs, and Background of the Clans and of Some Other Families Connected to Highland History*, rev. ed. (New York: C. N. Potter, 1982); D. Shambaugh, "The Soldier and the State in China: The Political Work System in the People's Liberation Army," *Chinese Quarterly* 127 (1991): 527–568.

26. L. L' Abate, ed., *Handbook of Developmental Family Psychology and Psychopathology* (New York: Wiley, 1993); J. A. Hostetler, *Communitarian Societies* (New York: Holt, Rinehart & Winston, 1974).

27. J. M. Lewis, "The Family System and Physical Illness," in *No Single Thread: Psychological Health in Family Systems* (New York: Brunner/Mazel, 1976).

28. D. Katz and R. L. Kahn, *The Social Psychology of Organizations*, 2nd ed. (New York: John Wiley, 1978); H. J. Leavitt, "Applied Organizational Change in Industry: Structural, Technological, and Humanistic Approaches," in J. G. March, ed., *Handbook of Organizations* (Chicago: Rand McNally, 1965): 1144–1170.

29. J. D. Thompson, *Organizations in Action* (New York: McGraw-Hill, 1967).

30. M. Malone, "The Twitter Revolution," *The Wall Street Journal* (April 18, 2009): A11.

31. P. E. Queen, "Enlightened Shareholder Maximization: Is This Strategy Achievable?" *Journal of Business Ethics* 127 (2015): 683–694.

31a. A. K. Schnackenberg and E. C. Tomlinson, "Organizational Transparency: A New Perspective on Managing Trust in Organization—Stakeholder Relationships," *Journal of Management*, 42, No. 7 (November 2016): 1753–1783.

32. F. J. Roethlisberger and W. J. Dickson, *Management and the Worker* (Cambridge, Mass.: Harvard University Press, 1939).

33. W. L. French and C. H. Bell, *Organization Development*, 4th ed. (Englewood Cliffs, N.J.: Prentice-Hall, 1990).

34. S. G. Barsade and D. E. Gibson, "Why Does Affect Matter in Organizations?" *Academy of Management Perspectives*, 21 (2007): 36–59.

35. J. P. Kotter, "Managing External Dependence," *Academy of Management Review* 4 (1979): 87–92.

36. H. K. Steensma and D. G. Corley, "Organizational Context as a Moderator of Theories on Firm Boundaries for Technology Sourcing," *Academy of Management Journal* 44 (2001): 271–291.

37. M. Yunus, F. Dalsace, D. Menasce, and B. Faivre-Tavignot, "Reaching the World's Poorest Consumers," *Harvard Business Review* 93 (March 2015): 46–53.

38. T. B. Lawrence and V. Corwin, "Being There: The Acceptance and Marginalization of Part-Time Professional Employees," *Journal of Organizational Behavior* 24 (2003): 923–943.

39. M. K. Gowing, J. D. Kraft, and J. C. Quick, *The New Organizational Reality: Downsizing, Restructuring and Revitalization* (Washington, D.C.: American Psychological Association, 1998); T. Tang and R. M. Fuller, "Corporate Downsizing: What Managers Can Do to Lessen the Negative Effects of Layoffs," *SAM Advanced Management Journal* 60 (1995): 12–15, 31.

40. L. E. Thurow, *Head to Head: The Coming Economic Battle among Japan, Europe, and America* (New York: William Morrow, 1992).

41. S. Ovide, "Microsoft CEO Nadella Hints at Organizational Changes; Chief Asks Top Staff to Simplify Operations; Defends Xbox Business," *Wall Street Journal* (July 10, 2014).

42. B. Dattée and J. Barlow, "Multilevel Organizational Adaptation: Scale Invariance in the Scottish Healthcare System," *Organizational Science*, 28, No. 2 (March–April 2017): 301–319.

43. D. Ciampa, *Total Quality* (Reading, Mass.: Addison-Wesley, 1992).

44. T. J. Douglas and W. Q. Judge Jr., "Total Quality Management Implementation and Competitive Advantage: The Role of Structural Control and Exploration," *Academy of Management Journal* 44 (2001): 158–169.

45. American Management Association, *Blueprints for Service Quality: The Federal Express Approach* (New York: American Management Association, 1991); P. R. Thomas, L. J. Gallace, and K. R. Martin, *Quality Alone Is Not Enough* (New York: American Management Association, 1992).

46. J. de Mast, "A Methodological Comparison of Three Strategies for Quality Improvement," *International Journal of Quality & Reliability Management* 21 (2004): 198–213.

47. M. Barney, "Motorola's Second Generation," *Six Sigma Forum Magazine* 1, No. 3 (May 2002): 13.

48. S. Shahabudin, "Six Sigma: Issues and Problems," *International Journal of Productivity and Quality Management* 3 (2008): 145–160.

49. J. A. Edosomwan, "Six Commandments to Empower Employees for Quality Improvement," *Industrial Engineering* 24 (1992): 14–15.

50. N. T. Duarte, J. R. Goodson, and T. P. Dougherty, "Managing Innovation in Hospitals and Health Systems: Lessons from the Malcolm Baldrige National Quality Award Winners," *Journal of Healthcare Management* 7 (2014): 21–34.

51. G. H. W. Bush, "Remarks at the Presentation Ceremony for the Malcolm Baldrige National Quality Awards" (speech, December 13, 1990).

52. See also the five articles in the Special Research Forum on Teaching Effectiveness in the Organizational Sciences, *The Academy of Management Journal* 40 (1997): 1265–1398.

53. L. Proserpio and D. A. Gioia, "Teaching the Virtual Generation," *Academy of Management Learning & Education* 6 (2007): 69–80.

54. L. W. Porter, G. A. Bigley, and R. M. Steers. *Motivation and Work Behavior*, 7th ed. (Burr Ridge, IL: Irwin/McGraw-Hill, 2003).

55. C. L. Cooper and J. C. Quick, *The Handbook of Stress and Health: A Guide to Research and Practice* (Chichester, UK: Wiley Blackwell, 2017).

56. D. L. Whetzel, "The Department of Labor Identifies Workplace Skills," *Industrial/Organizational Psychologist* 29 (1991): 89–90.

57. D. A. Whetton and K. S. Cameron, *Developing Management Skills,* 3rd ed. (New York: HarperCollins, 1995).

58. E. R. Kemery and L. T. Stickney, "A Multifaced Approach to Teamwork Assessment in an Undergraduate Business Program," *Journal of Management Education* 38 (2014): 462–479.

59. C. Argyris and D. A. Schon, *Organizational Learning: A Theory of Action Perspective* (Reading, Mass.: Addison-Wesley, 1978).

60. A. Y. Kolb and D. A. Kolb, "Learning Styles and Learning Spaces: Enhancing Experiential Learning in Higher Education," *Academy of Management Learning & Education* 4 (2005): 193–212.

2

1. M. A. Hitt, R. D. Ireland, and R. E. Hoskisson, *Strategic Management: Competitiveness & Globalization—Concepts and Cases, 12e* (Mason, OH: CENGAGE Learning, 2017).

2. H. G. Barkem, J. A. C. Baum, and E. A. Mannix, "Management Challenges in a New Time," *Academy of Management Journal* 45 (2002): 916–930.

3. S. C. Harper, "The Challenges Facing CEOs: Past, Present, and Future," *Academy of Management Executive* 6 (1992): 7–25; T. R. Mitchell and W. G. Scott, "America's Problems and Needed Reforms: Confronting the Ethic of Personal Advantage," *Academy of Management Executive* 4 (1990): 23–25.

4. K. Sera, "Corporate Globalization: A New Trend," *Academy of Management Executive* 6 (1992): 89–96.

5. K. Ohmae, *Borderless World: Power and Strategies in the Interlinked Economy* (New York: Harper & Row, 1990).

6. C. A. Bartlett and S. Ghoshal, *Managing across Borders: The Transnational Solution* (Boston: Harvard Business School Press, 1989).

7. F. Warner, "Learning How to Speak to Gen Y," *Fast Company* 72 (July 2003): 36–37.

8. K. R. Xin and J. L. Pearce, "Guanxi: Connections as Substitutes for Formal Institutional Support," *Academy of Management Journal* 39 (1996): 1641–1658.

9. P. S. Chan, "Franchise Management in East Asia," *Academy of Management Executive* 4 (1990): 75–85.

10. H. Weihrich, "Europe 1992: What the Future May Hold," *Academy of Management Executive* 4 (1990): 7–18.

10a. B. Schneider, V. Gonzalez-Roma, C. Ostroff, and M.A. West, "Organizational Climate and Culture: Reflection on the History of the Constructs in the *Journal of Applied Psychology*," *Journal of Applied Psychology* 102, No. 3 (2017): 468–482.

11. E. H. Schein, "Coming to a New Awareness of Organizational Culture," *MIT Sloan Management Review* 25 (1984): 3–16.

12. S. S. Sarwano and R. M. Armstrong, "Microcultural Differences and Perceived Ethical Problems: An International Business Perspective," *Journal of Business Ethics* 30 (2001): 41–56.

13. F. Warner, "Learning How to Speak to Gen Y," *Fast Company* 72 (July 2003): 36–37.

14. R. Sharpe, "Hi-Tech Taboos," *The Wall Street Journal* (October 31, 1995): A1.

15. G. Hofstede, *Culture's Consequences: International Differences in Work-Related Values* (Beverly Hills, Calif.: Sage Publications, 1980); G. Hofstede, "Motivation, Leadership, and Organization: Do American Theories Apply Abroad?" *Organizational Dynamics* (Summer 1980): 42–63.

16. G. M. Spreitzer, M. W. McCall, Jr., and J. D. Mahoney, "Early Identification of International Executive Potential," *Journal of Applied Psychology* 82 (1997): 6–29.

17. M. A. Hitt, L. Bierman, K. Uhlenbruck, and K. Shimizu, "The Importance of Resources in the Internationalization of Professional Service Firms: The Good, the Bad, and the Ugly," *Academy of Management Journal* 49 (2006): 1137–1157.

18. A. J. Michel, "Goodbyes Can Cost Plenty in Europe," *Fortune* (April 6, 1992): 16.

19. G. Hofstede, "Gender Stereotypes and Partner Preferences of Asian Women in Masculine and Feminine Countries," *Journal of Cross Cultural Psychology* 27 (1996): 533–546.

20. G. Hofstede, "Cultural Constraints in Management Theories," *Academy of Management Executive* 7 (1993): 81–94.

21. "IBM Offers Employees New 'Learning Accounts' and Global Training Programs," *InformationWeek* (July 26, 2007).

22. J. Sandberg, "Global-Market Woes Are More Personality Than Nationality," *The Wall Street Journal* (January 29, 2008).

23. L. R. Offerman and M. K. Growing, "Organizations of the Future," *American Psychologist* 45 (1990): 95–108.

24. J. Chatman, J. Polzer, S. Barsade, and M. Neale, "Being Different Yet Feeling Similar: The Influence of Demographic Composition and Organizational Culture on Work Processes and Outcomes," *Administrative Science Quarterly* 43 (1998): 749–780.

25. S. Caudron, "Task Force Report Reveals Coke's Progress on Diversity," *Workforce* 82 (2003): 40, http://www.workforceonline.com/section/03/feature/23/42/44/234246.html.

26. S. Prasso, "Google Goes to India," *Fortune* (October 29, 2007).

27. Women in the Labor Force: A Databook, http://www.bls.gov/opub/reports/cps/women-in-the-labor-force-a-databook-2014.pdf.

28. "Degrees Earned by Women," *Indicator* 27 (2008), http://nces.ed.gov/programs/coe/2008/section3/indicator27.asp.

29. Catalyst, *2007 Catalyst Census of Women Corporate Officers and Top Earners of the Fortune 500*, http://catalyst.org/publication/13/2007-catalyst-census-of-women-corporate-officers-and-top-earners-of-the-fortune-500.

30. "The 2015 NAFE Top 50 Companies for Executive Women," *Working Mother*, http://www.workingmother.com/best-companies/american-express-17.

31. U.S. Department of Labor, "Highlights of Women's Earnings in 2005," Report 995 (September 2006): 33; Catalyst, *Catalyst Census of*

Women Corporate Officers and Top Earners (2001).

32. A. M. Morrison, R. P. White, E. Van Velsor, and the Center for Creative Leadership, *Breaking the Glass Ceiling: Can Women Reach the Top of America's Largest Corporations?* (Reading, Mass.: Addison-Wesley, 1987).

33. Catalyst, "2014 S&P 500 Board Seats Held by Women by Race/Ethnicity," New York: Catalyst, March 17, 2105.

34. R. Soares, H. Foust-Cummings, C. Francoeur, and R. Labelle, *Companies Behaving Responsibly: Gender Diversity on Boards* (New York: Catalyst, 2015).

35. D. L. Nelson and M. A Hitt, "Employed Women and Stress: Implications for Enhancing Women's Mental Health in the Workplace," in D. C. Quick, L. R. Murphy, and J. J. Hurrell, Jr., eds., *Stress and Well Being at Work* (Washington, D. C.: American Psychological Association, 1992): 164–177.

35a. M. Little, V. S. Major, A. S. Hinojosa, and D. L. Nelson, "Professional Image Maintenance: How Women Navigate Pregnancy in the Workplace," *Academy of Management Journal* 58 (2015): 8–37.

36. L. L. Martins and C. K. Parsons, "Effects of Gender Diversity Management on Perceptions of Organizational Attractiveness: The Role of Individual Differences in Attitudes and Beliefs," *Journal of Applied Psychology* 92 (2007): 865–875.

37. A. Eyring and B. A. Stead, "Shattering the Glass Ceiling: Some Successful Corporate Practices," *Journal of Business Ethics* 17 (1998): 245–251.

38. Catalyst, *Advancing Women in Business: The Catalyst Guide* (San Francisco: Jossey-Bass, 1998).

39. Department of Health and Human Services, "A Profile of Older Americans: 2012," http://www.aoa.gov/Aging_Statistics/Profile/2012/docs/2012profile.pdf.

40. W. B. Johnston, "Global Workforce 2000: The New World Labor Market," *Harvard Business Review* 69 (1991): 115–127.

41. S. Needleman, "The Last Office Perk: Getting Paid to Volunteer," *The Wall Street Journal* (April 29, 2008): D1, D5.

42. J. Li, C. W. L. Chu, K. C. K. Lam, and S. Liao, "Age Diversity and Firm Performance in an Emerging Economy," *Human Resource Management* 50, No. 2 (March–April 2011): 247–270.

43. S. E. Jackson and E. B. Alvarez, "Working through Diversity as a Strategic Imperative," in S. E. Jackson, ed., *Diversity in the Workplace: Human Resources Initiatives* (New York: Guilford Press, 1992): 13–36.

44. "Managing Generational Diversity," *HR Magazine* 36 (1991): 91–92.

45. K. Tyler, "The Tethered Generation," *HR Magazine* (May 2007): 41–46.

46. S. R. Rhodes, "Age-Related Differences in Work Attitudes and Behavior: A Review and Conceptual Analysis," *Psychological Bulletin* 93 (1983): 338–367.

47. B. L. Hassell and P. L. Perrewe, "An Examination of Beliefs about Older Workers: Do Stereotypes Still Exist?" *Journal of Organizational Behavior* 16 (1995): 457–468.

48. U.S. Bureau of the Census, *Population Profile of the United States, 1997* (Washington, D.C.: U.S. Government Printing Office, 1997).

49. W. J. Rothwell, "HRD and the Americans with Disabilities Act," *Training and Development Journal* 45 (August 1991): 45–47.

50. J. J. Laabs, "The Golden Arches Provide Golden Opportunities," *Personnel Journal* (July 1991): 52–57.

51. Catalyst. "Quick Take: Lesbian, Gay, Bisexual & Transgender Workplace Issues," *Catalyst*, May 15, 2014.

52. B. A. Everly and J. L. Schwarz, "Predictors of the Adoption of LGBT-Friendly HR Policies," *Human Resource Management* 54 (2015): 367–384.

53. DiversityInc, "The Diversity Top 10 Companies for LGBT Employees," http://www.diversityinc.com/top-10-companies-lgbt-employees/.

54. A. N. Smith and S. V. Simms, "The Impact of Discrimination on Organizations." in A. J. Colella and E. B. King, eds., *Oxford Handbook of Workplace Discrimination* (New York: Oxford University Press, in press).

55. L. Armstrong, "What Men Say behind Closed Doors," *Working Mother* (June–July 2008): 87–90.

56. J. E. Rigdon, "PepsiCo's KFC Scouts for Blacks and Women for Its Top Echelons," *The Wall Street Journal* (November 13, 1991): A1.

57. P. A. Galagan, "Tapping the Power of a Diverse Workforce," *Training and Development Journal* 26 (1991): 38–44.

58. C. L. Holladay, J. L. Knight, D. L. Paige, and M. A. Quinones, "The Influence of Framing on Attitudes toward Diversity Training," *Human Resource Development Quarterly* 14 (2003): 245–263.

59. R. Thomas, "From Affirmative Action to Affirming Diversity," *Harvard Business Review* 68 (1990): 107–117.

60. T. H. Cox, Jr., *Cultural Diversity in Organizations: Theory, Research and Practice* (San Francisco: Berrett-Koehler, 1994).

61. "Business Ethics 100 Best Corporate Citizens 2004," http://www.business-ethics.com/BE100_2004, accessed June 23, 2008.

62. M. R. Fusilier, C. D. Aby, Jr., J. K. Worley, and S. Elliott, "Perceived Seriousness of Business Ethics Issues," *Business and Professional Ethics Journal* 15 (1996): 67–78.

62a. L. Huang and T. A. Paterson, "Group Ethical Voice: Influence of Ethical Leadership and Impact on Ethical Performance" *Journal of Management* 43, No. 4 (April 2017): 1157–1184.

63. J. S. Mill, *Utilitarianism, Liberty, and Representative Government* (London: Dent, 1910).

64. A. Smith, *An Inquiry into the Nature and Causes of the Wealth of Nations,* vol. 10 of The Harvard Classics, ed. C. J. Bullock (New York: P. F. Collier & Son, 1909).

65. A. Smith, *The Theory of Moral Sentiments* (Scotland: Glasgow Edition, 1790).

66. C. Fried, *Right and Wrong* (Cambridge, Mass.: Harvard University Press, 1978).

67. I. Kant, *Groundwork of the Metaphysics of Morals,* trans. H. J. Paton (New York: Harper & Row, 1964).

68. R. C. Solomon, "Corporate Roles, Personal Virtues: Aristotelean Approach to Business Ethics," *Business Ethics Quarterly* 2 (1992): 317–339; R. C. Solomon, *A Better Way to Think about Business: How Personal Integrity Leads to Corporate Success* (New York: Oxford University Press, 1999).

69. J. C. Quick and J. L. Goolsby, "Integrity First: Ethics for Leaders and Followers," *Organizational Dynamics* 42 (2010): 1–7; J. L. Goolsby, D. A. Mack, and J. C. Quick, "Winning by Staying in Bounds: Good Outcomes from Positive Ethics," *Organizational Dynamics* 39 (2010): 248–257.

70. M. Kouchaki and S. D. Desai, "Anxious, Threatened, and Also Unethical: How Anxiety Makes Individuals Feel Threatened and Commit Unethical Acts," *Journal of Applied Psychology* 100 (2015): 360–375.

71. W. Bulkeley, "Email Software Delves into Employees' Contacts," *The Wall Street Journal* (April 21, 2008): B9.

72. D. Kemp, "Employers and AIDS: Dealing with the Psychological and Emotional Issues of AIDS in the Workplace," *American Review of Public Administration* 25 (1995): 263–278.

73. J. J. Koch, "Wells Fargo's and IBM's HIV Policies Help Protect Employees' Rights," *Personnel Journal* (April 1990): 40–48.

74. J. C. Quick and M. A. McFadyen, "Sexual Harassment: Have We Made Any Progress?" *Journal of Occupational Health Psychology*, 22, No. 3 (July 2017).

75. L. F. Fitzgerald, F. Drasgow, C. L. Hulin, M. J. Gelfand, and V. J. Magley, "Antecedents and Consequences of Sexual Harassment in Organizations: A Test of an Integrated Model," *Journal of Applied Psychology* 82 (1997): 578–589.

76. E. Felsenthal, "Rulings Open Way for Sex-Harass Cases," *The Wall Street Journal* (June 29, 1998): A10; S. J. Adler, "Lawyers Advise Concerns to Provide Precise Written Policy to Employees," *The Wall Street Journal* (October 9, 1991): B1.

77. K. T. Schneider, S. Swan, and L. F. Fitzgerald, "Job-Related and Psychological Effects of Sexual Harassment in the Workplace: Empirical Evidence from Two Organizations," *Journal of Applied Psychology* 82 (1997): 401–415.

78. A. M. O'Leary-Kelly, R. L. Paetzold, and R. W. Griffin, "Sexual Harassment as Aggressive Behavior: An Actor-Based Perspective," *Academy of Management Review* 25 (2000): 372–388.

79. L. M. Goldenhar, N. G. Swanson, J. J. Hurrell, Jr., A. Ruder, and J. Deddens, "Stressors and Adverse Outcomes for Female Construction Workers," *Journal of Occupational Health Psychology* 3 (1998): 19–32; C. S. Piotrkowski, "Gender Harassment, Job Satisfaction and Distress among Employed White and Minority Women," *Journal of Occupational Health Psychology* 3 (1998): 33–42.

80. K. Aquino, L. Sheppard, M. B. Watkins, J. O'Reilly, and A. Smith, "Social Sexual Behavior at Work," *Research in Organizational Behavior* 34 (2014): 217–236.

81. R. A. Posthuma, C. P. Maertz, Jr., and J. B. Dworkin, "Procedural Justice's Relationship with Turnover: Explaining Past Inconsistent Findings," *Journal of Organizational Behavior* 28 (2007): 381–398.

82. D. Fields, M. Pang, and C. Chio, "Distributive and Procedural Justice as Predictors of Employee Outcomes in Hong Kong," *Journal of Organizational Behavior* 21 (2000): 547–562.

83. H. L. Laframboise, "Vile Wretches and Public Heroes: The Ethics of Whistleblowing in Government," *Canadian Public Administration* (Spring 1991): 73–78.

84. E. J. Epstein, "Was Snowden's Heist a Foreign Espionage Operation," *Wall Street Journal* (May 10, 2014): A13.

85. L. J. Christensen, A. Mackey, and D. Whetton, "Taking Responsibility for Corporate Social Responsibility: The Role of Leaders in Creating, Implementing, Sustaining, or Avoiding Socially Responsible Firm Behaviors," *The Academy of Management Perspectives* 28 (2014): 164–178.

86. S. Covel, "Tours to Fair-Trade Farms Help Coffee Sellers Spread Word," *The Wall Street Journal* (March 11, 2008): B5.

87. D. B. Turban and D. W. Greening, "Corporate Social Performance and Organizational Attractiveness to Prospective Employees," *Academy of Management Journal* 40 (1996): 658–672.

88. R. Walker, "Sex vs. Ethics," *Fast Company* (June 2008): 74–78.

3

1. K. Lewin, "Formalization and Progress in Psychology," in D. Cartwright, ed., *Field Theory in Social Science* (New York: Harper, 1951).

2. N. S. Endler and D. Magnusson, "Toward an Interactional Psychology of Personality," *Psychological Bulletin* 83 (1976): 956–974.

3. J. R. Terborg, "Interactional Psychology and Research on Human Behavior in Organizations," *Academy of Management Review* 6 (1981): 561–576.

4. C. Spearman, "General Intelligence: Objectively Determined and Measured," *American Journal of Psychology* 15 (1904): 201–293.

5. F. L. Schmidt and J. Hunter, "General Mental Ability in the World of Work: Occupational Attainment and Job Performance," *Journal of Personality and Social Psychology* 86, No. 1 (2004): 162–173; C. Bertua, N. Anderson, and J. F Salgado, "The Predictive Validity of Cognitive Ability Tests: A UK Meta-Analysis," *Journal of Occupational and Organizational Psychology* 78 (2004): 387–409.

6. T. J. Bouchard, Jr., "Twins Reared Together and Apart: What They Tell Us about Human Diversity," in S. W. Fox, ed., *Individuality and Determinism* (New York: Plenum Press, 1984); R. D. Arvey, T. J. Bouchard, Jr., N. L. Segal, and L. M. Abraham, "Job Satisfaction: Environmental and Genetic Components," *Journal of Applied Psychology* 74 (1989): 235–248.

7. G. Allport, *Pattern and Growth in Personality* (New York: Holt, 1961).

8. R. B. Cattell, *Personality and Mood by Questionnaire* (San Francisco: Jossey-Bass, 1973).

9. J. M. Digman, "Personality Structure: Emergence of a Five-Factor Model," *Annual Review of Psychology* 41 (1990): 417–440.

10. T. A. Judge, J. J. Martocchio, and C. J. Thoresen, "Five-Factor Model of Personality and Employee Absence," *Journal of Applied Psychology* 82 (1997): 745–755.

11. H. J. Bernardin, D. K. Cooke, and P. Villanova, "Conscientiousness and Agreeableness as Predictors of Rating Leniency," *Journal of Applied Psychology* 85 (2000): 232–234.

12. K. A. Leger, S. T. Charles, N. A. Turiano, and D. M. Almeida, "Personality and Stressor-Related Affect," *Journal of Personality and Social Psychology* 111 (2016): 917–928.

13. T. A. Judge and R. Ilies, "Relationships of Personality to Performance Motivation: A Meta-Analytic Review," *Journal of Applied Psychology* 87 (2002): 797–807.

14. G. M. Hurtz and J. J. Donovan, "Personality and Job Performance: The Big Five Revisited," *Journal of Applied Psychology* 85 (2000): 869–879.

15. K. A. Byrne, C. D. Silasi-Mansat, and D. A. Worthy. "Who Chokes Under Pressure? The Big Five Personality Traits and Decision-Making Pressure," *Personality and Individual Differences* 74 (2015): 22–28.

16. G. Bozionelos, "The Relationship of the Big Five With Workplace Network Resources: More Quadratic Than Linear," *Personality and Individual Differences* 104 (2017): 374–378.

17. J. F. Salgado, S. Moscoso, and M. Lado, "Evidence of Cross-Cultural Invariance of the Big Five Personality Dimensions in Work Settings," *European Journal of Personality* 17 (2003): S67–S76; C. Rodriguez and T. H. Church, "The Structure and Personality Correlates of Affect in Mexico: Evidence of Cross-Cultural Comparability Using the Spanish Language," *Journal of Cross-Cultural Psychology* 34 (2003): 211–230.

18. H. C. Triandis, "Cultural Influences on Personality," *Annual Review of Psychology* 53 (2002): 133–160.

19. M. Moody, "Adaptive Behavior in Intercultural Environments: The Relationship between Cultural Intelligence Factors and Big Five Personality Traits" (Ph.D. thesis, George Washington University, 2007).

20. M. R. Barrick and M. K. Mount, "The Big Five Personality Dimensions and Job Performance: A Meta-Analysis," *Personnel Psychology* 44 (1991): 1–26.

21. D. D. Clark and R. Hoyle, "A Theoretical Solution to the Problem of Personality-Situational Interaction," *Personality and Individual Differences* 9 (1988): 133–138.

22. D. Byrne and L. J. Schulte, "Personality Dimensions as Predictors of Sexual Behavior," in J. Bancroft, ed., *Annual Review of Sexual Research*, vol. 1 (Philadelphia: Society for the Scientific Study of Sex, 1990).

23. P. Harms, B. Roberts, and D. Wood, "Who Shall Lead? An Integrative Personality Approach to the Study of the Antecedents of Status in Informal Social Organizations," *Journal of Research in Personality* 41 (2007): 689–699.

24. T. A. Judge, E. A. Locke, and C. C. Durham, "The Dispositional Causes of Job Satisfaction: A Core Self-Evaluation Approach," *Research in Organizational Behavior* 19 (1997): 151–188.

25. M. Erez and T. A. Judge, "Relationship of Core Self-Evaluations to Goal Setting, Motivation and Performance," *Journal of Applied Psychology* 86 (2001): 1270–1279; R. F. Piccolo, T. A. Judge, K. Takahashi, N. Watanabe, and E. A Locke, "Core Self-Evaluations in Japan: Relative Effects on Job Satisfaction, Life Satisfaction, and Happiness," *Journal of Organizational Behavior* 26, No. 8 (2005): 965–984.

26. J. B. Rotter, "Generalized Expectancies for Internal vs. External Control of Reinforcement," *Psychological Monographs* 80, No. 609 (1966).

27. S. Aryee, F. O. Walumbwa, R. Mondejar, and C. W. L. Chu, "Core Self-Evaluations and Employee Voice Behavior: Test of a Dual-Motivational Pathway," *Journal of Management* 43 (2017): 946–966.

28. T. A. Judge and J. E. Bono, "Relationship of Core Self-Evaluations Traits—Self-Esteem, Generalized Self-Efficacy, Locus of Control, and Emotional Stability—With Job Satisfaction and Job Performance: A Meta-Analysis," *Journal of Applied Psychology* 86 (2001): 80–92.

29. Ibid.

30. S. S. K. Lam and J. Shaubroeck, "The Role of Locus of Control in Reactions to Being Promoted and to Being Passed Over: A Quasi Experiment," *Academy of Management Journal* 43 (2000): 66–78.

31. G. Chen, S. M. Gully, J. Whiteman, and R. N. Kilcullen, "Examination of Relationships among Trait-Like Individual Differences, State-Like Individual Differences, and Learning Performance," *Journal of Applied Psychology* 85 (2000): 835–847; G. Chen, S. M. Gully, and D. Eden, "Validation of a New General Self-Efficacy Scale," *Organizational Research Methods* 4 (2001): 62–83.

32. A. Bandura, *Self-Efficacy: The Exercise of Control* (San Francisco: Freeman, 1997).

33. D. R. Avery, "Personality as a Predictor of the Value of Voice," *Journal of Psychology* 137 (2003): 435–447.

34. T. A. Judge and J. E. Bono, "Relationship of Core Self-Evaluations Traits—Self-Esteem, Generalized Self-Efficacy, Locus of Control, and Emotional Stability—With Job Satisfaction and Job Performance: A Meta-Analysis," *Journal of Applied Psychology* 86 (2001): 80–92.

35. B. W. Pelham and W. B. Swann, Jr., "From Self-Conceptions to Self-Worth: On the Sources and Structure of Global Self-Esteem," *Journal of Personality and Social Psychology* 57 (1989): 672–680.

36. A. H. Baumgardner, C. M. Kaufman, and P. E. Levy, "Regulating Affect Interpersonally: When Low Esteem Leads to Greater Enhancement," *Journal of Personality and Social Psychology* 56 (1989): 907–921.

37. J. Schimel, T. Pyszczynski, J. Arndt, and J. Greenberg, "Being Accepted for Who We Are: Evidence That Social Validation of the Intrinsic Self Reduces General Defensiveness," *Journal of Personality and Social Psychology* 80 (2001): 35–52.

38. P. Tharenou and P. Harker, "Moderating Influences of Self-Esteem on Relationships between Job Complexity, Performance, and Satisfaction," *Journal of Applied Psychology* 69 (1984): 623–632.

39. R. A. Ellis and M. S. Taylor, "Role of Self-Esteem within the Job Search Process," *Journal of Applied Psychology* 68 (1983): 632–640.

40. J. Brockner and T. Hess, "Self-Esteem and Task Performance in Quality Circles," *Academy of Management Journal* 29 (1986): 617–623.

41. B. R. Schlenker, M. F. Weingold, and J. R. Hallam, "Self-Serving Attributions in Social Context: Effects of Self-Esteem and Social Pressure," *Journal of Personality and Social Psychology* 57 (1990): 855–863.

42. M. K. Duffy, J. D. Shaw, and E. M. Stark, "Performance and Satisfaction in Conflicted Interdependent Groups: When and How Does Self-Esteem Make a Difference?" *Academy of Management Journal* 43 (2000): 772–782.

43. T. Mussweiler, S. Gabriel, and G. V. Bodenhausen, "Shifting Social Identities as a Strategy for Deflecting Threatening Social Comparisons," *Journal of Personality and Social Psychology* 79 (2000): 398–409.

44. M. Snyder and S. Gangestad, "On the Nature of Self-Monitoring: Matters of Assessment, Matters of Validity," *Journal of Psychology and Social Psychology* 51 (1986): 125–139.

45. G. Toegel, N. Anand, and M. Kilduff, "Emotion Helpers: The Role of High Positive Affectivity and High Self-Monitoring Managers," *Personnel Psychology* 60, No. 2 (2007): 337–365.

46. A. Mehra, M. Kilduff, and D. J. Brass, "The Social Networks of High and Low Self-Monitors: Implications for Workplace Performance," *Administrative Science Quarterly* 46 (2001): 121–146.

47. W. H. Turnley and M. C. Bolino, "Achieving Desired Images while Avoiding Undesired Images: Exploring the Role of Self-Monitoring in Impression Management," *Journal of Applied Psychology* 86 (2001): 351–360.

48. M. Kilduff and D. V. Day, "Do Chameleons Get Ahead? The Effects of Self-Monitoring on Managerial Careers," *Academy of Management Journal* 37 (1994): 1047–1060.

49. A. H. Church, "Managerial Self-Awareness in High-Performing Individuals in Organizations," *Journal of Applied Psychology* 82 (1997): 281–292.

50. C. Douglas and W. L. Gardner, "Transition to Self-Directed Work Teams: Implications of Transition Time and Self-Monitoring for Managers' Use of Influence Tactics," *Journal of Organizational Behavior* 25 (2004): 45–67.

51. A. M. Isen and R. A. Baron, "Positive Affect and Organizational Behavior," in B. M. Staw and L. L. Cummings, eds., *Research in Organizational Behavior*, vol. 12 (Greenwich, Conn.: JAI Press, 1990).

52. D. Watson and L. A. Clark, "Negative Affectivity: The Disposition to Experience Aversive Emotional States," *Psychological Bulletin* 96 (1984): 465–490.

53. R. Ilies and T. Judge, "On the Heritability of Job Satisfaction: The Mediating Role of Personality," *Journal of Applied Psychology* 88 (2003): 750–759.

54. J. M. George, "State or Trait," *Journal of Applied Psychology* 76 (1991): 299–307.

55. J. M. George, "Mood and Absence," *Journal of Applied Psychology* 74 (1989): 287–324.

56. S. Lyubormirsky, L. King, and L. E. Diener, "The Benefits of Frequent Positive Affect: Does Happiness Lead to Success?" *Psychological Bulletin* 131, No. 6 (2005): 803–855.

57. S. Barsade, A. Ward, J. Turner, and J. Sonnenfeld, "To Your Heart's Content: A Model of Affective Diversity in Top Management Teams," *Administrative Science Quarterly* 45 (2000): 802–836.

58. J. M. Crant, "The Proactive Personality Scale and Objective Job Performance among Real Estate Agents," *Journal of Applied Psychology* 80 (1995): 532–537.

59. T. W. H. Ng, L. T. Eby, K. L. Sorensen, and D. C. Feldman, "Predictors of Objective and Subjective Career Success: A Meta Analysis," *Personnel Psychology* 58 (2005): 367–408; D. J. Brown, R. T. Cober, K. Kane, P. E. Levey, and J. Shalhoop, "Proactive Personality and the Successful Job Search: A Field Investigation with College Graduates," *Journal of Applied Psychology* 91 (2006): 717–726.

60. J. M. Crant and T. S. Bateman, "Charismatic Leadership Viewed from Above: The Impact of Proactive Personality," *Journal of Organizational Behavior* 21 (2000): 63–75.

61. H. Rorschach, *Psychodiagnostics* (Bern: Hans Huber, 1921).

62. C. G. Jung, *Psychological Types* (New York: Harcourt & Brace, 1923).

63. Consulting Psychologists Press, http://www.cpp.com/products/mbti/index.asp, accessed June 30, 2008.

64. R. Benfari and J. Knox, *Understanding Your Management Style* (Lexington, Mass.: Lexington Books, 1991).

65. O. Kroeger and J. M. Thuesen, *Type Talk* (New York: Delacorte Press, 1988).

66. S. Hirsch and J. Kummerow, *Life Types* (New York: Warner Books, 1989).

67. I. B. Myers and M. H. McCaulley, *Manual: A Guide to the Development and Use of the Myers-Briggs Type Indicator* (Palo Alto, Calif.: Consulting Psychologists Press, 1990).

68. G. P. Macdaid, M. H. McCaulley, and R. I. Kainz, *Myers-Briggs Type Indicator: Atlas of Type Tables* (Gainesville, Fla.: Center for Application of Psychological Type, 1987).

69. J. B. Murray, "Review of Research on the Myers-Briggs Type Indicator," *Perceptual and Motor Skills* 70 (1990): 1187–1202; J. G. Carlson, "Recent Assessment of the Myers-Briggs Type Indicator," *Journal of Personality Assessment* 49 (1985): 356–365.

70. A. Thomas, M. Benne, M. Marr, E. Thomas, and R. Hume, "The Evidence Remains Stable: The MBTI Predicts Attraction and Attrition in an Engineering Program," *Journal of Psychological Type* 55 (2000): 35–42.

71. C. Walck, "Training for Participative Management: Implications for Psychological Type," *Journal of Psychological Type* 21 (1991): 3–12.

72. G. Lawrence and C. Martin, *Building People, Building Programs: A Practitioner's Guide for Introducing the MBTI to Individuals and Organizations* (Center for Applications of Psychological Type, 2001); L. Berens, L. Ernst, M. Smith, *Quick Guide to the 16 Personality Types and Teams: Applying Team Essentials™ to Create Effective Teams* (Denbighshire, UK, Telos Publications, 2004).

73. J. Michael, "Using the Myers-Briggs Indicator as a Tool for Leadership Development: Apply with Caution," *Journal of Leadership & Organizational Studies* 10 (2003): 68–78.

74. E. C. Webster, *The Employment Interview: A Social Judgment Process* (Schomberg, Canada: SIP, 1982).

75. L. M. Little, V. S. Major, A. S. Hinojosa, and D. L. Nelson, "Professional Image Maintenance: How Women Navigate Pregnancy in the Workplace," *Academy of Management Journal* 58 (2015): 8–37.

76. N. Adler, *International Dimensions of Organizational Behavior*, 2nd ed. (Boston: PWS-Kent, 1991).

77. L. R. Offerman and M. K. Gowing, "Personnel Selection in the Future: The Impact of Changing Demographics and the Nature of Work," in Schmitt, Borman & Associates, eds., *Personnel Selection in Organizations* (San Francisco: Jossey-Bass, 1993).

78. H. G. Halvorson, "Managing Yourself: A Second Chance to Make the Right Impression," *Harvard Business Review* 98 (2015, January–February): 108–111.

79. J. Park and M. R. Banaji, "Mood and Heuristics: The Influence of Happy and Sad States on Sensitivity and Bias in Stereotyping," *Journal of Personality and Social Psychology* 78 (2000): 1005–1023.

80. M. W. Levine and J. M. Shefner, *Fundamentals of Sensation and Perception* (Reading, Mass.: Addison-Wesley, 1981).

81. R. L. Dipboye, H. L. Fromkin, and K. Willback, "Relative Importance of Applicant Sex, Attractiveness, and Scholastic Standing in Evaluations of Job Applicant Resumes," *Journal of Applied Psychology* 60 (1975): 39–43; I. H. Frieze, J. E. Olson, and J. Russell, "Attractiveness and Income for Men and Women in Management," *Journal of Applied Social Psychology* 21 (1991): 1039–1057.

82. P. Ekman and W. Friesen, *Unmasking the Face* (Englewood Cliffs, N.J.: Prentice-Hall, 1975).

83. J. E. Rehfeld, "What Working for a Japanese Company Taught Me," *Harvard Business Review* 68 (November–December 1990): 167–176.

84. M. W. Morris and R. P. Larrick, "When One Cause Casts Doubt on Another: A Normative Analysis of Discounting in Causal Attribution," *Psychological Review* 102 (1995): 331–355.

85. G. B. Sechrist and C. Stangor, "Perceived Consensus Influences Intergroup Behavior and Stereotype Accessibility," *Journal of Personality and Psychology* 80 (2001): 645–654; A. Lyons and Y. Kashima, "How Are Stereotypes Maintained through Communication? The Influence of Stereotype Sharedness," *Journal of Personality and Social Psychology* 85 (2003): 989–1005.

86. S. P. King and F. B. Bryant, "The Workplace Intergenerational Climate Scale (WICS): A Self-Report Instrument Measuring Ageism in the Workplace," *Journal of Organizational Behavior* 38 (2017): 124–151.

87. A. Feingold, "Gender Differences in Effects of Physical Attractiveness on Romantic Attraction: A Comparison across Five Research Paradigms," *Journal of Personality and Social Psychology* 59 (1990): 981–993.

88. M. Snyder, "When Belief Creates Reality," *Advances in Experimental Social Psychology* 18 (1984): 247–305.

89. M. Biernat, "Toward a Broader View of Social Stereotyping," *American Psychologist* 58 (2003): 1019–1027.

90. E. Burnstein and Y. Schul, "The Informational Basis of Social Judgments: Operations in Forming an Impression of Another Person," *Journal of Experimental Social Psychology* 18 (1982): 217–234.

91. T. DeGroot and S. Motowidlo, "Why Visual and Vocal Cues Can Affect Interviewers' Judgments and Predict Job Performance," *Journal of Applied Psychology* 84 (1999): 986–993; M. C. L. Greene and L. Mathieson, *The Voice and Its Disorders* (London: Whurr, 1989).

92. R. L. Gross and S. E. Brodt, "How Assumptions of Consensus Undermine Decision Making," *MIT Sloan Management Review* 42 (Winter 2001): 86–94.

93. R. Rosenthal and L. Jacobson, *Pygmalion in the Classroom: Teacher Expectations and Pupils' Intellectual Development* (New York: Holt, Rinehart & Winston, 1968).

94. D. Eden, "Pygmalion without Interpersonal Contrast Effects: Whole Groups Gain from Raising Manager Expectations," *Journal of Applied Psychology* 75 (1990): 394–398.

95. R. A. Giacalone and P. Rosenfeld, eds., *Impression Management in Organizations* (Hillsdale, N.J.: Erlbaum, 1990); J. Tedeschi and V. Melburg, "Impression Management and Influence in the Organization," in S. Bacharach and E. Lawler, eds., *Research in the Sociology of Organizations* (Greenwich, Conn.: JAI Press, 1984): 31–58.

96. A. Colella and A. Varma, "The Impact of Subordinate Disability on Leader–Member Exchange Relationships," *Academy of Management Journal* 44 (2001): 304–315.

97. D. H. M. Chng, M. S. Rodgers, E. Shih, and X. Song, "Leaders' Impression Management during Organizational Decline: The Roles of Publicity, Image Concerns, and Incentive Compensation," *The Leadership Quarterly*, published online January 2015.

98. S. Bozzolan, C. H. Cho, and G. Michelon, "Impression Management and Organizational Audiences: The Fiat Group Case," *Journal of Business Ethics* 126(2015): 143-165.

99. R. A. Baron, "Impression Management by Applicants during Employment Interviews: The 'Too Much of a Good Thing' Effect," in R. W. Eder and G. R. Ferris, eds., *The Employment Interview: Theory, Research, and Practice* (Newbury Park, Calif.: Sage Publications, 1989).

100. F. Heider, *The Psychology of Interpersonal Relations* (New York: Wiley, 1958).

101. S. Graham and V. Folkes, *Attribution Theory: Applications to Achievement, Mental Health, and Interpersonal Conflict* (Hillsdale: L. Erlbaum and Associates, 1990).

102. P. D. Sweeney, K. Anderson, and S. Bailey, "Attributional Style in Depression: A Meta-Analytic Review," *Journal of Personality and Social Psychology* 51 (1986): 974–991.

103. P. Rosenthal, D. Guest, and R. Peccei, "Gender Differences in Managers' Causal Explanations for Their Work Performance," *Journal of Occupational and Organizational Psychology* 69 (1996): 145–151.

104. J. Silvester, "Spoken Attributions and Candidate Success in Graduate Recruitment Interviews," *Journal of Occupational and Organizational Psychology* 70 (1997): 61–71.

105. L. Ross, "The Intuitive Psychologist and His Shortcomings: Distortions in the Attribution Process," in L. Berkowitz, ed., *Advances in Experimental Social Psychology* (New York: Academic Press, 1977); M. O'Sullivan, "The Fundamental Attribution Error in Detecting Deception: The Boy-Who-Cried-Wolf Effect," *Personality & Social Psychology Bulletin* 29 (2003): 1316–1327.

106. D. T. Miller and M. Ross, "Self-Serving Biases in the Attribution of Causality: Fact or Fiction?" *Psychological Bulletin* 82 (1975): 313–325.

107. J. R. Schermerhorn, Jr., "Team Development for High-Performance Management," *Training and Development Journal* 40 (1986): 38–41.

108. J. G. Miller, "Culture and the Development of Everyday Causal Explanation," *Journal of Personality and Social Psychology* 46 (1984): 961–978.

109. G. Si, S. Rethorst, and K. Willimczik, "Causal Attribution Perception in Sports Achievement: A Cross-Cultural Study on Attributional Concepts in Germany and China," *Journal of Cross-Cultural Psychology* 26 (1995): 537–553.

4

1. A. H. Eagly and S. Chaiken, *The Psychology of Attitudes* (Orlando, Fla.: Harcourt Brace Jovanovich, 1993).

2. M. Pounds, "Bring Positive Attitude to the Workplace Using Praise," in *South Florida Sun-Sentinel* (Fort Lauderdale, FL) (September 27, 2007), http://infotrac-college.thomson-learning.com, accessed July 2, 2008.

3. M. J. Rosenberg, C. I. Hovland, W. J. McGuire, R. P. Abelson, and J. H. Brehm, *Attitude Organization and Change* (New Haven, Conn.: Yale University Press, 1960).

4. L. Festinger, *A Theory of Cognitive Dissonance* (Evanston, Ill.: Row, Peterson, 1957).

5. R. H. Fazio and M. P. Zanna, "On the Predictive Validity of Attitudes: The Roles of Direct Experience and Confidence," *Journal of Personality* 46 (1978): 228–243.

6. A. Tversky and D. Kahneman, "Judgment under Uncertainty: Heuristics and Biases," in D. Kahneman, P. Slovic, and A. Tversky, eds., *Judgment under Uncertainty* (New York: Cambridge University Press, 1982): 3–20.

7. A. Bandura, *Social Learning Theory* (Englewood Cliffs, N.J.: Prentice-Hall, 1977).

8. I. Ajzen and M. Fishbein, "Attitude–Behavior Relations: A Theoretical Analysis and Review of Empirical Research," *Psychological Bulletin* 84 (1977): 888–918.

9. B. T. Johnson and A. H. Eagly, "Effects of Involvement on Persuasion: A Meta-Analysis," *Psychological Bulletin* 106 (1989): 290–314.

10. K. G. DeBono and M. Snyder, "Acting on One's Attitudes: The Role of History of Choosing Situations," *Personality and Social Psychology Bulletin* 21 (1995): 629–636.

11. I. Ajzen and M. Fishbein, *Understanding Attitudes and Predicting Social Behavior* (Englewood Cliffs, N.J.: Prentice-Hall, 1980).

12. I. Ajzen, "From Intentions to Action: A Theory of Planned Behavior," in J. Kuhl and J. Beckmann, eds., *Action-Control: From Cognition to Behavior* (Heidelberg: Springer, 1985).

13. I. Ajzen, "The Theory of Planned Behavior," *Organizational Behavior and Human Decision Processes* 50 (1991): 1–33.

14. A. Sagie and M. Krausz, "What Aspects of the Job Have Most Effect on Nurses?" *Human Resource Management Journal* 13 (2003): 46–62.

15. J. Kettle, "Factors Affecting Job Satisfaction in the Registered Nurse," *Journal of Undergraduate Nursing Scholarship*, http://juns.nursing.arizona.edu/Default.htm, accessed July 1, 2008.

16. C. P. Parker, B. B. Baltes, S. A. Young, J. W. Huff, R. A. Altman, H. A. LaCost, and J. E. Roberts, "Relationships between Psychological Climate Perceptions and Work Outcomes: A Meta-Analytic Review," *Journal of Organizational Behavior* 24 (2003): 389–416.

17. E. A. Locke, "The Nature and Causes of Job Satisfaction," in M. Dunnette, ed., *Handbook of Industrial and Organizational Psychology* (Chicago: Rand McNally, 1976).

18. P. C. Smith, L. M. Kendall, and C. L. Hulin, *The Measurement of Satisfaction in Work and Retirement* (Skokie, Ill.: Rand McNally, 1969).

19. R. Ilies and T. A. Judge, "On the Heritability of Job Satisfaction: The Mediating Role of Personality," *Journal of Applied Psychology* 88 (2003): 750–759.

20. T. A. Judge, R. F. Piccolo, N. P. Podsakoff, J. C. Shaw, and B. Rich, "The Relationship between Pay and Job Satisfaction: A Meta-Analysis of the Literature," *Journal of Vocational Behavior* 77 (2010): 157–167.

21. D. J. Weiss, R. V. Davis, G. W. England, and L. H. Lofquist, *Manual for the Minnesota Satisfaction Questionnaire* (Minneapolis: Industrial Relations Center, University of Minnesota, 1967).

22. C. D. Fisher, "Why Do Lay People Believe that Satisfaction and Performance Are Correlated? Possible Sources of a Commonsense Theory," *Journal of Organizational Behavior* 24 (2003): 753–777.

23. T. A. Judge, H. M. Weiss, J. D. Kammeyer-Mueller, and C. L. Hulin, "Job Attitudes, Job Satisfaction, and Job Affect: A Century of Continuity and Change," *Journal of Applied Psychology* (in press). Epub online January 26, 2017.

24. L. A. Bettencourt, K. P. Gwinner, and M. L. Meuter, "A Comparison of Attitude, Personality, and Knowledge Predictors of Service-Oriented Organizational Citizenship Behaviors," *Journal of Applied Psychology* 86 (2001): 29–41.

25. D. W. Organ, *Organizational Citizenship Behavior: The Good Soldier Syndrome* (Lexington, Mass.: Lexington Books, 1988).

26. P. M. Podsakoff, S. B. Mackenzie, and C. Hui, "Organizational Citizenship Behaviors and Managerial Evaluations of Employee Performance: A Review and Suggestions for Future Research," in G. Ferris, ed., *Research in Personnel and Human Resources Management* (Greenwich, Conn.: JAI Press, 1993): 1–40.

27. C. F. Lam, W. Wan, and C. J. Roussin, "Going the Extra Mile and Feeling Energized: An Enrichment Perspective of Organizational Citizenship Behaviors," *Journal of Applied Psychology*, 101 (2016): 379–391.

28. W. H. Bommer, E. W. Miles, and S. L. Grover, "Does One Good Turn Deserve Another? Coworker Influences on Employee Citizenship," *Journal of Organizational Behavior* 24 (2003): 181–196.

29. J. P. Trougakos, D. J. Beal, B. H. Cheng, I. Hideg, and D. Zweig, "Too Drained to Help: A Resource Depletion Perspective on Daily Interpersonal Citizenship Behaviors," *Journal of Applied Psychology* 100 (2015): 227–236.

30. M. C. Bolino, H. Hsiung, J. Harvey, and J. A. LePine, "Well, I'm Tired of Tryin! Organizational Citizenship Behavior and Citizen Fatigue," *Journal of Applied Psychology* 100 (2015): 56–74.

31. C. Ostroff, "The Relationship between Satisfaction, Attitudes and Performance: An Organizational Level Analysis," *Journal of Applied Psychology* 77 (1992): 963–974.

32. R. Griffin and T. Bateman, "Job Satisfaction and Organizational Commitment," in C. Cooper and I. Robertson, eds., *International Review of Industrial and Organizational Psychology* (New York: Wiley, 1986).

33. A. R. Wheeler, V. C. Gallagher, R. L. Brouer, and C. J. Sablynski, "When Person-Organization (Mis)Fit and (Dis)Satisfaction Lead to Turnover: The Moderating Role of Perceived Job Mobility," *Journal of Managerial Psychology* 22, No. 2 (2007): 203–219.

34. X. Huang and E. Van De Vliert, "Where Intrinsic Job Satisfaction Fails to Work: National Moderators of Intrinsic Motivation," *Journal of Organizational Behavior* 24 (2003): 133–250.

35. L. Sun, S. Aryee, and K. S. Law, "High-Performance Human Resource Practices, Citizenship Behavior, and Organizational Performance: A Relational Perspective," *Academy of Management Journal* 50 (2007): 558–577.

36. N. C. Carpenter and C. M. Berry, "Are Counterproductive Work Behavior and Withdrawal Empirically Distinct? A Meta-Analytic Investigation," *Journal of Management*, 43 (2017): 834–863.

37. J. C. Palmer, M. Komarraju, M. Z. Carter, and S. J. Karau, "Angel on One Shoulder: Can Perceived Organizational Support Moderate the Relationship Between the Dark Triad Traits and Counterproductive Work Behavior?" *Personality and Individual Differences*, 110 (2017): 31–37.

38. R. T. Mowday, L. W. Porter, and R. M. Steers, *Employee–Organization Linkages: The Psychology of Commitment* (New York: Academic Press, 1982).

39. N. Allen and J. Meyer, "Affective, Continuance, and Normative Commitment to the Organization: An Examination of Construct Validity," *Journal of Vocational Behavior* 49 (1996): 252–276.

40. J. P. Meyer, N. J. Allen, and C. A. Smith, "Commitment to Organizations and Occupations: Extension and Test of a Three-Component Model," *Journal of Applied Psychology* 78 (1993): 538–551.

41. J. P. Curry, D. S. Wakefield, J. L. Price, and C. W. Mueller, "On the Causal Ordering of Job Satisfaction and Organizational Commitment," *Academy of Management Journal* 29 (1986): 847–858; T. N. Bauer, T. Bodner, B. Erdogan, D. M. Truxillo, and J. S. Tucker, "Newcomer Adjustment during Organizational Socialization: A Meta-Analytic Review of Antecedents, Outcomes, and Methods," *Journal of Applied Psychology* 92 (2007): 707–721.

42. B. Benkhoff, "Ignoring Commitment Is Costly: New Approaches Establish the Missing Link between Commitment and Performance," *Human Relations* 50 (1997): 701–726; N. J. Allen and J. P. Meyer, "Affective, Continuance, and Normative Commitment to the Organization: An Examination of Construct Validity," *Journal of Vocational Behavior* 49 (1996): 252–276.

43. M. J. Somers, "Organizational Commitment, Turnover, and Absenteeism: An Examination of Direct and Interaction Effects," *Journal of Organizational Behavior* 16 (1995): 49–58; L. Lum, J. Kervin, K. Clark, F. Reid, and W. Sirola, "Explaining Nursing Turnover Intent: Job Satisfaction, Pay Satisfaction, or Organizational Commitment?" *Journal of Organizational Behavior* 19 (1998): 305–320.

44. F. Stinglhamber and C. Vandenberghe, "Organizations and Supervisors as Sources of Support and Targets of Commitment," *Journal of Organizational Behavior* 24 (2003): 251–270.

45. R. Eisenberger, S. Armeli, B. Rexwinkel, P. D. Lynch, and L. Rhoades, "Reciprocation of Perceived Organizational Support," *Journal of Applied Psychology* 86 (2001): 42–51; J. E. Finegan, "The Impact of Person and Organizational Values on Organizational Commitment," *Journal of Occupational and Organizational Psychology* 73 (2000): 149–169.

46. E. Snape and T. Redman, "Too Old or Too Young? The Impact of Perceived Age Discrimination," *Human Resource Management Journal* 13 (2003): 78–89.

47. J. A. Conger, "The Necessary Art of Persuasion," *Harvard Business Review* 76 (1998): 84–96.

48. J. Cooper and R. T. Croyle, "Attitudes and Attitude Change," *Annual Review of Psychology* 35 (1984): 395–426.

49. B. Martin, D. Wentzel, and T. Tomczak, "Effects of Susceptibility to Normative Influence and Type of Testimonial on Attitudes toward Print Advertising," *Journal of Advertising* (Spring 2008), http://infotrac-college.thomsonlearning.com, accessed July 2, 2009.

50. D. M. Mackie and L. T. Worth, "Processing Deficits and the Mediation of Positive Affect in Persuasion," *Journal of Personality and Social Psychology* 57 (1989): 27–40.

51. J. W. Brehm, *Responses to Loss of Freedom: A Theory of Psychological Reactance* (New York: General Learning Press, 1972).

52. D. DeSteno, R. E. Petty, and D. D. Rucker, "Discrete Emotions and Persuasion: The Role of Emotion-Induced Expectancies," *Journal of Personality & Social Psychology* 86 (2004): 43–56.

53. R. Petty, D. T. Wegener, and L. R. Fabrigar, "Attitudes and Attitude Change," *Annual Review of Psychology* 48 (1997): 609–647.

54. P. Brinol and R. E. Petty, "Overt Head Movements and Persuasion: A Self-Validation Analysis," *Journal of Personality and Social Psychology* 84 (2003): 1123–1139.

55. W. Wood, "Attitude Change: Persuasion and Social Influence," *Annual Review of Psychology* 51 (2000): 539–570.

56. A. Ortony, G. L. Clore, and A. Collins, *The Cognitive Structure of Emotions* (Cambridge, England: Cambridge University Press, 1988).

57. R. S. Lazarus, *Emotion and Adaptation* (New York: Oxford University Press, 1991).

58. X. Hu and S. Kaplan, "Is 'Feeling Good' Good Enough? Differentiating Discrete Positive Emotions at Work," *Journal of Organizational Behavior* 36 (2015): 39–58.

59. P. T. Van Katwyk, S. Fox, P. E. Spector, and E. K. Kelloway, "Using the Job-Related Affective Well-Being Scale to Investigate Affective Responses to Work Stressors," *Journal of Occupational Health Psychology* 52 (2000): 219–230.

60. B. L. Fredrickson, "The Role of Positive Emotions in Positive Psychology: The Broaden-and-Build Theory of Positive Emotions," *American Psychologist* 56 (2001): 218–226.

61. S. S. Kaplan, J. C. Bradley, J. N. Luchman, and D. Haynes, "On the Role of Positive and Negative Affectivity in Job Performance: A Meta-Analytic Investigation," *Journal of Applied Psychology* 94 (2009): 162–178; B. Lawrence and S. L. Robinson, "Ain't Misbehavin: Workplace Deviance as Organizational Resistance," *Journal of Management* 33, No. 3 (2007): 378–394.

62. B. L. Fredrickson and C. Brannigan, "Positive Emotions," in G. Bonnano and T. Mayne, eds., *Emotions: Current Issues and Future Directions* (New York: Guilford Press, 2001): 123–152.

63. D. Watson and L. A. Clark, "Affects Separable and Inseparable: On the Hierarchical Arrangement of Negative Affects," *Journal of Personality and Social Psychology* 62 (1992): 489–505.

64. A. M. Isen and R. A. Baron, "Positive Affect as a Factor in Organizational Behavior," *Research in Organizational Behavior* 13 (1991): 1–53; A. G. Miner and T. M. Glomb, "State Mood, Task Performance, and Behavior at Work: A Within-Persons Approach," *Organizational Behavior and Human Decision Processes* 112 (2010): 43–57.

65. M. Stolarski, K. S. Jankowski, G. Matthews, and J. Kawalerczyk, "Wise Birds Follow Their Clock: The Role of Emotional Intelligence and Morningness-Eveningness in Diurnal Regulation of Mood," *Chronobiology International*, 33 (2016): published online January 2016.

66. S. G. Barsade, "The Ripple Effect: Emotional Contagion and Its Influence on Group Behavior," *Administrative Science Quarterly* 47 (2007): 644–675.

67. J. E. Dutton, P. J. Frost, M. C. Worline, J. M. Lilius, and J. M. Kanov, "Leading in Times of Trauma," *Harvard Business Review* 80 (2002): 54–61.

68. T. A. Stewart, "The Highway of the Mind," *Harvard Business Review* 82 (2004): 116.

69. J. D. Mayer, P. Salovey, and D. R. Caruso, "Emotional Intelligence: Theory, Findings, and Implications," *Psychological Inquiry* 15 (2004): 197–215.

70. H. A. Elfenbein, S. G. Barsade, and N. Eisenkraft, "The Social Perception of Emotional Abilities: Expanding What We Know about Observer Ratings of Emotional Intelligence," *Emotion*, published online February 15, 2015.

71. A. R. Hochschild, *The Managed Heart: Commercialization of Human Feeling* (Berkeley: University of California Press, 1983).

72. A. A. Grandey, "When 'The Show Must Go On': Surface Acting and Deep Acting as Determinants of Emotional Exhaustion and Peer-Rated Service Delivery," *Academy of Management Journal* 46 (2003): 86–96; C. M. Brotherridge and A. A. Grandey, "Emotional Labor and Burnout: Comparing Two Perspectives of 'People Work'," *Journal of Vocational Behavior* 60 (2002): 17–39.

73. F. Navran, "Your Role in Shaping Ethics," *Executive Excellence* 9 (1992): 11–12.

74. K. Labich, "The New Crisis in Business Ethics," *Fortune* (April 20, 1992): 167–176.

75. L. S. Paine, *Value Shift: Why Companies Must Merge Social and Financial Imperatives to Achieve Superior Performance* (New York: McGraw-Hill, 2003).

76. D. B. Turban and D. M. Cable, "Firm Reputation and Applicant Pool Characteristics," *Journal of Organizational Behavior* 24 (2003): 733–751.

77. E. A. Lind, J. Greenberg, K. S. Scott, and T. D. Welchans, "The Winding Road from Employee to Complainant: Situational and Psychological Determinants of Wrongful-Termination Claims," *Administrative Science Quarterly* 45 (2000): 557–590.

78. "Stolen Birthrights; Australia's Aborigines," *The Economist* (US) (February 2, 2008), http://infotrac-college.thomsonlearning.com, accessed July 8, 2008; T. Johnston, "Australia Says 'Sorry' to Aborigines for Mistreatment," *The New York Times* (February 13, 2008), http://www.nytimes.com, accessed July 2, 2008.

79. Miriam Schulman, "Little Brother Is Watching You," Makkula Center for Applied Ethics, http://www.scu.edu/ethics/publications/iie/v9n2/brother.html, accessed July 1, 2008.

80. M. Oneal, P. Callahan, and E. Osnos, "Mattel Recalls 18 Million Toys," *Chicago Tribune* (August 15, 2007), http://www.chicagotribune.com/business/chi-toysaug15,0,7223810.story.

81. M. S. Baucus and D. A. Baucus, "Paying the Piper: An Empirical Examination of Longer-Term Financial Consequences of Illegal Corporate Behavior," *Academy of Management Journal* 40 (1997): 129–151.

82. J. O. Cherrington and D. J. Cherrington, "A Menu of Moral Issues: One Week in the Life of *The Wall Street Journal*," *Journal of Business Ethics* 11 (1992): 255–265.

83. B. L. Flannery and D. R. May, "Environmental Ethical Decision Making in the U.S. Metal-Finishing Industry," *Academy of Management Journal* 43 (2000): 642–662.

84. K. R. Andrews, "Ethics in Practice," *Harvard Business Review* (September–October 1989): 99–104.

85. M. Rokeach, *The Nature of Human Values* (New York: Free Press, 1973).

86. M. Rokeach and S. J. Ball-Rokeach, "Stability and Change in American Value Priorities, 1968–1981," *American Psychologist* 44 (1989): 775–784.

87. S. P. Eisner, "Managing Generation Y," *S.A.M. Advanced Management Journal* 70, No. 4 (2005): 4–15.

88. M. Henderson and D. Thompson, *Values at Work: The Invisible Threads between People, Performance, and Profit* (Auckland, New Zealand: HarperBusiness, 2003).

89. E. C. Ravlin and B. M. Meglino, "Effects of Values on Perception and Decision Making: A Study of Alternative Work Values Measures," *Journal of Applied Psychology* 72 (1987): 666–673.

90. E. C. Ravlin and B. M. Meglino, "The Transitivity of Work Values: Hierarchical Preference Ordering of Socially Desirable Stimuli," *Organizational Behavior and Human Decision Processes* 44 (1989): 494–508.

91. B. M. Meglino, E. C. Ravlin, and C. L. Adkins, "A Work Values Approach to Corporate Culture: A Field Test of the Value Congruence Process and Its Relationship to Individual Outcomes," *Journal of Applied Psychology* 74 (1989): 424–432.

92. T. A. Judge and R. D. Bretz, Jr., "Effects of Work Values on Job Choice Decisions," *Journal of Applied Psychology* 77 (1992): 261–271.

93. R. H. Doktor, "Asian and American CEOs: A Comparative Study," *Organizational Dynamics* 18 (1990): 46–56.

94. R. L. Tung, "Handshakes across the Sea: Cross-Cultural Negotiating for Business Success," *Organizational Dynamics* (Winter 1991): 30–40.

95. C. Gomez, B. L. Kirkman, and D. L. Shapiro, "The Impact of Collectivism and In-Group/Out-Group Membership on the Evaluation Generosity of Team Members," *Academy of Management Journal* 43 (2000): 1097–1106; J. Zhou and J. J. Martocchio, "Chinese and American Managers' Compensation Award Decisions: A Comparative Policy-Capturing Study," *Personnel Psychology* 54 (2001): 115–145.

96. A. J. Ali and M. Amirshahi, "The Iranian Manager: Work Values and Orientations," *Journal of Business Ethics* 40 (2002): 133–143.

97. R. Neale and R. Mindel, "Rigging Up Multicultural Teamworking," *Personnel Management* (January 1992): 27–30.

98. J. B. Rotter, "Generalized Expectancies for Internal versus External Control of Reinforcement," *Psychological Monographs* 80 (1966): 1–28.

99. L. K. Trevino and S. A. Youngblood, "Bad Apples in Bad Barrels: A Causal Analysis of Ethical Decision-Making Behavior," *Journal of Applied Psychology* 75 (1990): 378–385.

100. H. M. Lefcourt, *Locus of Control: Current Trends in Theory and Research,* 2nd ed. (Hillsdale, N.J.: Erlbaum, 1982).

101. N. Machiavelli, *The Prince,* trans. George Bull (Middlesex, England: Penguin Books, 1961).

102. R. Christie and F. L. Geis, *Studies in Machiavellianism* (New York: Academic Press, 1970).

103. R. A. Giacalone and S. B. Knouse, "Justifying Wrongful Employee Behavior: The Role of Personality in Organizational Sabotage," *Journal of Business Ethics* 9 (1990): 55–61.

104. S. B. Knouse and R. A. Giacalone, "Ethical Decision Making in Business: Behavioral Issues and Concerns," *Journal of Business Ethics* 11 (1992): 369–377.

105. L. Kohlberg, "Stage and Sequence: The Cognitive Developmental Approach to Socialization," in D. A. Goslin, ed., *Handbook of Socialization Theory and Research* (Chicago: Rand McNally, 1969): 347–480.

106. C. I. Malinowski and C. P. Smith, "Moral Reasoning and Moral Conduct: An Investigation Prompted by Kohlberg's Theory," *Journal of Personality and Social Psychology* 49 (1985): 1016–1027; M. Brabeck, "Ethical Characteristics of Whistleblowers," *Journal of Research in Personality* 18 (1984): 41–53; W. Y. Penn and B. D. Collier, "Current Research in Moral Development as a Decision Support System," *Journal of Business Ethics* 4 (1985): 131–136; L. K. Trevino and S. A. Youngblood, "Bad Apples in Bad Barrels: A Causal Analysis of Ethical Decision-Making Behavior," *Journal of Applied Psychology* 75 (1990): 378–385.

107. C. Gilligan, *In a Different Voice: Psychological Theory and Women's Development* (Cambridge, Mass.: Harvard University Press, 1982).

108. S. Jaffee and J. S. Hyde, "Gender Differences in Moral Orientation: A Meta-Analysis," *Psychological Bulletin* 126 (2000): 703–726.

109. G. R. Franke, D. F. Crown, and D. F. Spake, "Gender Differences in Ethical Perceptions of Business Practices: A Social Role Theory Perspective," *Journal of Applied Psychology* 82 (1997): 920–934.

5

1. R. Kanfer, M. Frese, and R. E. Johnson, "Motivation Related to Work," *Journal of Applied Psychology* 102, No. 3 (March 2017): 338–355.

2. J. P. Campbell and R. D. Pritchard, "Motivation Theory in Industrial and Organizational Psychology," in M. D. Dunnette, ed., *Handbook of Industrial and Organizational Psychology* (Chicago: Rand McNally, 1976): 63–130.

3. M. Weber, *The Protestant Ethic and the Spirit of Capitalism* (London: Talcott Parson, tr., 1930).

4. S. Freud, *Civilization and Its Discontents,* trans. and ed. J. Strachey (New York: Norton, 1961).

5. J. C. Quick, A. McFadyen, and D. L. Nelson, 2014, "No Accident: Health, Well-Being, and Performance at Work." *Journal of Organizational Effectiveness: People & Performance* 1 No. 1 (2014): 98–119.

6. T. A. Judge, L. S. Simon, C. Hurst, and K. Kelley, "What I Experienced Yesterday Is Who I Am Today: Relationship of Work Motivations and Behaviors to Within-Individual Variation in the Five-Factor Model of Personality," *Journal of Applied Psychology* 99 (2014): 199–221.

7. A. Smith, *An Inquiry into the Nature and Causes of the Wealth of Nations,* Vol. 10 of *The Harvard Classics,* C. J. Bullock, ed. (New York: Collier, 1909).

8. J. Jennings, *Less Is More: How Great Companies Use Productivity as a Competitive Tool in Business* (New York: Portfolio, 2002).

9. F. W. Taylor, *The Principles of Scientific Management* (New York: Norton, 1911).

10. Hearings before Special Committee of the House of Representatives to Investigate the Taylor and Other Systems of Shop Management under Authority of House Resolution 90, Vol. 3, 1377–1508 contains Taylor's testimony before the committee from Thursday, January 25, through Tuesday, January 30, 1912.

11. J. Breal, "Secret Sauce," *Fast Company* 115 (May 2007): 61–63.

12. F. J. Roethlisberger, *Management and Morale* (Cambridge, Mass.: Harvard University Press, 1941).

13. L. Van Dyne and J. L. Pierce, "Psychological Ownership and Feelings of Possession: Three Field Studies Predicting Employee Attitudes and Organizational Citizenship Behavior," *Journal of Organizational Behavior* 25 (2004): 439–459.

14. A. H. Maslow, "A Theory of Human Motivation," *Psychological Review* 50 (1943): 370–396.

15. W. James, *The Principles of Psychology* (New York: H. Holt & Co., 1890; Cambridge, Mass.: Harvard University Press, 1983); J. Dewey, *Human Nature and Conduct: An Introduction to Social Psychology* (New York: Holt, 1922); S. Freud, *A General Introduction to Psycho-Analysis: A Course of Twenty-Eight Lectures Delivered at the University of Vienna* (New York: Liveright, 1963); A. Adler, *Understanding Human Nature* (Greenwich, Conn.: Fawcett, 1927).

16. B. Litwiller, L. A. Snyder, W. D. Taylor, and L. M. Steele, "The Relationship Between Sleep and Work," *Journal of Applied Psychology*, 102, 4 (April 2017), 682–699.

17. N. K. Austin, "The Power of the Pyramid: The Foundation of Human Psychology and, Thereby, of Motivation, Maslow's Hierarchy Is One Powerful Pyramid," *Incentive* 176 (July 2002): 10.

18. D. M. McGregor, *The Human Side of Enterprise* (New York: McGraw-Hill, 1960).

19. D. M. McGregor, "The Human Side of Enterprise," *Management Review* (November 1957): 22–28, 88–92.

20. C. A. Fulmer and C. Ostroff, "Trust in Direct Leaders and Top Leaders: A Trickle-Up Model," *Journal of Applied Psychology*, 102, 4 (April 2017), 648–657.

21. Y. Berson, N. Halevy, B. Shamir, and M. Erez, "Leading from Different Psychological Distances: A Construal-Level Perspective on Vision Communication, Goal Setting, and Follower Motivation," *The Leadership Quarterly* 26 (2015): 143–155.

22. J. Boorstin, "No Preservatives. No Unions. Lots of Dough," *Fortune* 148 (September 15, 2003): 127–129.

23. C. P. Alderfer, *Human Needs in Organizational Settings* (New York: Free Press, 1972).

24. B. Schneider and C. P. Alderfer, "Three Studies of Need Satisfactions in Organizations," *Administrative Science Quarterly* 18 (1973): 489–505.

25. H. A. Murray, *Explorations in Personality: A Clinical and Experimental Study of Fifty Men of College Age* (New York: Oxford University Press, 1938).

26. D. C. McClelland, *Motivational Trends in Society* (Morristown, N.J.: General Learning Press, 1971).

27. D. C. McClelland, "Achievement Motivation Can Be Learned," *Harvard Business Review* 43 (1965): 6–24.

28. J. P. Chaplin and T. S. Krawiec, *Systems and Theories of Psychology* (New York: Holt, Rinehart & Winston, 1960); M. Stahl, *Managerial and Technical Motivation: Assessing Needs for Achievement, Power, and Affiliation* (Santa Barbara, CA: Praeger 1986).

29. J. S. Chun and J. N. Choi, "Members' Needs, Intragroup Conflict, and Group Performance," *Journal of Applied Psychology* 99 (2014): 437–450.

30. E. A. Ward, "Multidimensionality of Achievement Motivation among Employed Adults," *Journal of Social Psychology* 134 (1997): 542–544.

31. A. Sagie, D. Elizur, and H. Yamauchi, "The Structure and Strength of Achievement Motivation: A Cross-Cultural Comparison," *Journal of Organizational Behavior* 17 (1996): 431–444.

32. D. C. McClelland and D. Burnham, "Power Is the Great Motivator," *Harvard Business Review* 54 (1976): 100–111; J. Hall and J. Hawker, *Power Management Inventory* (The Woodlands, Tex.: Teleometrics International, 1988).

33. S. Schachter, *The Psychology of Affiliation* (Stanford, Calif.: Stanford University Press, 1959).

34. F. Herzberg, B. Mausner, and B. Snyderman, *The Motivation to Work* (New York: Wiley, 1959).

35. F. Herzberg, *Work and the Nature of Man* (Cleveland: World, 1966).

36. B. A. Scott, A. S. Garza, D. E. Conlon, and Y. J. Kim, "Why Do Managers Act Fairly in the First Place? A Daily Investigation of 'Hot' and 'Cold' Motives and Discretion," *Academy of Management Journal* 1015 (2015): 37–57.

37. G. van Houwelinger, M. van Dijke, and D. de Cremer, "Fairness Enactment as Response to Higher Level Unfairness," *Journal of Management*, 43, No. 2 (February 2017): 319–347.

37a. J. I. Menges, D. V. Tussing, A. Wihler, and A. M. Grant, "When Job Performance Is All Relative: How Family Motivation Energizes Effort and Compensates for Intrinsic Motivation," *Academy of Management Journal*, 60 (April 2017): 695–719.

38. R. Griffin, "Organizational Behavior," *Oxford Annotated Bibliographies: Management* (2013): www.oxfordbibliographies.com.

39. D. L. Nelson and B. L. Simmons, "Health Psychology and Work Stress: A More Positive Approach," in J. C. Quick and L. E. Tetrick, eds., *Handbook of Occupational Health Psychology* (Washington, D.C.: American Psychological Association, 2003): 97–119.

40. K. S. Cameron, J. E. Dutton, and R. E. Quinn, eds., *Positive Organizational Scholarship: Foundations of a New Discipline* (San Francisco: Berrett-Koehler, 2003).

41. J. Loehr and T. Schwartz, "The Making of a Corporate Athlete," *Harvard Business Review* 79 (2001): 120–129.

42. J. Loehr and T. Schwartz, *The Power of Full Engagement: Managing Energy, Not Time, Is the Key to High Performance and Personal Renewal* (New York: Free Press, 2003).

43. G. Kholreiser, "Engaging Employees Crucial for Their Morale," *The Nation* (November 29, 2010), http://www.nationmultimedia.com/2010/11/29/business/Engaging-employees-crucial-for-their-morale-30143355.html, accessed May 12, 2011.

44. P. M. Blau, *Exchange and Power in Social Life* (New York: Wiley, 1964); N. Horster, *Principles of Exchange and Power: Integrating the Theory of Social Institutions and the Theory of Value* (New York: P. Lang, 1997).

45. A. Etzioni, "A Basis for Comparative Analysis of Complex Organizations," in A. Etzioni, ed., *A Sociological Reader on Complex Organizations,* 2nd ed. (New York: Holt, Rinehart & Winston, 1969): 59–76.

46. S. S. Masterson and C. L. Stamper, "Perceived Organizational Membership: An Aggregate Framework Representing the Employee–Organization Relationship," *Journal of Organizational Behavior* 24 (2003): 473–490.

47. L. J. Song, A. S. Tsui, and K. S. Long, "Unpacking Employee Responses to Organizational Exchange Mechanisms: The Role of Social and Economic Exchange Perceptions," *Journal of Management* 35 (2009): 56–93.

48. J. S. Adams, "Inequity in Social Exchange," in L. Berkowitz, ed., *Advances in Experimental Social Psychology,* Vol. 2 (New York: Academic Press, 1965): 267–299; J. S. Adams, "Toward an Understanding of Inequity," *Journal of Abnormal and Social Psychology* 67 (1963): 422–436.

49. J. Nelson-Horchler, "The Best Man for the Job Is a Man," *Industry Week* (January 7, 1991): 50–52.

50. P. E. Downes and D. Choi, "Employee Reactions to Pay Dispersion: A Typology of Existing Research," *Human Resource Management Review* 24 (2014): 53–66.

51. R. C. Huseman, J. D. Hatfield, and E. A. Miles, "A New Perspective on Equity Theory: The Equity Sensitivity Construct," *Academy of Management Review* 12 (1987): 222–234.

52. G. Lemmon and S. J. Wayne, "Underlying Motives of Organizational Citizenship Behavior: Comparing Egoistic and Altruistic Motivations," *Journal of Leadership & Organization Studies* 22 (2015): 129–148.

53. K. E. Weick, M. G. Bougon, and G. Maruyama, "The Equity Context," *Organizational Behavior and Human Performance* 15 (1976): 32–65.

54. R. C. Huseman, J. D. Hatfield, and E. W. Miles, "A New Perspective on Equity Theory: The Equity Sensitivity Construct," *The Academy of Management Review* 12 (1987): 222–234.

55. J. Greenberg, "Equity and Workplace Status: A Field Experiment," *Journal of Applied Psychology* 73 (1988): 606–613.

56. J. Greenberg, "Losing Sleep over Organizational Justice: Attenuating Insomniac Reactions to Underpayment Inequity with Supervisory Training in Interactional Justice," *Journal of Applied Psychology* 91 (2006): 58–69.

57. J. Greenberg and B. Alge, "Aggressive Reactions to Workplace Injustice," in R. W. Griffin, A. O'Leary-Kelly, and J. Collins, eds., *Dysfunctional Behavior in Organizations, Vol. 1: Violent Behaviors in Organizations* (Greenwich, CT: JAI, 1998): 119–145.

58. R. A. Cosier and D. R. Dalton, "Equity Theory and Time: A Reformulation," *Academy of Management Review* 8 (1983): 311–319.

59. J. E. Martin and M. W. Peterson, "Two-Tier Wage Structures: Implications for Equity Theory," *Academy of Management Journal* 30 (1987): 297–315.

60. R. J. Sanchez, D. M. Truxillo, and T. N. Bauer, "Development and Examination of an Expectancy-Based Measure of Test-Taking Motivation," *Journal of Applied Psychology* 85 (2000): 739–750.

61. V. H. Vroom, *Work and Motivation* (New York: Wiley, 1964/1970).

62. U. R. Larson, "Supervisor's Performance Feedback to Subordinates: The Effect of Performance Valence and Outcome Dependence," *Organizational Behavior and Human Decision Processes* 37 (1986): 391–409.

63. M. C. Kernan and R. G. Lord, "Effects of Valence, Expectancies, and Goal-Performance Discrepancies in Single and Multiple Goal Environments," *Journal of Applied Psychology* 75 (1990): 194–203.

64. R. J. Sanchez, D. M. Truxillo, and T. N. Bauer, "Development and Examination of an Expectancy-Based Measure of Test-Taking Motivation," *Journal of Applied Psychology* 85 (2000): 739–750.

65. W. VanEerde and H. Thierry, "Vroom's Expectancy Models and Work-Related Criteria: A Meta-Analysis," *Journal of Applied Psychology* 81 (1996): 575–586.

66. E. D. Pulakos and N. Schmitt, "A Longitudinal Study of a Valence Model Approach for the Prediction of Job Satisfaction of New Employees," *Journal of Applied Psychology* 68 (1983): 307–312; F. J. Landy and W. S. Becker, "Motivation Theory Reconsidered," in L. L. Cummings and B. M. Staw, eds., *Research in Organizational Behavior* 9 (Greenwich, Conn.: JAI Press, 1987): 1–38.

67. J. Gibbs, K. Basinger, and D. Fuller, *Moral Maturity: Measuring the Development of Sociomoral Reflection* (Hillsdale, NJ: L. Erlbaum, 1992).

68. N. J. Adler, *International Dimensions of Organizational Behavior,* 4th ed. (Mason, Ohio: South-Western, 2001).

69. G. Hofstede, "Motivation, Leadership, and Organization: Do American Theories Apply Abroad?" *Organizational Dynamics* 9 (1980): 42–63.

70. G. H. Hines, "Cross-Cultural Differences in Two-Factor Theory," *Journal of Applied Psychology* 58 (1981): 313–317.

71. M. C. Bolino and W. H. Turnley, "Old Faces, New Places: Equity Theory in Cross-Cultural Contexts," *Journal of Organizational Behavior* 29 (2008): 29–50; M. C. Bolino and W. H. Turnley, "Erratum: Old Faces, New Places: Equity Theory in Cross-Cultural Contexts," *Journal of Organizational Behavior* 29 (2008): i.

6

1. I. Goodfellow, Y. Bengio, and A. Courville, *Deep Learning* (Cambridge, MA: Massachusetts Institute of Technology, 2016).

2. B. Cannon, "Walter B. Cannon: Reflections on the Man and His Contributions," in *Centennial Session,* (Washington, D.C., American Psychological Association Centennial Convention, 1992).

3. B. F. Skinner, *The Behavior of Organisms: An Experimental Analysis* (New York: Appleton-Century-Crofts, 1938).

4. B. F. Skinner, *Science and Human Behavior* (New York: Free Press, 1953).

5. F. Luthans and R. Kreitner, *Organizational Behavior Modification and Beyond* (Glenview, Ill.: Scott, Foresman, 1985).

6. A. D. Stajkovic and F. Luthans, "A Meta-Analysis of the Effects of Organizational Behavior Modification on Task Performance, 1975–95," *Academy of Management Journal* 40 (1997): 1122–1149.

7. C. B. Cadsby, F. Song, and F. Tapon, "Sorting and Incentive Effects of Pay for Performance: An Experimental Investigation," *Academy of Management Journal* 50 (2007): 387–405.

8. K. K. Merriman, "Lost in Translation: Cultural Interpretations of Performance Pay," *Compensation and Benefits Review* 42 (2010): 403–410.

9. J. Hale, "Strategic Rewards: Keeping Your Best Talent from Walking Out the Door," *Compensation and Benefits Management* 14 (1998): 39–50.

10. B. F. Skinner, *Contingencies of Reinforcement: A Theoretical Analysis* (New York: Appleton-Century-Crofts, 1969).

11. J. P. Chaplin and T. S. Krawiec, *Systems and Theories of Psychology* (New York: Holt, Rinehart & Winston, 1960).

12. L. Bareket-Bojmel, G. Hochman, and D. Ariely, "It's (Not) All about the Jacksons: Testing Different Types of Short-Term Bonuses in the Field," *Journal of Management* (Advanced online publication May 27, 2014).

13. M. Maccoby, J. Hoffer Gittell, and M. Ledeen, "Leadership and the Fear Factor," *Sloan Management Review* 148 (Winter 2004): 14–18.

14. A. Bandura, *Social Learning Theory* (Englewood Cliffs, N.J.: Prentice-Hall, 1977); A. Bandura, "Self-Efficacy: Toward a Unifying Theory of Behavioral Change," *Psychological Review* 84 (1977): 191–215.

15. J. J. Martocchio and E. J. Hertenstein, "Learning Orientation and Goal Orientation Context: Relationships with Cognitive and Affective Learning Outcomes," *Human Resource Development Quarterly* 14 (2003): 413–434.

16. A. Bandura, "Regulation of Cognitive Processes through Perceived Self-Efficacy," *Developmental Psychology* (September 1989): 729–735.

17. J. M. Phillips and S. M. Gully, "Role of Goal Orientation, Ability, Need for Achievement, and Locus of Control in the Self-Efficacy and Goal-Setting Process," *Journal of Applied Psychology* 82 (1997): 792–802.

18. M. Tims, A. B. Bakker, and D. Derks, "Daily Job Crafting and the Self-Efficacy-Performance Relationship," *Journal of Managerial Psychology* 29 (2014): 490–507.

19. J. C. Weitlauf, R. E. Smith, and D. Cervone, "Generalization Effects of Coping-Skills Training: Influence of Self-Defense Training on Women's Efficacy Beliefs, Assertiveness, and Aggression," *Journal of Applied Psychology* 85 (2000): 625–633.

20. A. D. Stajkovic and F. Luthans, "Social Cognitive Theory and Self-Efficacy: Going beyond Traditional Motivational and Behavioral Approaches," *Organizational Dynamics* (Spring 1998): 62–74.

21. T. M. Amabile and S. J. Kramer, "The Power of Small Wins," *Harvard Business Review* 38, No. 5 (July 8, 2008): 70–80.

22. V. Gecas, "The Social Psychology of Self-Efficacy," *Annual Review of Sociology* 15 (1989): 291–316.

23. E. A. Locke and G. P. Latham, *A Theory of Goal Setting and Task Performance* (Englewood Cliffs, N.J.: Prentice-Hall, 1990).

24. A. D. Stajkovic, E. A. Locke, and E. S. Blair, "A First Examination of the Relationships between Primed Subconscious Goals, Assigned Conscious Goals, and Task Performance," *Journal of Applied Psychology* 91 (2006): 1172–1180.

25. T. O. Murray, *Management by Objectives: A Systems Approach to Management* (Fort Worth, Tex.: Western Company, n.d.).

26. W. T. Brooks and T. W. Mullins, *High Impact Time Management* (Englewood Cliffs, N.J.: Prentice-Hall, 1989).

27. E. A. Locke, "Toward a Theory of Task Motivation and Incentives," *Organizational Behavior and Human Performance* 3 (1968): 157–189.

28. J. C. Quick, "Dyadic Goal Setting within Organizations: Role Making and Motivational Considerations," *Academy of Management Review* 4 (1979): 369–380.

29. D. McGregor, "An Uneasy Look at Performance Appraisal," *Harvard Business Review* 35 (1957): 89–94.

30. J. R. Hollenbeck, C. R. Williams, and H. J. Klein, "An Empirical Examination of the Antecedents of Commitment to Difficult Goals," *Journal of Applied Psychology* 74 (1989): 18–23.

31. R. C. Rodgers and J. E. Hunter, "The Impact of Management by Objectives on Organizational Productivity," unpublished paper (Lexington: University of Kentucky, 1989).

32. E. A. Locke, K. N. Shaw, L. M. Saari, and G. P. Latham, "Goal Setting and Task Performance: 1969–1980," *Psychological Bulletin* 90 (1981): 125–152.

33. D. B. Fedora, W. D. Davis, J. M. Maslync, and K. Mathiesond, "Performance Improvement Efforts in Response to Negative Feedback: The Roles of Source Power and Recipient Self-Esteem," *Journal of Management* 27 (2001): 79–98.

34. J. C. Quick, "Dyadic Goal Setting and Role Stress," *Academy of Management Journal* 22 (1979): 241–252.

35. G. S. Odiorne, *Management by Objectives: A System of Managerial Leadership* (New York: Pitman, 1965).

36. American Management Association, *Blueprints for Service Quality: The Federal Express Approach* (New York: American Management Association, 1991).

37. P. F. Drucker, *The Practice of Management* (New York: Harper & Bros., 1954).

38. R. D. Prichard, P. L. Roth, S. D. Jones, P. J. Galgay, and M. D. Watson, "Designing a Goal-Setting System to Enhance Performance: A Practical Guide," *Organizational Dynamics* 17 (1988): 69–78.

39. C. L. Hughes, *Goal Setting: Key to Individual and Organizational Effectiveness* (New York: American Management Association, 1965).

40. M. E. Tubbs and S. E. Ekeberg, "The Role of Intentions in Work Motivation: Implications for Goal-Setting Theory and Research," *Academy of Management Review* 16 (1991): 180–199.

41. Y. Gong, M. Wang, J.-C. Huang, S. Y. Cheung, "Toward a Goal Orientation-Based Feedback Seeking Typology: Implications for Employee Performance Outcomes," *Journal of Management*, 43, 4 (April 2017), 1234–1260.

42. J. R. Hollenbeck and A. P. Brief, "The Effects of Individual Differences and Goal Origin on Goal Setting and Performance," *Organizational Behavior and Human Decision Processes* 40 (1987): 392–414.

43. R. A. Katzell and D. E. Thompson, "Work Motivation: Theory and Practice," *American Psychologist* 45 (1990): 144–153; M. W. McPherson, "Is Psychology the Science of Behavior?" *American Psychologist* 47 (1992): 329–335.

44. A. S. DeNisi and K. R. Murphy, "Performance Appraisal and Performance Management: 100 Years of Progress?" *Journal of Applied Psychology*, 102, 3 (March 2017), 421–433.

45. F. L. Schmidt and J. Hunter, "General Mental Ability in the World of Work: Occupational Attainment and Job Performance," *Journal of Personality and Social Psychology* 86 (2004): 162–173.

46. D. L. Joseph, J. Jin, D. A. Newman, and E. H. O'Boyle, "Why Does Self-Reported Emotional Intelligence Predict Job Performance? A Meta-Analytic Investigation of Mixed EI," *Journal of Applied Psychology* 100 (2015): 298–342.

47. R. L. Cardy, *Performance Management: Concepts, Skills, and Exercises* (Armonk, New York, and London, England: M. E. Sharpe, 2004).

48. D. Hartley-Wilkins, "Getting the Best out of Your People: Managing Performance," *Human Resources* (April/May 2010): 26–27.

49. P. Cappelli and N. Rogovsky, "Employee Involvement and Organizational Citizenship: Implications for Labor Law Reform and 'Lean Production,'" *Industrial & Labor Relations Review* 51 (1998): 633–653.

50. L. D. Ordonez, M. E. Schweitzer, A. D. Galinskly, and M. H. Bazerman. "Goals Gone Wild: The Systematic Side Effects of Overprescribing Goal Setting," *Academy of Management Perspectives* 23 (2009): 6–16; E. A. Locke and G. P. Latham, "Has Goal Setting Gone Wild, or Have Its Attackers Abandoned

Good Scholarship?" *Academy of Management Perspectives* 23 (2009): 17–23.

51. M. E. Tubbs and M. L. Trusty, "Direct Reports of Motivation for Task Performance Levels: Some Construct-Related Evidence," *Journal of Psychology* 135 (2001): 185–205.

52. S. Ellis, R. Mendel, and M. Aloni-Zohar, "The Effect of Accuracy of Performance Evaluation on Learning from Experience: The Moderating Role of After-Event Reviews," *Journal of Applied Social Psychology* 39, No. 3 (2009): 541–563.

53. R. R. Kilburg, *Executive Coaching: Developing Managerial Wisdom in a World of Chaos* (Washington, D.C.: American Psychological Association, 2000).

54. K. Y. Wilson, "An Analysis of Bias in Supervisor Narrative Comments in Performance Appraisal," *Human Relations* 63 (2010): 1903–1933.

55. H. H. Meyer, E. Kay, and J. R. P. French, "Split Roles in Performance Appraisal," *Harvard Business Review* 43 (1965): 123–129.

56. W. Lam, X. Huang, and E. Snape, "Feedback-Seeking Behavior and Leader-Member Exchange: Do Supervisor-Attributed Motives Matter?" *Academy of Management Journal* 50 (2007): 348–363.

57. D. Motro and P. J. Aleksander, "Boys, Don't Cry: Gender and Reactions to Negative Performance Feedback," *Journal of Applied Psychology* 102, No. 2 (February 2017): 227–235.

58. J. S. Goodman, R. E. Wood, and M. Hendrickx, "Feedback Specificity, Exploration, and Learning," *Journal of Applied Psychology* 89 (2004): 248–262.

59. M. B. DeGregorio and C. D. Fisher, "Providing Performance Feedback: Reactions to Alternative Methods," *Journal of Management* 14 (1988): 605–616.

60. G. C. Thornton, "The Relationship between Supervisory and Self-Appraisals of Executive Performance," *Personnel Psychology* 21 (1968): 441–455.

61. A. S. DeNisi and A. N. Kluger, "Feedback Effectiveness: Can 360-Degree Appraisals Be Improved?" *Academy of Management Executive* 14 (2000): 129–140.

62. F. Luthans and S. J. Peterson, "360-Degree Feedback with Systematic Coaching: Empirical Analysis Suggests a Winning Combination," *Human Resource Management* 42 (2003): 243–256.

63. G. Toegel and J. A. Conger, "360-Degree Assessment: Time for Reinvention," *Academy of Management Learning and Education* 2 (2003): 297–311.

64. L. Hirschhorn, "Leaders and Followers in a Postindustrial Age: A Psychodynamic View," *Journal of Applied Behavioral Science* 26 (1990): 529–542.

65. F. M. Jablin, "Superior-Subordinate Communication: The State of the Art," *Psychological Bulletin* 86 (1979): 1201–1222.

66. T. C. Bednall, K. Sanders, and P. Runhaar, "Stimulating Informal Learning Activities through Perceptions of Performance Appraisal Quality and Human Resource Management Strength: A Two-Wave Study," *Academy of Management Learning & Education* 13 (2014): 45–61.

67. J. Pfeffer, "Six Dangerous Myths about Pay," *Harvard Business Review* 76 (1998): 108–119.

68. L. M. Leslie, C. F. Manchester, and P. C. Dahm, "Why and When Does the Gender Gap Reverse? Diversity Goals and the Pay Premium for High Potential Women," *Academy of Management Journal*, 60 (April 2017), 402–432.

69. "Six Employee Types Prefer Different Rewards," *HRFocus* 84, No. 4 (April 2007): 12.

70. M. Erez, "Work Motivation from a Cross-Cultural Perspective," in A. M. Bouvy, F. J. R. Van de Vijver, P. Boski, and P. G. Schmitz, eds., *Journeys into Cross-Cultural Psychology* (Amsterdam, Netherlands: Swets and Zeitlinger, 1994): 386–403.

71. G. T. Milkovich and J. M. Newman, *Compensation*, 4th ed. (Homewood, Ill.: Irwin, 1993).

72. T. Taylor, "The Challenge of Project Team Incentives," *Compensation and Benefits Review* 42 (2010): 411–419.

73. J. M. Bardwick, *Danger in the Comfort Zone* (New York: American Management Association, 1991).

74. D. F. Giannetto, "Get Your Money's Worth from Incentives," *Business Performance Management*, 7 (2009): 12.

75. J. H. Han, K. M. Bartol, and S. Kim, "Tightening Up the Performance-Pay Linkage: Roles of Contingent Reward Leadership and Profit-Sharing in the Cross-Level Influence of Individual Pay-for-Performance," *Journal of Applied Psychology* 100 (2015): 417–430.

76. K. N. Wexley, R. A. Alexander, J. P. Greenawalt, and M. A. Couch, "Attitudinal Congruence and Similarity as Related to Interpersonal Evaluations in Manager-Subordinate Dyads," *Academy of Management Journal* 23 (1980): 320–330.

77. H. H. Kelley, *Attribution in Social Interaction* (New York: General Learning Press, 1971); H. H. Kelley, "The Processes of Causal Attribution," *American Psychologist* 28 (1973): 107–128.

78. B. Raabe and T. A. Beehr, "Formal Mentoring versus Supervisor and Coworker Relationships: Differences in Perceptions and Impact," *Journal of Organizational Behavior* 24 (2003): 271–293.

79. A. M. Young and P. L. Perrewe, "What Did You Expect? An Examination of Career-Related Support and Social Support among Mentors and Protégés," *Journal of Management* 26 (2000): 611–633.

80. K. Doherty, "The Good News about Depression," *Business and Health* 3 (1989): 1–4.

81. K. E. Kram, "Phases of the Mentor Relationship," *Academy of Management Journal* 26 (1983): 608–625.

82. T. D. Allen, L. T. Eby, M. L. Poteet, E. Lentz, and L. Lima, "Career Benefits Associated with Mentoring for Protégés: A Meta-Analysis," *Journal of Applied Psychology* 89 (2004): 127–136.

83. L. T. Eby, M. M. Butts, B. J. Hoffman, and J. B. Sauer, "Cross-Lagged Relations between Mentoring Received from Supervisors and Employee OCBs: Disentangling Causal Direction and Identifying Boundary Conditions," *Journal of Applied Psychology* (Advanced online publication January 19, 2015).

84. S. J. Wells, "Choices Flourish at IBM," *HR Magazine* (May 2009): 52–57.

85. K. E. Kram and L. A. Isabella, "Mentoring Alternatives: The Role of Peer Relationships in Career Development," *Academy of Management Journal* 28 (1985): 110–132.

86. J. Greco, "Hey, Coach!" *Journal of Business Strategy* 22 (2001): 28–32.

7

1. P. D. Bliese, J. R. Edwards, and S. Sonnentag, "Stress and Well-Being at Work: A Century of Empirical Trends Reflecting Theoretical and Societal Influences," *Journal of Applied Psychology* 102, No. 3 (March 2017): 389–402.

2. M. Blake Hargrove, J. C. Quick, D. L. Nelson, and J. D. Quick, "The Theory of Preventive Stress Management: A 33-Year Review and Evaluation," *Stress and Health* 27 (2011): 182–193.

3. S. Benison, A. C. Barger, and E. L. Wolfe, *Walter B. Cannon: The Life and Times of a Young Scientist* (Cambridge, Mass.: Harvard University Press, 1987).

4. W. B. Cannon, *Bodily Changes in Pain, Hunger, Fear, and Rage: An Account of Recent Researchers into the Function of Emotional Excitement* (New York: Appleton-Century-Crofts, 1915).

5. W. B. Cannon, *The Wisdom of the Body* (New York: Norton, 1932).

6. R. S. Lazarus, *Psychological Stress and the Coping Process* (New York: McGraw-Hill, 1966).

7. M. R. Tuckey, B. J. Searle, C. M. Boyd, A. H. Winefield, and H. R. Winefield. "Hindrances Are Not Threats: Advancing the Multimensionality of Work Stress," *Journal of Occupational Health Psychology* 20 (2015): 131–147.

8. R. Rau, K. Morling, and U. Rosler, "Is There a Relationship between Major Depression and Both Objectively Assessed and Perceived Demands and Control?" *Work and Stress* 24 (2010): 88–106.

9. C. Liu, P. E. Spector, and L. Shi, "Cross-National Job Stress: A Quantitative and Qualitative Study," *Journal of Organizational Behavior* 28 (2007): 209–239.

10. J. Doron, Y. Stephan, C. Maiano, and C. LeScanff, "Motivational Predictors of Coping with Academic Examinations," *The Journal of Social Psychology* 151 (2011): 87–104.

11. J. D. Kammeyer-Mueller, T. A. Judge, and B. A. Scott, "The Role of Core Self-Evaluations

in the Coping Process," *Journal of Applied Psychology* 94 (2009): 177–195.

12. D. Katz and R. L. Kahn, *The Social Psychology of Organizations*, 2nd ed. (New York: Wiley, 1978): 185–221.

13. H. Levinson, "A Psychoanalytic View of Occupational Stress," *Occupational Mental Health* 3 (1978): 2–13.

14. L. Yang, J. Bauer, R. E. Johnson, M. W. Groer, and K. Salomon. "Physiological Mechanisms That Underlie the Effects of Interactional Fairness on Deviant Behavior: The Role of Cortisol Activity," *Journal of Applied Psychology* 99 (2014): 310–321.

15. G-H. Huang, N. Wellman, S. J. Ashford, C. Lee, and L. Wang. "Deviance and Exit: The Organizational Costs of Job Insecurity and Moral Disengagement," *Journal of Applied Psychology* 102, No. 1 (January 2017): 26–42.

16. T. L. Friedman, *The Lexus and the Olive Tree* (New York: Vintage Anchor, 2000).

17. S. Zuboff, *In the Age of the Smart Machine: The Future of Work and Power* (New York: Basic Books, 1988).

18. C. L. Cooper, A. Pandey, and J. C. Quick (Eds). 2012. *Downsizing: Is More Less?* (Chichester, UK: Cambridge University Press).

19. N. P. Podsakoff, J. A. LePine, and M. A. LePine, "Differential Challenge Stressor-Hindrance Stressor Relationships with Job Attitudes, Turnover Intentions, Turnover, and Withdrawal Behavior: A Meta-Analysis," *Journal of Applied Psychology* 92 (2007): 438–454.

20. R. L. Kahn, D. M. Wolfe, R. P. Quinn, J. D. Snoek, and R. A. Rosenthal, *Organizational Stress: Studies in Role Conflict and Ambiguity* (New York: Wiley, 1964).

21. C. Vandenberge, A. Panaciio, K. Bentein, K. Mignonac, and P. Roussel, "Assessing Longitudinal Change of and Dynamic Relationships among Role Stressors, Job Attitudes, Turnover Intention, and Well-Being in Neophyte Newcomers," *Journal of Organizational Behavior* 34 (2011): 652–671.

22. L. B. Hammer, T. N. Bauer, and A. A. Grandey, "Work-Family Conflict and Work-Related Withdrawal Behaviors," *Journal of Business and Psychology* 17 (2003): 419–436.

23. C. Nohe, L. L. Meier, K. Sonntag, and A. Michel, "The Chicken or the Egg? A Meta-Analysis of Panel Studies of the Relationship between Work-Family Conflict and Strain," *Journal of Applied Psychology* 100 (2015): 522–536.

24. S. Pal and P. O. Saksvik, "Work–Family Conflict and Psychosocial Work Environment Stressors as Predictors of Job Stress in a Cross-Cultural Study," *International Journal of Stress Management* 15, No. 1 (2008): 22–42.

25. A. Skogstad, S. Einarsen, T. Torsheim, M. S. Aasland, and H. Hetland, "The Destructiveness of Laissez-Faire Leadership Behavior," *Journal of Occupational Health Psychology* 12 (2007): 80–92.

26. P. D. Bliese and C. A. Castro, "Role Clarity, Work Overload and Organizational Support: Multilevel Evidence of the Importance of Support," *Work and Stress* 14 (2000): 65–74.

27. P. J. Frost, *Toxic Emotions at Work: How Compassionate Managers Handle Pain and Conflict* (Boston: Harvard Business School Press, 2003).

28. T. Nicholson and B. Griffin, "Here Today but Not Gone Tomorrow: Incivility Affects After-Work and Next-Day Recovery," *Journal of Occupational Health Psychology* 20 (2015) 218–225.

29. S. Grebner, N. K. Semmer, L. L. Faso, S. Gut, W. Kalin, and A. Elfering, "Working Conditions, Well-Being, and Job-Related Attitudes among Call Centre Agents," *European Journal of Work and Organizational Psychology* 12 (2003): 341–365.

30. M. P. Bell, J. C. Quick, and C. Cycota, "Assessment and Prevention of Sexual Harassment: An Applied Guide to Creating Healthy Organizations," *International Journal of Selection and Assessment* 10 (2002): 160–167.

31. L. T. Hosmer, "Trust: The Connecting Link between Organizational Theory and Philosophical Ethics," *Academy of Management Review* 20 (1995): 379–403; V. J. Doby and R. D. Caplan, "Organizational Stress as Threat to Reputation: Effects on Anxiety at Work and at Home," *Academy of Management Journal* 38 (1995): 1105–1123.

32. R. T. Keller, "Cross-Functional Project Groups in Research and New Product Development: Diversity, Communications, Job Stress, and Outcomes," *Academy of Management Journal* 33 (2001): 547–555.

33. M. F. Peterson and P. B. Smith, "Does National Culture or Ambient Temperature Explain Cross-National Differences in Role Stress? No Sweat!" *Academy of Management Journal* 40 (1997): 930–946.

34. R. S. DeFrank, "Executive Travel Stress: Perils of the Road Warrior," *Academy of Management Executive* 14 (2000): 58–72; M. Westman, "Strategies for Coping with Business Trips: A Qualitative Exploratory Study," *International Journal of Stress Management* 11 (2004): 167–176.

35. J. C. Quick, J. R. Joplin, D. A. Gray, and E. C. Cooley, "The Occupational Life Cycle and the Family," in L. L'Abate, ed., *Handbook of Developmental Family Psychology and Psychopathology* (New York: John Wiley, 1993).

36. S. Shellenbarger, "Work and Family," *The Wall Street Journal* (January 31, 1996): B1.

37. S. A. Lobel, "Allocation of Investment in Work and Family Roles: Alternative Theories and Implications for Research," *Academy of Management Review* 16 (1991): 507–521.

38. J. D. Quick, A. Henley, and J. C. Quick. "The balancing act—At work and at home," *Organizational Dynamics—Special Issue* 33 (2004): 426–438.

39. J. W. Pennebaker, C. F. Hughes, and R. C. O'Heeron, "The Psychophysiology of Confession: Linking Inhibitory and Psychosomatic Processes," *Journal of Personality and Social Psychology* 52 (1987): 781–793.

40. J. Loehr and T. Schwartz, "The Making of a Corporate Athlete," *Harvard Business Review* 79 (2001): 120–129.

41. J. D. Quick, R. S. Horn, and J. C. Quick, "Health Consequences of Stress," *Journal of Organizational Behavior Management* 8 (1986): 19–36.

42. R. M. Yerkes and J. D. Dodson, "The Relation of Strength of Stimulus to Rapidity of Habit-Formation," *Journal of Comparative Neurology and Psychology* 18 (1908): 459–482.

43. J. E. McGrath, "Stress and Behavior in Organizations," in M. D. Dunnette, ed., *Handbook of Industrial and Organizational Psychology* (Chicago: Rand McNally, 1976): 1351–1395.

44. T. A. Wright, R. Cropanzano, and D. G. Meyer, "State and Trait Correlates of Job Performance: A Tale of Two Perspectives," *Journal of Business and Psychology* 18 (2004): 365–383.

45. W. B. Cannon, *Bodily Changes in Pain, Hunger, Fear, and Rage* (New York: Appleton, 1915).

46. P. A. Herbig and F. A. Palumbo, "Karoshi: Salaryman Sudden Death Syndrome," *Journal of Managerial Psychology* 9 (1994): 11–16.

47. S. Sauter, L. R. Murphy, and J. J. Hurrell, Jr., "Prevention of Work-Related Psychological Distress: A National Strategy Proposed by the National Institute for Occupational Safety and Health," *American Psychologist* 45 (1990): 1146–1158.

48. R. Cropanzano, D. E. Rupp, and Z. S. Byrne, "The Relationship of Emotional Exhaustion to Work Attitudes, Job Performance, and Organizational Citizenship Behaviors," *Journal of Applied Psychology* 88 (2003): 160–169.

49. A. A. Grandey, "When 'The Show Must Go On': Surface Acting and Deep Acting as Determinants of Emotional Exhaustion and Peer-Rated Service Delivery," *Academy of Management Journal* 46 (2003): 86–96.

50. G. B. Hall, M. F. Dollard, M. R. Tuckey, A. H. Winefield, and B. M. Thompson, "Job Demands, Work–Family Conflict, and Emotional Exhaustion in Police Officers: A Longitudinal Test of Competing Theories," *Journal of Occupational and Organizational Psychology* 83 (2010): 237–250.

51. J. R. B. Halbesleben and W. M. Bowler, "Emotional Exhaustion and Job Performance: The Mediating Role of Motivation," *Journal of Applied Psychology* 92 (2007): 93–106.

52. I. Wylie, "Routing Rust-Out," *Fast Company Magazine* (January 2004): 40, www.fastcompany.com/magazine/78/5things.html.

53. H. Selye, *Stress in Health and Disease* (Boston: Butterworth, 1976).

54. B. G. Ware and D. L. Block, "Cardiovascular Risk Intervention at a Work Site: The Ford Motor Company Program," *International Journal of Mental Health* 11 (1982): 68–75.

55. D. B. Kennedy, R. J. Homant, and M. R. Homant, "Perceptions of Injustice as a Predictor of Support for Workplace Aggression," *Journal of Business and Psychology* 18 (2004): 323–336.

56. C. M. Barnes, J. A. Miller, and S. Bostock, "Helping Employees Sleep Well: Effects of Cognitive Behavioral Therapy for Insomnia on Work Outcomes," *Journal of Applied Psychology* 102, No. 1 (January 2017): 104–113.

57. W. F. Cascio, *Managing Human Resources: Productivity, Quality of Life, Profits*, 9th ed. (New York: McGraw–Hill, 2013).

58. F. K. Cocchiara and J. C. Quick, "The Negative Effects of Positive Stereotypes: Ethnicity-Related Stressors and Implications on Organizational Health," *Journal of Organizational Behavior* 25 (2004): 781–785.

59. J. M. Ivancevich, M. T. Matteson, and E. Richards, "Who's Liable for Stress on the Job?" *Harvard Business Review* 64 (1985): 60–72.

60. Frank S. Deus v. Allstate Insurance Company, civil action no. 88-2099, U.S. District Court, Western District of Louisiana.

61. R. S. DeFrank and J. M. Ivancevich, "Stress on the Job: An Executive Update," *Academy of Management Executive* 12 (1998): 55–66.

62. P. Wilson and M. Bronstein, "Employers: Don't Panic about Workplace Stress," *Personnel Today* (November 4, 2003): 10.

63. J. E. Bono and M. A. Vey, "Personality and Emotional Performance: Extraversion, Neuroticism, and Self-Monitoring," *Journal of Occupational Health Psychology* 12 (2007): 177–192.

64. C. S. Troutman, K. G. Burke, and J. D. Beeler, "The Effects of Self-Efficacy, Assertiveness, Stress, and Gender on Intention," *Journal of Applied Business Research* 16 (2000): 63–75.

65. S. E. Taylor, L. C. Klein, G. P. Lewis, T. L. Gruenewald, R. A. R. Burung, and J. A. Updegraff, "Biobehavioral Responses to Stress in Females: Tend-and-Befriend, Not Fight-or-Flight," *Psychological Review* 107 (2000): 411–429.

66. D. L. Nelson and J. C. Quick, "Professional Women: Are Distress and Disease Inevitable?" *Academy of Management Review* 10 (1985): 206–218; T. D. Jick and L. F. Mitz, "Sex Differences in Work Stress," *Academy of Management Review* 10 (1985): 408–420.

67. K. M. Rospenda, K. Fujishiro, C. A. Shannon, and J. A. Richman, "Workplace Harassment, Stress, and Drinking Behavior over Time: Gender Differences in a National Sample," *Addictive Behaviors* 33 (2008): 964–967.

68. L. Verbrugge, "Recent, Present, and Future Health of American Adults," *Annual Review of Public Health* 10 (1989): 333–361.

69. M. D. Friedman and R. H. Rosenman, *Type A Behavior and Your Heart* (New York: Knopf, 1974).

70. L. Wright, "The Type A Behavior Pattern and Coronary Artery Disease," *American Psychologist* 43 (1988): 2–14.

71. S. O. C. Kobasa, "Conceptualization and Measurement of Personality in Job Stress Research," in J. J. Hurrell, Jr., L. R. Murphy, S. L. Sauter, and C. L. Cooper, eds., *Occupational Stress: Issues and Developments in Research* (New York: Taylor & Francis, 1988): 100–109.

72. J. K. Ito and C. M. Brotheridge, "Predictors and Consequences of Promotion Stress: A Bad Situation Made Worse by Employment Dependence," *International Journal of Stress Management* 16, No. 1 (2009): 65–85.

73. J. Borysenko, "Personality Hardiness," *Lectures in Behavioral Medicine* (Boston: Harvard Medical School, 1985).

74. J. S. House, K. R. Landis, and D. Umberson, "Social Relationships and Health," *Science* 241 (1988): 540–545.

75. J. Bowlby, *A Secure Base* (New York: Basic Books, 1988).

76. C. Hazan and P. Shaver, "Love and Work: An Attachment-Theoretical Perspective," *Journal of Personality and Social Psychology* 59 (1990): 270–280.

77. J. C. Quick, D. L. Nelson, and J. D. Quick, *Stress and Challenge at the Top: The Paradox of the Successful Executive* (Chichester, England: Wiley, 1990).

78. "Partner Relationship Could Be a Buffer against Work-Related Stress," *Asian News International* (June 24, 2009).

79. J. C. Quick, J. R. Joplin, D. L. Nelson, and J. D. Quick, "Self-Reliance for Stress and Combat" (*Proceedings of the 8th Combat Stress Conference*, U.S. Army Health Services Command, Fort Sam Houston, Texas, September 23–27, 1991): 1–5.

80. J. C. Dvorak, "Baffling," *PC Magazine* 3 (November 4, 2003): 61, http://www.pcmag.com/article2/0,4149,1369270,00.asp.

81. O. Janssen, "How Fairness Perceptions Make Innovative Behavior More or Less Stressful," *Journal of Organizational Behavior* 25 (2004): 201–215; T. A. Judge and J. A. Colquitt, "Organizational Justice and Stress: The Mediating Role of Work–Family Conflict," *Journal of Applied Psychology* 89 (2004): 395–404.

82. K. Hickox, "Content and Competitive," *Airman* (January 1994): 31–33.

83. A. Drach-Zahavy and A. Freund, "Team Effectiveness under Stress: A Structural Contingency Approach," *Journal of Organizational Behavior* 28 (2007): 423–450.

84. R. W. Griffin, A. O'Leary-Kelly, and J. M. Collins, eds., *Dysfunctional Behavior in Organizations: Violent and Deviant Behavior* (Stamford, Conn.: JAI Press, 1998).

85. M. Kouchaki and S. D. Desai, "Anxious, Threatened, and Also Unethical: How Anxiety Makes Individuals Feel Threatened and Commit Unethical Acts," *Journal of Applied Psychology* 100 (2015): 360–375.

86. W. L. French and C. H. Bell, Jr., *Organizational Development: Behavioral Science Interventions for Organization Improvement*, 4th ed. (Englewood Cliffs, N.J.: Prentice-Hall, 1990).

87. C. Newton and S. Teo, "Identification and Occupational Stress: A Stress-Buffering Perspective," *Human Resource Management* 53 (2014): 89–113.

88. M. Macik-Frey, J. C. Quick, and J. D. Quick, "Interpersonal Communication: The Key to Unlocking Social Support for Preventive Stress Management," in C. L. Cooper, ed., *Handbook of Stress, Medicine, and Health*, rev. ed. (Boca Raton, FL: CRC Press).

89. J. C. Quick and C. L. Cooper, *FAST FACTS: Stress and Strain*, 2nd ed. (Oxford, England: Health Press, 2003).

90. M. E. P. Seligman, *Learned Optimism* (New York: Knopf, 1990).

91. F. Griva and F. Anagnostopoulos, "Positive Psychological States and Anxiety: The Mediating Effect of Proactive Coping," *Psychological Reports* 107 (2010): 795–804.

92. F. Luthans and C. M. Youssef-Morgan, "Psychological Capital: An Evidence-Based Positive Approach," *Annual Review of Organizational Psychology and Organizational Behavior* 4 (2017): 339–366.

93. W. T. Brooks and T. W. Mullins, *High-Impact Time Management* (Englewood Cliffs, N.J.: Prentice-Hall, 1989).

94. M. Westman and D. Eden, "Effects of a Respite from Work on Burnout: Vacation Relief and Fade-Out," *Journal of Applied Psychology* 82 (1997): 516–527.

95. C. P. Neck and K. H. Cooper, "The Fit Executive: Exercise and Diet Guidelines for Enhancing Performance," *Academy of Management Executive* 14 (2000): 72–84.

96. M. Davis, E. R. Eshelman, and M. McKay, *The Relaxation and Stress Reduction Workbook*, 3rd ed. (Oakland, Calif.: New Harbinger, 1988).

97. H. Benson, "Your Innate Asset for Combating Stress," *Harvard Business Review* 52 (1974): 49–60.

98. D. Ornish, *Dr. Dean Ornish's Program for Reversing Cardiovascular Disease* (New York: Random House, 1995).

99. J. W. Pennebaker, *Opening Up: The Healing Power of Expressing Emotions* (New York: Guilford, 1997).

100. M. E. Francis and J. W. Pennebaker, "Putting Stress into Words: The Impact of Writing on Physiological, Absentee, and Self-Reported Emotional Well-Being Measures," *American Journal of Health Promotion* 6 (1992): 280–287.

101. Z. Solomon, B. Oppenheimer, and S. Noy, "Subsequent Military Adjustment of Combat Stress Reaction Casualties: A Nine-Year Follow-Up Study," in N. A. Milgram, ed., *Stress and Coping in Time of War: Generalizations from the Israeli Experience* (New York: Brunner/Mazel, 1986): 84–90.

102. C. L. Cooper and J. C. Quick, *The Handbook of Stress and Health: A Guide to Research and Practice*. Chichester, UK: WileyBlackwell, 2017.

103. D. Gebhardt and C. Crump, "Employee Fitness and Wellness Programs in the

Workplace," *American Psychologist* 45 (1990): 262–272.

104. T. Wolf, H. Randall, and J. Faucett, "A Survey of Health Promotion Programs in U.S. and Canadian Medical Schools," *American Journal of Health Promotion* 3 (1988): 33–36.

105. S. Weiss, J. Fielding, and A. Baum, *Health at Work* (Hillsdale, N.J.: Erlbaum, 1990).

106. J. B. Bennett, R. F. Cook, and K. R. Pelletier, "Toward an Integrated Framework for Comprehensive Organizational Wellness: Concepts, Practices, and Research in Workplace Health Promotion," in J. C. Quick and L. E. Tetrick, eds., *Handbook of Occupational Health Psychology* (Washington, D.C.: American Psychological Association, 2003): 69–95.

8

1. D. L. Whetzel, "The Department of Labor Identifies Workplace Skills," *The Industrial/Organizational Psychologist* (July 1991): 89–90.

2. M. Macik-Frey, J. C. Quick, and J. D. Quick, "Interpersonal Communication: The Key to Unlocking Social Support for Preventive Stress Management," in C. L. Cooper, ed., *Handbook of Stress, Medicine, and Health, rev. ed.* (Boca Raton, FL: CRC Press), pp. 265–292.

3. *Richness* is a term originally coined by W. D. Bodensteiner, "Information Channel Utilization under Varying Research and Development Project Conditions" (Ph.D. diss., University of Texas at Austin, 1970).

4. T. J. Kiddie, "Text(ing) in Context: The Future of Workplace Communication in the United States," *Business and Professional Communication Quarterly* 77 (2014): 65–88.

5. B. Barry and I. S. Fulmer, "The Medium and the Message: The Adaptive Use of Communication Media in Dyadic Influence," *Academy of Management Review* 29 (2004): 272–292.

6. S. Aryee, F. O. Walumbwa, R. Mondejar, and C. W. L. Chu, "Core Self-Evaluations and Employee Voice Behavior: Test of a Dual-Motivational Pathway," *Journal of Management* 43, No. 3 (March 2017): 946–966.

7. E. Rautalinko and H. O. Lisper, "Effects of Training Reflective Listening in a Corporate Setting," *Journal of Business and Psychology* 18 (2004): 281–299.

8. A. G. Athos and J. J. Gabarro, *Interpersonal Behavior: Communication and Understanding in Relationships* (Englewood Cliffs, N.J.: Prentice-Hall, 1978).

9. A. D. Mangelsdorff, "Lessons Learned from the Military: Implications for Management" (Distinguished Visiting Lecture, University of Texas at Arlington, January 29, 1993).

10. D. A. Morand, "Language and Power: An Empirical Analysis of Linguistic Strategies Used in Superior–Subordinate Communication," *Journal of Organizational Behavior* 21 (2000): 235–249.

11. S. Bates, "How Leaders Communicate Big Ideas to Drive Business Results," *Employment Relations Today* 33 (Fall 2006): 13–19.

12. F. Luthans, "Successful versus Effective Real Managers," *Academy of Management Executive* 2 (1988): 127–132.

13. L. E. Penley, E. R. Alexander, I. E. Jernigan, and C. I. Henwood, "Communication Abilities of Managers: The Relationship of Performance," *Journal of Management* 17 (1991): 57–76.

14. J. A. LePine and L. Van Dyne, "Voice and Cooperative Behavior as Contrasting Forms of Contextual Performance: Evidence of Differential Relationships with Big Five Personality Characteristics and Cognitive Ability," *Journal of Applied Psychology* 86 (2001): 326–336.

15. F. M. Jablin, "Superior-Subordinate Communication: The State of the Art," *Psychological Bulletin* 86 (1979): 1201–1222; W. C. Reddin, *Communication within the Organization: An Interpretive Review of Theory and Research* (New York: Industrial Communication Council, 1972).

16. B. Barry and J. M. Crant, "Dyadic Communication Relationships in Organizations: An Attribution Expectancy Approach," *Organization Science* 11 (2000): 648–665.

17. J. Silvester, F. Patterson, A. Koczwara, and E. Ferguson, "'Trust Me . . .': Psychological and Behavioral Predictors of Perceived Physician Empathy," *Journal of Applied Psychology* 92 (2007): 519–527.

18. K. Mishra, L. Boynton, and A. Mishra, "Driving Employee Engagement: The Expanded Role of Internal Communications," *International Journal of Business Communications* 51 (2014): 183–202.

19. A. Furhham and P. Stringfield, "Congruence in Job-Performance Ratings: A Study of 360 Degree Feedback Examining Self, Manager, Peers, and Consultant Ratings," *Human Relations* 51 (1998): 517–530.

20. J. W. Gilsdorf, "Organizational Rules on Communicating: How Employees Are—and Are Not—Learning the Ropes," *Journal of Business Communication* 35 (1998): 173–201.

21. A. Malhotra and A. Majchrzak, "Enhancing Performance of Geographically Dispersed Teams through Targeted Use of Information and Communication Technologies," *Human Relations* 67 (2014): 389–411.

22. D. Tannen, *That's Not What I Mean! How Conversational Style Makes or Breaks Your Relations with Others* (New York: Morrow, 1986); D. Tannen, *You Just Don't Understand* (New York: Ballentine, 1990).

23. D. G. Allen and R. W. Griffeth, "A Vertical and Lateral Information Processing: The Effects of Gender, Employee Classification Level, and Media Richness on Communication and Work Outcomes," *Human Relations* 50 (1997): 1239–1260.

24. K. L. Ashcraft, "Empowering 'Professional' Relationships," *Management Communication Quarterly* 13 (2000): 347–393.

25. G. Hofstede, *Culture's Consequences: International Differences in Work-Related Values* (Beverly Hills, Calif.: Sage Publications, 1980).

26. G. Hofstede, "Motivation, Leadership, and Organization: Do American Theories Apply Abroad?" *Organizational Dynamics* 9 (1980): 42–63.

27. H. Levinson, *Executive* (Cambridge, Mass.: Harvard University Press, 1981).

28. B. M. Cole, "Lessons from a Martial Arts Dojo: A Prolonged Process Model of High-Context Communication," *Academy of Management Journal* 58 (2015): 567–591.

29. P. Benimadhu, "Adding Value through Diversity: An Interview with Bernard F. Isautier," *Canadian Business Review* 22 (1995): 6–11.

30. P. Schilpzand, I. E. de Pater, and A. Erez, "Workplace Incivility: A Review of the Literature and Agenda for Future Research," *Journal of Organizational Behavior* 37 (February 2016): S57–S88.

31. J. L. Welbourne, A. Gangadharan, and A. M. Sariol, "Ethnicity and Cultural Values as Predictors of the Occurrence and Impact of Experienced Workplace Incivility," *Journal of Occupational Health Psychology* 20 (2015): 205–217.

32. T. C. Reich and S. Hershcovis, "Observing Workplace Incivility," *Journal of Applied Psychology* 100 (2015): 203–215.

33. S. G. Taylor, A. G. Bedeian, M. S. Cole, and Z. Zhang, "Developing and Testing a Dynamic Model of Workplace Incivility Change," *Journal of Management* 43, No. 3 (March 2017): 645–670.

34. R. D. Laing, *The Politics of the Family and Other Essays* (New York: Pantheon, 1971).

35. H. S. Schwartz, *Narcissistic Process and Corporate Decay: The Theory of the Organizational Ideal* (New York: New York University Press, 1990).

36. W. R. Forrester and M. F. Maute, "The Impact of Relationship Satisfaction on Attribution, Emotions, and Behaviors Following Service Failure," *Journal of Applied Business Research* 17 (2000): 1–45.

37. T. Foulk, A. Woolum, and A. Erez, "Catching Rudeness Is Like Catching a Cold: The Contagion Effect of Low-Intensity Negative Behaviors," *Journal of Applied Psychology* 101, No. 1 (January 2016): 50–67.

38. A. M. Katz and V. T. Katz, eds., *Foundations of Nonverbal Communication* (Carbondale, Ill.: Southern Illinois University Press, 1983).

39. M. D. Lieberman, "Intuition: A Social Cognitive Neuroscience Approach," *Psychological Bulletin* (2000): 109–138.

40. E. T. Hall, *The Hidden Dimension* (Garden City, N.Y.: Doubleday Anchor, 1966).

41. E. T. Hall, "Proxemics," in A. M. Katz and V. T. Katz, eds., *Foundations of Nonverbal Communication* (Carbondale, Ill.: Southern Illinois University Press, 1983).

42. R. T. Barker and C. G. Pearce, "The Importance of Proxemics at Work," *Supervisory Management* 35 (1990): 10–11.

43. R. L. Birdwhistell, *Kinesics and Context* (Philadelphia: University of Pennsylvania Press, 1970).

44. K. I. Ruys and D. A. Stapel, "Emotion Elicitor or Emotion Messenger?" *Psychological Science*, 19 (2008): 593–600.

45. M. G. Frank and P. Ekman, "Appearing Truthful Generalizes across Different Deception Situations," *Journal of Personality and Social Psychology* 86 (2004): 486–495.

46. P. Ekman and W. V. Friesen, "Research on Facial Expressions of Emotion," in A. M. Katz and V. T. Katz, eds., *Foundations of Nonverbal Communication* (Carbondale, Ill.: Southern Illinois University Press, 1983).

47. H. H. Tan, M. D. Foo, C. L. Chong, and R. Ng, "Situational and Dispositional Predictors of Displays of Positive Emotions," *Journal of Organizational Behavior* 24 (2003): 961–978.

48. M. de Rond and J. Lok, "Some Things Can Never Be Unseen: The Role of Context in Psychological Injury at Ware," *Academy of Management Journal* 59 (December 2016): 1965–1993.

49. A. M. Katz and V.T. Katz, *Foundations of Nonverbal Communication* (Carbondale, IL: Southern Illinois University Press, 1983): 181.

50. J. J. Lynch, *A Cry Unheard: New Insights into the Medical Consequences of Loneliness* (Baltimore, MD: Bancroft Press, 2000).

51. J. C. Quick, J. H. Gavin, C. L. Cooper, and J. D. Quick, "Working Together: Balancing Head and Heart," in N. G. Johnson, R. H. Rozensky, C. D. Goodheart, and R. Hammond, eds., *Psychology Builds a Healthy World* (Washington, D.C.: American Psychological Association, 2004): 219–232.

52. J. C. Quick, C. L. Cooper, J. D. Quick, and J. H. Gavin, *The Financial Times Guide to Executive Health* (London, UK: Financial Times–Prentice Hall, 2003).

53. K. M. Wasylyshyn, "Coaching the Superkeepers," in L. A. Berger and D. R. Berger, eds., *The Talent Management Handbook: Creating Organizational Excellence by Identifying, Developing, and Positioning Your Best People* (New York: McGraw-Hill, 2003): 320–336.

54. J. C. Quick and M. Macik-Frey, "Behind the Mask: Coaching through Deep Interpersonal Communication," *Consulting Psychology Journal: Practice and Research* 56 (2004): 67–74.

55. R. Flinn, "Social Media: A New Jury Selection Tool," *Bloomberg Businessweek* (April 21, 2011).

56. B. J. Dunn, "Best Buy's CEO on Learning to Love Social Media," *Harvard Business Review* 88 (December 2010): 43–48.

57. D. Seetharaman, "Zuckerberg Lays Out Broad Vision for Facebook in 6,000-Word Mission Statement," *Wall Street Journal*, 17 Feb. 2017.

58. C. Brod, Technostress: *The Human Cost of the Computer Revolution* (Reading, Mass.: Addison-Wesley, 1984).

59. S. Kiesler, "Technology and the Development of Creative Environments," in Y. Ijiri and R. L. Kuhn, eds., *New Directions in Creative and Innovative Management* (Cambridge, Mass.: Ballinger Press, 1988).

60. S. Adams, "Being There," *Forbes* 187 (2011): 94.

61. S. Kiesler, J. Siegel, and T. W. McGuire, "Social Psychological Aspects of Computer-Mediated Communication," *American Psychologist* 39 (1984): 1123–1134.

62. P. Shachaf, "Cultural Diversity and Information and Communication Technology Impacts on Global Virtual Teams: An Exploratory Study," *Information & Management* 45 (2008): 131–142.

63. L. K. Barber and A. M. Santuzzi, "Please Respond ASAP: Workplace Telepressure and Employee Recovery," *Journal of Occupational Health Psychology* 20 (2015): 172–189.

9

1. J. E. Mathieu, J. R. Hollenbeck, D. van Knippenberg, and D. R. Ilgen, "A Century of Work Teams in the *Journal of Applied Psychology*," *Journal of Applied Psychology* 102, No. 3 (March 2017): 452–467.

2. S. S. Webber and R. J. Klimoski, "Crews: A Distinct Type of Work Team," *Journal of Business and Psychology* 18 (2004): 261–279.

3. J. L. Nemanich, S. Vélez-Castrillon, and S. Werner, "Knowledge-Based and Contextual Factors Associated with R&D Teams' Improvisation Capability," *Journal of Management* 42, No. 7 (November 2016): 1874–1903.

4. A. M. Towsend, S. M. DeMarie, and A. R. Hendrickson, "Virtual Teams: Technology and the Workplace of the Future," *Academy of Management Executive* 12 (1998): 17–29.

5. B. L. Kirkman, C. B. Gibson, and D. L. Shapiro, "'Exporting' Teams: Enhancing the Implementation and Effectiveness of Work Teams in Global Affiliates," *Organizational Dynamics* 30 (2001): 12–29.

6. A. Taylor and H. R. Greve, "Superman or the Fantastic Four? Knowledge Combination and Experience in Innovative Teams," *Academy of Management Journal* 49 (2006): 723–740.

7. S. Faraj and A. Yan, "Boundary Work in Knowledge Teams," *Journal of Applied Psychology* 94 (2009): 604–617.

8. P. Shaver and D. Buhrmester, "Loneliness, Sex-Role Orientation, and Group Life: A Social Needs Perspective," in P. Paulus, ed., *Basic Group Processes* (New York: Springer-Verlag, 1985): 259–288.

9. K. L. Bettenhausen and J. K. Murnighan, "The Development and Stability of Norms in Groups Facing Interpersonal and Structural Challenge," *Administrative Science Quarterly* 36 (1991): 20–35.

10. N. Ellemers, S. Pagliaro, M. Barreto, and C. W. Leach, "Is It Better to Be Moral Than Smart? The Effects of Morality and Competence Norms on the Decision to Work at Group Status Improvement," *Journal of Personality and Social Psychology* 95 (2008): 1397–1410.

11. I. Adarves-Yorno, T. Postmes, and S. A. Haslam, "Creative Innovation or Crazy Irrelevance? The Contribution of Group Norms and Social Identity to Creative Behavior," *Journal of Experimental Social Psychology* 43 (2007): 410–416.

12. D. Tjosvold and Z. Yu, "Goal Interdependence and Applying Abilities for Team In-Role and Extra-Role Performance in China," *Group Dynamics: Theory, Research, and Practice* 8 (2004): 98–111.

13. M. S. Cole, F. Walter, and H. Bruch, "Affective Mechanisms Linking Dysfunctional Behavior to Performance in Work Teams: A Moderated Mediation Study," *Journal of Applied Psychology* 93 (2008): 945–958.

14. V. U. Druskat and S. B. Wolff, "Building the Emotional Intelligence of Groups," *Harvard Business Review* 79 (2001): 80–90.

15. I. Summers, T. Coffelt, and R. E. Horton, "Work-Group Cohesion," *Psychological Reports* 63 (1988): 627–636.

16. D. C. Man and S. S. K. Lam, "The Effects of Job Complexity and Autonomy on Cohesiveness in Collectivistic and Individualistic Work Groups: A Cross-Cultural Analysis," *Journal of Organizational Behavior* 24 (2003): 979–1001.

17. Y. Shin and J. N. Choi, "What Makes a Group of Good Citizens? The Role of Perceived Group-Level Fit and Critical Psychological States in Organizational Teams," *Journal of Occupational and Organizational Psychology* 83 (2010): 531–552.

18. K. H. Price, "Working Hard to Get People to Loaf," *Basic and Applied Social Psychology* 14 (1993): 329–344.

19. M. C. Schippers, "Social Loafing Tendencies and Team Performance: The Compensating Effect of Agreeableness and Conscientiousness," *Academy of Management Learning & Education* 13 (2014): 62–81.

20. R. Albanese and D. D. Van Fleet, "Rational Behavior in Groups: The Free-Riding Tendency," *Academy of Management Review* 10 (1985): 244–255.

21. E. Diener, "Deindividuation, Self-Awareness, and Disinhibition," *Journal of Personality and Social Psychology* 37 (1979): 1160–1171.

22. S. Prentice-Dunn and R. W. Rogers, "Deindividuation and the Self-Regulation of Behavior," in P. Paulus, ed., *Psychology of Group Influence* (Hillsdale, N.J.: Erlbaum, 1989): 87–109.

23. B. M. Bass and E. C. Ryterband, *Organizational Psychology*, 2nd ed. (Boston: Allyn & Bacon, 1979).

24. W. G. Bennis and H. A. Shepard, "A Theory of Group Development," *Human Relations* 9 (1956): 415–438.

25. A. Joshi and A. P. Knight, "Who Defers to Whom and Why? Dual Pathways Linking

Demographic Differences and Dyadic Deference to Team Effectiveness," *Academy of Management Journal* 58 (2015): 59–84.

26. D. L. Fields and T. C. Bloom, "Employee Satisfaction in Work Groups with Different Gender Composition," *Journal of Organizational Behavior* 18 (1997): 181–196.

27. D. C. Lau and J. K. Murnighan, "Demographic Diversity and Faultlines: The Compositional Dynamics of Organizational Groups," *Academy of Management Review* 23 (1998): 325–340.

28. B. Tuckman, "Developmental Sequence in Small Groups," *Psychological Bulletin* 63 (1965): 384–399; B. Tuckman and M. Jensen, "Stages of Small-Group Development," *Group and Organizational Studies* 2 (1977): 419–427.

29. S. T. Bell and J. A. Belohlav, "The Power of 'We': The Effects of Psychological Collectivism on Team Performance over Time," *Journal of Applied Psychology* 96 (2011): 247–262.

30. D. Nichols, "Quality Program Sparked Company Turnaround," *Personnel* (October 1991): 24. For a commentary on Wallace's hard times and subsequent emergence from Chapter 11 bankruptcy, see R. C. Hill, "When the Going Gets Tough: A Baldrige Award Winner on the Line," *Academy of Management Executive* 7 (1993): 75–79.

31. S. Weisband and L. Atwater, "Evaluating Self and Others in Electronic and Face-to-Face Groups," *Journal of Applied Psychology* 84 (1999): 632–639.

32. C. J. G. Gersick, "Time and Transition in Work Teams: Toward a New Model of Group Development," *The Academy of Management Journal* 31 (1988): 9–41.

33. M. Hardaker and B. K. Ward, "How to Make a Team Work," *Harvard Business Review* 65 (1987): 112–120.

34. C. R. Gowen, "Managing Work Group Performance by Individual Goals and Group Goals for an Interdependent Group Task," *Journal of Organizational Behavior Management* 7 (1986): 5–27.

35. K. L. Bettenhausen and J. K. Murnighan, "The Emergence of Norms in Competitive Decision-Making Groups," *Administrative Science Quarterly* 30 (1985): 350–372; K. L. Bettenhausen, "Five Years of Groups Research: What We Have Learned and What Needs to Be Addressed," *Journal of Management* 17 (1991): 345–381.

36. N. Li, B. L. Kirkman, and C. O. L. H. Porter, "Toward a Model of Work Team Altruism," *Academy of Management Review* 39 (2014): 541–565.

37. J. E. McGrath, *Groups: Interaction and Performance* (Englewood Cliffs, N.J.: Prentice-Hall, 1984).

38. K. L. Gammage, A. V. Carron, and P. A. Estabrooks, "Team Cohesion and Individual Productivity," *Small Group Research* 32 (2001): 3–18.

39. W. J. Becker and R. Cropanzano, "Good Acting Requires a Good Cast: A Meso-Level Model of Deep Acting in Work Teams,"

Journal of Organizational Behavior 36 (2015): 232–249.

40. S. M. Klein, "A Longitudinal Study of the Impact of Work Pressure on Group Cohesive Behaviors," *International Journal of Management* 12 (1996): 68–75.

41. N. Steckler and N. Fondas, "Building Team Leader Effectiveness: A Diagnostic Tool," *Organizational Dynamics* 23 (1995): 20–35.

42. A. Carter and S. Holmes, "Curiously Strong Teamwork," *BusinessWeek* 4023 (February 26, 2007): 90–92.

43. W. R. Lassey, "Dimensions of Leadership," in W. R. Lassey and R. Fernandez, eds., *Leadership and Social Change* (La Jolla, Calif.: University Associates, 1976): 10–15.

44. B. Broysberg and L. Lee, "The Effect of Colleague Quality on Top Performance: The Case of Security Analysts," *Journal of Organizational Behavior* 29 (2008): 1123–1144.

45. J. D. Quick, G. Moorhead, J. C. Quick, E. A. Gerloff, K. L. Mattox, and C. Mullins, "Decision Making among Emergency Room Residents: Preliminary Observations and a Decision Model," *Journal of Medical Education* 58 (1983): 117–125.

46. J. Sieweke and B. Zhao, "The Impact of Team Familiarity and Team Leader Experience on Team Coordination Errors: A Panel Analysis of Professional Basketball Teams," *Journal of Organizational Behavior* 36 (2015): 382–402.

47. W. J. Duncan and J. P. Feisal, "No Laughing Matter: Patterns of Humor in the Workplace," *Organizational Dynamics* 17 (1989): 18–30.

48. L. Hirschhorn, *Managing in the New Team Environment* (Upper Saddle River, N.J.: Prentice-Hall): 521A.

49. G. Chen and R. J. Klimoski, "The Impact of Expectations on Newcomer Performance in Teams as Mediated by Work Characteristics, Social Exchanges, and Empowerment," *Academy of Management Journal* 46 (2003): 591–607.

50. B. Beersma, J. R. Hollenbeck, S. E. Humphrey, H. Moon, D. E. Conlon, and D. R. Ilgen, "Cooperation, Competition, and Team Performance: Toward a Contingency Approach," *Academy of Management Journal* 46 (2003): 572–590.

51. G. Parker, *Team Players and Teamwork* (San Francisco: Jossey-Bass, 1990).

52. N. R. F. Maier, "Assets and Liabilities in Group Problem Solving: The Need for an Integrative Function," *Psychological Review* 74 (1967): 239–249.

53. T. A. Stewart, "The Search for the Organization of Tomorrow," *Fortune* (May 18, 1992): 92–98.

54. P. Chattopadhyay, M. Tluchowska, and E. George, "Identifying the Ingroup: A Closer Look at the Influence of Demographic Dissimilarity on Employee Social Identity," *Academy of Management Review* 29 (2004): 180–202.

55. M. M. Stewart and P. Garcia-Prieto, "A Relational Demography Model of Workgroup

Identification: Testing the Effects of Race, Race Dissimilarity, Racial Identification, and Communication Behavior," *Journal of Organizational Behavior* 29 (2008): 657–680.

56. E. V. Hobman, P. Bordia, and C. Gallois, "Consequences of Feeling Dissimilar from Others in a Work Team," *Journal of Business and Psychology* 17 (2003): 301–325.

57. A. E. Randel and K. S. Jaussi, "Functional Background Identity, Diversity, and Individual Performance in Cross-Functional Teams," *Academy of Management Journal* 46 (2003): 763–774.

58. J. S. Bunderson, "Team Member Functional Background and Involvement in Management Teams: Direct Effects and the Moderating Role of Power Centralization," *Academy of Management Journal* 46 (2003): 458–474.

59. G. S. Van Der Vegt, E. Van De Vliert, and A. Oosterhof, "Informational Dissimilarity and Organizational Citizenship Behavior: The Role of Intrateam Interdependence and Team Identification," *Academy of Management Journal* 46 (2003): 715–727.

60. F. Balkundi, M. Kilduff, Z. I. Barsness, and J. H. Michael, "Demographic Antecedents and Performance Consequences of Structural Holes in Work Teams," *Journal of Organizational Behavior* 28 (2007): 241–260.

61. A. Pirola-Merlo and L. Mann, "The Relationship between Individual Creativity and Team Creativity: Aggregating across People and Time," *Journal of Organizational Behavior* 25 (2004): 235–257.

62. L. Thompson, "Improving the Creativity of Organizational Work Groups," *Academy of Management Executive* 17 (2003): 96–111.

63. J. Han, and D. J. Brass, "Human Capital Diversity in the Creation of Social Capital for Team Creativity," *Journal of Organizational Behavior* 35 (2014): 54–71.

64. C. Ford and D. M. Sullivan, "A Time for Everything: How the Timing of Novel Contributions Influences Project Team Outcomes," *Journal of Organizational Behavior* 25 (2004): 279–292.

65. N. M. Llorinkova and S. J. Perry, "When Is Empowerment Effective? The Role of Leader-Leader Exchange in Empowering Leadership, Cynicism, and Time Theft," *Academy of Management* 43, No. 5 (May 2017): 1631–1654.

66. R. R. Blake, J. S. Mouton, and R. L. Allen, *Spectacular Teamwork: How to Develop the Leadership Skills for Team Success* (New York: Wiley, 1987).

67. American Management Association, *Blueprints for Service Quality: The Federal Express Approach*, AMA Management Briefing (New York: AMA, 1991).

68. W. C. Byham, *ZAPP! The Human Lightning of Empowerment* (Pittsburgh, PA: Developmental Dimensions, 1989).

69. F. Shipper and C. C. Manz, "Employee Self-Management without Formally Designated Teams: An Alternative Road to Empowerment," *Organizational Dynamics* (Winter 1992): 48–62.

70. P. Block, *The Empowered Manager: Positive Political Skills at Work* (San Francisco: Jossey-Bass, 1987).

71. V. J. Derlega and J. Grzelak, eds., *Cooperation and Helping Behavior: Theories and Research* (New York: Academic Press, 1982).

72. G. S. Van der Vegt, J. S. Bunderson, and A. Oosterhof, "Expertness Diversity and Interpersonal Helping in Teams: Why Those Who Need the Most Help End Up Getting the Least," *Academy of Management Journal* 49 (2006): 877–893.

73. A. G. Athos and J. J. Gabarro, *Interpersonal Behavior: Communication and Understanding in Relationships* (Englewood Cliffs, N.J.: Prentice-Hall, 1978).

74. C. Douglas and W. L. Gardner, "Transition to Self-Directed Work Teams: Implications of Transition Time and Self-Monitoring for Managers' Use of Influence Tactics," *Journal of Organizational Behavior* 25 (2004): 47–65.

75. C. Douglas, J. S. Martin, and R. H. Krapels, "Communication in the Transition to Self-Directed Work Teams," *Journal of Business Communication* 43 (2006): 295–321.

76. J. L. Cordery, W. S. Mueller, and L. M. Smith, "Attitudinal and Behavioral Effects of Autonomous Group Working: A Longitudinal Field Study," *Academy of Management Journal* 34 (1991): 464–476.

77. G. Moorhead, C. P. Neck, and M. S. West, "The Tendency toward Defective Decision Making within Self-Managing Teams: The Relevance of Groupthink for the 21st Century," *Organizational Behavior and Human Decision Processes* 73 (1998): 327–351.

78. B. M. Staw and L. D. Epstein, "What Bandwagons Bring: Effects of Popular Management Techniques on Corporate Performance, Reputation, and CEO Pay," *Administrative Science Quarterly* 45 (2000): 523–556.

79. R. M. Robinson, S. L. Oswald, K. S. Swinehart, and J. Thomas, "Southwest Industries: Creating High-Performance Teams for High-Technology Production," *Planning Review* 19, published by the Planning Forum (November–December 1991): 10–47.

80. D. C. Hambrick and P. Mason, "Upper Echelons: The Organization as a Reflection of Its Top Managers," *Academy of Management Review* 9 (1984): 193–206.

81. C. Heavey and Z. Simsek, "Distributed Cognition in Top Management Teams and Organizational Ambidexterity," *Academy of Management*, 43, 3 (May 2017), pp. 919–945.

82. A. D. Henderson and J. W. Fredrickson, "Top Management Team Coordination Needs and the CEO Pay Gap: A Competitive Test of Economic and Behavioral Views," *Academy of Management Journal* 44 (2001): 96–117.

83. D. C. Hambrick and G. D. S. Fukutomi, "The Seasons of a CEO's Tenure," *Academy of Management Review* 16 (1991): 719–742.

84. J. C. Quick, D. L. Nelson, and J. D. Quick, "Successful Executives: How Independent?" *Academy of Management Executive* 1 (1987): 139–145.

85. A. A. Cannella, Jr, J. Park, and H. Lee, "Top Management Team Functional Background Diversity and Firm Performance: Examining the Roles of Team Member Colocation and Environmental Uncertainty," *Academy of Management Journal* 51(2008): 768–784.

86. J. W. Ridge, A. D. Hill, and F. Aime, "Implication of Multiple Concurrent Pay Comparisons for Top-Team Turnover," *Academy of Management* 43, No. 3 (May 2017): 671–690.

87. N. J. Adler, *International Dimensions of Organizational Behavior* (Mason, Ohio: South-Western, 2001).

88. I. D. Steiner, *Group Process and Productivity* (New York: Academic Press, 1972).

89. E. Kearney, D. Gebert, and S. C. Voelpel, "When and How Diversity Benefits Teams: The Importance of Team Members' Need for Cognition," *Academy of Management Journal* 52 (2009): 581–598.

90. T. Buyl, C. Boone, W. Hendriks, and P. Matthyssens, "Top Management Team Functional Diversity and Firm Performance: The Moderating Role of CEO Characteristics," *Journal of Management Studies* 48 (2011): 151–176.

10

1. H. A. Simon, *The New Science of Management Decision* (New York: Harper & Row, 1960).

2. R. Walker, "Brand Blue," *Fortune* (April 28, 2003): http://www.fortune.com/fortune/small-business/articles/0,15114,426909,00.html.

3. G. Huber, *Managerial Decision Making* (Glenview, Ill.: Scott, Foresman, 1980).

4. H. A. Simon, *Administrative Behavior* (New York: Macmillan, 1957).

5. E. F. Harrison, *The Managerial Decision-Making Process* (Boston: Houghton Mifflin, 1981).

6. R. L. Ackoff, "The Art and Science of Mess Management," *Interfaces* (February 1981): 20–26.

7. J. S. Lerner, Y. Li, P. Valdesolo, and K. S. Kassam, "Emotion and Decision Making," *Annual Review of Psychology* 66 (2015): 799–823.

8. B. M. Staw, "Knee-Deep in the Big Muddy: A Study of Escalating Commitment to a Chosen Course of Action," *Organizational Behavior and Human Performance* 16 (1976): 27–44; B. M. Staw, "The Escalation of Commitment to a Course of Action," *Academy of Management Review* 6 (1981): 577–587.

9. B. M. Staw and J. Ross, "Understanding Behavior in Escalation Situations," *Science* 246 (1989): 216–220.

10. R. L. Schaumberg and S. S. Wiltermuth, "Desire for a Positive Moral Self-Regard Exacerbates Escalation of Commitment to Initiatives with Prosocial Aims," *Organizational Behavior and Human Decision Processes* 123 (2014): 110–123.

11. L. Festinger, *A Theory of Cognitive Dissonance* (Evanston, Ill.: Row, Peterson, 1957).

12. B. M. Staw, "The Escalation of Commitment: An Update and Appraisal," in Z. Shapira, ed., *Organizational Decision Making* (Cambridge, England: Cambridge University Press, 1997).

13. D. M. Boehne and P. W. Paese, "Deciding Whether to Complete or Terminate an Unfinished Project: A Strong Test of the Project Completion Hypothesis," *Organizational Behavior and Human Decision Processes* 81 (2000): 178–194; H. Moon, "Looking Forward and Looking Back: Integrating Completion and Sunk Cost Effects within an Escalation-of-Commitment Progress Decision," *Journal of Applied Psychology* 86 (2000): 104–113.

14. J. A. Sonnenfeld, "How Rick Wagoner Lost GM," *BusinessWeek* (June 1, 2009), http://www.businessweek.com/managing/content/jun2009/ca2009061_966638.htm.

15. N. Sivanathan, D. C. Molden, A. D. Galinsky, and G. Ku, "The Promise and Peril of Self-Affirmation in the De-Escalation of Commitment," *Organizational Behavior and Human Decision Processes* 107 (2008): 1–14.

16. A. C. Hafenbrack, Z. Kinias, and S. G. Barsade, "Debiasing the Mind through Meditation: Mindfulness and the Sunk-Cost Bias," *Psychological Science* 25 (2014): 369–376.

17. G. Whyte, "Diffusion of Responsibility: Effects on the Escalation Tendency," *Journal of Applied Psychology* 76 (1991): 408–415.

18. D. van Knippenberg, B. van Knippenberg, and E. van Dijk, "Who Takes the Lead in Risky Decision Making? Effects of Group Members' Risk Preferences and Prototypicality," *Organizational Behavior and Human Decision Processes* 83 (2000): 213–234.

19. K. R. MacCrimmon and D. Wehrung, *Taking Risks* (New York: Free Press, 1986).

20. T. S. Perry, "How Small Firms Innovate: Designing a Culture for Creativity," *Research Technology Management* 28 (1995): 14–17.

21. A. Saleh, "Brain Hemisphericity and Academic Majors: A Correlation Study," *College Student Journal* 35 (2001): 193–200.

22. N. Khatri, "The Role of Intuition in Strategic Decision Making," *Human Relations* 53 (2000): 57–86.

23. H. Mintzberg, "Planning on the Left Side and Managing on the Right," *Harvard Business Review* 54 (1976): 51–63.

24. D. J. Isenberg, "How Senior Managers Think," *Harvard Business Review* 62 (1984): 81–90.

25. R. N. Beck, "Visions, Values, and Strategies: Changing Attitudes and Culture," *Academy of Managment Executive* 1 (1987): 33–41.

26. K. G. Ross, G. A. Klein, P. Thunholm, J. F. Schmitt, and H. C. Baxter, "The Recognition-Primed Decision Model," *Military Review, Fort Leavenworth* 84 (2004): 6–10.

27. C. I. Barnard, *The Functions of the Executive* (Cambridge, Mass.: Harvard University Press, 1938).

28. R. Rowan, *The Intuitive Manager* (New York: Little, Brown, 1986).

29. W. H. Agor, *Intuition in Organizations* (Newbury Park, Calif.: Sage, 1989).

30. D. J. Isenberg, "How Senior Managers Think" (Thousand Oaks, CA: Sage Publications, 1991).

31. H. A. Simon, "Making Management Decisions: The Role of Intuition and Emotion," *Academy of Management Executive* 1 (1987): 57–64.

32. J. L. Redford, R. H. McPhierson, R. G. Frankiewicz, and J. Gaa, "Intuition and Moral Development," *Journal of Psychology* 129 (1994): 91–101.

33. R. Wild, "Naked Hunch; Gut Instinct Is Vital to Your Business," *Success* (June 1998), http://www.findarticles.com/cf_dls/m3514/n6_v45/20746158/p1/article.jhtml.

34. W. H. Agor, "How Top Executives Use Their Intuition to Make Important Decisions," *Business Horizons* 29 (1986): 49–53.

35. O. Behling and N. L. Eckel, "Making Sense out of Intuition," *Academy of Management Executive* 5 (1991): 46–54.

36. L. R. Beach, *Image Theory: Decision Making in Personal and Organizational Contexts* (Chichester, England: Wiley, 1990).

37. E. Bonabeau, "Don't Trust Your Gut," *Harvard Business Review* 81 (2003): 116–126.

38. L. Livingstone, "Person-Environment Fit on the Dimension of Creativity: Relationships with Strain, Job Satisfaction, and Performance" (Ph.D. diss., Oklahoma State University, 1992).

39. G. Wallas, *The Art of Thought* (New York: Harcourt Brace, 1926).

40. H. Benson and W. Proctor, *The Break-Out Principle* (Scribner: New York, 2003); G. L. Fricchione, B. T. Slingsby, and H. Benson, "The Placebo Effect and the Relaxation Response: Neural Processes and Their Coupling to Constitutive Nitric Oxide," *Brain Research Reviews* 35 (2001): 1–19.

41. M. D. Mumford and S. B. Gustafson, "Creativity Syndrome: Integration, Application, and Innovation," *Psychological Bulletin* 103 (1988): 27–43.

42. T. Poze, "Analogical Connections—The Essence of Creativity," *Journal of Creative Behavior* 17 (1983): 240–241.

43. I. Sladeczek and G. Domino, "Creativity, Sleep, and Primary Process Thinking in Dreams," *Journal of Creative Behavior* 19 (1985): 38–46.

44. F. Barron and D. M. Harrington, "Creativity, Intelligence, and Personality," *Annual Review of Psychology* 32 (1981): 439–476.

45. R. J. Sternberg, "A Three-Faced Model of Creativity," in R. J. Sternberg, ed., *The Nature of Creativity* (Cambridge, England: Cambridge University Press, 1988): 125–147.

46. A. M. Grant and J. W. Berry, "The Necessity of Others Is the Mother of Invention: Intrinsic and Prosocial Motivations, Perspective Taking, and Creativity," *Academy of Management Journal* 54, No. 1 (2011): 73–96.

47. A. M. Isen, "Positive Affect and Decision Making," in W. M. Goldstein and R. M. Hogarth, eds., *Research on Judgment and Decision Making* (Cambridge, England: Cambridge University Press, 1997).

48. G. L. Clore, N. Schwartz, and M. Conway, "Cognitive Causes and Consequences of Emotion," in R. S. Wyer and T. K. Srull, eds., *Handbook of Social Cognition* (Hillsdale, N.J.: Erlbaum, 1994): 323–417.

49. B. L. Frederickson, "What Good Are Positive Emotions?" *Review of General Psychology* 2 (1998): 300–319; B. L. Frederickson, "The Role of Positive Emotions in Positive Psychology," *American Psychologist* 56 (2001): 218–226.

50. S. H. Harrison and D. T. Wagner, "Spilling Outside the Box: The Effects of Individuals' Creative Behaviors at Work on Time Spent with Their Spouses at Home," *Academy of Management Journal*, 59 (2016): 841–859.

51. J. Zhou, "When the Presence of Creative Coworkers Is Related to Creativity: Role of Supervisor Close Monitoring, Developmental Feedback, and Creative Personality," *Journal of Applied Psychology* 88 (2003): 413–422.

52. J. Peng, Y. Chen, Y. Xia, and Y. Ran, "Workplace Loneliness, Leader-Member Exchange and Creativity: The Cross-Level Moderating Role of Leader Compassion," *Personality and Individual Differences*, 104 (2017): 510–515.

53. B. Kijkuit and J. van den Ende, "The Organizational Life of an Idea: Integrating Social Network, Creativity and Decision-Making Perspectives," *Journal of Management Studies* 44, No. 6 (2007): 863–882.

54. T. M. Amabile, R. Conti, H. Coon, J. Lazenby, and M. Herron, "Assessing the Work Environment for Creativity," *Academy of Management Journal* 39 (1996): 1154–1184.

55. T. Tetenbaum and H. Tetenbaum, "Office 2000: Tear Down the Wall," *Training* (February 2000): 58–64.

56. L. Livingstone, D. L. Nelson, and S.H. Barr, "Person-Environment Fit and Creativity: An Examination of Supply-Value and Demand-Ability Versions of Fit," *Journal of Management* 23 (l997): 119–146.

57. R. L. Firestein, "Effects of Creative Problem-Solving Training on Communication Behaviors in Small Groups," *Small Group Research* (November 1989): 507–521.

58. R. Von Oech, *A Whack on the Side of the Head* (New York: Warner, 1983).

59. A. G. Robinson and S. Stern, *How Innovation and Improvement Actually Happen* (San Francisco: Berrett Koehler, 1997).

60. M. D. Mumford, E. M. Todd, C. Higgs, and T. McIntosh, "Cognitive Skills and Leadership Performance: The Nine Critical Skills," *The Leadership Quarterly*, 28 (2017): 24–39.

61. R. Y. J. Chua, Y. Roth, and J. Lemoine, "How Culture Impacts Creativity: Cultural Tightness, Cultural Distance, and Global Creative Work," *Administrative Science Quarterly* (in press), published online December 8, 2014.

62. G. Stasser, L. A. Taylor, and C. Hanna, "Information Sampling in Structured and Unstructured Discussion of Three- and Six-Person Groups," *Journal of Personality and Social Psychology* 57 (1989): 67–78.

63. E. Kirchler and J. H. Davis, "The Influence of Member Status Differences and Task Type on Group Consensus and Member Position Change," *Journal of Personality and Social Psychology* 51 (1986): 83–91.

64. R. F. Maier, "Assets and Liabilities in Group Problem Solving," *Psychological Review* 74 (1967): 239–249.

65. M. E. Shaw, *Group Dynamics: The Psychology of Small Group Behavior*, 3rd ed. (New York: McGraw-Hill, 1981).

66. P. W. Yetton and P. C. Bottger, "Individual versus Group Problem Solving: An Empirical Test of a Best Member Strategy," *Organizational Behavior and Human Performance* 29 (1982): 307–321.

67. W. Watson, L. Michaelson, and W. Sharp, "Member Competence, Group Interaction, and Group Decision Making: A Longitudinal Study," *Journal of Applied Psychology* 76 (1991): 803–809.

68. I. Janis, *Victims of Groupthink* (Boston: Houghton Mifflin, 1972); M. Kostera, M. Proppe, and M. Szatkowski, "Staging the New Romantic Hero in the Old Cynical Theatre: On Managers, Roles, and Change in Poland," *Journal of Organizational Behavior* 16 (1995): 631–646.

69. M. A. Hogg and S. C. Hains, "Friendship and Group Identification: A New Look at the Role of Cohesiveness in Groupthink," *European Journal of Social Psychology* 28 (1998): 323–341.

70. P. E. Jones and H. M. P. Roelofsma, "The Potential for Social Contextual and Group Biases in Team Decision Making: Biases, Conditions, and Psychological Mechanisms," *Ergonomics* 43 (2000): 1129–1152; J. M. Levine, E. T. Higgins, and H. Choi, "Development of Strategic Norms in Groups," *Organizational Behavior and Human Decision Processes* 82 (2000): 88–101.

71. A. L. Brownstein, "Biased Predecision Processing," *Psychological Bulletin* 129 (2003): 545–568.

72. C. P. Neck and G. Moorhead, "Groupthink Remodeled: The Importance of Leadership, Time Pressure, and Methodical Decision-Making Procedures," *Human Relations* 48 (1995): 537–557.

73. J. Schwartz and M. L. Ward, "Final Shuttle Report Cites 'Broken Safety Culture' at NASA," *The New York Times* (August 26, 2003), http://www.nytimes.com/2003/08/26/national/26CND-SHUT.html?ex=1077253200&en=882575f2c17ed8ff&ei=5070; C. Ferraris and R. Carveth, "NASA and the Columbia Disaster: Decision Making by Groupthink?" in Proceedings of the 2003 Convention of the Association for Business Communication Annual Convention, http://www.businesscommunication.org/conventions/Proceedings/2003/PDF/03ABC03.pdf.

74. W. P. Cheshire Jr., "Loopthink: A Limitation of Medical Artificial Intelligence," *Ethics & Medicine*, 33 (2017): 7–12.

75. A. C. Homan, D. van Knippenberg, G. A. Van Kleef, and K. W. C. De Dreu, "Bridging Faultlines by Valuing Diversity: Diversity Beliefs, Information Elaboration, and Performance in Diverse Work Groups," *Journal of Applied Psychology* 92, No. 5 (2007):1189–1199.

76. G. Moorhead, R. Ference, and C. P. Neck, "Group Decision Fiascoes Continue: Space Shuttle *Challenger* and a Revised Groupthink Framework," *Human Relations* 44 (1991): 539–550.

77. J. R. Montanari and G. Moorhead, "Development of the Groupthink Assessment Inventory," *Educational and Psychological Measurement* 49 (1989): 209–219.

78. P. Hart, "Irving L. Janis' Victims of Groupthink," *Political Psychology* 12 (1991): 247–278.

79. A. C. Mooney, P. J. Holahan, and A. C. Amason, "Don't Take It Personally: Exploring Cognitive Conflict as a Mediator of Affective Conflict," *Journal of Management Studies* 44, No. 5 (2007): 733–758.

80. J. A. F. Stoner, "Risky and Cautious Shifts in Group Decisions: The Influence of Widely Held Values," *Journal of Experimental Social Psychology* 4 (1968): 442–459.

81. S. Moscovici and M. Zavalloni, "The Group as a Polarizer of Attitudes," *Journal of Personality and Social Psychology* 12 (1969): 125–135.

82. G. R. Goethals and M. P. Zanna, "The Role of Social Comparison in Choice of Shifts," *Journal of Personality and Social Psychology* 37 (1979): 1469–1476.

83. A. Vinokur and E. Burnstein, "Effects of Partially Shared Persuasive Arguments on Group-Induced Shifts: A Problem-Solving Approach," *Journal of Personality and Social Psychology* 29 (1974): 305–315; J. Pfeffer, "Seven Practices of Successful Organizations," *California Management Review* 40 (1998): 96–124.

84. J. K. Palmer and J. M. Loveland, "The Influence of Group Discussion on Performance Judgments: Rating Accuracy, Contrast Effects and Halo," *The Journal of Psychology: Interdisciplinary and Applied* 142 (2008): 117–130.

85. P. Paulus, N. W. Kohn, L. E. Arditti, and R. Korde, "Understanding the Group Size Effect in Electronic Brainstorming," *Small Group Research* 44 (2013): 332–352.

86. N. Michinov, E. Jamet, N. Metayer, and B. L. Henaff, "The Eyes of Creativity: Impact of Social Comparison and Individual Creativity on Performance and Attention to Others' Ideas During Electronic Brainstorming," *Computers in Human Behavior* 42 (2015): 57–67.

87. A. Van de Ven and A. Delbecq, "The Effectiveness of Nominal, Delphi and Interacting Group Decision-Making Processes," *Academy of Management Journal* 17 (1974): 605–621.

88. R. A. Cosier and C. R. Schwenk, "Agreement and Thinking Alike: Ingredients for Poor Decisions," *Academy of Management Executive* 4 (1990): 69–74.

89. D. M. Schweiger, W. R. Sandburg, and J. W. Ragan, "Group Approaches for Improving Strategic Decision Making: A Comparative Analysis of Dialectical Inquiry, Devil's Advocacy, and Consensus," *Academy of Management Journal* 29 (1986): 149–159.

90. G. Whyte, "Decision Failures: Why They Occur and How to Prevent Them," *Academy of Management Executive* 5 (1991): 23–31.

91. L. Scholten, D. van Knippenberg, B. A. Nijstad, and K. W. C. De Dreu, "Motivated Information Processing and Group Decision-Making: Effects of Process Accountability on Information Processing and Decision Quality," *Journal of Experimental Social Psychology* 43, No. 4 (2007): 539–552.

92. E. E. Lawler III and S. A. Mohrman, "Quality Circles: After the Honeymoon," *Organizational Dynamics* (Spring 1987): 42–54.

93. T. L. Tang and E. A. Butler, "Attributions of Quality Circles' Problem-Solving Failure: Differences among Management, Supporting Staff, and Quality Circle Members," *Public Personnel Management* 26 (1997): 203–225.

94. J. Schilder, "Work Teams Boost Productivity," *Personnel Journal* 71 (1992): 67–72.

95. L. I. Glassop, "The Organizational Benefits of Teams," *Human Relations* 55 (2002): 225–249.

96. C. J. Nemeth, "Managing Innovation: When Less Is More," *California Management Review* 40 (1997): 59–68.

97. N. Adler, *International Dimensions of Organizational Behavior*, 3rd ed. (Mason, Ohio: South-Western, 1997).

98. K. W. Phillips and D. L. Lloyd, "When Surface- and Deep-Level Diversity Collide: The Effects on Dissenting Group Members," *Organizational Behavior and Human Decision Processes* 99, No. 2 (2006): 143–160.

99. T. Simons, L. H. Pelled, and K. A. Smith, "Making Use of Difference: Diversity, Debate, and Decision Comprehensiveness in Top Management Teams," *Academy of Management Journal* 42, No. 6 (1999): 662–673.

100. B. A. Livingston, P. Schilpzand, and A. Erez, "Not What You Expected to Hear: Accented Messages and Their Effect on Choice," *Journal of Management*, 43 (2017): 804–833.

101. J. Pfeffer, "Seven Practices of Successful Organizations," *California Management Review* 40 (1998): 96–124.

102. L. A. Witt, M. C. Andrews, and K. M. Kacmar, "The Role of Participation in Decision Making in the Organizational Politics–Job Satisfaction Relationship," *Human Relations* 53 (2000): 341–358.

103. J. He and W. R. King, "The Role of User Participation in Information Systems Development: Implications from a Meta-Analysis," *Journal of Management Information Systems* 25 (2008): 301–331.

104. C. R. Leana, E. A. Locke, and D. M. Schweiger, "Fact and Fiction in Analyzing Research on Participative Decision Making: A Critique of Cotton, Vollrath, Froggatt, Lengnick-Hall, and Jennings," *Academy of Management Review* 15 (1990): 137–146; J. L. Cotton, D. A. Vollrath, M. L. Lengnick-Hall, and K. L. Froggatt, "Fact: The Form of Participation Does Matter—A Rebuttal to Leana, Locke, and Schweiger," *Academy of Management Review* 15 (1990): 147–153.

105. T. W. Malone, "Is Empowerment Just a Fad? Control, Decision Making, and Information Technology," *Sloan Management Review* 38 (1997): 23–35.

106. IBM Customer Success Stories, "City and County of San Francisco Lower Total Cost of Ownership and Build on Demand Foundation" (February 3, 2004), http://www-306.ibm.com/software/success/cssdb.nsf/cs/LWRT-5VTLM2?OpenDocument&Site=lot usmandc.

107. T. L. Brown, "Fearful of 'Empowerment': Should Managers Be Terrified?" *Industry Week* (June 18, 1990): 12.

108. P. G. Gyllenhammar, *People at Work* (Reading, Mass.: Addison-Wesley, 1977).

109. R. Tannenbaum and F. Massarik, "Participation by Subordinates in the Managerial Decision-Making Process," *Canadian Journal of Economics and Political Science* 16 (1950): 408–418.

110. H. Levinson, *Executive* (Cambridge, Mass.: Harvard University Press, 1981).

111. R. F. Maier, "Assets and Liabilities in Group Problem Solving," Psychological *Review* 74 (1967): 239–249.

11

1. G. C. Homans, "Social Behavior as Exchange," *American Journal of Sociology* 63 (1958): 597–606.

2. R. D. Middlemist and M. A. Hitt, *Organizational Behavior: Managerial Strategies for Performance* (St. Paul, Minn.: West Publishing, 1988).

3. C. Barnard, *The Functions of the Executive* (Cambridge, Mass.: Harvard University Press, 1938).

4. J. R. P. French and B. Raven, "The Bases of Social Power," in D. Cartwright, ed., *Group Dynamics: Research and Theory* (Evanston, Ill.: Row Peterson, 1962); T. R. Hinkin and C. A. Schriesheim, "Development and Application of New Scales to Measure the French and Raven (1959) Bases of Social Power," *Journal of Applied Psychology* 74 (1989): 561–567.

5. K. D. Elsbach and G. Elofson, "How the Packaging of Decision Explanations Affects Perceptions of Trustworthiness," *Academy of Management Journal* 43, No. 1 (2000): 80–89.

6. P. M. Podsakoff and C. A. Schriesheim, "Field Studies of French and Raven's Bases of Power: Critique, Reanalysis, and Suggestions for Future Research," *Psychological Bulletin* 97 (1985): 387–411.

7. M. A. Rahim, "Relationships of Leader Power to Compliance and Satisfaction with Supervision: Evidence from a National Sample of

Managers," *Journal of Management* 15 (1989): 545–556.

8. C. Argyris, "Management Information Systems: The Challenge to Rationality and Emotionality," *Management Science* 17 (1971): 275–292; J. Naisbitt and P. Aburdene, *Megatrends 2000* (New York: Morrow, 1990).

9. P. P. Carson, K. D. Carson, E. L. Knight, and C. W. Roe, "Power in Organizations: A Look through the TQM Lens," *Quality Progress* (November 1995): 73–78.

10. K. Kruse, "Why Pepsi's CEO Writes to Her Employees' Parents," *Forbes*, February 6, 2014, accessed at http://www.forbes.com/sites/kevinkruse/2014/02/06/indra-nooyi-wholehearted-leader/.

11. J. Pfeffer and G. Salancik, *The External Control of Organizations* (New York: Harper & Row, 1978).

12. T. M. Welbourne and C. O. Trevor, "The Roles of Departmental and Position Power in Job Evaluation," *Academy of Management Journal* 43, No. 4 (2000): 761–771.

13. R. H. Miles, *Macro Organizational Behavior* (Glenview, Ill.: Scott, Foresman, 1980).

14. D. Hickson, C. Hinings, C. Lee, R. E. Schneck, and J. M. Pennings, "A Strategic Contingencies Theory of Intraorganizational Power," *Administrative Science Quarterly* 14 (1971): 219–220.

15. C. R. Hinings, D. J. Hickson, J. M. Pennings, and R. E. Schneck, "Structural Conditions of Intraorganizational Power," *Administrative Science Quarterly* 19 (1974): 22–44.

16. M. Velasquez, D. J. Moberg, and G. F. Cavanaugh, "Organizational Statesmanship and Dirty Politics: Ethical Guidelines for the Organizational Politician," *Organizational Dynamics* 11 (1982): 65–79.

17. D. E. McClelland, *Power: The Inner Experience* (New York: Irvington, 1975).

18. N. Shahinpoor and B. F. Matt, "The Power of One: Dissent and Organizational Life," *Journal of Business Ethics* 74, No. 1 (2007): 37–49.

19. N. Machiavelli, *The Prince*, trans. by G. Bull (Middlesex, England: Penguin Books, 1961).

20. S. Chen, A. Y. Lee-Chai, and J. A. Bargh, "Relationship Orientation as a Moderator of the Effects of Social Power," *Journal of Personality and Social Psychology* 80, No. 2 (2001): 173–187.

21. R. Kanter, "Power Failure in Management Circuits," *Harvard Business Review* (July–August 1979): 31–54.

22. F. Lee and L. Z. Tiedens, "Who's Being Served? 'Self-Serving' Attributions in Social Hierarchies," *Organizational Behavior and Human Decision Processes* 84, No. 2 (March 2001): 254–287.

23. M. Korda, *Power: How to Get It, How to Use It* (New York: Random House, 1975).

24. S. R. Thye, "A Status Value Theory of Power in Exchange Relations," *American Sociological Review* (2000): 407–432.

25. B. T. Mayes and R. T. Allen, "Toward a Definition of Organizational Politics," *Academy of Management Review* 2 (1977): 672–678.

26. M. Valle and P. L. Perrewe, "Do Politics Perceptions Relate to Political Behaviors? Tests of an Implicit Assumption and Expanded Model," *Human Relations* 53 (2000): 359–386.

27. W. A. Hochwarter, "The Interactive Effects of Pro-Political Behavior and Politics Perceptions on Job Satisfaction and Affective Commitment," *Journal of Applied Social Psychology* 33 (2003): 1360–1378.

28. W. A. Hochwarter, "The Interactive Effects of Pro-Political Behavior and Politics Perceptions on Job Satisfaction and Affective Commitment," *Journal of Applied Social Psychology* 33 (2003): 1360–1378.

29. W. A. Hochwarter, K. M. Kacmar, D. C. Treadway, and T. S. Watson, "It's All Relative: The Distinction and Prediction of Political Perceptions across Levels," *Journal of Applied Social Psychology* 33 (2003): 1955–2016.

30. D. A. Ralston, "Employee Ingratiation: The Role of Management," *Academy of Management Review* 10 (1985): 477–487; D. R. Beeman and T. W. Sharkey, "The Use and Abuse of Corporate Politics," *Business Horizons* (March–April 1987): 25–35.

31. C. O. Longnecker, H. P. Sims, and D. A. Gioia, "Behind the Mask: The Politics of Employee Appraisal," *Academy of Management Executive* 1 (1987): 183–193.

32. M. Valle and P. L. Perrewe, "Do Politics Perceptions Relate to Political Behaviors? Tests of an Implicit Assumption and Expanded Model," *Human Relations* 53, No. 3 (2000): 359–386.

33. D. Fedor, J. Maslyn, S. Farmer, and K. Bettenhausen, "The Contribution of Positive Politics to the Prediction of Employee Reactions," *Journal of Applied Social Psychology* 38, No. 1 (2008): 76–96.

34. D. Kipnis, S. M. Schmidt, and I. Wilkinson, "Intraorganizational Influence Tactics: Explorations in Getting One's Way," *Journal of Applied Psychology* 65 (1980): 440–452; D. Kipnis, S. Schmidt, C. Swaffin-Smith, and I. Wilkinson, "Patterns of Managerial Influence: Shotgun Managers, Tacticians, and Bystanders," *Organizational Dynamics* (Winter 1984): 60–67; G. Yukl and C. M. Falbe, "Influence Tactics and Objectives in Upward, Downward, and Lateral Influence Attempts," *Journal of Applied Psychology* 75 (1990): 132–140.

35. A. Wilhelmy, M. Kleinmann, C. J. Konig, K. G. Melchers, and D. M. Truxillo, "How and Why Do Interviewers Try to Make Impressions on Applicants? A Qualitative Study," *Journal of Applied Psychology*, 10 (2016): 313–332.

36. G. Yukl, P. J. Guinan, and D. Sottolano, "Influence Tactics Used for Different Objectives with Subordinates, Peers, and Superiors," *Groups & Organization Management* 20 (1995): 272–296.

37. C. A. Higgins, T. A. Judge, and G. R. Ferris, "Influence Tactics and Work Outcomes: A Meta-Analysis," *Journal of Organizational Behavior* 24 (2003): 89–106.

38. K. K. Eastman, "In the Eyes of the Beholder: An Attributional Approach to Ingratiation and Organizational Citizenship Behavior," *Academy of Management Journal* 37 (1994): 1379–1391.

39. K. J. Harris, K. M. Kacmar, S. Zivnuska, and J. D Shaw, "The Impact of Political Skill on Impression Management Effectiveness," *Journal of Applied Psychology* 92, No. 1 (2007): 278–285.

40. J. D. Westphal and G. Shani, "Psyched-Up to Suck-Up: Self-Regulated Cognition, Interpersonal Influence, and Recommendations for Board Appointments in the Corporate Elite," *Academy of Management Journal*, 59 (2016): 479–509.

41. G. D. Keeves, J. D. Westphal, and M. L. McDonald, "Those Closest Wield the Sharpest Knife: How Ingratiation Leads to Resentment and Social Undermining of the CEO," *Administrative Science Quarterly*, published January 10 (2017) at http://journals.sagepub.com/action/doSearch?SeriesKey=asqa&AllField=westphal

42. A. Drory and D. Beaty, "Gender Differences in the Perception of Organizational Influence Tactics," *Journal of Organizational Behavior* 12 (1991): 249–258.

43. S. Wellington, M. B. Kropf, and P. R. Gerkovich, "What's Holding Women Back?" *Harvard Business Review* (June 2003): 2–4.

44. P. Perrewe and D. Nelson, "Gender and Career Success: The Facilitative Role of Political Skill," *Organizational Dynamics* 33 (2004): 366–378.

45. R. Y. Hirokawa and A. Miyahara, "A Comparison of Influence Strategies Utilized by Managers in American and Japanese Organizations," *Communication Quarterly* 34 (1986): 250–265.

46. C. Anderson, S. E. Spataro, and F. J. Flynn, "Personality and Organizational Culture as Determinants of Influence," *Journal of Applied Psychology* 93 (May 2008): 702–710.

47. P. David, M. A. Hitt, and J. Gimeno, "The Influence of Activism by Institutional Investors on R&D," *Academy of Management Journal* 44, No. 1 (2001): 144–157.

48. G. R. Ferris, P. L. Perrewe, W. P. Anthony, and D. C. Gilmore, "Political Skill at Work," *Organizational Dynamics* 28 (2000): 25–37.

49. D. C. Treadway, W. A. Hochwarter, G. R. Ferris, C. J. Kacmar, C. Douglas, A. P. Ammeter, and M. R. Buckley, "Leader Political Skill and Employee Reactions," *Leadership Quarterly* 15 (2004): 493–513; K. K. Ahearn, G. R. Ferris, W. A. Hochwarter, C. Douglas, and A. P. Ammeter, "Leader Political Skill and Team Performance," *Journal of Management* 30, No. 3 (2004): 309–327.

50. P. L. Perrewé, K. L. Zellars, G. R. Ferris, A. M. Rossi, C. J. Kacmar, and D. A. Ralston, "Neutralizing Job Stressors: Political Skill as an Antidote to the Dysfunctional Consequences of Role Conflict Stressors," *Academy of Management Journal* 47 (2004): 141–152.

51. R. E. Frieder and K. J. Basik, "Political Skill, Behavioral Integrity, and Work Outcomes:

Test of a Multistage Model," *Journal of Leadership and Organizational Studies,* 24 (2017): 65–82.

52. G. Meisler, "Exploring Emotional Intelligence, Political Skill, and Job Satisfaction," *Employee Relations* 36 (2014): 280–293.

53. D. C. Treadway, G. Adams, T. J. Hanes, P. L. Perrewe, M. J, Magnusen, and G. R. Ferris, "The Roles of Recruiter Political Skill and Performance Resource Leveraging in NCAA Football Recruitment Effectiveness," *Journal of Management* 40 (2014): 1607–1626.

54. S. Y. Todd, K. J. Harris, R. B. Harris, and A. R. Wheeler, "Career Success Implications of Political Skill," *The Journal of Social Psychology* 149, No. 3 (June 2009): 179–204; I. M. Jawahar, J. A. Meurs, G. R. Ferris, and W. A. Hochwarter, "Self-Efficacy and Political Skill as Comparative Predictors of Task and Contextual Performance: A Two-Study Constructive Replication," *Human Performance* 21 (2008): 138–157.

55. K. Kumar and M. S. Thibodeaux, "Organizational Politics and Planned Organizational Change," *Group and Organization Studies* 15 (1990): 354–365.

56. D. Buchanan, "You Stab My back, I'll Stab Yours: Management Experience and Perceptions of Organization Political Behaviour," *British Journal of Management* 19 (March 2008): 49–64.

57. McClelland, *Power.*

58. D.R. Beeman and T.W. Sharkey, "Use and Abuse of Corporate Politics," *Business Horizons* 30 (1987): 26–30.

59. C. P. Parker, R. L. Dipboye, and S. L. Jackson, "Perceptions of Organizational Politics: An Investigation of Antecedents and Consequences," *Journal of Management* 21 (1995): 891–912.

60. S. J. Ashford, N. P. Rothbard, S. K. Piderit, and J. E. Dutton, "Out on a Limb: The Role of Context and Impression Management in Selling Gender-Equity Issues," *Administrative Science Quarterly* 43 (1998): 23–57.

61. J. Zhou and G. R. Ferris, "The Dimensions and Consequences of Organizational Politics Perceptions: A Confirmatory Analysis," *Journal of Applied Social Psychology* 25 (1995): 1747–1764.

62. M. L. Seidal, J. T. Polzer, and K. J. Stewart, "Friends in High Places: The Effects of Social Networks on Discrimination in Salary Negotiations," *Administrative Science Quarterly* 45 (2000): 1–24.

63. J. J. Gabarro and J. P. Kotter, "Managing Your Boss," *Harvard Business Review* (January–February 1980): 92–100.

64. P. Newman, "How to Manage Your Boss," *Peat, Marwick, Mitchell & Company's Management Focus* (May–June 1980): 36–37.

65. F. Bertolome, "When You Think the Boss Is Wrong," *Personnel Journal* 69 (1990): 66–73.

66. J. Conger and R. Kanungo, *Charismatic Leadership: The Elusive Factor in Organizational Effectiveness* (New York: Jossey-Bass, 1988).

67. G. M. Spreitzer, M. A. Kizilos, and S. W. Nason, "A Dimensional Analysis of the Relationship between Psychological Empowerment and Effectiveness, Satisfaction, and Strain," *Journal of Management* 23 (1997): 679–704.

68. L. D'Innocenzo, M. M. Luciano, J. E. Mathieu, M. T. Maynard, and G. Chen, "Empowered to Perform: A Multilevel Investigation of the Influence of Empowerment on Performance in Hospital Units," *Academy of Management Journal* 59 (2016): 1290–1307.

69. R. C. Ford and M. D. Fottler, "Empowerment: A Matter of Degree," *Academy of Management Executive* 9 (1995): 21–31.

70. M. R. Kukenberger, J. E. Mathieu, and T. Ruddy, "A Cross-Level Test of Empowerment and Process Influences on Members' Informal Learning and Team Commitment," *Journal of Management* 41 (2015): 987–1016.

71. X. Zhang and K. M. Bartol, "Linking Empowering Leadership and Employee Creativity: The Influence of Psychological Empowerment, Intrinsic Motivation, and Creative Process Engagement," *The Academy of Management Journal* 53 (2010): 107–128; S. Seibert, G. Wang, and S. Courtright, "Antecedents and Consequences of Psychological and Team Empowerment in Organizations: A Meta-Analytic Review," *The Journal of Applied Psychology* 96, No. 5 (2011): 981–1003.

72. S. Patel, "10 Examples of Companies with Fantastic Cultures," *Enterpreneur* (August 6, 2015), accessed at https://www.entrepreneur.com/article/249174.

12

1. J. P. Kotter, "What Leaders Really Do," *Harvard Business Review* 68 (1990): 103–111.

2. D. A. Plowman, S. Solansky, T. E Beck, L. Baker, M. Kulkarni, and D. V. Travis, "The Role of Leadership in Emergent, Self-Organization," *Leadership Quarterly* 18, No. 4 (2007): 341–356.

3. B. Stone, "Why Facebook Needs Sheryl Sandberg," *Bloomberg Businessweek* (May 12, 2011), accessed at http://www.businessweek.com/magazine/content/11_21/b4229050473695.htm.

4. A. Zaleznik, "HBR Classic—Managers and Leaders: Are They Different?" *Harvard Business Review* 70 (1992): 126–135.

5. "The World's 100 Most Powerful Women," *Forbes* (2016), accessed at https://www.forbes.com/profile/indra-nooyi/

6. R. M. Stogdill, "Personal Factors Associated with Leadership: A Survey of the Literature," *Journal of Psychology* 25 (1948): 35–71.

7. K. Lewin, R. Lippitt, and R. K. White, "Patterns of Aggressive Behavior in Experimentally Created 'Social Climates,'" *Journal of Social Psychology* 10 (1939): 271–299.

8. S. D. Sidle, "The Danger of Do Nothing Leaders," *The Academy of Management Perspectives* 21, No. 2 (2007): 75–77.

9. A. W. Halpin and J. Winer, "A Factorial Study of the Leader Behavior Description Questionnaire," in R. M. Stogdill and A. E. Coons, eds., *Leader Behavior: Its Description and Measurement,* research monograph No. 88 (Columbus, Ohio: Bureau of Business Research, The Ohio State University, 1957): 39–51.

10. E. A. Fleishman, "Leadership Climate, Human Relations Training, and Supervisory Behavior," *Personnel Psychology* 6 (1953): 205–222.

11. R. Kahn and D. Katz, "Leadership Practices in Relation to Productivity and Morale," in D. Cartwright and A. Zander, eds., *Group Dynamics, Research and Theory* (Elmsford, NY: Row, Paterson, 1960).

12. R. R. Blake and J. S. Mouton, *The Managerial Grid III: The Key to Leadership Excellence* (Houston: Gulf, 1985).

13. W. Vandekerckhove and R. Commers, "Downward Workplace Mobbing: A Sign of the Times?" *Journal of Business Ethics* 45 (2003): 41–50.

14. F. E. Fiedler, *A Theory of Leader Effectiveness* (New York: McGraw-Hill, 1964).

15. F. E. Fiedler, *Personality, Motivational Systems, and Behavior of High and Low LPC Persons,* tech. rep. No. 70-12 (Seattle: University of Washington, 1970).

16. J. T. McMahon, "The Contingency Theory: Logic and Method Revisited," *Personnel Psychology* 25 (1972): 697–710; L. H. Peters, D. D. Hartke, and J. T. Pohlman, "Fiedler's Contingency Theory of Leadership: An Application of the Meta-Analysis Procedures of Schmidt and Hunter," *Psychological Bulletin* 97 (1985): 224–285.

17. F. E. Fiedler, "The Contingency Model and the Dynamics of the Leadership Process," in L. Berkowitz, ed., *Advances in Experimental and Social Psychology,* vol. 11 (New York: Academic Press, 1978).

18. S. Arin and C. McDermott, "The Effect of Team Leader Characteristics on Learning, Knowledge Application, and Performance of Cross-Functional New Product Development Teams," *Decision Sciences* 34 (2003): 707–739.

19. F. E. Fiedler, "Engineering the Job to Fit the Manager," *Harvard Business Review* 43 (1965): 115–122.

20. R. J. House, "A Path–Goal Theory of Leader Effectiveness," *Administrative Science Quarterly* 16 (1971): 321–338; R. J. House and T. R. Mitchell, "Path–Goal Theory of Leadership," *Journal of Contemporary Business* 3 (1974): 81–97.

21. C. A. Schriescheim and V. M. Von Glinow, "The Path–Goal Theory of Leadership: A Theoretical and Empirical Analysis," *Academy of Management Journal* 20 (1977): 398–405; E. Valenzi and G. Dessler, "Relationships of Leader Behavior, Subordinate Role Ambiguity, and Subordinate Job Satisfaction," *Academy of Management Journal* 21 (1978): 671–678; N. R. F. Maier, *Leadership Methods and Skills* (New York: McGraw-Hill, 1963).

22. J. P. Grinnell, "An Empirical Investigation of CEO Leadership in Two Types of Small Firms," *S.A.M. Advanced Management Journal* 68 (2003): 36–41.

23. V. H. Vroom and P. W. Yetton, *Leadership and Decision Making* (Pittsburgh: University of Pittsburgh, 1973).

24. V. H. Vroom, "Leadership and the Decision-Making Process," *Organizational Dynamics* 28 (2000): 82–94.

25. P. Hersey and K. H. Blanchard, "Life Cycle Theory of Leadership," *Training and Development* 23 (1969): 26–34; P. Hersey, K. H. Blanchard, and D. E. Johnson, *Management of Organizational Behavior: Leading Human Resources*, 8th ed. (Upper Saddle River, N.J.: Prentice-Hall, 2001).

26. B. M. Bass, *Bass and Stogdill's Handbook of Leadership: Theory, Research, and Managerial Applications*, 3rd ed. (New York: Free Press, 1990).

27. G. B. Graen and M. Uhl-Bien, "Relationship-Based Approach to Leadership: Development of Leader–Member Exchange (LMX) Theory of Leadership over 25 Years," *Leadership Quarterly* 6 (1995): 219–247; C. R. Gerstner and D. V. Day, "Meta-Analytic Review of Leader–Member Exchange Theory: Correlates and Construct Issues," *Journal of Applied Psychology* 82 (1997): 827–844; R. C. Liden, S. J. Wayne, and R. T. Sparrowe, "An Examination of the Mediating Role of Psychological Empowerment on the Relations between the Job, Interpersonal Relationships, and Work Outcomes," *Journal of Applied Psychology* 85 (2001): 407–416.

28. J. Townsend, J. S. Phillips, and T. J. Elkins, "Employee Retaliation: The Neglected Consequence of Poor Leader–Member Exchange Relations," *Journal of Occupational Health Psychology* 5 (2000): 457–463.

29. D. Nelson, R. Basu, and R. Purdie, "An Examination of Exchange Quality and Work Stressors in Leader–Follower Dyads," *International Journal of Stress Management* 5 (1998): 103–112.

30. K. M. Kacmar, L. A. Witt, S. Zivnuska, and S. M. Gully, "The Interactive Effect of Leader–Member Exchange and Communication Frequency on Performance Ratings," *Journal of Applied Psychology* 88 (2003): 764–772.

31. C. C. Schermuly and B. Meyer, "Good Relationships at Work: The Effects of Leader-Member Exchange and Team-Member Exchange on Psychological Empowerment, Emotional Exhaustion, and Depression," *Journal of Organizational Behavior* 37 (2016): 673–691.

32. H. Liao, D. Liu, and R. Loi, "Looking at Both Sides of the Social Exchange Coin: A Social Cognitive Perspective on the Joint Effects of Relationship Quality and Differentiation on Creativity," *Academy of Management Journal* 53 (2010): 1090–1109.

33. P. Molenberghs, G. Prochilo, N. K. Steffens, and S. A. Haslam, "The Neuroscience of Inspirational Leadership: The Importance of Collective-Oriented Language and Shared Group Membership," *Journal of Management*, published online January 9, 2015.

34. J. M. Burns, *Leadership* (New York: Harper & Row, 1978); T. O. Jacobs, *Leadership and Exchange in Formal Organizations* (Alexandria, Va.: Human Resources Research Organization, 1971).

35. B. M. Bass, "From Transactional to Transformational Leadership: Learning to Share the Vision," *Organizational Dynamics* 19 (1990): 19–31; B. M. Bass, *Leadership and Performance beyond Expectations* (New York: Free Press, 1985).

36. P. M. Podsakoff, S. B. MacKenzie, and W. H. Bommer, "Transformational Leader Behaviors and Substitutes for Leadership as Determinants of Employee Satisfaction, Commitment, Trust, and Organizational Citizenship Behaviors," *Journal of Management* 22 (1996): 259–298.

37. W. Bennis, "Managing the Dream: Leadership in the 21st Century," *Training* 27 (1990): 43–48; P. M. Podsakoff, S. B. MacKenzie, R. H. Moorman, and R. Fetter, "Transformational Leader Behaviors and Their Effects on Followers' Trust in Leader, Satisfaction, and Organizational Citizenship Behaviors," *Leadership Quarterly* 1 (1990): 107–142.

38. "Starbucks Announces New Leadership Structure to Drive Global Growth," accessed at https://news.starbucks.com/news/starbucks-announces-new-leadership-structure.

39. X. H. F. Wang and J. M. Howell, "Exploring the Dual-Level Effects of Transformational Leadership on Followers," *Journal of Applied Psychology* 95 (2010): 1134–1144.

40. C. P. Egri and S. Herman, "Leadership in the North American Environmental Sector: Values, Leadership Styles, and Contexts of Environmental Leaders and Their Organizations," *Academy of Management Journal* 43 (2000): 571–604.

41. T. A. Judge and J. E. Bono, "Five-Factor Model of Personality and Transformational Leadership," *Journal of Applied Psychology* 85 (2001): 751–765.

42. H. J. Anderson, J. E. Baur, J. A. Griffith, and M. R. Buckley, "What Works for You May Not Work for (Gen)Me: Limitations of Present Leadership Theories for the New Generation," *The Leadership Quarterly* 28 (2017): 245–260.

43. The Jargon Dictionary, "The R Terms: Reality-Distortion Field," http://info.astrian.net/jargon/terms/r/reality-distortion_field.html.

44. R. J. House and M. L. Baetz, "Leadership: Some Empirical Generalizations and New Research Directions," in B. M. Staw, ed., *Research in Organizational Behavior*, vol. 1 (Greenwood, Conn.: JAI Press, 1979): 399–401.

45. G. C. Banks, K. N. Engemann, C. E. Williams, J. Gooty, K. D. McCauley, and M. R. Medaugh, "A Meta-Analytic Review and Future Research Agenda of Charismatic Leadership," *The Leadership Quarterly* (2017), accessed at http://www.sciencedirect.com/science/article/pii/S1048984316302971.

46. R. A. Brands, J. Menges, and M. Kilduff, "The Leader in Social Network Schema: Perceptions of Network Structure Affect Gendered Attributions of Charisma," *Organization Science* (in press).

47. F. Luthans and B. J. Avolio, "Authentic Leadership: A Positive Development Approach," in K. S. Cameron, J. E. Dutton, and R. E. Quinn, eds., *Positive Organizational Scholarship: Foundations of a New Discipline* (San Francisco: Berrett-Koehler, 2004): 241–261.

48. O. Epitropaki, R. Kark, C. Mainemelis, and R. G. Lord, "Leadership and Followership Identity Processes: A Multilevel Review," *The Leadership Quarterly*, 28 (2017): 104–129.

49. B. J. Avolio, W. L. Gardner, F. O. Walumbwa, F. Luthans, and D. R. May, "Unlocking the Mask: A Look at the Process by Which Authentic Leaders Impact Follower Attitudes and Behaviors," *The Leadership Quarterly* 15 (2004): 801–823.

50. S. Michie and J. Gooty, "Values, Emotions and Authentic Leadership Behaviors: Will the Real Leader Please Stand Up?" *The Leadership Quarterly* 16 (2005): 441–457.

51. S. Michie and D. L. Nelson, "The Effects of Leader Compassion Display on Follower Attributions: Building a Socialized Leadership Image" (Paper presented at the Academy of Management Conference Honolulu, Hawaii, 2005).

52. D. Yagil and H. Medler-Liraz, "Feel Free, Be Yourself: Authentic Leadership, Emotional Expression, and Employee Authenticity," *Journal of Leadership and Organizational Studies* 21 (2014): 59–70.

53. S. Liu, J. Laio, and H. Wei, "Authentic Leadership and Whistleblowing: Mediating Roles of Psychological Safety and Personal Identification," *Journal of Business Ethics*, published online January 8, 2015.

54. D. V. Day, J. W. Fleenor, L. E. Atwater, R. E. Sturm, and R. A McKee, "Advances in Leader and Leadership Development: A Review of 25 Years of Research and Theory," *The Leadership Quarterly* 25 (2014): 63–82.

55. D. Goleman, "What Makes a Leader?" *Harvard Business Review* 82 (2004): 82–91.

56. D. Goleman, "Never Stop Learning," *Harvard Business Review* 82 (2004): 28–30.

57. C. L. Gohm, "Mood Regulation and Emotional Intelligence: Individual Differences," *Journal of Personality and Social Psychology* 84 (2003): 594–607.

58. J. Useem, "A Manager for All Seasons," *Fortune* (April 30, 2001): 66–72.

59. R. C. Mayer, J. H. Davis, and F. D. Schoorman, "An Integrative Model of Organizational Trust," *Academy of Management Review* 20 (1995): 709–734.

60. R. S. Dooley and G. E. Fryxell, "Attaining Decision Quality and Commitment from Dissent: The Moderating Effects of Loyalty and Competence in Strategic Decision-Making Teams," *Academy of Management Journal* 42 (1999): 389–402.

61. J. Flint, "Why Rick Wagoner Had to Go," *Forbes* (March 30, 2009), http://www.forbes.com/2009/03/30/rick-wagoner-gm-jerry-flint-business-autos-backseat-driver.html.

62. S. A. Joni, "The Geography of Trust," *Harvard Business Review* 82 (2003): 82–88.

63. M. E. Heilman, C. J. Block, R. F. Martell, and M. C. Simon, "Has Anything Changed? Current Characteristics of Men, Women, and Managers," *Journal of Applied Psychology* 74 (1989): 935–942.

64. A. H. Eagly, S. J. Darau, and M. Makhijani, "Gender and the Effectiveness of Leaders: A Meta-Analysis," *Psychological Bulletin* 117 (1995): 125–145.

65. M. K. Ryan, S. A. Haslam, and T. Postmes, "Reactions to the Glass Cliff: Gender Differences in the Explanations for the Precariousness of Women's Leadership Positions," *Journal of Organizational Change Management* 20, No. 2 (2007): 182–197.

66. J. Hu and R. C. Liden, "Antecedents of Team Potency and Team Effectiveness: An Examination of Goal and Process Clarity and Servant Leadership," *Journal of Applied Psychology* 96, No. 4 (2011): 851–862.

67. R. K. Greenleaf, L. C. Spears, and D. T. Frick, eds., *On Becoming a Servant-Leader* (San Francisco: Jossey-Bass, 1996).

68. A. C. H. Schat, M. R. Frone, and E. K. Kelloway, "Prevalence of Workplace Aggression in the U.S. Workforce: Findings from a National Study," in E. K. Kelloway, J. Barling, and J. J. Hurrell, eds., *Handbook of Workplace Violence* (Thousand Oaks, CA: Sage, 2006): 47–89.

69. B. J. Tepper, C. A. Henle, L. S. Lambert, R. A. Giacalone, and M. K. Duffy, "Abusive Supervision and Subordinates' Organization Deviance," *Journal of Applied Psychology* 93 (2008): 721–732; P. A. Bamberger and S. B. Bacharach, "Abusive Supervision and Subordinate Problem Drinking: Taking Resistance, Stress and Subordinate Personality into Account," *Human Relations* 59 (2006): 1–30; B. J. Tepper, "Consequences of Abusive Supervision," *Academy of Management Journal* 43 (2000): 178–190; A. A. Grandey, J. Kern, and M. Frone, "Verbal Abuse from Outsiders Versus Insiders: Comparing Frequency, Impact on Emotional Exhaustion, and the Role of Emotional Labor," *Journal of Occupation Health Psychology* 12 (2007): 63–79.

70. B. J. Tepper, M. K. Duffy, C. A. Henle, and L. S. Lambert, "Procedural Injustice, Victim Precipitation and Abusive Supervision," *Personnel Psychology* 59 (2006): 101–123.

71. S. Thau and M. S. Mitchell, "Self-Gain or Self-Regulation Impairment? Tests of Competing Explanations of the Supervisor Abuse and Employee Deviance Relationship through Perceptions of Distributive Justice," *Journal of Applied Psychology* (in press).

72. S. H. Courtright, R. G. Gardner, T. A. Smith, B. W. McCormick, and A. E. Colbert, "My Family Made Me Do It: A Cross-Domain, Self-Regulator Perspective on Antecedents to Abusive Supervision," *Academy of Management Journal*, 59 (2016): 1630–1652.

73. E. P. Hollander and L. R. Offerman, "Power and Leadership in Organizations: Relationships in Transition," *American Psychologist* 45 (1990): 179–189.

74. H. P. Sims, Jr., and C. C. Manz, *Company of Heros: Unleashing the Power of Self-Leadership* (New York: John Wiley & Sons, 1996).

75. C. C. Manz and H. P. Sims, "Leading Workers to Lead Themselves: The External Leadership of Self-Managing Work Teams," *Administrative Science Quarterly* 32 (1987): 106–128.

76. L. Hirschhorn, "Leaders and Followers in a Postindustrial Age: A Psychodynamic View," *Journal of Applied Behavioral Science* 26 (1990): 529–542.

77. R. E. Kelley, "In Praise of Followers," *Harvard Business Review* 66 (1988): 142–148.

78. S. A. Eisenbeiss and D. van Knippenberg, "On Ethical Leadership Impact: The Role of Follower Mindfulness and Moral Emotions," *Journal of Organizational Behavior* 36 (2014): 182–195.

79. G. A. Yukl, *Leadership in Organizations*, 2nd ed. (Upper Saddle River, N.J.: Prentice-Hall, 1989).

80. D. A. Garvin and J. D. Margolis, "The Art of Giving and Receiving Advice," *Harvard Business Review* January–February (2015): 61–71.

13

1. Definition adapted from D. Hellriegel, J. W. Slocum, Jr., and R. W. Woodman, *Organizational Behavior* (St. Paul: West, 1992); and from R. D. Middlemist and M. A. Hitt, *Organizational Behavior* (St. Paul, Minn.: West, 1988).

2. D. Tjosvold, *The Conflict-Positive Organization* (Reading, Mass.: Addison-Wesley, 1991).

3. K. Thomas and W. Schmidt, "A Survey of Managerial Interests with Respect to Conflict," *Academy of Management Journal* 19 (1976): 315–318; G. L. Lippitt, "Managing Conflict in Today's Organizations," *Training and Development Journal* 36 (1982): 66–74.

4. M. Rajim, "A Measure of Styles of Handling Interpersonal Conflict," *Academy of Management Journal* 26 (1983): 368–376.

5. M. M. Hopkins and R. D. Yonker, "Managing Conflict with Emotional Intelligence: Abilities That Make a Difference," *Journal of Management Development* 34 (2015): 226–244.

6. Tjosvold, *The Conflict-Positive Organization* (Reading, MA: Addison-Wesley, 1991).

7. R. A. Cosier and D. R. Dalton, "Positive Effects of Conflict: A Field Experiment," *International Journal of Conflict Management* 1 (1990): 81–92.

8. D. Tjosvold, "Making Conflict Productive," *Personnel Administrator* 29 (1984): 121–130.

9. I. Janis, *Groupthink*, 2nd ed. (Boston: Houghton Mifflin, 1982).

10. A. C. Amason, W. A. Hochwarter, K. R. Thompson, and A. W. Harrison, "Conflict: An Important Dimension in Successful Management Teams," *Organizational Dynamics* 24 (1995): 25–35.

11. J. C. Quick, A. McFadyen, and D. L. Nelson, "No Accident: Health, Well-Being, Performance … and Danger," *Journal of Organizational Effectiveness: People and Performance* 1 (2014): 98–119.

12. R. Nibler and K. L. Harris, "The Effects of Culture and Cohesiveness on Intragroup Conflict and Effectiveness," *The Journal of Social Psychology* 143 (2003): 613–631.

13. R. Shaukat, A. Yousaf, and K. Sanders, "Examining the Linkages Between Relationship Conflict, Performance and Turnover Intentions: Role of Job Burnout as a Mediator," *International Journal of Conflict Management* 28 (2017): 4–23.

14. G. Walker and L. Poppo, "Profit Centers, Single-Source Suppliers, and Transaction Costs," *Administrative Science Quarterly* 36 (1991): 66–87.

15. R. Miles, *Macro Organizational Behavior* (Glenview, Ill.: Scott, Foresman, 1980).

16. H. Levinson, "The Abrasive Personality," *Harvard Business Review* 56 (1978): 86–94.

17. J. C. Quick and J. D. Quick, *Organizational Stress and Preventive Management* (New York: McGraw-Hill, 1984).

18. F. N. Brady, "Aesthetic Components of Management Ethics," *Academy of Management Review* 11 (1986): 337–344.

19. J. R. Ogilvie and M. L. Carsky, "Building Emotional Intelligence in Negotiations," *The International Journal of Conflict Management* 13 (2002): 381–400.

20. A. M. Bodtker and R. L. Oliver, "Emotion in Conflict Formation and Its Transformation: Application to Organizational Conflict Management," *International Journal of Conflict Management* 12 (2001): 259–275.

21. D. E. Conlon and S. H. Hunt, "Dealing with Feeling: The Influence of Outcome Representations on Negotiation," *International Journal of Conflict Management* 13 (2002): 35–58.

22. J. Schopler, C. A. Insko, J. Wieselquist, M. Pemberton, B. Witcher, R. Kozar, C. Roddenberry, and T. Wildschut, "When Groups Are More Competitive Than Individuals: The Domain of the Discontinuity Effect," *Journal of Personality and Social Psychology* 80 (2001): 632–644.

23. M. Sherif and C. W. Sherif, *Social Psychology* (New York: Harper & Row, 1969).

24. M. A. Zarate, B. Garcia, A. A. Garza, and R. T. Hitlan, "Cultural Threat and Perceived Realistic Group Conflict as Dual Predictors of Prejudice," *Journal of Experimental Social Psychology* 40 (2004): 99–105; J. C. Dencker, A. Joshi, and J. J. Martocchio, "Employee Benefits as Context for Intergenerational Conflict," *Human Resource Management Review* 17, No. 2 (2007): 208–220.

25. J. Wombacher and J. Felfe, "The Interplay of Team and Organizational Commitment in Motivating Employees' Interteam Conflict Handling," *Academy of Management Journal*, June 2016.

26. W. Tsai and S. Ghoshal, "Social Capital and Value Creation: The Role of Intrafirm Networks," *Academy of Management Journal* 41 (1998): 464–476.

27. K. J. Hurt and M. A. Abebe, "The Effect of Conflict Type and Organizational Crisis on Perceived Strategic Decision Effectiveness," *Journal of Leadership and Organizational Studies*, published online February 4, 2015.

28. D. L. Nelson and J. C. Quick, "Professional Women: Are Distress and Disease Inevitable?" *Academy of Management Review* 10 (1985): 206–218; D. L. Nelson and M. A. Hitt, "Employed Women and Stress: Implications for Enhancing Women's Mental Health in the Workplace," in J. C. Quick, J. Hurrell, and L. A. Murphy, eds., *Stress and Well-Being at Work: Assessments and Interventions for Occupational Mental Health* (Washington, D.C.: American Psychological Association, 1992).

29. E. C. Dierdorff and J. K. Ellington, "It's the Nature of Work: Examining Behavior-Based Sources of Work–Family Conflict across Occupations," *Journal of Applied Psychology* 93 (2008): 883–892.

30. M. G. Pratt and J. A. Rosa, "Transforming Work–Family Conflict into Commitment in Network Marketing Organizations," *Academy of Management Journal* 46 (2003): 395–418.

31. W. R. Boswell and J. B. Olson-Buchanan, "The Use of Communication Technologies after Hours: The Role of Work Attitudes and Work–Life Conflict," *Journal of Management* 33, No. 4 (2007): 592–610.

32. R. L. Kahn, D. M. Wolfe, R. P. Quinn, J. D. Noek, and R. A. Rosenthal, *Organizational Stress: Studies in Role Conflict and Ambiguity* (New York: Wiley, 1964).

33. J. R. B. Halbesleben, "A Meta-Analysis of Work Engagement: Relationships with Burnout, Demands, Resources, and Consequences," in A. Bakker and M. Leiter, eds., *Work Engagement: A Handbook of Essential Theory and Research* (New York: Psychology Press, 2010); M. Wang, S. Liu, Y. Zhan, and J. Shi, "Daily Work–Family Conflict and Alcohol Use: Testing the Cross-Level Moderation Effects of Peer Drinking Norms and Social Support," *Journal of Applied Psychology* 95 (2010): 377–386.

34. C. Nohe, A. Michel, and K. Sonntag, "Family-Work Conflict and Job Performance: A Diary Study of Boundary Conditions and Mechanisms," *Journal of Organizational Behavior* 35 (2014): 339–357.

35. J. L. Badaracco, Jr., "The Discipline of Building Character," *Harvard Business Review* (March–April 1998): 115–124.

36. B. Schneider, "The People Make the Place," *Personnel Psychology* 40 (1987): 437–453.

37. C. A. O'Reilly, J. Chatman, and D. F. Caldwell, "People and Organizational Culture: A Profile Comparison Approach to Assessing Person-Organization Fit," *Academy of Management Journal* 34 (1991): 487–516.

38. I. Dayal and J. M. Thomas, "Operation KPE: Developing a New Organization," *Journal of Applied Behavioral Science* 4 (1968): 473–506.

39. R. H. Miles, "Role Requirements as Sources of Organizational Stress," *Journal of Applied Psychology* 61 (1976): 172–179.

40. W. F. G. Mastenbroek, *Conflict Management and Organization Development* (Chichester, England: Wiley, 1987).

41. M. R. Frone, "Interpersonal Conflict at Work and Psychological Outcomes: Testing a Model among Young Workers," *Journal of Occupational Health Psychology* 5 (2000): 246–255.

42. K. Thomas, "Conflict and Conflict Management," in M. D. Dunnette, ed., *Handbook of Industrial and Organizational Psychology* (New York: Wiley, 1976).

43. H. H. Meyer, E. Kay, and J. R. P. French, "Split Roles in Performance Appraisal," *Harvard Business Review* 43 (1965): 123–129.

44. T. W. Costello and S. S. Zalkind, *Psychology in Administration: A Research Orientation* (Englewood Cliffs, N.J.: Prentice-Hall, 1963).

45. Snapshot Spy, "Employee Computer & Internet Abuse Statistics," http://www.snapshotspy.com/employee-computer-abuse-statistics.htm; data sources include U.S. Department of Commerce—Economics and Statistics Administration and the National Telecommunications and Information Administration—Greenfield and Rivet, "Employee Computer Abuse Statistics."

46. P. F. Hewlin, "And the Award for Best Actor Goes to . . . : Facades of Conformity in Organizational Settings," *Academy of Management Review* 28 (2003): 633–642.

47. C. A. Insko, J. Scholper, L. Gaertner, T. Wildschut, R. Kozar, B. Pinter, E. J. Finkel, D. M. Brazil, C. L. Cecil, and M. R. Montoya, "Interindividual–Intergroup Discontinuity Reduction through the Anticipation of Future Interaction," *Journal of Personality and Social Psychology* 80 (2001): 95–111.

48. D. Tjosvold and M. Poon, "Dealing with Scarce Resources: Open-Minded Interaction for Resolving Budget Conflicts," *Group and Organization Management* 23 (1998): 237–255.

49. R. Miles, *Macro Organizational Behavior* (Glenview, IL: Scott, Foresman, 1980). R. Steers, *Introduction to Organizational Behavior*, 4th ed. (Glenview, Ill.: Harper-Collins, 1991).

50. A. Tyerman and C. Spencer, "A Critical Text of the Sherrif's Robber's Cave Experiments: Intergroup Competition and Cooperation between Groups of Well-Acquainted Individuals," *Small Group Behavior* 14 (1983): 515–531; R. M. Kramer, "Intergroup Relations and Organizational Dilemmas: The Role of Categorization Processes," in B. Staw and L. Cummings, eds., *Research in Organizational Behavior* 13 (1991): 191–228.

51. N. Kercheval, "Dana Holgorsen Becomes West Virginia Coach after Bill Stewart Resigns," *Bloomberg* (June 11, 2011), http://bloomberg.com/news/2011-06-11/dana-holgorsen-becomes-west-virgiinia-coach-after-bill-stewart-resigns.html.

52. A. Carmeli, "The Relationship between Emotional Intelligence and Work Attitudes, Behavior and Outcomes: An Examination among Senior Managers," *Journal of Managerial Psychology* 18 (2003): 788–813.

53. R. Blake and J. Mouton, "Overcoming Group Warfare," *Harvard Business Review* 64 (1984): 98–108.

54. D. G. Ancona and D. Caldwell, "Improving the Performance of New Product Teams," *Research Technology Management* 33 (1990): 25–29.

55. M. A. Cronin and L. R. Weingart, "Representational Gaps, Information Processing and Conflict in Functionally Diverse Teams," *Academy of Management Review* 32, No. 3 (2007): 761–773.

56. C. K. W. DeDreu and L. R. Weingart, "Task versus Relationship Conflict, Team Performance, and Team Member Satisfaction: A Meta-Analysis," *Journal of Applied Psychology* 88 (2003): 741–749.

57. R. J. Lewicki, J. A. Litterer, J. W. Minton, and D. M. Saunders, *Negotiation*, 2nd ed. (Burr Ridge, Ill.: Irwin, 1994).

58. J. Brett and L. Thompson, "Negotiation," *Organizational Behavior and Human Decision Processes*, 136 (2016): 68–79.

59. G. Ku, C. S. Wang, and A. D. Galinsky, "Promise and Perversity: Towards a Comprehensive Model of Perspective Taking," *Research in Organizational Behavior* (in press).

60. S. Aslani, J. Ramirez-Marin, J. Brett, J. Yao, Z. Semnani-Azad, Z. Zhang, C. Tinsley, L. Weingart, and W. Adair, "Dignity, Face, and Honor Cultures: A Study of Negotiation Strategy and Outcomes in Three Cultures," *Journal of Organizational Behavior*, 37 (2016): 1178–1201.

61. J. Mazei, J. Huffmeier, P. A. Freund, A. F. Stuhlmacher, L. Bilke, and G. Hertel, "A Meta-Analysis on Gender Differences in Negotiation Outcomes and Their Moderators," *Psychological Bulletin* 141 (2015): 85–104.

62. C. K. W. De Dreu and A. E. M. Van Vianen, "Managing Relationship Conflict and the Effectiveness of Organizational Teams," *Journal of Organizational Behavior* 22 (2001): 309–328.

63. S. Steinberg, "Airbus Workers in France, Germany Strike against Massive Job Cuts," (March 1, 2007). http://www.wsws.org/articles/2007/mar2007/airb-m01.shtml.

64. R. A. Baron, S. P. Fortin, R. L. Frei, L. A. Hauver, and M. L. Shack, "Reducing Organizational Conflict: The Role of Socially Induced Positive Affect," *International Journal of Conflict Management* 1 (1990): 133–152.

65. S. L. Phillips and R. L. Elledge, *The Team Building Source Book* (San Diego: University Associates, 1989).

66. J. R. Curhan, M. A. Neale, L. Ross, and J. Rosencranz-Engelmann, "Relational Accommodation in Negotiation: Effects of Egalitarianism and Gender on Economic Efficiency and Relational Capital," *Organizational Behavior and Human Decision Processes* 107 (2008): 192–205.

67. T. N. Gladwin and I. Walter, "How Multinationals Can Manage Social and Political Forces," *Journal of Business Strategy* 1 (1980): 54–68.

68. http://www.greenpeace.org/usa/lego-got-awesome-savethearctic/

69. K. W. Thomas, "Toward Multidimensional Values in Teaching: The Example of Conflict Behaviors," *Academy of Management Review* 2 (1977): 484–490.

70. S. Alper, D. Tjosvold, and K. S. Law, "Conflict Management, Efficacy, and Performance in Organizational Teams," *Personnel Psychology* 53 (2000): 625–642.

71. A. Somech, H. S. Desvililya, and H. Lidogoster, "Team Conflict Management and Team Effectiveness: The Effects of Task Interdependence and Team Identification," *Journal of Organizational Behavior* 30 (2009): 359–378.

72. W. King and E. Miles, "What We Know and Don't Know about Measuring Conflict," *Management Communication Quarterly* 4 (1990): 222–243.

73. J. Barker, D. Tjosvold, and I. R. Andrews, "Conflict Approaches of Effective and Ineffective Project Managers: A Field Study in a Matrix Organization," *Journal of Management Studies* 25 (1988): 167–178.

74. K. A. Way, N. L. Jimmieson, and P. Bordia, "Shared Perceptions of Supervisor Conflict Management Style," *International Journal of Conflict Management* 27 (2016): 25–49.

14

1. S. K. Parker, F. P. Morgeson, and G. Johns, "One Hundred Years of Work Design Research: Looking Back and Looking Forward," *Journal of Applied Psychology* 102, No. 3 (March 2017): 403–420.

2. B. L. Berkelaar and P. M. Buzzanell, "Bait and Switch or Double-Edged Sword? The (Sometimes) Failed Promises of Calling," *Human Relations* 68 (2014): 157–178.

3. G. W. England and I. Harpaz, "How Working Is Defined: National Contexts and Demographic and Organizational Role Influences," *Journal of Organizational Behavior* 11 (1990): 253–266.

4. L. R. Gomez-Mejia, "The Cross-Cultural Structure of Task-Related and Contextual Constructs," *Journal of Psychology* 120 (1986): 5–19.

5. A. Wrzesniewski and J. E. Dutton, "Crafting a Job: Revisioning Employees as Active Crafters of Their Work," *Academy of Management Review* 26 (2001): 179–201.

6. D. T. Hall and M. Las Heras, "Reintegrating Job Design and Career Theory: Creating Not Just Good Jobs but Smart Jobs," *Journal of Organizational Behavior* 31 (2010): 448–462.

7. F. W. Taylor, *The Principles of Scientific Management* (New York: Norton, 1911).

8. T. Bell, *Out of This Furnace* (Pittsburgh: University of Pittsburgh Press, 1941); J. H. Gittell, D. B. Weinberg, A. L. Bennett, and J. A. Miller, "Is the Doctor in? A Relational Approach to Job Design and the Coordination of Work," *Human Resource Management* 47 (Winter 2008): 729–755.

9. N. D. Warren, "Job Simplification versus Job Enlargement," *Journal of Industrial Engineering* 9 (1958): 435–439.

10. T. Moller, S. E. Mathiassen, H. Franzon, and S. Kihlberg, "Job Enlargement and Mechanical Exposure Variability in Cyclic Assembly Work," *Ergonomics* 47 (2004): 19–40.

11. C. R. Walker and R. H. Guest, *The Man on the Assembly Line* (Cambridge, Mass.: Harvard University Press, 1952).

12. M. A. Campion, L. Cheraskin, and M. J. Stevens, "Career-Related Antecedents and Outcomes of Job Rotation," *Academy of Management Journal* 37 (1994): 1518–1542.

13. H. R. Nalbantian and R. A. Guzzo, "Making Mobility Matter," *Harvard Business Review* (March 2009): 76–84.

14. E. Santora, "Keep Up Production through Cross-Training," *Personnel Journal* (June 1992): 162–166.

15. S. Leroy, "Why Is It So Hard to Do My Work? The Challenge of Attention Residue When Switching between Work Tasks," *Organizational Behavior and Human Decision Processes* 109 (2009): 168–181.

16. R. P. Steel and J. R. Rentsch, "The Dispositional Model of Job Attitudes Revisited: Findings of a 10-Year Study," *Journal of Applied Psychology* 82 (1997): 873–879; C. S. Wong, C. Hui, and K. S. Law, "A Longitudinal Study of the Job Perception–Job Satisfaction Relationship: A Text of the Three Alternative Specifications," *Journal of Occupational & Organizational Psychology* 71 (Part 2, 1998): 127–146.

17. F. Herzberg, "One More Time: How Do You Motivate Employees?" *Harvard Business Review* 46 (1968): 53–62.

18. R. N. Ford, "Job Enrichment Lessons from AT&T," *Harvard Business Review* 51 (1973): 96–106.

19. R. J. House and L. A. Wigdor, "Herzberg's Dual-Factor Theory of Job Satisfaction and Motivation: A Review of the Evidence and a Criticism," *Personnel Psychology* 20 (1967): 369–389.

20. A. N. Turner and P. R. Lawrence, *Industrial Jobs and the Worker* (Cambridge, Mass.: Harvard University Press, 1965).

21. D. H. McKnight, B. Phillips, and B. C. Hardgrave, "Which Reduces IT Turnover Intention the Worst: Workplace Characteristics or Job Characteristics?" *Information & Management* 46 (2009): 167–174.

22. J. R. Hackman and G. R. Oldham, "The Relationship among Core Job Dimensions, the Critical Psychological States, and On-the-Job Outcomes," in *The Job Diagnostic Survey: An Instrument for the Diagnosis of Jobs and the Evaluation of Job Redesign Projects* (New Haven, Conn.: Department of Administrative Sciences, Yale University, 1974).

23. J. L. Pierce, I. Jussila, and A. Cummings, "Psychological Ownership within the Job Design Context: Revision of the Job Characteristics Model," *Journal of Organizational Behavior* 30 (2009): 477–496.

24. J. R. Hackman and G. R. Oldham, "Development of the Job Diagnostic Survey," *Journal of Applied Psychology* 60 (1975): 159–170.

25. E. Sadler-Smith, G. El-Kot, and M. Leat, "Differentiating Work Autonomy Facets in a Non-Western Context," *Journal of Organizational Behavior* 24 (2003): 709–731.

26. H. P. Sims, A. D. Szilagyi, and R. T. Keller, "The Measurement of Job Characteristics," *Academy of Management Journal* 19 (1976): 195–212.

27. H. P. Sims and A. D. Szilagyi, "Job Characteristic Relationships: Individual and Structural Moderators," *Organizational Behavior and Human Performance* 17 (1976): 211–230.

28. Y. Fried, "Meta-Analytic Comparison of the Job Diagnostic Survey and Job Characteristic Inventory as Correlates of Work Satisfaction and Performance," *Journal of Applied Psychology* 76 (1991): 690–698.

29. D. R. May, R. L. Gilson, and L. M. Harter, "The Psychological Conditions of Meaningfulness, Safety, and Availability and the Engagement of the Human Spirit at Work," *Journal of Occupational and Organizational Psychology* 77 (2004): 11–37.

30. D. DClercq, D. Bouckenooghe, U. Raja, and G. Matsyborska, "Unpacking the Goal Congruence-Organizational Deviance Relationship: The Roles of Work Engagement and Emotional Intelligence," *Journal of Business Ethics* 124 (2014): 695–711.

31. R. Wagner, "Nourishing Employee Engagement," *Gallup Management Journal* (February 12, 2004): 1–7, http://gmj.gallup.com/content/default.asp?ci=10504.

32. M. Soyars and J. Brusino, "Essentials of Engagement," *T&D* (March 2009): 62–65.

33. J. Loehr and T. Schwartz, *The Power of Full Engagement: Managing Energy, Not Time, Is the Key to High Performance and Personal Renewal* (New York: Free Press, 2003).

34. M. F. R. Kets de Vries, "Creating Authentizotic Organizations: Well-Functioning Individuals in Vibrant Companies," *Human Relations* 54 (2001): 101–111.

35. G. R. Salancik and J. Pfeffer, "A Social Information Processing Approach to Job Attitudes and Task Design," *Administrative Science Quarterly* 23 (1978): 224–253.

36. J. Pfeffer, "Management as Symbolic Action: The Creation and Maintenance of Organizational Paradigms," in L. L. Cummings and B. M. Staw, eds., *Research in Organizational Behavior*, vol. 3 (Greenwich, Conn.: JAI Press, 1981): 1–52.

37. C. Clegg and C. Spencer, "A Circular and Dynamic Model of the Process of Job Design," *Journal of Occupational & Organizational Psychology* 80 (2007): 321–339.

38. J. Thomas and R. Griffin, "The Social Information Processing Model of Task Design: A Review of the Literature," *Academy of Management Review* 8 (1983): 672–682.

39. D. J. Campbell, "Task Complexity: A Review and Analysis," *Academy of Management Review* 13 (1988): 40–52.

40. A. M. Grant, "Relational Job Design and the Motivation to Make a Prosocial Difference," *Academy of Management Review* 32 (2007): 393–417.

41. D. R. May, K. Reed, C. E. Schwoerer, and P. Potter, "Ergonomic Office Design and Aging: A Quasi-Experimental Field Study of Employee Reactions to an Ergonomics Intervention Program," *Journal of Occupational Health Psychology* 9 (2004): 123–135.

42. M. A. Campion and P. W. Thayer, "Job Design: Approaches, Outcomes, and Trade-Offs," *Organizational Dynamics* 16 (1987): 66–79.

43. J. Teresko, "Emerging Technologies," *Industry Week* (February 27, 1995): 1–2.

44. M. A. Campion and C. L. McClelland, "Interdisciplinary Examination of the Costs and Benefits of Enlarged Jobs: A Job Design Quasi-Experiment," *Journal of Applied Psychology* 76 (1991): 186–199.

45. B. Kohut, *Country Competitiveness: Organizing of Work* (New York: Oxford University Press, 1993).

46. D. Holman, S. Frenkel, O. Sorensen, and S. Wood, "Work Design Variation and Outcomes in Call Centers: Strategic Choice and Institutional Explanations," *Industrial and Labor Relations Review* 62 (July 2009): 510–532.

47. J. C. Quick and L. E. Tetrick, eds., *Handbook of Occupational Health Psychology, Second Edition* (Washington, D.C.: American Psychological Association, 2011).

48. W. E. Deming, *Out of the Crisis* (Cambridge, Mass.: MIT Press, 1986).

49. L. Thurow, *Head to Head: The Coming Economic Battle among Japan, Europe, and America* (New York: Morrow, 1992).

50. M. A. Fruin, *The Japanese Enterprise System—Competitive Strategies and Cooperative Structures* (New York: Oxford University Press, 1992).

51. W. Niepce and E. Molleman, "Work Design Issue in Lean Production from a Sociotechnical System Perspective: Neo-Taylorism or the Next Step in Sociotechnical Design?" *Human Relations* 51 (1998): 259–287.

52. S. K. Parker, "Longitudinal Effects of Lean Production on Employee Outcomes and the Mediating Role of Work Characteristics," *Journal of Applied Psychology* 88 (2003): 620–634.

53. E. Furubotn, "Codetermination and the Modern Theory of the Firm: A Property-Rights Analysis," *Journal of Business* 61 (1988): 165–181.

54. H. Levinson, *Executive: The Guide to Responsive Management* (Cambridge, Mass.: Harvard University Press, 1981).

55. B. Gardell, "Scandinavian Research on Stress in Working Life" (Paper presented at the IRRA Symposium on Stress in Working Life, Denver, September 1980).

56. L. Levi, "Psychosocial, Occupational, Environmental, and Health Concepts; Research Results and Applications," in G. P. Keita and S. L. Sauter, eds., *Work and Well-Being: An Agenda for the 1990s* (Washington, D.C.: American Psychological Association, 1992): 199–211.

57. L. R. Murphy and C. L. Cooper, eds., *Healthy and Productive Work: An International Perspective* (London and New York: Taylor & Francis, 2000).

58. J. Seigrist, "The Effort-Reward Imbalance Model," in C. L. Cooper and J. C. Quick. *The Handbook of Stress and Health: A Guide to Research and Practice*: pp. 24–35 (Chichester, UK: Wiley Blackwell, 2017).

59. A. B. Bakker and E. Demerouti, "Job Demands-Resources Theory: Taking Stock and Looking Forward," *Journal of Occupational Health Psychology*, 22, 3 (July 2017), 273–285.

60. M. Tims, A. B. Bakker, and D. Derks, "Examining Job Crafting from an Interpersonal Perspective: Is Employee Job Crafting Related to the Well-Being of Colleagues?" *Applied Psychology: An International Review*, published online March 2, 2015.

61. E. Carleton and J. Barling, "Sleep, Work, and Well-Being," in C. L. Cooper and J. C. Quick. *The Handbook of Stress and Health: A Guide to Research and Practice*. (Chichester, UK: Wiley Blackwell, 2017): 485–500; C. M. Barnes, J. A. Miller, and S. Bostock, "Helping Employees Sleep Well: Effects of Cognitive Behavioral Therapy for Insomnia on Work Outcomes," *Journal of Applied Psychology*, 102, 1 (Jan.), 2017, 104–113.

62. A. M. Grant, E. M. Campbell, G. Chen, K. Cottone, D. Lapedis, and K. Lee, "Impact and the Art of Motivation Maintenance: The Effects of Contact with Beneficiaries on Persistence Behavior," *Organizational Behavior and Human Decision Processes* 103 (2007): 53–67.

63. A. Idris, "Flexible Working as an Employee Retention Strategy in Developing Countries," *Journal of Management Research* 14 (2014): 71–86.

64. R. S. Gajendran, D. A. Harrison, and R. Delaney-Klinger, "Are Telecommuters Remotely Good Citizens? Unpacking Telecommuting's Effects on Performance via I-Deals and Job Resources," *Personnel Psychology*, published online August 15, 2014.

65. Y. Baruch, "The Status of Research on Teleworking and an Agenda for Future Research," *International Journal of Management Review* 3 (2000): 113–129.

66. K. E. Pearlson and C. S. Saunders, "There's No Place Like Home: Managing Telecommuting Paradoxes," *Academy of Management Executive* 15 (2001): 117–128.

67. S. Caudron, "Working at Home Pays Off," *Personnel Journal* (November 1992): 40–47.

68. D. S. Bailey and J. Foley, "Pacific Bell Works Long Distance," *HRMagazine* (August 1990): 50–52.

69. M. Virick, N. DaSilva, and K. Arrington, "Moderators of the Curvilinear Relationship between Extent of Telecommuting and Job and Life Satisfaction; The Role of Performance Outcome Orientation and Worker Type," *Human Relations* 63 (2010): 137–154.

70. I. Spieler, S. Scheibe, C. Stamov-Roßnagel, A. Kappas. "Help or Hindrance? Day-Level Relationships between Flextime Use, Work-Nonwork Boundaries, and Affective Well-Being," *Journal of Applied Psychology* 102, No. 1 (January 2017): 67–87.

71. S. A. Rogier and M. Y. Padgett, "The Impact of Utilizing a Flexible Work Schedule on the Perceived Career Advancement Potential of Women," *Human Resource Development Quarterly* 15 (2004): 89–106.

72. D. Derks, D. van Duin, M. Tims, and A. B. Bakker, "Smartphone Use and Work-Home Interference: The Moderating Role of Social Norms and Employee Work Engagement," *Journal of Occupational and Organizational Psychology* 88 (2015): 155–177.

73. S. Zuboff, *In the Age of the Smart Machine: The Future of Work and Power* (New York: Basic Books, 1988).

74. B. A. Gutek and S. J. Winter, "Computer Use, Control over Computers, and Job Satisfaction," in S. Oskamp and S. Spacapan, eds., *People's Reactions to Technology in Factories, Offices, and Aerospace: The Claremont Symposium on Applied Social Psychology* (Newbury Park, Calif.: Sage, 1990): 121–144.

75. L. M. Schleifer and B. C. Amick, III, "System Response Time and Method of Pay: Stress Effects in Computer-Based Tasks," *International Journal of Human-Computer Interaction* 1 (1989): 23–39.

76. K. Voight, "Virtual Work: Some Telecommuters Take Remote Work to the Extreme," *The Wall Street Journal Europe* (February 1, 2001): 1.

77. G. Salvendy, *Handbook of Industrial Engineering: Technology and Operations Management* (New York: John Wiley & Sons, 2001).

78. D. M. Herold, "Using Technology to Improve Our Management of Labor Market Trends," in M. Greller, ed., "Managing Careers with a Changing Workforce," *Journal of Organizational Change Management* 3 (1990): 44–57.

79. D. A. Whetten and K. S. Cameron, *Developing Management Skills,* 9th ed. (Upper Saddle River, N.J.: Pearson, 2015).

15

1. M. A. Hitt, R. D. Ireland, and R. E. Hoskisson, *Strategic Management: Competitiveness & Globalization—Concepts and Cases*, 12th ed. (Mason, OH: CENGAGE Learning, 2017).

2. J. Child, *Organization* (New York: Harper & Row, 1984).

3. P. Lawrence and J. Lorsch, *Organization and Environment: Managing Differentiation and Integration*, rev. ed. (Cambridge, Mass.: Harvard University Press, 1986).

4. J. Hage, "An Axiomatic Theory of Organizations," *Administrative Science Quarterly* 10 (1965): 289–320.

5. "The Army Reserve at 100: An Emerging Operational Force," *Army Logistician* (November–December, 2008): 15–16.

6. W. Ouchi and J. Dowling, "Defining the Span of Control," *Administrative Science Quarterly* 19 (1974): 357–365.

7. L. Porter and E. Lawler, III, "Properties of Organization Structure in Relation to Job Attitudes and Job Behavior," *Psychological Bulletin* 65 (1965): 23–51.

8. A. Ollier-Malaterre and A. Foucreault, "Cross-National Work-Life Research: Cultural and Structural Impacts for Individuals and Organizations," *Journal of Management* 43, No. 1 (January, 2017): 111–136.

9. R. Dewar and J. Hage, "Size, Technology, Complexity, and Structural Differentiation: Toward a Theoretical Synthesis," *Administrative Science Quarterly* 23 (1978): 111–136.

10. F. C. Vasoncelos and R. Ramirez, "Complexity in Business Environments," *Journal of Business Research* 64 (2011): 236–241.

11. Paul R. Lawrence and Jay W. Lorsch, "Differentiation and Integration in Complex Organizations," *Administrative Science Quarterly* 12, No. 1 (1967): 1–47.

12. J. R. R. Galbraith, *Designing Complex Organizations* (Reading, Mass.: Addison-Wesley-Longman, 1973).

13. W. Altier, "Task Forces: An Effective Management Tool," *Management Review* 76 (1987): 26–32.

14. P. Lawrence and J. Lorsch, "New Managerial Job: The Integrator," *Harvard Business Review* 45 (1967): 142–151.

15. J. Lorsch and P. Lawrence, "Organizing for Product Innovation," *Harvard Business Review* 43 (1965): 110–111.

16. D. Pugh, D. Hickson, C. Hinnings, and C. Turner, "Dimensions of Organization Structure," *Administrative Science Quarterly* 13 (1968): 65–91; B. Reimann, "Dimensions of Structure in Effective Organizations: Some Empirical Evidence," *Academy of Management Journal* 17 (1974): 693–708; S. Robbins, *Organization Theory: The Structure and Design of Organizations*, 3rd ed. (Englewood Cliffs, N.J.: Prentice-Hall, 1990).

17. M. C. Andrews, T. L. Baker, and T. G. Hunt, "The Interactive Effects of Centralization on the Relationship between Justice and Satisfaction," *Journal of Leadership & Organizational Studies* 15 (2008): 135–144.

18. A. Arora, S. Belenzon, and L. A. Rios, "Make, Buy, Organize: The Interplay Between Research, External Knowledge, and Firm Knowledge," *Strategic Management Journal* 35 (2014): 317–337.

19. H. Mintzberg, *The Structuring of Organizations* (Englewood Cliffs, N.J.: Prentice-Hall, 1979).

20. J. A. Kuprenas, "Implementation and Performance of a Matrix Organization Structure," *International Journal of Project Management* 21 (2003): 51–62.

21. Mintzberg, *Structuring of Organizations*.

22. K. Weick, "Educational Institutions as Loosely Coupled Systems," *Administrative Science Quarterly* (1976): 1–19.

23. D. Miller and C. Droge, "Psychological and Traditional Determinants of Structure," *Administrative Science Quarterly* 31 (1986): 540; H. Tosi, Jr. and J. Slocum, Jr., "Contingency Theory: Some Suggested Directions," *Journal of Management* 10 (1984): 9–26.

24. K. Singh, I. P. Mahmood, and S. Natarajan, "Capital Market Development and Firm Restructuring During an Economic Shock," *Organizational Science* 28, No. 3 (May–June, 2017): 552–573.

25. M. Meyer, "Size and the Structure of Organizations: A Causal Analysis," *American Sociological Review* 37 (1972): 434–441; J. Beyer and H. Trice, "A Reexamination of the Relations between Size and Various Components of Organizational Complexity," *Administrative Science Quarterly* 24 (1979): 48–64; B. Mayhew, R. Levinger, J. McPherson, and T. James, "Systems Size and Structural Differentiation in Formal Organizations: A Baseline Generator for Two Major Theoretical Propositions," *American Sociological Review* 37 (1972): 26–43.

26. M. Gowing, J. Kraft, and J. C. Quick, *The New Organizational Reality: Downsizing, Restructuring, and Revitalization* (Washington, D.C.: American Psychological Association, 1998).

27. M. Brauer and L. Laamanen, "Workforce Downsizing and Firm Performance: An Organizational Routine Perspective," *Journal of Management Studies* 51 (2014): 1311–1333.

28. L. Donaldson and G. Joffe, "Fit—The Key to Organizational Design," *Journal of Organization Design* 3 (2014): 38–45.

29. J. Werth and D. Fleming, "Creating a 'Super' Agency in San Diego County," *The Public Manager* (Fall 2008): 21–26.

30. J. Woodward, *Industrial Organization: Theory and Practices* (London: Oxford University Press, 1965).

31. C. Perrow, "A Framework for the Comparative Analysis of Organizations," *American Sociological Review* 32 (1967): 194–208; D. Rosseau, "Assessment of Technology in Organizations: Closed versus Open Systems Approaches," *Academy of Management Review* 4 (1979): 531–542.

32. C. Perrow, "A Framework for the Comparative Analysis of Organizations," *American Sociological Review* 32, No. 2 (1967): 194–208.

33. J. D. Thompson, *Organizations in Action* (New York: McGraw-Hill, 1967).

34. J. R. Baum and S. Wally, "Strategic Decision Speed and Firm Performance," *Strategic Management Journal* 24 (2003): 1107–1129.

35. Thompson, *Organizations in Action*.

36. H. Downey, D. Hellriegel, and J. Slocum, Jr., "Environmental Uncertainty: The Construct and Its Application," *Administrative Science Quarterly* 20 (1975): 613–629.

37. G. Dess and D. Beard, "Dimensions of Organizational Task Environments," *Administrative Science Quarterly* 29 (1984): 52–73.

38. J. A. Cogin and I. O. Williamson, "Standardize or Customize: The Interactive Effects of HRM and Environment Uncertainty on MNC Subsidiary Performance," *Human Resource Management* 53 (2014): 701–721.

39. G. G. Dess and D. W. Beard, "Dimensions of Organizational Task Environments," *Administrative Science Quarterly* 29, No. 1 (1984): 52–73.

40. T. Burns and G. Stalker, *The Management of Innovation* (London: Tavistock, 1961); Mintzberg, *Structuring of Organizations*.

41. M. Chandler and L. Sayles, *Managing Large Systems* (New York: Harper & Row, 1971).

42. M. Sanchez-Manzanares, R. Rico, and F. Gil, "Designing Organizations: Does Expertise Matter?" *Journal of Business Psychology* 23 (2008): 87–101.

43. R. E. Hoskisson, F. Chirico, J. (D.) Zyung, and E. Gambeta, "Managerial Risk Taking: A Multitheoretical Review and Future Research Agenda," *Journal of Management* 43, No. 1 (January 2017): 137–169.

44. R. Daft, *Organization Theory and Design*, 10th ed. (Mason, Ohio: South-Western, 2010).

45. R. S. Kaplan and D. P. Norton, "How to Implement a New Strategy without Disrupting Your Organization," *Harvard Business Review* (March 2006): 100–109.

46. L-H Lin, "Organizational Structure and Acculturation in Acquisitions: Perspectives of Congruence Theory and Task Interdependence," *Journal of Management* 40 (2014): 1831–1856.

47. N. J. Foss, J. Lyngsie, and S. A. Zahra, "Organizational Design Correlates of Entrepreneurship: The Roles of Decentralization and Formalization for Opportunity Discovery and Realization," *Strategic Organization* 13 (2015): 32–60.

48. W. R. Scott, *Organizations: Rational, Natural, and Open Systems*, 6th ed. (Upper Saddle River, N.J.: Prentice-Hall, 2006).

49. D. Miller and P. Friesen, "A Longitudinal Study of the Corporate Life Cycle," *Management Science* 30 (1984): 1161–1183.

50. S. Raisch, "Balanced Structures: Designing Organizations for Profitable Growth," *Long Range Planning* 41 (2008): 483–508.

51. M. H. Overholt, "Flexible Organizations: Using Organizational Design as a Competitive Advantage," *Human Resource Planning* 20 (1997): 22–32; P. W. Roberts and R. Greenwood, "Integrating Transaction Cost and Institutional Theories: Toward a

Constrained-Efficiency Framework for Understanding Organizational Design Adoption," *Academy of Management Review* 22 (1997): 346–373.

52. G. Davidson, "Organisation Structure: The Life Cycle of an Organization," *New Zealand Management* 56 (2008): 58–60.

53. C. W. L. Hill and G. R. Jones, *Strategic Management Theory,* 5th ed. (Boston: Houghton Mifflin, 2000).

54. F. Hoque, "Designing the Right Kind of Organization," *Baseline* (January/February 2009): 46.

55. Cengage Learning, 11e, 2013.

56. C. M. Savage, *5th Generation Management, Revised Edition: Co-creating through Virtual Enterprising, Dynamic Teaming, and Knowledge Networking* (Boston: Butterworth-Heinemann, 1996).

57. L-Q. Wei and C-M. Lau, "High Performance Work Systems and Performance: The Role of Adaptive Capability," *Human Relations* 63, No. 10 (October 2010): 1463L-Q. Wei and C-M. Lau, "High Performance Work Systems and Performance: The Role of Adaptive Capability," Human Relations 63, No. 10 (October 2010): 1463–1485.

58. D. Shin and A. M. Konrad, "Causality between High-Performance Work Systems and Organizational Performance," Journal of Management 43, No. 2 (February 2017): 455D. Shin and A. M. Konrad, "Causality between High-Performance Work Systems and Organizational Performance," Journal of Management 43, No. 2 (February 2017): 455–475.

59. B. Brown and S. D. Anthony, "How P&G Tripled Its Innovation Success Rate," *Harvard Business Review* 89 (June 2011): 64–72.

60. P. J. Brews and C. L. Tucci, "Exploring the Structural Effects of Internetworking," *Strategic Management Journal* 25 (2004): 429–451.

61. C. B. Gibson and J. L. Gibbs, "Unpacking the Concept of Virtuality: Geographic Dispersion, Electronic Dependence, Dynamic Structure, and National Diversity on Team Innovation," *Administrative Science Quarterly* 51 (2006): 451–495.

62. J. Fulk, "Global Network Organizations: Emergence and Future Prospects," *Human Relations* 54 (2001): 91–100.

63. The use of the theatrical troupe as an analogy for virtual organizations was first used by David Mack, circa 1995.

64. E. C. Kasper-Fuehrer and N. M. Ashkanasy, "Communicating Trustworthiness and Building Trust in Interorganizational Virtual Organizations," *Journal of Management* 27 (2001): 235–254.

65. R. Teerlink and L. Ozley, *More Than a Motorcycle: The Leadership Journey at Harley-Davidson* (Boston: Harvard Business School Press, 2000).

66. W. A. Cohen and N. Cohen, *The Paranoid Organization and 8 Other Ways Your Company Can Be Crazy: Advice from an Organizational Shrink* (New York: American Management Association, 1993).

67. P. E. Tetlock, "Cognitive Biases and Organizational Correctives: Do Both Disease and Cure Depend on the Politics of the Beholder?" *Administrative Science Quarterly* 45 (2000): 293–326.

68. M. F. R. Kets de Vries and D. Miller, "Personality, Culture, and Organization," *Academy of Management Review* 11 (1986): 266–279.

16

1. T. E. Deal and A. A. Kennedy, *Corporate Cultures* (Reading, Mass.: Addison-Wesley, 1982).

2. W. Ouchi, *Theory Z* (Reading, Mass.: Addison-Wesley, 1981).

3. T. J. Peters and R. H. Waterman, *In Search of Excellence* (New York: Harper & Row, 1982).

4. M. Gardner, "Creating a Corporate Culture for the Eighties," *Business Horizons* (January–February 1985): 59–63.

5. S. J. Hogan and L. V. Coote, "Organizational Culture, Innovation, and Performance: A Test of Schein's Model," *Journal of Business Research* 67 (2014): 1609–1621.

6. Definition adapted from E. H. Schein, *Organizational Culture and Leadership* (San Francisco: Jossey-Bass, 1985): 9.

7. C. D. Sutton and D. L. Nelson, "Elements of the Cultural Network: The Communicators of Corporate Values," *Leadership and Organization Development* 11 (1990): 3–10.

8. A. Gara, "Visa's CEO Charlie Scharf Steps Down After Four Years, Sick of San Francisco Travel," *Forbes* (October 17, 2016), accessed at https://www.forbes.com/sites/antoinegara/2016/10/17/visas-ceo-charlie-scharf-steps-down-after-four-years-sick-of-san-francisco-travel/#666533b199e0

9. J. Pagel, "Eskimo Joe's Getting Older, But Still Fun at 21," *Amarillo Business Journal* (November 20, 1996), http://www.businessjournal.net/entrepreneur1196.html.

10. A. Bandura, *Social Learning Theory* (Englewood Cliffs, N.J.: Prentice-Hall, 1977).

11. J. A. Chatman, "Leading by Leveraging Culture," *California Management Review* 45 (2003): 20–34.

12. J. M. Beyer and H. M. Trice, "How an Organization's Rites Reveal Its Culture," *Organizational Dynamics* 16 (1987): 5–24.

13. H. M. Trice and J. M. Beyer, "Studying Organizational Cultures through Rites and Ceremonials," *Academy of Management Review* 9 (1984): 653–669.

14. "Recap: The 2014 Berkshire Hathaway Annual Meeting," *The Wall Street Journal* (May 3, 2014), accessed at http://blogs.wsj.com/moneybeat/2014/05/03/live-blog-the-2014-berkshire-hathaway-annual-meeting/.

15. H. Levinson and S. Rosenthal, *CEO: Corporate Leadership in Action* (New York: Basic Books, 1984).

16. V. Sathe, "Implications of Corporate Culture: A Manager's Guide to Action," *Organizational Dynamics* 12 (1987): 5–23.

17. "Wal-Mart Culture Stories—The Sundown Rule," http://www.wal-martchina.com/english/walmart/rule/sun.htm.

18. J. Martin, M. S. Feldman, M. J. Hatch, and S. B. Sitkin, "The Uniqueness Paradox in Organizational Stories," *Administrative Science Quarterly* 28 (1983): 438–453.

19. J. Lofstock, "Applauding the QuikTrip Culture," http://www.quiktrip.com/aboutqt/news.asp.

20. "No layoffs—ever!" CNNMoney.com (August 12, 2011), http://money.cnn.com/galleries/2010/fortune/1001/gallery.bestcompanies_layoffs.fortune/.

21. S. R. Martin, "Stories About Values and Valuable Stories: A Field Experiment of Narratives to Shape Newcomers' Actions," *Academy of Management Journal,* 59 (2016): 1707–1724.

22. J. E. Vascellaro, "Facebook CEO in a Rush to 'Friend' Wall Street," *The Wall Street Journal* (March 3, 2010), http://online.wsj.com /article/SB100014240527487037873045750759428036 30712.html?mod=djem_jiewr_HR_domainid.

23. R. Goffee and G. Jones, "What Holds the Modern Company Together?" *Harvard Business Review* (November–December 1996): 133–143.

24. C. Argyris and D. A. Schon, *Organizational Learning* (Reading, Mass.: Addison-Wesley, 1978).

25 http://www.clifbar.com/article/the-five-aspirations

26. D. J. McAllister and G. A. Bigley, "Work Context and the Definition of Self: How Organizational Care Influences Organization-Based Self-Esteem," *Academy of Management Journal* 45 (2002): 894–905.

27. M. Peterson, "Work, Corporate Culture, and Stress: Implications for Worksite Health Promotion," *American Journal of Health Behavior* 21 (1997): 243–252.

28. http://www.capspire.com/careers/life-at-capspire/

29. L. Smircich, "Concepts of Culture and Organizational Analysis," *Administrative Science Quarterly* 28 (1983): 339–358.

30. Y. Weiner and Y. Vardi, "Relationships between Organizational Culture and Individual Motivation: A Conceptual Integration," *Psychological Reports* 67 (1990): 295–306.

31. M. R. Louis, "Surprise and Sense Making: What Newcomers Experience in Entering Unfamiliar Organizational Settings," *Administrative Science Quarterly* 25 (1980): 209–264.

32. T. L. Doolen, M. E. Hacker, and E. M. van Aken, "The Impact of Organizational Context on Work Team Effectiveness: A Study of Production Teams," *IEEE Transactions on Engineering Management* 50 (2003): 285–296.

33. O. A. O'Neill and N. P. Rothbard, "Is Love All You Need? The Effects of Emotional Culture, Suppression, and Work-Family Conflict on Firefighter Risk-Taking and Health," *Academy of Management Journal* 60 (2017): 78–108.

34. J. P. Kotter and J. L. Heskett, *Corporate Culture and Performance* (New York: Free Press, 1992); A. S. Boyce, L. R. G. Nieminen, M. A. Gillespie, A. M. Ryan, and D. R. Denison, "Which Comes First, Organizational Culture or Performance? A Longitudinal Study of Causal Priority with Automobile Dealerships," *Journal of Organizational Behavior*, published online January 15, 2015.

35. Deal and Kennedy, *Corporate Cultures.*

36. D. R. Katz, *The Big Store* (New York: Viking, 1987).

37. G. G. Gordon, "Industry Determinants of Organizational Culture," *Academy of Management Review* 16 (1991): 396–415.

38. G. Donaldson and J. Lorsch, *Decision Making at the Top* (New York: Basic Books, 1983).

39. R. H. Kilman, M. J. Saxton, and R. Serpa, eds., *Gaining Control of the Corporate Culture* (San Francisco: Jossey-Bass, 1986).

40. J. P. Kotter, *A Force for Change: How Leadership Differs from Management* (New York: Free Press, 1990); R. M. Kanter, *The Change Masters* (New York: Simon & Schuster, 1983).

41. J. A. Chatman, D. F. Caldwell, C. A. O'Reilly, and B. Doerr, "Parsing Organizational Culture: How the Norm for Adaptability Influences the Relationship Between Culture Consensus and Financial Performance in High-Technology Firms," *Journal of Organizational Behavior* 35 (2015): 785–808.

42. Schein, *Organizational Culture and Leadership.*

43. J. A. Pearce II, T. R. Kramer, and D. K. Robbins, "Effects of Managers' Entrepreneurial Behavior on Subordinates," *Journal of Business Venturing* 12 (1997): 147–160.

44. P. W. Braddy, A. W. Meade, and C. M. Kroustalis, "Organizational Recruitment Website Effects on Viewers' Perceptions of Organizational Culture," *Journal of Business and Psychology* 20, No. 4 (2006): 525–543.

45. A. Bryant, "Mitch Rothschild of Vitals: Pushing beyond Comfort Zones," *New York Times*, January 24, 2015, accessed at http://www.nytimes.com/2015/01/25/business/mitch-rothschild-of-vitalis-juggle-but-dont-tiptoe.html.

46. A. Xenikou and M. Simosi, "Organizational Culture and Transformational Leadership as Predictors of Business Unit Performance," *Journal of Managerial Psychology* 21, No. 6 (2006): 566–579.

47. D. C. Feldman, "The Multiple Socialization of Organization Members," *Academy of Management Review* 6 (1981): 309–318.

48. A. M. Ellis, T. N. Bauer, L. R. Mansfield, B. Erdogan, D. M. Truxillo, and L. S. Simon, "Navigating Uncharted Waters: Newcomer

Socialization through the Lens of Stress Theory," *Journal of Management* 41 (2015): 203–235.

49. D. L. Nelson, "Organizational Socialization: A Stress Perspective," *Journal of Occupational Behavior* 8 (1987): 311–324.

50. J. Fan and J. P. Wanous, "Organizational and Cultural Entry: A New Type of Orientation Program for Multiple Boundary Crossings," *Journal of Applied Psychology* 93 (2008): 1390–1400.

51. D. M. Cable, L. Aiman-Smith, P. W. Mulvey, and J. R. Edwards, "The Sources and Accuracy of Job Applicants' Beliefs about Organizational Culture," *Academy of Management Journal* 43 (2000): 1076–1085.

52. J. D. DeBode, K. W. Mossholder, and A. G. Walker. "Fulfilling Employees' Psychological Contracts: Organizational Socialization's Role," *Leadership and Organization Development Journal*, 38 (2017): 42–55.

53. D. L. Nelson, J. C. Quick, and M. E. Eakin, "A Longitudinal Study of Newcomer Role Adjustment in U.S. Organizations," *Work and Stress* 2 (1988): 239–253.

54. N. J. Allen and J. P. Meyer, "Organizational Socialization Tactics: A Longitudinal Analysis of Links to Newcomers' Commitment and Role Orientation," *Academy of Management Journal* 33 (1990): 847–858.

55. T. N. Bauer, E. W. Morrison, and R. R. Callister, "Organizational Socialization: A Review and Directions for Future Research," *Research in Personnel and Human Resources Management* 16 (1998): 149–214.

56. D. M. Cable and C. K. Parsons, "Socialization Tactics and Person–Organization Fit," *Personnel Psychology* 54 (2001): 1–23.

57. S. H. Harrison, D. M. Sluss, and B. E. Ashforth, "Curiosity Adapted the Cat: The Role of Trait Curiosity in Newcomer Adaption," *Journal of Applied Psychology* 96 (2011): 211–220; M. Wang, Y. Zhan, E. McCune, and D. Truxillo, "Understanding Newcomers' Adaptability and Work-Related Outcomes: Testing the Mediating Roles of Perceived P-E Fit Variables," *Personnel Psychology* 64 (2011): 163–189.

58. A. M. Saks, J. A. Gruman, and H. Cooper-Thomas, "The Neglected Role of Proactive Behavior and Outcomes in Newcomer Socialization," *Journal of Vocational Behavior* 79 (2011): 36–46.

59. D. M. Rousseau, "Assessing Organizational Culture: The Case for Multiple Methods," in B. Schneider, ed., *Organizational Climate and Culture* (San Francisco: Jossey-Bass, 1990).

60. R. A. Cooke and D. M. Rousseau, "Behavioral Norms and Expectations: A Quantitative Approach to the Assessment of Organizational Culture," *Group and Organizational Studies* 12 (1988): 245–273.

61. R. H. Kilmann and M. J. Saxton, *Kilmann-Saxton Culture-Gap Survey* (Pittsburgh: Organizational Design Consultants, 1983).

62. W. J. Duncan, "Organizational Culture: 'Getting a Fix' on an Elusive Concept,"

Academy of Management Executive 3 (1989): 229–236.

63. P. Bate, "Using the Culture Concept in an Organization Development Setting," *Journal of Applied Behavior Science* 26 (1990): 83–106.

64. K. R. Thompson and F. Luthans, "Organizational Culture: A Behavioral Perspective," in B. Schneider, ed., *Organizational Climate and Culture* (San Francisco: Jossey-Bass, 1990).

65. S. Seren and U. Baykal, "Relationships between Change and Organizational Culture in Hospitals," *Journal of Nursing Scholarship* 39, No. 2 (2007): 191–197.

66. V. Sathe, "How to Decipher and Change Corporate Culture," in R. H. Kilman et al., *Managing Corporate Cultures* (San Francisco: Jossey-Bass, 1985).

67. M. E. Johnson-Cramer, S. Parise, and R. L. Cross, "Managing Change through Networks and Values," *California Management Review* 49, No. 3 (2007): 85–109.

68. S. Lee, J. Kim, and B. Park, "Culture Clashes in Cross-Border Mergers and Acquisitions: A Case Study of Sweden's Volvo and South Korea's Samsung," *International Business Review*, November 20, 2014, accessed at http://www.sciencedirect.com/science/article/pii/S0969593114001772.

69. N. J. Adler, *International Dimensions of Organizational Behavior*, 2nd ed. (Boston: PWS Kent, 1991).

70. A. Laurent, "The Cultural Diversity of Western Conceptions of Management," *International Studies of Management and Organization* 13 (1983): 75–96.

71. P. C. Earley and E. Mosakowski, "Creating Hybrid Team Cultures: An Empirical Test of Transnational Team Functioning," *Academy of Management Journal* 43 (2000): 26–49.

72. D. Lei, J. W. Slocum, Jr., and R. W. Slater, "Global Strategy and Reward Systems: The Key Roles of Management Development and Corporate Culture," *Organizational Dynamics* 19 (1990): 27–41.

73. L. K. Trevino and K. A. Nelson, *Managing Business Ethics: Straight Talk about How to Do It Right* (New York: John Wiley & Sons, 1995).

74. M. Kaptein, "Understanding Unethical Behavior by Unraveling Ethical Culture," *Human Relations* (in press).

75. P. J. Zak, "The Neuroscience of Trust," *Harvard Business Review* January/February (2017), accessed at https://hbr.org/2017/01/the-neuroscience-of-trust.

76. P. Zoghbi-Manrique-de-Lara and M. Viera-Armas, "Corporate Culture as a Mediator in the Relationship Between Ethical Leadership and Personal Internet Use," *Journal of Leadership and Organizational Studies* (2017), accessed at http://journals.sagepub.com/doi/pdf/10.1177/1548051817696877.

77. M. Jin, J. Lee, and M. Lee, "Does Leadership Matter in Diversity Management? Assessing the Relative Impact of Diversity Policy

and Inclusive Leadership in the Public Sector," *Leadership and Organization Development Journal* 38 (2017), accessed at http://www.emeraldinsight.com/doi/abs/10.1108/LODJ-07-2015-0151.

78. L. Quast, "6 Tips for an Inclusive Organizational Culture," *Forbes* (April 17 2017), accessed at https://www.forbes.com/sites/lisaquast/2017/04/17/combating-gender-discrimination-6-tips-for-an-inclusive-organizational-culture/#12deecabf5da.

79. J. Kell, "Meet the Workplace Culture Warriors," *Fortune* (March 15, 2017), accessed at http://fortune.com/2017/03/14/best-companies-to-work-for-culture/.

80. S. A. Hewlett and K. Yoshino, "LGBT-Inclusive Companies are Better at 3 Big Things," *Harvard Business Review* (February 2, 2016), accessed at https://hbr.org/2016/02/lgbt-inclusive-companies-are-better-at-3-big-things.

81. http://about.att.com/sites/diversity/our_people

17

1. J. H. Greenhaus, *Career Management* (Hinsdale, Ill.: CBS College Press, 1987).

2. D. T. Hall, *Careers in Organizations* (Pacific Palisades, Calif.: Goodyear, 1976).

3. Greenhaus, *Career Management;* T. G. Gutteridge and F. L. Otte, "Organizational Career Development: What's Going on Out There?" *Training and Development Journal* 37 (1983): 22–26.

4. M. B. Arthur, P. H. Claman, and R. J. DeFillippi, "Intelligent Enterprise, Intelligent Careers," *Academy of Management Executive* (November 1995): 7–22.

5. M. Lips-Wiersma and D. T. Hall, "Organizational Career Development Is Not Dead: A Case Study on Managing the New Career during Organizational Change," *Journal of Organizational Behavior* 28, No. 6 (2007): 771–792.

6. D. Jemielniak, "Managers as Lazy, Stupid Careerists?" *Journal of Organizational Change Management* 20, No. 4 (2007): 491–508.

7. D. E. Super, *The Psychology of Careers* (New York: Harper & Row, 1957); D. E. Super and M. J. Bohn, Jr., *Occupational Psychology* (Belmont, Calif.: Wadsworth, 1970).

8. J. L. Holland, *The Psychology of Vocational Choice* (Waltham, Mass.: Blaisdell, 1966); J. L. Holland, *Making Vocational Choices: A Theory of Careers* (Englewood Cliffs, N.J.: Prentice-Hall, 1973).

9. F. T. L. Leong and J. T. Austin, "An Evaluation of the Cross-Cultural Validity of Holland's Theory: Career Choices by Workers in India," *Journal of Vocational Behavior* 52 (1998): 441–455.

10. C. Morgan, J. D. Isaac, and C. Sansone, "The Role of Interest in Understanding the Career Choices of Female and Male College Students," *Sex Roles* 44 (2001): 295–320.

11. J. K. Hellerstein and M. S. Morrill, "Dads and Daughters: The Changing Impact of Fathers on Women's Occupational Choices," *Journal of Human Resources* 46, No. 2 (2011): 333–372; S. H. Osipow, *Theories of Career Development* (Englewood Cliffs, N.J.: Prentice-Hall, 1973).

12. J. P. Wanous, T. L. Keon, and J. C. Latack, "Expectancy Theory and Occupational/Organizational Choices: A Review and Test," *Organizational Behavior and Human Performance* 32 (1983): 66–86.

13. P. O. Soelberg, "Unprogrammed Decision Making," *Industrial Management Review* 8 (1967): 19–29.

14. J. P. Wanous, *Organizational Entry: Recruitment, Selection, and Socialization of Newcomers* (Reading, Mass.: Addison-Wesley, 1980).

15. S. L. Premack and J. P. Wanous, "A Meta-Analysis of Realistic Job Preview Experiments," *Journal of Applied Psychology* 70 (1985): 706–719.

16. http://www.timewarnercable.com/corporate/about/careers.

17. http://www.dads.state.tx.us/providers/job-preview/idd-video.html

18. P. W. Hom, R. W. Griffeth, L. E. Palich, and J. S. Bracker, "An Exploratory Investigation into Theoretical Mechanisms Underlying Realistic Job Previews," *Personnel Psychology* 41 (1998): 421–451.

19. J. A. Breaugh, "Realistic Job Previews: A Critical Appraisal and Future Research Directions," *Academy of Management Review* 8 (1983): 612–619.

20. G. R. Jones, "Socialization Tactics, Self-Efficacy, and Newcomers' Adjustment to Organizations," *Academy of Management Journal* 29 (1986): 262–279.

21. M. R. Buckley, D. B. Fedor, J. G. Veres, D. S. Wiese, and S. M. Carraher, "Investigating Newcomer Expectations and Job-Related Outcomes," *Journal of Applied Psychology* 83 (1998): 452–461.

22. J. Oliver, R. T. Erk, A. Koch, T. L. Russell, N. E. Babin, S. A. Ardison, and M. C. Young, "Identification and Accessioning of Individuals for Officer Candidate School: Developing Realistic Job Previews," technical report, United States Army Research Institute for Behavioral and Social Sciences (2014), accessed online.

23. A. De Vos and C. Freese, "Sensemaking During Organizational Entry: Changes in Newcomer Information Seeking and the Relationship with Psychological Contract Fulfillment," *Journal of Occupational and Organizational Psychology* 84 (2011): 288–314.

24. P. Buhler, "Managing in the '90s," *Supervision* (July 1995): 24–26.

25. D. T. Hall and J. E. Moss, "The New Protean Career Contract: Helping Organizations and Employees Adapt," *Organizational Dynamics* (Winter 1998): 22–37.

26. S. A. Zahra, R. L. Priem, and A. A. Rasheed, "Understanding the Causes and Effects of Top Management Fraud," *Organizational Dynamics* 36, No. 2 (2007): 122–139.

27. A. Fisher, "Don't Blow Your New Job," *Fortune* (June 22, 1998): 159–162.

28. D. Goleman, *Working with Emotional Intelligence* (New York: Bantam, 1998); A. Fisher, "Success Secret: A High Emotional IQ," *Fortune* (October 26, 1998): 293–298.

29. N. Libbrecht, F. Lievens, B. Carette, and S. Cote, "Emotional Intelligence Predicts Success in Medical School," *Emotion* 14 (2014): 64–73.

30. K. V. Petrides, A. Furnham, and G. N. Martin, "Estimates of Emotional and Psychometric Intelligence," *Journal of Social Psychology* 144 (April 2004): 149–162.

31. C. Chermiss, "The Business Case for Emotional Intelligence," *The Consortium for Research on Emotional Intelligence in Organizations* (2003), http://www.eiconsortium.org/research/business_case_for _ei.htm; L. M. Spencer, Jr., and S. Spencer, *Competence at Work: Models for Superior Performance* (New York: John Wiley & Sons, 1993); L. M. Spencer, Jr., D. C. McClelland, and S. Kelner, *Competency Assessment Methods: History and State of the Art* (Boston Hay/McBer, 1997).

32. J. O. Crites, "A Comprehensive Model of Career Adjustment in Early Adulthood," *Journal of Vocational Behavior* 9 (1976): 105–118; S. Cytrynbaum and J. O. Crites, "The Utility of Adult Development in Understanding Career Adjustment Process," in M. B. Arthur, D. T. Hall, and B. S. Lawrence, eds., *Handbook of Career Theory* (Cambridge: Cambridge University Press, 1989): 66–88.

33. D. E. Super, "A Life-Span, Life-Space Approach to Career Development," *Journal of Vocational Behavior* 16 (1980): 282–298; L. Baird and K. Kram, "Career Dynamics: Managing the Superior/Subordinate Relationship," *Organizational Dynamics* 11 (1983): 46–64.

34. D. J. Levinson, *The Seasons of a Man's Life* (New York: Knopf, 1978); D. J. Levinson, *The Seasons of a Woman's Life* (New York: Knopf, 1996).

35. D. J. Levinson, "A Conception of Adult Development," *American Psychologist* 41 (1986): 3–13.

36. D. L. Nelson, "Adjusting to a New Organization: Easing the Transition from Outsider to Insider," in J. C. Quick, R. E. Hess, J. Hermalin, and J. D. Quick, eds., *Career Stress in Changing Times* (New York: Haworth Press, 1990): 61–86.

37. J. P. Kotter, "The Psychological Contract: Managing the Joining Up Process," *California Management Review* 15 (1973): 91–99.

38. D. M. Rousseau, "New Hire Perceptions of Their Own and Their Employers' Obligations: A Study of Psychological Contracts," *Journal of Organizational Behavior* 11 (1990): 389–400; D. L. Nelson, J. C. Quick, and J. R. Joplin, "Psychological Contracting and Newcomer Socialization: An Attachment Theory Foundation," *Journal of Social Behavior and Personality* 6 (1991): 55–72.

39. H. Zhao, S. Wayne, B. Glibkowski, and J. Bravo "The Impact of Psychological Breach on

Work-Related Outcomes," *Personnel Psychology* (2007): 647–680.

40. S. S. Nifadakr and T. N. Bauer, "Breach of Belongingness: Newcomer Relationship Conflict, Information, and Task-Related Outcomes During Organizational Socialization," *Journal of Applied Psychology* 101 (2016): 1–13.

41. D. J. Levinson," A conception of adult development," *American Psychologist* 41, No. 1 (January 1986): 3–13.

42. J. W. Walker, "Let's Get Realistic about Career Paths," *Human Resource Management* 15 (1976): 2–7.

43. E. H. Buttner and D. P. Moore, "Women's Organizational Exodus to Entrepreneurship: Self-Reported Motivations and Correlates," *Journal of Small Business Management* 35 (1997): 34–46; Center for Women's Business Research Press Release, "Privately Held, 50% or More Women-Owned Businesses in the United States," 2004, http://www.nfwbo.org/pressreleases/nationalstatetrends/total.htm.

44. D. G. Collings, H. Scullion, and M. J. Morley, "Changing Patterns of Global Staffing in the Multinational Enterprise: Challenges to the Conventional Expatriate Assignment and Emerging Alternatives," *Journal of World Business* 42, No. 2 (2007): 198–213.

45. B. Filipczak, "You're on Your Own," *Training* (January 1995): 29–36.

46. K. E. Kram, *Mentoring at Work: Developmental Relationships in Organizational Life* (Glenview, Ill.: Scott, Foresman, 1985).

47. T. D. Allen, L. T. Eby, G. T. Chao, and T. N. Bauer, "Taking Stock of Two Relational Aspects of Organizational Life: Tracing the History and Shaping the Future of Socialization and Mentoring Research," *Journal of Applied Psychology*, 102 (2017): 324–337.

48. J. Arnold and K. Johnson, "Mentoring in Early Career," *Human Resource Management Journal* 7 (1997): 61–70.

49. B. P. Madia and C. J. Lutz, "Perceived Similarity, Expectation–Reality Discrepancies, and Mentors' Expressed Intention to Remain in the Big Brothers/Big Sisters Programs," *Journal of Applied Social Psychology* 34 (March 2004): 598–622.

50. "A Guide to the Mentor Program Listings," *Mentors Peer Resources*, http://www.mentors.ca/mentorprograms.html.

51. http://www.diversityinc.com/mentoring/why-mentoring-is-not-an-option-at-ibm/

52. R. Friedman, M. Kan, and D. B. Cornfield, "Social Support and Career Optimism: Examining the Effectiveness of Network Groups among Black Managers," *Human Relations* 51 (1998): 1155–1177.

53. S. E. Seibert, M. L. Kraimer, and R. C. Liden, "A Social Capital Theory of Career Success," *Academy of Management Journal* 44 (2001): 219–237.

54. http://corporate.exxonmobil.com/en/company/careers/employment-policies/diversity

55. M. A. Covaleski, M. W. Dirsmuth, J. B. Heian, and S. Samuel, "The Calculated and the Avowed: Techniques of Discipline and Struggles over Identity in Big Six Public Accounting Firms," *Administrative Science Quarterly* 43 (1998): 293–327.

56. B. R. Ragins and J. L. Cotton, "Easier Said Than Done: Gender Differences in Perceived Barriers to Gaining a Mentor," *Academy of Management Journal* 34 (1991): 939–951; S. D. Phillips and A. R. Imhoff, "Women and Career Development: A Decade of Research," *Annual Review of Psychology* 48 (1997): 31–43.

57. Ibid.

58. A. Ramaswami, G. F. Dreher, R. Bretz, and C. Wiethoff, "Gender, Mentoring and Career Success: The Importance of Organizational Context," *Personnel Psychology* 63, No. 2 (2010): 385–405.

59. W. Whiteley, T. W. Dougherty, and G. F. Dreher, "Relationship of Career Mentoring and Socioeconomic Origin to Managers' and Professionals' Early Career Progress," *Academy of Management Journal* 34 (1991): 331–351; G. F. Dreher and R. A. Ash, "A Comparative Study of Mentoring among Men and Women in Managerial, Professional, and Technical Positions," *Journal of Applied Psychology* 75 (1990): 539–546; T. A. Scandura, "Mentorship and Career Mobility: An Empirical Investigation," *Journal of Organizational Behavior* 13 (1992): 169–174.

60. G. F. Dreher and T. H. Cox, Jr., "Race, Gender and Opportunity: A Study of Compensation Attainment and Establishment of Mentoring Relationships," *Journal of Applied Psychology* 81 (1996): 297–309.

61. D. D. Horgan and R. J. Simeon, "Mentoring and Participation: An Application of the Vroom-Yetton Model," *Journal of Business and Psychology* 5 (1990): 63–84.

62. B. R. Ragins, J. L. Cotton, and J. S. Miller, "Marginal Mentoring: The Effects of Type of Mentor, Quality of Relationship, and Program Design on Work and Career Attitudes," *Academy of Management Journal* 43 (2000): 1177–1194.

63. C. Buengeler, A. C. Homan, and S. C. Voelpel, "The Challenge of Being a Young Manager: The Effect of Contingent Reward and Participative Leadership on Team-Level Turnover Depend on Leader Age," *Journal of Organizational Behavior*, 37 (2016): 1224–1245.

64. C. R. Masterson and J. M. Hoobler, "Care and Career: A Family Identity-Based Typology of Dual-Earner Couples," *Journal of Organizational Behavior* 36 (2015), accessed online, doi:10.1002/job.1945.

65. A. Croft, T. Schmader, K. Block, and A. S. Baron, "The Second Shift Reflected in the Second Generation," *Psychological Science* (2015), accessed online, doi:10.1177/0956797614533968.

66. B. Morris, "Is Your Family Wrecking Your Career? (And Vice Versa)," *Fortune* (March 17, 1997): 70–80.

67. Ibid.

68. L. K. Barber, S. G. Taylor, J. P. Burton, and S. F. Bailey, "A Self-Regulatory Perspective of Work-to-Home Undermining Spillover/Crossover: Examining the Roles of Sleep and Exercise," *Journal of Applied Psychology* 102 (2017): 753–763.

69. E. McGrath, H. D. Cooper-Thomas, E. Garrosa, A. I. Sanz-Vergel, and G. W. Cheung, "Rested, Friendly, and Engaged: The Role of Daily Positive Collegial Interactions at Work," *Journal of Organizational Behavior* (2017), accessed at http://onlinelibrary.wiley.com/doi/10.1002/job.2197/full.

70. R. G. Netemeyer, J. S. Boles, and R. McMurrian, "Development and Validation of Work–Family Conflict and Family–Work Conflict Scales," *Journal of Applied Psychology* 81 (1996): 400–410.

71. B. Livingston and T. A. Judge, "Emotional Responses to Work-Family Conflict: An Examination of Gender Role Orientation among Working Men and Women," *Journal of Applied Psychology* 93 (2008): 207–216.

72. N. Yang, C. C. Chen, J. Choi, and Y. Zou, "Sources of Work–Family Conflict: A Sino–U.S. Comparison of the Effects of Work and Family Demands," *Academy of Management Journal* 43 (2000): 113–123.

73. A. Iris Aaltion and H. Jiehua Huang, "Women Managers' Careers in Information Technology in China: High Flyers with Emotional Costs?" *Journal of Organizational Change Management* 20, No. 2 (2007): 227–244.

74. See http://www.ehow.com/info_7737471_companies-great-benefits.html.

75. Mitchell Gold Co., "Day Care," http://www.mitchellgold.com/daycare.asp.

76. http://www.mgbwhome.com/OurDaycare.aspx

77. H. Zacher and H. Schultz, "Employees' Eldercare Demands, Strain, and Perceived Support," *Journal of Managerial Psychology* 30 (2015): 183–198.

78. Cincinnati Area Senior Services, "Corporate Elder Care Program," http://www.senserv.org/elder.htm.

79. E. E. Kossek, J. A. Colquitt, and R. A. Noe, "Caregiving Decisions, Well-Being, and Performance: The Effects of Place and Provider as a Function of Dependent Type and Work–Family Climates," *Academy of Management Journal* 44 (2001): 29–44.

80. http://www.parentsinapinch.com/sitters-and-nannies/

81. B. Schulte, "Aging Population Prompts More Employers to Offer Elder-Care Benefits to Workers," *The Washington Post*, November 16, 2014, accessed at http://www.washingtonpost.com/local/aging-population-prompts-more-employers-to-offer-elder-care-benefits-to-workers/2014/11/16/25f9c8e6-6847-11e4-a31c-77759fc1eacc_story.html.

82. L. J. Barham, "Variables Affecting Managers' Willingness to Grant Alternative Work Arrangements," *Journal of Social Psychology* 138 (1998): 291–302; J. Kaplan, "Hitting the Wall at Forty," *Business Month* 136 (1990): 52–58.

83. K. E. Kram, "Phases of the Mentoring Relationship," *Academy of Management Review* 26 (1983): 608–625.

84. B. Rosen and T. Jerdee, *Older Employees: New Roles for Valued Resources* (Homewood, Ill.: Irwin, 1985).

85. J. W. Gilsdorf, "The New Generation: Older Workers," *Training and Development Journal* (March 1992): 77–79.

86. J. F. Quick, "Time to Move On?" in J. C. Quick, R. E. Hess, J. Hermalin, and J. D. Quick, eds., *Career Stress in Changing Times* (New York: Haworth Press, 1990): 239–250.

87. D. Machan, "Rent-an-Exec," *Forbes* (January 22, 1990): 132–133.

88. S. Kim and D. C. Feldman, "Working in Retirement: The Antecedents of Bridge Employment and Its Consequences for Quality of Life in Retirement," *Academy of Management Journal* 43 (2000): 1195–1210.

89. http://www.gallup.com/poll/168707/average-retirement-age-rises.aspx

90. T. A. Beehr, "To Retire or Not to Retire: That Is Not the Question," *Journal of Organizational Behavior* 35 (2014): 1093–1108.

91. E. Schein, *Career Anchors* (San Diego: University Associates, 1985).

92. G. W. Dalton, "Developmental Views of Careers in Organizations," in M. B. Arthur, D. T. Hall, and B. S. Lawrence, eds., *Handbook of Career Theory* (Cambridge: Cambridge University Press, 1989): 89–109.

93. D. C. Feldman, "Careers in Organizations: Recent Trends and Future Directions," *Journal of Management* 15 (1989): 135–156.

18

1. M. A. Verespej, "When Change Becomes the Norm," *Industry Week* (March 16, 1992): 35–38.

2. P. Mornell, "Nothing Endures but Change," *Inc.* 22 (July 2000): 131–132, http://www.inc.com/magazine/20000701/19555.html.

3. H. J. Van Buren, III, "The Bindingness of Social and Psychological Contracts: Toward a Theory of Social Responsibility in Downsizing," *Journal of Business Ethics* 25 (2000): 205–219.

4. "The Mystery of the Chinese Consumer," *The Economist* (July 7, 2011), http://www.economist.com/node/18928514?story_id=189285148.

5. See http://www.tata.com/htm/Grou-_MnA_YearWise.htm.

6. http://www.fool.com/investing/general/2014/01/04/costco-expands-its-global-reach.aspx

7. L. R. Offerman and M. Gowing, "Organizations of the Future: Changes and Challenges," *American Psychologist* (February 1990): 95–108.

8. http://www.fool.com/investing/general/2014/01/04/costco-expands-its-global-reach.aspx

9. http://www.pewresearch.org/fact-tank/2014/01/07/

number-of-older-americans-in-the-workforce-is-on-the-rise/

10. http://www.siemens.com/about/sustainability/en/core-topics/employees/ management-and-facts/index.php

11. http://www.cnet.com/how-to/apple-pay-vs-google-wallet-vs-paypal/

12. https://www.currencycloud.com/news/blog/currency-cloud-reviews-apple-pay-google-wallet-and-paypal

13. R. M. Kanter, "Improving the Development, Acceptance, and Use of New Technology: Organizational and Interorganizational Challenges," in *People and Technology in the Workplace* (Washington, D.C.: National Academy Press, 1991): 15–56.

14. http://www.gapinc.com/content/attachments/gapinc/GPS_AR13.pdf

15. "Gap Inc. 2003 Social Responsibility Report," *Gap Inc.* (September 17, 2004), http://ccbn.mobular.net/ccbn/7/645/696/index.html.

16. S. A. Mohrman and A. M. Mohrman, Jr., "The Environment as an Agent of Change," in A. M. Mohrman, Jr., et al., eds., *Large-Scale Organizational Change* (San Francisco: Jossey-Bass, 1989): 35–47.

17. T. D'Aunno, M. Succi, and J. A. Alexander, "The Role of Institutional and Market Forces in Divergent Organizational Change," *Administrative Science Quarterly* 45 (2000): 679–703.

18. M. Jarman, "Intel Opens 'Leading-Edge Fab: Plant to Build Most Powerful Chips," *The Arizona Republic* (October 21, 2007), http://www.azcentral.com/arizonarepublic/business/articles/1021biz-intel1021.html.

19. Q. N. Huy, "Emotional Balancing of Organizational Continuity and Radical Change: The Contribution of Middle Managers," *Administrative Science Quarterly* 47 (March 1, 2002): 31–69.

20. D. Nadler, "Organizational Frame-Bending: Types of Change in the Complex Organization," in R. Kilmann and T. Covin, eds., *Corporate Transformation* (San Francisco: Jossey-Bass, 1988): 66–83.

21. R. Winkler, "YouTube: 1 Billion Viewers, No Profit," *The Wall Street Journal* (February 15, 2015), accessed at http://www.wsj.com/articles/viewers-dont-add-up-to-profit-for-youtube-1424897967.

22. L. Ackerman, "Development, Transition, or Transformation: The Question of Change in Organizations," *OD Practitioner* (December 1986): 1–8.

23. T. D. Jick, *Managing Change* (Homewood, Ill.: Irwin, 1993): 3.

24. J. M. Bloodgood and J. L. Morrow, "Strategic Organizational Change: Exploring the Roles of Environmental Structure, Internal Conscious Awareness, and Knowledge," *Journal of Management Studies* 40 (2003): 1761–1782.

25. D. Miller and M. J. Chen, "Sources and Consequences of Competitive Inertia. A Study of the U.S. Airline Industry," *Administrative Science Quarterly* 39 (1994): 1–23.

26. S. L. Brown and K. M. Eisenhardt, "The Art of Continuous Change: Linking Complexity

Theory and Time-Paced Evolution in Relentlessly Shifting Organizations," *Administrative Science Quarterly* 42 (1997): 1–34.

27. J. Child and C. Smith, "The Context and Process of Organizational Transformation: Cadbury Ltd. in Its Sector," *Journal of Management Studies* 12 (1987): 12–27.

28. M. Uhl-Bien and M. Arena, "Complexity Leadership: Enabling People and Organizations for Adaptability," *Organizational Dynamics* 46 (2017): 9–20.

29. R. M. Kanter, *The Change Masters* (New York: Simon & Schuster, 1983).

30. J. R. Katzenbach, *Real Change Leaders* (New York: Times Business, 1995).

31. J. L. Denis, L. Lamothe, and A. Langley, "The Dynamics of Collective Leadership and Strategic Change in Pluralistic Organizations," *Academy of Management Journal* 44 (2001): 809–837.

32. M. Beer, *Organization Change and Development: A Systems View* (Santa Monica, Calif.: Goodyear, 1980): 78.

33. K. Whalen-Berry and C. R. Hinings, "The Relative Effect of Change Drivers in Large-Scale Organizational Change: An Empirical Study," in W. Passmore and R. Goodman, eds., *Research in Organizational Change and Development* 14 (New York: JAI Press, 2003): 99–146.

34. J.L. Denis, L. Lamothe, and A. Langley, "The Dynamics of Collective Leadership and Strategic Change in Pluralistic Organizations," *Academy of Management Journal*, 44 (2001): 809–837.

35. J. W. Brehm, *A Theory of Psychological Reactance* (New York: Academic Press, 1966).

36. J. A. Klein, "Why Supervisors Resist Employee Involvement," *Harvard Business Review* 62 (1984): 87–95.

37. B. L. Kirkman, R. G. Jones, and D. L. Shapiro, "Why Do Employees Resist Teams? Examining the 'Resistance Barrier' to Work Team Effectiveness," *International Journal of Conflict Management* 11 (2000): 74–92.

38. D. L. Nelson and M. A. White, "Management of Technological Innovation: Individual Attitudes, Stress, and Work Group Attributes," *Journal of High Technology Management Research* 1 (1990): 137–148.

39. S. Elias, "Employee Commitment in Times of Change: Assessing the Importance of Attitudes Toward Organizational Change," *Journal of Management* 35 (2009): 37–55; J. B. Avey, T. S. Wernsing, and F. Luthans, "Can Positive Employees Help Positive Organizational Change? Impact of Psychological Capital and Emotions on Relevant Attitudes and Behaviors," *Journal of Applied Behavioral Science* 44 (2008): 48–70.

40. T. Diefenbach, "The Managerialistic Ideology of Organisational Change Management," *Journal of Organizational Change Management* 20, No. 1 (2007): 126–144.

41. A. E. Rafferty, N. L. Jimmieson, and A. A. Armenakis, "Change Readiness: A

Multilevel Review," *Journal of Management* 39 (2013): 110–135.

42. T. G. Cummings and E. F. Huse, *Organizational Development and Change* (St. Paul, Minn.: West, 1989).

43. N. L. Jimmieson, D. J. Terry, and V. J. Callan, "A Longitudinal Study of Employee Adaptation to Organizational Change: The Role of Change-Related Information and Change-Related Self Efficacy," *Journal of Occupational Health Psychology* 9 (2004): 11–27.

44. N. DiFonzo and P. Bordia, "A Tale of Two Corporations: Managing Uncertainty during Organizational Change," *Human Resource Management* 37 (1998): 295–303.

45. J. de Vries, C. Webb, and J. Eveline, "Mentoring for Gender Equality and Organisational Change," *Employee Relations* 28, No. 6 (2006): 573–587.

46. A. H. Hon, M. Bloom, and J. M. Crant, "Overcoming Resistance to Change and Enhancing Creative Performance," *Journal of Management* 40 (2014): 919–941.

47. A. Shatte, A. Perlman, B. Smith, and W. D. Lynch, "The Positive Effect of Resilience on Stress and Business Outcomes in Difficult Work Environments," *Journal of Occupational and Environmental Medicine* 59 (2017): 135–140.

48. K. Lewin, "Frontiers in Group Dynamics," *Human Relations* 1 (1947): 5–41.

49. C. Bareil, A. Savoie, and S. Meunier, "Patterns of Discomfort with Organizational Change," *Journal of Change Management* 7, No. 1 (2007): 13–24.

50. W. Mc Whinney, "Meta-Praxis: A Framework for Making Complex Changes," in A. M. Mohrman, Jr., et al., eds., *Large-Scale Organizational Change* (San Francisco: Jossey-Bass, 1989): 154–199.

51. M. Beer and E. Walton, "Developing the Competitive Organization: Interventions and Strategies," *American Psychologist* 45 (1990): 154–161.

52. B. Bertsch and R. Williams, "How Multinational CEOs Make Change Programs Stick," *Long Range Planning* 27 (1994): 12–24.

53. J. Amis, T. Slack, and C. R. Hinings, "Values and Organizational Change," *Journal of Applied Behavioral Science* 38 (2002): 356–385.

54. W. L. French and C. H. Bell, *Organization Development: Behavioral Science Interventions for Organization Improvement*, 4th ed. (Englewood Cliffs, N.J.: Prentice-Hall, 1990); W. W. Burke, *Organization Development: A Normative View* (Reading, Mass.: Addison-Wesley, 1987).

55. A. O. Manzini, *Organizational Diagnosis* (New York: AMACOM, 1988).

56. M. R. Weisbord, "Organizational Diagnosis: Six Places to Look for Trouble with or without a Theory," *Group and Organization Studies* 1 (December 1976): 430–444.

57. H. Levinson, *Organizational Diagnosis* (Cambridge, Mass.: Harvard University Press, 1972).

58. J. Nicholas, "The Comparative Impact of Organization Development Interventions," *Academy of Management Review* 7 (1982): 531–542.

59. G. Odiorne, *Management by Objectives* (Marshfield, Mass.: Pitman, 1965).

60. E. Huse, "Putting in a Management Development Program that Works," *California Management Review* 9 (1966): 73–80.

61. J. P. Muczyk and B. C. Reimann, "MBO as a Complement to Effective Leadership," *Academy of Management Executive* (May 1989): 131–138.

62. L. L. Berry and A. Parasuraman, "Prescriptions for a Service Quality Revolution in America," *Organizational Dynamics* 20 (1992): 5–15.

63. T. A. Stewart, and A. P. Raman, "Lessons from Toyota's Long Drive," *Harvard Business Review* 85, No. 7/8 (2007): 74–83.

64. W. G. Dyer, *Team Building: Issues and Alternatives*, 2nd ed. (Reading, Mass.: Addison-Wesley, 1987).

65. E. Stephan, G. Mills, R. W. Pace, and L. Ralphs, "HRD in the Fortune 500: A Survey," *Training and Development Journal* 42 (January 1988): 26–32.

66. A. Edmondson, "Psychological Safety and Learning Behavior in Work Teams," *Administrative Science Quarterly* 44 (1999): 350–383.

67. See http://www.teambuildinginc.com/services4_teamconcepts.htm; http://www.teambuildinginc.com/services5.htm.

68. https://www.teambonding.com/programs/team-food-truck-challenge/

69. L. L. Gilson, M. T. Maynard, N. C. J. Young, M. Vartiainen, and M. Hakonen, "Virtual Teams Research: 10 Years, 10 Themes, and 10 Opportunities," *Journal of Management*, published online before print on November 24, 2014, accessed at http://jom.sagepub.com.argo.library.okstate.edu/content/early/2014/11/21/0149206314559946.full.

70. E. Schein, *Its Role in Organization Development, Process Consultation*, vol. 1 (Reading, Mass.: Addison-Wesley, 1988).

71. H. Hornstein, "Organizational Development and Change Management: Don't Throw the Baby Out with the Bath Water," *Journal of Applied Behavioral Science* 37 (2001): 223–226.

72. K. A. Aikens, J. Astin, K. R. Pelletier, K. Levanovich, C. M. Baase, Y. Y. Park, and C. M. Bodnar, "Mindfulness Goes to Work: Impact of an Online Workplace Intervention," *Journal of Occupational and Environmental Medicine* 56 (2014): 721–731.

73. I. L. Goldstein, *Training in Organizations*, 3rd ed. (Pacific Grove, Calif.: Brooks/Cole, 1993).

74. J. A. Conger and R. M. Fulmer, "Developing Your Leadership Pipeline," *Harvard Business Review* 81 (2003): 76–84.

75. J. Reb, J. Narayanan, and S. Chaturvedi, "Leading Mindfully: Two Studies on the Influence of Supervisor Trait Mindfulness on Employee Well-Being and Performance," *Mindfulness* 5 (2014): 36–45.

76. M. Jay, "Understanding How to Leverage Executive Coaching," *Organization Development Journal* 21 (2003): 6–13; D. Goleman, R. Boyaysis, and A. McKee, *Primal Leadership: Learning to Lead with Emotional Intelligence* (Harvard Business School Press, 2004).

77. K. M. Wasylyshyn, "Executive Coaching: An Outcome Study," *Consulting Psychology Journal* 55 (2003): 94–106.

78. J. W. Smither, M. London, R. Flautt, Y. Vargas, and I. Kucine, "Can Working with an Executive Coach Improve Multisource Feedback Ratings over Time? A Quasi-Experimental Field Study," *Personnel Psychology* 56 (2003): 23–44.

79. P. Petrou, E. Demerouti, and D. Xanthopoulou, "Regular versus Cutback-Related Change: The Role of Employee Job Crafting in Organizational Change Contexts of Different Nature," *International Journal of Stress Management* 24 (2017): 62–85.

80. W. N. Burton, C. Chen, A. Schultz, and X. Li, "Association Between Employee Sleep with Workplace Health and Economic Outcomes," *Journal of Occupational and Environmental Medicine* 59 (2017): 177–183.

81. American Psychological Association, "Psychologically Healthy Workplace Awards," http://apahelpcenter.mediaroom.com/file.php/mr_apahelpcenter/spinsite_docfiles/134/phwa_magazine_2007.pdf.

82. R. A. Katzell and R. A. Guzzo, "Psychological Approaches to Worker Productivity," *American Psychologist* 38 (1983): 468–472.

83. P. F. Sorenson, T. Yaeger, and R. Narel, "The New Golden Age of Organization Development Research and Knowledge," *Organization Development Journal* 35 (2017): 47–55.

INDEX

A

ABC model, 53–54
Abilities, 35, 200
Ability diversity, 25–26, 222
Abrasiveness, 222
Absenteeism, 113, 152, 155, 214
Abusive supervision, 214
Accenture, 102
Acceptability of work, 247
Acceptance and confirmation, 301
Accepting responsibility, 14
Accidents, 112, 113
Accommodating style of conflict management, 233, 234
Accounting firms, 261, 302
Acculturation stress, 286
Accuracy, of self-performance evaluation, 95
Achievement, 66
Achievement, need for, 75–76, 85
Achievement-oriented individuals, 50
Achievement-oriented style of leadership, 206
Achilles' heel phenomenon, 114
Acquisition strategies, 266
Action learning, 324
Action Tank (France), 9
Active listening, 318
Active participation, 14
Actual performance, 95
ADA (Americans with Disabilities Act), 25, 30
Adams, Stacy, 80–81
Adams's theory of inequality, 80–81
Adaptability, 212
Adaptation culture, 279
Adaptive culture, 279
Adaptiveness, 310
Adhocracy, 259, 261
Adjourning stage, 147, 148
Adkins, Joyce, 117
Adler, Alfred, 73
Administrative orbiting, 230
Administrative science, 5.
  See also Management
Advancement stage of career, 297, 298, 299–305
Adversaries, 155
Aetna, 318
Affect, 36–40, 53, 54, 56, 57
Affective commitment, 59
Affective conflict, 172
Affiliation, need for, 75, 76, 77
Affirming contact, 127

African Americans, 23
Age, 66, 306
Age bias, 25
Age cohorts, 25
Age Discrimination in Employment Act (1967), 306
Age diversity, 24–25, 153, 158
Age-fifty transition, 306
Ageism, 48
Agent, 180–181
Aggressive mechanisms, 228
Agile workforce, 239
Agor, Weston, 167–168
Agreeableness, 36–37
Agreement, in groups, 147
AIDS, 30
Airbus, 233
Airline industry, 265, 266.
  See also specific airlines
Alcoa, 295
Alcon Laboratories, 23, 27
Alderfer, Clayton, 74, 76, 80
Alfred P. Sloan Award, 277
Algorithms, 11
Alienated follower, 215
Alienated relationships, 79
Allies, 155
Allport, Gordon, 36
Allstate, 114
Alternative work patterns, 248, 249–250, 304, 305
Altruism, 84, 186
Amazon, 58, 320
Amazon Go, 320
Ambiguity, 93, 168
Ambition, 66
America. *See* United States
American Airlines, 82, 311
American Apparel, 32
American Express, 23, 62, 75, 297, 325
Americans with Disabilities Act (ADA), 25, 30
Amygdala highjack, 63
Annual performance reviews, 94
Anthrocentric approach to job design, 246–247
Anthropology, 5
Anticipatory socialization, 281–282
Anxiety, 72, 117
Apologies, 191
Appearance, 47, 50
Apple, 138, 211, 266, 313, 324
Apple Pay, 313
Applied psychology, 236
Appointments, 20
ARCO, 31
Aristotle, 29
Armstrong World Industries, 45

Artifacts, 273–276
Artificial intelligence, 86, 88, 171–172
Artistic occupation, 293
Assertiveness, 232, 233
Assigned group, 146
Assumptions, 273, 274, 277, 284, 317
AT&T
  diversity, 288
  employment policy, 27
  Foundry for Connected Health, 169
  job enrichment, 241
  telecommuting, 249, 325
  use of MBTI, 43
AT&T National Running Team, 146, 148
Atlantic Richfield (ARCO), 31
Attachment theory, 115
Attitude
  ABC model, 53–54
  behavior associated with, 55–56
  change through persuasion, 59–61
  cognitive dissonance, 54
  components of, 53–54
  cultural differences, 56
  decision making, 166
  defined, 52
  formation, 54–56
  job satisfaction, 56–57
  social perception, 46
  work attitudes, 56
Attitude formation, 54–56
Attractiveness, 47, 48
Attribution model, 101
Attribution theory, 50–51, 100–101
Attributional biases, 51
Auditory learner, 13
Australia, 18, 21, 64, 170, 182, 297
Authentic leadership, 212
Authority, 176, 180, 196
Authority issues, 146
Authority relationships, 222
Authority system, 186
Authority-compliance manager, 203, 204
Autocratic style of leadership, 201
Automation, 241
Automotive industry, 10, 11, 165, 240, 260, 263. *See also specific companies*
Autonomous work group, 155–156
Autonomy, 77, 194, 243
Avnet, Inc., 98

Avoiding style of conflict management, 233, 234

B

B Corp (Certified Benefit Corporation), 64
Baby boomers, 25, 66
Baby boomlet. *See* Generation Y
Baby bust generation, 25, 66
Baldridge, Malcolm, 12
Bandura, Albert, 91, 274
Bangladesh, 284
Bank of America, 167, 288
Barnard, Chester, 167
Barriers to communication, 130–132
Basic design dimensions, 258–259
Beatrice, John, 305
Beck, Robert, 167
Behavior
  attitude change and, 59–61
  attitudes and, 52–56
  attitudes predictive of, 55
  communication technologies effect, 139–141
  emotions and moods effects, 61–63
  ethical behavior, 63–65
  group, 145–146
  job satisfaction, 56–57
  motivations, 70–85
  norms of, 145
  organizational citizenship behavior, 57–59
  in times of change, 5–6
  values, 65–67, 69
Behavioral intent, 53, 54
Behavioral measures of personality, 40
Behavioral models of learning, 86–91
  classical conditioning, 87–88
  operant conditioning, 88
  punishment, 90–91
  reinforcement theory, 88–90
Behavioral norms, 145, 148–149
Behavioral problems, 112
Behavioral theories of leadership, 201–204
Belgium, 238
Ben & Jerry's, 64
Benefits, discrimination and, 26–27
Benevolent friction, 220
Benevolents, 82
Benson, Herbert, 121
Berkshire Hathaway, Inc., 275

Better Work Program, 314
Beyond Meat, 278
Bezos, Jeff, 185, 320
Bias, 25, 176
Bicultural group, 158
Big Five personality traits,
  36–37, 40
Binney & Smith, 265
Biological approach to job
  design, 245
Bisexuals, 26–27
BJ Services Company, 92, 98
Black & Decker, 5
"Black Belt" (Six Sigma), 11
Black Employee Success
  Team (BEST), 302
Blackmail, 192
Blake, Robert, 202
Blanchard, Kenneth, 209
Blood, Milton, 72
Bloomberg, Michael, 185
Blue Man Group, 162
Blumenthal, Neil, 313
BMW, 280
Boards, gender diversity on, 182
Boise Cascade, 306
Bonuses, 88
Borden, 305
Borderless company, 312
Boss-employee relationship,
  222
Bounded rationality model,
  163
BP oil spill, 174
Brain, hemisphere dominance
  and, 166, 167
Brain-lateralization, 166
Brainstorming, 173–174
Branson, Richard, 170
Brazil, 170
Breaking Bad, 275
Breaks, 119
Bridge employment, 307, 308
Briggs, Katherine, 41
British Petroleum, 31
Brown, Eric, 5
Brown, Ethan, 278
Buffett, Jimmy, 275
Buffett, Warren, 42, 185, 274,
  275
Bureaucracy, 258
Burke, James, 63, 216
Burnout, 112, 113
Bush, George H. W., 12, 31
Bush, George W., 157
Business Ethics, 28
Business model innovation, 259
Busyness, 305

C

Calculated relationships, 79
Cambodia, 284
Campbell Soup, 304
Campion, Michael, 244
Canada, 18, 122, 182
Cannon, Walter B., 87,
  105–106, 111
Capital, 255

CapSpire, 277
Career, 236, 290
Career anchors, 308
Career coach, 296
Career development, 97
Career enhancement, 97
Career functions, 300
Career ladder, 300
Career lattice, 300
Career management, 290–308
  advancement stage, 299–305
  career anchors, 308
  career stage model, 297–298
  defined, 290
  establishment stage,
    298–299
  foundations for success,
    296–297
  maintenance stage, 305–306
  new vs. old paradigms, 292
  occupational and
    organizational choice,
    291–296
  withdrawal stage, 298,
    306–308
Career path, 300
Career planning, 326–327
Career plateau, 306
Career progress, 109
Career stage model
  advancement stage, 297,
    298, 299–305
  establishment stage, 297,
    298–299
  maintenance stage, 297, 298,
    305–306
  withdrawal stage, 297,
    306–308
Career stress, 109
Caribbean, 135
Caribou Coffee, 10, 11
Categorical imperative, 29
Cattell, Raymond, 36
Cell phones, 250
El Celler de Can Roca, 106
Center for Creative
  Leadership, 299
Central route to persuasion,
  60–61
Centrality, 184
Centralization, 258, 262, 264,
  266, 267, 268, 269. See
  also Decentralization
CEO, 16, 24. See also Leader/
  leadership; Manager/
  management
  crisis situations, 310
  decision speed, 264
  diversity of upper echelons,
    158
  mentors, 101
  narcissistic, 201
  personality of, 270
  seasons of tenure, 156, 157
  teams effect on, 157
  women as, 213, 214
Ceremonies and rites,
  274–275
Certified Benefit Corporation
  (B Corp), 64

Chade-Meng Tan, 62
Challenge, 4, 115
Challenge stressors, 109
Challenger, 152
Challenger shuttle disaster,
  171
Challenges for managers,
  16–33. See also Manager/
  management
  competing in the global
    economy, 16–20
  cultural difference and
    work-related attitudes,
    18–22
  diverse workforce, 22–28
  ethical dilemmas, 29–33
  ethics, character, and
    personal integrity, 28–29
Change. See also Change
  management
  behavior in times of, 5–6
  defined, 4
  opportunity creator, 9–12
  stress related to, 109
Change agent, 316
Change and acquisition, 281,
  282, 283
Change management,
  310–327
  determining need for
    organization development
    interventions, 320–321
  forces for change in
    organizations, 310–315
  group-focused techniques
    for OD intervention,
    321–323
  individual-focused
    techniques for OD
    intervention, 323–327
  Lewin's model, 318–320
  organization development
    cycle, 321
  resistance to change,
    316–318
  scope of, 315–316
The Change Masters (Kanter),
  316
Channel Etiquette, 141
Chaparral Steel, 4
Character assassination, 230
Character theories of ethics,
  29
Characteristics of effective
  goals, 92
Charisma, 211
Charismatic leadership, 182,
  211–212
Chesapeake Energy Co., 326
Chevron, 288
Chief executive officers. See
  CEO
Chief marketing officers
  (CMOs), 241, 242
Child care, 304
Child-rearing/day care
  arrangements, 109, 110
China
  attribution errors, 51
  communication barriers, 131

corporate social
  responsibility, 265
decision making, 176
feedback, 96
guanxi, 17, 304
individuals as element of
  team, 98
job satisfaction, 58
monitoring performance, 96
negotiation style, 232
perception of job stress, 106
regional armies, 6
team rewards, 98
time orientation, 22
U.S. companies and, 17
values, 67
Western firms in, 312, 314
work-family conflict, 304
Chrysler Corporation, 156
Churchill, Winston, 5
Circle coach, 270
Circle organization, 270
Cisco Systems, 304, 307
Citicorp, 158
Civic work, 111
Civility, 132–134
Clarifying the implicit, 127,
  128
Clark, Stan, 274
Classical conditioning, 87–88
Clif Bar, 276
Climate change, 190
Clinton, Bill, 211
Clinton, Hillary, 42
Clockwork metaphor, 2, 3, 7
Clothing, 46
Coaching
  executive coaching, 324–325
  leader's role in, 280
  mentoring, 101, 301
  performance enhancement,
    97
  personal integrity
    development, 137
  self-coaching, 296
  self-efficacy development, 91
Coalition tactics, 188, 189, 190
Coca-Cola, 18
  differentiation, 256
  ethical behavior, 63
  human resource system, 23
  worldwide operations, 16
Co-CEO arrangement, 158
Codes of ethics, 32–33, 145
Coercive power, 182–183, 184
Coffee industry, 10
Cognition, 53–54, 57
Cognitive appraisal approach
  to stress, 106
Cognitive behavior therapy,
  112
Cognitive conflict, 172
Cognitive dissonance, 54, 164
Cognitive dissonance theory,
  164
Cognitive moral development,
  68–69, 167
Cognitive process theory, 83
Cognitive routes to
  persuasion, 60–61

Cognitive structure, 46
Cognitive style, 165
Cognitive theories of learning, 91–92
Cohesiveness, 28
Collaborating style of conflict management, 234, 235
Collaboration skills, 14, 148
Collaborator, 152
Collectivism
  decision making, 175–176
  direction of OCBs, 58
  equity theory, 85
  expectancy theory, 85
  in Hofstede's dimensions of cultural differences, 19, 21
  individual as element of team, 98
  job satisfaction, 59
  need for achievement, 76
  negotiation style, 232
  values, 67
Columbia shuttle disaster, 171
Combat situations, 111–112
Comfort zones, 135
Command-and-control management, 59
Commerce Department, U.S., 12
Commitment, 115, 152, 224–225
Committed relationships, 79
Common resources, 221–222
Communication, 124–141
  barriers/gateways, 130–132, 223
  civility/incivility, 132–134
  computer-mediated, 138–139
  cultural diversity and, 28
  defensive/nondefensive, 132, 133
  defined, 124
  of in-group vs. out-group members, 210
  information richness, 126
  interpersonal communication model, 125–126
  leaders and, 280
  managing organizational politics, 192
  new managers and, 299
  nonverbal, 134–137
  one-way/two-way, 129
  overcoming resistance to change, 318
  positive, healthy, 137
  skills for effective managers, 129–130
  social media, 138–141
  technological innovations, 138–139
  written, 138
Communication gatekeepers, 151
Communication skills, 155
Communicative disease, 137
Communicator, 125, 152

Company-sponsored day care, 304
Comparison other, 81, 82
Compensation, 77, 88, 228–229
Compensation awards, 113–114
Competence, 65, 194
Competence norms, 145
Competence skills, 154
Competing style of conflict management, 233–234
Competition, in global economy, 16–20
Competitive norms, 148
Competitive people, 155
Competitive strategy of conflict management, 229–230
Complexity, 256, 257, 258, 262, 264, 266, 267
Comprehensive approach to motivation, 71
Comprehensive health promotion, 122. *See also* Wellness programs
Compromise mechanisms, 228–229
Compromising style of conflict management, 234–235
Compulsive behavior, 72
Compulsive constellation, 270
Computational learning theory, 86
Computerized monitoring of employees, 30, 64, 250
Computer-mediated communication, 138–139
Conceptual component of communication, 126
Concern for others, 66
Confession, 122
Confidentiality, 30
Confirmation, 301
Conflict, 218–235
  causes, 221–224
  consequences of, 220
  defined, 218
  diagnosing, 220–221
  formal-informal, 8
  forms of group conflict, 224–225
  goal setting reducing, 92
  individual conflict in organizations, 225–229
  interpersonal, 227–228
  intrapersonal, 225–229
  labor-management, 73
  management strategies and techniques, 227–228, 229–232
  management styles, 232–235
  nature of, 218–221
  during organizational entry, 294
  union-management strife, 8
Conflict management strategies, 229–232
Conflict management styles, 232–235

Conflict reduction, rites of, 275
Confrontation, 231–232
Conger, Jay, 194
Congruence, 282
Conscientiousness, 36–37
Consensus, 100, 147
Consensus building, 169
Consequences of stress, 111–114
Consequential theories of ethics, 28–29
Consideration, 202
Consistency, 100
Consult group, 208
Consult individually, 208
Consultation, 188, 189
Context of organizations, 267
Contextual variables, 261–267, 270
Contingency theories, 204–210
Contingent reward of leadership behaviors, 99
Continuance commitment, 59
Continuous schedule of reinforcement, 90
Contributions, 80
Contributor, 152
Control, 109, 115, 164
Control Data Services, Inc., 10
Conventional level of moral development, 68
Conventional occupation, 293
Conversion, 229
Cooper, Kenneth, 121
Cooperative and helping behaviors, 155
Cooperative strategy of conflict management, 229–230
Cooperative teamwork skills, 152
Cooperativeness, 232, 233
Coordination, 260
Coping methods
  emotion- and problem-focused, 106
  transformational and regressive, 115
Corcoran, Barbara, 295
Corcoran Group, 295
Core feelings, 127, 128
Core job characteristics, 242, 243
Core self-evaluation (CSE), 37–40
Coronary-prone behavior, 114
Corporate allegiance, 293
Corporate capital, 255
Corporate competition, 10
Corporate culture. *See* Organizational (corporate) culture
Corporate Cultures (Deal/ Kennedy), 272
Corporate Equality Index, 288
Corporate social performance (CSP), 24

Corporate social responsibility, 7, 32, 265
Corporate stories, 275–276
Corporate warfare, 10
Corporation, as dominant organizational form, 6
Correcting poor performance, 99–102
Costco, 312
Counseling, 91, 101, 301
Counterdependence, 115
Counterproductive work behavior (CWB), 59
Country club manager, 203, 204
Courage, 66
Creativity
  decision making process, 168–170
  defined, 168
  of in-group vs. out-group members, 210
  organizational influences, 169
  work groups, 153–154
Credit cards, 313
Crisis, 280
Critical feedback, 96–97
Critical psychological states, 242, 243
Critical resources, 183
Critical thinking, 13
Critical-incident technique, 78
Cross-cultural task forces, 22
Cross-functional team, 231
Cross-training, 240–241
Crowdsourcing, 173
Crowdthink, 173
CSE (core self-evaluation), 37–40
Cultivation stage of mentoring, 302
Cultural assumptions and values, 317
Cultural differences
  attitude formation, 55
  attribution errors, 51
  business guide, 20
  comfort zones, 135
  communication, 131–132
  conflict caused by, 223–224
  cost of layoffs, 19
  creativity and, 170
  cross-cultural sensitivity, 22
  cultural intelligence, 37
  decision making, 175–176
  direction of OCBs, 58
  eye contact, 128, 136
  global economy and, 18–19
  individualism vs. collectivism, 19, 21
  influence tactics, 190
  in Japan, Mexico, Saudi Arabia, 20
  job satisfaction, 58
  masculinity vs. femininity, 19, 21–22
  motivation, 84–85
  negotiations, 232
  nonverbal communication, 47, 135, 136

perception, 46
perception of job stress, 106
power distance, 19, 21
relaxation training, 121
short-term vs. long-term
    orientation, 19
time orientation, 22
uncertainty avoidance, 19,
    21
values, 67
work definitions, 238
work-home conflicts, 304
Cultural diversity, 146. *See
    also* Diversity
Cultural intelligence, 37
Cultural relativisim, 29
Cultural sensitivity training, 22
Culture. *See* Cultural
    differences;
    Organizational
    (corporate) culture
Customer focus, 10–12
CWB (counterproductive
    work behavior), 59
Cyberloafing, 287–288
Czech Republic, 302

D

Daimler Benz, 16, 280
Dana-Farber Cancer Institute,
    148
Dao, David, 227
Data, 126
Data capacity, 127
Data loss, 5
Deal, Terry, 272
Decentralization, 259, 260
Decide, 207
Decision making, 160–178
    algorithms and, 11
    computer-mediated
        communication and, 139
    diversity and culture in, 28,
        175–176
    empowerment and self-
        managed team, 177–178
    escalation of commitment,
        164–165
    ethical, 63–65, 68–69
    group decision-making
        process, 170–175
    individual influences,
        165–170
    models and limits of,
        162–165
    normative decision model,
        207–209
    organizational design and
        structure, 266
    organizational size and, 262
    over job content, 195
    participation in, 176–178
    personality preference, 92
    process of, 160–162
    programmed/
        nonprogrammed decision,
        160
    time taken for, 165

Decision-making process,
    160–162
Deep acting, 63
Deepwater Horizon, 174
De-escalation, 165
Defense mechanisms,
    228–229
Defensive communication,
    132, 133
Defensive tactics, 133–134
Deficiency problem
    (performance
    measurement), 95, 96
Defining moments, 226
Degradation, rites of, 275
Delegate, 208
Delegating style of leadership,
    210
Deloitte, 102
Delphi technique, 174
Delta Airlines (Northwest
    Airlines), 10
Demands, 79–80
Deming, W. Edwards, 246
Democratic style of
    leadership, 201
Demographic dissimilarity,
    152
Demographic trends, 23
Denial of responsibility, 14
Denmark, 21
Departmentalization, 255
Dependency, 183, 184
Depression, 106, 112, 113, 120
Depressive constellation, 270
Design of work. *See* Job and
    work design
Desperate Housewives, 275
Deus, Frank, 114
Devil's advocacy, 174
Dewey, John, 73
Diagnosing conflict, 220–221
Diagnosis, 321
Dialectical inquiry, 174
Diet, 120, 121
Differentiation, 239, 253–256,
    267
Difficult conversations, 127
Digital detox, 280
Digital technology, 262
Dignity cultures, 232
Direct experience, 54–55
Disability, 23, 25–26
Disabled workers, 23
Disagreement, 95
Discipline, 186
Discounting principle, 47
Discrete exchange, 292
Discrimination, 26, 27, 59,
    287, 306
Disney Institute, 169
Displacement, 228
Display rules, 63
Dispositions, 37
Dissatisfied workers, 58
Dissemination of misleading
    information, 134
Dissimilarity, 152–153,
    157–158
Distinctiveness, 100

Distress, 78, 79, 105, 112–113,
    116
Distributive bargaining, 232
Distributive justice, 31
Divergent thinking, 168
Diverse Slate Approach, 31
Diversity. *See also* Cultural
    differences
    ability, 25–26
    age, 24–25
    benefits and problems,
        27–28
    on boards, 182
    decision making, 175–176
    defined, 22
    ethnic, 23
    gender, 23–24
    at Google, 8
    in group formation, 146
    mentoring and, 301–302
    organizational, 9
    organizational change,
        312–313
    organizational culture and,
        286–287
    organizational workforce, 12
    potential for conflict, 218
    sexual orientation and
        gender identity, 26–27
    stereotyping, 25, 27
    teams and groups, 146,
        152–153, 171
    top management team,
        156–158
    valuing, 27
    of workforce, 22–28
Diversity training, 27,
    131–132, 224
Divisionalized form, 259, 261
Domain, 264–265
Dominant defensiveness, 133
Dot-com boom (Silicon
    Valley), 23
Doubt, 165
Dow Chemical Company, 16,
    324
Downsizing, 10, 19, 109, 262,
    311
Dramatic constellation, 270
DreamBox Learning, 220
Dreaming sessions (GE
    Capital), 177
Dress, cultural differences
    in, 20
DriveSavers, 117
Drucker, Peter, 93
Drug Resistance Education
    Program (D.A.R.E.), 164
Dual-career partnership, 303
Due process nonaction, 230
Dugan, Regina, 176
Dynamic equilibrium, 256
Dysfunctional conflict, 220, 224
Dysfunctional turnover, 113

E

EAP (employee assistance
    program), 122

Earning, 98–99
Eastern Airlines, 150
Eastman Kodak, 8, 63, 81
Edison, Thomas, 263
Education, 13, 14–15
Educational opportunities, 88
Effective decision, 162–163
Effective follower, 215
Efficacy, 121
Egalitarian people, 155
Ego lens, 46
Ego-ideal, 106
Egypt, 243
EI. *See* Emotional intelligence
    (EI)
Einstein, Albert, 89
Eisenhower, Dwight, 138
Elaboration likelihood model
    of persuasion, 60–61
Eldercare, 304, 307
Electronic brainstorming, 174
Eli Lilly, 240, 324
Ellison, Larry, 185
E-mail, 126, 131, 138, 139,
    280
Emergency response, 105
Emergent groups, 146
Emotional component of
    communication, 126
Emotional contagion, 62
Emotional dissonance, 63, 110
Emotional exhaustion, 112
Emotional intelligence (EI),
    27
    career success and, 296–297
    conflict management and,
        219
    defined, 62
    employee engagement, 243
    of leaders, 212–213
    managers and, 130
    measurement, 63
    performance ability, 94–95
    political skill and, 192
    positive organizational
        behavior, 121
    reflecting core feelings and,
        128
Emotional labor, 63
Emotional stability, 36–37
Emotional support, 299
Emotional toxins, 107, 109
Emotion-focused coping, 106
Emotions, 61–63, 223
Empathy
    as communication skill, 127,
        129–130
    component of emotional
        intelligence, 212, 219,
        296, 297
    emotional competence, 151
    forgiveness and, 224
    overcoming resistance to
        change, 318
Employee appraisal. *See*
    Performance appraisal
Employee assistance program
    (EAP), 122
Employee attrition, 5
Employee development, 97

Employee empowerment, 91
Employee empowerment grid, 195–196
Employee participation, 93
Employee rights, 30
Employee voice behavior, 126
Employee-boss relationship, 193–194, 222
Employee-oriented style of leadership, 202
Employees. *See also* Career management
  hiring and firing process, 280–281
  organizational socialization, 281–283
Empowerment
  decision making, 177–178
  defined, 194
  dimensions, 194
  employee empowerment grid, 195–196
  guidelines for, 194
  organizational, 286
  self-managed teams and, 154–156
  skills required, 154–155
  through team work, 91
Enacted values, 276
Encounter, 282
Endurability of work, 247
ENFJ type, 44
ENFP type, 44
Engagement, 243–244
Engineering, 5
Enhancement, rites of, 275
Enlightened self-interest, 73, 74
Enterprising occupation, 293
Entitleds, 82
Entitlement, 99
ENTJ type, 44
ENTP type, 44
Entrepreneurs, 19
Entrepreneurship, 84
Environment, 261, 264–266, 279, 311
Environmental uncertainty, 265
Equal Employment Opportunity Commission, 30
Equal Pay Day, 277
Equal versus equal power network, 227, 228
Equitability, 97
Equity, 80–81
Equity sensitives, 81–82
Equity theory, 79–82, 85
ERG theory, 74–75
Ergonomics, 5, 244–246
Ernst & Young, 24, 304, 305
Escalation of commitment, 164–165
ESFJ type, 44
ESFP type, 44
Eskimo Joe's, 274
Espoused values, 276
Essential skills, 14
Establishment stage of career,

297, 298–299
Esteem needs, 73
ESTJ type, 43, 44
ESTP type, 44
Ethical behavior
  character theories, 29
  codes of ethics, 32–33, 145
  cognitive moral development, 68–69
  consequential theories, 28–29
  corporate social responsibility, 32
  cultural relativism, 29
  defined, 63
  employee rights, 30
  ethical decision making, 63–65
  factors affecting, 65–69
  individual/organizational model of, 66
  locus of control, 67
  Machiavellianism, 67–68
  management of, 28–29, 313–314
  monitoring performance, 96
  organizational behavior management, 12
  organizational justice, 31
  power use, 184–186
  review of /i1Wall Street Journal/i0, 64–65
  rule-based theories, 29
  sexual harassment, 30–31
  values, 65–67
  virtue ethics, 29
  whistle-blowing, 31–32
Ethical decision making, 29–33, 63–65
Ethical organizational culture, 287–288
Ethical theories, 28–29
Ethicon Endo-Surgery, 169
Ethics, 184–186, 222–223
Ethics violations, 109
Ethnic diversity, 23, 146
Etiquette on social media, 141
Etzioni, Amitai, 79, 80
Europe, 10, 135, 283
European Union, 17–18, 312
Eustress, 78–79, 111
Evaluation component of goal setting, 94
Evaluation systems, 83
Evaluative support, 299
Exchange tactic, 188, 189, 190
Executive coaching, 101, 137, 324–325. *See also* Coaching
Executive tenure, 156
Exercise, 120, 121
Existence need, 74, 76
Expatriate managers, 19, 131
Expectancy, 82–84
Expectancy theory of motivation, 82–84, 85, 293
Experience diversity, 158
Experiential learning, 14
Expert power, 182, 183, 184

Expressiveness, 129
External attribution, 50, 100–101, 187
External change agents, 316
External forces of change, 312–314
External incentives, 72–73
External perspective of human behavior, 4
External pressure, 150
External task environment, 7
External theories of motivation, 70
Externals, 38, 67
Extinction, 88, 90–91
Extraversion (E), 36–37, 41, 42, 91, 114, 190
Extreme environments, 110
ExxonMobil, 43, 302
Eye contact, 127, 128, 134, 136–137, 139

F

Face cultures, 232
Facebook
  channel etiquette, 141
  Diverse Slate Approach, 31
  mindfulness and, 63
  rituals, 276
  Sandberg and, 199
  wellness program, 325
  Zuckerberg and, 138, 207
Facial expressions, 47, 134, 136–137, 139
Facilitate, 208
Facilitation of exposure and visibility, 301
Facsimile (fax) machines, 138
Fade-out effects, 121
Failure, fear of, 317
Failure-oriented individuals, 50
Fairness, 66
False-consensus effect, 49
Family expectations, 110
Family organizations, 6
Fannie Mae, 304–305
Fantasy, 229
Fatalistic cultures, 51
Fatigue, 108
Federal Arbitration Act, 155
Federal Aviation Administration, 283
FedEx, 93, 97, 154
Feedback
  360-degree, 97
  acceptance of, 228
  as core job characteristic, 243
  interpersonal communication, 126
  managing up, 194
  on performance, 89, 92
  performance enhancement, 89, 96–97
  survey, 321–322
Feedback component, 97
Feelers, 92

Feeling, 43, 125–126, 127
Feeling type (F), 41, 91, 164
Femininity, 19, 21–22, 176
Fielder, Fred, 205–206
Fielder's contingency theory, 205–206
Fight-or-flight response, 104, 105
Financial reinforcement, 88
Firefighters, 278
Firing employees, 280–281
First impressions, 48–49
First-impression error, 48
First-shift rule, 170
Fisher, Eileen, 190
Fisher, George, 12
Fit perspective, 279
Five structural configurations, 259–261
Five-stage model of group development, 146–148
Fixation, 228
Fixed interval schedule of reinforcement, 90
Fixed ratio schedule of reinforcement, 90
Flat structure, 255, 257
Flexibility, 97, 310
Flexibility training, 121
Flexible jobs, 239
Flexible work schedule, 304, 305
Flextime, 54, 248, 249–250
Flight, 229
Focal role, 118
Follower maturity, 209, 210
Follower readiness, 209, 210
Followership, 214–215
Food Truck Challenge, 323
Force field analysis, 319
Forces for change in organizations, 310–315
Ford Motor Company, 18, 62, 112, 257, 288, 325
Forecasts, 11
Forgiveness, 66, 224
Formal group, 146
Formal leadership, 198
Formal mentoring programs, 302
Formal organization, 7–8
Formality of structure, 255
Formalization, 258, 260, 262, 264, 266, 267, 268
Forming stage, 147
Forms, 138
Foundational behavioral research, 201–202
Foundations for successful career, 296–297
Foundry for Connected Health, 169
Four-day workweek, 249
Four-way test, 32
Fox, Michael J., 183
Framing, 184
France, 9, 67, 182, 280
Free market system, 72
Free riding, 145
Freedom, 66

French, John, 182, 184
Freud, Sigmund, 72, 73
Friendship, 301
Fukutomi, G. D. S., 156
Full engagement, 79
Function of organizational culture, 277–278
Functional background, 152, 176
Functional conflict, 219–220
Functional turnover, 113
Fundamental attribution error, 51

G

Gain-sharing plans, 98
Gallup's Q12 survey, 243
Gandhi, Mahatma, 212
Gap Inc., 314
Garr, Stacia Sherman, 102
Gates, Bill, 185, 275
Gates, Melinda, 185
Gateways to communication, 130–132
Gay people, 26–27
GE Capital, 176–177
GE Healthcare, 323
GE Medical Systems Group (GEMS), 22
Gender bias, 48, 287
Gender differences. *See also* Women
  on boards, 182
  charisma, 212
  communication, 130–131
  conflict and, 223
  ethical behavior, 69
  in groups, 146
  leadership, 213, 214
  mentoring relationships, 302
  moral development, 69
  negotiation styles, 232
  organizational politics, 190
  risk aversion, 166
  stress, 114
Gender diversity, 23–24, 146
Gender harassment, 30. *See also* Sexual harassment
Gender identity, 26–27
Gender pay gap, 98
Gender roles, 12
Geneen, Harold, 143, 239
Genentech, 324
General attitudes, 55
General Electric (GE), 102
  employee response to feedback, 96
  management by objectives, 322
  multinational corporation, 312
  Six Sigma, 11, 15
  WorkOut sessions, 310
General mental ability (GMA), 35, 94
General Mills, 324, 325
General Motors (GM), 5, 165, 178, 199, 213

General self-efficacy, 38
General theory of relativity (GTR), 89
Generation X, 25, 66
Generation Y, 17, 18, 25, 66
Geographically dispersed teams, 130
Gerber, 63
Gerdau Ameristeel, 97
Germany
  authoritarian tradition, 178
  communication barriers, 131
  definition of work, 238
  design of work, 246–247
  global competition, 312
  women on boards, 182
Gersick, Connie, 148
Gestalt school of thought, 91
Gestures, 136, 139
Gifts, cultural differences in, 20
Gilboa, Dave, 313
Gilligan, Carol, 69
Gilmartin, Ray, 158
The Giving Pledge, 185
Glass ceiling, 23–24, 213
Glass cliff, 213
Global Citizens Portfolio (IBM), 22
Global competition
  concerns for leaders, 12
  cost of layoffs in various countries, 19
  cultural differences, 18–22
  developing cross-cultural sensitivity, 22
  driver of change, 9, 10
  social and political changes, 17–18
  trade barriers, 17
Global economy, competition in, 16–20
Global human resource management, 22
Global Leadership Program (GE Medical Systems Group), 22
Global organizational culture, 287
Global travel, 110
Globalization, 16
  competing in global economy, 16–20
  organizational change, 312
  organizational design and structure, 268
  pay equity, 81
  potential for conflict, 218
  staffing issues, 300
  task demands, 107
Globalization of operating territory, 12
GMA (general mental ability), 35, 94
Goal differences, 222
Goal setting, 92–94, 118, 121
Goal setting programs, 93–94
Goals
  characteristics, 92
  relationship to

organizational structure, 261, 266–267
  task performance related to, 92–93
Goal-setting theory, 92
Goldman Sachs, 102, 318
Goleman, Daniel, 61, 296
Google, 259
  acquisition of YouTube, 315
  corporate culture, 273–274
  diversity of employees, 8
  mindfulness training, 62, 324
  reference checks, 296
Google Pixel, 139
Google Wallet, 313
Goolsby Leadership Academy (University of Texas), 29, 146, 148
Government sectors, 9
GP³ method of time management, 121
Graceful exit, 165
Grant, Jody, 151
Graphic Controls Corporation, 240–241
Gratitude, 61
Great Britain, 21, 135. *See also* United Kingdom
Greece, 317
Green Eileen, 190
Green Mountain Coffee Roasters, 326
Green movement, 165
Greenleaf, Robert, 213–214
Greenpeace, 233, 235
Group, 142. *See also* Work teams and groups
Group behavior, 145–146
Group cohesion, 145, 149–150, 171
Group decision-making
  advantages/disadvantages, 171
  limits of, 171–173
  techniques, 173–174
Group development stages, 146–148
Group dynamics, and technology, 139
Group formation, 146
Group polarization, 172–173
Group-Atmosphere Scale, 205
Group-focused techniques of OD intervention, 321–323
Groupthink, 156, 158, 171–172, 175, 220
Growth need, 74, 76
Growth need strength, 242, 243
Guanxi, 17, 304

H

Habits, 6
Hackman, Richard, 242–243
Haiti, 17
Hall, Edward, 135
Hallmark Cards, 152

Hambrick, D., 156
Hampton Inn hotels, 176
Happiness, 66
Harassment, 26
Hardee's Food Systems, 117
Hardy personality, 115
Harley-Davidson, 270
Harvard University, 304
Hawthorne studies, 8, 73, 272
Hayward, Tony, 213
Hazardous substances, 110
Headaches, 108
Healing dialogue, 137
Health
  communication, and, 137
  comprehensive health promotion, 122
  culture of, 284
  stress. *see* Stress
  wellness program, 325, 326
  work design and, 248
Health promotion programs, 326
Healthcare, 169
Heart disease, 108
Heartfelt communication, 137
Heim, Piet, 89
HERO (hope, efficacy, resilience, and optimism), 121
Hersey, Paul, 209
Herzberg, Frederick, 77, 80, 238, 241
Herzberg's two-factor theory, 77–78, 80, 85, 238, 241
Heskett, James, 279
Heuristics, 163
Hewlett-Packard, 28, 45, 276, 316
Hewson, Marillyn, 214
Hierarchy of authority, 258, 260, 262, 264, 267, 268, 269
High achievers, 75–76
High vs. low power network, 227, 228
High vs. middle versus low power network, 227–228
High-context communicators, 131
Highly consequential decisions, 171
High-Machs, 67–68, 186
High-performance work systems (HPWS), 269
High-trust cultures, 287
Hindrance stressor, 106
Hippocratic oath, 32
Hiring and firing employees, 280–281
Hirschhorn, Larry, 144
Hispanic Americans, 23, 301, 312
Hitler, Adolf, 211
HIV-infected workers, 30
H.J. Heinz, 286
Hofstede, Geert, 18, 19, 22, 175
Hofstede's dimensions of cultural differences, 18, 19

Holgorsen, Dana, 230
Holiday, 55
Holland, John, 293, 307
Home demands, 107, 110
Home Depot, 312
Homeostasis, 106
Homeostatic/medical
    approach to stress,
    105–106
Homestead Works of U.S.
    Steel, 8
Homogeneous groups, 158,
    171
Honda, 16
Honesty, 66
Honeywell, 43
Hong Kong, 145
Honor cultures, 232
Hope, 78–79, 121
Horizontal differentiation,
    255, 261, 268
Horizontal integration
    mechanisms, 257
Horizontal teams, 257
Hospitals, 11, 12, 260, 261,
    285
Hostile jokes, 134
House, Robert, 206
HPWS (High-performance
    work systems), 269
Human activity, nature of, 274
Human behavior, in
    organizations, 2–5
Human capital diversity, 153
Human nature, 274
Human relationships, nature
    of, 274
Human resource (HR)
    practices, 269
Human Rights Campaign, 288
Humane Society, 278
Humor, 151
Hungary, 170
Hygiene factors, 77, 78, 85

I

Iacocca, Lee, 156, 168
IBM
    cultural sensitivity program,
        22
    Hofstede's research, 18
    job enlargement program,
        240
    leadership training, 324
    mentoring program, 101, 301
    organizational culture, 276,
        278
    performance feedback, 102
    process quality
        management, 148
    product and service quality,
        10
    resilience training, 318
    social responsibility, 32
    subsidiaries in EU, 18
    Taylor's notion of
        performance standards, 5
    women executives, 24

ICTs (Information and
    communication
    technologies), 130, 131,
    139–141
Identification, 229
Illumination, 168
Immigrants, 19, 75
Impact, 194
Implicit memory, 6
Implicit thoughts and feelings,
    127, 128
Impoverished manager, 203,
    204
Impression management,
    49–50, 188
In Search of Excellence
    (Peters/Waterman), 272
Incivility, 3, 132–134
Inclusion and Diversity of
    Employees (PRIDE), 302
Inclusive culture, 288
Income inequality, 185
Incremental change, 315
Incubation stage of creativity,
    168
India, 21, 51, 135, 175, 182,
    223–224
Indirect experience, 54
Individual and group
    alternative reward
    systems, 98
Individual differences
    attitudes, 52–54
    defined, 34
    emotions and moods, 61–63
    ethical behavior, 63–65
    eye contact, 128
    job satisfaction, 56–57
    organizational citizenship
        behavior, 57–59
    skills and abilities, 34
    stress-strain relationship,
        114–116
    values, 69
Individual distress, 112–113
Individual influences on
    creativity, 168–169
Individual reward systems,
    98
Individual stress prevention,
    120–122
Individual-focused techniques
    of OD intervention,
    323–327
Individualism
    decision making, 175–176
    direction of OCBs, 58
    equity theory, 85
    expectancy theory, 85
    in Hofstede's dimensions
        of cultural differences,
        19, 21
    individual as element of
        team, 98
    job satisfaction, 59
    need for achievement, 76
    negotiation style, 232
    values, 67
Individualistic people, 155
Individuality, loss of, 145–146

Individualized consideration,
    211
Individual-organization fit,
    and creativity, 169–170
Individual-organizational
    exchange relationship, 80
Indonesia, 175
Inequality Theory, 80–81
Inequity, 80–81
INFJ type, 44
Influence, 176, 180, 188, 299
Influence tactics, 188–191
Informal group, 146
Informal leadership, 198
Informal mentoring programs,
    301–302
Informal organization, 8–9
Information, 126
Information and
    communication
    technologies (ICTs), 130,
    131, 139–141
Information database, 138
Information gathering, 92
Information management
    skills, 14
Information overload, 139
Information power, 184
Information richness, 126, 127
Informational cues, 100, 101
Informational support, 299
Information-processing
    technologies, 268–269
Informative managing style,
    130
INFP type, 44
ING Direct, 323
Ingratiation, 188, 189, 190
In-group member, 210
Initiating structure, 202
Initiation stage of mentoring,
    302
Inputs, 7
Insomnia, 112
Inspirational appeals, 188, 189
Inspirational leadership
    theories, 210–212
Inspirational motivation, 211
Instant messaging, 138, 139
Instrumental values, 66, 67
Instrumentality, 83
Integrated involvement, 144
Integrated role expectations,
    118
Integration, 239, 253,
    256–258, 267
Integration, rites of, 275
Integrative approach, 37
Integrative negotiation, 232
Integrator, 152, 231, 257
Intel, 315
Intelligence, stereotypes and,
    49
Intentions, 47, 94
Interactional psychology
    approach, 34–35
Interdependence, 115, 221,
    238–239, 263
Interdisciplinary framework
    for work design, 244–246

Interdisciplinary influences,
    4–5
Intergenerational conflict,
    25, 48
Intergroup conflict, 224–225
Intergroup power, 183–184
Interim reviews, 94
Intermittent schedule of
    reinforcement, 90
Internal attribution, 50, 101
Internal change agents, 316
Internal competition, 150
Internal forces of
    organizational change,
    314–315
Internal needs, 72
Internal perspective of human
    behavior, 4
Internal theories of
    motivation, 70
Internals, 38, 67
International activity, 16
International Coach
    Federation, 325
International executives, 19
International perspectives on
    work design, 246–248
Internet, 5
Internet surfing (at work), 229
Internet-based cognitive
    behavior therapy, 112
Internetworking, 269
Interorganizational conflict,
    224
Interpersonal communication,
    124–129
    defined, 124
    employee voice behavior,
        126
    model of, 125–126
    reflective listening, 126–129
Interpersonal conflict, 28, 112,
    227–228
Interpersonal demands, 107,
    109–110, 282
Interpersonal diversity, 146
Interpersonal influence, 191
Interpersonal issues, 146
Interpersonal orientation, 255
Interpersonal power, 182–183
Interpersonal relationships,
    fear of disruption of, 317
Interpersonal skills, 296
Interrole conflict, 109,
    225–226
Interviews, 295
Intimate space, 135, 136
INTJ type, 44
INTP type, 44
Intragroup conflict, 225
Intrapersonal conflict,
    225–229
Intrarole conflict, 109, 226
Intrinsic motivation, 72, 73
Introversion (I), 41, 42, 91
Intuition, 166–168
Intuitive types (N), 41, 43, 44,
    91, 164, 167
Intuitors, 92
Invalidity, 96

Investigative occupation, 293
Invisible hand, 72
Iran, 67
Ireland, 19
Isautier, Bernard, 131
Isenberg, Daniel, 167
ISFJ type, 44
ISFP type, 44
Islam, 67
Israel, 21, 89, 238
ISTJ types, 44
ISTP type, 44
Italy, 19, 21
Ivancevich, John M., 92

J

J. P. Morgan Chase, 288
J. Willard Marriott Award of
    Excellence, 89
Jackson, Jesse, 227
Jago, Arthur, 207–209
James, LeBron, 119
James, William, 4, 73
Janis, Irving, 171–172
Japan
    communication barriers, 131
    cultural differences in, 20,
        21
    definition of work, 238
    design of work, 246
    distributive justice, 31
    facial expressions, 136
    global competition, 10, 312
    group decisions, 176
    importance of social context,
        47
    individuals as element of
        team, 98
    influence tactics, 190
    loyalty, 67
    monitoring performance, 96
    negotiation style, 232
    team rewards, 98
    tsunami, 111
    uncertainty avoidance, 21
    women on boards, 182
Jargon, 132
JCI (Job Characteristics
    Inventory), 243
JDI (job descriptive index),
    56, 57
JDS (Job Diagnostic Survey),
    242–243
Job, 236, 238–239
Job and work design, 236–251
    alternate work patterns,
        249–250
    alternative approaches to job
        design, 244–248
    contemporary issues in,
        248–251
    decision making, 177–178
    international perspectives,
        246–248
    job enrichment, 241
    telecommuting, 226,
        248–249, 250, 304, 305,
        307, 325–326

traditional approaches to job
    design, 239–244
work in organizations,
    236–239
Job change rate, 84
Job Characteristics Inventory
    (JCI), 243
Job Characteristics Model,
    242
Job characteristics theory,
    241–244
Job choice, 66
Job content, 195–196
Job context, 195–196, 238
Job decision latitude, 117–118
Job descriptive index (JDI),
    56, 57
Job design. *See* Job and work
    design
Job Diagnostic Survey (JDS),
    242–243
Job enlargement, 240–241
Job enrichment, 77, 241
Job insecurity, 107
Job redesign, 117–118,
    325–326
Job rotation, 170, 240–241
Job satisfaction
    cultural differences, 58
    defined, 56
    dimensions and
        measurement, 56–57
    emotions and moods, 61
    evaluation of work, 247
    job enlargement and
        enrichment, 240–241
    motivation and hygiene
        factors, 78
    organizational citizenship
        behavior, 57–59
    organizational commitment,
        59
    person-organization fit, 58
    realistic job previews, 294
    socialization improving, 283
    work values and, 66
    workplace deviance
        behavior, 58
Job sharing, 248, 249, 305
Job strain model, 117, 118
Job-demand-resources (JD-R)
    model, 248
Jobs, Steve, 211, 266
Johnson & Johnson, 145
    credo, 32, 33
    ethical behavior, 63, 109
    health promotion program,
        122
    psychology research on
        military personnel, 4
    on-site day-care center, 304
    Tylenol tampering incident,
        216
    wellness program, 5, 326
Joint Ethics Regulation, 32
Joking behaviors, 151
Judging, 41, 43
Jung, Carl, 40–45, 91
Jurisdictional ambiguity, 222
Just Coffee Cooperative, 32

Justice, 186
Just-in-time management, 12

K

Kahn, Robert, 6, 106
Kalanick, Travis, 202
Kant, Immanuel, 29
Kanter, Rosabeth Moss,
    186–187, 316
Karoshi (death by overwork),
    112
Katz, Daniel, 6
Kauss, Sarah, 204
Kelley, Harold, 100–101
Kennedy, Allan, 272
Kentucky Fried Chicken
    (KFC), 17, 27, 312
Kibbutzim, 21
Kilmann-Saxton Culture-Gap
    Survey, 283–284
KIND, 297
Kinesics, 134, 136
King, Rodney, 146
Klean Kanteen, 64
Klein, Gary, 167
Knowledge of results, 242, 243
Knowledge-based
    organizations, 268–269
Kohlberg, Lawrence, 68–69
Kohl's, 24
Kopp, Wendy, 42
Korda, Michael, 186, 187
Korea, 67, 131, 232, 282
Koresh, David, 211
Kotter, John, 199, 279
Kraft Foods, 117, 286
Kraft Heinz, 286

L

Labeling, 133–134
Labor Department, U.S., 14
Labor efficiency, 72
Labor laws, 155
Lack of trust, 110
Laissez-faire style of
    leadership, 109, 201–202
Landy, Frank, 248
Language, 126, 132
Language styles, 147
Late adulthood transition, 307
Lateral moves, 306
Latham, Gary, 92
Law of effect, 88
Lawrence, Paul R., 255, 256
Lawrence Livermore National
    Labs (LLNL), 307–308
Layoffs, 19, 59, 64, 311, 314
Lazarus, Richard, 106
Leader effectiveness, 205–206
Leader/leadership, 198–216
    abusive supervision, 214
    behavioral theories, 201–204
    contingency theories,
        204–210
    contributions of, 200
    defined, 198

early trait theories, 200–201
emerging issues, 212–214
followership, 214–215
gender difference, 213, 214
guidelines for, 215–216
informal/formal leadership,
    198
inspirational leadership
    theories, 210–212
introversion and, 42
leader-member exchange
    theory, 210
leadership process, 199
management compared to,
    199–200
role in shaping and
    reinforcing organizational
    culture, 280–281
servant leadership, 213–214
Leader-member exchange
    (LMX) theory, 210
Leader-member relations, 205
Leadership and strategy
    council (LSC), 270
Leadership Grid, 202–204
Leadership identity, 37
Leadership process, 199
Leadership training and
    development, 324
Lean production, 246
Leaner organizations, 109
Learned optimism, 120
Learning
    behavioral models, 86–91
    defined, 86
    experiential, 14
    lifelong, 15
    observing a model, 55
    organizational knowledge,
        13–15
    social, 55
    social and cognitive theories,
        91–92
    structured, 14–15
    from structured activity, 14
    structured activity, 14–15
    students as coproducers, 14
Learning environment, 15
Learning process, 14–15
Learning styles, 13
Learning teams, 322, 323
Least preferred coworker
    (LPC), 205, 206
Leavitt, H., 6
Left-brain skills, 166, 167
Legal rights, 29
Legitimate power, 182, 183,
    184
LEGO, 233
Leisure time activities, 121
Lesbians, 26–27
Letters, 138
Levi, Lennart, 247
Levi Strauss and Co., 284, 326
Levinson, Daniel J., 297
Levinson, Harry, 106, 321
Lewin, Kurt, 4, 34, 201,
    318–320
Lewin's model for managing
    change, 318–320

LG Group, 282
LGBT, 26–27, 288
Liaison devices, 261
Liaison role, 257
Liberty Mutual, 262
Life cycles in organizations, 267–268
Life stages, 297–298
Lifelong learning, 15
Linkage mechanisms, 258
LinkedIn, 141
Listening, 126–129
"Live for Life Program" (Johnson & Johnson), 5
LMX (leader-member exchange theory), 210
Locke, Edwin, 92
Lockheed Martin, 214
Locus of control, 38, 67, 69
Loehr, Jim, 79
Long-term orientation, 19, 22
Loose cultures, 170
Lorenzo, Frank, 150
Lorsch, Jay W., 255, 256
Loss, fear of, 317
Love, 66
Love (social) needs, 73
Low-context communicators, 131
Low-Machs, 67
Loyalty, 67
LPC (least preferred coworker), 205, 206
LSC (leadership and strategy council), 270
Lubetsky, Daniel, 297
Lululemon, 191
Luna, 277
Luthans, Fred, 88, 91
Lynch, James, 137
Lyons, Dan, 322–323

M

Machiavelli, Niccolò, 67, 68, 186
Machiavellianism, 67–68, 69, 186
Machine bureaucracy, 259, 260
Machine learning, 86, 88
Macik-Frey, Marilyn, 137
Mackey, John, 74
Maintenance functions, 150, 151
Maintenance stage of career, 297, 298, 305–306
Majority-wins rule, 170
Malaysia, 170, 175, 248
Malcolm Baldridge National Quality Award, 12
Management, 5
Management and managers career management. see Career management challenges, 16–33
change management, 317–318
co-CEO arrangement, 158

command-and-control management, 59
communication skills, 129–130
competition in global economy, 16–20
conflict management skills, 219
contributions of, 200
cultural differences and work-related attitudes, 18–22
decision making. see Decision making
diverse workforce leadership, 22–28
employee attitudes and, 52–54
employee empowerment, 91
encouraging ethics, character, and personal integrity, 28–29
ethical behavior, 63–65
ethics, 63–65
leadership compared to, 199–200
management by exception, 257
management by objectives, 93, 322
Maslow's need hierarchy, 73–75
modeling behavior, 274
power of. see Power
structural roles of managers, 269
struggles of new managers, 299
team leaders, 158
top management team, 156–158
Management by exception, 257
Management by objectives (MBO), 93, 98, 322
Management development component, 97
Management process, 199
Managerial grid. See Leadership Grid
Manager's goal orientation, 255
Managing change. See Change management
Managing political behavior, 192–196
Managing up, 193–194
Mandela, Nelson, 212
Manifest needs, 75
Manuals, 138
Manufacturing sector, 9
March, James, 5
Marriott International, 89
Martin, Joanne, 275
Masculinity, 19, 21–22, 176
Maslach, Christina, 112
Maslow, Abraham, 73–75

Maslow's need hierarchy, 73–75, 76, 80, 283
Mass production jobs, 240
Mass technology, 263
Mastenbroek, W.F.G., 227
Matrix organization, 259
Mattel, 64
Mature group, 148–150
MBO (management by objectives), 93, 98, 322
MBTI (Myers-Briggs Type Indicator), 40–45, 163–164
MBTI Atlas, 43
McClelland, David, 75–77, 185–186, 188
McClelland's need theory, 75–77, 80
McDonald's, 26, 262
McGrath, Joseph, 111
McGregor, Douglas, 74, 75, 76
McJOBS, 26
McRaven, William, 31
Meaning, 194
Meaning of work, 237–238
Meaningfulness of work, 242, 243
Measured performance, 95
Mechanistic approach to job design, 245
Mechanistic structure, 265, 268
Medical illnesses, 112
Medicine, 5
Meditation, 165
Medium of communication, 126, 127
Memorandums (memos), 138
Mental locks, 169–170
Mentor/mentoring
  becoming a mentor, 306
  career development, 300–303
  definitions, 101, 300–301
  gender difference, 302
  importance of, 303
  managing resistance to change, 318
  phases, 101, 302–303
Merck & Company, 28, 158
Mergers and acquisitions, 286–287, 318
Merit raises, 99
Merrill Lynch, 325
Message, 125
Message characteristics of persuasion, 60
Mexico, 18, 20, 21, 67, 317
Meyer, M., 262
Michael J. Fox Foundation, 183
Microcultural differences, 18
Middle East, 135
Middle level, 259–260, 261
Middle-of-the road management, 203
Militaristic response, 105
Military code of ethics, 32
Military organizations, 4, 6, 150, 255, 257, 295

Mill, John Stuart, 28
Millennials, 17, 18, 25, 211
Mindfulness, 62, 63, 165, 324, 326
Minnesota Multiphasic Personality Inventory (MMPI), 40
Minnesota Satisfaction Questionnaire (MSQ), 56, 57
Minorities, 8, 23, 91, 96, 301, 312
Mintzberg, Henry, 166–167, 258, 259–260
Mintzberg's five basic structural configurations, 259–261
Misinformation, 192
Misleading information, 134
Mission, 148, 195–196
Mitchell Gold + Bob Williams, 304
MMPI (Minnesota Multiphasic Personality Inventory), 40
Mobil, 322
Mobile payment market, 313
Modeling, 55, 274, 280, 299
Monetary bonuses, 89
Monsanto, 320
Mood, 46, 61–62
Moral development theory, 68–69
Moral maturity, 84
Moral rights, 29
Morgan Stanley, 102
Mortality norms, 145
Motivating Potential Score (MPS), 242
Motivation, 70–85
  Adams's theory of inequality, 80–81
  creativity and, 168
  cultural differences, 84–85
  defined, 70
  equity theory, 79–82
  ERG theory, 74–75
  eustress, strength, and hope, 78–79
  expectancy theory, 82–84
  external incentives, 72–73
  external theories, 70
  goal setting, 92–93
  Herzberg's two-factor theory, 77–78
  internal needs, 72
  internal theories, 70
  intrinsic factors, 72
  Maslow's need hierarchy, 73–75
  McClelland's need theory, 75–77
  needs theories, 72–75
  participation in decision making, 178
  performance and, 112
  positive energy and full engagement, 79
  process theories, 70

social exchange and equity theory, 79–82
work behavior, 70–73
Motivation factors, 77–78
Motivation programs, 83
Motivational approach to job design, 245
Motivational problems, 83–84
Motivation-hygiene theory of motivation, 77–78
Motley Fool, 326
Motorola, 11, 12, 23, 143
Mouton, Jane, 202
Moving, 319
MPS (Motivating Potential Score), 242
MSQ (Minnesota Satisfaction Questionnaire), 56, 57
Multicultural group, 158
Multicultural top teams, 158
Multinational organizations, 16. *See also* Transnational organizations
Multitasking, 140
Munger, Charles, 275
Munoz, Oscar, 227
Murray, Henry, 75
Murray Thematic Apperception Test (TAT), 75–76
Musk, Elon, 42
Mutual aid and protection, 155
Myers, Isabel Briggs, 41, 163–164
Myers-Briggs Type Indicator (MBTI), 40–45, 163–164

N

Nadella, Staya, 10
Name Our Ship campaign, 173
Name-dropping, 50
Narcissism, 201
National Aeronautics and Space Administration (NASA), 5, 7, 171, 261
National Association for Female Executives (NAFE), 23
National Environment Research Council (NERC), 173
National Football League (NFL), 224
National Labor Relations Act, 155
National Union of Journalists, 247
Natural liberty, 29
Nature, work attitudes and, 58
Need hierarchy, 73
Needs analysis, 321
Needs theories of motivation, 72–75
Negative affect, 37, 39–40, 56
Negative consequences, 88, 89, 91

Negative emotions, 61, 62
Negative inequity, 81
Negative moods, 61
Negative power, 185–186
Negative reinforcement, 89
Negative stress, 111–114
Negativism, 228
Negotiation, 20, 231–232
Neiman Marcus, 264
NEO Personality Inventory, 40
Nestlé, 312
Netherlands, 21, 67, 238
Network groups, 301–302
Network organization, 270
Networking, 192
Networking ability, 191
Networking technology, 5
Neuroticism, 114
New team environment, 144
New Zealand, 85, 283
Nike, 276
Nissan, 16
No discretion (employee empowerment grid), 195
Nominal group technique (NGT), 174
Nonaction, 230
Nonadaptive culture, 279
Nondefensive communication, 132, 133, 134
Nonfinancial reinforcement, 88
Nonmonetary bonuses, 89
Nonprofit sector, 9
Nonprogrammed decisions, 160
Nonsubstitutability, 184
Nonverbal communication, 47, 62, 134–137, 139. *See also* Eye contact
Nonwork demands, 110–111
Nooyi, Indra, 183, 200
Normative commitment, 59
Normative decision model, 207–209
Norming stage, 147
Norms of behavior, 145, 148–149
North American Free Trade Agreement (NAFTA), 18
Northern Telecom (Nortel Networks), 175
Northwest Airlines (now Delta), 10
Norway, 21, 109, 170, 182
Notice period payment, 19
Nous Group, 262

O

Obama, Barack, 42, 210
Objective element of career, 290
Objective knowledge, 13–14, 15
Objective knowledge acquisition, 13–14
OBM (organizational behavior modification), 88

OCB (organizational citizenship behavior). *See* Organizational citizenship behavior (OCB)
Occupational choice, 293
Occupational excellence, 292–293
OCI (organizational culture inventory), 283
OD (organizational development), 320–321
Office design, 110, 169
Officer effectiveness reports (1813), 96
Official group, 146
Older workers, 9, 25
Oldham, Greg, 242
One-way communication, 129
On-site day-care center, 304
Opening up, 121–122
Open-minded discussion, 230
Open-mindedness, 66
Openness, 14, 36–37
Open-plan offices, 169
Open-systems view of organization, 6–7
Operant conditioning, 88
Operating level, 259–260
Operational support planning, 94
Opponents, 155
Opportunistic management, 203
Opportunistic what's-in-it-former manager (Opp), 204
Opportunities, 4, 9–12
Optimism, 120, 121, 164
Optimization, 163
Organic structure, 265, 268
Organization
circle, 270
clockwork metaphor, 2, 3, 7
diversity, 9
formal, 7–8
informal, 8–9
network, 270
as open systems, 6–7
snake pit metaphor, 2, 7–8
transnational, 16–20
virtual, 270
Organization man manager, 203
Organizational (corporate) culture, 272–288
anthropology, 5
assessing, 283–284
behavior norms, 145
challenges to developing a positive, cohesive culture, 286–288
changing, 284–286
decision making, 177–178
defined, 272–273
functions, 277–278
leader's role in shaping and reinforcing, 280–281
levels of, 272–277
organizational socialization, 281–283

relationship to performance, 278–279
Organizational behavior, 2–15
application of knowledge and skills, 15
attitudes, 52–54
defined, 4
diversity of, 9
individual differences, 34
interdisciplinary influences, 4–5
learning about, 13–15
objective knowledge acquisition, 13–14
personality and, 36–40
quality at work and, 12
skill development, 14–15
Organizational behavior modification (OBM), 88, 91
Organizational change. *See* Change management
Organizational chart, 253, 254
Organizational choice and entry, 293–296
Organizational citizenship behavior (OCB), 80
dissimilarity and, 152
employee involvement programs enhancing, 95
group cohesion and, 145
of in-group vs. out-group members, 210
leadership fostering, 214
mentoring and, 101
moods and, 61
workplace deviance vs., 57–59
Organizational commitment, 59, 93, 224–225
Organizational context, 6–7
Organizational culture inventory (OCI), 283
Organizational design and structure, 252–271
basic design dimensions, 258–259
contextual variables, 261–267
definitions, 252
emerging organizational structures, 269–270
factors adversely affecting structure, 270–271
five structural configurations, 259–261
forces reshaping organizations, 267–269
key organizational design processes, 253–258
relationship among key organizational design elements, 267
Organizational development cycle, 321
Organizational development (OD), 320–321
Organizational distress, 112, 113–114

Organizational empowerment, 292, 293
Organizational forms, 6
Organizational Health Center (OHC), 117
Organizational influences, on creativity, 169
Organizational justice, 31, 117
Organizational life cycle, 267–268
Organizational performance, 157
Organizational politics
    defined, 188
    influence tactics, 188–191
    managing political behavior, 192–196
    political skill, 191–192
    resistance to change, 317
Organizational position, 236
Organizational processes, 269–270
Organizational psychology, 4
Organizational reward systems, 88, 90
Organizational socialization, 281–283
Organizational stress, 117
Organizational stress prevention, 117–120
Organizational structure, 252. See also Organizational design and structure
Organizational transparency, 7
Organizational wellness, 122
Ornish, Dean, 121
Ortega, Amancio, 185
Other-enhancing techniques, 50
Other-negative feedback, 94
Other-positive feedback, 94
Oticon, 169
Ouchi, William, 272
Outcomes of socialization, 282, 283
Out-group member, 210
Outputs, 7
Outsourcing, 5, 261
Overdependence, 115–116
Oxytocin, 79

P

Pacific Bell, 249
Paid volunteerism, 25
Pakistan, 170
Panic, Milan, 30
Paralanguage, 134, 137
Paranoid constellation, 270
Paraphrasing the expressed, 127–128
Parental care, 110
Parents in a Pinch, Inc., 304
Participating style of leadership, 210
Participation, 318
Participation problems, 113
Participative decision making, 176–177

Participative management, 192
Participative style of leadership, 206
Participatory empowerment, 195–196
Part-time professionals, 10
Paschal, Carolyn Smith, 305–306
Passage, rites of, 275
Passive attitude, 14
Patagonia, 64
Paternalism/maternalism management, 203
Paternalistic father-knows-best manager, 204
Path-goal theory, 206–207
Pattern recognition, 86
Pavlov, Ivan, 87, 91
Pay dispersion, 81
Pay equity, 81
Pay for performance, 88
Pay inequality, 81
Pay secrecy, 230
PayPal, 313
Peer relationships, 101
People, 6, 7
PepsiCo, 200
Perceiver, 45–46
Perceiving, 41, 43
Perception, 45–47, 244. See also Social perception
Perception-shaping mechanisms, 281
Perceptual differences, 222
Perceptual lenses, 45–46
Perceptual screen, 125
Perceptual/motor approach to job design, 245
Perdue Farms, 304
Perez, Bill, 150
Performance
    correction of poor performance, 99–102
    defining, 95
    emotional intelligence and, 62–63, 94–95
    general mental ability and, 94
    goal setting increasing, 92–93
    intrinsic factors and external incentives, 72–73
    job satisfaction and, 56
    measuring, 95–96
    moods and, 61
    motivation and, 112
    organizational commitment and, 59
    positive and negative consequences affecting, 88–89
    predicting, 94–96
    rewards for, 98–99
Performance appraisal, 95, 188
Performance arousal, 111
Performance decrements, 113
Performance evaluation, 92, 93–94, 102

Performance feedback, 93, 96–97
Performance management, 95, 99
Performance management system, 95
Performance measurement, 95–96
Performance norms, 145
Performance planning, 83
Performance reviews, 94
Performance standards, 250
Performance-monitoring systems, 95–96
Performing stage, 147–148
Peripheral route to persuasion, 60, 61
Permoral level of moral development, 68
Perrow, Charles, 263–264
Person, 35
Personal and work outcomes, 243
Personal demands, 107, 110, 111
Personal distance, 136
Personal element of communication, 126–127
Personal enactment, 274
Personal factors of conflict, 221, 222–224
Personal freedom, 284
Personal integrity, 137
Personal interaction skills, 14
Personal payoff, 178
Personal power, 186, 192
Personality
    application of theory, 40–45
    attitude-behavior link affected by, 55
    Big Five traits, 36–37, 40
    creativity and, 168
    decision making, 166
    defined, 36
    integrative approach, 37
    of leaders and managers, 200
    learning, and, 91–92
    locus of control, 38
    measurement tools, 40
    Myers-Briggs Type Indicator, 40–45
    occupational choice and, 293
    positive/negative affect, 37, 39–40
    proactivity, 40
    resistance to change, 317
    self-efficacy, 38
    self-esteem, 38–39
    self-monitoring, 39
    trait theory, 36–37
Personality conflicts, 222
Personality hardness, 115
Personality measurement tools, 40
Personality preference, 92
Personality theory application, 36–40
    types, 40–45
Personality-organization constellations, 270

Personalized power, 76–77
Person-environment fit approach to stress, 106
Person-job fit approach, 241–242, 243
Personnel changes for conflict management, 230
Person-organization fit, 58
Person-role conflict, 109, 226
Persons with disabilities, 25–26
Persuasion, 59–61
Persuasive arguments view, 173
Persuasiveness, 130
Pessimism, 120
Peters, Thomas, 272
Phased retirement, 307
Philippines, 143
Phoenix, Arizona, 167
Physical appearance, 46, 50
Physical demands, 107, 110
Physical exercise, 120, 121
Physiological needs, 73, 74
Pillsbury Company, 64
Pitney Bowes, 63
Planned change, 311–312
Planning component of goal setting, 94
Planning goal attainment, 121
Pleasure, 66
POB (Positive organizational behavior), 78, 121
Polaroid, 316
Political behavior
    defined, 188
    influence tactics, 188–191
    management of, 192–196
    political skill, 191–192
Political changes, globalization and, 17–18
Political skill, 191–192, 226
Politics in organizations. See Organizational politics
Polyphasic activity, 140
Poor leadership, 109, 110
Position power, 205, 206
Positive affect, 37, 39–40, 168
Positive competitive teamwork skills, 152
Positive consequences, 88, 89
Positive emotions, 61, 62, 63
Positive energy, 79
Positive inequity, 81
Positive moods, 61, 63
Positive organizational behavior (POB), 78, 121
Positive power, 185–186
Positive reinforcement, 89
Positive stress, 111–112
Positive thinking, 120–121
Poverty, 185
Powell, Colin, 157
Power
    defined, 180–181
    ethical use, 184–186
    forms and sources in organizations, 181–184
    need for, 75, 76–77

personalize and socialized, 76–77
symbols of, 186–187
Power distance, 19, 21, 175
Power dynamic, 129
Power lens, 46
Power networks, 227–228
Power of earning, 98–99
Power plays, 133
Powerlessness, 187
Praise, 121
Predictability of work, 247
Preferences, in Myers-Briggs Type Indicator, 41
Prejudice, 26, 27
Preparation stage of creativity, 168
Pressure, 189, 190
Pressure tactic, 189
Prestige, 150
Preventive stress management, 116–122
Price war, 164
PricewaterhouseCoopers (PwC), 302
Primacy effect, 48
Primary prevention, 116, 120
The Prince (Machiavelli), 67, 186
Principled dissent, 186
Principled level of moral development, 68
Prioritizing, 121
Privacy issues, 30, 64
Private sector, 9
Proactive personality, 40
Problem analyzability, 263, 264
Problem solving, 89
Problem-focused coping, 106
Procedural justice, 31
Process consultation, 323
Process orientation, 269
Process production, 263
Process skills, 154–155
Process theories of motivation, 70
Procter & Gamble, 262, 269, 312
Product, 10
Product and service quality programs, 322
Production-oriented style of leadership, 202
Productivity norms, 148–150
Professional bureaucracy, 259, 261
Professional help, 122
Professional Role Behaviors Survey, 5
Programmed decisions, 160
Progression hypothesis, 73–74
Project allegiance, 292, 293
Project team, 306
Projection, 49
Projective tests, 40
Protection, 301
Protestant ethic, 72
Proxemics, 134, 135–136
Psychoanalysis, 72

Psychoanalytic approach to stress, 106
Psychological breaches, 299
Psychological capital (PsyCap), 120–121
Psychological contract, 298–299
Psychological distress, 112
Psychological intimacy, 144, 151
Psychological ownership, 73
Psychological Types (Jung), 40–41
Psychology, 4
Psychosocial functions of mentors, 301
Psychosomatic disorders, 112
Public distance, 136
Puerto Rico, 122
Puig, Imma, 106
Punctuated equilibrium model, 148
Punishment, 87, 89, 90–91
Purpose, of organizational forms, 5
Purpose of groups, 148
Pygmalion effect, 49, 194

Q

QATs (Quality action teams), 154
QIP (Quality improvement process), 154
Qualitative assessment methods, 283
Qualitative goals, 92
Quality, customer focus and, 10–12
Quality action teams (QATs), 154
Quality circle, 175
Quality improvement, 12
Quality improvement process (QIP), 154
Quality management, 12
Quality programs, 322
Quality team, 175
Quantitative assessment methods, 283
Quantitative goals, 92
Quatar, 232
Queen bee syndrome, 223
Questioning, probing attitude, 14
Quick, James Campbell, 137
Quick, Jonathan D., 77
QuikTrip, 276

R

Racial dissimilarity, 152
Rational model of decision making, 163
Rational persuasion, 188, 189
Rationality, 163
Rationalization, 229
Raven, Bertram, 182, 184
Reactance, 316–318

Reagan, Ronald, 137, 211
Realism, 281, 282
Realistic job preview (RJP), 294–296
Realistic occupation, 293
Reality, nature of, 274
Reality-distortion field, 211
Receiver, 125
Recruitment, 64, 66
Redefinition stage of mentoring, 303
Referent power, 182, 183, 184
Reflecting core feelings, 127, 128
Reflective listening, 126–129
Reframing problems, 154
Refreezing, 319–320
Regression hypothesis, 74–75
Regressive coping, 115
Reinforcement, 87, 89
Reinforcement theory, 88–90
Relatedness need, 74, 76
Relationship to environment, 274
Relationship-oriented leader, 205, 206
Relationships, 283
Relaxation response, 121
Relaxation training, 120, 121
Relevance, 55
Reliability, 97
Reliability engineering, 12
Reliability problems (performance measurement), 95
Religious organizations, 6
Renewal, rites of, 275
Reports, 138
Resilience, 121
Resilience training, 318
Resistance to change, 316–318
Resource expansion for conflict management, 231
Resource management skills, 14, 192
Response to communication, 127
Responsibility, 66
Responsibility for work outcomes, 242, 243
Responsiveness, 97, 310
Restaurants, nonverbal communication in, 135
Restructuring, 10
Results-oriented performance appraisal methods, 96
Resumés, 25, 295
Retirement, 306–308
Retirement plan, 74
Revitalization, 10
Reward power, 182, 183, 184
Rewards
    allocation, 280
    creativity and, 170
    employee motivation, 77, 99
    entitlement to, 99
    expectancy theory, 82–84
    individual vs. team, 98
    job performance enhanced by, 73

job satisfaction and, 56–57
for performance, 98–99
power of earning, 99
strategic, 88
Rhodes, Rocky, 110
Richness, 126, 127
Right to privacy, 64
Right-brain skills, 166, 167
Riots, 146
Risk, 165–166
Risk aversion, 166
Risk takers, 166, 168
Rites and ceremonies, 274–275
Rites of passage, 275
Rites of renewal, 275
Rituals, 274, 276
RJP (realistic job preview), 294–296
Rodney King verdict, 146
Rodriguez, Gina, 277
Rokeach, Milton, 65, 66
Role, 225
Role ambiguity, 107, 109, 202, 227–228, 282
Role analysis, 226
Role clarity, 93
Role conflict, 107, 109, 110, 227, 282
Role demands, 107, 109, 282
Role incumbent, 225
Role modeling, 301
Role negotiation, 118, 325
Role overload, 109
Role senders, 225
Role set, 225
Role stress, 93, 109
Rooney, Dan, 31
Rooney Rule, 31
Rorschach ink blot test, 40
Rote memorization, 13
Rothschild, Mitch, 281
Routineness, 264
Royal Dutch/Shell Group, 256
Rudd, Kevin, 64
Rudeness, 134
Rules-based theories of ethics, 29
Russia, 17, 22
Rust-out, 112

S

Safety and security needs, 73
Samsung Galaxy, 139
Samsung Heavy Industry, 286
San Diego County Government, 262
San Francisco, city/county, 177
Sandberg, Sheryl, 199, 200, 207
Sanger-Harris, 92
SAP, 288
SAS, 276
Satisfaction questionnaire, 57
Satisfice, 163, 294
Saudi Arabia, 20
Scandinavian approach to design of work, 247–248

Schedules of reinforcement, 90

Schein, Edgar, 18, 273, 277, 280, 308, 323

Schizoid constellation, 270

Schultz, Howard, 211

Schwartz, H., 5

Schwarzenegger, Arnold, 275

Scientech, 10

Scientific approaches of labor sciences, 247

Scientific management, 73, 239–240

Scope of change, 315–316

Scully, John, 266

Search Inside Yourself Leadership Institute (SIYLI), 62

Sears, 255, 279

The Seasons of a Man's Life (Levinson), 297

The Seasons of a Woman's Life (Levinson), 297

Seating dynamics, 135–136, 137

Secondary prevention, 116, 120

Secrecy, 230

Security, need for, 74, 84–85

Selection interview, 45

Selective perception, 47–48

Self-actualization, 73, 74, 76, 84–85

Self-awareness, 212, 296

Self-categorization theory, 152

Self-concept, 46

Self-confidence, 65, 212, 296

Self-control, 127, 296

Self-determination, 194

Self-directed team, 154–156

Self-efficacy, 38, 50, 91

Self-enhancing techniques, 50

Self-esteem, 38–39, 60, 74, 152

Self-evaluations, 97

Self-fulfilling prophecy, 49

Self-image, 106

Self-imposed performance expectation, 82

Self-interest, 72, 73, 74, 188

Self-leadership, 214, 215

Self-led followers, 214

Self-managed team, 154–156, 175, 194, 196, 214

Self-management, 196

Self-monitoring, 38, 39, 55, 192

Self-negative feedback, 94

Self-performance evaluation, 95

Self-positive feedback, 94

Self-promotion, 192

Self-reliance, 115–116, 296

Self-report questionnaire, 40, 53, 63

Self-respect, 66

Self-serving bias, 51

Self-sufficiency, 66

Selling style of leadership, 209

Sense-making, 169

Sensing type (S), 41, 43, 44, 91, 164

Sensitivity, 129–130

Sensors, 92

Separation stage of mentoring, 302–303

Servant leadership, 213–214

Service quality, 10

Service sector, 9, 15

Sexism, 48

Sexual coercion, 30

Sexual harassment
  as abuse of personal power, 186
  abusive supervision, 214
  emotional dissonance and, 110
  as emotional toxin, 109
  ethical dilemmas, 30–31
  internationally, 12
  at Sterling Jewelers, 287
  stress and, 114

Sexual orientation, 26–27

Shainin system of quality improvement, 12

Sharf, Charles, 274

Shark Tank, 295

Sheep, 215

Shell Oil Company, 233, 235, 256

Short-term orientation, 19, 22

Siemens, 313

Silence, 128

Silent generation, 25

Simon, Herbert, 5, 163

Simple structure, 259, 260, 261

Sims, Henry, 243

Sincerity, 191

Singhal, Amit, 186

SIP model, 244

Situation, 35, 47

Situation favorableness, 205

Situational cues, 47

Situational leadership model, 209–210

Situations, 38

Six Sigma, 11–12, 15

SIYLI (Search Inside Yourself Leadership Institute), 62

Size, as contextual variable, 261–262, 267

Skill development, 13, 14–15, 248, 251

Skill diversity, 222

Skill variety, 243

Skills, 35

Skills training, 323–324

Skinner, B. F., 87, 91

Slater, Steven, 63

Sleep, 74, 248

Slim, Carlos, 185

Sloan, Alfred P., 199

SMART goals, 92

Smartphone, 138–139

Smith, Adam, 29, 72, 84

Smith, Fred, 97

Smith & Wesson, 263

Smyth, Michael, 64

Snake pit metaphor, 2, 7–8

Snowden, Edward, 32

Social astuteness, 191

Social changes, globalization and, 17–18

Social comparison approach, 173

Social constraints, 55–56

Social context, 47

Social decision schemes, 170

Social distance, 135, 136

Social identity theory, 152

Social information processing (SIP) model, 244

Social learning, 55

Social learning theory, 91, 274

Social loafing, 145

Social media, 63, 138–141

Social needs, 74

Social occupation, 293

Social perception, 45–47
  barriers to, 47–50
  cultural differences, 45
  perceiver, characteristics of, 45–46
  situation, characteristics of, 47
  target, characteristics of, 46–47

Social power, 185, 186, 192

Social reinforcement, 88, 91

Social relationships, 284

Social responsibility, 7, 32

Social sexual behavior, 31

Social support systems, 117, 118–119, 299

Socialization process, 281–283

Socialized power, 76–77

Sociology, 4–5

Sociotechnical system (STS), 246

Solomon, Robert, 29

Sony, 300

Source characteristics of persuasion, 60

South America, 135

South Korea, 182

Southwest Airlines, 10, 196, 276

Southwest Industries, 156

Southwestern Bell, 274–275, 300, 317

Span of control, 255, 257, 258, 259, 262

Spatial differentiation, 255–256

Spearman, Charles, 35

Special decision-making groups, 175

Specialization, 221, 255, 258, 262, 264, 267, 268, 269

Specific attitudes, 55

Specific environment, 264

Sponsorship, 300–301

St. Mary's/Duluth Clinic Health System, 243–244

Stages of moral development, 68–69

Stagnation, 10

Stajkovic, Alexander, 91

Stalker, G. M., 265

Standardization, 258, 261, 262, 264, 267, 268, 269

Standing by, 187

Starbucks, 10, 211

Statistical modeling techniques, 12

Status, need for, 74

Status inconsistencies, 222

Status status, 150

Status structure, 150

Stereotypes
  about women, 27, 48, 49, 114, 137, 223
  disadvantage to organizations, 25, 27
  effect on work teams, 48
  increase in stereotype behavior, 26
  mentoring affected by, 301
  unconscious bias and, 31
  of U.S., 131
  of women, 114

Sterling Jewelers, 287

Stewart, Bill, 230

Stock options, 88

Stories, 275–276

Storming stage, 147

Strain, 105, 108

Strategic apex, 260. *See also* Upper echelons

Strategic change, 315

Strategic contingencies, 183, 184

Strategic leader, 200

Strategic rewards, 88

Strategies, 266–267

Strength, 78–79

Strenuous activities, 110

Stress, 104–122
  body movement/posture, 136
  cognitive appraisal approach, 106
  comprehensive health promotion, 122
  consequences, 111–114
  cultural differences, 110
  defined, 104
  distress, 78, 79, 105
  effect on performance, 94
  effects on the body, 108
  e-mail and, 280
  eustress, 78–79, 111
  goal setting reducing, 92, 93
  of in-group vs. out-group members, 210
  homeostatic/medical approach, 105–106
  individual differences, 114–116
  individual distress, 111–114
  nonwork demands, 110–111
  organizational distress, 112
  person-environment fit approach, 106
  positive, 111–112
  preventive stress management, 116–122
  psychoanalytic approach, 106

psychophysiology of, 106, 117

technology induced, 250

work demands, 107–110

Yerkes-Dodson law, 111

Stress audit, 110

Stress leave, 113

Stress response, 104, 105, 107, 112, 116, 121

Stress-management strategies, 116

Stressors, 104, 108, 299

Stroke, 108

Strong culture, 278–279

Strong situation, 38

Structural changes for conflict management, 231

Structural configurations, 259–261

Structural dimensions of organizations, 258, 267

Structural diversity, 153

Structural factors of conflict, 221–222

Structural holes, 153

Structure, 5, 7

Structured activity, learning from, 14

Structured learning, 14–15

STS (sociotechnical system), 246

Students, as coproducers in learning, 14

Stumpf, John, 314

Subjective element of career, 290

Suboptimization, 227–228

Subordinate defensiveness, 133

Substance abuse, 112–113

Suicide, 72

Superficial conformity, 320

Superleadership, 215

Superordinate goal, 231

Supervisory goal commitment, 93

Support, 318

Support staff, 259–260, 261

Supportive style of leadership, 206

Supreme Court, U.S., 30

Surface acting, 63

Surveillance, 247

Survey feedback, 321–322

Survivors, 215

Sustainable design, 190

Swearing, 132

Sweatshop, 110

Sweden, 21, 96, 175, 247–248

Swedish Worker Life Fund, 247

S'Well, 204

Switzerland, 241

Symbolic rehearsal, 55

Symbols, 18, 272, 274, 276, 277

Synergy, 170

Systems behavior and performance skills, 14

Szilagyi, Andrew, 243

T

Tactile learner, 13

Taguchi's methods of quality improvement, 12

Tall structure, 255, 257

Target, 46–47, 180–181, 325

Target characteristics of persuasion, 60

Task accomplishment, 94. *See also* Performance; Task performance

Task demands, 107–109, 282

Task environment, 7, 264–265

Task force, 257

Task functions, 150–151

Task identity, 243

Task innovation, 284

Task issues, 146

Task performance, 92–93. *See also* Performance

Task setting, 195

Task significance, 243

Task structure, 205

Task support, 283–284

Task uncertainty, 248

Task variability, 263, 264

Task-authority structure, 238

Task-oriented leader, 205, 206

Tasks, 6, 7

Task-specific self-efficacy, 38, 91

TAT (Murray Thematic Apperception Test), 75–76

Taylor, Frederick W., 5, 73, 94, 239–240, 246

Taylor, Herbert J., 32

TCEs (team coordination errors), 151

Team building, 117, 322–323

Team coordination errors (TCEs), 151

Team creativity, 153–154

Team manager, 203, 204

Team reward systems, 98

Teambuilding, Inc., 322–323

Team-oriented work design, 177–178

Teams. *See* Work teams and groups

Teamwork, 14, 144. *See also* Work teams and groups

Technical language, 132

Technical staff, 259–260, 261

Technocentric approach to job design, 246

Technological interdependence, 263, 264

Technology

classification schemes, 263–264

communication through, 138–141

as component of open systems, 7

defined, 263

fear of change, 317

as means to wealth, 72

organizational change, 313

outsourcing through, 5

privacy issues, 30

productivity of labor, 72

recruitment practices, 280–281

relationship to organizational structure, 262–264

spending on, 262

stress created by, 109

task demands and, 107

virtual office, 250

at work, 250

Technology utilization skills, 14

Technostress, 109, 248, 250

Technostructure, 260

Telecommuting

at Cisco, 307

design of work, 248–249, 250

job redesign, 325–326

work-home conflicts, 226, 304, 305

Teleconferencing, 139

Telegraph, 247

Tele-surveillance, 250

Telling style of leadership, 209

Temporal pressure, 121

Temporary personal factors, 95

Temporary top-level executive, 306

Tenneco, 322

Terminal values, 66, 67

Territorial space, 135, 136

Tertiary prevention, 116–117, 120

Testimonials, 60

Texas Capital Bancshare, 151

Texas Department of Aging and Disability Services, 295

Text messaging, 126, 131

Thailand, 283

Thayer, Paul, 244

Theory of occupational choice, 293

Theory of personality differences, 91–92

Theory X and Theory Y, 73, 74, 75, 76

Theory Z (Ouchi), 272

Thinkers, 92

Thinking type (T), 41, 43, 91, 164

Thompson, James, 7, 263, 264

Thompson, Leigh, 153

Thorndike, Edward, 88

Thought, 125

Threat perception, 117

Threat stressor, 106

3M, 16, 63

360-degree feedback, 97

Throughputs, 7

Thumbs-up sign, 18

Thurow, Lester, 10

Tight cultures, 170

Timberland, 64

Time constraints, 171

Time management, 121

Time orientation, 22, 176, 255

Time power, 187

Time pressure, 109

Time Warner Cable, 294–295

Time-bound goals, 92

Time-driven model of leadership, 208

Timing of measurement, 55

Tocqueville, Alexis de, 84

Token group, 158

Token woman syndrome, 223

Top management team, 156–158

Torre, Joe, 213

Total quality, 11, 12

Total quality management (TQM), 11, 156

Total rewards, 98

Tough-mindedness, 65

Toyota

global thinking, 16

quality of products, 11

relating to Generation Y, 18

technological innovations, 322

TQM (total quality management), 11, 156

Trade barriers, 17

Training, 14, 69, 88

Trait theory, 36–37, 200–201

Transactional leader, 210

Transformational change, 315

Transformational coping, 115

Transformational leadership, 210–211

Transgender people, 26–27

Transnational organizations, 16–20

Transparency, 7

Traumatic events, 111

Travelers Group, 249

Triangulation, 284

True assessment, 95

Trump, Donald, 138, 275

Trust, 146, 213, 270, 287

Trust lens, 46

Trustworthiness, 296

Truth-wins rule, 170

Tuckman, Bruce, 146–147

Turkey, 284

Turnover, 113, 152, 155

Twelve-step problem-solving method, 12

Twitter, 7, 138, 141

Two-factor theory of motivation, 77–78, 80, 85, 238, 241

Two-thirds-majority rule, 170

Two-way communication, 129

TXI Chaparral Steel, 196, 245

Tylenol tampering incident, 216

Type A behavior pattern, 114

Type B behavior pattern, 114

Tyson Foods, 278

U

Uber, 186, 202

Ulcers, 108

Uncertainty, 183–184, 192, 295
Uncertainty avoidance, 19, 21, 175
Unconscious bias, 31
Unconscious processes, 168
Unfreezing, 319, 320
Unilever, 286
Union-management strife, 8
Unit technology, 263
United Airlines, 227
United Kingdom, 131. *See also* Great Britain
United Services Automobile Association (USAA), 249
United States
  business culture, 22
  businesses owned by women, 300, 307
  communication barriers, 131
  cost of layoffs, 19
  definition of work, 238
  disabled workers, 26
  economy, 15
  extraverts, 42
  GDP, 15
  global competition, 10
  graying of the workforce, 24
  group cohesion, 145
  group decisions, 175, 176
  Hofstede's dimensions of cultural differences, 19, 22
  home demands, 110
  influence tactics, 190
  information and communication technologies, 131
  loyalty, 67
  monitoring performance, 96
  motivation, 84–85
  NAFTA, 18
  need for achievement, 76
  negotiation style, 232
  nonverbal communication, 136
  perception of job stress, 106
  retirement age, 307
  reward systems, 98
  sensing types, 43
  thinking/feeling types, 43
  thumbs-up sign, 18
  values, 67
  wellness program, 122
  women in workforce, 12, 23–24, 312
  women on boards, 182
  work-home conflicts, 303–304
  workplace stress, 117
  work-related psychological disorders, 112
  zones of territorial space, 136
Universities, 261
Unknown, fear of, 317
Unofficial group, 146
Unplanned change, 312
Unwanted sexual attention, 30
Upper echelon theory, 156

Upper echelons, 156–158, 174, 260, 261
Upward appeals, 188, 189
U.S. Air Force Thunderbirds, 150
U.S. Army, 295
U.S. Army Reserve, 255
U.S. Department of Labor, 14
U.S. Navy Blue Angels, 149, 150
U.S. Steel, 8, 15
Utilitarianism, 28

V

Vacation, 121, 277, 305
Valeant Pharmaceuticals International, 30
Valence, 83
Valero Energy, 4, 325
Validity, 97
Validity problem (performance measurement), 96
Value congruence, 282
Value judgment, 223
Values
  conflict, and, 222–223
  cultural differences, 67
  decision making, 166
  defined, 65
  espoused/enacted, 276
  instrumental/terminal, 66, 67
  organizational change, 320
  organizational culture, 273, 274, 276–277
  resistance to change, 317
  rewards consistent with, 280
  stability, 69
  work values, 66
Variable interval schedule of reinforcement, 90
Variable ratio schedule of reinforcement, 90
Variety, 240
Venezuela, 21
Verbal communication, 47
Verification stage of creativity, 168
Verizon Communications, 249
Vertical differentiation, 255, 260, 268
Vertical integrators, 257
Vertical linkages, 257
Violence, 26, 72
Violence prevention programs, 117
Virgin Group, 170
Virtual office, 250
Virtual organization, 270
Virtual teams, 143, 148
Virtue ethics, 29
Visa, 274
Visual learner, 13
Vitals, 281
Vocal pitch, 49
The Voice, 165
Voice behavior, 126
Voice mail, 138

Volkswagen, 280
Volunteer work, 111
Volunteerism, paid, 25
Volvo, 178, 286
Vroom, Victor, 83, 207–209
Vroom-Yetton-Jago normative decision model, 207–209

W

Wagoner, Rick, 165, 213
Wall Street Journal, 64–65
Wallace Supply Company, 147
Walmart, 264, 312
Walmart China, 275
Walt Disney Enterprises, 167
Warby Parker, 64, 313
Wasylyshyn, Karol, 137
Waterman, Robert, 272
Watson, Tom, Sr., 276
Weak organ hypothesis, 114
Weak situation, 38
Weber, Max, 72
WebEx, 250
Welch, Jack, 312
Well-being, 104. *See also* Health
Wellness programs, 5, 325, 326
Wells Fargo, 288, 314
Western Company of North America, 92, 98
Weyerhaeuser, 5
Whataburger, 73
WhataGames, 73
Whistle-blowers/whistle-blowing, 31–32, 186
Whole Foods, 320
"Whole-system" change, 10
Wild turkey, 157
Wilson, Chip, 191
Windows icon, 18
Win-lose strategies, 229–230
Win-win-strategy, 229–230
Withdrawal, 229
Withdrawal mechanisms, 229
Withdrawal stage of career, 297, 298, 306–308
Wm. Wrigley Jr. Company, 150
Women. *See also* Gender differences; Sexual harassment
  on boards, 182
  business ownership, 300, 307
  change agents, 316
  conflict and, 223
  conversational style, 130–131
  executive positions, 24
  gender pay gap, 98
  as leaders, 213, 214, 300
  mentoring relationships, 302
  negotiation style, 232
  pay inequity, 81
  political leadership, 24
  response to diversity, 27
  response to stress, 114

  risk aversion, 166
  self-efficacy, 91
  stereotype, 27, 48, 49, 114, 137
  view of organizational politics, 190
  in workforce, 12, 23–24, 312–313
  work-home conflicts, 303–304
Women's Interest Network (WIN), 302
Woodward, Joan, 263
Woolley-Wilson, Jessie, 220
Work
  defined, 236
  meaning of, 237–238
  in organizations, 236–239
Work attitudes, 56
Work autonomy, 243
Work behavior, 70–73
Work breaks, 119
Work content, 238
Work definition patterns, 237–238
Work demands, 107–110
Work design. *See* Job and work design
Work design parameters, 248
Work overload, 109, 111
Work repetitiveness, 240
Work simplification, 239–240
Work stress
  consequences, 111–114
  sources, 107–111
Work team process, 152
Work team structure, 151–152
Work teams and groups, 142–158
  benefits of, 143–144
  benefits to organizations, 144
  building for organizational development, 322–323
  characteristics of a mature group, 148–150
  definitions, 142–143
  effectiveness, factors in, 151–154
  empowerment and self-managed teams, 154–156, 175, 196
  five-stage model, 146–148
  group behavior, 145–146
  group decision making, 170–175
  group formation and development, 146–150
  horizontal integration, 257
  learning teams, 322, 323
  new managers and, 299
  new team environment, 144
  norms of behavior, 145
  under old career paradigm, 293
  organizational citizenship behavior in, 57
  punctuated equilibrium model, 148
  rewards, 99

self-managed teams, 154–156

social benefits to individuals, 144

stress prevention, 117

task and maintenance functions, 150–151

upper echelons, 156–158, 174

virtual teams, 143

Work value scales (WVS), 238

Work values, 66

Workaholism, 111

Work-at-home professionals, 226

Worker Well-Being initiative of Levi Strauss, 284

Workforce diversity, 312–313

Work-home conflict, 226, 303–305

Working together, 137

Working Together (Alcon Laboratories), 27

Work-life balance, 226, 248, 249, 277

Workplace aggression, 112

Workplace civility, 132–134

Workplace design, 58

Workplace deviance behavior (WDB), 90

Workplace injustice, 82

Workplace telepressure, 140

Work-related psychological disorders, 112

Work-related tension, 149

World Trade Organization (WTO), 253, 254

Wright brothers, 315

Wrigley, Bill, 150

Wriston, Walter, 158

Written communication, 138

WTO (World Trade Organization), 253, 254

WVS (work value scales), 238

Wyeth Corporate Communications, 323

Y

Yerkes-Dodson law, 111

Yes people, 215

Yetton, Phillip, 207–209

YouTube, 141, 315

Yum! Brands, 27

Z

Z problem-solving model, 163–164

Zaleznik, Abraham, 200

Zingerman's Deli, 162

Zinn, Jon Kabat, 61

Zone of indifference, 181

Zuckerberg, Mark, 42, 138, 185, 207, 276

TEST YOUR KNOWLEDGE

CHAPTER 1 Organizational Behavior and Opportunity

1. Define *organizational behavior*. What is its focus?
2. Identify the four action steps for responding positively to change.
3. What is an organization? What are its four system components? Give an example of each.
4. Briefly describe the elements of the formal and the informal organization. Give examples of each.
5. Describe how competition and total quality are affecting organizational behavior.

CHAPTER 2 Challenges for Managers

1. What are Hofstede's five dimensions of cultural differences that affect work attitudes?
2. What are the primary sources of diversity in the U.S. workforce?
3. What are the potential benefits and problems of diversity?
4. What are some of the ethical challenges encountered in organizations?
5. Describe the difference between distributive and procedural justice.

CHAPTER 3 Personality, Perception, and Attribution

1. What are individual differences, and why should managers understand them?
2. Define *personality* and describe its origins.
3. Describe two theories of personality and explain what each contributes to our knowledge of personality.
4. What factors influence social perception? What are the barriers to social perception?
5. Describe the errors that affect the attribution process.

CHAPTER 4 Attitudes, Emotions, and Ethics

1. Discuss cultural differences in job satisfaction and organizational commitment.
2. Define *values*. Distinguish between instrumental values and terminal values.
3. What is the relationship between values and ethics?
4. How does locus of control affect ethical behavior?
5. What is Machiavellianism, and how does it relate to ethical behavior?

CHAPTER 5 Motivation at Work

1. What are the five categories of motivational needs described by Maslow? Give an example of how each can be satisfied.
2. What are the Theory X and Theory Y assumptions about people at work? How do they relate to the hierarchy of needs?
3. What three manifest needs does McClelland identify?
4. How do hygiene and motivational factors differ?
5. What are two new ideas in motivation that managers are using?

CHAPTER 6 Learning and Performance Management

1. Define the terms *learning, reinforcement, punishment,* and *extinction*.
2. What are the differences in the way introverted and extraverted and intuitive and sensing people learn?
3. What are the five characteristics of well-developed goals?
4. What are the benefits of 360-degree feedback?
5. What are the two possible attributions of poor performance? What are the implications of each?

CHAPTER 7 Stress and Well-Being at Work

1. Define *stress, distress,* and *strain*.
2. Describe four approaches to understanding stress.
3. What are the four changes associated with the stress response?
4. What is a nonwork demand? How does it affect an individual?
5. What are primary prevention, secondary prevention, and tertiary prevention?

CHAPTER 8 Communication

1. Why is reflective listening important in interpersonal communication?
2. What are the five communication skills of effective supervisors and managers?
3. What are the costs of incivility and blessings of civility?
4. How does nonverbal communication affect interpersonal relationships?
5. What is communicative disease?

CHAPTER 9 Work Teams and Groups

1. What is the difference between a group and a team?
2. What are the components of Tuckman's Five-Stage Model?
3. Describe the four characteristics of mature groups.
4. Describe five task and five maintenance functions that effective work teams must perform.
5. What are the benefits and potential drawbacks of selfmanaged teams?

CHAPTER 10 Decision Making by Individuals and Groups

1. List and describe Jung's four cognitive styles.
2. What are the individual and organizational influences on creativity?
3. What are the individual and organizational foundations of empowerment and teamwork?
4. Describe the advantages and disadvantages of group decision making.
5. Describe the symptoms of groupthink, and identify actions that can be taken to prevent it.

CHAPTER 11 Power and Political Behavior

1. What are the five types of power according to French and Raven? What are their effects?
2. What is information power?
3. What are the intergroup sources of power?
4. What are the four power-oriented characteristics of the best managers?
5. What are the symbols of power according to Kanter?

CHAPTER 12 Leadership and Followership

1. Define leadership and followership.
2. Distinguish between formal leadership and informal leadership.
3. Define transformational, charismatic, and authentic leadership.
4. Describe the differences between autocratic and democratic work environments. How do they differ from a laissez-faire workplace?
5. Define initiating structure and consideration as leader behaviors.

CHAPTER 13 Conflict and Negotiation

1. Discuss the differences between functional and dysfunctional conflict.
2. Identify the structural and personal factors that contribute to conflict.
3. Discuss the four major forms of conflict in organizations.
4. What defense mechanisms do people use in interpersonal conflict?
5. Identify five styles of conflict management.

CHAPTER 14 Jobs and the Design of Work

1. Describe six patterns of working that have been studied in different countries.
2. Describe four traditional approaches to the design of work in America.
3. What are the salient features of the social information-processing (SIP) model of job design?
4. How do the Japanese, German, and Scandinavian approaches to work differ from one another and from the American approach?
5. What are five emerging issues in jobs and the design of work?

CHAPTER 15 Organizational Design and Structure

1. Define differentiation and integration.
2. Describe the six basic dimensions of organizational design.
3. Identify four forces that are reshaping organizations today.
4. Discuss the nature of emerging organizational structures.
5. List four symptoms of structural weakness.

CHAPTER 16 Organizational Culture

1. Explain the three levels of organizational culture.
2. Describe five artifacts of culture and give an example of each.
3. Explain three theories about the relationship between organizational culture and performance.
4. Contrast adaptive and nonadaptive cultures.
5. Describe the three stages of organizational socialization. How is culture communicated in each stage?

CHAPTER 17 Career Management

1. What is a realistic job preview, and why is it important?
2. What are psychological contracts?
3. What stressors are associated with socialization?
4. What are the career functions provided by a mentor?
5. What are the two key issues to deal with during the maintenance career stage?

CHAPTER 18 Managing Change

1. What are the major external and internal forces for change in organizations?
2. Contrast incremental, strategic, and transformational change.
3. Name the four behavioral reactions to change.
4. Describe force field analysis and its relationship to Lewin's change model.
5. What is organization development? Why is it undertaken by organizations?

1-1 **Define organizational behavior.** Organizational behavior is individual behavior and group dynamics in organizations. The foundation of organizational behavior is human behavior, so the study of OB involves understanding workers' behavior in terms of their history and personal value systems and examining the external factors to which a person is subject. Organizational behavior has grown out of contributions from psychology, sociology, engineering, anthropology, management, and medicine.

opportunities Favorable times or chances for progress and advancement. (p. 4)

change The transformation or modification of an organization and/or its stakeholders. (p. 4)

challenge The call to competition, contest, or battle. (p. 4)

organizational behavior The study of individual behavior and group dynamics in organizations. (p. 4)

psychology The science of human behavior. (p. 4)

sociology The science of society. (p. 4)

1-2 **Identify four action steps for responding positively in times of change.** Change is an opportunity when one has a positive attitude, asks questions, listens, and is committed to succeed. People in change situations often become rigid and reactive, rather than open and responsive. This behavior works well in the face of gradual, incremental change. However, rigid and well-learned behavior may be counterproductive responses to significant change.

engineering The applied science of energy and matter. (p. 5)

anthropology The science of human learned behavior. (p. 5)

management The study of overseeing activities and supervising people in organizations. (p. 5)

medicine The applied science of healing or treating diseases to enhance an individual's health and well-being. (p. 5)

1-3 **Identify the important system components of an organization.**

task An organization's mission, purpose, or goal for existing. (p. 6)

people The human resources of an organization. (p. 6)

technology The tools, knowledge, and/or techniques used to transform inputs into outputs. (p. 7)

structure The systems of communicaation, authority and roles, and workflow. (p. 7)

1-4 **Describe the formal and informal elements of an organization.** Organizations have formal and informal elements within them. The formal organization is the official, legitimate, and most visible part that enables people to think of organizations in logical and rational ways. The informal organization is unofficial and less visible. The informal elements of the organization are often points of diagnostic and intervention activities in organization development.

formal organization The official, legitimate, and most visible part of the system. (p. 7)

informal organization The unofficial and less visible part of the system. (p. 8)

Hawthorne studies Studies conducted during the 1920s and 1930s that suggested the importance of the informal organization. (p.8)

1-5 **Identify factors that contribute to the diversity of organizations in the economy.** The United States has the largest economy in the world. It is composed of manufacturing organizations, service organizations, privately owned companies, and nonprofit organizations; all contribute to our national well-being. Understanding a variety of organizations will help you develop a greater appreciation for your own organization and for others in the world of private business enterprises and nonprofit organizations.

1-6 **Describe the opportunities that change creates for organizational behavior.** The changes and challenges that managers face are driven by international competition and customer demands. Managers in this environment must be aware of the risks associated with downsizing and the marginalization of part-time workers. Organizations also face regular challenges in the areas of globalization, workforce diversity, ethics and character, and technological innovation.

1-7 **Demonstrate the value of objective knowledge and skill development in the study of organizational behavior.** Although organizational behavior is an applied discipline, a student is not "trained" in organizational behavior. Rather, one is "educated" in organizational behavior and is a coproducer in learning. To enrich your study of organizational behavior, take the learning style inventory on this card.

objective knowledge Knowledge that results from research and scientific activities. (p. 13)

skill development The mastery of abilities essential to successful functioning in organizations. (p. 13)

WHAT ABOUT YOU?

Learning style inventory

Directions: This 24-item survey is not timed. Answer each question as honestly as you can. Place a check on the appropriate line after each statement.

	OFTEN	SOMETIMES	SELDOM
1. Can remember more about a subject through the lecture method with information, explanations, and discussion.	___	___	___
2. Prefer information to be written on the chalkboard, with the use of visual aids and assigned readings.	___	___	___
3. Like to write things down or to take notes for visual review.	___	___	___
4. Prefer to use posters, models, or actual practice and some activities in class.	___	___	___
5. Require explanations of diagrams, graphs, or visual directions.	___	___	___
6. Enjoy working with my hands or making things.	___	___	___
7. Am skillful with and enjoy developing and making graphs and charts.	___	___	___
8. Can tell if sounds match when presented with pairs of sounds.	___	___	___
9. Remember best by writing things down several times.	___	___	___
10. Can understand and follow directions on maps.	___	___	___
11. Do better at academic subjects by listening to lectures and tapes.	___	___	___
12. Play with coins or keys in pockets.	___	___	___
13. Learn to spell better by repeating the word out loud than by writing the word on paper.	___	___	___
14. Can better understand a news development by reading about it in the paper than by listening to the radio.	___	___	___
15. Chew gum, smoke, or snack during studies.	___	___	___
16. Feel the best way to remember is to picture it in my head.	___	___	___
17. Learn spelling by "finger spelling" words.	___	___	___
18. Would rather listen to a good lecture or speech than read about the same material in a textbook.	___	___	___
19. Am good at working and solving jigsaw puzzles and mazes.	___	___	___
20. Grip objects in hands during learning period.	___	___	___
21. Prefer listening to the news on the radio rather than reading about it in the newspaper.	___	___	___
22. Obtain information on an interesting subject by reading relevant materials.	___	___	___
23. Feel comfortable touching others, hugging, hand-shaking, etc.	___	___	___
24. Follow oral directions better than written ones.	___	___	___

Scoring Procedures:

Score 5 points for each OFTEN, 3 points for each SOMETIMES, and 1 point for each SELDOM.

Visual Preference Score: 5 points each for questions 2 + 3 + 7 + 10 + 14 + 16 + 19 + 22 = ___

Auditory Preference Score: 5 points each for questions 1 + 5 + 8 + 11 + 13 + 18 + 21 + 24 = ___

Tactile Preference Score: 5 points each for questions 4 + 6 + 9 + 12 + 15 + 17 + 20 + 23 = ___

Source: Adapted from J. N. Gardner and A. J. Jewler, Your college experience: Strategies for Success, Third concise edition (Belmont, CA: Wadsworth/ITP, 1998), 62–63; E. Jensen, Student Success Secrets, 4th ed. (Hauppauge, NY: Barron's, 1996), 33–36.

CHAPTER 2 LEARNING OBJECTIVES / KEY TERMS

2-1 **Describe the factors that affect organizations competing in the global economy.** Globalization suggests that the world is free from national boundaries. In transnational organizations, the global viewpoint supersedes national issues; organizations operate across long distances and employ a multicultural mix of workers. Social and political issues affect global operations and strategy development.

transnational organization An organization in which the global viewpoint supersedes national issues. (p. 17)

guanxi The Chinese practice of building networks for social exchange. (p. 17)

expatriate manager A manager who works in a country other than her or his home country. (p. 19)

2-2 **Explain how cultural differences form the basis of work-related attitudes.** Individualistic cultures emphasize and encourage individual achievement, whereas collectivist cultures view group loyalty and unity as paramount. Other factors affecting work-related attitudes are power distance, uncertainty avoidance, masculinity versus femininity, and time orientation. Developing cross-cultural sensitivity training, cultural task forces, and global human resource management is critical to success.

individualism A cultural orientation in which people belong to loose social frameworks and their primary concern is for themselves and their families. (p. 21)

collectivism A cultural orientation in which individuals belong to tightly knit social frameworks and depend strongly on extended families or clans. (p. 21)

power distance The degree to which a culture accepts unequal distribution of power. (p. 21)

uncertainty avoidance The degree to which a culture tolerates ambiguity and uncertainty. (p. 21)

masculinity A cultural orientation in which assertiveness and materialism are valued. (p. 21)

femininity A cultural orientation in which relationships and concern for others are valued. (p. 21)

time orientation Whether a culture's values are oriented toward the future (long-term orientation) or toward the past and present (short-term orientation). (p. 22)

2-3 **Describe the challenges and positive influences diversity brings to today's business environment.** Diversity encompasses all forms of differences among individuals, including culture, gender, age, ability, religion, personality, social status, and sexual orientation. The benefits of diversity are human talent, marketing, creativity and innovation, problem solving, and flexibility. Potential problems are resistance to change, lack of cohesiveness, communication, conflicts, and decision making.

diversity All forms of difference among individuals, including culture, gender, age, ability, religion, personality, social status, and sexual orientation. (p. 22)

glass ceiling A transparent barrier that keeps women from rising above a certain level in organizations. (p. 23)

2-4 **Discuss the role of ethics, character, and personal integrity in the organization.** Ethical theories help us understand, evaluate, and classify moral arguments; make decisions; and defend conclusions about what is right and wrong. Ethical theories can be classified as consequential, rule based, or character.

consequential theory An ethical theory that emphasizes the consequences or results of behavior. (p. 28)

rule-based theory An ethical theory that emphasizes the character of the act itself rather than its effects. (p. 29)

character theory An ethical theory that emphasizes the character, personal virtues, and intent of the individual. (p. 29)

2-5 **Explain five issues that pose ethical dilemmas for managers.** Organizations experience a variety of ethical and moral dilemmas such as employee rights, sexual harassment, organizational justice, whistleblowing, and social responsibility. Managers can use ethical theories to guide them through moral choices and ethical decisions.

distributive justice The fairness of outcomes that individuals receive in an organization. (p. 31)

procedural justice The fairness of the process by which outcomes are allocated in an organization. (p. 31)

whistle-blower An employee who informs authorities of the wrongdoings of her or his company or coworkers. (p. 31)

social responsibility The obligation of an organization to behave ethically in its social environment. (p. 32)

WHAT ABOUT YOU?

Planning for a Global Career

Think of a country you would like to work in, do business in, or visit. Find out about its culture, using Hofstede's dimensions as guidelines. You can use a variety of sources to accomplish this, particularly your school library, government offices, faculty members, or others who have global experience.

Answer the following questions:

1. Is the culture individualistic or collectivist?
2. Is the power distance high or low?
3. Is uncertainty avoidance high or low?
4. Is the country masculine or feminine in its orientation?
5. Is the time orientation short term or long term?
6. How did you arrive at your answers to the first five questions?
7. How will these characteristics affect business practices in the country you chose to investigate?

3-1 **Describe individual differences and explain why they are important in understanding organizational behavior.** Individual differences are skills, abilities, personalities, perceptions, attitudes, emotions, and ethics. To understand human behavior, we must know something about the person and something about the organization, work group, personal life situation, job characteristics, and environmental influences.

interactional psychology The psychological approach to understanding human behavior that involves knowing something about the person and about the situation. (p. 34)

individual differences The way in which factors such as skills, abilities, personalities, perceptions, attitudes, values, and ethics differ from one individual to another. (p. 34)

3-2 **Articulate key personality traits and explain how they influence behavior in organizations.** Personality is an individual difference that lends consistency to a person's behavior. Two major theories, integrative approach and trait theory, state that personality affects attitude, performance, attendance, motivation, satisfaction, commitment, and occupational success at work.

personality A relatively stable set of characteristics that influence an individual's behavior. (p. 36)

trait theory A personality theory that advocates breaking down behavior patterns into a series of observable traits in order to understand human behavior. (p. 36)

integrative approach The broad theory that describes personality as a composite of an individual's psychological processes. (p. 37)

strong situation A situation that overwhelms the effects of individual personalities by providing strong cues for appropriate behavior. (p. 38)

locus of control An individual's generalized belief about internal control (self-control) versus external control (control by the situation or by others). (p. 38)

general self-efficacy An individual's general belief that he or she is capable of meeting job demands in a wide variety of situations. (p. 38)

self-esteem An individual's general feeling of self-worth. (p. 38)

self-monitoring The extent to which people base their behavior on cues from other people and situations. (p. 39)

positive affect An individual's tendency to accentuate the positive aspects of herself or himself, other people, and the world in general. (p. 39)

negative affect An individual's tendency to accentuate the negative aspects of himself or herself, other people, and the world in general. (p. 40)

3-3 **Discuss how personality theories may be applied in organizations.** Managers assess the personalities of their organizations' members with projective tests, behavioral measures, and self-report questionnaires. These tests give practical insight into the personality and psychological traits of workers such as decisionmaking skills, management style, thought processes, diversity, and tolerance.

projective test A personality test that elicits an individual's response to abstract stimuli. (p. 40)

behavioral measures Personality assessments that involve observing an individual's behavior in a controlled situation. (p. 40)

self-report questionnaire A common personality assessment that involves an individual's responses to a series of questions. (p. 40)

Myers-Briggs Type Indicator® (MBTI) instrument An instrument developed to measure Carl Jung's theory of individual differences. (p. 41)

Extraversion Being energized by interaction with other people. (p. 42)

Introversion Being energized by spending time alone. (p. 42)

Sensing Gathering information through the five senses and focusing on what actually exists. (p. 42)

Intuition Gathering information through a "sixth sense" and focusing on what could be. (p. 42)

Thinking Making decisions in a logical, objective fashion. (p. 43)

Feeling Making decisions in a personal, value-oriented way. (p. 43)

Judging Preferring closure and completion in making decisions. (p. 43)

Perceiving Preferring to explore many alternatives with flexibility and spontaneity. (p. 43)

3-4 **Define social perception and explain the factors that affect it.** Social perception is the process of interpreting information about another person. Management perceptions are affected by perceptual lenses, attitude, mood, and cognitive structure. The target's physical appearance, communication skills, and perceived intentions as well as characteristics of the situation influence perception. In an organization, virtually all management activities rely on perception.

social perception The process of interpreting information about another person. (p. 45)

discounting principle The assumption that an individual's behavior is accounted for by the situation. (p. 47)

3-5 **Identify five common barriers to social perception and explain the difficulties they cause.** In organizations, expectations of an individual affect both the manager's behavior toward the individual and the individual's response. Five barriers to social perception are selective perception, stereotyping, first-impression error, projection, and self-fulfilling prophecies. Understanding social perception in organizations may lead to favorable performance evaluations, salary increases, and help individuals compete for jobs.

selective perception The tendency to select information that supports our individual viewpoints while discounting information that threatens our viewpoints. (p. 47)

stereotype A generalization about a group of people. (p. 48)

first-impression Forming lasting opinions about an individual based on initial perceptions. (p. 48)

projection Overestimating the number of people who share our own beliefs, values, and behaviors. (p. 49)

self-fulfilling prophecy Allowing expectations about people to affect our interaction with them in such a way that those expectations are fulfilled. (p. 49)

impression management The process by which individuals try to control the impressions others have of them. (p. 49)

3-6 **Explain the attribution process and how attributions affect managerial behavior.** Attribution theory explains how we pinpoint the causes of our own behavior (and performance) and that of others. Attribution theory has many applications in the workplace. We can attribute events to an internal source of responsibility or an external source. In other words, when we succeed, we take credit for it (internal source); when we fail, we blame the situation on other people (external source).

attribution theory A theory that explains how individuals pinpoint the causes of their own and others' behavior. (p. 50)

fundamental attribution error The tendency to make attributions to internal causes when focusing on someone else's behavior. (p. 51)

self-serving bias The tendency to attribute one's successes to internal causes and one's failures to external causes. (p. 51)

4-1 **Explain the ABC model of an attitude.** Attitudes are closely linked to behavior and are an integral part of the world of work. Attitudes are a response to an entity (person, object, situation, or issue) on an affective, cognitive, or behavioral basis. People prefer consistency between attitudes and behavior. Disruption causes tension, which motivates individuals to change attitudes or behavior to maintain consistency. The tension produced by a conflict between attitudes and behavior is *cognitive dissonance.*

attitude A psychological tendency expressed by evaluating something with a degree of favor or disfavor. (p. 53)

affect The emotional component of an attitude. (p. 53)

cognitive dissonance A state of tension produced when an individual experiences conflict between attitudes and behavior. (p. 54)

4-2 **Describe how attitudes are formed.** Attitudes are learned. Influences on attitudes are direct experience and social learning. Culture also plays a definitive role in attitude development. Attitude–behavior correspondence depends on five things: attitude specificity, attitude relevance, timing of measurement, personality factors, and social constraints. Attitudes affect work behavior. Demanding jobs over which employees have little control negatively affect their work attitudes. A positive psychological climate can generate positive attitudes and good performance.

social learning The process of deriving attitudes from family, peer groups, religious organizations, and culture. (p. 55)

4-3 **Identify sources of job satisfaction and commitment.** *Job satisfaction* is a pleasurable or positive emotional state resulting from the appraisal of one's job or job experiences. It has been treated as a general attitude and as satisfaction with five specific dimensions of the job: pay, the work itself, promotion opportunities, supervision, and coworkers. Rewards are key to influencing both job satisfaction and work performance if valued by employees and tied directly to performance.

job satisfaction A pleasurable or positive emotional state resulting from the appraisal of one's job or job experiences. (p. 56)

4-4 **Distinguish between organizational citizenship and workplace deviance behaviors.** Individuals who identify strongly with the organization are more likely to perform *organizational citizenship behavior*—behavior above and beyond the call of duty. A misfit between an individual's and the organization's values is called a lack of person–organization fit. Dissatisfied workers are likely to skip work and quit jobs. *Workplace deviance behavior* is a result of negative attitudes and consists of counterproductive behavior that violates organizational norms and harms others or the organization.

organizational citizenship behavior (OCB) Behavior that is above and beyond the call of duty. (p. 57)

counterproductive work behavior Behavior that violates organizational norms and causes harm to the organization and/or employees. (p. 59)

organizational commitment The strength of an individual's identification with an organization. (p. 59)

affective commitment Organizational commitment based on an individual's desire to remain in an organization. (p. 59)

continuance commitment Organizational commitment based on the fact that an individual cannot afford to leave. (p. 59)

normative commitment Organizational commitment based on an individual's perceived obligation to remain with an organization. (p. 59)

4-5 **Identify the characteristics of the source, target, and message that affect persuasion.** Through persuasion, one individual (the source) tries to change the attitude of another person (the target). Three major characteristics of the source affect persuasion: expertise, trustworthiness, and attractiveness. Targets with low selfesteem or in a good mood are easier to persuade. Individuals with extreme attitudes or high self-esteem are more resistant. The elaboration likelihood model proposes that persuasion occurs either through a central route or peripheral route, differentiated by the amount of elaboration, scrutiny, or motivation in the message.

4-6 **Discuss the definition and importance of emotions at work.** Emotions are mental states including feelings, physiological changes, and the inclination to act and are normal parts of human functioning and decision making. Positive emotions that travel through a work group produce cooperation and task performance. The opposite also occurs when negative emotions destroy morale and performance.

emotions Mental states that include feelings, physiological changes, and the inclination to act. (p. 61)

emotional contagion A dynamic process through which the emotions of one person are transferred to another, either consciously or unconsciously, through nonverbal channels. (p. 62)

4-7 **Contrast the effects of individual and organizational influences on ethical behavior.** *Ethical behavior* is behavior that is consistent with one's personal values and the commonly held values of the organization and society. Firms with better reputations attract more applicants, creating a larger hiring pool, and evidence suggests that respected firms can choose higher-quality applicants. Unethical behavior by employees can affect individuals, work teams, and even the organization.

ethical behavior Acting in ways consistent with one's personal values and the commonly held values of the organization and society. (p. 63)

4-8 **Identify the factors that affect ethical behavior.** Factors that influence an individual's ethical behavior are values, locus of control, *Machiavellianism* (one's willingness to do whatever it takes to get one's own way), and an individual's level of *cognitive moral development*. Organizations can offer guidance by encouraging ethical behavior through codes of conduct, ethics committees, ethics communication systems, training, norms, modeling, and rewards and punishments.

values Enduring beliefs that a specific mode of conduct or end state of existence is personally or socially preferable to an opposite or converse mode of conduct or end state of existence. (p. 65)

instrumental values Values that shape the acceptable behaviors that can be used to achieve some goal or end state. (p. 66)

terminal values Values that influence the goals to be achieved or the end states of existence. (p. 66)

Machiavellianism A personality characteristic involving one's willingness to do whatever it takes to get one's own way. (p. 67)

cognitive moral development The process of moving through stages of maturity with regard to making ethical decisions. (p. 68)

CHAPTER 5 LEARNING OBJECTIVES / KEY TERMS

5-1 **Define motivation and articulate different views of how individuals are motivated at work.** *Motivation* is the process of arousing and sustaining goaldirected behavior. Motivation theories may be broadly classified into internal, process, and external theories. A comprehensive approach to understanding motivation, behavior, and performance must consider three elements of the work situation—the individual, the job, and the work environment—and how these elements interact.

motivation The process of arousing and sustaining goal-directed behavior. (p. 71)

psychoanalysis Sigmund Freud's method for delving into the unconscious mind to better understand a person's motives and needs. (p. 72)

self-interest What is in the best interest of and benefit to an individual. (p. 72)

5-2 **Explain Maslow's hierarchy of needs and its two main modifications.** Douglas McGregor used Maslow's need theory to explain motivation. McGregor's Theory X assumptions are appropriate for employees motivated by lower order needs—physiological and safety needs. Theory Y assumptions apply to employees motivated by higher order needs—social, esteem, and self-actualization. Clayton Alderfer's ERG theory of motivation grouped human needs into three basic categories: existence, relatedness, and growth. He explains both progressive need gratification and regression when people face frustration.

Theory X A set of assumptions managers might apply to individuals who are motivated by lower-order needs. (p. 74)

Theory Y A set of assumptions managers might apply to individuals who are motivated by higher-order needs. (p. 74)

ERG theory A theory that organizes human needs into the categories of existence, relatedness, and growth. (p. 74)

5-3 **Discuss how the needs for achievement, power, and affiliation influence an individual's behavior in the workplace.** David McClelland identified three learned or acquired needs, called manifest needs. The *need for achievement* encompasses excellence, competition, challenging goals, persistence, and overcoming difficulties. The *need for power* includes the desire to influence others, the urge to change people or events, and the wish to make a difference in life. The *need for affiliation* means an urge to establish and maintain warm, close, intimate relationships with others.

manifest needs Learned or acquired needs that are easily perceived. (p. 75)

need for achievement A manifest need that concerns excellence, competition, challenging goals, persistence, and overcoming difficulties. (p. 75)

need for power A manifest need that concerns the desire to influence others, change people or events, and make a difference in life. (p. 76)

need for affiliation A manifest need to establish and maintain warm, close, intimate relationships with other people. (p. 77)

5-4 **Describe the two-factor theory of motivation.** Frederick Herzberg's two-factor theory examined experiences that satisfied or dissatisfied people at work. Motivation factors relate to job satisfaction; hygiene factors relate to job dissatisfaction. Motivation factors are responsibility, achievement, recognition, advancement, and the work itself. Hygiene factors are company policy and administration, technical supervision, salary, interpersonal relations with one's supervisor, working conditions, salary, and status. Excellent hygiene factors result in employees being *not dissatisfied*.

motivation factor A work condition that satisfies the need for psychological growth. (p. 77)

hygiene factor A work condition that generates dissatisfaction due to discomfort or pain. (p. 77)

5-5 **Explain two new ideas in human motivation.** Positive organizational scholarship links eustress to investing in strengths, finding positive meaning in work, displaying courage and principled action, and drawing on positive emotions at work. A second idea, by Jim Loehr, centers on positive energy and full engagement. This approach suggests that individuals do not need to be activated by fulfilling unmet needs but are already activated by their own physical, emotional, mental, and spiritual energy.

eustress Healthy, normal stress. (p. 78)

CHAPTER REVIEW

CHAPTER 5 LEARNING OBJECTIVES / KEY TERMS

5-6 **Describe the role of inequity in motivation.** Equity theory is a social exchange process theory of motivation that focuses on the individual–environment interaction. Individuals and organizations want an equitable arrangement for both members of the relationship. Inequity occurs when a person receives more, or less, than the person believes is deserved based on effort and/or contribution.

inequity A situation in which a person perceives that he or she is receiving less than he or she is giving or is giving less than he or she is receiving. (p. 80)

equity sensitive An individual who prefers an equity ratio equal to that of his or her comparison other. (p. 81)

benevolent An individual who is comfortable with an equity ratio less than that of his or her comparison other. (p. 82)

entitled An individual who is comfortable with an equity ratio greater than that of his or her comparison other. (p. 82)

5-7 **Describe the expectancy theory of motivation.** Vroom's expectancy theory of motivation focuses on personal perceptions of the performance process. The key constructs in the expectancy theory of motivation are *valence, expectancy,* and *instrumentality.* Valence is the value or importance one places on a particular reward. Expectancy is the belief that effort leads to performance. Instrumentality is the belief that performance is related to rewards.

valence The value or importance one places on a particular reward. (p. 83)

expectancy The belief that effort leads to performance. (p. 83)

instrumentality The belief that performance is related to rewards. (p. 83)

moral maturity The measure of a person's cognitive moral development. (p. 84)

5-8 **Describe the cultural differences in motivation.** Most motivation theories in use today have been developed by and about Americans. When researchers have examined the universality of these theories, they have found that the studies did not replicate the results found in the United States due to cultural differences.

6

CHAPTER 6 LEARNING OBJECTIVES / KEY TERMS

6-1 **Describe behavioral theories of learning.** The behaviorist approach to learning assumes that observable behavior is a function of its consequences. Behaviorists argue that learning stems from classical and operant conditioning. *Classical conditioning* is the process of modifying behavior so that pairing a conditioned stimulus with an unconditioned stimulus elicits an unconditioned response. *Operant conditioning* is the process of modifying behavior by following specific behaviors with positive or negative consequences. Reinforcement enhances desirable behavior, while punishment and extinction diminish undesirable behavior.

learning A change in behavior acquired through experience. (p. 87)

classical conditioning Modifying behavior by pairing a conditioned stimulus with an unconditioned stimulus to elicit an unconditioned response. (p. 87)

operant conditioning Modifying behavior through the use of positive or negative consequences following specific behaviors. (p. 88)

positive consequences Results of a behavior that a person finds attractive or pleasurable. (p. 88)

negative consequences Results of a behavior that a person finds unattractive or aversive. (p. 88)

reinforcement A strategy to cultivate desirable behavior by either bestowing positive consequences or withholding negative consequences. (p. 89)

punishment A strategy to discourage undesirable behavior by either bestowing negative consequences or withholding positive consequences. (p. 90)

extinction A strategy to weaken a behavior by attaching no consequences to it. (p. 90)

6-2 **Describe social and cognitive theories of learning.** The social learning theory occurs when we observe other people and model their behavior. Central to the theory is the notion of *task-specific self-efficacy*, an individual's beliefs and expectancies about his or her ability to perform a task effectively. In the cognitive theory, the personality functions of intuition, sensing, thinking, and feeling have learning implications. Each person has a preferred mode of gathering, evaluating, and making decisions about information.

task-specific self-efficacy An individual's internal expectancy to perform a specific task effectively. (p. 91)

6-3 **Explain how goal setting can be used to direct learning and performance.** *Goal setting* is the process of establishing desired results that guide and direct behavior. Goals often increase employee effort and motivation, which in turn improve task performance. Goal setting also reduces the role of stress associated with conflicting and confusing expectations because it clarifies the task–role expectations for employees. The third major function of goal setting is improving the accuracy and validity of performance evaluation.

goal setting The process of establishing desired results that guide and direct behavior. (p. 92)

management by objectives (MBO) A goal-setting program based on interaction and negotiation between employees and managers. (p. 93)

6-4 **Define performance and identify the tools used to measure it.** Performance is most often called task accomplishment. *Performance management* is a process of defining, measuring, appraising, providing feedback on, and improving performance. Performance appraisals give employees feedback on performance, identify the employees' developmental needs, and influence promotion and reward decisions, demotion and termination decisions, and information about selection and placement decisions. Electronic performance-monitoring systems, goal setting, and MBO are performance appraisal methods.

performance management A process of defining, measuring, appraising, providing feedback on, and improving performance. (p. 95)

performance appraisal The evaluation of a person's performance. (p. 95)

CHAPTER REVIEW

CHAPTER 6 LEARNING OBJECTIVES / KEY TERMS

6-5 **Explain the importance of performance feedback and how it can be delivered effectively.** Good performance appraisal systems develop people, enhance careers, and boost individual and team achievements in an organization. Effective performance appraisal systems have five key characteristics: validity, reliability, responsiveness, flexibility, and equitability. The supervisor must establish mutual trust, be vulnerable and open to challenge, and be a skilled, empathetic listener who encourages employees to discuss their aspirations.

360-degree feedback A process of self-evaluation and evaluations by a manager, peers, direct reports, and possibly customers. (p. 97)

6-6 **Identify ways managers can reward performance.** Performance rewards can be pay, rewards, trust, fun, and meaningful work. Individual reward systems foster autonomous, independent behavior; and encourage creativity, problem solving, and distinctive contributions. At the individual level, these include skill-based and pay-for-knowledge systems. Team reward systems encourage cooperation, joint efforts, and the sharing of information and expertise. At the group level, gain-sharing plans emphasize collective cost reduction by allowing workers to share in the gains achieved by reducing production costs.

6-7 **List several strategies for correcting poor performance.** Harold Kelley's attribution theory aims to explain behavior based on shared perceptions and attitudes between supervisors and employees. Internal attributions might include low effort, lack of commitment, or lack of ability. External attributions might include equipment failure or unrealistic goals. Supervisors may express personal concern, reprimand the employee, or provide training. They may provide coaching, counseling, mentoring, or refer the employee to trained professionals

consensus An informational cue indicating the extent to which peers in the same situation behave in a similar fashion. (p. 100)

distinctiveness An informational cue indicating the degree to which an individual behaves the same way in other situations. (p. 100)

consistency An informational cue indicating the frequency of behavior over time. (p. 100)

mentoring A work relationship that encourages development and career enhancement for people moving through the career cycle. (p. 101)

CHAPTER 7 LEARNING OBJECTIVES / KEY TERMS

7-1 **Define stress, distress, and strain.** *Stress*, or the stress response, is the unconscious preparation to fight or flee experienced when faced with any demand. A *stressor*, or demand, is the person or event triggering the stress response. *Distress* or *strain* refers to adverse psychological, physical, behavioral, and organizational consequences that may occur as a result of stressful events.

stress The unconscious preparation to fight or flee that a person experiences when faced with any demand. (p. 104)

stressor The person or event that triggers the stress response. (p. 104)

distress The adverse psychological, physical, behavioral, and organizational consequences that may arise as a result of stressful events. (p. 105)

strain Distress. (p. 105)

7-2 **Compare four different approaches to stress.** There are four principal approaches to stress. Walter B. Cannon developed the homeostatic/medical approach because he believed stress resulted when an external, environmental demand upset the *homeostasis*. Richard Lazarus's cognitive appraisal approach saw stress as a result of a person–environment interaction, yet emphasized cognitive appraisal in classifying persons or events as stressful. Robert Kahn's person–environment fit approach claimed that confusing and conflicting expectations of social roles create stress. Harry Levinson's psychoanalytic approach believed the *ego-ideal* and the *self-image* interact to cause stress.

homeostasis A steady state of bodily functioning and equilibrium. (p. 106)

ego-ideal The embodiment of a person's perfect self. (p. 106)

self-image How a person sees himself or herself, both positively and negatively. (p. 106)

7-3 **Explain the psychophysiology of the stress response.** The stress response begins with the release of chemical messengers, primarily adrenaline, into the bloodstream. These messengers activate the sympathetic nervous system and endocrine (hormone) system to trigger mind–body changes to prepare the person for fight or flight. As the body responds, the person shifts from a neutral posture to an offensive posture.

7-4 **Identify work and nonwork causes of stress.** Major categories of work demands that cause stress are role conflict, role ambiguity, task demands, role demands, interpersonal demands, and physical demands. Nonwork demands may broadly be identified as home demands from an individual's personal life environment and personal demands that are self-imposed

workaholism An imbalanced preoccupation with work at the expense of home and personal life satisfaction. (p. 111)

7-5 **Describe the consequences of stress.** Positive stress can create *eustress*, while negative stress, or distress, can erode morale and performance. Three forms of individual distress are: *psychological distress*, *medical illnesses*, and *behavioral problems*. The symptoms of *organizational stress* are: low morale, dissatisfaction, communication breakdowns, and disruption of working relationships. Three major costs of *organizational distress* are: participation problems, performance decrements, and compensation awards.

participation problem A cost associated with absenteeism, tardiness, strikes and work stoppages, and turnover. (p. 113)

performance decrement A cost resulting from poor quality or low quantity of production, grievances, and unscheduled machine downtime and repair. (p. 113)

compensation award An organizational cost resulting from court awards for job distress. (p. 113)

7-6 **Discuss individual factors that influence a person's response to stress and strain.** Individual differences, such as gender and Type A behavior pattern, enhance vulnerability to strain under stressful conditions. Other individual differences, such as personality hardiness and self-reliance, reduce vulnerability to strain under stressful condition.

Type A behavior pattern A complex of personality and behavioral characteristics, including competitiveness, time urgency, social status insecurity, aggression, hostility, and a quest for achievements. (p. 114)

personality hardiness A personality characterized by commitment, control, and challenge and, hence, resistant to distress. (p. 115)

transformational coping A way of managing stressful events by changing them into less subjectively stressful events. (p. 115)

self-reliance A healthy, secure, interdependent pattern of behavior related to how people form and maintain supportive attachments with others. (p. 115)

counterdependence An unhealthy, insecure pattern of behavior that leads to separation in relationships with other people. (p. 115)

overdependence An unhealthy, insecure pattern of behavior that leads to preoccupied attempts to achieve security through relationships. (p. 115)

CHAPTER REVIEW

CHAPTER 7 LEARNING OBJECTIVES / KEY TERMS

7-7 **Identify the stages and elements of preventive stress management for individuals and organizations.** The three stages of prevention are primary, secondary, and tertiary prevention. *Primary prevention* is intended to reduce, modify, or eliminate the demand or stressor causing stress. *Secondary prevention* is intended to alter or modify the individual's or the organization's response to a demand or stressor. *Tertiary prevention* is intended to heal individual or organizational symptoms of distress and strain.

preventive stress management An organizational philosophy according to which people and organizations should take joint responsibility for promoting health and preventing distress and strain. (p. 116)

primary prevention The stage in preventive stress management designed to reduce, modify, or eliminate the demand or stressor causing stress. (p. 116)

secondary prevention The stage in preventive stress management designed to alter or modify the individual's or the organization's response to a demand or stressor. (p. 116)

tertiary prevention The stage in preventive stress management designed to heal individual or organizational symptoms of distress and strain. (p. 116)

8-1 **Describe the interpersonal communication process and the role of listening in the process.** Interpersonal communication is reflective, objective, and perceptual. The conceptual and emotional component of messages is affected by verbal and nonverbal communication and is key to understanding and verifying the message. Reflective listening enables the listener to understand the communicator's meaning, reduce perceptual distortions, and overcome interpersonal barriers that lead to communication failures.

communication The evoking of a shared or common meaning in another person. (p. 124)

interpersonal communication Communication between two or more people in an organization. (p. 124)

communicator The person sending a message. (p. 125)

receiver The person accepting a message. (p. 125)

perceptual screen A window through which one interacts with others. It influences the quality, accuracy, and clarity of the communication. (p. 125)

message The thoughts and feelings that the communicator is attempting to evoke in the receiver. (p. 125)

feedback Information fed back that completes two-way communication. (p. 126)

language The words, their pronunciations, and the methods of combining them used and understood by a group of people. (p. 126)

data Uninterpreted and unanalyzed elements of a message. (p. 126)

information Data that have been interpreted, analyzed, and have meaning to some user. (p. 126)

richness The ability of a medium to convey meaning to a receiver. (p. 126)

employee voice behavior communication of suggestions, concerns, information about problems, or work-related opinions to effect constructive changes in the workplace. (p. 126)

reflective listening Carefully listening to message and immediately repeating it back to the speaker. (p. 126)

two-way communication An interactive form of communication in which there is an exchange of thoughts, feelings, or both. (p. 129)

one-way communication Communication in which a person sends a message to another person and no feedback, questions, or interaction follows. (p. 129)

8-2 **Describe the five communication skills of effective supervisors.** Five communication skills that distinguish "good" from "bad" supervisors include being expressive speakers, empathetic listeners, persuasive leaders, sensitive people, and informative managers.

8-3 **Explain five communication barriers and the gateways through them.** Barriers to communication in the workplace are physical separation, status differences, gender differences, cultural diversity, and language. Awareness and recognition are the first steps to overcoming barriers. Other gateways are recognizing differences in gender-specific conversation style, understanding cultural differences, and avoiding technical terms and jargon.

barriers to communication Factors that distort, disrupt, or even halt successful communication. (p. 130)

gateways to communication Openings that break down communication barriers. (p. 130)

8-4 **Distinguish between civility and incivility, and defensive and nondefensive communication.** *Civility* is communication that respects the integrity and dignity of the individual. It carries the potential to avoid hurt feelings, prevent harm and damage to working relationships, and contribute to well-being in the workplace. *Incivility* is communication that respects the integrity and dignity of the individual. It can create a barrier between people and jar emotions, though the consequences of incivility depend on its source. *Defensive communication* includes aggressive and angry communication as well as passive, withdrawing communication. *Nondefensive communication* is an assertive, direct, powerful form of communication.

incivility Discourteous communication and rude behavior that are disrespectful, hurtful, or injurious. (p. 132)

civility Communication and behavior that respect the integrity and dignity of the individual. (p. 132)

defensive communication Messages that are aggressive, malevolent, passive, or withdrawn. (p.133)

nondefensive communication Messages that are assertive, direct, and powerful. (p. 133)

CHAPTER REVIEW

CHAPTER 8 LEARNING OBJECTIVES / KEY TERMS

8-5 Explain the impact of nonverbal communication. Most meaning in a message is conveyed nonverbally. *Nonverbal communication* includes all elements of communication, such as gestures and the use of space, that do not involve words or language. The four basic kinds of nonverbal communication that managers need to understand and read are proxemics, kinesics, facial and eye behavior, and paralanguage.

nonverbal communication All elements of communication that do not involve words or language. (p. 134)

proxemics The study of an individual's perception and use of space. (p. 135)

territorial space Bands of concentric space radiating outward from the body. (p. 135)

kinesics The study of body movement and posture. (p. 136)

8-6 Explain positive, healthy communication. James Lynch suggests that heartfelt communication may be equally or more important than cognition in the communication process. According to Lynch, positive, healthy communication is exemplified by trust and truthfulness, core values and beliefs, strong ethical character, personal integrity, openness, and simplicity in communication.

communicative disease Loneliness and social isolation resulting from the absence of heartfelt communication in relationships. (p. 137)

8-7 Identify how new communication technologies and social media affect the communication process. Technologies such as cell phones, e-mail, voice mail, faxes, computers, and informational databases provide instant exchange of volumes of information and render geographic boundaries and time zones irrelevant. Lack of personal interaction and nonverbal cues alter the social context of exchange and remove organizational barriers. The potential for information overload, constant accessibility to work, and multitasking also affects behavior.

information communication technology (ICT) An extensive category of new developments in interpersonal communication that allow fast, even immediate, access to information. (p. 139)

CHAPTER 9 LEARNING OBJECTIVES / KEY TERMS

9-1 **Define group and work team.** A *group* is two or more people having common interests, objectives, and continuing interaction. A *work team* is a group of people with complementary skills who are committed to a common mission, performance goals, and approach for which they hold themselves mutually accountable.

group Two or more people with common interests, objectives, and continuing interaction. (p. 143)

work team A group of people with complementary skills who are committed to a common mission, performance goals, and approach for which they hold themselves mutually accountable. (p. 143)

9-2 **Explain the benefits organizations and individuals derive from working in teams.** Teams are very useful in performing work that is complicated, complex, interrelated, and/or more voluminous than one person can handle. Teams combine the knowledge, talent, skills, and abilities of individual members and integrate effort for task accomplishment. On an individual level, members benefit from psychological intimacy and achieving integrated involvement.

teamwork Joint action by a team of people in which individual interests are subordinated to team unity. (p. 144)

psychological intimacy Emotional and psychological closeness to other team or group members. (p. 144)

integrated involvement Closeness achieved through tasks and activities. (p. 144)

9-3 **Identify the factors that influence group behavior.** *Group norms* of cooperative behavior facilitate team performance and effectiveness. *Group cohesion* can enhance job satisfaction and improve productivity. *Social loafing*—member failure to contribute time, effort, thoughts, or other resources to a group—may negate the group's efforts and achievements. With loss of individuality, members may lose their sense of accountability, inhibition, and responsibility for individual behavior.

norms of behavior The standards that a work group uses to evaluate the behavior of its members. (p. 145)

group cohesion The interpersonal glue that makes members of a group stick together. (p. 145)

Social loafing The failure of a group member to contribute personal time, effort, thoughts, or other resources to the group. (p. 145)

loss of individuality A social process in which individualgroup members lose self-awareness and its accompanying sense of accountability, inhibition, and responsibility for individual behavior. (p. 145)

9-4 **Describe how groups form and develop.** Groups, formal and informal, go through stages of development to become mature and productive units. Mature groups work through the necessary interpersonal, task, and authority issues to achieve at high levels. According to this group development model, a group addresses three issues: interpersonal issues, task issues, and authority issues.

status structure The set of authority and task relations among a group's members. (p. 150)

FIGURE 9.1 **TUCKMAN'S FIVE-STAGE MODEL OF GROUP DEVELOPMENT**

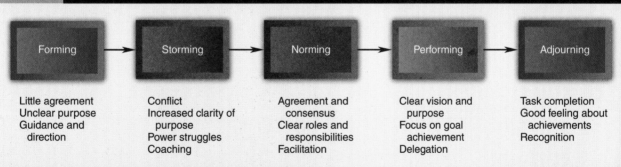

Forming	Storming	Norming	Performing	Adjourning
Little agreement Unclear purpose Guidance and direction	Conflict Increased clarity of purpose Power struggles Coaching	Agreement and consensus Clear roles and responsibilities Facilitation	Clear vision and purpose Focus on goal achievement Delegation	Task completion Good feeling about achievements Recognition

9-5 **Explain how task and maintenance functions influence group performance.** Effective groups carry out various task functions to perform work successfully and do maintenance functions to ensure member satisfaction and a sense of team spirit. Teams that successfully fulfill these functions afford members the potential for the social benefits of psychological intimacy and integrated involvement.

task function An activity directly related to the effective completion of a team's work. (p. 150)

maintenance function An activity essential to effective, satisfying interpersonal relationships within a team or group. (p. 151)

9-6 **Discuss the factors that influence group effectiveness.** Work team effectiveness in the new team environment requires management's attention to both work team structure and work team process. In addition to how the team is structured and what the team does, diversity and creativity are two areas with significant impact on team performance.

9-7 **Describe how empowerment relates to self-managed teams.** Empowerment, an organizational attribute, encourages participation, an essential ingredient for teamwork. Empowered *self-managed teams*, designed to take on responsibilities and address issues traditionally reserved for management, succeed through development of competence skills, process skills, communication skills, and cooperative and helping behaviors.

self-managed team A team that makes decisions that were once reserved for managers. (p.155)

9-8 **Explain the importance of upper echelons and top management teams.** Self-managed teams at the top of the organization are referred to as *upper echelons*. Organizations are often a reflection of these *upper echelons*. Upper echelon theory argues that background characteristics of the top management team can predict organizational characteristics and set standards for values, competence, ethics, and unique characteristics throughout the organization.

upper echelon A top-level executive team in an organization. (p. 156)

CHAPTER 10 LEARNING OBJECTIVES / KEY TERMS

10-1 **Identify the steps in the decision-making process.** The decision-making process involves *programmed decisions* and *nonprogrammed decisions*. The first step is recognizing the problem or realizing a decision must be made. Second, the objective of the decision is identified. The third step is gathering information relevant to the problem. The fourth step is listing and evaluating alternative courses of action. Finally, the manager selects the alternative that best meets the decision objective.

programmed decision A simple, routine matter for which a manager has an established decision rule. (p. 160)

nonprogrammed decision A new, complex decision that requires a creative solution. (p. 160)

10-2 **Describe various models of decision making.** The *rational model* of decision making contends that the decision maker is completely rational in his or her approach. *Bounded rationality* theory suggests that constraints force decision makers to be less rational and assumes that managers satisfice and develop heuristics. The *Z problem-solving model* capitalizes on the strengths of four separate preferences (Sensing, Intuiting, Thinking, and Feeling), allowing managers to use preferences and nonpreferences to make decisions

effective decision A timely decision that meets a desired objective and is acceptable to those individuals affected by it. (p. 162)

rationality A logical, step-by-step approach to decision making, with a thorough analysis of alternatives and their consequences. (p. 163)

bounded rationality A theory that suggests that there are limits to how rational a decision maker can actually be. (p. 163)

satisfice To select the first alternative that is "good enough," because the costs in time and effort are too great to optimize. (p. 163)

heuristics Shortcuts in decision making that save mental activity. (p. 163)

escalation of commitment The tendency to continue to support a failing course of action. (p. 164)

10-3 **Discuss the individual influences that affect decision making.** Decisions reflect the people who make them. The individual influences that affect decision making are comfort with risk, cognitive style, personality, intuition, and creativity.

cognitive style An individual's preferred method for gathering information and evaluating alternatives. (p. 165)

risk aversion The tendency to choose options that entail fewer risks and less uncertainty. (p. 166)

intuition A fast, positive force in decision making that is utilized at a level below consciousness and involves learned patterns of information. (p. 166)

creativity A process influenced by individual and organizational factors that results in the production of novel and useful ideas, products, or both. (p. 168)

FIGURE 10.1 **THE DECISION-MAKING PROCESS**

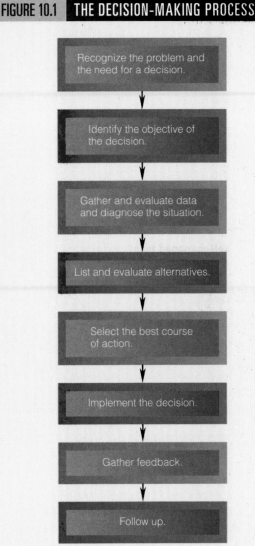

Recognize the problem and the need for a decision.

Identify the objective of the decision.

Gather and evaluate data and diagnose the situation.

List and evaluate alternatives.

Select the best course of action.

Implement the decision.

Gather feedback.

Follow up.

© Cengage Learning

10-4 **Explain how groups make decisions.** Group decisions are utilized for several reasons: to achieve *synergy*, to gain commitment to a decision, and to maximize knowledge and experience in problem-solving situations. Seven techniques utilized in group decisions are brainstorming, nominal group technique, devil's advocacy, dialectical inquiry, quality circles and quality teams, and self-managed teams.

synergy A positive force that occurs in groups when group members are stimulated to produce new solutions to problems through the process of mutual influence and encouragement within the group. (p. 170)

social decision schemes Simple rules used to determine final group decisions. (p. 170)

groupthink A deterioration of mental efficiency, reality testing, and moral judgment resulting from pressures within the group. (p. 171)

group polarization The tendency for group discussion to produce shifts toward more extreme attitudes among members. (p. 173)

brainstorming A technique for generating as many ideas as possible on a given subject while suspending evaluation until all the ideas have been suggested. (p. 173)

nominal group technique (NGT) A structured approach to group decision making that focuses on generating alternatives and choosing one. (p. 174)

devil's advocacy A technique for preventing groupthink in which a group or individual is given the role of critic during decision making. (p. 174)

dialectical inquiry A debate between two opposing sets of recommendations. (p. 174)

quality circle A small group of employees who work voluntarily on company time, typically one hour per week, to address work-related problems such as quality control, cost reduction, production planning and techniques, and even product design. (p. 175)

quality team A team that is part of an organization's structure and is empowered to act on its decisions regarding product and service quality. (p. 175)

10-5 **Describe the role culture plays in decision making.** Styles of decision making vary greatly among cultures and affect the way people view decisions. The dimensions proposed by Hofstede in Chapter 2 that affect decision making are: uncertainty avoidance, power distance, individualism/collectivism, time orientation, masculinity/femininity, cultural diversity, functional background, and strategic decision making.

10-6 **Explain how organizations can improve the quality of decisions through participation.** *Participative decision making* can include employees identifying problems, generating alternatives, selecting solutions, planning implementations, and/or evaluating results. Participative management can increase employee creativity, job satisfaction, and productivity, and improve a company's economic performance.

participative decision making. Decision making in which individuals who are affected by decisions influence the making of those decisions. (p. 176)

CHAPTER 11 LEARNING OBJECTIVES / KEY TERMS

11-1 **Describe the concept of power.** Power is the ability to influence others. Influence is the process of affecting the thoughts, behavior, and feelings of others. Authority is the right to influence others. Power is an exchange relationship.

power The ability to influence another person. (p. 180)

influence The process of affecting the thoughts, behavior, and feelings of another person. (p. 180)

authority The right to influence another person. (p. 180)

zone of indifference The range in which attempts to influence a person will be perceived as legitimate and will be acted on without a great deal of thought. (p. 181)

11-2 **Identify forms and sources of power in organizations.** Power in organizations can be categorized simply as interpersonal or intergroup. French and Raven's five forms of interpersonal power are reward, coercive, legitimate, referent, and expert power. Information power is another form of interpersonal power. Intergroup power derives from control of critical resources and of strategic contingencies. To have control over contingencies, a group must be able to cope with uncertainty, have a high degree of centrality, and perform a function indispensable to the organization.

reward power Power based on an agent's ability to control rewards that a target wants. (p. 182)

coercive power Power that is based on an agent's ability to cause an unpleasant experience for a target. (p. 182)

legitimate power Power that is based on position and mutual agreement; agent and target agree that the agent has the right to influence the target. (p. 182)

referent power An elusive power that is based on interpersonal attraction. (p. 182)

expert power The power that exists when an agent has specialized knowledge or skills that the target needs. (p. 182)

strategic contingencies Activities that other groups depend on in order to complete their tasks. (p. 183)

11-3 **Describe the role of ethics in using power.** The key to using all of these types of power well is to use them ethically. McClelland believes personal power is negative and social power is positive. That is, when power is used for the good of the group rather than for individual gain, the power is positive.

information power Access to and control over important information. (p. 184)

personal power Power used for personal gain. (p. 186)

social power Power used to create motivation or to accomplish group goals. (p. 186)

11-4 **Identify symbols of power and powerlessness in organizations.** Two theorists examine symbols of power: Rosabeth Moss Kanter's list of symbols is grounded in doing things for others: for people in trouble, for employees, for bosses. There is an active, other-directed element in her symbols. Michael Korda's list focuses on status and whether there are more people for whom you would inconvenience yourself than people who would inconvenience themselves for you.

powerlessness A lack of power. (p. 187)

11-5 **Define organizational politics and understand the role of political skill and major influence tactics.** Organizational politics is an inevitable feature of work life. Political behavior consists of actions not officially sanctioned that are taken to influence others in order to meet personal goals. Managers should take a proactive role in managing politics. Political skill is the ability to get things done through favorable interpersonal relationships outside formally prescribed organizational mechanisms.

organizational politics The use of power and influence in organizations. (p. 188)

political behavior Actions not officially sanctioned by an organization that are taken to influence others in order to meet one's personal goals. (p. 188)

political skill The ability to get things done through favorable interpersonal relationships outside formally prescribed organizational mechanisms. (p. 191)

11-6 **Identify ways to manage political behavior in organizations.** To manage political behavior in their employees, managers can: use open communication; clarify expectations regarding employee performance; use participative management techniques; encourage cooperation among work groups; manage scarce resources well; and provide a supportive organizational climate. Individuals must also manage up—that is, manage the boss. The biggest trump to political behavior is empowerment.

empowerment Sharing power in such a way that individuals learn to believe in their ability to do the job. (p. 194)

FIGURE 11.1 **EMPLOYEE EMPOWERMENT GRID**

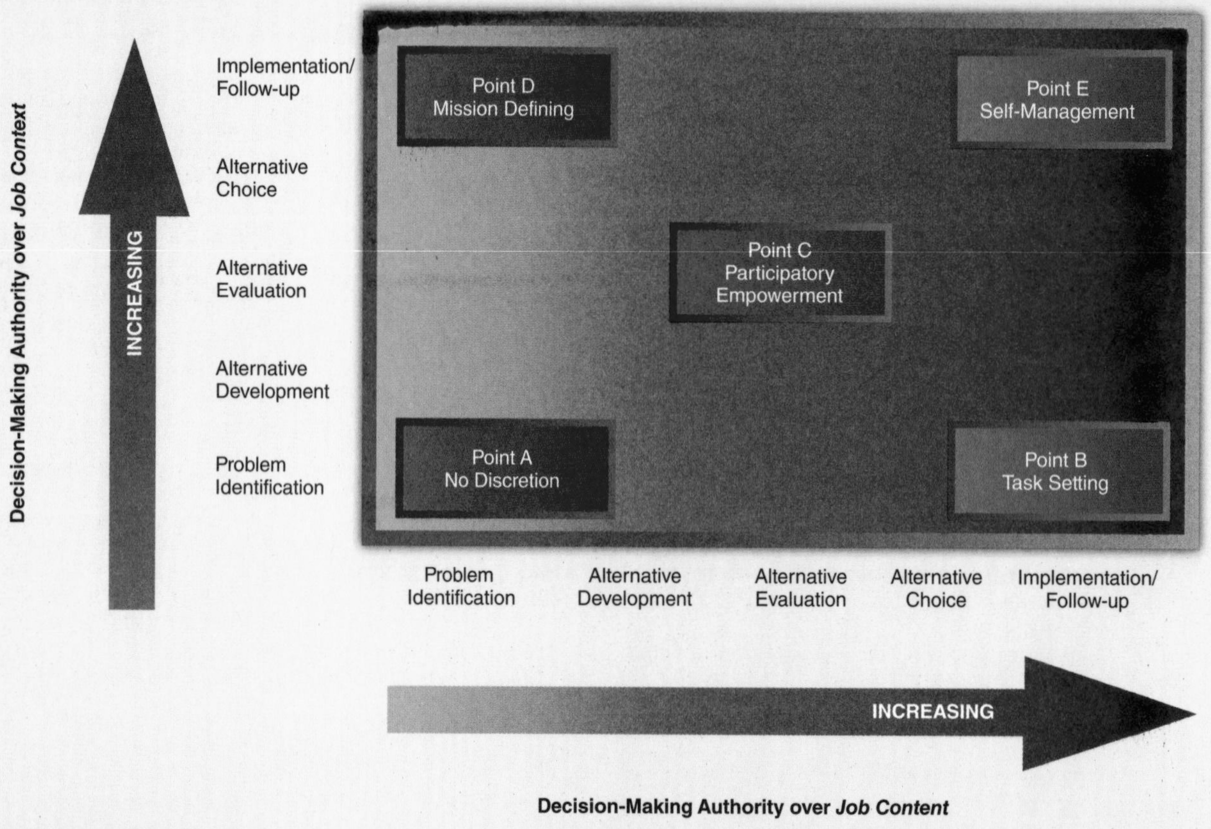

Decision-Making Authority over *Job Context*

INCREASING

- Implementation/ Follow-up
- Alternative Choice
- Alternative Evaluation
- Alternative Development
- Problem Identification

Point D
Mission Defining

Point E
Self-Management

Point C
Participatory
Empowerment

Point A
No Discretion

Point B
Task Setting

| Problem Identification | Alternative Development | Alternative Evaluation | Alternative Choice | Implementation/ Follow-up |

INCREASING

Decision-Making Authority over *Job Content*

12-1 **Discuss the differences between leadership and management and between leaders and managers.** Leadership is the process of guiding and directing behavior of people in the work environment. The management process reduces uncertainty and stabilizes an organization. *Leaders* agitate for change and new approaches; in contrast, *managers* advocate stability and the status quo. They differ along four separate dimensions of personality: attitudes toward goals, conceptions of work, relationships with other people, and sense of self.

leadership The process of guiding and directing the behavior of people in the work environment. (p. 198)

formal leadership Officially sanctioned leadership based on the authority of a formal position. (p. 198)

informal leadership Unofficial leadership accorded to a person by other members of the organization. (p. 198)

leaders An advocate for change and new approaches to problems. (p. 200)

managers An advocate for stability and the status quo. (p. 200)

12-2 **Explain the role of trait theory in describing leaders.** The first studies of leadership attempted to identify what physical attributes, personality characteristics, and abilities distinguished leaders from other members of a group. The trait theories have had very limited success in being able to identify the universal, distinguishing attributes of leaders.

12-3 **Describe the role of foundational behavioral research in the development of leadership theories.** Behavioral theories address how leaders behave. The Lewin, Lippitt, and White studies identified three basic leadership styles: autocratic, democratic, and laissez-faire. Ohio State University measured specific leader behaviors—initiating structure and consideration. The University of Michigan studies suggested two styles of leadership: employee oriented and production oriented.

autocratic style A style of leadership in which the leader uses strong, directive actions to control the rules, regulations, activities, and relationships in the work environment. (p. 201)

democratic style A style of leadership in which the leader uses interaction and collaboration with followers to direct the work and work environment. (p. 201)

laissez-faire style A style of leadership in which the leader has a hands-off approach. (p. 201)

initiating structure Leader behavior aimed at defining and organizing work relationships and roles, as well as establishing clear patterns of organization, communication, and ways of getting things done. (p. 202)

consideration Leader behavior aimed at nurturing friendly, warm working relationships as well as encouraging mutual trust and interpersonal respect within the work unit. (p. 202)

leadership grid An approach to understanding a leader's or manager's concern for results (production) and concern for people. (p. 202)

organization man manager (5,5) A middle-of-the-road leader. (p. 203)

authority-compliance manager (9,1) A leader who emphasizes efficient production. (p. 204)

country club manager (1,9) A leader who has great concern for people and little concern for production, attempts to avoid conflict, and seeks to be well liked. (p. 204)

team manager (9,9) A leader who builds a highly productive team of committed people. (p. 204)

impoverished manager (1,1) A leader who exerts just enough effort to get by. (p. 204)

paternalistic father-knows-best manager (9+9) A leader who promises reward and threatens punishment. (p. 204)

opportunistic what's-in-it-for-me manager (Opp) A leader who uses whichever style will maximize self-benefit. (p. 204)

12-4 **Describe and compare the four contingency theories of leadership.** Fiedler's contingency theory proposes that the fit between the leader's need structure and the favorableness of the leader's situation determine the team's effectiveness in work accomplishment. The role of the leader in path–goal theory is to clear the follower's path to the goal. In normative decision theory, leaders and managers determine the appropriate level of employee participation in decision making, and the Situational Leadership theory suggests that the leader's behavior should be adjusted to the maturity level of the followers.

least preferred coworker (LPC) The person a leader has least preferred to work with. (p. 205)

task structure The degree of clarity, or ambiguity, in the work activities assigned to the group. (p. 205)

position power The authority associated with the leader's formal position in the organization. (p. 205)

leader–member relations The quality of interpersonal relationships among a leader and the group members. (p. 205)

12-5 **Discuss the recent developments in leadership theory of leader–member exchange and inspirational leadership.** With leader–member exchange theory (LMX), leaders form *in-groups* whose members work within the leader's inner circle and *out-groups* whose members are outside the circle. In-group members receive greater responsibilities, more rewards, and more attention. Inspirational leadership theories—*transformational leadership, charismatic leadership,* and *authentic leadership*—can result in positive, productive member behavior because followers are inspired by the leader to perform well.

charismatic leadership A leader's use of personal abilities and talents to have profound and extraordinary effects on followers. (p. 211)

12-6 **Discuss how issues of emotional intelligence, trust, gender, and servant leadership are informing today's leadership models.** All workers must be aware of emerging leadership issues such as emotional intelligence, trust, women leaders, and servant leadership. These trait studies can affect leaders' decision-making skills, strategy implementation, and ability to build organizational citizenship behaviors. For women as leaders, the focus is shifting to behaviors and style rather than gender stereotypes.

12-7 **Define followership and identify different types of followers.** The follower role has alternatively been cast as one of *self-leadership* in which the follower assumes responsibility for influencing his or her own performance. Five types of followers are *effective, alienated, sheep, yes people,* and *survivors.* They are identified based on two dimensions: (1) activity versus passivity and (2) independent, critical thinking versus dependent, uncritical thinking.

followership The process of being guided and directed by a leader in the work environment. (p. 214)

12-8 **Synthesize historical leadership research into key guidelines for leaders.** Leaders and organizations appreciate the unique attributes, predispositions, and talents of each leader. Leaders challenge the organizational culture, when necessary, without destroying it. Participative, considerate leader behaviors demonstrate a concern for people. Different leadership situations call for different leadership talents and behaviors. Good leaders are likely to be good followers.

Describe the nature of conflicts in organizations. *Conflict* is defined as any situation in which incompatible goals, attitudes, emotions, or behaviors lead to disagreement or opposition between two or more parties. *Functional conflict* is a healthy, constructive disagreement between two or more people. *Dysfunctional conflict* is an unhealthy, destructive disagreement between two or more people.

functional conflict A healthy, constructive disagreement between two or more people. (p. 219)

dysfunctional conflict An unhealthy, destructive disagreement between two or more people. (p. 220)

13-2 Explain the role structural and personal factors play in causing conflict in organizations. Conflict can be classified into categories: *structural factors* and *personal factors*. Structural factors include specialization, interdependence, common resources, goal differences, authority relationships, status inconsistencies, and jurisdictional ambiguities. The causes of conflict that arise from individual differences include skills and abilities, personalities, percept.

jurisdictional ambiguity The presence of unclear lines of responsibility within an organization. (p. 222)

FIGURE 13.1 CAUSES OF CONFLICT IN ORGANIZATIONS

13-3 Discuss the nature of group conflict in organizations. *Interorganizational conflict* occurs between two or more organizations. Conflict occurring between groups or teams is known as *intergroup conflict*. Possible positive effects include increased group cohesiveness, task focus, and group loyalty. Possible negative consequences include extreme competition, hostility, and decreased communication between groups. *Intragroup conflict* is within groups or teams and can serve to avoid groupthink.

interorganizational conflict Conflict that occurs between two or more organizations. (p. 224)

intergroup conflict Conflict that occurs between groups or teams in an organization. (p. 224)

intragroup conflict Conflict that occurs within groups or teams. (p. 225)

13-4 Describe the factors that influence conflict between individuals in organizations. *Intrapersonal conflict* occurs within an individual. Tips for managing intrapersonal conflict are to analyze and match your values with the organization's, understand expectations, and develop political skills. Conflict between two or more people, or *interpersonal conflict*, can arise from individual differences. To manage interpersonal conflict, it is helpful to understand power networks in organizations, defense mechanisms exhibited by individuals, and ways to cope with difficult people.

intrapersonal conflict Conflict that occurs within an individual. (p. 225)

interrole conflict A person's experience of conflict among the multiple roles in his or her life. (p. 225)

intrarole conflict Conflict that occurs within a single role, such as when a persvon receives conflicting messages from role senders about how to perform a certain role. (p. 226)

person–role conflict Conflict that occurs when an individual in a particular role is expected to perform behaviors that clash with his or her personal values. (p. 226)

interpersonal conflict Conflict that occurs between two or more individuals. (p. 227)

fixation An aggressive mechanism in which an individual keeps up a dysfunctional behavior that obviously will not solve the conflict. (p. 228)

displacement An aggressive mechanism in which an individual directs his or her anger toward someone who is not the source of the conflict. (p. 228)

negativism An aggressive mechanism in which a person responds with pessimism to any attempt at solving a problem. (p. 228)

compensation A compromise mechanism in which an individual attempts to make up for a negative situation by devoting himself or herself to another pursuit with increased vigor. (p. 228)

identification A compromise mechanism whereby an individual patterns his or her behavior after another's. (p. 229)

rationalization A compromise mechanism characterized by trying to justify one's behavior by constructing bogus reasons for it. (p. 229)

flight/withdrawal A withdrawal mechanism that entails physically escaping (flight) or psychologically escaping (withdrawal) a conflict. (p. 229)

conversion A withdrawal mechanism in which emotional conflicts are expressed in physical symptoms. (p. 229)

fantasy A withdrawal mechanism that provides an escape from a conflict through daydreaming. (p. 229)

13-5 **Describe effective and ineffective techniques for managing conflict.** Effective conflict management techniques include appealing to superordinate goals, expanding resources, changing personnel, changing structure, and confronting and negotiating. Ineffective techniques include nonaction, secrecy, administrative orbiting, due process nonaction, and character assassination.

nonaction Doing nothing in hopes that a conflict will disappear. (p. 230)

secrecy Attempting to hide a conflict or an issue that has the potential to create conflict. (p. 230)

administrative orbiting Delaying action on a conflict by buying time. (p. 230)

due process nonaction A procedure set up to address conflicts that is so costly, time-consuming, or personally risky that no one will use it. (p. 230)

character assassination An attempt to label or discredit an opponent. (p. 230)

superordinate goal An organizational goal that is more important to both parties in a conflict than their individual or group goals. (p. 231)

distributive bargaining A negotiation approach in which the goals of the parties are in conflict, and each party seeks to maximize its resources. (p. 232)

integrative negotiation A negotiation approach in which the parties' goals are not seen as mutually exclusive, but the focus is on both sides achieving their objectives. (p. 232)

13-6 **Identify five styles of conflict management.** Managers have at their disposal a variety of conflict management styles: avoiding, accommodating, competing, compromising, and collaborating. One way of classifying styles of conflict management is to examine the styles' assertiveness (the extent to which you want your goals met) and cooperativeness (the extent to which you want to see the other party's concerns met).

14-1 **Differentiate between job and work.** A *job* is an employee's specific work and task activities in an organization. *Work* is effortful, productive activity resulting in a product or a service. A job is composed of a set of specific tasks, each of which is an assigned piece of work to be done in a specific time period. Work is an especially important human endeavor because it has a powerful effect in binding a person to reality.

job A set of specified work and task activities that engage an individual in an organization. (p. 236)

work Mental or physical activity that has productive results. (p. 236)

meaning of work The way a person interprets and understands the value of work as part of life. (p. 237)

14-2 **Discuss the traditional approaches to job design.** Good job design differentiates and integrates tasks, improves productivity, and enhances employee well-being. Approaches to job design that were developed during the twentieth century are job enlargement/job rotation, job enrichment, and the job characteristics theory. Each approach offers unique benefits to the organization, the employee, or both, but each also has limitations and drawbacks.

work simplification The standardization and the narrow, explicit specification of task activities for workers. (p. 239)

job enlargement A method of job design that increases the number of activities in a job to overcome the boredom of overspecialized work. (p. 240)

job rotation A variation of job enlargement in which workers are exposed to a variety of specialized jobs over time. (p. 240)

cross-training A variation of job enlargement in which workers are trained in different specialized tasks or activities. (p. 240)

job enrichment Designing or redesigning a job by incorporating motivational factors into it. (p. 241)

Job Characteristics Model A framework for understanding person–job fit through the interaction of core job dimensions with critical psychological states within a person. (p. 242)

Job Diagnostic Survey (JDS) The survey instrument designed to measure the elements in the Job Characteristics Model. (p. 242)

engagement The expression of oneself as one performs in work or other roles. (p. 243)

14-3 **Identify and describe alternative approaches to job design.** Several alternative approaches to job design have emerged over the past couple of decades: the social information-processing model; ergonomics and the interdisciplinary framework of Michael Campion and Paul Thayer; the international perspectives of the Japanese, Germans, and Scandinavians; and the health and well-being aspects of work design. Healthy work enables individuals to adapt, function well, and balance work with private life activities.

social information-processing (SIP) model A model that suggests that the important job factors depend in part on what others tell a person about the job. (p. 244)

ergonomics The science of adapting work and working conditions to the employee or worker. (p. 244)

lean production Using committed employees with ever expanding responsibilities to achieve zero waste and 100% good product, delivered on time, every time. (p. 246)

sociotechnical systems (STS) Giving equal attention to technical and social considerations in job design. (p. 246)

technocentric Placing technology and engineering at the center of job design decisions. (p. 246)

anthropocentric Placing human considerations at the center of job design decisions. (p. 246)

14-4 **Identify and describe contemporary issues facing organizations in the design of work.** Contemporary job design issues include telecommuting, alternative work patterns, techno-stress, and skill development. Work is relationally designed to provide opportunities and increase flexibility for employees. Companies use these and other approaches to the design of work as ways to manage a growing business while contributing to a better balance of work and family life for employees.

job sharing An alternative work pattern in which more than one person occupies a single job. (p. 249)

flextime An alternative work pattern that enables employees to set their own daily work schedules. (p. 249)

virtual office A mobile platform of computer, telecommunication, and information technology and services. (p. 250)

technostress The stress caused by new and advancing technologies in the workplace. (p. 250)

WHAT ABOUT YOU?

Is your work environment a healthy one?

To determine whether your work environment is a healthy one, read the text section on "Work Design and Well-Being" on page 248, then complete the following four steps.

Answer each question in the five steps "yes" or "no."

Step 1. Control and Influence
_____ Do you have influence over the pace of your work?
_____ Are system response times neither too fast nor too slow?
_____ Do you have a say in your work assignments and goals?
_____ Is there an opportunity for you to comment on your performance appraisal?

Step 2. Information and Uncertainty
_____ Do you receive timely information to complete your work?
_____ Do you receive complete information for your work assignments?
_____ Is there adequate planning for changes that affect you at work?
_____ Do you have access to all the information you need at work?

Step 3. Conflict at Work
_____ Does the company apply policies clearly and consistently?
_____ Are job descriptions and task assignments clear and unambiguous?
_____ Are there adequate policies and procedures for the resolution of conflicts?
_____ Is your work environment an open, participative one?

Step 4. Job Scope and Task Design
_____ Is there adequate variety in your work activities and/or assignments?
_____ Do you receive timely, constructive feedback on your work?
_____ Is your work important to the overall mission of the company?
_____ Do you work on more than one small piece of a big project?

Scoring

Count the number of "yes" answers in Steps 1 through 4: _____
If you have ten to sixteen "yes" answers, this suggests that your work environment is a psychologically healthy one.
If you have seven or fewer "yes" answers, this may suggest that your work environment is not as psychologically healthy as it could be.

15-1 **Define differentiation and integration as organizational design processes.** *Differentiation* is the design process of breaking the organizational goals into tasks. Three different forms of differentiation are horizontal, vertical, and spatial. *Integration* is the design process of linking the tasks together to form a structure that supports goal accomplishment. Vertical linkage devices include hierarchical referral, rules and procedures, plans and schedules, added positions, and management information systems. The horizontal linkages are liaison roles, task forces, integrator positions, and teams.

organizational design The process of constructing and adjusting an organization's structure to achieve its business strategy and goals. (p. 252)

organizational structure The linking of departments and jobs within an organization. (p. 252)

differentiation The process of deciding how to divide the work in an organization. (p. 253)

integration The process of coordinating the different parts of an organization. (p. 256)

15-2 **Discuss the basic design dimensions managers must consider in structuring an organization.** Basic design dimensions combine to yield various structural configurations. Structural dimensions include the following: formalization, centralization, specialization, standardization, complexity, and hierarchy of authority. Levels of structural dimensions determine bureaucratic (high) or flexible and loose (low) organizations. Henry Mintzberg's alternative approach is to describe what is and is not important to the success of the organization and design structures that fit each organization's unique set of circumstances.

formalization The degree to which the organization has official rules, regulations, and procedures. (p. 258)

centralization The degree to which decisions are made at the top of the organization. (p. 258)

specialization The degree to which jobs are narrowly defined and depend on unique expertise. (p. 258)

standardization The degree to which work activities are accomplished in a routine fashion. (p. 258)

complexity The degree to which many different types of activities occur in the organization. (p. 258)

hierarchy of authority The degree of vertical differentiation across levels of management. (p. 258)

business model innovation The innovative processes and rationale for how an organization creates, delivers, and captures value. (p. 258)

15-3 **Describe five structural configurations for organizations.** Henry Mintzberg proposed five structural configurations: the simple structure, the machine bureaucracy, the professional bureaucracy, the divisionalized form, and the adhocracy. The five basic parts of the organization, for Mintzberg, are the upper echelon, and/or strategic apex; the middle level, or middle line; the operating core; the technical staff, or technostructure; and the support staff. The organization's goals and levels of differentiation, integration, and formalization determine the structural configuration.

simple structure A centralized form of organization that emphasizes a small technical and support staff, strong centralization of decision making in the upper echelon, and a minimal middle level. (p. 260)

machine bureaucracy A moderately decentralized form of organization that emphasizes support staff differentiated from the line operations of the organization, limited horizontal decentralization of decision making, and a well-defined hierarchy of authority. (p. 260)

professional bureaucracy A decentralized form of organization that emphasizes the expertise of the professionals in the operating core of the organization. (p. 261)

divisionalized form A loosely coupled, composite structural configuration composed of divisions, each of which may have its own structural configuration. (p. 261)

adhocracy A selectively decentralized form of organization that emphasizes the support staff and mutual adjustment among people. (p. 261)

15-4 **Describe four contextual variables that influence organizational structure.** Four variables influence the success of an organization's design: size, technology, environment, and strategy and goals. These variables provide a manager with key considerations for the right organizational design. The amount of change in the contextual variables throughout the life of the organization influences the amount of change needed in the basic dimensions of the organization's structure.

contextual variables A set of four characteristics that influence the success of an organization's design: size, technology, environment, and strategy and goals. (p. 261)

technological interdependence The degree of interrelatedness of the organization's various technological elements. (p. 264)

environment Anything outside the boundaries of an organization. (p. 264)

task environment The part of the environment that is directly relevant to the organization. (p. 264)

environmental uncertainty The amount and rate of change in the organization's environment. (p. 265)

mechanistic structure An organizational design that emphasizes structured activities, specialized tasks, and centralized decision making. (p. 265)

organic structure An organizational design that emphasizes teamwork, open communication, and decentralized decision making. (p. 265)

15-5 **Explain the forces reshaping organizations.** Several forces reshaping organizations are causing managers to go beyond the traditional frameworks and to examine ways to make organizations more responsive to customer needs. Some of these forces include shorter organizational life cycles, globalization, and rapid changes in information technology. These forces together increase the demands on process capabilities within the organization and emerging organizational structures. To successfully retain their health and vitality, organizations must function as open systems that are responsive to their task environment.

organizational life cycle The differing stages of an organization's life from birth to death. (p. 267)

15-6 **Identify and describe emerging organizational structures.** Network organizations are weblike structures that contract some or all of their operating functions to other organizations and then coordinate their activities through managers and other employees at their headquarters. Virtual organizations are temporary network organizations consisting of independent enterprises. The circle organization, crafted by Harley-Davidson in its drive to achieve teamwork without teams, is a more open system and an organic structure for customer responsiveness.

15-7 **Identify factors that can adversely affect organizational structure.** If organizational structure is out of alignment with its contextual variables, one or more of the following symptoms appears: delayed decision making, low-quality decision making, non-response to changing environment, and interdepartmental conflict. Also, managers' personal cognitive biases and political ideologies affect their good judgment and decision-making abilities and may adversely affect the structure of the organization.

CHAPTER 16 LEARNING OBJECTIVES / KEY TERMS

16-1 **Identify the three levels of organizational culture and evaluate the roles they play in an organization.** *Organizational culture* is a pattern of basic assumptions considered valid and taught to new members as the way to perceive, think, and feel in the organization. *Artifacts* are cultural symbols in the physical and social work environments, such as personal enactment, ceremonies and rites, stories, rituals, and symbols. Deeper level *values* reflect inherent beliefs, and *assumptions* guide behavior and tell members of an organization how to perceive situations and people.

organizational (corporate) culture A pattern of basic assumptions that are considered valid and that are taught to new members as the way to perceive, think, and feel in the organization. (p. 273)

artifacts Symbols of culture in the physical and social work environments. (p. 273)

espoused values What members of an organization say they value. (p. 276)

enacted values Values reflected in the way individuals actually behave. (p. 276)

assumptions Deeply held beliefs that guide behavior and tell members of an organization how to perceive situations and people. (p. 277)

FIGURE 16.1 **LEVELS OF ORGANIZATIONAL CULTURE**

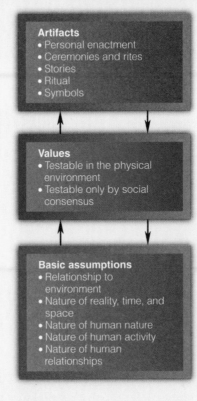

Artifacts
- Personal enactment
- Ceremonies and rites
- Stories
- Ritual
- Symbols

Visible but often not decipherable

Values
- Testable in the physical environment
- Testable only by social consensus

Greater level of awareness

Basic assumptions
- Relationship to environment
- Nature of reality, time, and space
- Nature of human nature
- Nature of human activity
- Nature of human relationships

Taken for granted Invisible Preconscious

SOURCE: From Edgar H. Schein, *Organizational Culture and Leadership: A Dynamic View.* Copyright © 1985 Jossey-Bass, Inc. Reprinted by permission of John Wiley & Sons, Inc.

16-2 **Evaluate the four functions of organizational culture within an organization.** Organizational culture serves four basic functions. First, culture provides a sense of identity to members and increases commitment to the organization. Second, culture provides a way for employees to interpret the meaning of organizational events. Third, culture reinforces the values in the organization. Finally, culture serves as a control mechanism for shaping behavior.

16-3 **Explain the relationship between organizational culture and performance.** A *strong-culture* organization acts with a consensus on the values that drive the company and with an intensity that is recognizable even to outsiders. The "fit" perspective (*fit culture*) argues that a culture is good only if it fits the industry or the firm's strategy. Three particular industry characteristics may affect culture: the competitive environment, customer requirements, and societal expectations. An *adaptive culture* is a culture that encourages confidence and risk taking among employees, has leadership that produces change, and focuses on the changing needs of customers.

strong culture An organizational culture with a consensus on the values that drive the company and with an intensity that is recognizable even to outsiders. (p. 278)

adaptive culture An organizational culture that encourages confidence and risk taking among employees, has leadership that produces change, and focuses on the changing needs of customers. (p. 279)

16-4 **Describe five ways leaders reinforce organizational culture.** Leaders play a critical role in shaping and reinforcing organizational culture. Managers need to create a positive culture through what they pay attention to how they react to crises, how they behave, how they allocate rewards, and how they hire and fire employees. Transformational leaders create a more adaptive culture, which in turn increases business unit performance.

16-5 **Describe the three stages of organizational socialization and the ways culture is communicated in each step.** Newcomers are transformed from outsiders to participating, effective members of the organization through *organizational socialization*. Three stages in the socialization process are *anticipatory socialization, encounter,* and *change and acquisition*. Through positive effective socialization, newcomers understand and adopt values and norms ensuring the company's culture and central values survive. Results can be good performance, high job satisfaction, and the intention to stay with the organization.

organizational socialization The process by which newcomers are transformed from outsiders to participating, effective members of the organization. (p. 281)

anticipatory socialization The first socialization stage, which encompasses all of the learning that takes place prior to the newcomer's first day on the job. (p. 281)

encounter The second socialization stage, in which newcomers learn the tasks associated with the job, clarify their roles, and establish new relationships at work. (p. 282)

change and acquisition The third socialization stage, in which the newcomer begins to master the demands of the job. (p. 282)

16-6 **Discuss how managers assess their organization's culture.** Both qualitative and quantitative methods can be used to assess organizational culture. The Organizational Culture Inventory (OCI) and the Kilmann-Saxton Culture-Gap Survey are quantitative tools. In the hopes of generating a more accurate assessment of organizational culture, managers combine multiple instruments, a practice called *triangulation*.

triangulation The use of multiple methods to measure organizational culture. (p. 284)

16-7 **Explain actions managers can take to change organizational culture.** Managers can use two approaches to change organizational culture: help current members buy into a new set of values, or add newcomers and socialize them into the organization and remove current members appropriately. Managers must send consistent messages about the new values and beliefs, provide credible communication, and live the new values. Cultural change can be assumed to be successful if new behavior is intrinsically motivated.

16-8 **Identify the challenges organizations face developing positive, cohesive, cultures.** Achieving a positive, cohesive corporate culture may be difficult in mergers, acquisitions, and globalization due to possible conflicts between organizations and cultural diversity on a geographic level. Developing an ethical culture requires management modeling, promoting ethical norms, and trust. Developing a culture of empowerment and quality involves including employees in decision making, removing obstacles to their performance, and reinforcing the value of product and service.

CHAPTER 17 LEARNING OBJECTIVES / KEY TERMS

17-1 Explain occupational and organizational choice decisions. Today most workers no longer work in one organization for the length of their working lives. The new career model is characterized by discrete exchange, occupational excellence, organizational empowerment, and project allegiance. When building a career, individuals first select an occupation that meets their needs, values, abilities, and preferences.

career The pattern of work-related experiences that spans the course of a person's life. (p. 290)

career management A lifelong process of learning about self, jobs, and organizations; setting personal career goals; developing strategies for achieving the goals; and revising the goals based on work and life experiences. (p. 290)

realistic job preview (RJP) Both positive and negative information given to potential employees about the job they are applying for, thereby giving them a realistic picture of the job. (p. 294)

17-2 Identify foundations for a successful career. Two foundations for a successful career are becoming your own career coach and developing your emotional intelligence. To become your own career coach, you must acquire multiple skills, develop self-reliance, and cultivate a flexible, team-oriented attitude. Emotional competencies are of equal or greater importance than technical skills.

17-3 Explain the career stage model. The career stage model shows that individuals pass through four stages in their careers: establishment, advancement, maintenance, and withdrawal. Timing of career transitions varies greatly among individuals.

establishment The first stage of a person's career in which the person learns the job and begins to fit into the organization and occupation. (p. 297)

advancement The second, high achievement-oriented career stage in which people focus on increasing their competence. (p. 297)

maintenance The third stage in an individual's career in which the individual tries to maintain productivity while evaluating progress toward career goals. (p. 297)

withdrawal The final stage in an individual's career in which the individual contemplates retirement or possible career changes. (p. 297)

17-4 Explain the major tasks facing individuals in the establishment stage of the career stage model. *Establishment* is the first stage of a person's career. The activities that occur in this stage center around learning the job and fitting into the organization and occupation. Individuals in this stage begin to work out their psychological contract with the organization and form attachment relationships with coworkers.

psychological contract An implicit agreement between an individual and an organization that specifies what each is expected to give and receive in the relationship. (p. 298)

17-5 Identify the issues confronting individuals in the advancement stage of the career stage model. *Advancement* is a high achievement-oriented stage in which people focus on increasing their competence. A hallmark of this stage is the exploration of career paths, or sequences of job experiences along which employees move during their careers. Some companies use career lattices that move employees laterally through the organization in an attempt to build diverse skills. A mentor provides numerous sponsorship, facilitating, and psychosocial functions for the protégé. Dualcareer partnerships are common now and can lead to work–home conflicts.

career path A sequence of job experiences that an employee moves along during his or her career. (p. 300)

career ladder A structured series of job positions through which an individual progresses in an organization. (p. 300)

mentor An individual who provides guidance, coaching, counseling, and friendship to a protégé. (p. 300)

dual-career partnership A relationship in which both people have important career roles. (p. 303)

flexible work schedule A work schedule that allows employees discretion in order to accommodate personal concerns. (p. 304)

eldercare Assistance in caring for elderly parents and/or other elderly relatives. (p. 304)

17-6 **Describe how individuals can navigate the challenges of the maintenance stage of the career stage model.** The *maintenance* stage finds the individual trying to maintain productivity while evaluating progress toward career goals. Individuals sustain their performance and continue to grow, although at a slower rate. Individuals in this stage may also become mentors.

career plateau A point in an individual's career at which the probability of moving farther up the hierarchy is low. (p. 306)

17-7 **Explain how individuals withdraw from the workforce.** The *withdrawal* stage involves contemplation of retirement or possible career change. Increasingly, individuals in this stage are opting for phased retirement, which is a gradual cessation of work. To help workers at this stage of their careers, organizations should provide opportunities for continued involvement with the organization, such as mentoring to other employees making career transitions.

phased retirement An arrangement that allows employees to reduce their hours and/or responsibilities in order to ease into retirement. (p. 307)

bridge employment Employment that takes place after a person retires from a full-time position but before the person's permanent withdrawal from the workforce. (p. 307)

17-8 **Explain how career anchors help form a career identity.** Career anchors are self-perceived talents, motives, and values that guide an individual's career decisions. Five main anchors are technical/functional competence, managerial competence, autonomy and independence, creativity, and security/stability.

career anchors A network of self-perceived talents, motives, and values that guide an individual's career decisions. (p. 308)

18-1 Identify the major external and internal forces for change in organizations. When organizations are in a state of turmoil and transition, all members are affected. *External* forces that demand change are globalization, workforce diversity, technological change, and managing ethical behavior. *Internal* pressures for change are generally recognizable: declining effectiveness, crisis, changes in employee expectations, and a changed work climate. Adaptiveness, flexibility, and responsiveness are characteristics of the organizations that will succeed in meeting the challenges of change.

planned change Change resulting from a deliberate decision to alter the organization. (p. 311)

unplanned change Change that is imposed on the organization and is often unforeseen. (p. 312)

18-2 Describe how different types of change vary in scope. Change can be of a relatively small scope, such as a modification in a work procedure (an *incremental change*) or of a larger scale, such as the restructuring of an organization (a *strategic change*). The most massive scope of change is *transformational change*, in which the organization moves to a radically different, and sometimes unknown, future state. One of the toughest decisions faced by leaders is the "pace" of change. Researchers agree that pace is important; however, they can't agree on which pace of change is most beneficial.

incremental change Change of a relatively small scope, such as making small improvements. (p. 315)

strategic change Change of a larger scale, such as organizational restructuring. (p. 315)

transformational change Change in which the organization moves to a radically different, and sometimes unknown, future state. (p. 315)

change agent The individual or group that undertakes the task of introducing and managing a change in an organization. (p. 315)

18-3 Discuss methods organizations can use to manage resistance to change. The contemporary view holds that resistance is simply a form of feedback and that this feedback can be used very productively to manage the change process. Three key strategies for managing resistance to change are communication, participation, and empathy and support.

18-4 Explain Lewin's organizational change model. Lewin's model, the idea of force field analysis, contends that a person's behavior is the product of two opposing forces; one force pushes toward preserving the status quo and the other force pushes for change. Lewin's change model is a three-step process: *unfreezing*—encouraging individuals to discard old behaviors, *moving*—new attitudes, values, and behaviors are substituted for old ones, and *refreezing*—new attitudes, values, and behaviors are established as the new status quo.

unfreezing The first step in Lewin's change model, in which individuals are encouraged to discard old behaviors by shaking up the equilibrium state that maintains the status quo. (p. 319)

moving The second step in Lewin's change model, in which new attitudes, values, and behaviors are substituted for old ones. (p. 319)

refreezing The final step in Lewin's change model, in which new attitudes, values, and behaviors are established as the new status quo. (p. 319)

18-5 Explain how companies determine the need to conduct an organization development intervention. *Organization development (OD)* is a systematic approach to organizational improvement. The first step, the diagnosis, should pinpoint specific problems and areas in need of improvement. Six areas to examine carefully are the organization's purpose, structure, reward system, support systems, relationships, and leadership. A needs analysis then determines the skills and competencies that employees must have to achieve the goals of the change.

organization development (OD) A systematic approach to organizational improvement that applies behavioral science theory and research in order to increase individual and organizational well-being and effectiveness. (p. 320)

18-6 **Discuss the major group-focused techniques for organization development intervention.** Some OD intervention methods emphasize changing the organization itself or changing the work groups within the organization. Intervention methods in this category include survey feedback, management by objectives, product and service quality programs, team building, and process consultation. All the preceding OD methods focus on changing the organization or the work group.

survey feedback A widely used intervention method whereby employee attitudes are solicited using a questionnaire. (p. 321)

management by objectives (MBO) An organization-wide intervention technique that involves joint goal setting between employees and managers. (p. 321)

quality program A program that embeds product and service quality excellence in the organizational culture. (p. 322)

team building An intervention designed to improve the effectiveness of a work group. (p. 322)

process consultation An OD method that helps managers and employees improve the processes that are used in organizations. (p. 323)

18-7 **Discuss the major individual-focused techniques for organization development intervention.** Managers have a host of organization development techniques to facilitate organizational change. Development efforts include skills training, leadership training and development, executive coaching, role negotiation, job redesign, health promotion programs, and career planning. Success depends on techniques used, competence of the change agent, the organization's readiness for change, and top management commitment. Programs do not drive change; business needs do.

skills training Increasing the job knowledge, skills, and abilities that are necessary to do a job effectively. (p. 323)

leadership training and development A variety of techniques that are designed to enhance individuals' leadership skills. (p. 323)

executive coaching A technique in which managers or executives are paired with a coach in a partnership to help them perform more efficiently. (p. 324)

role negotiation A technique whereby individuals meet and clarify their psychological contract. (p. 325)

job redesign An OD intervention method that alters jobs to improve the fit between individual skills and the demands of the job. (p. 325)